Born in Madrid in 1897, Arturo Barea lived in England from 1939 until his death in 1957. The story of his years in Spain is the subject matter of this remarkable autobiographical trilogy *The Forging of a Rebel*. The first volume, *The Forge*, describes his childhood and youth. *The Track* takes him from the age of twenty to twenty-eight – years spent as a conscript soldier in Spanish Morocco, as a businessman and as a husband and father. *The Clash* describes the Spanish Civil War and his own part in that struggle.

Forced to leave Spain, he and Ilsa, the Austrian socialist and journalist who became his second wife, settled in the village of Eaton Hastings near Faringdon in Berkshire. He worked for the BBC during the war, and contributed articles to journals such as *Horizon*, *London Forum* and *The Times Literary Supplement*. Barea published novels and short stories as well as books of criticism, including *Lorca, the Poet and His People* (1944) and *Unamuno* (1952).

Nigel Townson is Senior Lecturer in History at the European University of Madrid. He has edited the latest edition of *The Forging of a Rebel* in Spanish and compiled the *Cuentos Completos* (*Complete Short Stories*) as well as a selection of Arturo Barea's other writings, *Palabras Recobradas* (*Recovered Words*). He is also the author of *The Crisis of Democracy in Spain: Centrist Politics Under the Second Republic, 1931–1936* (Sussex Academic Press, 2000).

D0880204

THE
FORGING
OF A REBEL

ARTURO BAREA

Translation by
ILSA BAREA

Introduction by
NIGEL TOWNSON

Walker & Company
New York

First published in Great Britain by Faber & Faber: *The Forge*
© 1941 Arturo Barea; *The Track* © 1943 Arturo Barea; *The Clash*
© 1946 Arturo Barea. An omnibus edition of *The Forge, The
Track,* and *The Clash* was first published in the United States by
Reynal & Hitchcock, Inc., in 1946 © Reynal & Hitchcock. An
omnibus edition was published in Great Britain in 1972 by Doris-
Poynter Limited © 1970 Arturo Barea; translation © Ilsa Barea. In
1972 in the United States, The Viking Press published an omnibus
edition copyright © 1970 by Arturo Barea, translation copyright
© 1972 by Ilsa Barea. Reprinted by permission of the Author's
Estate. This edition published in Great Britain in 2001 by
Granta Books and in the United States of America in 2002 by
Walker Publishing Company.

Published simultaneously in Canada by Fitzhenry and Whiteside,
Markham, Ontario L3R 4T8

For information about permission to reproduce selections from
this book, write to Permissions, Walker & Company,
435 Hudson Street, New York, New York 10014

Library of Congress Cataloging-in-Publication Data
Barea, Arturo, 1897–1957.
[Forja de un rebelde. English]
The forging of a rebel / Arturo Barea ; translation by Ilsa Barea ;
introduction by Nigel Townson.
p. cm.
In 3 pts.; each pt. also published separately under the titles:
The forge, The track, and The clash.
ISBN 0-8027-7615-9 (pbk. : alk. paper)
1. Barea, Arturo, 1897–1957. 2. Spain—Social life and
customs. 3. Rif Revolt, 1921–1926—Personal narratives.
4. Spain—History—Civil War, 1936–1939—Personal
narratives. I. Title.

DP236.B3 A2 2001
946.08'092—dc21 2001045466

Printed in Canada

2 4 6 8 10 9 7 5 3 1

CONTENTS

INTRODUCTION

Few books on the Spanish Civil War of 1936–39 and its origins have been as acclaimed as *The Forging of a Rebel* by Arturo Barea. The first volume of this autobiographical trilogy, *The Forge*, published in June 1941, was lauded by Stephen Spender for its 'great artistic merits' and 'rare poetic feeling', while *The Times* declared that 'it is doubtful if there has yet appeared a more convincing picture of the anvil on which a rebel was forged'. The second book, *The Track*, which appeared in July 1943, was eulogized for its 'great beauty and vivid detail'. Cyril Connolly singled out the author for being 'something rarely found these days', as he 'thinks and feels clearly and honestly'. Published in February 1946, the third tome, *The Clash*, was declared by George Orwell 'an exceptional book' of 'considerable historical interest'. Altogether, as one critic summed up, the trilogy was 'as essential to an understanding of twentieth-century Spain as the reading of Tolstoy is indispensable to the comprehension of nineteenth-century Russia'.

Such success notwithstanding, Arturo Barea had come late to writing. *The Forge*, his first novel, was published when he was forty-three years of age, *The Clash* at forty-eight. Indeed, had it not been for the Civil War, Barea would probably not have become a writer at all. However, this was not due to a lack of motivation. During his early life he was torn between his artistic aspirations and the exigencies of earning a living. He was born on 20 September 1897 into a lower-class family in the Extremaduran town of Badajoz, near the Portuguese border. The sudden death of his father, an army recruiting agent, caused the family to move to Madrid just two months later. There, his mother worked as a maid in her brother's household and as a washerwoman on the banks of the river Manzanares. Unlike his two brothers and sister, Arturo lived with his well-to-do uncle and aunt. At the weekend, he would rejoin the family in the working-class district of El Avapiés. Thus the young Barea was caught between two worlds: an unresolved tension that would contribute to his sense of being an outsider and ultimately shape his work as a writer.

Following the sudden death of his uncle, Arturo had to start work at the age of thirteen. He undertook a succession of poorly-paid jobs before making some money as a commercial traveller for a diamond dealer during the First World War – the outbreak of which marks the end of *The Forge*. By this stage, he had become afflicted, he recounts in his autobiographical notes, by 'the literary microbe', attending literary *peñas*, or discussion groups, at the cafés in the centre of Madrid. More time, he discovered to his horror, had to be dedicated to 'praising and "sucking up" to the chosen master' than to writing. This 'vileness and endless mental torture' might lead to the publication of an unremunerated article, but the process would then continue for months and even years until one managed to join a newspaper on a mere pittance. Such a drawn-out and humiliating route to literary success clashed violently with Barea's prickly pride. He thereupon abandoned the literary scene, his ambitions buried. In short, he could not earn a living as a writer, especially as he was determined to support his mother, to whom he was devoted. This contradiction is manifest in *The Forging of a Rebel*, but is crystallized in the short story 'The Centre of the Ring', which takes place between 1914 and 1920, the period which falls between the first and second volumes of the trilogy.

In 1920, Barea, now fully-grown, of a lithe, tallish build, was called up for military service in Spanish Morocco, the country's one remaining colony, an experience that constitutes the core of *The Track*. Here, he was a witness to the ubiquitous cupidity and incompetence of the Spanish army, of the wretchedness of the rank-and-file, and of the degradations of the Moroccan population. He also came to know personally many of the generals who later headed the insurgency of July 1936 against the democratic Republic. While in Morocco, Barea did not entirely abandon his literary aspirations. He wrote some poetry along with the occasional short story, though only a single story, 'La Medalla' ('The Medal') of 1922, has come to light. Nonetheless, on leaving the army in 1923, Barea did not attempt to pursue a career as a writer. On the contrary, he followed a highly conventional path: he married, became a father, and secured a steady job in the patents business. By the end of the 1920s, he had become the technical director of a leading firm, thereby allowing him to provide for both his immediate family and his mother, now in old age. The marriage to Aurelia Grimaldos, however, was, in his own words, a 'depressing failure' that led him to take ever greater refuge in his work.

The eruption of mass politics with the establishment in 1931 of Spain's first democratic regime, the Second Republic, partly assuaged Barea's restless spirit. He became involved, as in the 1910s, with the socialist trade union movement. Still, his union activities represented, he later noted, 'a constant and bitter contradiction' in relation to his work at the patent office, where he dealt on a quotidian basis with big businesses.

By the outbreak of the Civil War in July 1936, Barea had published nothing except a little poetry, a few short stories, and the occasional political piece. The war – the cornerstone of *The Clash* – was to change all that. First, having joined the Office of Foreign Press Censorship at the Ministry of Foreign Affairs in August 1936, he came into contact with journalists and writers, including figures such as Ernest Hemingway and John Dos Passos – both of whom would strongly shape Barea's later literary work. He was also influenced by a short, plump Austrian with a mass of curly hair by the name of Ilsa Kulcsar. She, like many other foreigners, had gone to Spain to defend the republican cause, having been an activist in the Austrian Social Democratic Party. Appointed as Barea's assistant, when, upon the departure of the government for Valencia in November 1936, he had been made head of the censorship office, she was not only of inestimable help to him in his work as a censor – she spoke five languages extraordinarily well, albeit with a Viennese accent – but also encouraged him to write. Within weeks, moreover, they had become lovers. The fact that for much of 1937 Barea, as the 'Unknown Voice of Madrid', had to give daily radio talks of a literary and propagandistic nature was a further stimulus. The catalyst, however, was the nervous breakdown which he suffered in the summer of 1937. This was a result of the sixteen-hour days, the unremitting bombardments, the collapse of his marriage, and the increasingly ugly battle with the Communist-dominated bureaucracy in Valencia. Barea strove to transcend this all-enveloping crisis through writing. On 17 August 1937, he published a story in the *Daily Express* under the headline 'This was written under shell fire' – a curious coincidence given that the great bulk of what he produced thereafter, as a republican exile in England, would appear first in English. In 1938, he published his first book, a collection of slight, propagandistic short stories – many of which drew on his radio talks and which concerned the everyday struggle of the common people against 'fascism' – entitled *Valor y Miedo* (*Courage and Fear*). According to Barea, it was the last tome to be printed in Barcelona before Franco's troops entered the Catalan capital.

By the end of 1937, the Communists had effectively forced Barea to abandon not only the censorship office and his radio work, but, worse still, in February 1938, Spain itself. Once in Paris, he started work on the first draft of *The Forge* in an effort to alleviate the hunger, the dire living conditions, and the pain of the Republic's protracted defeat. Shocked by France's 'inner decay' and convinced of the 'coming catastrophe', Arturo and Ilsa – who had married just a week before leaving Spain – fled to England. They reached their destination the month that the Republic fell to the Nationalists: March 1939. The Civil War had transformed Arturo Barea's life: he had left his wife for another woman, gone into exile, and finally committed himself to writing.

'More than I expected', Arturo underlines in the autobiographical notes, 'and more than seemed likely in a Spaniard, I took to English life at once, and fell in love with the English countryside'. Thus it was in 'the peace of the country' that he achieved his first literary triumph in England – the short story 'A Spaniard in Hertfordshire', which appeared in the *Spectator* in June 1939. The following year, he began work for the Latin American section of the BBC's World Service. He wrote and presented a fifteen-minute talk on an aspect of British life, under the pseudonym of 'Juan de Castilla', virtually every week up until his death; that is to say, over 850 programmes. These reflective monologues proved extremely popular, 'Juan de Castilla' coming top of the listeners' annual poll on numerous occasions, and became his principal source of income. Accordingly, Arturo Barea's work at the BBC not only provided him with a certain measure of material security but also added to his renown as a writer – albeit in countries other than his own.

In 1941, Barea enjoyed his first critical success with the essay 'Not Spain but Hemingway', a searing indictment of the American novelist's *For Whom the Bell Tolls*. The same year, he published *Struggle for the Spanish Soul*, a dissection of the ideas and forces that underpinned the Franco dictatorship, which appeared alongside George Orwell's *The Lion and the Unicorn* in the 'Searchlight' series at Secker & Warburg. Editor Tosco Fyvel assured Barea in a letter that the book would make him 'a famous man'. Arturo, he predicted, would be known as '*the* Spanish writer in the country before the end of the summer'.

Barea did indeed become famous in 1941, but not as a result of *Struggle for the Spanish Soul*. That year, *The Forge* was published. Edited by T.S. Eliot at Faber & Faber, the book was translated by Sir Peter Chalmers-Mitchell, the former British consul in Malaga and a republican sympathizer, who had helped get the novel published. His rendering of *The Forge*, as Stephen Spender discreetly put it, was 'not all that could be desired'. As a result, the next two volumes, *The Track* and *The Clash*, made available in 1943 and 1946 respectively, were translated by Ilsa. 'Any English writer,' author Gerald Brenan observed in a letter to Arturo, 'would be pleased to write as well', while *The Times* commented approvingly that *The Track* 'is so well translated that it reads as though it had been written in English and were in fact the product of an English mind'. Not surprisingly, Ilsa also produced a new version of *The Forge*, in 1946. That same year the three novels went on sale in the USA in a one-volume edition entitled *The Forging of a Rebel*. Acclaimed as a 'masterpiece' and as 'an invaluable contribution to our knowledge of modern Spain, as well as a work of high literary distinction', the trilogy, Bertram Wolfe pronounced ringingly, was 'one of the great autobiographies of the twentieth century'. The book sold 4,000 copies in the first month.

Barea had two, interrelated aims in writing *The Forging of a Rebel*. First, he endeavoured to expose, as he explains in the English introduction to *The Track*, 'the dark psychological and social undercurrents of the Spanish War'.

Second, he sought to do so by giving 'voice' to the 'common people', having been 'one of them'. He therefore rejected the first draft of the book as too abstract and ideologically-led, preferring instead to focus on the concrete lives of individual people. 'I can talk of what I've seen, of what I've lived', as he put it in a letter. 'Living beings', he emphasised, 'interest me much more than theory and analysis'. Characterized by its spare style, the photographic quality of its descriptions, its close attention to local detail and the corresponding colloquialism of the language, and by its uncompromising emotional honesty as well as by a remarkable absence of bitterness, *The Forging of a Rebel* is, as the *Guardian* observed, 'a Spanish masterpiece which illuminates an entire historical epoch'.

The first Spanish edition was published in 1951 by Losada of Buenos Aires. Since Arturo had lost most, if not all, of the original manuscript, he and Ilsa had to re-translate the English version back into Spanish. This was evidently done with a certain haste as the text is plagued by grammatical errors and anglicisms. In Spain itself, Barea's republican past, his self-proclaimed socialism, and *The Forging of a Rebel*'s unflinching critique of the *ancien régime* ensured that only clandestine copies circulated under the Franco regime. Once the transition to democracy got under way, the trilogy was at last published in Spain in 1978; that is to say, thirty-seven years after *The Forge* first appeared. Although new editions were brought out in 1980 and 1985–86, it was not until the Debate edition of 2000 that the Losada text was finally corrected.

Arguably, *The Forging of a Rebel*'s English version, despite being produced by a non-native speaker, is more polished and fluent than the re-translated Spanish one. What is more, this was the basis for the trilogy's translation, as Ilsa explains in a letter, into 'nearly all' other languages as 'virtually no translator' was familiar enough with Arturo's 'very un-academic, direct and colloquial vocabulary'. Altogether, the book has been published in ten languages. For the translation, as for so much else, Arturo had Ilsa to thank. She was, as Arturo recognized, 'my collaborator in everything . . . my companion in the most ample sense of the word'.

Recognition of Barea's worth as a writer was reflected in the tour which he undertook of Denmark in 1946. The following year, he was put forward for the Nobel prize, and, according to Ilsa, was shortlisted for the award. In 1952, he was invited to lecture at the State University of Pennsylvania on nineteenth- and twentieth-century Spanish literature – quite an achievement for an autodidact. Moreover, such was the popularity of the BBC talks that the Corporation sent him in 1956 on a 48-day tour of Argentina, Chile and Uruguay, where he gave numerous lectures and interviews and attended a host of banquets and multitudinous book signings. He was fêted not just for his broadcasting work but also because of *The Forging of a Rebel*. The Losada edition, for example, had sold 10,000 copies in a matter of months. Despite the

malevolent efforts of the Francoist embassies to smear him as 'Arturo Beria' –
a reference to Stalin's brutal security chief which hinted at Arturo's allegedly
Communist past – the tour was an unqualified triumph.

Barea's interest as a writer is far from restricted to the trilogy alone. Often
portrayed as a down-to-earth, working-class writer without literary or intellectual pretensions, his work as a critic has been unjustly neglected. In 1944,
he published *Lorca, the Poet and His People*, a path-breaking analysis of the
Andalusian poet that is still of value today. Admittedly, the later study of
Miguel de Unamuno, the irascible Basque polymath – undertaken in collaboration with Ilsa – is of much less interest. Nonetheless, Arturo wrote some
extremely stimulating literary criticism, characterized by its accessibility, by the
sheer soundness of its judgement, and by a determination to place the novels
within their social and historical context. In short, Barea was an independently-
minded and thought-provoking critic.

Only one novel was completed by Arturo following *The Forging of a Rebel*.
Published in English in 1951 and in Spanish four years later, the revealingly-
titled *The Broken Root* can be regarded as a sequel to the trilogy insofar as it
concerns a Spaniard, who, like Barea, is exiled in England, but who, unlike
Barea, returns home; in other words, the book concerns the aftermath of
the Civil War. While replicating many of the virtues of *The Forging of a Rebel*,
the novel lacks the structural coherence and narrative impact of the trilogy's
first-hand testimony. In the meantime, Arturo continued to write short stories
right up until his death. A posthumous collection, *El Centro de la Pista* (*The
Centre of the Ring*), was published in Spain in 1960, but it was not until 2001
that the *Cuentos Completos* (*Complete Short Stories*), finally appeared. Many of
the stories complement *The Forging of a Rebel*. Virtually all, moreover, concern
Spain, despite the fact that the author spent the last half of his adult life in
England. Yet this is true of all Arturo Barea's work – the literary criticism, the
historical accounts, the political commentaries, the novels, and the short
stories – with the exception of his journalistic assignments.

The pain of exile, for a writer whose work was centred almost exclusively
on his home country, is more than evident in *The Broken Root*. Yet it was in
England, and in the company of Ilsa, that Arturo Barea encountered the
peace and stability necessary to become a writer. Furthermore, he wrote, 'I do
not intend ever to return permanently to Spain, even after the overthrow of
the Fascist regime, but hope to live "somewhere in England"'. He died
during the night of 24 December 1957 from a heart attack. He left behind an
unfinished novel, *His Brother's Keeper*, which, like all his previous novels, was
set in Spain.

Undoubtedly, the variety and quality of Arturo Barea's output as a writer,
ranging from his literary criticism and political analyses to his short stories and
journalism, has not been fully appreciated. Still, his greatest work remains *The*

Forging of a Rebel. In part, this is because the trilogy tackles the origins and course of the conflict of 1936–39. What distinguishes *The Forging of a Rebel*, however, is its first-hand testimony, its emotional integrity, and its effort to relate the untold story of the mass of ordinary Spaniards. If, to this, one adds the graphic descriptions, the penetrating observations, and the compelling narrative, it is evident why *The Forging of a Rebel* remains one of the greatest accounts of twentieth-century Spain's greatest tragedy: the Civil War.

Nigel Townson

ARTURO BAREA

THE
FORGE

To
Two Women
my mother, the Señora Leonor
and
my wife, Ilsa

CONTENTS

PART I

PART II

What the hammer? What the chain?
In what furnace was thy brain?
What the anvil?

1. River and Attic

THE wind blew into the two hundred pairs of breeches and filled them. To me they looked like fat men without a head, swinging from the clothes-lines of the drying-yard. We boys ran along the rows of white trousers and slapped their bulging seats. Señora Encarna was furious. She chased us with the wooden beater she used to pound the dirty grease out of her washing. We took refuge in the maze of streets and squares formed by four hundred damp sheets. Sometimes she caught one of us; then the others would begin to throw mud pellets at the breeches. They left stains as though somebody had dirtied his pants, and we imagined the thrashing some people would get for behaving like pigs.

In the evening, when the breeches had dried, we helped to count them in tens. All the children of the washerwomen went with Señora Encarna up to the top story of the washhouse. It was a big loft with a roof like a V turned upside down. Señora Encarna could stand upright in the middle, but her top-knot nearly touched the big beam. We would stand at the sides and bang our heads against the sloping roof.

Señora Encarna had in front of her the heaps of breeches, sheets, pants, and shirts. The pillow-cases were apart. Everything had its number. Señora Encarna sang it out and threw the piece to the boy in charge of the set of ten to which it belonged. Each of us looked after two or three groups, the "twenties," or the "thirties," or the "sixties," and had to drop each piece on the right heap. Last of all we stuffed into each pillow-case, as into a sack, one pair of breeches, two sheets, one pair of pants, and one shirt, all marked with the same number. Every Thursday, a big cart drawn by four horses came down to the river to fetch the two hundred bundles of clean linen and leave another two hundred of dirty washing behind.

It was the linen of the men of the Royal Horse Guards, the only soldiers who had sheets to sleep in.

Every morning, soldiers of the Guards rode over the King's Bridge escorting an open carriage in which the Prince of Asturias used to sit, or sometimes the Queen. But first a rider would come out of the tunnel which led to the Royal Palace, to warn the guards on the bridge. They would chase away the people, and the carriage with its escort would pass when the bridge was empty. As we were children and so could not be anarchists, the police let us stay while they went by. We were not afraid of the Horse Guards, because we knew their breeches too well.

The Prince was a fair-haired boy with blue eyes, who looked at us and laughed like a ninny. People said he was dumb and had to go for a walk in the Casa de Campo every day, between a priest and a general with white mustaches. It would have been better for him to come and play with us by the river. And then we would have seen him with nothing on when we were bathing, and would have known what a prince looks like inside. But apparently they did not want him to come. Once we discussed it with Uncle Granizo, the owner of the washhouse, because he was friends with the head keeper of the Casa de Campo, who sometimes spoke to the Prince. Uncle Granizo promised to see to it, but later he told us that the general would not give his permission.

Those military were all alike. A general who had been in the Philippines often came to visit my Uncle José. He had brought back with him an old Chinese who was very fond of me, a pink wooden walking-stick, which he said had been the spine of a fish called the manatee and was the death of anyone who got a whack with it, and a cross which was not a real cross but a green star with many rays, which he wore everywhere, embroidered on his vest and shirt and as an enamel button in his coat-lapel.

Every time this general came to visit my uncle, he grunted, cleared his throat and asked me whether I was already a little man. He would at once begin to scold me: "Keep quiet, boy, a little man mustn't do that. . . . Leave that cat alone, boy, you're a little man now." I used to sit down on the floor between my uncle's legs while they talked about politics and the war of the Russians and Japanese. The war had finished long before, but the general liked to speak of it because he had been in China and Japan himself. When they talked about that, I used to listen, and every time I heard how the Japanese had beaten up the Russians I was glad. I could not stand the Russians. They had a very nasty king who was the Tsar and a police chief called Petroff, Captain Petroff, who was a brute and lashed people with his whip. My uncle bought me a new number of the *Adventures of Captain Petroff* every Sunday. They threw a lot of bombs at him, but he never got killed.

When they stopped speaking of the war they bored me and I went to play on the dining-room carpet.

That other general who was with the Prince must have been just the same. He had to teach the Prince how to make wars when he became king, because all kings must know how to make wars, and the priest taught him how to speak. I didn't understand that. How could he speak if he was dumb? Perhaps he could, because he was a prince; but the dumb people I knew could only talk by signs. And it was not for lack of priests.

It was a nuisance that no ball came floating down, when we needed one to play with that evening.

It was quite easy to fish a ball. There was a small wooden bridge in front of Uncle Granizo's house. It was made of two old rails with planks on top and a railing, all painted green. Underneath flowed a black stream which came out of a tunnel; and that tunnel and that stream were the big sewer of Madrid. All the balls which the children of Madrid dropped into the gutters came floating down there, and we fished for them from our bridge with a net made of a stick and the wire guard of a brazier. Once I caught one made of rubber; it was painted red. Next day at school, Cerdeño took it away from me and I had to keep my mouth shut because he was bigger than I was. But I made him pay for it. In the *Corrala,* the square in front of the school where we used to play, I threw a stone at his head from the top of the railing, so that he went about with a bandage for two days and they had to sew up his brain with stitches. Of course, he did not know who had done it. But I carried a sharp stone in my pocket after that, just in case, and if he had tried to beat me, they would have had to sew him up a second time.

Antonio, the one who limped, once fell from the bridge and nearly drowned. Señor Manuel, the handyman, pulled him out and squeezed his tummy with both hands until Antonio began to spit up dirty water. Afterwards they gave him tea and brandy to drink. Señor Manuel, who was a tippler, took a good swill out of the bottle because his trousers were all wet and he said he was cold.

Nothing doing, no ball came down. I went to dinner, my mother was calling me. That day we had our meal in the sun, sitting on the grass. I liked it better than the cold days with no sun, when we had to eat at Uncle Granizo's. His house was a tavern with a tin-covered bar and some round tables which were all wobbly. The soup would spill over and the brazier stank. It was not really a brazier, but a big portable stove, with an open fire in the middle and all the stewing-pots of the washerwomen placed round it. My mother's was small, because there were only the two of us, but Señora Encarna's pot was as big as a wine-jar. There were nine of them, and they ate out of a washbowl instead of a plate. All nine sat on the grass round their bowl and dipped in their spoons in turn. When it rained and they had to eat indoors, they sat at two tables and divided their stew between the washbowl and a very big earthenware casserole which Uncle Granizo used for stewing snails on Sundays. For on Sundays the washhouse was shut and Uncle Granizo cooked snails. In the evening, men and women came down to the river and they danced, ate snails and drank wine. Once Uncle Granizo invited my mother and me, and I stuffed. The snails were caught in the grass round there, especially after the rain, when they came out to sun themselves. We boys collected them, painted their houses in many colors and let them run races.

The *cocido* tasted better here than at home.

First you cut bread into very thin bits and poured over them the soup of the stew, yellow with saffron. Then you ate the chick-peas, and after them the meat together with fresh tomatoes cut in half and sprinkled with plenty of salt. For dessert we had salad, juicy green lettuce with tender hearts such as you could not have got anywhere in town. Uncle Granizo grew the lettuces on the banks of the sewer, because he said that they grew better on sewage water. And it was true. It sounded nasty. But people spread dung on the corn-fields and chickens eat muck, and in spite of all that, bread and chickens are very good.

The chickens and ducks knew our meal-time. They arrived as soon as my mother turned over her washing-board. A big, fat earthworm had been underneath and now it wriggled. One of the ducks saw it at once. He ate the worm just as I used to eat thick noodles: he dangled it in his bill, sucked—plff—and down it went. Then he plucked at the feathers of his neck, as if some crumbs had fallen there, and waited for me to throw him my piece of bread. I would not give it him in my fingers because he was a brute and pinched. He had a very hard bill and it hurt.

With the washing-board for a table we ate, my mother and I, sitting on the grass.

My mother's hands were very small. As she had been washing since sunrise, her fingers were covered with little wrinkles like an old woman's skin, but her nails were bright and shining. Sometimes the lye would burn right through her skin and make pin-prick holes all over her finger-tips. In the winter her hands used to get cut open; as soon as she took them out of the water into the cold air, they were covered with sharp little ice crystals. The blood would spurt as though a cat had scratched her. She used to put on glycerine, and her hands healed at once.

After the meal we boys went to play at Paris-Madrid Motor Races with the wheelbarrows used for the washing. We had stolen four of them from Señor Manuel, without his noticing, and kept them hidden in the meadow. He did not like us playing with them, because they were heavy and he said one of us would have his leg broken one day. But they were great fun. Each barrow had an iron wheel in front which screeched as it rolled. One boy would get into a wheelbarrow and another would push it at top speed until he had enough of it. Then he would suddenly tip up the barrow, and the passenger would topple out. One day we played at train-crashes, and lame Antonio squashed his finger. He was always unlucky. He was lame because of a thrashing his father had given him. He fell into the sewer, too. As he wore out one of his shoes more quickly than the other, his mother made him wear both shoes of a pair on both feet, changing them each day, so that he used up the two equally quickly. When he wore his left shoe on his right foot, which was the sound one, he limped with both legs and it was very funny to see him hopping on his crutches.

I had seen the real Paris-Madrid races in the Calle del Arenal, at the corner of the street where my uncle lived. There were many policemen lined up so that people should not get run over. The cars were not allowed to finish in the Puerta del Sol as they had wanted to, and the goal was at the Puente de los Franceses. Three or four cars crashed there. I had never seen a racing-car before. All the cars in Madrid looked like carriages without their horses, but those racing-cars were different. They were long and low and the driver crouched right down in them so that you saw nothing but his head—a fur cap and goggles with big glasses like a diver's. The cars had thick pipes which let off explosions like cannon-shots and puffs of smoke with a horrid smell. The papers said they could go up to fifty-five miles an hour. The train to Méntrida, which is thirty-five miles from Madrid, took from six in the morning till eleven, so that it was not surprising if some of those racing men smashed themselves up on the road.

But I liked driving very fast. In our quarter we boys had a car of our own. It was a packing-case on four wheels, and you could steer the front wheels with a rope. We used to race it down the long slope of the Calle de Lepanto. At the bottom we went so fast that we kept on rolling along the asphalt of the Plaza de Oriente. The only danger was a lamp-post at the corner there. Manolo, the son of the pub-keeper, ran into it one day and broke his arm. He yelled, but it was not really bad; they put his arm in plaster and he went on driving with us as before. Only then he was afraid. When he got to the bottom of the slope he always braked with his foot against the curb.

The meadow where we had our races that day was called the "Park of Our Lady of the Port." The grass was thick, and many poplars and horse-chestnut trees grew in it. We used to peel the bark off the poplars; it left a clear green patch which seemed to sweat. The chestnut trees grew prickly balls with a chestnut inside which you could not eat, because it gave you a tummy-ache. When we found any of those balls we hid them in our pockets. Then, when one of the boys stooped, the rest of us would throw chestnuts at his behind, and the prickles would prick him, and he would jump. Once we split one of the green balls open, took out the chestnut and stuck the shell under the tail of a donkey grazing in the meadow. The donkey went crazy, rushed all over the place, kicked, and would not even let his master come near him.

I never knew why the meadow was named after Our Lady of the Port. There was a Holy Virgin in a little chapel; a fat priest lived there who used to take his walks in the meadow and sit down under the poplars. A very pretty girl lived with him. The washerwomen said she was his daughter, but he said she was his niece. One day I asked him why the place was called "Our Lady of the Port," and he told me that she was the patroness of the fishermen. When they were shipwrecked they prayed to her and she saved them. If they drowned, they went to Heaven. But I could not understand why they kept this Holy Virgin in Madrid instead of taking her to San Sebastian, where there was the sea and fishermen. I had seen them myself two years before, when my uncle took me along in the summer. But here in the Manzanares were no boats and no fishermen, and nobody could have drowned there, because the water reached just to one's waist in the deepest spot.

It seemed that the Virgin was there because of all the men from Galicia who lived in Madrid. Every August, all Gallegos and Asturians went to this meadow; they sang and danced to their bagpipes, ate, and got drunk. Then they carried the Virgin round the meadow in a procession, and all the bagpipes went along. The boys from the Orphanage came down too and played in the procession. They were children without father or mother who lived there in the Home and had to learn music. If one of them played his trumpet badly, the teacher would knock it up with his fist and break the boy's teeth. I had seen a boy who had no teeth left, but he blew the trumpet beautifully. He could even play the couplets of the *jota* all by himself. The others would stop playing, and he would blow the *copla* on his trumpet. The people clapped and he bowed. Then the women and some of the men gave him a few centimos, but secretly, so that the Director should not see it and take them away. For the orphans were paid for playing in the procession, but the teacher took the money and the boys got nothing but the garlic soup in the Home. They all had lice and an eye-sickness called trachoma, which looked as though their eyelids had been smeared with sausage meat. And the heads of some of them were bald from mange.

Many of them had been dumped in the foundlings' home by the

mothers when they were still infants-in-arms. That was one of the reasons why I loved my mother very much. When my father died, there were four of us children, and I was four months old. People wanted to make my mother put us into the foundlings' home—so I was told—because she would never be able to keep all of us alive. My mother went down to the river as a washerwoman. I was taken in by my Uncle José and Aunt Baldomera. On the days when my mother was not washing she worked as their servant; she cooked for them, did all the housework, and at night she went back to the attic where she lived with Concha, my sister. José, my eldest brother, at first got his meals in the *Escuela Pía.* When he was eleven, my mother's eldest brother took him into his shop in Cordova. Concha got her meals at the nuns' school. My second brother, Rafael, was a boarder at the College of San Ildefonso, which is an institution for orphan boys born in Madrid.

Twice a week I slept in the attic, because my Uncle José said I was to be the same as my brothers and sister and should not think myself the young gentleman of the family. I did not mind, I enjoyed myself better there than in my uncle's flat. Uncle José was very good, but my aunt was a grumpy old bigot and would not leave me alone. Every evening I had to go with her to Rosary in the Church of Santiago; and that was too much praying. I believed in God and the Holy Virgin. But that did not mean that I wanted to spend the day at prayer or in church. Every day at seven in the morning—Mass at school. Before lessons began—prayers. Then the lesson in religion. In the afternoons, before and after school—prayers. And then, when I was quite happy playing in the street, my aunt would call me to go to Rosary, and on top of it she made me pray before I went to sleep and before I got up. When I was in the attic, I did not go to Rosary, and I did not pray either in the evening or in the morning.

As it was summer then, there was no school. Every Monday and Tuesday I went to the attic; those were the days when my mother went down to the river to wash, and I went with her to play in the fields. When my mother had finished packing up her washing, we went home uphill, up the Cuesta de la Vega. I liked that road because it passed under the Viaduct, a high iron bridge which spanned the Calle Segovia. It was from the top of this viaduct that people threw themselves down if they wanted to take their own lives. I knew a stone slab in the pavement of the Calle Segovia which had cracks because a man had smashed his head on it. His head was squashed like a pie, and the stone broke into four pieces. A little cross was engraved on the slab, so that people should know and remember. Each time I passed under the viaduct, I looked up to see if someone was not just about to jump down. It would have been no joke if anyone had squashed my mother or me. If he had fallen on the sack of washing which Señor Manuel carried home for my mother, it would have hurt no-one. The sack was huge, bigger than a man.

I knew exactly what was in it, because I had helped my mother to count the linen: twenty sheets, six tablecloths, fifteen shirts, twelve nightshirts, ten pairs of pants—a great many things. Poor Señor Manuel had to stoop under it when he wanted to get through the door of our attic. He let the sack slide down gently so that it should not burst, and leaned against the wall, breathing very fast, with sweat running down his face. My mother always gave him a very full glass of wine and asked him to sit down. If he had drunk water he would have died, for it would have stopped him sweating.

He would drink his wine, and then draw a handful of stubs and big coarse cigarette papers out of his blouse, and roll himself a fat, untidy cigar out of the stubs. One day I stole one of Uncle José's good cigars with a gold band and gave it to Señor Manuel. He told my mother, and she scolded me and told my uncle about it. He scolded me too, but then he gave me a kiss and took me to the pictures, because he said my heart was in the right place. After that I did not know whether it had been right or wrong to give Señor Manuel a cigar. I thought it was right, though, because he had been very happy. He smoked it after his meal and kept the stump which he cut up to roll a special cigarette from it. Afterwards my uncle gave me a cigar for Señor Manuel from time to time, and he had never done that before.

The Viaduct was all of iron, like the Eiffel Tower in Paris, only not so high. The Eiffel Tower was a huge iron tower built by a French engineer in Paris for an exhibition, in the year in which I was born. I knew that story very well, because my uncle had the old numbers of *La Illustración* with photographs of the tower and the engineer, a gentleman with a long beard like all Frenchmen. Apparently they never managed to take the tower to pieces after the exhibition was over, so they left it standing so that it should fall down by itself. For one day it would fall into the Seine, the river which flows through Paris, and destroy many houses. They said people in Paris were very much afraid of it; a lot of those who lived in the neighborhood had moved away so as not to get crushed.

It was just the same with our Viaduct: it was sure to fall one fine day. When soldiers had to ride over it, they went very slowly, and even so the whole bridge trembled. If you stood in the middle, you could feel it swaying up and down, like in an earthquake. My uncle said the bridge would crack if it vibrated less; but naturally it would have to break if it vibrated too much, and that was what would happen one day. I thought I would not like to be standing underneath just then, but that it would be interesting to look on. The year before, on *Inocentes* Day, the *A.B.C.*,

which always had very good pictures, published a photograph of the
Viaduct in ruins. It was an All Fools' joke that time, but many people
went to look with their own eyes, because they thought it had to be true
when there was a picture of it. Afterwards they were angry with the paper; but I thought it was the same with them as with me: they were
angry because it was not true.

At each end of the Viaduct was a policeman on patrol, to keep people
from throwing themselves over. If anyone wanted to do it he had to wait
until late at night, when the guards were asleep. Then he could jump.
The poor men must have got terribly bored, wandering round the streets
until they could kill themselves. And then they still had to climb over
the railing. The Viaduct was no good for old people because they could
not climb. They had to hang themselves or jump into the big lake in the
Retiro Park, but someone nearly always pulled them out from there and
massaged their stomach, like lame Antonio's, until they spat out the water
and did not die.

My mother said they wanted to kill themselves because they had not
enough money to buy food, but I would not have killed myself for that.
I would have stolen some bread and run away. They could not have put
me in prison as I was a child. But if people did not want to do that, why
didn't they work? My mother who was a woman worked. Señor Manuel
worked too, and he was a very old man. He carried the heavy sacks with
the washing, although he had a rupture through which his bowels stuck
out. Once he carried a big bundle of linen up to the attic and when he
got upstairs he felt very ill. My mother put him on the bed and pulled
down his trousers. She had a great fright and called for Señora Pascuala,
the concierge, and both together quickly pulled off his trousers and pants.
He had a swarthy belly full of hairs which were nearly all white, and a
bulgy lump rather like a bullock's was hanging down from his parts. My
mother and Señora Pascuala pushed this lump back into his belly with
their fists and fastened his truss over it, a kind of belt which had a pad
over the hole where his bowels slipped out. Then Señor Manuel dressed
and drank a cup of tea and a glass of brandy. Señora Pascuala boxed my
ears because I had been watching, and said children should never see such
things. But I was glad because now I would know how to push Señor
Manuel's bowels back again if ever they slipped out while I was alone
with him. The worst would be if it happened in the street and his bowels
fell right out, for then he would have to die.

Now, Señor Manuel, who had a ruptured belly and smoked nothing
but fag-ends, had no wish to kill himself. He was always cheerful and
played with me. He used to let me ride on his shoulders and tell me that
he had grandchildren like myself in Galicia. He smoked stubs so that

he could visit them every year. My uncle used to get him what they called a charity ticket, and he traveled almost for nothing. When he came back he always brought butter in a round pig's bladder for my uncle. It was sweet, fresh butter which I liked to spread on my bread and sprinkle with sugar. Once I asked him why he did not commit suicide, and he said he wanted to die at home in Galicia. I wondered whether he would kill himself there one summer, but then I thought he probably would not. Besides, he said that people who commit suicide go to hell, and everybody else told me the same.

Our attic was in a large house in the Calle de las Urosas. The ground floor was all stables, with more than a hundred fine carriages and their horses. The boss of the stables was an old man with a queer, flattened-out nose. My mother said he had picked it like I did, and because his nails were dirty, the tip of his nose started rotting one day. They had to cut it off and take a piece off his behind to sew on it instead. Once I wanted to make him angry and asked if he really had a piece of his behind sewn on to his nose, and he threw a scotch at me: one of those heavy wooden wedges which keep the wheels from running backwards on a slope. It missed me and struck the printing-shop opposite. There it hit a rack on which they kept their little boxes with letters and knocked one of them over. The A's and T's got mixed up, and all the boys of our street sat and sorted them out into little heaps.

The gateway of our house was so big that we could play with tops, and at hopscotch and ball there, when Señora Pascuala was not about. Her lodge was very small, squeezed in under the staircase, and the stairs were as big as the gateway; they had a hundred and one steps. When I went down, I jumped them three at a time. Sometimes I used to slide down the banisters; but once I lost my seat and was left dangling outside the railing over the second floor. Nobody saw it, but it gave me a fright so that I thought my heart would burst, and my legs trembled. If I had fallen then, the same would have happened to me as to our water jar. There was no running water in our attic and we had to fetch it from the stables. My mother had bought a very big jar, and even when I went down with it, it was heavy; but when I carried it upstairs filled with water, I had to rest at every landing. And once I dropped it from the second floor and it exploded like a bomb down there. It was from the same spot that I nearly fell myself. When I passed it afterwards, I always kept away from the banisters.

Upstairs there was a large round window with small panes, like some church windows. When the powder-magazine at Carabanchel exploded, the glass broke and was strewn all over the stairs. I was very small then, but I remember how my mother carried me down and into the street in her arms. She ran, because she did not know what had happened. People were very frightened at that time, because so many things had occurred one after the other: a few years earlier a huge meteor had come down in Madrid. Then Mount Vesuvius, the big volcano in Italy, had an outburst, and afterwards came the Halley Comet. There was also an earthquake in San Francisco, a city much bigger than Madrid, and another one in Messina. Many people believed that the end of the world would come after the end of the nineteenth century. I saw the Halley Comet myself, but I was not frightened. It was beautiful. My uncle and I watched it from the Plaza de Palacio. It was a ball of fire with a tail of sparks, rushing along the sky. My aunt had not come out with us because she was too much afraid. She kept all the candles burning before a Virgin we had at home and prayed there the whole night. When we went to bed she closed the wooden shutters very tight, and my uncle asked her if she was afraid of the comet entering our balcony. At that time, a ship with dynamite, the *Machichaco,* had exploded in Santander and blown up half the town. An iron girder had pierced two houses before it stuck fast. *Sucesos* printed a picture in colors, which showed chunks of the ship and arms and legs flying in the air.

Opposite the round window began the passage which led to all the attic flats. The first belonged to Señora Pascuala, it was the biggest and had seven rooms; then came Señora Paca with her four rooms, and across the passage Señora Francisca who had only one room, like all the rest.

Paca and Francisca are the same name, but Señora Paca was one thing and Señora Francisca another. Señora Francisca was an old lady who had been a widow for many years. As she had no money she sold things for children on the Plaza del Progreso, a whole lot of things for two coppers, such as monkey-nuts, hazel-nuts, jacks-in-the-box, and bengal lights. But she was a lady. The other was a big fat woman who walked about in a dressing jacket so thin that you could see her breasts with very black nipples through it. One day I saw a few black hairs sticking through the stuff of her jacket and afterwards I always had to think of her when I saw bristles on a bacon-rind. It did not matter, because I did not like bacon. Señora Paca always went round shouting and screaming; once Señora Pascuala, who had quite a good voice herself, told her that she would get herself chucked out.

Señora Paca was a washerwoman too, but she did not wash at Uncle Granizo's place—only at a laundry in the Ronda de Atocha, where there is no river and they had to do their washing in basins filled with water from a tap. I had been there once. I did not like it. It looked like a factory, with rows of basins full of wash, steam hanging in the air over

them, and the women jostling each other alongside and screaming like
mad. There was no sun and no grass and the linen stank. The drying-
yard with the clothes-lines was a bit of waste ground at the back. Tramps
used to climb over the hoardings and steal the washing. Of course they
sometimes tried to do the same down by the river, but they were less
cheeky there because it was open ground, where the women could run
and throw stones after them, and they always got caught. In fact, the decent washerwomen were at the river, opposite the Casa de Campo; but
from the Toledo Bridge downstream and in the laundries of the *Rondas*
there were only slatterns.

Our passage made a bend, and then came a straight bit, thirty-seven
meters long; I had measured it myself, meter by meter, with my
mother's tape-measure. There was a small window in the corner which
let the sun through, and a large window in the middle of the ceiling,
where the water came in when it rained. It came through the small window too, whenever a strong wind was blowing from the front. That
made two puddles in the passage. When a tile was missing on the roof,
the rain trickled through into the attic, and you put a pan underneath
where it dripped. The passage and the attics were floored with bricks, or
rather with tiles of burnt clay which looked like bricks. They were very
cold in winter time, but our attic had a rush-mat with straw underneath
and so we could play on the floor.

Our attic was Number 9 in the passage. Next door was the attic of the
powder-woman who made up rockets and squibs for children. The
neighbors said she could make bombs and was an Anarchist. She had a
lot of books and was very kind. One night the police came. They went
away without arresting her, but they woke up all the rest of us, because
they turned her room upside down and threw things about.

In the attic next to hers lived Señora Rosa and her husband. He was
a harness-maker and she was shortsighted; she could not have seen
seven-on-a-donkey. They were tiny and very thin and loved each other
very much. They always spoke in a low, soft voice and you hardly noticed
them. They would have liked to have a child, and their room was a
refuge for us when we were afraid of a beating. Then Señora Rosa would
stand in front of her door and not let anyone in, nor us out, until they
promised her not to touch us. She had a very small, very white face, and
very light blue eyes with lashes so fair that you scarcely saw them. She
wore spectacles with thick glasses and my mother said she could see well
in the dark. When she looked at you, her eyes were like a bird's.

Then there was still another attic, the smallest of all. An old woman
lived there, called Antonia, and nobody knew anything about her because
nobody wanted to have anything to do with her. She went begging in

the streets and came home at eleven at night, just before the front door was locked. She would come up muttering to herself, drunk with gin. Upstairs she would bolt her door and start talking to her cat. Once she was sick on the stairs and Señora Pascuala made her scrub the staircase from top to bottom.

At the end of the passage lived the cigarette-maker. She and her daughter worked together making cigarettes for the Queen. They were very long cigarettes on to which they stuck cardboard holders with a fine brush dipped into a dusty little pot of gum. And that was what the Queen put in her mouth. The little pot was of thick green glass, and as they used to wipe their brush on its rim, it always had some hardened drops of gum sticking to its outside, like the wax drops on church candles. When they ran short of gum, Señora Maria scraped off the dried blobs, put them into the pot and poured some hot water over them. Once, she had no hot water ready and used stock from her stewing-pot; and her cigarettes got spotted with grease.

In a corner of the passage was the lavatory. At night I was afraid of going there, for a lot of fat cockroaches came crawling out and ran about in the passage to feed on the garbage cans which all the neighbors put in front of their attic doors. In summer, when you had to leave the door open, you heard them running about in the passage outside, making a small noise like crackling paper. They did not get into our room because my mother had nailed a strip of linoleum along the bottom of the door, the kind of linoleum rich people had in their houses. But lots of them got into the room of Señora Antonia, the drunkard, because it was next door to the lavatory and had no linoleum. Her cat ate them, and it made you feel sick, because when she crunched them they sounded like monkey-nuts.

Big rats from the stables used to get into the house and sometimes came up to the attics. In the stables they had many rat-traps and dogs of the ratter kind. In the mornings, the traps were taken out into the street, often with four or five live rats in them. Sometimes the neighbors and all the children of our street would make a circle, and they would open the traps and let loose the dogs to chase and kill the rats. At other times they poured paraffin over the rats and burnt them inside the wire traps, but only rarely because it made the whole street smell of burnt hair and roasted flesh. Once a rat bit a dog in the muzzle and got away. A piece was missing out of the dog's nose after that. He belonged to Señor Paco, the one who had his behind stitched on to his nose. So the two of them looked alike, and the men at the printers' called them the "pugs."

We had arrived home, and my mother was very tired. Downstairs the milkman lent her a can to carry her milk, so that we had not to go up and down again for it, and she began at once to cook our supper. We were having fried potatoes with fresh sardines and an egg, and afterwards a little coffee, I with milk, my mother black and boiling hot. I never understood how she could stand it like that. While she was cooking, I sat down to read *The Children of Captain Grant* by Jules Verne. From time to time, I stole one of the potato slices just out of the frying-pan. Then she fried the sardines. They smelled good. But my mother would not let me steal one of them, because they were few.

2. Café Español

B Y the time my uncle and aunt had walked down from the third floor and reached our front door, I had already raced down the stairs, banged the glass door, got cursed for it by the concierge, run all the way to the entrance of the Café Español, told Angel I would be with him in a moment, and got back in time for my aunt to take me by the hand, so that I could walk the same way over again with them, very decorously.

The gas jet above our house-door burned with an open flame like a small slice of melon. A little farther on, the pipe from a water main, left without its cap, spilt over on the side-walk. I stepped on it and blocked its round mouth with my sole. The water spluttered out and splashed my aunt's stockings, which made her furious.

It was a clear night with a moon of polished tin plate, which lit up the streets white on black. In the Calle del Arenal, the new street-lamps with their gas mantles seemed to fill the whole street with moonlight. The old jets in our own street looked like the pale yellow flames of matches on the white moonlit side, and on the black moonless side like blobs of quivering light.

When we came to the corner, Angel stopped crying out the evening papers and came up to bid a good evening to my uncle and aunt, cap in hand, his long straight hair falling round his pumpkin-shaped head; he moved like a little old man. He handed my uncle a paper and, as usual,

Uncle told him to keep the small change. We winked at each other, Angel and I, because we knew how and when we were going to meet and play. My aunt was annoyed when I played with Angel, and his mother did not like it during selling hours because then he left off crying out his papers. Our best time was when I had come to the café before the *Heraldo* was out. By the time the paper arrived all damp and smelly from the press, I had wrung permission out of my aunt to go with Angel, after having driven her into her worst temper. My uncle invariably cut short the dispute by saying: "Oh, let the boy run along!" I would take myself off while she went on grumbling to my uncle about how she was afraid of my being run over and how she hated people seeing me run round with a newspaper boy who was, after all, nothing but a street urchin, a ragamuffin who might teach me the Lord only knew what.

Angel would take the pile of newspapers, while his mother stayed in the doorway of the café shouting *"Heraldo!,"* and we started on our expedition through the almost deserted streets of the quarter. We ran, because you have to be on the spot if you want to sell your paper before your competitors arrive. Here and there, maids would open a front door and shout through the dark: "Here, an *Heraldo!"* Angel and I would run across the streets, to and fro from door to door, doubling back on our tracks twenty times. Papers for regular customers had to be delivered to their homes. Angel would enter the front door and run up the stairs, while I waited for him outside. More maids kept coming out of housedoors calling for the *Heraldo,* and then I had to go, as I was left with the armful of papers. If I had had to sell papers, I should have felt ashamed, but as I was not the newspaper-seller myself, it amused me. Most of the servant-girls knew that I was Angel's friend, but all new maids were flabbergasted when they saw a newspaper boy in a starched white collar, silk bow tie, sailor blouse with gold braid, and shining patent leather boots. That was how my aunt made me dress up when we were going to the café, because all the people who met there were better class; and it was also one of her reasons against my going with Angel. In daytime, when I played in the street in my drill blouse and rope-soled sandals, she did not mind Angel, who wore a grown man's jacket given him by one of his customers. It had been taken in to fit him, but it was still too big and the weight of the coppers had pulled the pockets out of shape, so that they dragged along the ground when he stooped.

Our rounds through the quarter by night were an adventure, like the adventures in books. While we were running along, cats would jump up and shoot across the street like bullets, scared by our pounding steps and more scared when we clapped our hands to make them run still faster. They would scramble up a wall and dive into a window. There were garbage heaps at the street corners; the gaunt dogs who burrowed there watched us and growled, so that we went out of their way. Sometimes they would run after us and we had to stop and drive them off with stones. On the steps of the Church of Santiago the tramps were getting their bed-chamber ready; children were bringing up theater bills torn from hoardings, which they used as mattresses. The men sat on the church steps while the boys made the beds. Sometimes they would go into a huddle and send out boys to keep watch on all the street corners. Then they would play cards and the boys had to warn them when the police or the night-watchman were coming. At other times they spread a newspaper on the ground with all the food people had given them, and everybody ate from it. They used their fingers or wooden spoons with a short handle, such as they had in jail or in barracks. In the winter they used to make a bonfire of straw and planks torn from hoardings. They sat round the fire and often the night-watchman or the police patrol would join them for a while to get warm. When it rained very heavily, the big wrought-iron gates of the church would be thrown open and they would sleep under the porch. We never stopped with them, because they often stole children.

Milkmen passed on galloping horses, their milk-cans clattering, and they seemed to us the cowboys of American tales. Sometimes we met the Viaticum. In front walked the priest in his embroidered cope, beside him the sacristan carrying a great square lantern. After them went the neighbors in double file, with burning candles in their hands. There were always a great many old women among them, and all the tramps who had been sleeping at the church gate went along too. They kept the candle-ends they had been given and later sold them to the wax-chandler opposite the church; they bought wine with the money. So the tramps were very pleased when anybody in the neighborhood was dying.

They did very much the same with timber from the hoardings: they tore it off and took it to a bakery in the Calle del Espejo. The master used it to kindle his oven and in exchange gave them great heaps of "crisps"—broken buns and biscuits. As everybody know that the planks of the hoardings got stolen by the tramps, we boys of the neighborhood tore off planks, too, and took them to the same bakery. And the tramps got all the blame.

That night, the *Heraldo* was already out and there were no adventures. It was a pity, because the night was very beautiful.

In the entrance to the café, between the outer and the inner door, there was a square space, some two yards by two. Against one of the walls stood a red-painted cupboard with glass panes, full of matchboxes, cigars, packets of cigarettes, and bundles of toothpicks. In the lower half there were two shelves with piles of newspapers. The glass panes of the entrance door were plastered with illustrated papers and instalments of boys' serials. Señora Isabel, Angel's mother, sat on a low stool squeezed in between the cupboard and the outer door. In that corner she cooked meals on a spirit lamp, mended Angel's trousers or her own vests, counted newspapers, and made toothpicks, whittling down small sticks of wood with a very sharp knife which pared off minute shavings like grated cheese. There was hardly room for her in the corner. But when her eldest daughter and her son-in-law visited her, with a baby-in-arms and two toddlers, they all packed themselves in there so as not to block the passage, and they all got in. Angel's mother was a bundle of nerves; when she was alone she never stopped gesticulating, talking to herself and swearing. When she was angry, she was like a mad cat and Angel would not go near her.

As we passed by her, she greeted us and gave me a whole heap of matchboxes with colored pictures for my collection.

Most of our party was already sitting round our regular table, a table with a round, white marble top, which had room for twelve people: there was Don Rafael, the architect, who was eternally cleaning his glasses with a handkerchief he kept in his breast-pocket. When he got into a discussion, his handkerchief and his spectacles were constantly between his pocket, his nose, and his hands. Don Ricardo—Maestro Villa, the conductor of the Madrid Municipal Orchestra—short, pot-bellied, and always merry, was the only one to drink beer, while the others took white coffee. Then there was Don Sebastian, the father of Esperancita, a little girl who used to play with Angel and me, and Don Emilio, the parish priest of the Church of Santiago, a fat, hairy man; the hairs on his finger-joints were tight little curls which looked like ink-stains, and his stubble pricked my cheeks when he kissed me.

There was Doña Isabel and her sister, Doña Gertrudis. Doña Isabel was the mistress, and Doña Gertrudis her servant, because ever since she had been a widow, she had lived in her sister's house and been supported by her. Doña Isabel wore bright silk dresses and always had a fur or a feather boa round her shoulders. The other dressed in mourning. Doña Gertrudis had a black scarf round her head, and Doña Isabel a huge hat with dyed plumes of the kind known as *pleureuses* which danced like a feather duster when she talked or moved her head. Doña Isabel had a round face and a sagging, lumpy skin. She used a lot of white powder with rouge on top of it, and she painted her eyes and lips. Her dresses were cut so low that it left her whole neck free, and her throat hung in a pouch like a pigeon's crop. The face of Doña Gertrudis was like a church candle, long and yellow. The two sisters had a flat on the same floor as my uncle.

Finally, there were Modesto and Ramiro, the pianist and the violinist of the café; they were paid five pesetas a day, and got their supper and white coffee.

The cleverer of the two was Ramiro, the violinist. He could walk between the tables without using his stick, and when he went up to the piano no one could have told that he was blind. He recognized everybody by their voice and their step, and could tell false money with his fingers. I was very fond of him, but he made me afraid when he took off his dark glasses, because his eyes were like the white of an egg; he wore the spectacles so as not to frighten people. His hands were small and chubby and they seemed to search you. At times he would call me and pass his hands over my head, face, and body. When his fingers touched my eyelashes, nose, lips, ears, neck, and hair, it seemed to me as if his fingertips had tiny eyes which were looking closely into my skin. Afterwards, he used to tell me with great conviction that I was a handsome boy, and I believed him because he never made mistakes. I had two silk bow ties, exactly alike, both with little white spots, but one was blue and the other red; and Ramiro could tell with his fingers which one I was wearing.

Modesto had empty eye-sockets with glass eyes in them; when they looked at you, they made you uncomfortable because they did not move. He was very grave, Ramiro very gay. Modesto was tall and thin, and Ramiro short and round, so the two looked like a blind Don Quixote and a blind Sancho Panza. Modesto often petted me, but he never looked at me with his hands.

My aunt sat down beside Don Emilio, the priest, and began to talk to him about the church. The rest of the men were talking politics and my aunt would not let Don Emilio join in. Whatever she said, he always answered: "Yes, Doña Baldomera. . . . No, Doña Baldomera," until in the end she left him alone and started discussing the neighbors in our house with Doña Isabel. In the meantime, she was preparing my special cup of coffee, which was one of my aunt's tricks to save money. The waiter brought a cup for my uncle, another for my aunt, and two glasses of water. I got a thick breakfast-cup of the kind used for chocolate. Manolo, the boy, came with the big coffee-pots and filled my uncle's cup with black coffee and my aunt's with milk. Then he poured a little coffee and a little milk into each of their glasses, and my aunt gave him a copper. She got to work with the two cups and two glasses until she had the same mixture in all of them; then she filled my big cup with white coffee and still had two full cups left for my uncle and herself.

As soon as the mixing was over, I gulped down my coffee and went off with Esperancita who had been pinching me from behind my chair because she wanted to play. We plunged into the labyrinth of screens, chairs, and sofas. The sofas ran along the walls, and we loved to scramble on all fours through the sunk lane between their backs and the tables. When we banged our heads against a table and got bruised, we stood up on a sofa to look at ourselves in the big mirrors. Our shoe-soles left marks on the seat and Señor Pepe, the head-waiter, came and scolded us. We tried to wipe out the marks by slapping the sofa, but clouds of dust rose up and our hands left red patches outlined in dusty white. Señor Pepe became 'angry and cleared away the dust with his napkin, without slapping.

At other times we scratched the red velvet the wrong way and drew letters and faces which we rubbed out by stroking down the pile with our palms. When we made our drawings, the little hairs of the velvet tickled our fingertips as if a cat were licking them, and they turned into a cat's back when we smoothed them.

The manager of the café was watching us from behind the counter. We slipped away, up the small staircase to the billiard room, opened the green baize door and crept in.

I see it today with eyes I did not then possess:

A huge room with many windows along three of its walls and all the lights out. Yet, coming in through the windows on the one side, the white glare of the arc-lamps in their wire-screened globes, which frightened the moths with the splutters and sparks of their carbon and the sudden crackle of their mechanism, and from the other side the livid flares from the old gas jets in the Calle de Vergara with their hissing, melon-slice flames. In the middle of the room eight massive tables, their square shadows swaying with the shifting, varying lights, their varnish throwing sparks, the blotting-paper of their green cloth sucking in the rays. The long shadows of the window frames, sketching black crosses at broken angles on floor, tables, and walls. All asleep, all silent, and so resonant that a low word wakes murmurs in every corner and the gently pattering noise of a fleeing mouse startles us, as we stand timidly on the threshold. The padded door closes softly behind us.

The sight of the balls, glittering through the netting of their little sacks, encouraged us to carry on our adventure. The sound of the first balls knocking against each other broke the heavy silence, and we snapped out of our tension into mad canters round the tables, snatching all the balls from their pockets, and pouring our booty on to the central table which seemed to us the most dignified, the mother of all the tables. Running round and round its six elephant feet, we jumped through the weaving lights and dipped our hands into the living sea of balls which were running over the green cloth, lighting it up with white and red glints and banging their heads against each other with the dry rap of bones.

The sudden glare from the lamps in the room being switched on all at once, and the black sweep of the manager's ferocious mustache caught us perched on the top of the green lawn and turned us to stone, while the last balls were still running out their course and knocking against their neighbors just when we wanted them to stop and be silent. We leaped from the table like monkeys in flight and rushed down the narrow staircase up which we had come on tip-toes, jumping the steps three at a time, pursued by the threats of the ogre. We tumbled into the café with faces scarlet from excitement and fright.

My mother had come. When we got near our table, Esperancita ran and hid behind the red curtain over the entrance. I went after her, and through the glass panes saw my mother talking with Angel's mother and Señor Pepe, the waiter. Esperancita was in the secret and we talked things over quickly. She ran out from behind the curtain towards the other door of the café, further down the room, and I followed her. Esperancita disappeared behind the curtain of the other door, and so did I, but instead of hiding there we ran out into the street and went round to the front entrance where the newspapers were. My mother was still there in the little lobby. We kissed and hugged each other, and I told her in a rush all about the trick we had invented so that I could come and kiss her without my aunt seeing it.

We ran back the same way we had come, and went on romping all over the café as though nothing had happened. But I explained to Esperancita once again why we so often had to act a little comedy:

"You see, my aunt gets very angry if she sees me kissing my mother. She wants me only to kiss her, and she doesn't want me to love my mother at all. And when she's angry she says I'm an ungrateful boy, because it's she who's keeping me, and then she has a row with my mother and says my mother's behaving as if she was afraid of my being stolen from her. So if my mother and I want to kiss, we always hide."

In the meantime my mother had come in and sat down beside my aunt. Pepe had brought her a cup and a little dish with sugar; I went to their table, just gave her a pat on the shoulder, said "Hullo!" and took one of her lumps of sugar. Then I ran away to go on playing. My aunt was pleased.

We found a set of dominoes on a table near by and began building houses with the stones. I could see my mother quietly drinking her coffee and my aunt talking away to Doña Isabel, probably the same old stories about our neighbors.

My mother was a very small woman, rather plump, with quick movements. Her skin was very fair, her eyes gray like a cat's, and her brown hair had only a few white strands on the temples; she did not look her fifty-odd years. She was wearing a black skirt, a gray calico blouse, a striped kerchief on her head, and a striped apron.

My aunt was sixty years old. She had a black dress with embroidered flowers and a black veil over her white hair. Her face was old, but it looked like fine porcelain and she was proud of the natural pink of her cheeks and the silkiness of her hands. But my mother had hands as soft as my aunt's and even smaller. Sometimes that annoyed my aunt who used to put cream on her hands and rub them with lemon and glycerine; she would tell my mother that she did not understand how anyone could keep such hands, working as my mother did.

My aunt was the mistress and my mother the servant, just like Doña Isabel and Doña Gertrudis. She came and sat down to drink her coffee with the others after she had cleared my uncle and aunt's supper table, scrubbed the pots and pans and swept the dining-room and kitchen. Sometimes she would join in the general conversation, because the others liked her very much and kept asking her questions, but usually she kept silent and waited for an occasion to slip away and have a talk with Angel's mother or Señor Pepe.

The party broke up at eleven o'clock and we went home, my aunt and I in front, my uncle and my mother behind. It was earlier than usual and we had missed our game with Angel who had just finished selling his papers and looked ruefully after us, for our going meant that he would be alone until closing time. We had to get up very early the next morning, because in the afternoon, my uncle, my aunt, and I were going into the country for the summer holidays. My mother was going to sleep in the flat that night. Although the coach only left in the afternoon, my aunt had to start packing and preparing the food already in the morning. She was sure not to leave us in peace all day with her restlessness. As usual, it would be my mother who would have to put up with her, because my uncle would take me along to see the changing of the guard in the morning and we would not come back until lunchtime. That was his method of getting away from her every Sunday.

When we got home, my cat and I drank my milk together on the dining-room table, as we did every night. My uncle sat down opposite us, while my aunt pottered round in the bedroom next door, preparing the night-light which also had to serve instead of a lamp for her Virgin. Then it suddenly occurred to me to say to my uncle:

"I want to sleep with my mother tonight, because we're going away tomorrow."

"All right, go to bed with her."

My aunt appeared in the bedroom door and burst out: "The child will sleep in his own bed, just as he does every night!"

"But, my dear——" said my uncle.

"None of your 'my dears', and none of your 'buts'! It's better for the child to sleep alone."

"But if the boy is going away tomorrow and wants to sleep with his mother for once, why can't you let him? After all, doesn't he sometimes sleep in our bed because you happened to have a fancy for it, and I'm sure he must sleep worse in a bed with two people than with one."

My aunt bridled and began to scold: "I said 'no,' and 'no' it is! The boy would never have dreamed of wanting to sleep with his mother if she hadn't put the idea into his head." And she called shrilly for my mother: "Leonor, Leonor, the child will sleep in his own bed, because I want him to! There's been quite enough pampering already, and the child gets his own way far too much."

My mother, who did not know the reason for this to-do, came in looking baffled and said: "Well, his bed's ready."

At my mother's quiet voice, my aunt sank into a chair and began to shed tears on to the table.

"You're all trying to kill me by breaking my heart! You're all in league to make me suffer! Even you"—she turned to my uncle—"you're in the conspiracy with them. Of course, you say 'yes,' and then there's nothing to be done about it. I know what it is—you've worked it out between you, and I, poor thing, have to swallow it and say nothing."

My mother, tense with anger, took me by the arm and said: "Come along, now, say good night to your uncle and aunt, and go to bed."

My aunt had another explosion:

"So that's it! Everything's settled! Well, the child will not go to his bed tonight, he will come to bed with me!"

My uncle banged his fist on the table and got up, furious: "The woman's crazy and she'll drive us all crazy"

I got violently excited, clutched my mother's skirts and shrieked: "I want to go to bed with my mother tonight!"

The tears and cries of my aunt redoubled, and in the end she got her way with the help of my mother, who restrained her own emotion and pushed me towards my aunt.

In their bedroom I wept, feeling deserted by my mother and hating my aunt who insisted on undressing me between sobs and cuffs, changing from bursts of tenderness, which smeared my face with tears and slavers, to attacks of rage in which she pinched and shook me. In the end my uncle lost what patience he had left and told her firmly to shut up. We went to bed, and I lay between the two. My aunt began to say her rosary and I had to say it with her, while my uncle read the *Heraldo* by the light of a candle on his night-table. As usual, my aunt went to sleep before she came to the second decade of the rosary; her mouth hung half open and showed the gap left by the two front teeth which were swimming in a glass on her night-table. After a while, I turned cautiously to my uncle and whispered:

"She's asleep now, I want to go to my mother."

My uncle placed a finger to his lips and very softly asked me to wait. He blew out the candle and we both lay in the semi-darkness of the night-light which threw fearful shadows on the ceiling. After a long while my uncle lifted me carefully out of bed, gave me a kiss and told me to go off without making a noise.

I crept along the passage into my mother's room, next door to the kitchen, touching the bedclothes in the dark, and said that it was me, so that she should not be afraid. She asked me anxiously to go back. But when I told her that my uncle had helped me to get out, she made room for me in her bed. And there I lay with my back to her, rolled into a ball in the crook of her arm. The cat jumped on to the bed and butted his way under the top sheet, as he always did. The three of us stayed very quiet, so as to fall asleep.

A drop of water fell on my neck and the cat licked my face.

3. Roads of Castile

AN HOUR before the coach was to start, my uncle, my aunt, and I were already sitting in a corner of the taproom, beside us two suitcases and a basket with food and water bottles, for once on the road one could get nothing but well-water. My uncle took his thick silver watch with its tiny little key from his pocket, opened the case and showed the dial to my aunt:

"Now see how unreasonable you are! We're an hour early."

"Maybe, but at least I don't have to worry."

I went into the doorway of the inn where the coach was standing, still without its mules, the wheels cluttered with lumps of mud from the road. Many of the passengers were waiting there, leaning against the wall, baskets and saddle-bags stuffed with parcels at their feet. All were country people: a fat man, made still fatter by his saddle-bags; a little old woman with a blackish face; a big, stout woman with child, accompanied by a big and a little girl; and a few more men and women. I wondered which of them were going with us in the coach and which had come to see their people off. The grooms led the mules out of the gateway in pairs and harnessed them to the coach. The rear pair had to be backed into their place and were tied to the pole with a lot of tackle. It was interesting to see how difficult it is for animals to go backwards.

As soon as the mules were harnessed, all the suitcases and parcels were put on the top of the coach and the people began to take their seats. Of course, my aunt had to be among the first to enter the coach and wanted my uncle and me to get in as well. My uncle left her to grumble all by herself and took me to the confectioner's shop to buy sweets for my cousins in the village. We bought a lot of green peppermint drops which stain your fingers like wet paint and burn your tongue because they are so strong. But the country people like them best of all. We also bought two pounds of *paciencias,* small round biscuits the size of a copper, of which they gave us a big bagful. We took our parcels to my aunt who at once started to scold because we would not get in; she was afraid the coach would leave without us. My uncle paid no attention to her and went with me to the tavern, to drink beer with lemon fizz.

Among all the people in the tavern, my uncle was the only gentleman from Madrid. Everybody was in country clothes except us: my uncle had his black alpaca suit, his starched shirt, and bowler hat, my aunt wore her embroidered black dress and black mantilla, and I my white sailor suit. That morning my uncle had had a row with my aunt because of our clothes. He wanted to put on an old jacket and an old pair of trousers, and to travel in a cap and carpet slippers, and he wanted me to go in my blouse and rope-soled sandals. But she protested and said that, thank God, we were not beggars. And as usual, she had her way. My uncle, who was stout, already had to push a silk handkerchief under his stiff collar to be less bothered by sweating, and from time to time he took off his hat and wiped the sweat from his bald head. With his starched shirt front, cuffs, and collar, he was cursing the "stupid ideas" of my aunt, as he said. If I had been in his place, I thought, I would have dressed just as I liked, and if she had been angry, she would have had to swallow it. But he was so good that he put up with all her whims rather than annoy her.

When we entered the coach at long last, it was not easy to squeeze in. All the seats except my uncle's were occupied, and we had to push through all the people to get there. I had to stand between my uncle's knees and we waited for the coach to start. The heat was unbearable. The people were wedged together and their heads almost touched the low roof of the coach. On the top, the handyman was tying the bundles fast and loading up the last pieces of luggage; and every step of his shook down dust on our heads and sounded as though the boards were going to crack. The coach was completely full and the groom for the mules had to get on to the left mule in the lead, because three women went on the box-seat beside the driver, packed as close as sardines. Two men, who only wanted to go to Campamento, were standing on the footboard; they paid fifty centimos fare.

The coach screeched while we were rolling down the steep slope of the Calle de Segovia. The brakes were put on so hard as almost to stop the wheels from turning, and still the coach nearly ran into the mules. It sometimes happened that the coach overturned half-way down the hill and the journey came to an end.

After crossing the Segovia Bridge, we went uphill again along the Extremadura Road. At the Segovia Bridge, Madrid ended and the country began. To call it country was only a manner of speaking, though, because there was nothing but a few shriveled little trees along the road, without leaves and covered in dust, fields of yellow grass with black patches from bonfires, and a number of shacks built by the rag-pickers out of the sheet-metal from old tins, with big garbage dumps outside the door, which you could smell from the road.

My aunt did what she always did on a journey. As soon as the coach began to move, she crossed herself and started saying the Rosary. Her beads were of olive-wood which had come from Palestine, from the Garden of Olives, and had been blessed by the Pope. At home she had another rosary of silver beads, and a third one of agates which she had brought from France, from Lourdes; its cross had a small crystal set in the middle, and when you looked through it you saw Our Lady in the Grotto.

The road was full of ruts and dust. The coach went bumping along and the dust came in through the open windows so that we were enveloped in a cloud. When you moved your jaws your teeth chewed sand. But the sun was so fierce that we could not have shut the windows without getting stifled. One of the women felt sick. She knelt on the seat and stuck her head out of the window to vomit. In the intervals between vomiting, her head bounced up and down in the window like the head of a stuffed doll. By the time we arrived she would have spat out the lining of her bowels, for she started being sick twenty minutes after we left Madrid, and we still had over four hours to go.

I began to feel hungry. With all that fuss and hurry not to be too late for a seat in the coach, I had not had a bite since lunch. I said so to my aunt, and she got cross with me. She told me to wait until she had said her Rosary, but she was only half-way through. Opposite us sat a fat man. He had taken out a loaf of bread with a *tortilla*—a potato-omelette—inside, sandwich-fashion. It smelled very good. He kept on cutting off pieces with his clasp-knife and eating them, and it made me ravenously hungry to watch him. I would have loved to beg a bite off him. Again I asked my aunt for something to eat, this time in a loud voice; surely the fat man would let me have a piece of his *tortilla* if she did not give me anything. And I wanted to make her so angry that she would refuse to let me eat, for she had taken nothing but bread and chocolate along, and what I wanted was the omelette. She did get angry. She pinched my thigh and gave me nothing. The fat man cut off a large chunk of bread and a slice of *tortilla* the size of half a brick, and offered them to me. My uncle let me take them and scolded my aunt: "Must you always make a fool of yourself?" Then she produced the bread and chocolate, but I did not want them any more. The *tortilla* was fine, and the man gave me a few slices of dry sausage on top of it. I enjoyed it even more because I had got my way and my uncle had taken my side. He got out the leather bottle with the wine for our supper, accepted the *tortilla* himself, and so the three of us ate and drank. The two men started discussing me; the fat man took my uncle to be my father.

He told us he had a son who was studying law in Madrid, but had failed in his exams, and now was cramming to have another go at them in September. My uncle said that I was a very good scholar, and the fat man answered that his boy was a young rascal who cost him all the money he was earning from his farm. Then the two went on to talk of the crops. The man had a good deal of land in a village near Brunete and knew our whole family there; he had known my uncle's father and grandparents.

After the row about the food, my aunt had started telling the woman with the little girl, who was sitting opposite her, all about the worry and annoyance I caused her. I did not want to hear what she said, because otherwise I would have had to answer back and tell all about how she kept nagging me.

Our coach was going downhill into the valley of the Guadarrama, a river very much like the Manzanares, with hardly any water, nothing but a bed full of sand and a little stream running through rushes. The road made many bends and twists between the town of Móstoles and the river; there we had to cross a very old wooden bridge, so old that the passengers had to get out of the coach to lessen its weight. And then up another long slope, ending in Navalcarnero.

In the market square of Móstoles there stood a half-finished monument hidden under scaffolding and white sheets. It was a statue of the Mayor of Móstoles, and was meant to be inaugurated the following year, 1908, the Centenary of the War of Independence. That Mayor of Móstoles had been in office when Napoleon tried to conquer Spain. He was an old fellow in a coffee-brown cloak with tiers of shoulder-capes, a big, wide-brimmed hat, and a tall staff. When he heard the French were in Madrid, he called the town-crier and gave him a proclamation to read to all the people of the town. And in it he, the Mayor of Móstoles, declared war on Napoleon. Of course it was foolish to think that a little place like that could make war against the armies of Napoleon. But if Napoleon had come to Móstoles and the Mayor had got hold of him all by himself, he would certainly have beaten him to death with his mayor's staff. In my *History of Spain* there was a picture of the Mayor reading out his proclamation, and a portrait of Napoleon in his greatcoat with white lapels, white trousers, and his hand thrust between the buttons of his coat.

Father Joaquín, my history master, a very tall Basque, told us that Napoleon could not conquer Spain because there were many people like the Mayor of Móstoles who were not afraid of him. In Madrid, two artillery lieutenants, Daoiz and Velarde, took a cannon and put themselves at the head of the people. In Saragossa, a woman, Agustina of Aragon, egged on the men and started firing off a cannon against the French. In Bailén, all the goadsmen—the herdsmen who kept watch over the wild bulls, riding on a horse and carrying a goad—got together and went out against the cuirassiers. They had nothing but their wooden goads with steel points, while the cuirassiers had strong lances, a plated steel cuirass and a steel helmet with a feather bush. The cowboys just wore their jackets and their flat-brimmed hats, and there were far less of them than of the cuirassiers. But they gave Napoleon's cuirassiers such a thrashing that an Englishman called Wellington, who came to Spain to help us, was quite taken aback. The people in his country would not believe him when he told them about it.

My grandmother, my mother's mother, was a very small child when Napoleon's soldiers came to those villages. The French killed children with their bayonets, sticking them into their bottoms. So my grandmother's parents put her in a basket, let her down the well of the house, which had a vaulted side-shaft, and hid her there. Her mother went down to give her the breast whenever the soldiers were not looking. My grand-mother was ninety-nine years old now. My brother and sister and I called her "Little Grandmother," for she was a tiny, wrinkled old woman, her face and hands covered with coffee-colored spots. Our other grand-mother we called "Big Grandmother," because she was much taller than a man and very big. We were going to meet her in Navalcarnero.

The mules were changed at the coaching-inn, and in the meantime the people had supper, either their own food or a meal from the kitchen of the inn. We had hake fried in batter and pork fillets with fried red pep-pers, and my uncle invited the fat man to eat with us, because we had eaten up his *tortilla*. We also had black coffee which my aunt had taken along in a bottle wrapped in a thick layer of newspapers, so that it was still hot.

Big Grandmother sat down with us and lifted me on to her lap. It was like sitting in an easy-chair. She and my aunt began to chat, and as usual, they soon quarreled. When both were little girls, they had played to-gether in their village; they still called each other the first thing that came into their minds. My aunt was a bigot, and my grandmother an atheist. When they were both about twelve years old, their parents sent them to Madrid into service. My grandmother served in many houses before she married. My aunt started as a maid with a very old, very pious lady and stayed with her until she married my uncle. It was being with her old mistress which turned her into a bigot for good.

The two were different even in their manner of eating. My aunt ate tiny morsels, and my grandmother tucked in as much as the fat man, who stuffed as though he had never eaten the *tortilla* and the loaf of bread. And during the meal they discussed me.

"It's high time the boy got a bit of fresh air and stopped being tied to your apron-strings," said my grandmother. "You're turning him into a ninny with all your priests and prayers. Just look what a booby-face he has! It's a good job he's going to stay with me for a few days. I'll soon shake him awake!"

"Well, there's nothing the matter with the child," my aunt bridled. "The only trouble with him is that he's very naughty, and that's why he doesn't put on weight. As to his education, I can't imagine what you can have against it. Except, of course, that you would like the boy to become an unbeliever like yourself. It would be better for you if you remembered your age, as I do, and that you will go straight to hell if you carry on like this."

"All the better, it's warmer there. And anyhow, all good-humored people go to hell, and all tiresome bigots like you go to heaven. And I can tell you frankly, I prefer to be with amusing people. You simply smell of wax."

"Jesus Christ, you're always saying blasphemous things, and you'll come to a very bad end."

"I'll be damned! If I say anything blasphemous, it's because somebody's trodden on my corn in the street, or because I pinch my finger in a door. After all, one's a woman, and not a carter! What I am not, and what I don't want the boy to become is a hysterical woman like yourself, who can't get away from the skirts of the priests and sacristans!"

My aunt started to sob, and then my grandmother felt quite miserable. In the end, they made it up and my grandmother said:

"Now, look here, Baldomera, of course I know that you're very kind and that the boy has a very good home with you, but all the same, you're turning him into a fool. You go on praying as much as you like, but let the boy play. Because that's what you want, isn't it," she added, turning to me, "to play?"

I did not want to make my aunt even more annoyed with me, so I said that I liked going to church very much. And then my grandmother exploded:

"You're a sissy, that's what you are!" And she squeezed me in her big arms and crushed me against her breasts, and it was as if I was being smothered by a feather-bed. I felt hurt and said nothing, but two big tears ran down my face. And then my grandmother lost her head. She took me in her arms, kissed me, hugged me, shook me like a doll, and made me promise to come and stay with her in September and to give her my word that I wasn't angry with her. She took me along to the bar-table of the tavern, filled my pockets with monkey-nuts and roasted chick-peas, bewildered me with a stream of questions, and only calmed down after I had assured her again and again that I was not angry, but that I wasn't a sissy either, and that, if she called me a sissy again, I would not visit her at Navalcarnero.

We arrived in Brunete at ten o'clock that night. I was completely worn out and only wanted to go to bed.

The village was a heap of houses, deep black shadows on very white walls gleaming with the same light as the moon itself. People were sitting or lying in the doorways to get a breath of air, a few chatting, but most of them asleep. When we walked through the village to the house of Uncle Hilario, my Uncle José's brother, the people got up to welcome us, and some offered us doughnuts and brandy. I didn't want any, the only thing I wanted was to sleep. The night watchman of the village came up to us, slapped my uncle on the shoulder, patted me and said:

"So, you're a man now!"

Then he stood on tip-toe, stretching his neck like a cock about to crow, put one hand to his mouth and shouted:

"Eleven o' the clock, and clear!"

4. Wheat Lands

T H E sunlight, speckled with flies, streamed through the small square window over the head of my bed. The room smelled of village, of sundried grain in the corn-loft opposite, of furze burning in the kitchen, of clinging reek from the chicken-coop and of dung in the stables, and of the mud walls of the house, baked dry by the sun and covered with whitewash.

I dressed and went down the stairs, massive logs hewn with the adze.

The ground floor was a huge room floored with small river pebbles. Beside the doorway were the water-racks which carried eight big-bellied pitchers of white clay, beaded with moisture; their linen cover had a centerpiece with initials a span long, embroidered in red wool. In the middle of the room stood the table of stout pine planks, white from being scrubbed with sand and big enough to seat the whole family and the farm-hands, some twenty in all. Seeds which had to be sorted out were spread out on it, and when Aunt Braulia ironed the household linen, her ironing blanket covered no more than one of its corners. Along the walls stood a great number of chairs of plaited straw, a heavy mahogany commode, and a chest with a rounded lid covered by a tawny-haired hide and studded with gilt nails and a lock like an old door knocker. Above the chest was the cuckoo-clock, its brass weights hanging from gilded chains, its pendulum running from one side to the other without ever bumping against the wall, a little bunch of flowers painted in each of the four corners of the wooden dial, and above it, the little window of the cuckoo, a small wooden bird which chanted the hours and half-hours. When the hand of the clock was about to reach the full hour, it stopped as though it had found a pebble in its path. Then it made a sudden jump on the dial and one of the weights fell down very fast, setting the whole machinery turning so that it rattled like a box full of nails. The din frightened the cuckoo; he opened the door of his little house and began to sing, curtseying and stretching out his neck to see whether this time the weight had not got smashed on the floor. When he had sung the hour he went back and shut the door until the half-hour, when he came out, but only gave a single cry in a surly way, as if he had been disturbed for something silly which was not worth his while.

The cuckoo-clock always reminded me of the village night-watchman, and the night-watchman reminded me of the cuckoo-clock. The man walked to and fro in the village street the whole night, watching the clock on the church tower and the sky. Every time the clock struck the hour, he had to cry it out and announce the weather: "Two o' the clock, and clear. . . . Two o' the clock, and cloudy. . . .Two o' the clock, and raining." In times of drought, when people were afraid of losing their crops, neighbors would wake each other up as soon as the night-watchman sang out the hour and "raining." They would go and stand under their doorways to get wet, and some would go out to their fields to make sure that the water was falling on them and not only on the fields of their neighbors.

At the far end of the room there was the hearth, with the larder on one side and the door to the stables on the other. The hearth was a circle of tiles, flanked by two stone benches. Above it was a bell-shaped chimney lined with soot; you could see the sky through the hole at the top. On the wall hung the pots and pans, ancient copper and iron pots, blue-and-white Talavera jars and kitchen irons, spits, grills, and so on. The wide shelf of the mantelpiece was stacked with dishes, bowls, and crocks, in their middle a big, round platter like a sun. It was an earthenware platter half an inch thick, with dirty blue flowers on a greenish-yellow ground and a rim of metallic blue. This was the oldest piece of crockery in the kitchen. On the back it had a curious sign like a tattoo mark and an inscription in blue old-fashioned lettering which said "Talavera 1742."

Aunt Braulia used to scour her metal things with lye made from dung ash. Her iron looked like silver and her copper like gold. The ash came from the hearth, for the fire was a big heap of dried dung with a heart of embers smoldering day and night. If you thrust a shovel through the crust you saw a ball of fire red as a pomegranate. You stuck the iron point of a huge pair of bellows into its middle, blew on it, and a flame would leap up. Then you threw furze into the flame to keep it burning, and put the three-legged frying-pan on top of the fire. When you had finished that part of your cooking, you closed the fire-hole with the shovel and nothing was left but the yellow, smoking heap of dry dung and the ring of pots round it, in which the stews were slowly simmering. Red sausages and black-puddings were hung inside the bell of the chimney to be dried and cured by the smoke.

When I came down there was nobody in the room but Aunt Braulia, who was sitting on a low stool beside the fire. The first thing she said was that I must be hungry and she would get me my breakfast at once. They were all crazy about my food whenever I stayed in the village. They had got it into their heads that they had to stuff me and fatten me up. But in reality there were far less things to be had in Brunete than in Madrid. In Brunete, the only fruit was grapes from the grape vines on the house walls, and they were not yet ripe. The only meat they ever saw was lamb and pork from the last slaughtering, laid in pickle or smoke-cured. I knew beforehand the kind of meals I would get: fried eggs for breakfast, a stew of chick-peas with bits of red sausage, bacon and mutton at midday, and potatoes boiled with a piece of meat or dried cod in the evening. Occasionally a man with a donkey brought a few cases of sardines or hake from Madrid, but not in the summer, for the fish would have gone bad on the journey. So the only fish they got in the village were dried-up sardines out of the grocer's barrel, their eyes and bellies yellow with oil, or dried salt cod. There were no green vegetables. Brunete lies in a dry plain without trees or water, where nothing grows but wheat, barley, chickpeas, and vetch. They had to fetch their water with donkeys from two miles away, from a ravine which was just a kind of crack in the ground, petering out in the far distance towards the Sierra.

For food I preferred Méntrida and Navalcarnero to Brunete, above all Méntrida, where my mother's people lived and where I was going to stay after Brunete. Méntrida had orchards and gardens, game, partridges, and rabbits, and there were fine fish and eels in the river near by, the Alberche. They also got fish by train from Madrid. And the village always had plenty of beautiful grapes and tomatoes, cucumbers, and lettuce. In a place called Valdiguera there were hundreds of very old fig-trees which had round, fat figs with bright red flesh and a taste of honey; people called them *melares,* "honey-sweets." Every family owned two or three of those fig-trees, and when I came to visit them, they would all invite me to pick myself figs early in the morning when the chill of the night was still on them.

Méntrida had all those things because it lies in the valley of a little river flowing into the Alberche, which has a strip of poplar-grown meadowland with many garden plots.

Brunete had a few wells, but they were very deep and the water was brackish. In Méntrida, every house had a well of its own, and many had to make a ditch from the well to the street, because the water would overflow in winter. It was very cold, sweet water.

Navalcarnero was different again. It lies on the top of a hill and in the town itself there is nothing, but its fields, which all lie on the slope down to the river Guadarrama, produce grapes, fruit, and vegetables as well. Moreover it is so near to Madrid that it gets most of the things to be had in town.

Yet with all that, it was Aunt Braulia who prided herself most on her cooking. Other people in Brunete had nothing but an onion and bread in the morning before going to work in the fields, a *gazpacho*—bread, onions, and cucumber in vinegar and water with very little oil—at midday, and a stew in the evening, made just of chick-peas and a slice of bacon. They tasted meat only two or three times a year. But Uncle Hilario, Aunt Braulia's husband and the eldest brother of my Uncle José, had become one of the richest men in the village.

There had been six brothers, and all escaped when lots were drawn for the call-up, except my Uncle José. At that time, conscript soldiers stayed in barracks eight years. When Uncle José was called up, he was just a yokel like the others and could not read or write. They had been a very poor family, as there were so many children; they only got chick-pea and bacon-rind stews, and at that the poorest chick-peas which they had kept back for seed, because the picked ones fetched more money and they sold them. In barracks, Uncle José learned to read and write. In the meantime his parents died and his brothers worked their land in common and married. Although my Uncle José had left his share of the land to them, they were starving, what with all the wives and the children who soon arrived. In those years it sometimes happened that they had no money to hire mules or donkeys to till their fields, and then the men and women would draw the plow. Aunt Braulia had drawn it many times. But meanwhile Uncle José, who had no intention of going back to the plow, had become a sergeant and after his discharge he got a post in the War Ministry, because he had beautiful handwriting and was good at figures. Then he began to save up money and to lend it to his brothers, so that they had no more need to beg loans from the village usurer to whom they had to pay a peseta for every five he lent them. And after the wheat harvest they no longer sold the grain to the usurer either, because my uncle sold it in Madrid for them. They all shared in the profits. Then came the Cuban war. My uncle had lent money to other people in the village as well. One day he went there, called all his relations and the older men of the village together and told them that, if they let him have their wheat, he would sell it for them to the army people in Madrid at a much higher price than they got from the usurer. Then they became rich, and my uncle gave them enough money to buy more land and mules. They all worked together under Uncle Hilario, but it was my Uncle José who was in command. The other half of the village lands belonged to the people who were in debt with the usurer.

The usurer was a distant relative of ours, Don Luis Bahía, who had left the village when he was a little boy and later became a millionaire through the Jesuits. He was one of their agents; my Uncle José said he himself really had no money, and the money he lent to people belonged to the Jesuits, who got hold of the land in that way.[1] I knew him from Madrid, for he had dealings with my uncle and I went along to his office a few times; but he scared me. He was old, bald, with a big head and a very fleshy nose curved like the beak of a parrot, and he watched you out of very cold eyes. His skin was like yellow wax. He always wore a black suit, with black office-sleeves up to his elbows, and a round silk cap with a tassel. His office was papered a dark green and the crocheted net curtains on his balcony windows were green too, so that the whole room was in darkness and his face looked like the head of a slimy beast in its lair. Once, in Méntrida, I had seen a big toad sitting among the water weeds, and I thought of him.

I ate the fried eggs and red sausage Aunt Braulia put before me, and then went out to the threshing-floors.

The village was a single street through which the main road passed. The fields, already cut, were yellow with stubble. In a place where the ground rose lay the threshing-floors. They were flat circular spaces paved with round cobbles, which had to be swept very clean before the sheaves were spread out. Then a stout plank studded with spiky flint-stones, a kind of harrow, dragged by a mule, went round and round the carpet of wheat ears, separating the grain from the straw. The boys rode on the plank, one to guide the mule and all the others as a game. We would jostle and push each other from the rocking plank and tumble on to the mattress of straw. The only risk was of falling in front of the plank and being run over by the harrow. This had happened to one of my small cousins, and it left scarred lines all over his back as though he had been tattooed by Indians.

Farther away on the threshing-floors, men winnowed the crushed straw, tossing it into the air against the wind, so that the chaff was blown away and the heavy grains left. We boys ran into the cloud of chaff, rowing with our arms and shutting our eyes, and our skin got full of tiny needles which stuck and would not let us sleep at night. Then we rolled in the hills of clean wheat until the hard grains filled our ears, mouth, and nostrils, and slipped into our socks and pockets. At least, that was what

---

[1] After the death of Don Luis Bahía, a lawsuit, widely discussed all over Spain, was fought over his will by which he left over thirty million pesetas to the Society of Jesus.— *Author's Note.*

happened to me. But my cousins' skin was so tanned by the sun and dust that the straw needles did not prick them, and they had neither socks nor sandals, for they all went barefoot, and no pockets either, such as I had in my blouse. They wore nothing but a shirt and a pair of knickers tied with string round their middle. What bothered me most was the sun. During the first days in the country my skin always went pink, my nose and cheeks peeled, and I kept on changing my skin like a lizard, until I was nearly as brown as my cousins by the time I went back to Madrid. But I never went as brown as Uncle Hilario.

Uncle Hilario was a tall old man with large bones, very much dried-up. He had a completely bald head full of lumps, with a wen on top which looked like a plum; but the skin of his skull was so dark you hardly noticed that he had no hair at all. The skin at the back of his neck was coarse and dry, and seamed by deep wrinkles which looked as if they had been carved with a knife. He used to shave on Thursdays and Sundays, as priests do, and then the shaved part of his face was so much whiter than the rest of his head that it looked as though it had been rubbed with emery paper. Sometimes he took one of my hands, which were rather soft and thin, laid it on one of his own big, broad hands with broken nails, and made a bewildered face. Then he would press my hand between both of his, and I imagined what would happen if he were to rub his hands: he would skin my hand with the hard, calloused lumps on his palms. The wood of the plow-handle shone like the varnished rails of our staircase at home, because Uncle Hilario had rubbed his hard palms over it so often.

At noon the church clock struck twelve, and we all went back to the house to eat. Aunt Braulia had laid the table and put a deep dish in the middle, into which she poured stew from an iron pot over a hundred years old. It had been burned by the fire until it looked like black porous clay. On each side of the table stood a big, long-spouted flagon of wine, but only my uncle, my aunt, and I had glasses. The others drank from the free jet, holding the flagon at arm's length and tipping the spout. It was the same with the food. The six children all ate from one bowl. The grown-ups ate from the big dish. But as we were there, they had put plates for the three of us, and for Uncle Hilario and Aunt Braulia. The children and farm-hands ate what was left over when we had been served.

After the meal it was too hot to go back to work at once, and all took a short siesta. Some simply lay down on the stones in the doorway which was very cool because the entrances from the street and from the stable were both covered with a thick curtain, so that the sun was shut out but a current of air let through. And the two stone benches by the fire were very cool, for they were in the strong draft that swept up through the chimney.

At two the men went back to the fields, but they left me behind because the sun was too strong for me while I was still not used to it. So nobody woke me, until I wakened by myself at five o'clock.

Both my aunts were standing in the doorway with three other women, telling all the stories of the village since they had been young. I would have liked to play, but my cousins were working now and I was afraid of going out into the street. As there was not a tree in the village and all the houses were white, the street was like an oven and even the stones were too hot to be touched. So I made a voyage of discovery all round the house.

In the corn-loft, which the village people simply called "the loft," were three big heaps, wheat, barley, and vetch, piled up to the rafters. There were big, dense spiders' webs, and for a time I amused myself catching flies. I tore their wings off and threw the flies into the spiders' webs.

A fly got entangled in the web, and the spider stuck her head out of her hidey-hole. After a short while she came running out, her body like a black chick-pea slung high on legs like bent wires. She wrapped a leg or so round the fly and carried it off. When she was running across her web, I thought she was going to jump on me and bite me. I felt sick and scared, so I took a broom and started to smash up all the cobwebs. From one of them a fat yellow spider with a body like a boiled clam fell on to the floor, ran along the boards and came very near to my feet. I stamped on her and ran down the ladder of the loft. Downstairs I wiped my shoe-sole on the hearth stones. Some bits of hairy legs came off it, still jerking.

There were swallows' nests on the rafters near the doorway. I put a chair on the chest and climbed up to see one of them from close to. I wondered how the Chinese were able to eat swallows' nests; they were nothing but small bowls of hard mud. Inside they were lined with wheat straw. Nobody would have hurt a swallow, for the swallows eat vermin in the fields, and when Christ was crucified, the swallows picked thorns out of His brow.

Once my Uncle José caught a swallow and tied a thin silver wire round one of her legs, and she came back the next year. But after that she never came back again. She had probably died in the meantime, for swallows have a short life. But storks live very long. It was because of the story of the village stork that Uncle José had tried to find out about the swallow.

On the roof of the church there was a stork's nest like a heap of firewood. Once the priest who was in the village at the time, a very old man who used to collect wild insects, caught a stork and put a big copper ring with the inscription "Spain" round one of his legs. When the stork came back the next year, he had round his other leg a silver ring with letters nobody could read; but a professor who came from Madrid specially to see it said they were in Arabic and read "Istanbul," which meant a province in Turkey. Then the priest tied a little ribbon with the national colours to the ring, and the stork came back with a red ribbon instead. That stork died in Brunete, and the priest kept the two rings and seven red ribbons in the sacristy of his church.

There were other birds in Brunete too, but none of them could be eaten. There were the black-and-white magpies which liked to walk about in the road, stepping like little women. There were the crows, a smaller kind of raven, which came in flocks and called "ca-ca-ca-ca." They turned up when a dead mule had been thrown into the ravine, and ate it. For whenever a mule or donkey died in the village it was taken out to the ravine where the spring was and thrown into a deep hollow there. This hollow was far away from the spring and from the village, but I went there once, and it was full of white skeletons of mules and donkeys. The crows were sitting round the ravine and cackling. They were like malicious old women grousing and grumbling. When you came near they rose into the air and kept flying in circles over your head, cawing and calling until you went away.

There was still another kind of bird, the bats. They came out in the dusk and began to fly through the village street and to bang against the house walls because they were white. We boys hunted them with a tablecloth or other white cloth tied to two sticks which we held over our heads. When the bat bumped against the white cloth, we clapped the sticks together, and the bat was caught in the folds. Then the bats were nailed to a wall by their wings. Their wings were like the thin fabric of an umbrella, but hairy, and tore without bleeding, as easily as an old rag; their body looked like a mouse with a little pig's snout and pointed ears, like the devil's. When they were wrapped in their wings, they seemed old women in big shawls, and when they were hanging asleep from the rafters, they seemed little children such as the storks carry in their bills in fairy-tales.

When the bats were stuck on a wall, the men used to light a cigarette and make them smoke it. The bats got drunk with the smoke and made funny movements with their nose and belly and eyes, which filled with water. We laughed a lot. But when I saw them nailed to the wall, drunken with smoke, I was sorry for them and I thought they were a bit human, like a baby that has slipped out of its swaddling clothes, with its little tummy naked. And once I tried to explain to the people what I had

learned at school: that the bats eat vermin. But they laughed at me and
said they were foul beasts which sucked the blood of sleeping people,
biting them behind the ears. And they said a girl had died that way; or
rather, not quite died—but she had grown whiter and whiter, with no
blood left in her, and nobody knew what was the matter with her until
they found a bat in her bed, and a small drop of blood behind her ear.
They burned the bat and gave the girl its ashes to eat mixed with wine,
on an empty stomach. And she got well. For this reason, they killed all
the bats they could, so they said.

But when they grew tired of torturing a bat, one of the lads tore it
from the wall, and the poor beast lay on the gutter stones, moving the
tatters of its thin wings and wrinkling its little nose, and I could not
believe that it had ever been capable of killing anyone.

Brunete was a boring village. Its fields had no trees, and no fruit, and
no flowers, and no singing birds, and men and children were rough and
taciturn. Now, when the wheat was harvested and they had made some
money, was the only time when they had a little fun, at the fairs. But they
were the poorest fairs I knew. A few traders set up stalls in the market
square, lighted by small oil lamps or candles, where they sold trash for
two coppers. But nobody bought anything, so they used to raffle it for
what they could get, which was the only way to get rid of their stuff. A
fireworks-man came to the fair and let off fifteen or twenty rockets in
front of the church every night between ten and twelve, that was all; only
on the very last day he lighted five or six catherine wheels.

The only things that amused those people were the bulls. And even
this amusement showed the kind of brutes they were.

The village square was unpaved, full of ruts, with an iron lamppost
on a stone base in the middle. Round this plaza people would draw up
their carts on the eve of a bullfight; the shaft of each cart was riding on
the bottom planks of the next and all of them were roped together so
that they should not slide apart. This was a sort of barrier and a gangway
with an uneven floor, where people could stand. The village lads and the
children would squat between the wheels, in reach of the bull's head,
and from there they would watch the fight or sally to take part in it.
The bulls were kept penned up in a blind alley opening into the square,
where the butcher had his corral. It was called Christ Alley.

The fiesta started on the first day of the fair with what they called the
"Bull of the First Drop," because he was let loose almost at dawn, at the
time when the men took their early morning glass of spirits. The carts
filled with women, old men, and children who shouted when the bull
came out—a bull-calf, good enough to be played by the village lads.

At first the little bull attacked and threw the lads. But he was so small and young that they managed to hold him by the horns, drag him to the ground, kick him with their heavy boots and beat him with their sticks. At eleven in the morning he reeled on his legs and gave no more fight, but fled from the gang of lads and boys who by then all dared to come out into the plaza. He backed against the wheels of the carts, but from there they pricked at him with knives and the old men held their burning cigar butts against his haunches to make the beast attack again in blind rage. And so it went on till noon.

We watched from the balcony of the Town Hall, where we stood with the mayor, the doctor, the apothecary, and the priest. The mayor and the priest were both fat men, they roared with laughter and slapped each other on the back as they pointed out each detail to one another.

At four in the afternoon the real bulls began. First the village lads fought two young bulls which had learned cunning in other village bull-fights and tossed the boys against the carts as though they wanted to avenge the bull-calf of the morning. They stayed in the ring a long time until there was no one left who cared to brave them. Then they were driven driven back into the corral, and the "bull of death" was released.

He had to be killed by a team of four *maletillas,* torero-apprentices who went round the villages fighting bulls, and starving. As they did not come from this village, the mayor had bought a huge old bull with enormous horns, taller than any of the little bull-fighters. The poor lads cowered when he came into the square and they saw his bulk, but the village people began to shout and some of the young men jumped into the ring, brandishing their sticks.

It was a pitiful thing to see those lads in their shabby, patched-up bull-fighter's costume, its gold spangles tarnished or missing, running round the bull's head in little spurts and flicking their cape under his nose, only to flee, and then to clamber up the lamppost when they were driven away with sticks from the cart barrier. But there was worse to come.

The bugle of the band sounded the banderilla tune, and the public bellowed with joy. For now it was not enough to make little dashes at the bull. Now the banderillas had to be placed, and that meant being at the very horns of the bull. And the little toreros knew only too well that their hope of gain lay in this feat, and in the killing.

It was the custom to dedicate each pair of banderillas to one of the rich men of the place. Then, if they had been placed well, that is to say, in the nape of the bull's thick neck, the rich man would shell out two *duros*—ten pesetas—or even five *duros,* and when the team made the round of the carts to collect, people would fill the cape with big coppers and one or the other silver coin thrown in. If the banderillas were not

placed, there was no money, and if all banderillas failed, they usually
got stones instead of cash.

The lean and hungry little torero takes up his stand at the far end
of the plaza. He turns his pallid face and looks back distrustfully at the
sticks of the village lads threatening his back, some with a spike and
some with a knife tied to their points; and he turns again in panic to
look at the savage beast in front of him up to whose horns he must get,
so as to raise his arms, stretch his belly and chest in a single movement,
and drive home the be-ribboned sticks before the horns are driven into
his own body.

And there is the "pass of death." The matador is as a rule a young
lad of seventeen or eighteen, more suicidally inclined than his comrades,
with the face of a mystic. He needs an inspired skill to fight bulls in those
villages. If he were to kill the bull by a clean sword thrust, so that it is
felled without having to be finished off, the people would feel defrauded.
He must play the bull for a long time, he must thrust to kill, not once
but many times, with art and courage. He must not jab at the bull's ribs
or shoulder blades from the side, but hurl himself at its horns. And only
then, when he has demonstrated his valor and made the women shriek
with fear ten times over, may he lunge and thrust in his sword, to the hilt,
if he can, wounding the bull in its entrails so that it is left standing in
the ring on four straddled legs, vomiting blood in dark gushes until it
crumples up, turning over on its back, its legs thrashing the air.

Then the public goes mad with enthusiasm. Silver coins, cigars, and
pieces of sausage rain down, and uncorked wine bottles pour wine on the
people in gushes as the bull had vomited its blood, and the little torero
must drink from those bottles to quench his thirst and to bring some
color back into his cheeks.

For the occasions when the bull gores young flesh, there is a little door
in the Town Hall, which says "First Aid." Inside is a pine table, scrubbed
with sand and lye, and a few pitchers of hot water. On a straw-bottomed
chair in a corner lie the doctor's case with a few old instruments and, for
safety's sake, the butcher's carving knives and meat saw. The wounded
lad is laid on the table, naked, and given a rough and ready treatment.
The blood is staunched with wads of cotton wool, soaked in iodine as
one might soak sponge-fingers in wine, and pressed on with bare fingers,
and the gash is stitched up with thick needles and coarse, twisted silk
yarn reeled off a ball, which the old women of the village prepare, just
as they prepare the thread to tie the umbilical cord. Then the boy is put
on a mattress and taken in a cart to Madrid, along a road full of sun and
of dust.

As a quiet little boy, perched on the chair with the doctor's case, I have seen one of those butcher's cures done to a lad with his head dangling from the table, his eyes glazed, his hair dripping sweat, whose torero dress had been slit open with a knife, so that they could get at a gash in his thigh so deep that there was room in it for the doctor's hand. When the bull-fights are over, the people dance and drink.

5. Wine Lands

THE square iron rod of the axle passed right through the middle of the cart. It had no springs and leaped so violently every time the wheels bumped over a hole or stone in the road that you had to take care not to get a knock. Uncle José and Uncle Hilario sat in the front seats and passed each other the reins of the mule from time to time. My aunt and I sat at the back, facing each other. The small, two-wheeled cart had two lateral wooden seats covered with rush mats, a roof of curved canes with a white canvas tilt, and a pair of canvas curtains in front and at the back. We were going to Méntrida, but Uncle Hilario was going to drive back in his cart that evening so as to sleep at home in Brunete.

When you reach the crest of the hill you see the road-mender's hut and a whitewashed well with a cone-shaped roof. It has a window with an iron grille that can be locked and inside a bucket and chain so that all who pass by on the road may drink. From there the hill slopes down, and you can see Méntrida.

The yellow and gray fields of the dry earth, without trees and without water, stay behind, and the green land begins. From the mountains of the Escorial, purple in the distance, to the hills of Toledo at the end of a horseshoe of far-away ridges, the land is utterly green, green with trees and green with gardens. The cornfields are yellow patches and the vineyards white patches flecked with green; for the soil of the vineyards is whiter and sandier than that of the wheat lands. Scattered between the vines in many of the vineyards are olive trees, large posies of silver green amongst the bright green of the grape vine.

Méntrida is ringed by a chain of hills, all of them tunneled: they are

its wine-cellars. For if Brunete is the land of bread, Méntrida is the land
of wine. When you look at the hills from afar they seem pitted with
black holes. Each of these holes has a low oaken door with a padlock and
above it a small, square window with crossbars through which the wine
draws its breath, the wine in the fat-bellied earthen jars standing in the
niches of the cave. If you put your face close to one of the little windows,
the hill smells drunk.

The streets of Méntrida climb up the hills around the ravine which
passes through the middle of the village and is its sewer. On the highest
hill, at the far end of a street too steep for carts, stands the church. The
house of my grandmother, my mother's mother, was in the little square
before the porch, and our cart had to make a loop round the village to
get there.

It was a small house. If you looked at it from the church terrace it had
one story, and if you looked at it from the street on the hillside it had
two stories. If you went in by the front door you had a basement under
your feet, and if you walked in by the side door you had a story over
your head, so nobody ever quite knew which floor he was on. The door on
the hillside was always locked, and the door on to the church terrace
was a swing door with a sign-board on top of it, which showed a high
ladies' boot with innumerable buttons and the lettering "Shoemaker."

The shoemaker was my Uncle Sebastian, a tiny old man with many
wrinkles—but not so many as my grandmother had—who was married
to my mother's sister, Aunt Aquilina. Uncle Sebastian made and repaired
boots and shoes, but by this time he took in only little work, because he
suffered from asthma. Apart from Grandmother, there lived in the house
his daughter Elvira with her husband Andrés, and their two children who
were much younger than I was. My brother Rafael and my sister Concha
were staying there for a time too.

When our cart stopped in the little church square, they all came out of
the door, one after the other. Rafael and Concha were first, they came
running out to greet Uncle and Aunt to see whether they had brought
them anything from Madrid. Then came my two little cousins, shuffling
along like two funny little animals. The boy was very thin, with a big
tummy and a big head; he was called Fídel and had a yellow face with
ears which looked as if they had no blood in them and were of wax.
The girl was called Angelita and when she moved, her steel corset and
the steel joints of the boots she had to wear creaked. After them came
their parents, he a big, strong man and she a woman who was always
ailing and limped from an ulcer on her leg. Then Aunt Aquilina and
Uncle Sebastian came out arm in arm, a cheery old couple, always happy.
And last of all came Grandmother Eustaquia in her black dress, with her

nobbly stick, little gray eyes, chin and nose almost touching each other, and a skin like brown parchment, as wrinkled as a dried fig. Next year she would have her hundredth birthday, if she did not die before. But it was more likely that she would bury all the rest. She was up at five every morning, sweeping the house, lighting the fire and making breakfast. She could never keep still for a second and went trotting about from one floor to the other, tapping with her stick so that nobody could go on sleeping. As soon as she saw that our eyes were open, she would chase us out of bed, calling us sluggards and saying that beds were made for sleeping, not for dawdling. And you had to jump out of bed if you did not want to risk a whack from her stick.

Uncle José and Aunt Baldomera were going to spend the night there, but they had to catch the train to Madrid at six in the morning. It was a most boring day, because they were treated like fine folk from Madrid. We stayed in the house all the time, my brother and sister wore their best clothes, and the grown-ups spent the whole afternoon telling each of us in turn to keep quiet and not to quarrel. We would have liked to get out and run about, but as we could not do that, we had a number of rows which all ended with my brother's and sister's ears getting boxed, because of course it had to be their fault. Nobody would have dared to smack me in front of my aunt. But my sister pinched me and whispered:

"You just wait till tomorrow, I'll rub your nose in the dirt for you. You'd better make the best of it while your dear auntie's here!"

And I made the best of it, of course, by repeating her threats out loud, which earned her some more cuffs. In the end they turned the pair of them out into the street so that we should get some peace. I stayed indoors, very cross because I could not go out with them, and at the same time very pleased because everyone had taken my part.

Andrés was a master mason, and he told my uncle stories about how things were going in his trade. Uncle Sebastian was sitting on his cobbler's bench and did nothing but cough and grunt. As he liked me very much and I liked him very much too, I went to him and asked him what was the matter.

"This damned cough's choking me, my boy," he said between two wheezes, "and your aunt won't let me smoke, which is the only thing that helps my cough. . . . As though at my age anything mattered anyhow."

I went to Uncle José and asked him:

"Give me a cigarette for Uncle Sebastian, please."

They all cried out, but I explained that Uncle's Cuban cigarettes were so mild that they could not do him any harm. So they let him smoke. He stopped coughing and they had to admit I was right. Uncle José gave him a whole pack of cigarettes. Uncle Sebastian smoked them hungrily, one after the other, and at nightfall he had a very bad fit of coughing, I did not know whether because he had run out of cigarettes and wanted some more, or because he had smoked too many.

Next morning we all went down to the station with my uncle and aunt. It was more than three miles from the village and we had to go in the cart of Old Neira, the mail carrier, who took passengers to and from the station. He also owned an inn and wagons which carted wine to Madrid. It was still night when we got up, for the train passed through at half-past six and we had to make our journey to the station in the dawn.

The truth of it was that I was already waiting for my uncle and aunt to be gone. I would have been glad if Uncle had stayed on by himself, for he left me alone, but my aunt was impossible. On the other hand I was afraid that my brother and sister would get even with me for the cuffs of the day before. At the very last moment my aunt started giving good advice to Aunt Aquilina and me: about the right food for "the child"; about what "the child" liked best and what disagreed with him; about the clothes I ought to put on; about my going to Mass on Sundays and saying my morning and evening prayers; and that they must take great care so that I should not be run over or be bitten by a dog. When the train started moving, I thought they all were glad to see the last of her; she was still leaning out of the window and shouting instructions.

On our way back to the village, Old Neira stopped at a market garden he had by the roadside, and brought us a heap of cucumbers, tomatoes, and purple-skinned, mild onions. He took bread, dry sausages and a leather bottle of wine from his saddlebags, and we had breakfast there in his garden. The cucumbers and tomatoes still had the night chill on them and they were good to eat, sprinkled with salt. If my aunt had seen me, she would have cried to heaven, for I ate five or six cucumbers, and she would have thought I was going to die on the spot.

We had only just got home, when Aunt Rogelia, another of my mother's sisters, entered in great excitement:

"It's past belief that you shouldn't have come to see us yet! It's one thing that you can't stand my Luis"—she addressed my grandmother— "but it's quite another thing that the boy shouldn't even be allowed to visit his aunt!"

They told her it had not been their fault; that my uncle and aunt had not gone out all afternoon and that we had just seen them off to Madrid; that in any case I should have gone to see all my relatives that day.

My Aunt Rogelia, who was a plump little woman, strong and energetic, took me by the hand and said firmly:

"Well, all right then, he's coming to eat with me."

Aunt Aquilina protested, saying she had already prepared a meal, but all her arguments were in vain. I was pleased, because Uncle Luis's place was wonderful. So we trotted through the village and stopped at every house, because my aunt had to show me off to I don't know how many relations and neighbors.

When we got to their house, we found my Uncle Luis surrounded by village lads, sharpening plowshares. He did not interrupt his work. We had to step gingerly around the crowd, or we should have risked a knock on the head from one of the hammers they were all swinging. In the little house at the back my two girl cousins were just tidying up, and they hugged me and kissed me. Aunt Rogelia brought out some buns and I ate a couple of them, but then I slipped away to the forge.

My Uncle Luis was the village blacksmith, and his two sons, Aquilino who was nineteen, and Feliciano who was sixteen, were his assistants. He was a big, tall, stout man in a leather apron and rolled-up sleeves. The skin of his arms was very white, with black smudges all over. In one hand he would hold the great tongs which gripped the end of a red-hot horseshoe, and in the other hand a little hammer, with which he beat time for the sledge hammers wielded by Aquilino and the other lads and struck the hot iron when he wanted to shape it. That was always a marvelous thing to me.

He would put a piece of iron in the furnace, and Feliciano and I would pull the chain of the bellows—a bellows big enough to hold the two of us—in a regular rhythm, so that it fanned the coal until the iron was glowing white and throwing sparks. He would place the iron on the anvil and the lads struck one after the other with their heavy sledge hammers, flattening and lengthening the iron which spat glowing chunks and grew first red and then purple. Uncle Luis shifted it with his tongs so that each blow struck the right place. Suddenly he would smite a few light blows on the nose of the anvil which rang like a bell, and start hammering the iron all alone until it changed shape, curved, fined down at the points, and became a horseshoe. Last of all he struck a small flap out of the curve itself, which became the calk for the toe of the hoof. Then he gripped the punch in another pair of tongs, and Aquilino struck it home with his sledge hammer, one blow for each nail-hole. Uncle Luis always had seven holes made, for he said that it brought good luck to find a horseshoe with seven holes, and he wanted to bring good luck to the whole world.

My Uncle Luis belonged to a race of men which has almost disappeared; he was a craftsman and gentleman. He was so deeply in love with his craft that to him the iron was something alive and human. At times he talked to it. Once he was commissioned to make the wrought-

iron railings and window-screens for the "castle" as people called the
house of the richest landowner in the place. The masterpiece, a screen for
a tall window, as large as a balcony, was to be placed in the middle of
the façade over the doorway. He took no money for it, so as to have the
right to let his imagination run riot with his hammer and to shape the
iron to his taste. Into that screen he poured his vision of a fancy world
of leaves and tendrils twining round stout bars, perhaps influenced by
his visits to the great silver screen in Toledo Cathedral, which he knew
by heart.

Physically he was a Castilian of the old breed, a man with a cast-iron
stomach. He rose with the dawn and "killed the worm," as he said, with
a glass of brandy which he himself had distilled in a patched and mended
copper still, from the crushed grapes out of which he had pressed the
juice for his wine. Then he went to work in the forge. At seven he had
his breakfast, a stewed rabbit, or a brace of pigeons, or something on that
scale, with a big bowl of salad. After that he forged his iron until noon
when, with the stroke of the bell, he stopped and went to eat, even if
the iron had just left the fire.

His midday meal was either the true Castilian *cocido,* chick-peas
studded with chunks of bacon, red sausage, and ham, with bits of chicken
and large, greasy marrow bones, or else a rich potato stew, with more
chunks of meat than potatoes. For dessert he ate half a melon—and the
average melon weighed four pounds in Méntrida—or two pounds of
grapes, or a platter full of sliced tomatoes. At five he had an afternoon
snack, as solid a meal as his breakfast, which only whetted his appetite
for a supper as substantial as his midday meal. All day long a gallon jar
with red, frothing wine stood by his anvil, to spare its master the taste of
water which, as he said, "bred frogs."

He owned a field of wheat, a strip of garden land, a vineyard and six
fig trees. In the course of the year he found time and means to till his
land, to mill his wheat, to make his wine and to dry his figs in the sun
for the coming winter. His house was an ever-full larder. To add to its
riches and to please his own palate, he would go out in the dark of night
and come home in the small hours, two or three rabbits in his pouch, or
his wicker basket filled with fish from the Alberche, still alive.

He had married my Aunt Rogelia against the considered opinion of
both their families, for at that time he was half starved and had nothing.
The two went to work like donkeys and in time grew more comfortably
off than the rest of their relations. The woman, small in stature but strong
in body, tackled the job which had fallen to her with inexhaustible energy
and gaiety. To cope with his meals alone seemed a miracle, but she also
looked after the food and the house, the chickens, and the pigs, she baked

the bread and she took care of their four children who arrived one after the other, as though she wanted to waste no time in childbirth. My aunt never took to her bed before giving birth. When she was big with child, she went on washing, scrubbing, and cooking tirelessly, as always. Suddenly she would say to her husband: "Luis, it's coming." She would lie down while he called a neighboring woman who understood about such matters. On the following day a cup of chocolate and a good chicken broth, thick as though stirred with flour, put her on her legs again, and she went back to her cooking and scrubbing as if nothing had happened.

They were a happy couple and had no problems. She was woman enough for all the needs of her powerful male, and in their youth, when the two of them were building up the forge between them, it was no rare thing for the door to be locked and the pair to turn a deaf ear to the knocking of customers. When they opened again, he would stand there, filling the doorway with his mighty body, smiling slyly at his neighbors' jokes. He used to plant his huge hand on her plump shoulder with a smack, wink at the joker, and say: "Just look at her—small and round, but as hot as red pepper!"

When I came to the forge, the men were still hammering away at the broad blade of the plowshare, and Feliciano was pulling the bellows-chain without stopping, so that the second plowshare should be ready when they had finished the first. As I knew that nobody would take any notice of me just then, I took hold of the chain and pulled in time with Feliciano, who slapped my shoulder with his free hand and said: "Hullo, Madrileño!" That was all; his brain could never hold more than three words at a time. He was the stupidest of the whole family.

When they had finished the plowshare we had been heating with the bellows, Uncle Luis lifted the gallon jar with one hand, and filled a tall, thick glass with wine. It made the round of the lads and each wiped his lips with the back of his dirty hand. My uncle drank last, filled the glass again and handed it to me: "Come here, sparrow!"

It was his first word of greeting. He lifted me on to the anvil with only one hand.

"Here, drink it up, you need some blood in you." He turned to the lads and said: "I don't know what the blasted hell they give the kids in Madrid to keep them as thin as spooks. Look at the calves he's got!" He squeezed my leg between his forefinger and thumb until I thought my flesh would split. "You ought to stay here in the forge as my apprentice in your holidays. And no more petticoats for you. What with the old women and the priests, they'll be turning you into a sniffling sissy."

I drank down the whole glass of wine, like a man. It was a dry, strong wine which made you feel hot. Aquilino, in a gust of affection, picked me up from the anvil and swung me through the air, round and round, like a rag doll. When he set me on the ground I was half choked with fright and wine.

"This afternoon," he said, "I'll buy you a spinning top and make you a point with the lathe."

Making points for spinning tops was something Aquilino was very proud of, and all the village children ran after him for them.

The points he made had a long, square spike at one end which he stuck red-hot into the wood of the top. The other end he either turned on the lathe until it had the shape of an acorn, or else filed it down to a narrow point with a groove spiraling down it. It was not easy to fix a point. You had to get it right into the center of the top, and then it would hum and "go to sleep," as we used to say. Otherwise it would wobble and scratch you if you put it on your palm.

I never got bored at Uncle Luis's. Beside the door of the forge stood a work-bench with a vise, and there were rows of tools on the wall, and odd bits of iron all over the floor. You only had to pick up one, fix it in the vise, and start filing it. I liked mechanics; I was going to be an engineer when I was older. This time I wanted to make a wheel. I made a circle on a piece of sheet iron with the big calipers, and then began to file it down. But my brother and sister turned up. First they went into the house to see our aunt and get their buns, and then they came back for me. Concha took me by the arm and said:

"Come along and let's play. I've told Aunt."

The forge lay at the end of the village. We only had to climb the slope of a little ravine and were in the open country. Concha went first and I followed. She was very thin and had her hair twisted into a tiny little bun at the back of her neck. Her legs showed under her petticoats; they were sunburned and her muscles moved like cords while she climbed, Rafael came behind me, silent and sulky. When we reached the top we followed the edge of a harvested field along the wall of brambles which bordered it on the side of the ravine.

I knew my brother and sister better than they thought. I knew that the storm was going to break. Concha would shout at me and shake me until she got tired of it. If I answered back, we would come to blows and then I would get it. I was the smallest and weakest. If I gave her time to let off steam, she would not beat me up in cold blood.

And so it was. When we came to the clearing where the old trees stood round the source of the stream which ran through the village, Concha turned round and clutched my arm:

"Well, now we've got him, the spoiled little baby. But there aren't any aunts or nephews here, nor any petticoats to hide under. So you think because we live in the attic and you at the flat, dressed up like a little gentleman, that we aren't as good as you are? Well, you'd better get it into your head that you're no better than us. You're the son of Señora Leonor the washerwoman, and now I'll bash your mug in so you remember!"

She shook me like an old rag and pinched my arm until it stung. I said nothing and hung my head. Rafael stood watching us with his hands in his pockets. Concha grew more and more excited: "Look at him, just like a silly old hen. Well, that's just what he is. Now you're not crowing any more, are you? Now you're like a dead fly! Grandmother Inés is right when she says you're a lying Jesuit. Now you dare to hit me, I'm a girl, you just dare!" And she stuck her fists under my eyes.

"Shall I shake him?" asked Rafael.

Concha looked me up and down contemptuously: "What for? Can't you see he's a sissy?"

The insult struck home, coming on top of my grandmother's insult which I had not forgotten, and I saw red. The three of us rolled on the ground, kicking, hitting, and biting. After a while the big hands of a man cuffed us apart and held my sister and me firmly separated, one on each side of him, while we kicked at one another behind his back. Rafael had become perfectly quiet and glared spitefully at the man. Concha stamped on his foot—he wore only rope-soled canvas shoes—and he swore and boxed her ears. He was my ally then, so I kicked her on the shins. We both wrenched ourselves free and got at each other, I pulling her hair, she clutching my neck. I grabbed handfuls of hair, she dug her nails into me.

The man carried us to the forge, one under each arm, our legs threshing the air. Rafael followed behind us without a word. The man took us in and explained to my uncle:

"Here, take 'em, they're like a pair of wild cats."

Uncle Luis looked at us calmly. Both our faces and legs were covered with scratches and we glowered at each other under half-shut lids.

"You do look pretty." He turned to Rafael and said: "And what have you got to say, Pussyfoot?"

"Me? Nothing."

"So I see. So it was the two of you against the smallest, was it? You're a nice pair of heroes."

"He's just a nasty, dirty louse," screamed my sister.

"They're jealous because I live with Uncle," screamed I.

"I'll settle this," said Uncle Luis. "You make it up now, at once, d'you hear? You've got all worked up, but now you'll be friends again. And the first time I catch you making another shindy, I'll give each of you such a hiding that you'll go lame for a week."

We washed our faces in the water of the trough where the iron was cooled. Uncle Luis put a thick cobweb over a gash in my knee: "Now, leave it on, it stops the bleeding and it'll heal your scratch." And so the plaster stayed there, a web full of dust and blood which grew as hard as clay.

We ate stewed rabbit in a dark, strong sauce of garlic and bay leaf cooked with wine, and the meal meant peace. When we left we were friends, the three of us, but I was the master because I had a silver *duro* in my pocket, and the market square and streets around were full of stalls. A *duro* was five pesetas or a lot of big coppers, and the things on sale did not cost more than ten centimos each. Village people, who recognized me and knew I had just come from Madrid, called me and bought me so many monkey-nuts, hazel-nuts, and roasted chick-peas that all my pockets were full of them. Concha insisted on buying blackberries and got her mouth and fingers stained with purple. Then she stood there, like a silly fool, with her hands sticky and her fingers spread out stiffly, and could not get at her handkerchief to wipe them clean, for fear of making stains on her white dress. In the end she washed in a puddle at the side of the square and dried her fingers on her handkerchief. Rafael stuffed himself with fresh nuts which were sold in their green shells to make them weigh more. But he and I had the same idea, and Concha was in our way: we wanted to smoke aniseed-and-cocoa cigarettes just as the men smoked their tobacco. If we had said so to Concha, she would have told Aunt Aquilina who would have made a fuss. So at first we tried to think out a way of getting rid of her because she was a nuisance, but then I found a solution.

You could buy little squibs which went off with a loud bang, fifty for ten centimos. I suggested our buying a hundred of them and Concha liked the idea. We would let them off in the streets and throw them under doorways to frighten people. But of course, after we had bought them, we still had to light them before they could go off. Every squib had a fuse, a piece of string soaked in gunpowder. We could have lit them with matches, but that would have meant buying several boxes. I proposed quite innocently that we should buy aniseed cigarettes to light the fuses with. So we bought a packet of ten cigarettes, and Rafael asked a young man for a light. He laughed when he let Rafael have it. We lit ours from Rafael's cigarette, for Concha wanted to throw squibs too. I had to light a cigarette for her, and she carried it hidden in her hand. She only sucked it now and then, with her face to the wall so that people

should not see her. The aniseed tickled your throat and eyes and made
you cough, but we smoked like men. Then we began to throw the squibs
under doorways. At houses where Rafael and Concha knew the people
and said some nasty old woman lived there, we all three lit squibs and
threw them inside in a bunch. When the first one exploded, all the
women ran out to see what had happened, and then the other two went
off and frightened them even more. We laughed, hidden round the next
corner, ready to bolt if they came after us.

But all girls are fools. When we were going through a street where
there was no one about, Concha had to stick her cigarette into her mouth
and puff smoke, and of course a fussy old woman came out of her house
and saw us. She smacked Concha's face so that the cigarette jumped out
of her mouth, and raised hell, calling her names—pig, beast, hussy, strum-
pet, and God knows what else. She would not let go of her arm because
she wanted to take her home and tell Aunt Aquilina all about it. And
the old meddler did drag Concha along, weeping and trying to get away
and yelling for us to come with her. The old woman called us names too
and said we were shameless good-for-nothings. At every house she passed
she told the story to all the women she met, and they all started screaming and slapping Concha's face and shouting at us. Rafael thought of
bashing in the old witch's head with a stone. When we came to our house
they went inside, and we could hear Concha screaming, but we did not
go in. Then Aunt Aquilina came out and hauled us in. We did not like
it, but we had to go and then we got it. Aunt Aquilina started dealing
out cuffs, mainly to Rafael and Concha, for she said it was their fault.
Suddenly she saw that Rafael's pockets were bulging:.

"Where are the cigarettes? Empty your pockets at once, all of them,
so I can see what's there."

Rafael, who was sometimes malicious, dug his hands into his pockets
and brought out hazelnuts, walnuts, and roasted chick-peas. But when
my aunt screamed, "The cigarettes, where are the cigarettes?" he pulled
out a handful of cigarettes mixed with a lot of squibs and threw them
into the kitchen fire. My aunt, who did not notice what it was, kept on:
"Throw them all in, all of them!" So Rafael dropped all his squibs into
the fire, and I did too. My aunt cried:

"Tonight you'll not go and see the fireworks!"

But then the fuses of the squibs caught fire, and things got going.
There were bangs, and ashes and burning straw flew all over the room.
Grandmother jumped up from her stool, dragging after her the ball of
wool with which she was knitting socks. A frying pan on the hearth was
blown full of cinders, sparks fell on the chairs and on the curtains of the
kitchen shelf, and my aunt could not understand what was happening.

The two women shrieked and Uncle Sebastian, who had tumbled to it, stayed behind his shoemaker's bench and laughed. We ran out into the street and did not go back until late in the evening. The table was laid and everybody was most serious. Nobody said a word, only Little Grandmother pattered around muttering, and we watched her out of the corner of our eyes in case she tried to hit us with her stick. We sat down at the table and Aunt Aquilina brought the meal.

"No supper for the wicked children tonight," she said sternly and handed each of us a chunk of bread. "That's all you're going to get."

We said not a word. I was mad with rage. I had never been left without a meal, and my eyes filled with tears of fury. But I did not want to cry. Only my tears trickled down my face, and then Aunt Aquilina saw them and began heaping meatballs on my plate.

"Well, I'll let you off this once. . . . There's the fiesta tonight and I don't want to get angry, but . . ." and she launched forth into a sermon while she was filling our plates. Uncle Sebastian chuckled and said:

"When all's said and done, it was a funny trick the children played on us!"

Aunt and Grandmother went for him like two wasps:

"That's right, you would go and take their side!"

And a violent row began, so that our poor uncle did not know where to hide from the onslaught. Meanwhile, we finished our meal and got away. We agreed to buy Uncle Sebastian a packet of cigarettes and a roll of cigarette paper. When the fireworks started and everyone had gone to the stone parapet which overlooked the market square, we gave him them in secret. He let me sit on his knee and gave me a kiss, and we watched the rockets burst in the sky. Suddenly he said to Aunt:

"Take the child, I must go to the lavatory."

When he came back he had a cigarette in his mouth and said a friend had given it him and after all, everybody had to celebrate one day in the year. Aunt grumbled but she left him alone. His eyes sparkled merrily, he winked at us and chuckled behind her back.

The square was full of dancing couples and on the terrace before the church, where we were, was the man with the fireworks, a fat Valencian in a black blouse and round hat, with a cigar in his mouth. In his left hand he held a rocket, which looked like a thick candle, and with his right he put his burning cigar to it. When it spluttered, he suddenly opened his fingers and the rocket went swishing up into the air. We children stood round him in a circle and stared at the sky until we saw it burst into many colored stars. The empty shell of the rocket fell down, its last sparks crackling, and bounced over the rooftops. One year a house was set on fire by a rocket.

That day was the Feast of Our Lady, and our aunt began to dress us up in our best clothes very early in the morning. Mine were the finest in the village, of course, for all the others wore country things, while I had Madrid clothes. Rafael had a suit from Madrid, too, but his was cheap, ready-made, and did not fit him; the cloth was so harsh that he could hardly move. Concha also had a cheap dress from Madrid, starched until it was as stiff as a board, and she looked ridiculous with a big blue ribbon in her plait. Both had heavy boots, Rafael's with brass toecaps, and they found it hard to walk in them, and they looked with envy at my sailor suit and patent leather shoes. Concha called me Señorito, because she said I was playing the young gentleman again, and managed to give me a kick so that the varnish of my shoe got all scratched. I pulled her plait and untied her ribbon and we had a fight. But then we all went with Uncle Sebastian to look at the auction for Our Lady's stand.

The Virgin, wrapped in an embroidered velvet cloak and surrounded by burning candles, was carried out of the church on a platform decorated with the heads of little angels painted in natural colors. They stopped with her under the porch and the mayor, dressed in his cape, holding his staff with the gold knob, cried out:

"This year, as every year, we are going to hold an auction for the stand of Our Lady."

The highest bidders were given the six places at the shafts and the right to carry Our Lady on their shoulders to the hermitage of Berciana, a hill three miles from the village. All the rich men of the place and all those who had made a vow started bidding. The two places in front were the best. One shouted:

"Forty *reales!*" [1]

"Fifty!"

This set them going. When only four bidders for the right shaft in front were left, the mayor cried:

"One hundred and fifty *reales* have been offered. Does nobody offer more?"

After he had repeated it a couple of times, someone offered a hundred and seventy-five, and the bids went up slowly until only two were left who insisted on carrying the Virgin. Then everybody was anxious to see which of the two considered himself the most important man in the place.

"Two hundred and fifty *reales*," said one pompously.

"Three hundred," the other snapped.

[1] At the time, about 1901, small sums of money were often given in the obsolete coinage of the *real*. 1 real = 25 centimos.—*Translator's Note.*

"Damnation, three hundred and fifty! Don't you go and think you'll carry her off!" the first shouted back.

In the end they quarreled about who was going to carry Our Lady, cursing and swearing and calling each other cuckolds. The priest took the auction money.

After the auction, the procession to Berciana started, with Our Lady in front, behind her the priest in a golden cope and saying Latin prayers. After him came the mayor, the judge, the doctor, the schoolmaster, and, in a double file, all the neighbors who wanted to carry a lighted candle. Then came the rest of the village in a huddle, the men carrying their hats in their hands, the women with a silk kerchief on their heads. They all wore their best clothes, most of them their wedding-dress, which was too tight for some and too big for others.

The funniest of all were the boys and girls. The boys were dressed like the men, in corduroy suits, a shirt with a collar and silk bow, a straw hat and heavy boots. The girls had stiffly starched dresses in loud colors, showing their very white, starchy petticoats and the edging of their panties. They had bright silk bows in their hair, stockings knitted in very thick wool, and boots with toecaps of metal. None of them knew how to move, because they were used to wearing a smock or knickers, and to going barefoot or in rope-soled sandals. Before we were half-way there, most of the children had to be dragged along by their parents, stumbling over each stone in the road.

When we came to the little Berciana river, the procession crossed through the stream instead of passing over the wooden bridge; I wondered whether they did it because they were afraid the bridge would break or because they wanted to make a sacrifice to Our Lady. They all took off their shoes, and turned up their trousers and skirts. Most of the children and many of the grown-ups did not put on their shoes again afterwards. Some said they had made a vow to Our Lady to walk barefoot to the Hermitage, but it was really because their boots hurt them.

The Hermitage was on the top of a hill which rose up from the stream, at its foot a big meadow of short grass where oak-trees grew. Mass was said in the chapel, but most of the people stayed outside because there was no room for them. In the meantime, loaded carts, mules, and bullocks arrived from the village and were installed on the meadow. The people who came with them unpacked, and out of the carts and hampers came frying pans and casseroles, rabbits, chickens, lambs, and pigeons. Someone had taken along a calf, cinnamon-colored, with a white muzzle, which was tied to the back of the cart and strained against the rope round its short horns. Some had brought chairs and set them in a circle in the grass. The best spots were in the shade of the oaks, and people slung ropes between the trees and put blankets on them to get more shade. Away from the trees kitchens were set up, with earthen stewing pots, plates, glasses, and frying-pans. The big wine skins and leather bottles were left in the shade of the tree-trunks; some people dug holes in the ground near the brook, where they buried their bottles to keep them cool.

After Mass the people came down to the meadow. First everybody had to sample the wine and take a drink from the free jet of a leather bottle, or out of a jar filled from a wine skin. Then everyone, children and grown-ups, collected firewood in the oak copses. The men and women lopped off branches with little axes, and the children carried armfuls of kindling sticks to their own camp fires. Quickly a hundred fires were blazing in the open and the air was full of floating chicken and pigeon feathers. Sheep and rabbits were strung up in trees and skinned by men in shirt sleeves. Tablecloths were spread on the ground and laid with platters of sliced sausages, olives, and gherkins, with tomatoes cut in half and dressed in salt and oil; and everybody had a bite and a drink of wine. We children went from spread to spread and picked out whatever we liked best and drank secretly from the wine jars. Soon all the valley smelled of roast meat and of smoke from burning thyme and broom. People began to feel hungry and to hurry up the cooks.

I remembered the description of the wedding feast of the rich Camacho in *Don Quixote de la Mancha* and it seemed to me that Don Quixote himself might suddenly appear on the crest of one of those hills, astride Rocinante, with Sancho Panza behind him smacking his lips at the good smell.

The children of the fireworks-man went round selling rockets which burst high in the air with bangs like rifle shots. Wafer-sellers had come from Madrid to the fiesta, young boys from Galicia who made the journey on foot with a tin box full of thin rolled wafers slung round their shoulders, and the people flocked round them trying their luck at the lottery-wheel and smacking the children who wanted to turn the wheel too.

Even the dogs seemed to have got wind of the fiesta, for everywhere you saw village dogs slinking round the bonfires, with hanging heads and their tails between their legs. A few people threw them a bone, others threw a stone or a log at them, and then they ran off to find another group. Sometimes a few dogs chose the same fire and sat down on their haunches, very tense, their noses in the air, their eyes glued to the hands of the woman who did the cooking. When she threw them a bite, the cleverest caught it and the others growled at him.

Little Grandmother had arrived in Uncle Luis's cart, and both the families joined in one group. We were fifteen in all, and Grandmother began to tell us how one year all her sons with their wives and children, and some with their grandchildren, had come to a fiesta in the village. There had been over a hundred of them. Grandmother had had eighteen children, of whom fourteen were still living. Her eldest son had great-grandchildren at the time of the fiesta, and arrived from Cordova with a family of twenty-odd. Grandmother had married a tailor, and since they did not earn enough money to keep all their children, they had sent them out into the world as they grew up, the girls into service in Madrid, the boys either to Madrid or to Andalusia. One of them went to Barcelona and one to America, but neither of them had ever come back to the village and people knew them only from photographs. The Barcelona one was a man with a broad black beard and a bowler hat, who looked like a secret service agent, and the American was a dried-up man with a clean-shaven face, who looked like a priest. Grandmother had never gone further away from the village than Madrid, and then she had to be taken by cart, because she did not want to get into the train. She said the train was a thing of the devil. And she would die without having been in a train.

Aquilino had fixed up a swing between two trees, and so had many of the others. The girls sat in the swings and the lads pushed them so that they swung high up into the air, shrieking and showing their legs. The lads had their fun out of looking at them, they nudged each other in the ribs, winked and said: "Did you see? A fine lass, eh?" They laughed a lot and sometimes they pinched the girls' legs or bottoms. Some girls laughed and shrieked and some turned angry. After the meal, when all of them were stuffed and full of wine, the lads pinched more and the girls shrieked less.

That was how courtships started, and quarrels. In the middle of the afternoon they were all a little drunk. The older men stretched themselves on the ground to take their siesta, and the young lads tumbled themselves down beside the girls who were sitting on the grass, but not to go to sleep. The girls played with the lads' hair, and sometimes they slapped at them, if one had touched a girl's leg or thigh or breast. Later, when the sluggishness of digestion had passed, they danced, and danced on into the night. Many of the couples went for a stroll on the other side of the hills.

One couple walked off, their arms wound tightly round each other's waists, and Andrés shouted good advice after them, such as telling them not to drink from the stream because it made big bellies. And everybody laughed.

My Uncle Luis had slept through his siesta and awakened with a parched throat, he said. As a little refreshment he ate a bowl of salad·

and half a dozen oil doughnuts, solid and floury. Then he tucked me under his arm like a parcel and took me for a round.

We went to the top of the hill. The valley with the picnickers disappeared and the land was lonely. Far away you saw the white snow peaks of the Sierra de Guadarrama and the towers of the monastery of El Escorial.

Suddenly Uncle Luis, who was walking behind me, gave a wild howl: "Uh-huh-huuuh!"

I turned round, frightened. A couple came out of a little gully, she with her blouse unbuttoned, he with his jacket dangling. Uncle Luis held his sides and laughed so that his belly heaved with the laughter. He lifted me on to his shoulders and ran through the gullies, howling his howl. Couples dashed out of thickets and hollows and fled down to the valley, pursued by our shouts and laughter.

When we came back to the crowd, Uncle Luis swung me from his shoulders and lifted a full jar to his mouth, and again his laughter burst out so that the wine spluttered. Everyone turned towards him. He caught the little round figure of Aunt Rogelia in his arms and plastered her face with kisses. Then he lifted her up on his hands, stretching his arms as though he meant to fling her far into the air.

"Huh-huh-huuuh!" he shouted, and his chest and shoulders resounded.

At his cry all the valley fell silent and the echo answered beyond the darkening hills.

6. Outhouse of Madrid

I T ' S good to be here. My head between my mother's knees, on the softness of her thighs under the soft linen of her apron. To look at the flames twisting and dancing in the air. My mother is peeling potatoes at the side of the kitchen fire and talking to Grandmother. She tells her about her life in my uncle's flat, her work and her worries, and about how my aunt is jealous of her because of me. And I watch her face from below, without her seeing me. Her face in the red glow of the flames. Her face tired from work and worry. I bury my head in her apron like a cat. I would like to be a cat. I would jump on her lap and roll myself into a ball there. I'm sick of everybody, sick of my aunt, of school, sick of all the stupid people who think I am only a child, while I know I'm more than they and see everything and swallow down everything and keep it to myself. Jump on her lap, roll myself into a ball, doze, hearing my mother talk without listening to her words, feeling her warmth and the glow of the fire and the smell of burning broom. Stay there quiet, so quiet.

"How tiresome the child is—go and play with your brother and sister."

"I don't want to."

I curl up more tightly, trying to get still closer to her. My mother is stroking my head, my tousled hair, my unruly cowlick, and her fingers pass idly over my head, but I feel them inside me. When her hand lies still, I take it and look at it. So very tiny, so thin, worn by the water of the river, with small tapering fingers, the fingertips pricked by the lye, with twisted blue veins, nervous and alive. Alive with warmth and blood, alive in quick motion, always ready to leap and fly, to scrub vigorously, to stroke gently. I love to press them to my cheeks and rub my skin against them, to kiss and nibble her fingertips, here where I have no need to hide behind a door when I want to kiss my mother, with my aunt shouting:

"Where are you, child?"

"Here in the kitchen, Aunt."

"What are you doing there?"

"I'm going to the lavatory."

And in the meantime my mother clattering with the pots and pans and I slamming the lavatory door. . . .

What rights has my aunt over me? She keeps me in her house, but then my mother is her servant. Why hasn't she had children? For she is jealous because she has no child of her own, and she would like to take me away from my mother. But not my uncle. My uncle loves me, but he doesn't want to take me away from my mother. Why can't he be my father? My aunt could die, and then my uncle would marry my mother just to be my father. He said so once as a joke, but I think it's true. He too is fed up with my aunt, with her prayers and her crotchets. Once my aunt was cross and said: "I ought to be dead, then you would be rid of me!" "Fine," said my uncle, "when you're dead I'll marry Leonor and become the boy's papa. What do you think of it, Leonor? Do you accept my snow-white hand?" He said it to my mother with a laugh, and she answered smiling: "Well, let me think it over in the meantime." My goodness, what a row! My aunt sobbed and wept, clutching me to her, and I cried too. My uncle furious at my aunt's stupidity, my mother trying to calm her down and bearing with her affronts. "You ungrateful person, that's the reward I get from all of you for my goodness! That's what you would like—me to go to my grave so that the three of you can do what you like." And so on. We had no evening meal and did not go to the café. And we were in bed before ten. The day after, everyone went round with sour faces.

Here in the village we are alone. Sometimes I get hold of her and kiss her hungrily. "Now let go, you wheedling rascal!" she says and pushes me away. But I can see that it makes her happy and that she puts up with my aunt for my sake, so that I can get on well and become an engineer soon, because my uncle will pay for my studies and I want to be an engineer. And nothing is too hard for her as long as I kiss her and love her, and she kisses me and loves me more than anyone else. When I'm grown up she won't have to go down to the river, and I'll be rich so that she's happy and can have all she wants, and she'll be a grandmother like our Little Grandmother, a tiny little granny with lots of wrinkles, in a black dress, an old woman's dress, on which I'll rest my head when I'm tired after work.

Good things do not last. The day before yesterday my mother came, and tomorrow we must both go away, I to Navalcarnero and she to Madrid, back to work.

As the train stopped for a quarter of an hour in the station, I dragged my mother off to look at the engine. It was a small Belgian engine, painted green and almost square, and no good at all. I had been in a big railway engine. Uncle José had a cousin who was an engine-driver at the North Station and always drove the Paris Express. Once he took my uncle and me to Segovia in an engine without a train. The engine was so big that they had to lift me up to the cabin where the driver and stoker were. We went off with nothing but the tender and did not stop at any station until Segovia. The stoker kept on shoveling coal into the open mouth of the furnace so that the flames licked out, and we passed through the country with the track free before and behind us, racing along the rails so fast that it was like flying through the air. In the innards of the engine was a big handle which was the brake. My uncle told me that an engine driver once tried to save his train from crashing into another and turned the handle so hard that he thrust it through his stomach. He saved the train but he died, spiked by the brake. Then there were thermometers and pressure gages and level-tubes with little nickeled taps, and the iron chain of the whistle. When you pulled it the steam whistled and you went deaf with the noise. All the taps were dripping water or oil. There was one which dripped a lot and I wanted to turn it off, but hot oil spurted out in a fan and made spots on all our clothes. When we passed over an iron bridge, everything bounced, the rails, the bridge, and the engine, and I wanted the engine to go faster so that we should be past the bridge when it smashed. We went back by train, but the journey in a carriage was boring.

The train from Méntrida was just as small as its engine. The carriages were matchboxes with dirty wooden seats, full of country people with their saddlebags, baskets, and chickens tied by the legs, which they shoved under the seat. Some carried rabbits with their bowels slit open so that you could see the purple kidneys, and some carried small wine casks or baskets full of eggs bedded in straw. Sometimes, when we came to a station, we saw people running on the road from the village and making signs for the train to stop. The station master always waited for them. Then they tumbled into the carriage, pushing each other and stamping on other people's feet or knocking them over with their bundles, and slumped down in their seats, sweating after their run with the baskets and saddlebags.

Navalcarnero was the biggest station on the line. It had a goods shed with a zinc roof and three lines for shunting. Just beside the station was the flour mill, and a special siding led to the mill from the station itself, made a curve and passed under the iron factory gate. When the gate was closed it made me think that if they pulled the wrong switch, we would run straight through the railing, train and all, and land inside the mill.

Grandmother Inés was waiting for us in the station. Concha had come along with my mother and me; she and I were going to stay in Navalcarnero until the end of the month. When the train with my mother had gone, Grandmother laid her arms on each of our shoulders, her hands hanging down over our chests, and so she walked to the town, with us glued to her sides.

Grandmother's hand was as large as a man's and her arm was a bulky mass. It was right to call her Big Grandmother. She weighed over two hundred pounds and was taller than most men. Her strength was enormous and she ate and drank like a farm-hand. Every time she came to Madrid, Aunt Baldomera invited her to have her meals with us, and she always said no. She used to go to Botín's, a very old Madrid restaurant, and order roast sucking pig. When none of us was with her, she would eat the sucking pig all by herself, together with a huge bowl of lettuce salad, and drink two pints of wine with it. She would have been a good match for Uncle Luis.

Navalcarnero was different from the other villages. It was very close to Madrid and the market town of its district. Many of the gentry lived there. They would not have been called gentry in Madrid, but they were gentry in Navalcarnero. The town was divided into two races of people:

those who dressed as they did in Madrid, and those who wore blouses and corduroy trousers. There were the women in hat or mantilla, and the women with wide petticoats and apron, with a kerchief round their heads. There was a Poor Man's Casino, a large tavern full of flies, and a Rich Men's Casino, a kind of café with marble-topped tables. In the church there were two rows of benches in the middle, with chairs placed in front of them. The gentlemen sat ón the benches and their ladies on the chairs. The rest of the church was for the farmers and the poor. Farmers with money spread out a round mat of esparto grass and put a straw-covered chair on it for the wife. The poor knelt on the flagstones.

I knew this because I sometimes went to church, although my grandmother never took me there. On Sundays she asked:

"Well now, do you want to go to Mass?"

I usually said·yes, for two reasons: first, if I did not go it would be a sin, and secondly, it was an odd experience to go by myself. Mass in Navalcarnero was different from other places. At school all the boys heard Mass together, and we filled the whole church. When I went to church with my aunt, I was tied to her and to her caprices, and she spent the whole time telling me to be quiet, to kneel down, to get up, not to cough, not to sneeze, to keep my hands still, and not to disturb her in her devotions.

Here in Navalcarnero it was quite another thing. I went alone, even when one of Grandmother's neighbors had asked me to go with her, because I knew what old women were like. I stayed under the porch, in the little yard behind the iron gate and watched the people going in. When they were all inside, I entered, alone. They were all clustering round the High Altar and I came in very softly and stayed at the back of the church between the pillars. I was always afraid that one of the old women might call me and make me kneel down beside her.

The floor, the pillars, and the lower part of the walls of the church were of stone, the rest whitewashed. In the middle was a chandelier shaped like a pear and covered with glass crystals which sparkled like diamonds when the sun shone on them. I did not know why, but that chandelier, which hung on a very long cord from the center of the cupola, was nearly always swinging very slowly from one side to the other. I liked to watch it moving and filling with colored sparks whenever it passed through one of the sunbeams which shone through the windows in the lantern of the dome.

At the entrance there was a Christ on the Cross, naked, very thin, and yellow, almost green, in color. The bloodstains were quite black, because he had not been repainted for many years. His lower parts were covered by a little velvet apron with a gold fringe. Some people lifted the apron and looked underneath. The paint of the toes had peeled off because the women had kissed them so much, and the bare wood showed. There was a black knot in the wood on the big toe of the left foot, which looked like a corn. His head was dangling as if his neck had been broken and he had a dirty, chocolate-colored beard with cobwebs between hair and throat. Tears were running from his eyes, and they looked like the hardened wax drippings on a candle. The only beautiful thing about him were the eyes, blue glass eyes which stared at the peeled toes.

At the side of the Christ was the Holy Water stoup, with a puddle underneath where the yokels stamped with their rope-soles—plff! But the ladies took great care not to step in it and leaned over on tiptoe to dip their fingers into the holy water. Fine people wetted their fingertips, and country folk put their whole hand in. They had made the puddle.

There was a Virgin of solid silver in the church. She was life-size and was standing on a moon, a mass of clouds and many heads of little angels with pigeon's wings. People said she weighed a ton. One day I watched two old women smearing the Virgin full of metal polish and rubbing her with an old rag until she shone. They got the cheeks and chin bright like glass, but some of the white stuff stuck in the eyes and the mouth, and one of the old women tried hard to polish them, spitting on her handkerchief and wiping the eyes of Our Lady just as people do when children have sand in their eyes. The other old woman was rubbing the angels' heads as angrily as if she wanted to smack them. But they hadn't any bottoms.

Up in the choir they had an organ with a keyboard in a very old wooden case, like a barrel-organ. There were two bellows under the keyboard, on which the organist had to pedal; they looked like two old books which had fallen open. Sometimes the organist stepped on one of the books out of time, and then, when he pressed down the keys, there was no sound from the organ but only a blast of air, as when a mule lets off wind. As soon as the blast stopped short, one of the organ pipes mewed out of tune.

Apart from these things the church was nothing but a cold barn where one could stay comfortably only in summer. But it had some real death skulls. When somebody had died and the Mass for the Dead had to be read, they put in the middle of the church a bier covered by a black, silver-embroidered cloth, surrounded by tall candles. On the black cloth they laid a skull and cross-bones. The skull and bones were real. An old, huge chest in the sacristy was filled with skulls and bones which weighed practically nothing because they were hollowed out by worms. They felt like cardboard. When there was a Mass for the Dead, they took out a skull and two long bones. If the dead man had been rich, the priest selected a skull himself, and the sacristan scraped its pate and rubbed it with oil to make it shine. When a skull was cracked they mended it with a drop of wax. One had four or five wax teeth in its jaw. When there was no Mass for the Dead and the priest and sacristan were away, all of us boys who were friends with the altar-boys played with the bones in the little garden behind the church.

I did not like Navalcarnero as much as Méntrida. It lies high on a hill, on the great trunk road from Madrid to Extremadura. From the town, the road leads downhill towards Madrid on one side, and downhill towards Valmojado on the other. Once you came to the foot of the hill on either side there were trees, but the whole hill of Navalcarnero itself had no trees except the few meager little trees in the Station Avenue, many of which were crippled. On the hillside were cornfields, now shorn and dry, and vines laden with black grapes. The wheat was harvested, but they were just gathering in the grapes for the wine. Big, heavy wagons went along the Extremadura Road with baskets full of grapes, high as a man. The grapes at the bottom of the baskets were crushed and the wagons dripped fat red blobs which mixed with the dust of the street and became purple-black little balls.

The people made their wine, pouring their grapes into a big shallow trough of stone or cement and crushing them there; the trough had a hole through which the must ran down into a huge jar in the cellar. Two or three houses had a hand-press for their grapes, and one house had a hydraulic press. The whole town went to look at it.

When we came to my grandmother's house, we were met by her sister, Aunt Anastasia. She was as tall as my grandmother, but much heavier, for she was older and her legs were swollen from rheumatism. The two sisters were inseparable, but at the same time they could never stay together, for they were both very bossy. Aunt Anastasia lived upstairs and Grandmother on the ground floor. When they had a quarrel, Aunt Anastasia walked up the straight wooden staircase which creaked under her weight, and slammed her door so that bits of plaster fell from the ceiling and the whole house shook. They would not speak to each other for two or three days. Then either Grandmother went upstairs and banged at her sister's door, shouting that the row was now over, or her sister came down and walked into the sitting-room, asking Grandmother if she wasn't ashamed of herself for not having been up to see her sister in three days; and saying that she must be dying before Grandmother's conscience told her to bring her sister a glass of water. So they had to quarrel for another half-hour before they could make peace.

There were also my grandmother's wards. When my father had died

—he was the last of her twenty-five children to die—and my mother had gone to stay with my uncle and aunt, Grandmother went as a housekeeper to Señor Molina, a wealthy man of Navalcarnero who had been left a widower with four children. Grandmother, who herself had been a widow for many years, stayed with him. And in his will he made her the guardian and trustee of his four children.

Each of them was a calamity in himself. The eldest, Fernando, was twenty years old and spent the whole day in the Casino; he had a mistress in the town and something on his lungs. The next one, Rogelio, was fifteen, and he was downright bad. He talked of nothing but girls and did all sorts of things. But he had got it into his head that he wanted to become a monk in the monastery of El Escorial and spent his day with the parish priest. Antonio, the youngest, was rickety, and looked like a hunchback, with his head sunk deep between his shoulders. He had small, red-rimmed eyes, always smeared with a yellow ointment. The girl, Asunción, had had smallpox as a child and her face was pitted with marks. The edges of her nostrils were frayed as though birds had pecked them away.

The first thing Grandmother did was to show us where we were going to sleep. Concha had to share a bed with Asunción and I with Rogelio.

My grandmother's house was the house of big beds. Every room had a tall iron bedstead heaped with two or three mattresses so that you had to climb on a chair to get in. When Grandmother wanted to get into her bed, Asunción and Concha pushed at her behind to help her up, and I laughed when I saw her in her white nightdress: she looked just like a big lumpy mattress herself. When she let herself fall on to her bed, all the springs screeched. They were spiral springs, tapering in the middle, and when they were flattened down they squealed.

From Grandmother's house we went to Señor Molino's farm where they were crushing grapes. A ring of men and women, all barefoot, walked round and round in the stone trough and stamped on the grapes so that their legs were spattered with must. We joined them, but I got out quickly because the grape-stalks pricked my feet. The others stayed, I went off with Grandmother.

We crossed the town and came out on the road to Valmojado. Grandmother walked with long steps and slowed down only when we had passed the houses. The road dipped downhill between two steep earthbanks; we sat down on the ridge and watched the wagons with grapes pass below us. Then Grandmother began to talk to herself:

"I'm getting old and they"—she meant Señor Molina's children—"don't matter to me. My sister'll die before me, and then you'll be the only ones left. You'll become house-owners. You know I've got two houses in this town. You'll have the same trouble with them as I've got now, you'll have to put new tiles on the roofs every year and you'll never get your rents. And then people say there's a God. Like hell there is."

She looked at me and burst out laughing:

"Now I'm perverting the little angel—if your aunt heard me we'd have a fight! But look, whatever your aunt and her priests may tell you, there isn't a God, except in the collection boxes in church. Well, anyhow, you'll find that out for yourself, because you can't deny the blood in your veins. Your father was one of the sergeants of the Villacampa rising, and it was a miracle he wasn't executed. And I once threw a priest down the stairs because he insisted on his pious tricks and was killing off the only one of your uncles that was left me. When your mother became a widow, all God did for her was to leave her alone in the hotel with two *duros* in her pocket and your father stiff and cold in his bed. Afterwards God was sorry for her, it's true, so He turned her into a servant and washerwoman, and found her an attic and a few priests and nuns to ladle out soup to your brothers. And then there are still people who thank God for His mercy!"

When my grandmother spoke like that in earnest she made me very sad. I wanted to believe in God and the Virgin, but the things she said were true. If God can do everything, He could have treated us more kindly, because my mother was very good. Really, He might have treated my grandmother worse instead, for she was always saying blasphemous things, but still she was rich and had what she wanted.

Grandmother was silent for a while and changed the subject:

"Well, you've come here to have a good time and not to hear sermons. But—don't forget, the priests are scoundrels!"

She took me by the hand and we walked back to town, she striding ahead and I trotting behind. When we came to the market square she gave me two pesetas and said: "Run along, and when you hear it strike twelve, you come home for the meal." And she walked down the street in the middle of the gutter, straight-backed and muttering blasphemies, or so I thought.

Here in the market square of Navalcarnero was a house that belonged to me. Or rather, it was going to belong to me when Grandmother died. It had three stories and a portico with heavy wooden posts which were greasy from the backs of the men who leaned against them. Each post had a square stone base, and the roof of the portico was made of smoke-blackened beams. There the butcher had his shop, with the carcass of a cow, half covered by a white cloth with bloodstains on it, and cuts of meat, liver, and lungs in white china dishes, set out on little marble slabs. In one dish there was the whole heart of a cow. The butcher's daughter chased the flies away with a duster made of long, colored paper strips; and at the back of the shop hung a whole pig with a tin pail fastened to its tusks, to catch the blood which dripped from its snout.

The butcher called me:

"Hello, Madrileño, have you come for the grape-harvest?"

When I entered his shop I knocked against the pig which was swinging heavily on its hook and it hit me with its greasy back. I pushed it away with my hand; its fatty bacon-flesh was loathsome.

"Come in, come in, I'll give you something for your granny to fry for you."

He gave me three thick, black blood-puddings shiny with fat, which made grease stains in the newspaper he wrapped round them so that you could read the printed letters on the other side of the sheet. I had to take the warm, flabby parcel, which I hated having to grip with my fingers, and on top of it I had to submit to a kiss from the butcher and another from his wife, both of whom were as fat and greasy as their pig and their black-puddings. Their daughter stood in the doorway; she was a very pretty girl with a delicate face, and she stroked my hair, but did not kiss me. When I went out of the butcher's shop I felt greasy all over.

Next door in the portico was the tavern, where they invited me to have some sweets and a peppermint soda. The tavern smelled of wine, of the pitch of wine skins, and of the tobacco and sweat of the men who drank at the tin-sheathed bar table. Some who knew me explained to the others that I was the grandson of "Old Anés." They did not pronounce it Inés. One of the men said he did not know her, and the tavern-keeper cried:

"But you must know her, she's known in all Spain! Now look, you'll remember who she is at once if I tell you she's the fattest woman in town, the only one who doesn't go to Mass,, and the owner of this house."

Then a little old man who was sipping from a half-pint jar, said:

"Hell, she was a fine lass, she was, when she was come twenty. We were all after her, and she boxed all our ears for us. There wasn't one of us who could have said he'd pinched one of her teats. Before you lifted your hand, she whipped round and slapped your face and left you all of a daze. Then she married old Vicente who was a wagon-maker along the road. He was a good soul—a short little man—and he liked a good meal better than working with his plane. When they were married, Anés plunked herself down in his workshop, and then Vicente worked as if he'd been paid by the hour. It wasn't that she said anything to him, she just sat there on a chair and sewed, but old Vicente wouldn't look up from his pegs. So the workshop went up and up like foam. But Anés had a child every year, or I should say every ten months, and it was lucky they all died off, because if they hadn't she'd have filled the town with them.

A good breeding doe, she was. When the two got older, Vincente just died, like a little bird, I should say because he couldn't cope with so much woman."

The church bell rang twelve and the men went home to eat. The little old man said I should greet Grandmother from him and told me a few times: "She was a fine lass, she was!"

After the siesta, Concha went with Asunción to visit her girl friends and I went out with Rogelio. We passed through the town and walked downhill through the harvested fields, following the little footpaths along their edges, towards the river Guadarrama. Rogelio said to me: "You'll see what fun we'll have. All the boys meet here by the river."

When we came to the stream, whose water did not reach to one's ankles, there were seven or eight boys rolling naked in the sand or splashing in the pools. They were burned black as cinders from the sun and spurted sand and water at us. Rogelio and I got out of our clothes and joined them. I felt funny with my white skin among all those nigger-boys. Rogelio was the biggest, his under-belly was already grown with black hair. Some of the other boys had hair growing there too, and they were very proud of looking as hairy as men.

When we were tired of playing and running, Rogelio called us together and took the photograph of a naked woman out of his jacket, and showed it to me before the others.

"Fernando gave it to me. He says she's been his girl, but I don't believe it, he's such a liar."

I did not believe it either, for it was simply the picture of an undressed *artiste*, such as you could see often in Madrid, a woman with one foot on a stool so that you saw her thighs, and nothing on but an embroidered chemise, black stockings, and her hair in a coil on the top of her head. The picture went from hand to hand among the boys, but we were watching Rogelio, who was stroking his member with one hand. The bigger boys were in the same way. The photograph did not do anything to me, nor to the little boys; but it seemed ridiculous to us not to be like the older boys, so we began to play too. We laughed, but we felt nervous and watched one another to see what happened. When the big boys came to the end, they jeered at us because we could not do what men did. When we dressed we were all very tired and very sad.

On the way back to the town we bound ourselves by an oath not to tell anybody, and Rogelio swore he would break the head of the first boy who said anything. Then he explained to us about women, and the blood mounted to my head with shame and suffocation. In the street, when the other boys went away to their houses, Rogelio told me in confidence:

"Tonight we'll have fun together, you and I alone."

I felt a mixture of shame at what had happened in the afternoon, and of curiosity about what Rogelio wanted to do that night. I was absent-minded and did not look anyone in the face, least of all Grandmother. At supper she noticed it and asked me whether I was ill. I said no, but I knew I was getting scarlet in the face, because I felt my cheeks burning. She got up, put her hand on my forehead, and said:

"You're very hot. In a little while you'll go to bed, because you must be tired after the journey."

After supper, Fernando, the eldest, said he was going to the Casino, and Grandmother made a row. To keep her quiet he got hold of Rogelio and me and said he would take us along, he was only going to have some coffee and would come back with us at once. As it was very early, Grand-mother let us go. On the way, Fernando told us what he had in mind:

"You come along and have something, coffee or whatever you like. Afterwards I'm going to see my girl, and you go home and tell Anés that old Paco's come to see me and I've stayed with him to settle about the grapes."

I thought we were going to have coffee in the lounge with the marble-topped tables, but Fernando took us up a small, steep wooden staircase at the back. Before I could ask he explained to me:

"The lounge is only the public bar. There's another room upstairs for us members."

The room upstairs was as big as the lounge; it had two billiard-tables with patched-up tops, a few round marble tables and some square tables with a green cloth where people played cards. At the back, a number of people were huddled round yet another table, under two green-shaded lamps, where you heard the rattling of money. Fernando went straight there.

The table was covered with the same kind of green cloth, and two men were seated there on high stools, one at each side. One held a pack of cards, and the other had big heaps of cash and banknotes in front of him. Rogelio said:

"They're playing 'Monte.' The man with the cards is the banker and the other with all the money is the cashier. You see, the banker puts four cards on the table, and everyone places his bet on one of them, whatever he likes. The card which comes out first when the pack is dealt wins, and all the others lose."

The banker spread out four cards and said: "Make your bets!"

All hastened to put their pesetas and duros by the side of the card they favored, and then the banker said: "Nothing more goes!"

He began to deal cards from the pack which he had turned face upwards, until one of the four cards on the table came out. Then the other man, the cashier, raked in most of the money and paid the people who had bet on the winning card as much money as they had staked. Fernando lost two duros. When the banker spread another four cards on the table, Fernando again bet two duros. And so he went on losing duros. Suddenly he turned round and said we should drink some coffee. Rogelio called the waiter who gave us two glasses of very bad coffee. Fernando kept losing, and Rogelio asked him to let him play instead; but Fernando did not listen to him. He called me:

"Come here, you, Madrileño!"

He put a heap of money in front of me, sat me on his knees and said to me, while the banker spread out his four cards:

"Take as much of this money as you want and put it beside the card you like best."

There was a knave of spades. I took a peseta and put it on a corner. Fernando said:

"Don't be afraid, put duros, or put as much as you want."

So I took a heap of duros, four or five, and put them beside the knave. All the men round the table watched me, but I was sure that the knave would come out first. Many who had already laid their bets took them away from their own cards and put them beside mine. The banker said grumpily:

"Now, have we all finished? Nothing more goes."

He turned the pack face upwards, and there was a knave. Fernando got paid three times as much as I had laid, and the banker, in a very bad temper, had to pay all the others. He turned to Fernando and said:

"Now look here, children can't play."

Everybody protested, but the banker insisted that I could not play, or he would take away his cards and leave the others to carry on alone. Rogelio and I had to sit down at a little table in the corner, bored and annoyed.

After a long while Fernando and a fat man whom I did not know came to our table. They started talking about land, vineyards, and promissory notes. The fat man told Fernando that he had already given him a lot of money although he was a minor. Fernando answered:

"What does that matter to you? If I give you a note post-dated for when I come of age, there's no hitch in it."

The fat man said:

"But supposing you die in the meantime? Because, you know you've got the face of a man with T.B., and one can't be sure of you."

"You needn't be afraid of my dying. A sick cat never dies," answered Fernando with a grin.

The fat man took banknotes and a stamped form from his pocket. Fernando signed, and the man gave him the money. It astonished me that there was nothing else written on the paper. Fernando said to the fat man: "You see I trust your word!"

"Now, when have I ever cheated you?"

Fernando went back to the gaming table and the man started to give us explanations: "You're the grandson of Inés, aren't you? You're already a man now. Here, buy yourself something." He gave me a duro. "Are you jealous?" he asked Rogelio. "Here's one for you, too. Fernando's a good lad. We had to settle this affair with the grapes, and it's all settled now. Your father was a fine man." He put a hand on Rogelio's shoulders: "A nice lot of duros we made together, your father and me, my boy. But when he took that Inés into his house, it was all over. She had a grouch against me, because your grandmother"—he nodded towards me—"never could stand me, and so in the end your father and I quarreled. She knew which side of her bread was buttered all right."

Rogelio stared into the man's face.

"Give me five duros," he said suddenly.

"But what do you want five duros for, shaver?"

"You give me five duros, or I'll tell Inés that you're giving Fernando money. I'm not a child like him"—he meant me—"and either you give me the money or I'll tell Inés. Everybody knows that you lend money and then seize people's lands."

"Boy, those are things one doesn't say out loud. You must show respect for your elders and betters. Here's another duro and shut up. And you too," he said to me. "Here's another for you—and don't say anything to your grandmother."

He got up angrily and pulled Fernando away from the table. They began to dispute, first in a low voice and then loudly:

"Go to bed with children, and you wake up mucky," said the man. "If only you hadn't brought those babes along! Especially that grandson of hers. It's not so bad with your brother, after all; you give him a duro and he keeps his mouth shut. But I don't trust that little leech. As soon as he gets home he'll tell his grandmother and we'll have a row."

Fernando answered:

"Don't you worry—what does he know?"

He turned to us and sent us away.

"And remember—I'm staying here because I've got to buy grapes."

Outside in the street, Rogelio said:

"I get a duro out of that fellow every time, it's a good trick. But don't say a word to Anés, or she'll take all the money away from us."

I promised silence and we tied our duros into our handkerchiefs so that they should not clink. When we came home, Grandmother grumbled and groused because Fernando was not back, and then we went to bed.

We slept in a whitewashed room with cross beams, an enormous bed, under it a chamber pot almost as big as the bed, two chairs and a chest with a rounded lid. The huge window that gave on to the street had an iron grille with a close leaf pattern. The room was chilly, the sheets damp; the stone tiles of the floor were icy cold and sweated moisture. We undressed in haste and clambered on to the bed, which was as high as ourselves. Inside the sheets we slowly got warm, but then it soon became intolerably hot under the blanket. Rogelio asked me:

"Are you hot?"

"I'm almost in a sweat."

"We must take off everything." He pulled off his pants and undervest and stayed quite naked.

I felt ashamed. But if we had bathed without anything on, why shouldn't we lie without any clothes now? So we both stayed naked in the bed. Rogelio pressed himself against me. His skin burned. He passed his hand over my body and said:

"You're so cool."

He began to stroke my sexual organs. I pushed his hand away, but he insisted: "Let me, don't be silly, you'll see how much you'll like it."

I let him go on, dazed with shame, burning hot. Suddenly something happened in me, I did not know what; but I went mad with rage and kicked him furiously in his ribs, while he clutched and pulled at my member in the greatest excitement, without letting go. I jumped out of bed. I had hung my belt over the iron bedrail. Now I seized it and started hitting out at his head, sides, buttocks, and belly. He yelled and rolled in the bed. A little trickle of blood ran down his forehead over one eye. Grandmother came into the room in her nightdress, a candlestick in her hand, and big slippers on her feet. She caught us as he was writhing on the bed and I lashing out at him, blind with fury, anger and loathing. Grandmother boxed my ears and I crumpled up in a corner, weeping.

Then, while she stood there in her nightgown and we in our nakedness, came the explanations. Rogelio sat in a chair and did not say a word. I talked and talked, mixing everything up.

"You see, Grandmother, he's a pansy. He's been touching me and wanting to do dirty things. And his brother's a gambler. And all the boys here play with themselves when they're together. He's got a post card with a naked woman. . . ."

I cried and fumbled for my trousers, to haul the duros out of my pocket, hiccoughing. Grandmother took the money and carried me to her own bed, wrapped me up, let me lie in the curve of her belly, and there I went to sleep. But before that she had given Rogelio a kick on his naked bottom, and her slipper had come off and sailed through the air. I had laughed through my tears.

I woke when the outer door slammed. Fernando was back. It was dawning, and Grandmother shouted at him from the top of her bed. Fernando was drunk.

"Now there, there, Anés. Leave me alone. I'm too sleepy."

He sat down in the dining room, drank a glass of brandy and fell asleep on the dining-room table. Grandmother got up in her nightgown, lifted him in her arms and carried him to his bedroom. It was funny to see my grandmother in the half light of the morning, big as she was, her white nightgown billowing down to her feet, carrying Fernando on her arms like a stuffed doll. I heard him fall on to his bed like a sack, and snore so that you heard it through the whole house.

A wagon passed by in the street, and all the window panes rattled. The carter was singing. And my grandmother came back into her bed, gathered me in her arms, laid my head on her breast and began to hum a tune.

7. Madrid

MADRID smells better. It does not smell of mules, or of sweat, or of smoke, or of dirty farmyards with the warm reek of dung and of chickens. Madrid smells of sun. On the balcony of our flat, which is on the third floor, you can sun yourself in the mornings. The cat stays in a corner of the balcony on his square of rug, peers down into the street over the edge of the board placed against the foot of the railings, and sits down and sleeps. From time to time, he opens his golden eyes and looks at me. Then he shuts them again and goes on sleeping. In his sleep he twitches his nostrils and smells everything.

When they water the street below, the fresh scent of moist earth rises up to the balcony just as when it is raining. When the wind blows from the north you smell the trees in the Casa de Campo. When the air is still and the whole quarter lies quiet, the wood and plaster of the old houses smell, the clean linen spread out on the balconies, and the sweet basil in the flower-pots. The old walnut and mahogany furniture sweats beeswax; you smell it through the open balconies while the women are cleaning. In the basement of our house is a smart carriage yard, and in the mornings, when the lacquered carriages are taken out into the street, sluiced and brushed, you can smell them. The horses, white and cinnamon brown, come out for their walk covered with a blanket and they smell of warm hair.

Near our house is the Plaza de Oriente with its bronze horses in the middle and the stone kings round it, with its two marble basins full of water, and of frogs, toads, tadpoles, and fishes, and with two little public gardens at the sides. The whole square smells of trees, water, stone and bronze. Farther on is the Royal Palace with its square courtyard, the Plaza de Armas, carpeted with sand, treeless, flanked with a row of balconies. The sun beats down on it from sunrise to sunset, and it is like a sandy beach without its sea. Two cannon point their muzzles towards the open country, and a soldier with white leather straps and shining black cartridge-cases paces between them day and night. The balconies are on the further side of a vaulted gallery with six stone arches, and after crossing the sun-filled yard, you feel as if you were in a cold cellar. The fresh air from the Campo del Moro and the Casa de Campo sweeps through the balconies and cools the sand of the courtyard.

When you look out from one of the balconies, everything is green; when you turn your back to it, everything is yellow. The lawns and woods are green, the grains of sand and the stone blocks are yellow.

There is a clock, so old that it has only one hand, because at the time it was made people did not yet count the minutes. Above the clock is a small turret with the bells and hammers hanging free in the air, always ready to strike the hours. Just under it are sentry boxes of thick stone with slits for windows and a roof like a colander. And there are three great gates which no one ever enters except ambassadors and foreign kings. Then the soldiers, who are on guard in their sentry boxes so that nobody should pass, let them through and present arms.

Swallows swoop and chatter over the heads of the sentries. There are thousands of them. Every corner of the hundred windows of the façade holds a nest, or even two or three, glued to each other, each with its little opening as if it were a pocket. There are so many of them that the swallows who came later because they were born after the others had to pile their nests into the arches of the two stone galleries. On summer evenings, when the sun is setting, they make you giddy as they flash in and out. They return a thousand times to their nests where their broods shrill, waiting with wide-open beaks for their mothers who in passing leave an insect as though it were a kiss.

Once a day, at eleven sharp, the soldiers come marching into the court-yard in slow step, in full-dress uniform. At the head of the infantry walk the four sappers, their nickeled shovels and picks on their shoulders, then the drummers, the buglers, and the band with their brass instruments sparkling and shining in the sun, and then the commanding officer, sit-ting very straight on his horse with his decorations and his sword, and behind him the flag. The cavalry in silver plated cuirasses or fur dolmans, in metal helmets or shaggy busbies with death-head badges. Last of all come the two guns drawn by eight square-crouped horses, the iron gun-carriages loaded with cannon balls, their muzzles covered with a leather cap shined with blacking. On the other side of the yard, the soldiers who are coming off guard are lined up. The two flags salute one another across the empty square and the two officers ride slowly forward, meet in the middle and whisper to each other the secret password of those who may enter or leave the palace. They salute each other with their naked swords, raising them to their foreheads and lowering them to their feet, filling the square with flashes of light. Then those who are coming off guard march through the courtyard in the same order as those who had come on, and the sound of their bugles dies away in the streets. The people stream into the yard once more, and the new soldiers play with the nurse-maids and the children.

During the night, the square stands empty, the heavy clanking iron gates are closed, the birds go to sleep and everything turns white in the moonlight. From outside the railings you hear the steps of the sentries on the flagstones of the entrance sounding across the huge courtyard. The street lamps on the wide pavements of the Calle de Bailén dazzle with their white light the hundreds of hawk-moths that come up from the parks.

Our quarter—for this was our quarter—stretched farther on through a maze of old alley-ways as far as the Calle Mayor. They were narrow, twisting streets, as our forefathers had built them for some reason or other. They had wonderful names: the names of saints, like Saint Clara and Saint James; then heroic names of wars like Luzon, Lepanto, Inde-pendence; and lastly fancy names—Street of the Mirror, of the Clock, of the Stoop—which were the oldest and most winding alleys, those which were best for playing at "Thieves and Robbers." There were bits of waste ground with broken hoardings and ruins inside, old houses with empty doorways, stone courtyards with solitary trees, little squares narrower even than the streets. They twisted and intertwined so that it was easy to hide and to escape in them.

There we used to play at "I spy." The one who was left over waited until he heard the shouts of the gang which scattered into the alleys. "I see you-oo-oo!"

He would start to run and behind his back the boys who had been crouching in the corners came out from the doorways, calling: "Past and safe!"

He would run on, smelling out the holes like a dog until he caught one of the boys squatting on the ground or behind some worm-eaten door: "I spy!"

Sometimes they both shouted at the same time, and then a quarrel would start and end in blows.

We had our quarter and our law. At times, the gang of a neighboring quarter invaded our territory, and then we defended our right with stones which ricocheted from the corners. The war usually lasted for days, and cost bumps and bruises. In the end, the attackers would get tired and leave us in peace. At other times, we ourselves attacked a neighboring quarter because the boys there were stinkers or because they had beaten up one of our gang who was passing through their territory.

Everything in our quarter was ours: the holes in the street where we played marbles: the railings of the square where we played hopscotch: the frogs and the toads in the fountain of the Plaza de Oriente: the right to the planks of the hoardings which we could exchange for broken biscuits at the pastrycook's in the Calle del Espejo: the right to catch the hawk-moths round the street lights of the Calle del Arenal, to chuck stones at the gas lamps, to jump down the high steps leading up to the Church of Santiago, and to light bonfires in the Plaza de Ramales.

That was our law.

Our council meetings took place in the doorway of the plasterer's yard. Pablito was the son of the plasterer, and the doorway belonged to him. We sat down, and the plaster fallen from the sacks made our trousers white all over. Pablito was very fair, very thin and very small, but he was the brainiest of us. Eladio, the son of the tavern keeper of the Calle de la Independencia, was the strongest brute. Between the two of them they settled all our problems, and organized our games and our pranks. Sometimes one of them undid what the other had started, because they were opposites.

In the Calle de Lemus was a piece of waste ground with a broken fence. In the ground were the cellars of a tumbledown house which nobody looked after. One day Eladio dared us all: "I'm going in there. I won't be beaten until I say I am. But I tell you, don't cry if I bash somebody's head in—and you can bash in mine for all I care."

He slipped through one of the holes in the fence and disappeared in the cellars, where the grass was growing and bricks piled up together with the muck of all the people who used them as lavatories. We laid a plan of attack. He was the bandit Vivillo and we were the Civil Guard. When we tried to get in through the holes in the hoarding, Eladio received us with a shower of stones which knocked against the planks; we retreated and fetched a supply of bricks and rubble. People went to the other side of the street so as not to get hit by our stones, and shouted at us. Eladio defended himself in his holes like a hero, and each time we invaded the waste ground we had to get out again, because he hit hard, with all the strength of the son of a tavern keeper from the hills of Asturias.

Pablito sat down behind the fence and started thinking. He got a clue from the *Adventures of Dick Navarro*. We quickly lit a bonfire in the street and wrapped our stones in smouldering paper. When the paper began to burn we threw the stones at Eladio who called us cowards, so as to dare us to invade his territory. The ground was littered with old paper, rags, straw, and rubbish thrown in by the neighbors, and soon bonfires flared up all over the place. Some of us threw stones wrapped in burning paper, some just threw stones, thick as hail, and Eladio paid us back by throwing whole bricks and bounding between the flames in a great fury. In the end we entered in a pack, our pockets full of stones, and carrying burning planks torn from the fence.

Eladio surrendered, and the neighbors kicked us out of the grounds. The ruins of the house had begun to catch fire, and the butcher, the coal merchant, the milkman, and the tavern keeper had to hurry up with pails of water. Our blouses were full of holes burned by sparks. Eladio screamed at the neighbors from behind the next corner: "Dirty pigs, bastards!"

Then we showered all the stones we were carrying in our pockets on the men, and the whole quarter was in an uproar, with doors and balconies banging while they were chasing us. The French baker from the Calle del Espejo came after us with a knobstick and thrashed Antoneja, who was always unlucky.

The next day, the ruins were full of mud and smoke fumes. The Frenchman's loaves got a broadside of horse droppings. We collected them in the stables of the house where I lived, and then our whole gang chucked them on to the rolls and buns heaped on the counter. The Frenchman caught a boy and gave him a hiding with one of the sticks of broom which he used for heating the oven. The boy's mother made a frightful row, she came down with a knife and wanted to kill the Frenchman. All the women and some of the men in the quarter wanted to storm the baker's shop.

"That dirty Frenchie dared to hit my boy!"

We boys bombarded the shop with stones, and the people cheered. Nobody remembered about the ruined house. An old woman said to a man: "You know, my father—God grant he's in heaven now, poor man— used to tell us that the French stuck their bayonets into schoolboys' bottoms and carried them round the streets like that."

The baker did not lose his customers, because he baked the best bread in the quarter. But for weeks he had to put up with people handling his rolls and loaves, and saying: "Christ, this loaf's not baked through—and that's burned—I want a decent loaf of bread."

We made peace with the baker when he got a cartload of broom for his oven. The branches were hung with pointed little seeds which danced just like a teetotum. We swarmed up the stack of scented, sticky broom, took all the sticks we wanted and filled our pockets with the tight, resinous, acorn-like pods. The man let us do it without interfering, and after that we went back to his shop to buy rolls warm from the oven, and told him it had all been our fault.

It was only a few days till my school term, and I spent them with Uncle José. In the mornings he took his stick with the silver knob—he had another one with a gold knob—and brushed his silky bowler hat with a tiny brush of very soft bristles, which he passed gently over the rounded crown and the stiff, curved brim. Then he walked slowly in the sun up the Calle de Campomanes and talked. He told me stories of when he was a boy. I could not imagine him as a child, I thought that he had always been as I was seeing him then.

"When I was your age, I was earning my bread. At eight years I was just like the boys you have seen in Brunete. I clambered on to the croup of a donkey and went to the spring to fetch water. I took their meals to my father and my elder brothers, to where they were working in the fields, and looked after the water jars so that they always had fresh water. Of course, I couldn't handle the plow, but I drove the harrow on the threshing floor and weeded the fields with a small hoe. I mowed with a sickle and tied the sheaves which the men left in a heap for me to tie. At night I got up by starlight and went out into the corral. The well bucket was so big that there was nearly room enough for me to sit in it, and it stood on the curb of the well. I had to let it down the well and haul it up when it was full. It bumped against the wall and was so heavy that I was sometimes afraid the rope would drag me down into the well shaft. When the bucket was at the height of the curbstone I dragged it on to the edge, and then I tipped it and filled the pails for the cattle which were waiting for me in the stable and turning their heads. When it was very cold I picked up my blanket from the hearthstone and lay down between the mules until dawn."

As I listened to him, I thought this was a marvelous life for a boy, a great game.

He used to speak slowly of men and things, with the leisurely, inexorable, measured pace of an old Castilian accustomed to see the hours pass by with the flat lands before him, forced to seek knowledge from the swaying grass blade and the leaping insect.

"When I was a small boy, I already worked like a man. Our food was bad. There were many of us, and my father used to pick out the black chick-peas, and the ones yellow with rust, for us to eat. He left the good ones for seed, and they were rosy chick-peas with a skin like the dry skin of a man. Our best meals were the cool *gazppacho* in the summer and potato stew in the evenings. None of my brothers were called up to the Army, but I was, and then, when I was twenty, I started to do what you are doing now: I started studying. I had big clumsy fingers stiff with horny skin, and I wept with rage because I couldn't write. The penholders slipped through my fingers, until I made one for myself. At that time only rich people used pens as you know them. The others had quills which had to be sharpened with a penknife, and I couldn't write with them. We also used canes trimmed like quills. I took a stout cane and made myself a pen that didn't slip through my fingers. I studied hard, but I never came so far as to know half of what you know already now. I learned about figures, but I never could learn algebra." He added, as though speaking to himself: "How is it possible to add up letters?"

"It's quite easy, Uncle," I answered. "Just as you add up figures." Proudly I began to give him a lesson in elementary algebra.

He listened, but he did not understand. He strained himself to follow my reasoning, and I grew almost angry when he would not understand such simple things. He dropped my hand and put his own hand on my shoulder, stroking my neck.

"It's no good. We can't do anything about it, you and I. What you don't learn as a boy, you won't learn as a man. It's just as if one's brain got hardened."

The Plaza de Callao was full of bookstalls. Every year before the opening of the school term, there was a book fair and Madrid was littered with stalls. The greatest number of them was here, in the booksellers' quarter, and at the Puerta de Atocha, where they filled the Paseo del Prado. My uncle and I liked to go from stall to stall looking for bargains. Between the fairs we went into the bookshops of the Calle de Mesonero

Romanos, the Calle de la Luna, and the Calle de la Abada. Most of the shops were just wooden sheds set up on empty building sites. The biggest bookshop was at the corner of the Calle de la Luna and the Calle de la Abada, a green-painted wooden shed as big as a coach mews. The owner, an old man, was a friend of my uncle's and had worked on the land like him. They always started to talk hard about old times and the land. Meanwhile I burrowed in the books and put those I liked in a heap. They were cheap: most of them cost ten or fifteen centimos. Every time my uncle saw the heap of books he grumbled, but I knew very well that the bookseller would not let me go away without them, and would not let my uncle discard half of them either. If my uncle did not buy them, the bookseller would give them to me. At times, though, he would take away books which I ought not to read yet, as he said. The only bad thing about it was that I could not sell those books to him afterwards. When I had read them, we took them back to the bookseller and let him have them for nothing. I also bought books in the Calle de Atocha, but the booksellers there bought them back for half the price I had paid.

There was a Valencian writer called Blasco Ibáñez who had written all these books. The priests at my school said that he was one of the worst anarchists, but I did not believe it. Once he had said that nobody read books in Spain because the people had not enough money to buy them; and I thought he was right, because our school books were very expensive. Then he said: "I will give the Spaniards something to read." And he opened a bookshop in the Calle de Mesonero Romanos and started making books. Not his own books, since he said that would not be fair, but the best books you could find in the world, and every copy was sold at thirty-five centimos. People bought them by the thousand and when they had read a book, they sold it to the second-hand bookstalls where the children and the poor bought them. That was how I had read Dickens, Tolstoi, Dostoevski, Dumas, Victor Hugo, and others.

People started at once to imitate Blasco Ibáñez. The publisher Calleja, who used to print all the school books and fairy tales, began a series called "The Novel of Today"—*La Novela de Ahora*—so as to fight against Blasco Ibáñez's series which was called "The Illustrated Novel"—*La Novela Ilustrada*. In that series Calleja published many adventure stories by Mayne Reid and Salgari, as well as Spanish classics. The two firms were fighting each other, but most people bought the issues of both every week. Then the Catalans became jealous and the publisher Sopena started printing very thick volumes on very bad paper, but with a brightly colored cover. They found less buyers, because there were not many people who could afford to spend one peseta, which was the price of a volume. The masons who were the workers with the highest wages since the strike organized by Pablo Iglesias—one of the revolutionaries like Blasco Ibáñez—earned no more than four pesetas per day at the most, that is to say, if they were skilled workers, and 1.75 pesetas if they were simple laborers. Of course many of them bought books at the second-hand shops, but only books at fifteen centimos.

As it was a long way from our house to school, I always took with me two or three novels to read and to exchange afterwards with the other boys. But we had to take care because of the Fathers at the school. If they caught us with a book of the "Illustrated Novel" series, they took it away and tore it to bits. We were only allowed a "Novel of Today" or one of the thrillers for a few coppers.

I had a funny experience because of this. Both series published one and the same book by Balzac, the "Illustrated Novel" under the title of *Eugenie Grandet* and the "Novel of Today" under the title *Los Avaros de Provincias*. I showed them both to Father Vesga, the most bigoted of all our teachers, and asked him whether I ought to tear up this "Illustrated Novel" edition as well, although it was the same book as the other one. He got as angry as a wild cat, punished me, and confiscated both books. After that he mounted the dais, banged his fist on the table and on the two books, and explained:

"Here you see how they poison the minds of young children! Yes, gentlemen! So as to make people confuse this edition of Calleja, as you all know, a Christian firm which would never lower itself to printing such filth as Blasco Ibáñez publishes in his dirty 'Illustrated Novel,' that man, who was excommunicated by the Holy Father, dares to copy the same work with another title! No, gentlemen, it is not permitted to buy a single volume of the 'Illustrated Novel,' whatever it may be, because that only means furnishing arms to Satan! And if by misfortune you should find books of this kind at home it is your duty to talk to your parents about it and tear them up, even if your parents get angry."

At this the priest had a fit of mad rage; I believe he would have killed Blasco Ibáñez if he had been there. He spoke of him as of a monster who murdered people. In the end he turned to me and said "You"—he used "you" in place of "thou" only when he was furious—"you will stay on your knees in the classroom for a fortnight, and by then you will have learned not to read such books!"

We went to my uncle's office which was in the building of the church of San Martín in the Calle de la Luna. That church owned an ancient cemetery in the grounds of Amaniel, in which the members of the Confraternity of Saint Martin used to be buried. Later on the State decreed the closing of the cemetery and prohibited any more burials there, as it was already full. Then many of the people whose relatives were buried there had them dug up and removed to another cemetery, so that they all could be buried in the same grave. Since my uncle was in charge of the cemetery office, people came to him to get the permit to dig up their father or mother or grandfather and take them to another place. It was a very expensive business, because as soon as you fiddled with a dead body, everyone cashed in. You had to pay dues to the State, to the Madrid Town Council, to both cemeteries, the one from which the body was removed, and the other in which it was going to be buried; to the Church of San Martín, to the parish in which the relatives lived, to all the parishes through which the coffin would have to pass; the cost of the exhumation, the fee of the forensic doctor who had to attend the opening of the grave, and the price of the new grave site. Thus it cost more than a thousand duros, or five thousand pesetas, to transfer a body.

People gave gratuities up to five hundred pesetas to my Uncle José so that he would speed up the dispatch of the necessary papers. He ran round to the Town Council, the cemeteries, and the parish offices for them and settled everything.

Often, when my school was closed, I went with him and listened to the conversations; many of them were very curious. Most removals were to the cemeteries of San Isidro and San Lorenzo. In the cemetery of San Lorenzo there was a very fat and jolly chaplain who exclaimed every time we arrived: "Hullo, Pepe—how many new lodgers are you bringing me?" Then he would produce a bottle of old sweet wine and some biscuits. "Well, let's drink to the health of the dead!" He would fill his glass first, drink it, smack his tongue, thump my uncle on the back, and say: "That's the good one, you know, the one I use at Mass! You see, we've always got a few crazy old women who give me things. They pay the three pesetas for the responsories, and then from time to time they bring a little bottle as well to make the recommendation of the defunct to Divine Mercy more effective!"

When we said good-by to him the bottle was always empty, although my uncle and I had drunk only a small glass each.

My uncle's office was at the end of a very dark corridor which began at a side door of the church and ran alongside a garden neglected for many years. The garden was full of odd plants which grew between the grass and entangled your feet. Some of them had climbed the trees and the walls, and the trees and the walls were covered with leaves. In the middle was a round basin which must have been a fountain once upon a time. The rain water had collected there and it had rotted the stone. Plants had grown in the broken fountain and hung over its rim down to the ground; and from the ground, plants had climbed up, twined with the others, and crept into the basin, so that you did not know which were growing from the fountain. In spring every corner of the garden was full of flowers. On the walls, on the trees, and in the basin of the fountain bells opened, white or purple with yellow pistils. There were red and orange poppies and there were roses of a very dark red, difficult to pick, because they had thorns like hooks. After rain, snails covered the garden. They came up in thousands, and I never understood from where they came and where they went. There were green lizards a foot long, and from the office window we could see rats big as small cats crossing the garden. The church was full of rats.

In autumn the trees turned yellow and the leaves heaped up in the garden. When you walked on them they crackled like old paper. After the rains they rotted, and then the ground of the garden was as soft as a thick carpet. The trees were very old and very big, and hundreds of birds lived in them; all the birds from the whole quarter, because the children never went into the garden. I was the only one to go there, I and a very old priest who had belonged to the church for many years and who liked to sit in the garden reading his breviary. In winter he used to sit in the sun and at times he fell asleep there. As the black cloth of his robes grew very hot, the small lizards sometimes climbed on to his knees. When he woke and saw them, he stroked them gently and they lifted their heads as though they were looking into his face.

Once there was a new parish priest who wanted to tidy up the garden, and the old priest made a row in the sacristy, shaking his stick and crying aloud:

"Damnation, if he touches the garden I'll whack him!"

He was so old that they left his garden as he wanted it. Whenever he saw me, he called me and told the story. "Those fools," he would say, "they think they can do better than God. Wouldn't this garden be nice with a few little pebbled paths and a few small trees with their hair trimmed as if the barber came every morning? You see, all those gardeners only want to correct the works of God, and so they clip the leaves off the trees until they look like a wedding cake. What's your opinion?" he would ask me.

"You see, Father Cesareo, for me this is the best garden in the world. Here I can walk on the grass and pick the flowers I like, but in the Retiro where the trees are trimmed as you say, you mustn't walk on the grass or take a flower. If you do the park keeper beats you with his stick, or if you are with a grown-up he fines you five pesetas. And then there is barbed wire, and if you don't take care your legs get all torn and scratched. That's why I like going to the Moncloa, where you can run about on the grass and there are flowers and pines, or coming here to this garden."

But not all priests were like Padre Cesareo. In the sacristy they used to quarrel over the Masses and the confessional. There was a big priest who had a very bad temper; he liked playing cards so much that whenever he had to stay on duty in the church, he went to my uncle's office to play Tresillo. He always boxed the altar boys' ears and had rows with everybody. He quarreled even with the women who came to the sacristy to bring candles for the altars. When the candle was thin, he took it between the tips of his fingers and said: "Madam, this is just a match stick. Either you've very little piety, or very little money. But I suppose it's little piety you have, because you've got money enough for trinkets and paint." When the candle was thick, he grew just as angry: "Where do you want us to place this pole? Of course, you buy a fat taper so that it should last on the altar many days and you can point it out to all your neighbors and say: 'Do you see that big, tall candle in the middle of all the small ones? That's my candle!' So you have a good reason for a little gossip and for showing off. What you're spending on wax you ought to give to our Church, which is in sore need of it."

The funny thing was that in this way he squeezed money out of everybody. Then he would show the duro or the two pesetas to the other priests and say: "See what idiots you are. The only argument that helps with these people is a good kick in the pants. With your 'Madam this' and 'Madam that' and kissing hands you don't get money out of them. If you want to milk a cow you've got to pull her teats."

He kept the money for himself and the others never dared to say anything. Only once Don Rafael, a small timid priest, went out of his way to tell him that those donations should go into the common pool. The other looked him up and down as if he were going to hit him, and pulled a duro out of his cassock. He flicked it on the palm of his hand and said: "It's me who's earned this duro. Everyone who likes duros can earn them for himself. It would be a nice thing for me to fill your pockets! *Nequaquam!*" And he put the duro back into his cassock.

There was a seat attendant in the church who was also the janitor of the sacristy and the offices, a kind of watchman. During services he walked about in the church among the people with a collecting box and made everybody pay the five centimos for his seat. It was a good job, because many people gave him ten centimos or more for keeping a prie-dieu instead of a straw-bottomed chair reserved for them, and others gave him letters or messages for their sweethearts and tipped him a peseta or two. Then, when the girl came to hear Mass, he went to her to cash in the copper for the chair, winked, and gave her the letter; and so he would get another tip. The priests took the money out of the collecting boxes by opening the padlock, but the seat attendant kept on filching money. He did it with a corset whalebone. He stuck a little pellet of hot pitch on the point of the bone, pushed it through the slit of the box and left it inside to let the pitch cool. Then the money stuck to it, and he fished out the coins one by one.

In the afternoon, when my uncle left his office, we went to the Callao Cinema. It was a big, ugly shed of wood and canvas. In the entrance stood a barrel-organ with many drums, flutes, and trumpets, and some figures dressed up as pages, which turned round and round on one foot, nodded their heads to make a bow, and struck an instrument with their hands. One of them had a drum, another a lyre with little bells, and a third a tambourine. Highest of all stood a figure with a baton which conducted the music. Behind them was the machinery; there was a tall box with a very long strip of paper covered with holes, which passed over a cylinder and then fell into another box alongside. When the roll ran over the cylinder, which was also covered with holes, the air passed through the holes of the paper into the hollow inside and made the instruments of the organ sound.

The shed was filled with wooden benches, and at the far end was the screen and the speaker. The speaker was a very amusing man who explained the whole film and cracked jokes at the things which appeared on the screen. The people applauded him very much, especially when one of Toribio's films was running. They called him Toribio, but in reality he was a French actor by the name of André Deed, who always did things that made you laugh. They also gave Pathé films about animals and flowers, which showed you how animals live and how flowers grow. Once I saw a hen's egg with its white and yolk, so large that it filled the whole screen. It began to move slowly and to change its form. First something like an eye appeared, and then the little chick began to shape, and in the end it was already formed, pecked at the shell of the egg, broke it, and came out with a bit of the shell stuck to its behind. You also saw films of the King and Queen looking at horse races, and of foreign kings and lots of other people.

The owner of the cinema knew us; he was a very kind man who had lived in France for many years. His name was Gimeno. On Thursday afternoons, when there was no class, he did not charge the boys more than five centimos for a ticket. When he saw a boy hanging round the organ he asked him why he did not come in. The boy would say: "I haven't got the money." Then Gimeno would take a look at him, and if he wasn't a ragamuffin he would say: "Come on, get in." Other boys who had no money begged for it from the people who were passing by, and many bought a five-centimo ticket for them. So the cinema filled with boys on Thursdays; even the passages were full of those who could not squeeze on to the benches. Grown-ups disliked going there on Thursdays because of the row going on, with all the boys squealing and making noises. But Señor Gimeno enjoyed the Thursdays more than any other day, and so did the speaker; on Thursdays he cracked more jokes and told more crazy stories than ever.

Sometimes my uncle and I went to other places in Madrid, to the Retiro Park, when the band was playing there, or to the gardens of the Buen Retiro outside the Park. There in the gardens another band used to play and usually a circus with animals was set up there in summer. A lion-tamer called Malleu, a Spaniard, who was said to be the best lion-tamer in the world, had a lion into whose cage nobody else ever dared to enter. The Circus Parish had another lion-tamer, and Malleu offered him 1,000 pesetas if he dared to enter the cage of his lion. We went sometimes to the Circus Parish, but only when there was no dangerous show on. Once a young girl called Minna Alice who turned somersaults in a wooden hoop mounted on a car had got killed, and my uncle did not want me to go to anything where I might see someone killing himself.

It is difficult to turn back.

You look into the sky, and see cloud cavalcades heaped up by the air which never tires of giving them new shape, or you see but the blue dome aquiver with sunlight. It is the same at night, although the sun is hidden and the light comes only from the stars and the moon. Invisibly, the waves ride on in that sky by day and by night.

All over the earth voices and songs are thrown into the air at random, mixed, massed as the clouds are massed by the wind. A copper wire slung across the roof of a house catches them all, and its frail thread of a body shudders at the impact. An anode and a cathode hurl those voices and songs at each other, as they arrive in mingled surging waves, and the patient hand of the listener regulates the mad leap of the electrons so as to single out a voice or a symphony. But there is always one strain of sound which dominates everything else, a wave more tenacious than the others, to which you have to listen.

Old Madrid, the Madrid of my childhood, is a great surge of clouds or of waves, I do not know which. But beyond all those whites and blues, beyond all the songs and sounds and vibrations, there is one predominant strain:

EL AVAPIES.

At that time it was the frontier of Madrid. It was the end of Madrid, and the end of the world. With that critical instinct for the right word, which two thousand years since earned the tag of *vox populi, vox dei,* the people had baptized the limits of El Avapies; there were the *Americas* and there was *El Mundo Nuevo,* the New World. It was another world indeed. So far civilization and the city reached, and there they ended.

There began a world of abstruse things and beings. There the city cast its ash and spume, and so did the nation. The seething waters of Madrid threw their scum from the center to the periphery, and the scum of the seething waters of Spain was sucked from the periphery to the center. The two waves met and formed a belt which spanned the town. Only the initiated, the Civil Guards, and we children penetrated into that live barrier.

Gullies and slopes bearded with rough ears of grass eternally yellow, dry, and harsh. Fumes from factory chimneys and evil-smelling trickles from stables. Allotments with lumpy soil, black and putrid; foul streams and parched cracks in the earth. Epileptic trees, hostile thistles and thorns, gaunt dogs with angular ribs, dusty telegraph poles with their white china cups broken, goats browsing on waste paper, empty rusted tins, huts sunk to their knees in the ground. Gypsies with bold side-whiskers, gypsy women in motley, grease-stained petticoats, beggars with abundant beards and lice, children all bottom and belly, filth trickling down their legs, the navel button protruding from their dusky paunches. This was called the "Quarter of the Injuries."

It was the lowest rung in the social ladder that began at the Plaza de Oriente, in the Royal Palace with its gates open to plumed helmets and diamond-spangled *décolletés,* and ended in El Avapies, which then spewed out the last dregs and deposited them in the other world, in the Americas and the *Mundo Nuevo.*

Thus El Avapies was the pointer of the scales, the crucial point between existence and non-existence. One came to El Avapies from above or from below. Whoever came from above had stepped down the last step left to him before the final and absolute fall. Whoever came from below had scaled the first step upwards, which might lead to anywhere and anything. Millionaires have passed through El Avapies before crossing the outer belt of the Rondas and turning into drunken beggars. Rag-pickers, collectors of cigarette stubs and waste paper, filthy from spittle and trampling feet, have climbed the step of El Avapies and come to be millionaires. In El Avapies, all the prides exist side by side, the pride of having been everything and no longer wanting to be anything, and the pride of having been nothing and wanting to be everything.

If those tremendous and wantonly cruel forces were to clash, life would be impossible. But the two waves never break against each other. Between them lies a firm, calm beach which absorbs the impact of both and converts them into currents which ebb and flow: all Avapies works.

In its houses built with prison galleries running round their courtyards, passages open to the winds, a single lavatory for all the inmates, a door and a window per cell, live the plasterer, the smith, the carpenter, the newspaper vendor, the blind beggar from the corner, the bankrupt, the rag-and-bone man, and the poet. In those courtyards with their pavement of rounded pebbles, a dripping water-tap in the middle, all the tongues of one language meet: the refined accent of the gentleman, the shameless talk of the pimp, the slang of thieves and beggars, the high-flown rhetorics of the budding writer. You hear horrifying blasphemies and exquisitely tender phrases.

Every day during many years of my childhood I walked from the gates of the Palace down to the gates of the New World, and scaled the slope on my way back. At times I went into the Palace and watched from the marble galleries guarded by halberdiers the pageant of the royalty, the princes and the grandees of Spain. At times I crossed the frontier into the no-man's world beyond the New World and watched naked gypsies squatting in the sun and killing the lice which the swarthy fingers of their mother or sister plucked from their hair, one by one. I watched the rag-pickers separating the mountain of refuse into heaps of food for themselves and their animals, and heaps of rubbish which they would be able to sell for a few coppers.

I fought battles with stones against the brats of the gypsies and the rag-pickers, and I played decorously at quoits or at hopscotch with boys in braided sailor suits, with curled hair and white collars and silk scarves.

If El Avapies still resounds in me through all the echoing strains of my life, there are two reasons:

There I learned all I know, the good and the bad, to pray to God and to curse Him, to hate and to love, to see life crude and bare as it is, and to feel an infinite longing to scale the next step upwards and to help all others to scale it. That is one of the two reasons.

The other is that my mother lived there. But this reason is my own.

8. School and Church

I MADE more friends among the other boys of our form, among the
rich boys, than the two other scholarship pupils. Although Sastre and
Cerdeño came to school with better suits than before they had gone to
class upstairs, I was still better dressed than either of them. Also, they
lived in tenement houses in El Avapies, while I lived in a wealthy quarter
and knew many thing they did not know. Sometimes they accused me
to my face of avoiding them so as to be with the others. And it was not
true. What really happened was that I could get on with the rich boys
and they could not, because they remained what they were, street urchins
of the slums. When I was with the rich boys, I felt more as if I was with
my own kind. When I was with the other two, it always annoyed me
that they did not realize we were no longer downstairs and could neither
say nor do the same things as before. They came to school with their
pockets full of green wheat-ears and nibbled them during the lessons and
told stories of how they had been throwing stones together with the
Ronda gang in a battle against the boys of the New World, how the Civil
Guard had come riding and how all the boys had got together, two hundred of them, to throw stones at the Civil Guard. One day Cerdeño arrived with his hands blackened, and when Father Joaquín asked him
why he hadn't washed them, he said that the day before, a Sunday, he
had been gleaning at the "Flea Station." The Flea Station was what they
called the shunting station of Las Delicias—The Delights—on the suburban line, where the trains from the North Station were linked with
trains from the South Station. The children and women of the quarter
went there to the coal dumps with little baskets and collected bits of good
coal from among the cinders of the railway engines. They also used to
pinch what real coal they could get, and burn it at home or sell it. Cerdeño went there because it was fun for him.

It sometimes happened that he and Sastre produced *gallinejas* for break
at eleven: cow's tripe fried in tallow at street stalls and put between two
chunks of bread. Whenever they were eating them, they stank from the
smell of hot grease. And apart from all that, it was impossible to teach
them not to speak as people spoke in El Avapies; they still used any kind
of bad word that came to their mind.

It was difficult for me. When I was with the two of them, I was more
at my ease, but they looked at me as though I were different. When I

was with the others, I found it more pleasant, but they knew that I was different from them, that I was the son of a washerwoman, that I was with them only because I had won the scholarship and the priests paid for my studies. So it happened that when they wanted to insult me, the rich boys called me "Washerwoman's Son," and the poor boys "Little Gentleman."

The oddest thing was that there were many poor boys who were not poor and many rich boys who were not rich. In the non-paying forms there were sons of tradesmen from the quarter, whose fathers had a very good business, and in the forms upstairs there were sons of civil servants whose fathers had to starve themselves so that their boys could shine at school among the rich pupils. And these two groups showed off most, one as being poor and the other as being rich.

It was a Sunday. After Mass I went with Father Joaquín up to his room to collect some books he wanted to lend me. Then we walked down to the cloisters on the first floor, where the relatives of the boarders stayed with the boys after Mass until mealtime. That day it was Father Joaquín's turn to receive the parents and tell them how their boys had done.

Nieto, the Asturian, was with his father, a broad, strong man with the face of a bulldog. Nieto called me, and Father Joaquín and I went over together.

"Look, Papa," he said, "this is Barea."

His father looked me up and down with little gray eyes glinting under shaggy eyebrows.

"Oh yes, that's the son of the washerwoman you told me about. You should learn from him, considering you have cost me good money, only to turn out more of a brute than a washerwoman's son."

Nieto went quite pale and I felt that I had grown red. Father Joaquín put one hand on my head and took Nieto by the arm, saying: "Run away for a while." Then he turned to Nieto's father, very gravely, and said:

"Here the two of them are equal, or rather, here the son of a washerwoman is more than the son of a mine-owner who pays three hundred pesetas per month."

He turned on his heel and walked away calmly, without bowing his head. The old man gazed after him and then called his son. The two began a discussion, sitting there on the bench.

I passed by them and said to the boy:

"See you tomorrow." And I walked on without bowing to his father. Father Joaquín stood by the door. He said nothing to me. I said nothing to him. I kissed his hand and went away.

I went down the steps of the entrance without seeing them, for my eyes
filled with water. What Father Joaquín had done was against the rules
of the school, where people with money were never treated that way. If
he were found out, he would be alone against all the other priests. Because things were like that, he played his oboe for the birds and talked to
them.
I was alone as he was. Both of us were different from the others.

Once a month all those of us who had already been to their 'first
Communion went to confession. The priests distributed themselves over
the church and the thousand pupils distributed themselves among the
priests just as they pleased because nobody could force us to confess to
a priest we did not like. Some priests, such as Father Joaquín and Father
Fidel, had very long queues waiting at their confessionals; by looking at
the size of the files you could see which of the priests were liked by the
boys. Those who had confessed joined their form in the file in front of
the High Altar, to say their penitential prayers, to hear Mass and to
take Communion. Thus the Church was filled with the sound of coming
and going, of mumbled prayers and the patter of shoe soles. The Father
Préfect went round to keep order.
Every month it was the same. Father Vesga was left with no more
than the six or eight boys whom he had made promise that they would
confess to him. Although he took longer over each confession than any
of the other priests, he was always left alone before the others had finished. Then the Father Prefect would go from file to file and ask one
or the other boy whether he would not go to Father Vesga for his confession. We liked him so much that he usually collected enough boys to
form a queue. That day he had done the trick with me, and I went to
Father Vesga because I did not really mind.
Father Vesga put his arm round my shoulder and neared his head to
mine. The confession began. The questions about the Commandments
came one by one, and I was proud to be able to answer them all.
"Do you love God? Do you go to Mass on Sundays? Do you love your
parents? Do you speak the truth?"
We reached the Sixth Commandment. All the priests used to ask us
whether we did dirty things or not; as we knew what they meant by
that, we answered "yes" or "no," mostly "yes," because we all did those
things or thought we had been doing them. Then the priests said: "Look
here, my son, you mustn't do that. It's a sin and very bad for you. Children who do it become consumptive and die." They told us to say a few
penitential Paternosters, and that was that.
With Father Vesga it was different.

"You know what the Sixth Commandment says, my son?"

"Yes, Father. It says: Thou shalt not fornicate."

"Tell me what 'fornicate' means."

I did not know and could not tell him. I knew that it was a bad thing which was done between men and women, but that was all I knew. Father Vesga turned very grave.

"You must not lie in the Holy Tribunal of Penance. First you tell me that you know the Sixth Commandment, and now you contradict yourself and tell me that you don't know what fornication means."

"Fornication, Reverend Father, fornication is—well, things men and women do, which are a sin."

"So, so. Things men and women do. And what is it men and women do, you shameless boy?"

"I don't know, Father. I've never fornicated."

"And a nice thing it would be if you had, you shaver. I'm not asking if you have fornicated or not, I'm asking you what it means to fornicate."

"I don't know. The boys say that fornication is when a man makes a woman be with child. When they're married it's not a sin, and when they're not married it is."

"Now, come, what I want you to do is to tell me how men and women make children."

"I wouldn't know. They get married and sleep together and then they get children. That's all I know."

"So, that's all you know, eh? What a very innocent babe, it doesn't know more than that! But what you do know is how to play with your parts."

"Sometimes, Father."

"Well, that's fornication." There followed a sermon of which I did not understand a word, or rather, which threw me into endless confusion. Woman is Sin. For the sake of Woman the human race fell from grace, and all the saints suffered the temptations of evil. They had apparitions of naked women with bare breasts and lewd movements. And nowadays Satan does not even spare the children. He comes to drive away their sleep and to show them naked women to sully the purity of their minds. And so on and on for half an hour. He spoke to me of flowing hair, quivering bosoms, lascivious hips, of King Solomon, of obscene dances, of women at street corners, in a torrent of angry words which all went to say that Woman was a sack of uncleanliness and evil, and that men slept with women and therefore went to Hell.

When I got away from the priest to say my penitential prayers, I could not pray. My brain was full of naked women and of the curiosity to know what it was they did with men.

But nobody knew it. I asked my mother, my uncle, my aunt, and they answered my questions in an odd manner. What is fornicating? How are children made? Why do women get pregnant? Some people told me that children ought not to speak of such things, and others said that it was a sin, and a few said I was a shameless boy.

In one of the bookstalls of the Calle de Atocha I found a book which explained everything. It told of a man and a woman who went to bed together and of everything they did. The book made the round of my class and all the boys read it. So as not to be caught by the priests, the boys took it to the lavatory to read and to look at the pictures, which showed the man and the woman fornicating. I read the book many times and it excited me. The same happened to me whenever I saw picture postcards of naked women.

Now I understood why the Holy Virgin had the Child Jesus without doing dirty things with Saint Joseph. The Holy Ghost made her pregnant without their having to do them. But because my father and my mother slept together they had me, and therefore my mother was not a virgin. What I did not know, however, was why my uncle and aunt had no children, although they did sleep together. Perhaps my aunt was so pious that they did not do any dirty things and so could not have children. But they would have liked to have some. On the other hand, God had said: "Increase and multiply."

I did not understand.

Father Vesga said it was sin to come near a woman. But Don Juan, a very kind priest in the church of San Martín, was once in the sacristy together with a woman. She was sitting on his knees and he had his hands between her breasts. When I came in they both got very red. The priest came up to me and said I should go away, he was just hearing her confession. I told Uncle José about it and he said those were things young children should not discuss and I was on no account to tell my aunt.

Men said things to women in the streets, and women at street corners invited men to go and sleep with them, and the men gave them money.

I was in a terrible muddle about it all and did not know what was good and what was bad.

But there were many other things I found I did not understand. The church of San Martín had many collection boxes, like all churches; it said on them "For the Poor Souls in Purgatory," "For the Cult of the Faith," "For the Poor." The priests opened those boxes every evening, took out the money, made little piles of a duro out of the big coppers and piles of half a duro out of the small coppers, distributed the piles among themselves, and played cards in the sacristy. One day Don Tomás lost all the cash which had fallen to his lot, as well as five duros out of his own cassock. When he got up from the table, he said:

"Today the Blessed Souls have done the dirty on me."

He took the bottle with sweet strong wine, the sacramental wine, and drank down a big glass.

"One must take life in gulps, as it comes," he said and went away.

The dead are hallowed and the soil of the cemeteries is holy ground. In the Cemetery of San Martín, the walls of the vaults had crumbled and the coffins with the bones stuck out. The chaplain and the keepers of the cemetery collected the rotten planks and used them as firewood. Often they threw in the bones as well, because they were so worm-eaten than they burned like wood. But when people had arranged for one of the dead to be dug out and transferred to another cemetery, the priest put on his embroidered cope and carried the aspergillum, and the grave-diggers dug most carefully so as not to crush the coffins. They took out the bones, laid them tenderly on a white sheet, the priest said his Latin and the sacristan gave the responses. Then the priest sprinkled Holy Water over the bones and they were carried off to be buried elsewhere, all because the family of that particular corpse had the money to take it away. The other corpses were only good enough for bonfires, and their bones were broken up with a hammer before being thrown to the flames.

On some days more people died than on others. Two women would come to the sacristy and order a Requiem Mass to be said for their husbands, or fathers; their names were noted down on a list, and they had to pay a stipend of three pesetas for the Mass. "Tomorrow at eleven," said the priest. Then the other women would arrive and ask for another Mass. The priest would note their names and pocket his three pesetas. "Tomorrow at eleven," he would say. Sometimes three or four families met in church, each in its corner, to listen to a Mass each family had paid for its own departed. When the priest read the oration for the deceased, he reeled off from a slip of paper the names of the three or four people who had died, so that the dead could share the Mass among themselves.

Once an Obsequial Mass was ordered costing two hundred and fifty pesetas; three priests were to celebrate and a black catafalque was to be set up in the middle of the church. It so happened that three more Masses for the Dead were paid and registered for the same day. "Tomorrow at ten," said the priest to everybody. At ten the church was full of people who listened to the Solemn Mass being sung. But then, when no Requiem Mass was read, the three families went into the sacristy one after the other to inquire about it. The priest asked:

"Weren't you at the Solemn Mass?"

"Yes, Father," they all answered.

"Well, that was the Mass for your dear departed. By a coincidence several families came together at the same hour, and as we have not so many priests as to be able to oblige everyone, we agreed to hold a Solemn Mass for the families together. So you have gained by it, really."

The people walked away through the sacristy corridor and one said with great satisfaction: "Who could have foretold this to poor Juanito? There you see, my girl, he was lucky all his life and even after his death they let him have a whole Solemn Mass for three pesetas."

And mysteries: everything in religion was a mystery.

A Saint was walking by the sea shore when he saw a child sitting on the sand. The child held a shell in his hand and filled it with water from the sea and then poured the water into a hollow in the sands.

"What are you doing, child?" the Saint asked.

"I am emptying the sea into this hollow," answered the child.

"That is impossible. How can you expect the water of the sea to find room in this little hollow? It is impossible."

"It is more impossible to find out why God is One and Three," replied the child, "and yet you keep on trying to find out."

At that the Saint realized that he was speaking to an Angel whom the Lord had sent him.

It did not interest me why God was One and Three at the same time. But I wondered why he had to be One and Three to be God. It only seemed to be so as to make things difficult for us.

"How many Gods are there?" asked the teacher.

"One."

"Yes, but that's not the right answer."

"Three."

"Yes, but that's not the right answer either."

The right answer was to say that there were three deities, Father, Son, and Holy Ghost, but only One True God. Then the teacher was satisfied; but I was not, because I still did not know which was the true God, nor did the teachers.

My aunt wanted to have the Pope's Benediction. For ten pesetas she got a Benediction which was for her personally, and she put it in a frame. Some years later they gave her another for one hundred pesetas, which was valid for her and all the members of her family down to the fifth generation. She took the old benediction out of the frame and threw it in the dustbin. Then she put the new Benediction in its place, and so I was blessed by Leo XIII.

The more I learned about religion, the more problems arose. The worst of it was that I could not discuss them with anyone, because my teachers only grew angry and punished me. One day in the Scripture lesson we came to the the story of Joshua, who stopped the sun in its course until the end of the battle. I asked Father Vesga how that could be, for our geography teacher had told us that the sun stands still and the earth revolves, and therefore it would be impossible to stop the sun. Father Vesga answered grumpily:

"You should not ask forward questions. This is laid down in the Holy Scriptures and that ought to be enough for you. Faith moveth mountains and detaineth the sun. If you had the right faith you would understand these matters which are as clear as daylight."

Then I asked Father Joaquín about it. He put his hand on my head and said with a great smile:

"Now, what shall I say to you, my boy? In olden times many odd things happened. As you know, there was a time when the animals spoke and everybody understood them. Doubtless in Joshua's time the sun moved."

Father Fidel said more:

"Listen, my boy, what happened was that it was not the sun that stopped, but the earth, only it looked as though the sun had stopped. It's just like when you are in a train, you think the telegraph poles move and then stop. When the Bible was written, people didn't yet know that the earth moved, they only saw the sun moving just as we see it now. For that reason they put down that the sun stood still, although it was really the earth."

"But, Father, according to what we learned in Physics the earth could not stop because if it did we would all be thrown into space. Besides, the earth would burn if it suddenly stopped."

He looked at me with great seriousness and said:

"But, my dear boy, who told you that it stopped suddenly? It stopped slowly, of course, like a tram stops. And now run away, I've got a lot of work to do."

Little by little I realized that I was not alone in wanting to know the truth about God and Faith. The books I was reading raised the same questions. The Church put those books on the Index, but it did not answer them. The only person with whom I could speak about them was Father Joaquín, who neither grew angry nor took the books away from me. We had many discussions. Only once did he convince me. I sat at his desk and he stood in front of his music-stand, the oboe in his hand and the birds on the window sill. He looked out into the courtyard, into the sky, as though he were seeing nobody, and he began to speak not to me but to himself.

"None of us knows anything about anything. The only certainty is that we exist. That the earth exists, and the sun, and the moon, and the stars, and the birds and fishes and plants and all things, and that every-

thing lives and dies. There must have been a beginning once, the first
hen or the first egg must have arrived, but I don't know which. The first
tree and the first bird. Someone made them. After that everything carried
on under a law. This is what I call God and in Him I believe, in Him
who rules all this. Beyond God I only believe in goodness."

He was silent, and then he gave me a book:
"Take it and read it. And believe in what you like. Even if you don't
believe in God—as long as you're good, it is just as though you did."

He gave me *The Life of Saint Francis of Assisi.*

I had a shoe box with holes in the top so that the caterpillars inside
could breathe. They were silkworms. I had the Chinese kind, with coffee-brown spots, and the white kind. When I threw mulberry leaves into
the box, the silkworms first stayed hidden. Then they began to climb up
and nibble the edges of the leaves; they cut out round bits with the two
dark teeth at the point of their head, holding on to the edge of the leaf
with their legs and moving their head up and down. As they went on
eating they made tiny cylindrical droppings. From time to time they
wrinkled their forehead between the two little black eyes, and the bluish
band running along their body began to undulate from tail to head, as
though a blood stream were passing through it. Then they changed their
position and found themselves another part of the leaf to nibble. Sometimes two of them came nose to nose while they were gnawing their way
through; then they lifted their heads and seemed to be looking and saying something to one another. One of them would wrinkle its forehead
and they would change places.

I picked them up in my fingers. They were soft and warm, they twisted
their bodies round my finger with their hairy little legs and seemed to
sample its skin, quite astonished that there existed such a kind of leaf.
Then they noticed the box beneath them, rolled up into a tight ball and
let themselves drop to start eating again.

If I put the leaf of any other tree among the mulberry leaves they did
not touch it. They stepped across and went to the other leaves. They
knew, smelled, and saw it. I wondered if they knew and smelled and
saw me. Did they know who I was and what I was like? When I watched
them in their box and they lifted their heads, they seemed to look at me.
Then I took one, laid it along one finger and passed the tip of another
of my fingers over the soft, tender body. It stretched, and raised its head
and front legs. Suddenly it wrinkled its forehead. I dropped it into the
box, and it resumed eating. But now and again it lifted its head to look
at me.

Later on they crept into a corner of the box, fastened their legs to the cardboard and started swiveling their heads round, and a thin thread of spittle dripped out of their mouths. Their bodies became very small and the silk thread wrapped itself round them, until the only thing to be seen was a little shadow still moving its head in the shell of the cocoon. In the end the cocoon-egg lay there, yellow or white, fastened to a corner of the box. Every day I opened another cocoon to see what was inside. The skin of the silkworms had turned hard, as if made of horn, dark as an olive stone, ringed all round, with the snout and the two black teeth left. They were fast asleep and did not waken, and the only thing that moved gently were the rings. Later on they grew real legs, a head, and wings, they turned white and developed two shaggy horns formed like silken half-moons. In the end they bored a hole through the cocoon and crept out on the white cloth I had prepared for them at the bottom of the box. The females fluttered their wings very quickly and flew round and round. Then the male came and they fastened on to each other by their tails. They stuck together for hours. The belly of the female swelled to a ball and she sprinkled the white cloth with minute yellow eggs which looked first golden and later turned black. And then the moths died. They stayed in the box, dried up, their wings sticking to their small bodies as though they had sweated in death.

I kept the white cloth under a stack of sheets. It was full of thousands of eggs. My aunt put apples between the linen, which dried and crumpled like the face of an old woman. Next year the white cloth smelled of apples and out of every little egg came a black thread which turned into a silkworm.

I was sitting on the balcony with the shoe box standing in the sun so that the silkworms should be warm. Beside me I had a heap of books which I picked up one by one to go through them. It was almost June, and I had to pass the examinations for two matriculation courses at the same time, and then to compete for an honors certificate. They were all pushing me: the priests of the school crammed me and occupied themselves with hardly anyone else in the form, examining me about the same things in a thousand different ways. My uncle promised me that I could study engineering if I got through the exams with honors. My poor mother stroked my hair and asked me to make an effort; she could do nothing for me, but my uncle and aunt would do everything if I was a good boy. My aunt dressed me up in my best clothes and took me visiting; she showed me off to her friends as a phenomenon, and bald gentlemen and old ladies, rather like my aunt herself, plied me with silly questions.

"Very nice, Arturito, very nice! And now tell me, how are you getting on with your studies?"

Once Doña Isabel made me so furious with that kind of question that I began to speak at great speed about logarithms, the binomial theory, parabolic curves, and produced a spate of nonsensical algebraic formulas with lots of "*a.s*" and "*x.s*" and symbols and phantastic figures. Doña Isabel stared at me and her chin sagged until I stopped short and said solemnly: "And that's all I know."

"What a marvel, Doña Baldomera, what a marvel of a child! Just like my husband. When poor Juan sat down to work with figures he was simply marvelous. D'you know that he did sums in his head? In his head! This boy will go far. Just as my poor Juan would have gone far if he had only lived."

I felt like calling her idiot, old sow, bitch, beast, and all sorts of things. I would have liked to tear the false plait out of her top-knot and scour her face, covered in butter-yellow face-cream mixed with powder as it was, with a swab soaked in dish-water.

My future! I was going to be an engineer so as to make everybody happy, but above all so that my mother no longer needed to go on washing and to be somebody's servant. They were all very good to me. They all dished out charity to me. Yet I felt tired and did not want to eat or play. I only wanted to see: to see things and beings as Saint Francis had seen them.

The cat settled down on my knees. He looked at the box with the silk-worms and at the books; he looked at me with his golden eyes. Then he turned those eyes inwards, curled up into a ball, his body folded between his legs and his tail stroking his nose, and purred. I thought that he understood me and knew about things. I too understood him. But when he sat there looking at me and looking at things, I did not know what he wanted to say. He said nothing, but I could see in his eyes that his head was as full of thoughts as my own. He slept so as to avoid thinking. The same happened to me. Often I was suddenly so overwhelmingly sleepy that I lay down on the carpet of our dining room, or on the floor of the balcony, and slept.

The two dogs of the coach yard were white and lively. I had seen them when they were just born and small as a fist; they knew me and liked me. When I went out into the street they came up, wagging their tails, barking and jumping. I used to collect lumps of sugar in the café and they always begged for them. I squatted down on my haunches and they thrust their black noses into the pocket of my blouse to get at the sugar. The cat looked down from the balcony through the bars of the railing and saw me playing with the dogs. Then, when I went upstairs, the cat refused to play with me; he was angry. I opened the cupboard and produced a bag of biscuits. We both ate, I sitting on the floor and he sitting between my knees, and made it up. Later on my aunt was annoyed, but she was wrong. The cat and I were right.

People were astonished at the things Malleu could do with his lions in the Buen Retiro Gardens. I was not astonished. He had a large round iron cage which he filled with wooden stools. The lions came filing out, and one after the other jumped on a stool, sat down, its head high, and watched Malleu. He was a tall, lean, green-eyed man with frizzy hair like a Cuban's. He talked to the lions and they understood. They roared, and people thought they were going to attack him, but Malleu knew that the lions were only answering him, and I knew too. After that they did their tricks, leaping and running through the cage. The biggest lion opened his jaws wide and Malleu stuck his head inside. The others leaped at him and stretched out their paws with thick toes and curved claws, as though they wanted to devour him. But they only wanted to play, because Malleu never beat them.

I watched him while he was feeding them. He did it himself. An assistant brought a wheelbarrow loaded with chunks of meat and Malleu went into the cages. He speared each lump of meat on a big, long fork and fed it to them. Then he scratched their manes just above the eyes and patted them gently on the head. The lions would growl softly and sometimes one of them would throw itself on the floor on its back, waving its paws in the air. I once saw a lion whom he had not patted come growling after him, grumbling because it had been forgotten.

When Malleu left the cage he petted the children outside and asked us boys if we liked lions. He took us to see lion cubs like woolly poodles. They nibbled his hands and scratched him. Some of us stuck our hands through the bars and petted them too. They did not mind us, but when a grown-up man tried to touch them they got angry. They showed their teeth, growled, and put out their claws.

"Brother Wolf—Brother Stone!" said Saint Francis.

I had sown stringbeans in an empty pimento tin and chick-peas in another. I wanted to see them grow. Every day I dug up the earth to take the seeds out, and afterwards I put them back. They sprouted; each threw up a shoot like a little white horn; then they grew small roots; and in the end they had leaves. They grew as if they had understood me and wanted to give me pleasure, by showing me how they were and how they grew.

I hammered a piece of iron and it grew warm as if it felt pain.

Then the examinations were over and I had been entered for the matriculation course with honors. They took me to a doctor. I was very thin and had no appetite. I only wanted to read, to sleep, and to watch animals. The doctor examined my chest and said:

"There's nothing wrong with him. It's his age. He's growing. The best thing is to send him to the country and give him a tonic."

I went to Méntrida to run about by the river and to take spoonfuls of cod-liver oil, black and thick; it made me so sick that they had to stop giving it me.

I had a prospectus of my school with me; it said that tuition there was so good that in the final examinations of the year the Institute had obtained so-and-so many honors and matriculation certificates. My Aunt· Aquilina showed it to all the women in the village: "That's my nephew, you know, Leonor's son. He's very clever." Then the women stuffed me with cake and gave me small glasses of strong wine to strengthen me.

The best physicians were my Uncle Luis, the schoolmaster of the village, and Saint Francis.

When they told Uncle Luis about my studies, he put his heavy hand on my shoulder and said:

"So what? Have you come to pull the bellows-chain for a bit? What you need is good food and exercise. Come along tomorrow and I'll teach you the craft."

So I pulled the bellows-chain, and hammered and filed lumps of iron in the vice at the workshop. I stained my face and hands black with soot. I went shooting with my uncle at dusk. He filled me with food and wine, but I was angry and almost in tears when I was not able to lift the smallest of the hammers with my thin arms.

"Damnation," said my uncle, "what the boy needs is less school and more play. As it is he'll get T.B. and then we'll see what comes of all that cursed school-learning."

He set out to shoot partridges and rabbits for me and when he did not get any he killed a pigeon. Aunt Rogelia made a broth of it for me alone. I developed an appetite and Uncle Luis was happy when he saw me eat. The rabbits and partridges tasted of the herbs of the hills.

Aunt Aquilina took me to the village school teacher. He was a small, friendly, gay old man. My aunt started explaining, he listened and read the school prospectus. Then he put his hand on my head.

"My poor little fellow—and tell me, what would you really like to do?"

I told him that I was going to be an engineer and that I liked animals and plants. I told him about Saint Francis and he smiled. I spoke to him with all confidence because he listened very attentively, without saying a word, and looked at me all the time as though he wanted to know what was inside me.

When I had finished, he said:

"Come and fetch me tomorrow morning, we'll go and catch butterflies together."

There we were in the meadow by the river, the schoolmaster and I. I didn't know how to catch butterflies, but he ran after them with a gauze net on the end of a long stick and caught them in their flight. Then he took them very carefully between the tips of his fingers and put them into a round tin box. He showed me lizards, little tortoises, and chameleons. We watched green cicadas dry themselves in the sun, escape from their jacket, and fly off, while the old sheath which showed the outlines of legs, wings, and head was left lying on the ground.

He explained the animals to me one by one. He took a lizard and told me what lizards were like, how they ate, how they lived. Then, when I thought he would put it into his tin box too, he stroked its head with one finger. The lizard shut its tiny eyes as though it liked the touch. Then he opened his hand and set it free. The lizard stayed there on the hand, green and glittering in the sun, and instead of leaping to the ground it climbed up the sleeve and rested on the schoolmaster's shoulder, waving its long tail like a whip. The schoolmaster walked on with the lizard, which poked its head into the hair on his neck from time to time.

When we returned to the village and reached the edge of the meadow, the schoolmaster picked up the lizard, put it on the ground, scratched its back, and said:

"Now be off with you, we're going. You go home."

The lizard stayed quietly in the grass and then went slowly away, its head swaying above its forelegs.

I ate a meager *cocido* in the schoolmaster's house, with only one piece of meat and one piece of bacon, no sausage and no other dish to go with it, served in old, yellow-and-green pottery bowls. It was very well cooked. The school had a farmyard and there the schoolmaster's wife, a quiet, clean old woman, shook out the crumbs. The hens and the sparrows came for them; they knew that they got them every day at that hour.

The village priest gave a lecture on Religious Doctrine for young girls and lads every Sunday afternoon. Everybody had to go, because otherwise the priest would have been angry and there would have been trouble with the Mayor and with the farms which employed labor during the wheat and grape harvests. The school teacher had tried to hold daily evening classes for the young people, where they could learn to read and write, which hardly any of them knew how to do. But the priest was furious and the Mayor forbade the classes.

The school teacher stayed on for nothing except to teach the small children how to read. That was all he could do, because after they were seven to nine years old, the children were used to work in the fields. In the summer they even used the little boys of five and six to glean wheat-ears and to pull up onions. So the schoolmaster devoted his time to collecting animals in the meadow. He had a collection of cases full of butterflies, moths, and beetles and a few stuffed birds. The neighbors brought him their canaries and their decoy partridges when they were sick or had broken a leg, and he cured them.

I brought him the *Life of Saint Francis*. He had read it already. He merely said that Saint Francis was made a Saint because he had been that kind of man. But nowadays there were no Saints any more.

When I went alone to the meadow I sat down in the grass and watched. After I had kept still for a while, all the animals moved as though I did not exist, and I looked at them playing and working while I thought.

Up till then I had believed in God as everybody, the priests and my family, had taught me to believe in Him: as a very kind man who saw everything and put everything right. The Virgin and the Saints commended to Him all those who prayed to them in their need, and begged God to grant them the things they wanted.

But now I could not help comparing everything I saw with this idea of an absolutely just God, and I was frightened, for I could not discover His justice anywhere.

Certainly, it was very good that I could stay with my uncle and aunt and become an engineer. But my mother had to go washing down by the river and be the servant of my uncle and aunt, and she had to leave my sister with Señora Segunda and my brother as a boarder in a charity school, because if she had not done that, she would not have been able to support us all, even working as she did. It would have been much easier if my father had not died. They were giving me the chance to study for a career, but I had to pay for it by going crazy with all the books and obtaining honors in the matriculation course so that the school could put it into their prospectus, otherwise they would not give me free education. Then I would be just like all the other boys.

God rewarded those who were good.

Poor Angel got up at five in the morning to sell newspapers in his torn canvas shoes and then, when the sales hours were over at midnight, he went to sleep in the entrance of the Royal Theater so as to be able to sell the first place in the queue. He and his mother together hardly earned enough for their meals, and they worked the whole day long. But Don Luis Bahía owned half Brunete by driving the poor people to whom he had lent money from the land which belonged to them. Not only did God not punish him, but when he came to San Martín, the priests there made much of him and took him to be an excellent man, because he paid for Masses and Novenas. What happened with me at school happened everywhere. The only good people were those who had money, all the others were bad. When they protested, they were told to be patient because they would go to Heaven; therefore all the evil that happened to them in this world did not matter; on the contrary, it was really a merit and their lot was enviable. But I did not notice rich people making themselves into poor people so as to go to Heaven.

I wanted to know things, to know much, because this was the only way to become rich, and if you were rich you had everything, you even went to Heaven.

For money the priests said Mass and gave indulgences for millions and millions of days. If a poor man died and God condemned him to a hundred thousand years in Purgatory, and if his widow could not spare more than three pesetas for a Mass, only two or three thousand days would be taken off his time in Purgatory. But when a rich man died and his people paid for a first-class funeral, it did not matter if God condemned him to millions of years in Purgatory; three priests would celebrate Mass; there would be a choir and the organ and everything, and he would be granted a plenary indulgence. If somebody was lame and had a thousand pesetas so that he could go to Lourdes, he had a chance of coming back on straight legs. But if he was poor and could not go to Lourdes, he had to stay lame all his life, because the Virgin worked miracles only for those who went there.

When the poor people had to go in ragged clothes and one saw their naked skin, just because they had nothing else to wear, they were not allowed into church to pray, and if they insisted the police were fetched and detained them. But the big chests in the sacristy were filled with good clothes and jewels for the Saints, and the wooden images were clothed and decked with diamonds and velvet. Then all the priests would come out, just as in the Royal Theater, in silver and golden robes, while the candles were lighted and the organ played and the choir sang; and during the singing the sacristans would pass round the collection boxes. When everything was over they locked up the church and the poor people stayed under the porch to sleep in their nakedness. Inside was the Virgin, still in her golden crown and velvet mantel, very snug and warm, because the church was carpeted and the stoves burning. The Child Jesus was dressed in gold-embroidered little pants and he also had a velvet cloak and a crown of diamonds. Under the porch was a poor woman for whom my mother had once bought ten centimos' worth of hot milk because she showed us her wrinkled, dried-up breasts, while her baby was crying, half naked. She sat in the porch of the church of Santiago, on a litter of waste paper, and said to my mother:

"May God reward you, my dear."

My mother went home and came back with an old shawl which she used to wrap round her waist when she was washing by the river in winter, and the woman bundled her child up in the shawl, for they were going to sleep there in the open all night. The woman said she would cover herself with old theater bills.

On the following day my aunt took me to the Novena and said how beautiful the Virgin was with her mantle and crown and all the candles. I remembered the poor woman of the night before. When we came out of church I told my aunt about her.

"My boy," she said, "there are many unfortunate people, but God knows what He is doing. Maybe she was a bad woman, because, you see, all the women who walk about in the streets are lost creatures. I suppose she had no milk because she drinks too much."

The Novena was in honor of Our Lady, the Most Holy Virgin of Mothers' Milk and Good Delivery.

The meadow by the river was alive with animals which had been coming up softly and slowly while I was thinking. They took no notice of me. Two lizards were playing between the grasses in the sun, moving their tails and flicking their tongues. Frogs were leaping in the stream and chasing each other. There was a black patch of ants which were coming and going with loads of grains for their ant heap. Dung-beetles had surrounded a heap of droppings and were fabricating little balls out of it. They worked in couples, a male and female together, each pushing their ball, which sometimes toppled and rolled over them. They were all playing and all working, both things alike.

I wished to be like them, I wished all people to be like them. I tried to speak of those matters to Uncle Luis and he listened, trying to follow. After I had explained, he said:

"Now look here, all that's just a lot of rubbish they've put into your head. God once set out to create the world. Every time he had made a little ball, like our earth, and taken it out of his oven still red-hot, he gave it a flick and sent it spinning through the air. From time to time he amused himself making people and beasts, and so he let one of the little balls cool and let all the people and animals on top of it grow. He watched the creatures growing and taught them how to live. One day he got tired of all the worlds, among them our earth, took the lot and kicked them into space. Then he went to sleep and nobody has heard a word from him since."

Of course he said it to tease me. But I was unhappy because he would not understand that I needed God.

I went back to Madrid, I continued to go to Church, at school and with my aunt. But I could not pray.

Part II

1. Death

EVERY morning, when my uncle was going to shave, he hung his mirror on a nail in the balcony frame, tied the loop of his razor strop to the window catch and ranged his bowl of hot water, his brush, cut-throat razor, and the little squares of paper he used to wipe off the lather, on the dining-room table. His razors were German; the mark engraved on their blades showed three little men holding hands, as if they were dancing and singing. The blades were honed so that they curved inwards from back to edge, sat loosely in their horn grip, and were so thin that they looked as though they were going to snap. They had a little curved tail like a dog's tail, where you put your thumb, and the handle stuck out stiffly.

He smeared his face with the soap which he used to grate himself off a big cake, set the blade at an angle and started to shave. The razor rasped on the hard hairs of his throat, and curly white waves of lather, flecked with fine black lines of cut hair, collected in the hollow of the blade. Whenever the heap grew too big, he wiped it off with a piece of paper. The sun shone through our balcony in the mornings, and when it fell on the paper, the tiny bubbles of the lather turned from white to mother-of-pearl.

I had torn off yesterday's pages from the three calendars in our house, and as the sun shone on the lather, I twisted a page into a tube, dipped its end into the foam and blew softly. The bubbles grew into a bunch of grapes, they swelled and quivered, and I caught one on the tip of my tube. In the sunlight it turned blue, red, purple, and orange, until it burst and spat little drops on my nose. Sometimes there was a hair on the top of the little globe, and it slid softly downwards as if it was falling.

I watched him while he gravely shaved his throat before the mirror. His hairs puzzled me. Why has he got hairs? Why haven't women any? I shall have hairs like his one day, but my sister never. Girls don't grow hairs. Old women often have some on their upper lip or on their chin. When my uncle stands there in his vest, his shirt sleeves rolled up, he has a smell. It is the smell of a man. When people begin to smell like that they grow hair on their faces.

Uncle José stood with his head thrown back, his throat taut, and looked in the mirror out of the corner of his eyes. The up-stroke of the blade cut his hairs with a rasping sound—riss, riss! The noise stopped. Blood splashed bright over the white lather, ran down his throat and painted a river with all its streams on his vest. My uncle stayed with his arm hanging down, the razor dangling as though it were broken, his other hand dabbing at the wound, a cut like a small mouth. You could see the sound of the gurgle, as little blobs of blood came out of the lips of the wound and became a trickle which ran down between the gray hair on his chest and his vest. Uncle José put the razor on the table and sat down in the rocking chair. He let himself drop, and then for the first time I saw how heavy he was. His face was yellow as the wax of a church candle, his hair glued to his temples, his bald head covered with little sweat drops, his mustache limp, his lips purple.

"Call your mother," he said.

My mother had a shock when she saw his yellow face and the red stream which had made trickles all over his vest. My aunt was at Mass.

"Don't be scared, Leonor, it's nothing really. I've cut myself, and the sight of the blood made me feel sick."

My mother washed him. She drew his undervest over his limp arms and left his gray-haired chest bare. In the groove of his chest, the sweat collected in glistening drops. A glass of brandy. My uncle rested in the rocking chair, breathing slowly, his mouth half open, and stroked my head. I was sitting on the curved chair arm. Rocking chairs like ours were made in Vienna; they dipped branches in boiling water, and when the wood got soft, they bent it into any form they wanted.

The steaming hot tea and the brandy revived him, and I could see the drops of blood coming back into his face and his bald pate so that the skin reddened. The cut was no longer bleeding, it was covered with a strip of taffeta and one could not see anything. When my aunt came back, my uncle told her that he had cut himself, as if it were of no importance.

I went into the kitchen and asked my mother in a low voice: "Mother, is Uncle going to die?"

"Silly, don't you see it was nothing serious? Many people feel sick when they see blood, and so your uncle was a bit sick."

But I knew he was dead. I didn't know what it was to die. But I knew he was dead. "Rabbit," my cat, also knew that Uncle was dead. I had told him so. He mewed very softly, plaintively, opening his mouth slowly, as if he wanted to yawn. I hugged his head and he looked at me with his yellow eyes. Then he went out on the balcony, sat down on his haunches, and began to stare into the darkness, rigid, with his eyes turned inwards.

My uncle had gone to the office, as he did every day, and I stayed on the balcony, for it was a holiday and I was not going to school. The cat was with me, curled up on his little mat. From time to time, he lifted his head, scented the air, and looked as if he were waiting. Inside the house, my mother and my aunt were cleaning up and clattering with their pots. The smell of food seeped out to the balcony.

A carriage turned the street corner, and the cat and I got up to look. The horse came up the short slope and stopped before our house door. A man and a priest got out, they entered our house in a hurry, and came out again with Señor Gumersindo, our concierge. The coachman climbed down from his seat. Between the four of them they lifted Uncle José out of the carriage. The black roof of the coach tilted under their weight, and in the sun it looked like a black mirror throwing its glints up into my face. The four carried him into the house, and I ran out of the room and hurtled myself down the stairs.

Watching them, and walking backwards, I climbed the stairs again in front of them. How heavy my uncle was! His legs doubled up against his stomach, head lolling, arms hanging down, shirt open and damp with sweat, foam on his half-open lips. He was breathing hard and blowing out the foam, as if it were he who had to carry the four upstairs, not they him. His eyes were half closed, the whites showing, and the pupils hidden in the inside of his head.

Upstairs, they dropped him on the bed—how heavy he was! My aunt shrieked and wept, my mother ran to the kitchen to fetch tea, to fetch hot water, to fetch I don't know what. I took one of his hands, it folded up in mine like an empty glove. The cat was restlessly weaving in and out between my feet. Together they dragged off his boots and opened his trousers, his coat, his waistcoat, his shirt. After they had taken off his socks, they lifted him up to take away his clothes from under him, and left him there on the under sheet in his pants and vest. Then they covered him up to his throat, and there his head remained, like Saint Peter's, with a fringe of gray hair round a bald skull, sweating and snoring. The cat jumped on to the foot of the bed and sat down to look at him with serious eyes. He stayed there because nobody dared to chase him away. I wanted to chase him off, and he looked at me. I left him. My mother wanted to chase him away, and without turning round he bristled his fur and growled softly, as though not wanting to wake my uncle. He showed his fangs and his red tongue.

What is angina pectoris? They didn't know, or they didn't want to tell.

In the evening, when the sun had gone and the lamps were not yet lit, the neighboring women came together and sat in a circle, in silence.

"God give him back his health, or whatever may be best for him," said one of them.

"Our Father which art in Heaven . . ."

We all prayed, very low, so that he should not hear us, while my aunt pressed herself into the armchair and let her tears run over her face. I prayed—oh, how I prayed! God and the Virgin and all the Saints must hear me! When the old women stopped, I went on praying, very softly and secretly so that they could not see me. God must hear me!

The bedroom was full of strong apothecary smells, of the patter of feet on tiptoe, of the clatter of cups and bottles on the marble tops of the night table. Don Tomás, the doctor, came out and said in a low voice to all of us and to nobody in particular:

"What a man. He is made of iron. Anyone else would have been dead by now."

Then he stayed in the bedroom clutching my uncle's wrist, and felt his pulse. My uncle slowly opened his eyes, looked at us, and he stretched out a hand and stroked my neck. Thus we passed the night, he sleeping and breathing deeply, his hand on my neck, and I fighting. If I fall asleep, he will die, I kept telling myself. As they could not get me away, my mother made me drink strong black coffee with a drop of brandy. When I woke up I found myself on my feet, half lying on the pillows, with a blanket wrapped round me and my uncle's hand on my neck. My mother was sitting on a stool at the foot of the bed and my aunt was sleeping in the armchair. The light of dawn came through the balcony. All my bones were aching. Mother lifted me up as I was, wrapped in the blanket, and carried me to my bed. She began to untie my shoes, but I never knew whether she got them off, for I sank down into blackness.

Then came better days. Uncle José left his bed and wandered slowly round the house, in slippers. But we three, the cat, he, and I, we knew it, he was dead.

One day he started looking for things in the chest of drawers, and called me:

"Take this," he said. "My silver watch with the two little keys. I've tied them with a bit of string so that they shouldn't get lost. My cufflinks. The walking stick with the golden handle. My signet ring." He took it off his finger where it sat loosely; he had become much thinner. "Give it all to your mother and tell her to keep it for you." He kissed me.

I took the things to my mother.

"Why did your uncle give you all this?" she asked.

"I don't know. He told me you would keep them for me until I'm older." I did not want to tell her that he was dead. She went to my uncle.

"Why did you give the boy all this?"

"Listen, Leonor, you're somebody to whom I can tell the truth. I'll never wear them again. I know it. I'm dead." And he said it serenely, his gray eyes looking at my mother, at me, and the cat, as if he were ashamed of his dying.

"Don't talk such nonsense, you'll soon be well again. You're very strong and healthy."

"Maybe you want to deceive me, or maybe you don't see it, just like the doctor. But it's true. I know that I've very few days left. I feel it inside here." He gently tapped his chest. "Look, the boy knows it too, don't you?" And he looked at me. When the cat lifted his head, watching him, he added: "And the cat too. Children and animals feel what we others can't feel."

At night I went down to fetch the milk, and in the stables a dog was howling, as dogs do when there is death in the house. Señor Pedro held its muzzle. "Keep still, blasted dog."

I went back with my milk can and thought of what my uncle has said. The dogs knew it too. My uncle was already in bed. He took a glass of hot milk with some drops of the medicine that smelled so strongly. I sat down on his bed and he spoke to me, but I did not know what he was saying. He had his meal all by himself; then he turned down the wick of the lamp which was mirrored on the oilcloth of the table like a little yellow sun. They sent me to sleep, but first I kissed his face many times; it was prickly. They had given him my bed so that he should have quiet, and I slept in the back room next door on a camp bed.

The cat came with me, crept under the sheet where it folded over the blanket, and fell asleep, purring. We both slept.

The cat woke me. He sat up on the bed and mewed softly. A strip of light shone from under the door of Uncle's bedroom and all was quiet. The cat and I listened. And suddenly the house was full of cries.

The blood relatives were sitting round the dining-room table. My aunt sat at the head, and I by her side. There they were: Uncle Hilario with his bald mahogany-colored skull, and the wen like a ripe tomato on top of it. Aunt Braulia in the fourteen green, yellow, and black petticoats of her Sunday dress. Uncle Basilio, another brother of my uncle's, with a big square head on a massive body, squeezed into a suit of thick, black cloth which smelled of moth balls. Aunt Basilisa, sister of my aunt, a very small, wrinkled, grumpy old woman with a mustache of sparse gray hairs like the clipped whiskers of a cat. Her husband, Uncle Anastasio, very impressive in his black suit, like a retired Captain, with black-lacquered mustache and beetling, shoe-polish-black eyebrows. My Grandmother Inés, who was here because my aunt had asked her to come and help her, as Grandmother understood about this sort of thing, being the trustee of Señor Molina's Estate. And then there was Father Dimas, my aunt's spiritual adviser, who had heard my uncle's last confession.

My grandmother and the priest sat next to each other. The two big fat ones together. The priest belonged to the class of flabby fat people who are made of rolls of lard; he was all fat: his many chins, the pouches under his eyes, his wrists, his chest, his stomach and the enormous belly which stretched his cassock and made it look like a shiny balloon. My grandmother belonged to the other class of fat people, who have big solid bones never quite buried in flesh. She had a heavy jawbone, a big, broad nose; the knobs of her bones stuck out of her skin at the wrists and elbows of her colossal arms. The priest was unctuous, Grandmother was sharp and prickly like a hedgehog. Don Dimas did not yet know her, and he would never have imagined that there existed in such a Christian family as ours so deadly an enemy as she was.

Uncle Hilario put his heavy hand, racked by the plow, on the table and asked:

"Well, Baldomera, and what do you intend to do now?"

"That's why I asked you to còme. So that you can advise me. I—I've an idea."

"I'm surprised to hear it," said my grandmother, who was put out of gear by the presence of the priest and only waited for an occasion to explode.

"Let me speak, Inés," my aunt went on. "As my poor Pepe fortunately left enough for my modest needs, and as I've nobody in the world except the child"—she gave me four kisses wet with tears—"I'd thought of retiring into a Holy Establishment where the Sisters take ladies like myself as boarders; and the child would go to a boarding school."

Father Dimas tenderly contemplated the nails on his hands which he held folded over his paunch. The country cousins looked at one another without quite taking in what she had said. Uncle Anastasio, who was standing, probably so as not to spoil the creases in his trousers, nervously twisted his mustache.

Grandmother Inés rose heavily from her chair, and from the towering height of her eyes she looked down on all their heads. Then she faced her victim, my aunt:

"Look, Baldomera. Just now I said I was surprised to hear you'd had an idea, and I say it again. Where did you get this idea of yours from?"

"Father Dimas advised it," said my aunt with bowed head.

"I see. So that's how you do it, is it, Father Sausage?"

"Madam," began the Father, red with anger.

"The devil take your 'Madams.' Don't come to me with your sticky sweet stuff. D'you think I'm a suckling? Look, Baldomera, you don't know this sort and I do. You go into a convent and they treat you very nicely; the Reverend Father—yes, this one here—will visit you piously every day. At the school they will take good care of the boy—from what you just said it wouldn't be the school he goes to now, would it?"

"No. I had thought of sending him to school at Areneros."

"Precisely. Father Sausage thought of putting him into Areneros. There you have the whole bag of tricks. The boy to be turned into a Jesuit, and his aunt made to leave a will with the boy as sole heir! And so the whole thing stays within the family—isn't that so, Father Sausage?"

"Doña Baldomera, I withdraw. This is intolerable. My sacred office forbids me to dispute with a vulgar woman. I was not aware that such persons were to be found in this most Christian household."

My grandmother caught the priest's arm and dug in her powerful fingers.

"Of course, his Illustrious Reverence believed there were only fools here, like this poor soul. But you've made a mistake, I am here. The boy will *not* go to the Jesuits' College, simply because I'm his grandmother and I don't want him to. Baldomera can go to the Convent if she likes, for I'm neither her mother nor her grandmother—if I were, I'd spank her bottom in spite of all her gray hairs. And as to 'vulgar woman,' Father Greasebag, it's the first and last time I'll let you get away with it, and that only out of respect for the deceased. Next time, I'll make your fat cheeks swell to double their size."

The family had by now realized that this was an attempt to get hold of my aunt and make her cut everybody out of her will. Through the story of Don Luis Bahía, they all knew what the Jesuits were like. And all of them shouted agreement with Grandmother, while Father Dimas wrapped himself into his cape, filling the room with whirlwinds. Grandmother carefully opened the door for him. When he was already on the stairs, she could no longer restrain her rage.

"Off with you," she shouted, "back to your hole, you cockroach!"

And she slammed the door so that the glass cups on the sideboard danced and tinkled like little bells.

My aunt was scared.

"But, Inés, what have you done?"

"What have I done? Swallowed my wish to slap that fellow's face. Well, that's that. Now we can talk as a family, without false Fathers."

Uncle Hilario, that shrewd peasant, spoke up first.

"I think, if nobody else has a better idea"—nobody meaning my grandmother who was watching him with intense seriousness—"you ought, for a time at least, to come with us to the village until you've got over your first sorrow. Later on you can stay there in peace without anything to worry you. The girls will do all the work for you and you'll live like a queen. The boy—well, if you wish he can go on with his studies and visit you in the summer."

Uncle Anastasio stopped twisting his mustache, placed one hand on the edge of the table, crossed one leg over the other, and started to stroke his chins.

"I'm of a different opinion, from beginning to end. Of course you must be surrounded with warmth and affection. But you can't hide away in a village. You need distraction, you must see things, go out, meet people. You will have that nowhere better than with your own sister and your niece—your godchild," he stressed. "You know well what it would be like staying with us. As to Arturo, you simply give his mother whatever is needed for his studies and he can come to our house whenever he likes. I don't say he can sleep there because there is no room, but he can stay with you the whole day if you like."

My grandmother kept silent, she looked from one to the other and nobody said a word. My aunt waited for Grandmother to speak, and when she still said nothing, asked her timidly:

"And you, Inés, what do you think?"

"Me? What would I advise, you mean? Now listen, I'm going to tell you, because it will make me sick if I can't speak out. And let him scratch who feels the itch. What I advise you is not to be a fool. The departed has left you enough cash to lead an easy life. You just stay in your house together with the boy, as you've done all your life, keep Leonor to do your work, and you yourself do what you like without asking anybody's leave. Are you really so silly as not to understand what this pack wants? The priest wants to separate you from the boy and the family. The family wants to separate you from the boy and from other relatives, and all—now get this straight—all of them want to get at your money."

There was a chorus of protests:

"But, Inés, the only thing we want is her welfare."

"What you want is her money. If the departed had left her with one old rag in front and another behind, I'd like to see who would be the perfect gentleman and take her into his house, old, bigoted, and touchy as she is. Of all of us who are here, maybe the only one to take her in would be me, because I've enough bread left to give her a piece of mine. Listen," she added and turned to my aunt, "stop asking the family for advice. Families and old junk are all right—at a distance. Ask advice from people who have nothing to do with you, and you'll see that they tell you that you ought to stay at home and tie the strings of your purse tight to keep off the spongers who will come over you like flies after honey. Do you realize what it means to be a good soul like you, who is foolish out of sheer goodness, with a hundred and fifty thousand pesetas in a family of starvelings? You'll know in time, only wait."

Uncle Hilario made a dignified protest:

"There is nobody here who wants to take anything away from her."

"Is that so? How much did you owe Pepe? Must have been more than five hundred pesetas. And of course, when you heard that your brother had died, you came here with the cash in case Baldomera needed some at once, didn't you? Yes, and that's why I had to give her a thousand pesetas yesterday so that she could pay for things without having to worry."

Uncle Hilario sat down in confusion and grunted:

"That's no way of discussing things."

"Of course not. The only thing one can do if one's got any decency is to open the door and go."

"That would be rude," objected Uncle Hilario.

"Well, then swallow your pill. Truth is always painful. And the truth is that you've all come here like carrion crows at the smell of death, to see which bit you can carry off for yourselves."

Aunt Baldomera had begun to weep and to cry, and Grandmother cut short the discussion with a simple recipe:

"Well, the matter is closed. And you stop crying, the departed will not come back for all your tears. Let's say a Paternoster, perhaps it will do him good—I'll pray too, though I don't believe in it—and afterwards every owl back to its own olive tree!"

My aunt began the Paternoster, half smiling, half crying. When the two old women were left alone, they fell into each other's arms, both weeping. Suddenly Grandmother broke away, opened the balcony doors wide, and said:

"Let's have some air. It smells of rot in here."

The gusts of fresh air carried off the smell of many sweaty people, and the clouds of cold cigar smoke, blue in the light of the lamp, drifted out in long thin ribbons.

The days became monotonous. Early in the mornings, my aunt, more pious than ever, used to go to church and did not return before eleven or so. My mother put the house in order and in the afternoons went home to the attic. My aunt and I stayed alone, I reading at the dining-room table, she slumbering in the rocking chair, the cat on her lap. At eleven or twelve at night she woke up with a start, looked at the clock, and we went to bed, my aunt, the cat, and I.

Her affection for me and her jealousy of my mother had sharpened. She would not leave us alone for a minute. On Thursdays and Sundays, when I was free, she would not have me go with my mother, but went out with me herself, to the Plaza de Oriente or the Plaza de Palacio. There she sat on a seat, and every time she would find another old woman to whom she could tell the story of my uncle, and shed some tears. In one of the attics of the house lived Señora Manuela who had a refreshment stand in the Plaza de Oriente; we often went there, my aunt took some refreshment and exchanged with Señora Manuela memories of their respective husbands.

Since my uncle had died, the family showed a fervent love for my aunt. The Brunete family came to town nearly every month. Aunt Baldomera had torn up all the receipts of their debts to Uncle José, because they had had such a bad year. When they arrived they used to bring a couple of chickens and some dozens of big, fresh eggs. When they went, they would take with them 50 or 100 duros. My aunt's sister, Aunt Basilisa, often came to keep her company in the afternoon; at other times, Baldomerita, my aunt's godchild, would come and be received with a shower of kisses and hugs. My aunt gave her things, because she herself would not wear them again in her mourning which she intended to wear "until God took her home to her Pepe." One day she gave Baldomerita her gold and diamond earrings; another, her golden chain; another, her brooch; another, her rings. All the valuable things disappeared one by one, the high tortoiseshell combs, the waving mantillas with their dense lace, the Manila shawl with its ivory Chinese figures, the embroidered silk dresses. Every time the day of a patron saint or another holiday arrived, the family was short of money and unable to celebrate it. And my aunt took a big banknote, folded it quite small and put it in the bodice of her niece's dress. Late in the afternoon, when my mother had gone or was about to go, Aunt Eulogia would arrive together with her daughter Carmen; they were relatives of my aunt in just the same degree as my mother and I. Each time they found something to do in the house, something to sew or to iron. Between flattery and caresses they got one hundred peseta note after the other out of my aunt.

They all did the same things; they spoiled me and made much of me, and they ran down my mother, fanning my aunt's dislike of her. The situation between my mother, my aunt, and myself became increasingly tense, the smallest causes produced discussions which stung like needles. My aunt wept in the dining room and my mother in the kitchen. Then the end came; my mother said:

"Listen, Aunt, things can't go on like this. You and I don't understand each other. You've been very kind to us, but there has to be an end somewhere. I will go back to my attic, you have others who will serve you gladly, and we'll all live in peace."

"And the child, what will you do with the child?"

"You will have to decide what you want to do about him."

I was a mere nothing in their discussion, neither of them asked me what I wanted.

"If you don't want to stay in my house," said my aunt, "I won't force you. The child can stay until he has finished school and then we shall see to it, if God gives me good health, that he makes his career as his uncle wished."

"Agreed," said my mother. "You find somebody to help you and as soon as you say the word, I'll leave the house."

In the afternoon, Aunt Eulogia and Carmen promised to come from the next day onwards.

"Of course, of course, Baldomera, you'll see how well we'll look after you. You and the boy will have everything you need."

Aunt Basilisa spoke seriously to my aunt:

"What in the world is this? You're jumping from the frying pan into the fire; you chuck out Leonor and take in Eulogia. Haven't you burned your fingers often enough? These women are coming here to sponge. What you ought to do is to live with us—after all, I am your sister. If you are worried for the boy's sake because our house is not big enough to have him there, why, we could come here and live with you; this flat is very big."

But my aunt had no wish to have Uncle Anastasio in her house and decided for Aunt Eulogia. Carmen would sleep in the flat, her mother would come in the morning and leave at night.

All these conversations went on in my presence. Nobody restrained himself in what he said. Why should they? My aunt was going to make me an engineer. What more could I want? Moreover, they were not concerned about me. Once inside my aunt's home, they would arrange to get rid of me, sooner or later.

My mother packed her clothes and Señor Manuel came to fetch the big and heavy box. While he went down the stairs, my mother entered the dining room.

"Well, Aunt, I'm going. I hope you'll keep well. When you need anything from me, send me a message through the boy."

And then I said—and the tears choked me:

"She can't send you messages through me, because I'm coming with you." I turned to my aunt and said in a white fury: "My mother won't stay here and I won't either. I'm going with her to the attic and you can keep your money and your career for yourself. I can work. If you've had no children, that's your bad luck. I won't desert my mother. You can stay here with your Baldomerita and your Carmencita and give them what you like, the mantillas and the money, because you're a selfish woman. My mother has been your servant for twelve years. That's what she was, but you talk big and say you've kept her and me out of charity, because we were starving. And now these filthy women come and you give them the money, I've seen it, and the jewels and the dresses and everything, because they flatter you and kiss you all over."

I was filled with anger and rage at seeing my mother scorned, rage at losing my career, rage at seeing strangers loot the house, and nobody · could have made me shut my mouth.

"Just count your money. . . . Yes," I was glaring at my aunt, "the money you keep in the notecase in the cupboard. Where you've got your five thousand pesetas and the bank receipts. Just count it, and you'll see what's missing. Later on they'll say my mother took it, but I know who filched the money."

Aunt Eulogia and her daughter were clattering with the pots and pans in the kitchen. My aunt, deeply disturbed, went to the cupboard; five hundred pesetas were missing.

"There you see. My grandmother was right when she said you were a fool. Do you know who took them?"

I dragged Carmen out of the kitchen.

"It was her, she took them yesterday. I saw it, yes, I saw it. I was hiding here"—I hid behind the curtain—"and her mother was on the lookout in case you moved out of the armchair. Go on, now say it's a lie."

Carmen, who was hardly older than I, a child herself, started to cry.

"Was it you?" demanded my aunt.

"Yes, Señora. I don't know anything about it. My mother told me to."

I took my mother by the arm.

"Let's go. Now you know."

We went, my mother shocked, I trembling with rage and excitement and with tears running down my face. When we were down in the street, my mother kissed me. From the balcony my aunt called out:

"Leonor, Leonor! Arturito!"

We turned the first corner of the Calle de la Amnistia and then walked slowly, without speaking, through the sun-filled streets, until we were up in the attic. There my mother began to unpack the clothes from the box. I watched her, without saying a word. She stopped and said gently:

"We must fetch your clothes from your aunt's."

"Let her go to hell with them," I gave back furiously.

And I threw myself on to my mother's big iron bed, weeping into the pillows so that they got wet, shaken by spasms. My mother had to lift me and slap my face, because I could not speak. Señora Pascuala, the concierge, made me drink a cup of lime-blossom tea with brandy. I lay there like a trussed bundle.

"We'd better put him to bed properly," said Señora Pascuala.

Between them they undressed me, and I let them. I watched the little square of sunlight under the window. Afterwards I fell asleep.

Mother went to my school with me to say good-by to the Fathers. One after another came and spoke to her. At last, the Father Rector came and joined the Father Prefect and us.

"It's a pity," he said. "He's a particularly gifted boy. Now look. We quite understand your position. We'll give the boy free tuition and food, because it suits us to, and it would be a pity to lose him."

"But the clothes, Father," said my mother.

"Don't worry, we'll see to that. The boy will not go without clothes."

My mother was inclined to leave me in the school. She had borne with my aunt for so many years. What would she not have done for me? The Father Rector ended the discussion:

"Well, we're going to take the boy as another boarder. Where one hundred are fed, there's enough for a hundred and one. As to clothing and books, we'll arrange for them. Don't you worry."

And I? Was I nothing? Was the whole world to dispose of me at its pleasure? Everyone wanted to give me charity and then to exploit it. I had to stay in the school, shut up there, always hearing people say that I was there on charity, studying like a mule, so that later on the priests could use my successes in their advertisements in order to attract fathers like Nieto's who would call me son of a washerwoman.

"I want to go to work," I said suddenly.

"All right, all right," said the Father Rector. "Don't you worry about anything, you will have what you need."

"I don't want any more charity. D'you believe I don't know it?" Through my tears the words came tumbling out: "I know very well what it means to be the son of a washerwoman—I know what it means to be told about the charity you've received—I know all about the school prospectus—I know what it means that my mother has to scrub floors in my aunt's house without being paid for it. I know about the rich and the poor. I know I am one of the poor and I don't want anything from the rich."

They brought me a cup of tea from the College kitchen and the Father Rector kept on patting me on the shoulder. Finally, they had to leave me for a long time on one of the plush-covered sofas in the visitors' hall. The Fathers came one by one to see me and be kind. Father Joaquín sat down beside me, lifted my head and asked me what was the matter with me. I answered him hysterically, but he rapped me over the fingers and said:

"No, no, slowly, as if you were making your Confession."

The Father Rector pushed my mother to the other end of the hall, and we two stayed alone. I told the priest everything; he was holding my hands in his own big hands and squeezed them gently to encourage me. When I had finished, he said:

"You're right." He went up to the Father Rector and my mother, and said gravely:

"You can't do anything. Between the lot of them they have smashed the boy. The best thing is to let him have a taste of life."

When we left, he crushed my hand in his, in a handshake as between men, and said:

"Now you must be brave. You're a man now."

We walked up the slope of Mesón de Paredes, my mother thoughtful and I proud: I was right. Father Joaquín had said so.

That afternoon, Aunt Basilisa came up to the attic to speak to my mother.

"Baldomera wants to see the boy," she told her.

Before she could answer, I replied:

"Tell her I don't want to. And what's more, you've no business to come here to the attic. You've managed to get rid of us anyhow. This here is not Aunt's place. This is my place, and I don't want you or anybody else to come here. Tell Aunt Baldomera that I won't come because I don't want to. It's as far from us to her as from her to us. If only poor Uncle José could see it!" Again rage blinded me, and I caught her by the arm.

"Off with you, off, out in the street, you old hag, tale-bearer, lick-spittle! Out with you, go back and steal your sister's jewels and money and clothes until she's left naked! Thief!"

She attempted to shout back. But Señora Pascuala, who knew the whole story and had arrived because of the noise, caught hold of her.

"Go away. The boy's right, yes, Señora, he's absolutely right. The best thing you can do is to get out. And don't give me any of your back-chat! I'm the doorkeeper here, and I won't stand for any scandals. D'you understand, you beggar? What you've got, you toffs, is hunger and greed. And that's enough of it. Out with you. Out of this house!"

She shoved her along the corridor of the attics, and Aunt Basilisa never dared to say a word. If she had opened her mouth, Señora Pascuala would have beaten her up, what with her old wish to get square with one of these fine ladies.

2. Return to School

T H E tall oak wardrobe was still full of the clothes which belonged to someone else: the two sailor suits, the blue and the white one, on their curved clothes hangers. The short knickers with the elastic band over the knee, which left a red welt on one's skin. The row of striped drill blouses, each stripe a chain of tiny checks. The cream colored piqué shirt fronts. The silk neckties. The flat, starched collars. The round sailor caps with their gold lettering and dangling strings. The tartan caps and the beret for the street. The red school folder.

My aunt took out piece after piece and laid everything out on the bed. I recognized them all, one by one, as one recognizes what one has worn on one's own body, but they seemed foreign things, things that belonged to someone else.

"What shall we do with them?" she asked me.

With the pride of the possessor of a man's suit made to measure, with no more wrinkles than those round the bulge of my uncle's silver watch anchored to its plaited gold chain, I answered:

"It doesn't matter, we'll find some boy who can make use of them."

My aunt folded up each piece of clothing and stored it away in the bottom drawer of the wardrobe, with moth balls between the folds.

"Well, I think we will keep the things. They may come in handy," she said.

Did she think that I would ever put on those clothes again? I glanced at myself in the big looking-glass of the sitting-room, a looking-glass in a gilt frame which reached up to the ceiling and was slightly inclined as though bowing to the floor. In my soft hat I was taller than many men, only I was very thin and the face was the face of a boy.

"I'm going out," I told my aunt.

"Take care of yourself and be careful where you go and what you do and don't be late."

"I'm going to see my friends, and I'll be back soon."

When I started walking down the stairs I whistled loudly, as I always did. At the next landing I fell silent. Was it right to whistle and jump down stairs as I did when I went down to play in the street, with my packet of sandwiches in my hand? Señor Gumersindo, the concierge, saw me in the doorway and stopped me:

"You're looking very smart, young sir."

He no longer called me Arturito. I was "young sir." I walked up the street and looked for my friends. The gang was playing at hopscotch in the Plaza de Ramales and having an argument as to whether Pablito, the plasterer's son, had touched the line or not. My arrival stopped their dispute. I had to tell them all my recent adventures, and all about my soon entering a bank as an employee. The boys were thrilled. When they had enough of listening to me, the boy whose turn it was picked up a pebble, put his hands behind his back, made a few secretive movements, and then held his two closed fists under my nose.

"Come on, say which. Are you going to play?"

I would have liked to be in the game. But how could I play in a grown-up suit, with a silver watch in my pocket, and a gold chain across my waistcoat?

"No," I said, and added, to tone down my refusal: "You can't jump in this sort of suit."

For a while I stayed there, watching their jumps, somewhat shame-faced, for I felt a fool, and then I left with a "See you later" which really meant "never." I walked down to the sunlit Plaza de Oriente, across the wide yard of the Plaza de la Armería to the balconies which opened on to the Casa de Campo. Boys much bigger than I were playing in the square with bare legs, in blouses and smocks. But I could no longer play. I was a man, I had to be serious. In a few months' time I would work in the Bank. For I was certain to win the competition for the job.

Everything was settled. Don Julian, the man from the Bank who always came to the Café Español, was going to recommend me to the directors. He was one of the heads of their Stock Exchange Department and had worked in the bank for thirty years. The directors thought much of him, and with his recommendation it would be quite enough if I passed the entrance test. For this I had to learn simple bookkeeping, which was easy and also arranged for. The Escuela Pía, my old school, had a commercial class for poor pupils, and I was going to take it.

Matters with my aunt were settled as though nothing had ever happened. My mother went there in the mornings and left late in the evenings. ·She could have slept at my aunt's, because Concha and Rafael got bed and board where they worked, but she did not want to. She said she had her own home and would not leave it a second time, and I thought she was right.

It was as though nothing had ever happened; but many things had happened. When I wanted to go out, I no longer had to ask if I could go and play. I simply took my hat and said: "I'm going out now." I no longer had any need to open the sideboard in secret to get at the biscuits, and then to leave the door open and crumbs on the carpet so that my aunt should think that it had been the cat. Now I opened the sideboard, put three or four biscuits on a plate and ate them. Then I poured myself out a glass of strong wine and drank it. My aunt looked on and beamed. When I was going out she asked me if I had any cash with me in case I wanted to buy something, and I always carried two or three pesetas in my waistcoat pocket. Before, it had always been necessary to tell her a long tale before I could get a single peseta out of her. .

I had to see Angel. Here on the balcony of the Palace there was nothing for me·to do, except to stare at the Campo del Moro and the Casa de Campo like an idiot. It was quiet at the café about that time. I found Angel sitting by himself in the corner of the entrance lobby, making parcels of the papers he had not sold the day before and had to return to the distribution agents. When he saw me I thought his face turned sad.

"Hullo, Arturo, and how are you?"

I quickly told him the story of the last few changes in my life: my aunt, the bank, Don Julian. He listened in silence, with his old man's face wrinkled. When I had finished he patted me on the shoulder with a hand blackened by coppers and printers' ink.

"Now we won't cry out the *Heraldo* at night any more."

He dragged a bundle of cheap novels out of the bottom of the cupboard and offered them to me.

"Take all the ones you haven't read yet."

I went through the series of the *Illustrated Novel* and picked out those I did not know. Angel only watched me.

"Well, look, I'm taking these here. Come up to us later on and take all you want of my books."

"I'm not going up to your place because your aunt won't like it."

"You're silly," I said. "Now look here. From tonight on you simply bring us the paper upstairs, because I told you to. And then you stay with me for a bit. I'll arrange everything with my aunt."

Pepe, the waiter, came out. When he saw me he was surprised.

"Well, well, Arturito, it's a long time since I saw you last. And now you're a young man." He gave me a long look. "And how's Doña Baldomera?"

"All right. Poor woman, she thinks of my uncle's death all the time."

"Poor Don José. Your uncle was a very good man. How time passes. When you came to the café the first time you were still in swaddling clothes and I hadn't any gray hairs yet. Of course you and your family won't come here now, but I do hope you'll come from time to time to see your old friends. Manuel, my boy—you know him—is a young man too by now. He does everything at our little wine shop, together with his mother."

"But, Pepe," I said, half amused and half ashamed, "you speak to me so solemnly. Now, are you going to address me as 'Arturo' or as 'sir' in future?"

"I don't know, it's just that I'm used to it, you know. Of course, there it is, you're used to seeing young Arturo and so you can't get into a new habit overnight."

"But I'm what I was, and I want you to go on as before, Pepe."

The old man embraced me and kissed me on my mouth with his gray mustache, far more affectionately than he had done on the nights I had come with my uncle. Then he sat down on Angel's stool and wiped his eyes with the white napkin hanging over his sleeve.

I went away with my bunch of books under my arm. I did not want to go home. I wanted to see the quarter, and the boys, and—well, I wanted to play.

In the Plaza de Isabel II, I turned round on my heels and walked slowly home.

"What's the matter with you, my boy? You look irritated," said my aunt.

"Nothing's the matter. Nothing."

I sat down in a chair to read one of the new novels. The cat was sitting on his square of rug, watching me. There was nothing else on the balcony. But I could not go on reading. I got up and went into the bedroom. There I took a pair of shorts from the bottom drawer of the wardrobe, undressed, and put them on. In shirt sleeves I went back to the dining room, and I noted the coolness of the air on my bare legs.

"I've changed, because I didn't want to crumple my suit," I told my aunt.

And I threw myself down full length on the balcony floor, an open book between me and the cat. My hair touched the cat's head and every time I turned a page he stretched out his paw .and gave the paper a lightning rap. He wanted to play and turned over on his back, his white belly stretched. I stuck my head into the hollow between his four legs, and he mussed my hair because it tickled him.

Doña Emilia called from the balcony opposite me:

"Arturito, sweetie, so you've come back?"

The cat jumped up and ran off. I was ashamed of my childish games. I gave her a brief answer, went inside and shut the balcony door. Then I changed slowly back into the grown-up suit and resumed my reading, sitting at the dining-room table and not taking in a word of what the book said.

The Commercial Class started at ten and lasted till half-past eleven in the morning, and there was a shorthand class in the afternoon. Father Joaquín took the morning class and a parliamentary stenographer of the Senate took the afternoon class.

I went before ten o'clock and called on Father Joaquín in his room. It was open to the four winds as always, there was his music stand, there were his birds fluttering round the window. He was reading a book and said mechanically: "Come in," when I knocked softly. ."Ah, it's you." He stood up and hugged me. "So you want very much to start studying again? It won't be difficult for you. In a few months you'll have caught up. You will go to the lectures downstairs with all the others, so that you keep in step with them, but I'm going to explain things to you outside class hours, much more quickly and simply than I could do it with the other boys. And then it will be work and earning a living for you, because you're a man now, aren't you, boy?"

We went downstairs to the class together. All the boys rose.

"Sit down," said Father Joaquín.

He went with me to the platform, turned round, and said:

"From today you're going to have a new classmate who's known to a good many of you anyhow. He won't stay with us long, only long enough to study bookkeeping which he needs because he's already working. Now, all move down and make room for him. As you know there isn't a first or last pupil in this class, but we'll have to give him the first place because he's earned it."

There I stayed, at the beginning of the first row, and he began with the lesson. It seemed intended to give me an outline of the matters already studied by the class, so that I should be able to follow. I found it easy to pick up the main threads with the help of the syllabus Father Joaquín had given me. The boys watched me and whispered among themselves.

Many of them stared at my hat which was hanging on a peg among their caps and berets. None of them spoke to me. They were all poor boys from the quarter. I knew some of them, but when I tried to speak with them they shut up like clams and answered me with a "huh," a "yes," or a "no."

After the end of the lesson I followed Father Joaquín back to his room. "What do you think of it?" he asked me.

"It's difficult to say." I found it hard to speak. With my hat between my fingers, I was standing on the other side of the desk, facing him. Father Joaquín rose, walked round the desk, put his hand on my shoulder and drew me gently nearer.

"Now come, tell me. What's the matter with you?"

"I don't know. It's very funny. Everything seems changed. Even the stones of the cloisters, which I know by heart, one by one. Everybody seems changed to me, the boys, you, the school. Even Mesón de Paredes Street. When I walked through it this morning I found it changed. To me, the men, the women, the kids, the houses, everything—absolutely everything—seems changed. I don't know how, and I can't explain it."

Father Joaquín looked straight into my eyes for a short while.

"Of course, you see everything changed. But everything is just the same as before, only you have changed. Let's see what you've got in your pockets—show me." I was bewildered, but he insisted. "Yes, I mean it, show me everything you carry in your pockets"

In confusion, I pulled a silk handkerchief out of my breast pocket, then my smart, new leather wallet, the silver watch, the folded handkerchief, two pesetas, a fancy magazine pencil, a small notebook. There was nothing else.

"Haven't you anything else?"

"No, sir."

"Well, well. And what have you done with your marbles and your spinning-top? Don't you carry brass chips, or matchboxes, or printed pictures, or string for playing thieves and robbers? Haven't you a single torn pocket, isn't there a button missing somewhere, haven't you got ink-stains on your fingers?"

I must have made a very silly face. He took the things piece by piece, mockingly, and stowed them back into my pockets.

"Here's the nice silk handkerchief, to look elegant. So you ogle the girls already, do you? The nice wallet to keep the money safe. There aren't any banknotes in it yet, but they'll come, never mind. Everything takes time. Here's the silver watch so you know the time, and you don't have to look at the clocks in shops any more and then sprint through the streets because it's getting late. And you don't have to wait for the clock in the bell tower to strike any more."

He put both hands on my shoulders, the two big hands of a man, and again looked straight into my face.

"Do you understand now what has happened to you?"

"Yes, sir," I said.

"If you go now to see Father Vesga," he added quizzically, "he'll tell you that you have lost the condition of purity. I tell you simply that you're no longer a child"

I met nobody but my aunt and my mother, and Father Joaquín was the only person with whom I could talk and have discussions. Least of all we spoke of bookkeeping, which came to me very easily indeed. Sometimes we went together to hunt for books in the Prado, or to go to a Museum, and we talked. We talked as though we had been father and son in the flesh. Then one day Father Joaquín said:

"It's Communion today. Have you already dropped the practice of going to Communion once a month?"

"Yes, sir."

"Of course, it's quite natural. Anyhow, if you feel like it you can come to Communion tomorrow."

On the following day I went to school and accompanied Father Joaquín into church.

"Now what do you intend doing?"

"I'm going to take Communion," I answered.

"If you like, stay here and wait for me, and then I'll hear your Confession."

When I was in the confessional, in front of him, he said: "Now tell me your sins."

"But what could I tell you, Father?"

What could I have told the man who knew my innermost thoughts, as my mother did not know them, as I did not know them myself, since it was often he who had explained them to me?

"That's true enough," he answered. "Let's pray a Paternoster together for the soul of your uncle."

We broke fast in his room, with a cup of thick chocolate, buns, and a glass of lemonade.

When I walked home, there was light everywhere.

I was separated from everybody else, except Father Joaquín. I saw this very clearly. The people I knew stopped treating me as a child, but nobody thought of treating me as a man. I realized that there were many things of which they could not talk to me. Yet I needed to talk, I needed people to talk to me, I needed to understand things. The grown-up people never realized that their behavior to me was ridiculous. If they were talking of women when I happened to come in, they stopped and changed the conversation, so that I should not hear that kind of thing, since I was still a child. They did not realize that I knew everything they could have told me. They were hypocrites and fools, all of them. Didn't they see that I was lonely?

I needed to play. I bought a heap of tools and started to construct a small steam engine. I made the drawings and cut out the pieces from sheet-brass. I had bought a treatise on steam engines and copied its drawings. The book was old and described engines of thirty years ago, but it suited me. I wanted to make a very simple engine. My aunt was annoyed because I stained my hands and made a mess in the flat.

On Sundays I went down to the *Rastro,* the Junk Market, to buy the pieces I could not make myself. It was in El Avapies, near my school.

The steep slope which leads from the Plaza de Cascorro down to the New World is called *Ribera de Curtidores,* Curriers' Bank. From the near-by slaughterhouses the hides of all the cattle which Madrid consumes wander into the tanners' workshops. On both sides of the sloping street are the tan-yards with timber structures of four or five tiers, where the hides hang from rafters to dry in the air and sun which enter freely from all sides. The skins carry an acrid smell of rotting flesh, which fills the whole quarter and clutches at your throat. On that slope, the street-hawkers set up their junk stalls and you can buy everything, except what you set out to buy.

There they sell every used thing people get rid of. There are old clothes worn out fifty years ago, skirts still spread on crumbling wicker hoops, uniforms from the time of Ferdinand VII. There are paintings, furniture, carpets, tapestries, dented musical instruments, pots and pans of all sizes, rusty surgical knives, old bicycles with twisted wheels, absurd clocks, iron railings, tombstones with blurred names, old carriages with broken spokes or a hole in the roof through which the sun shines onto the tattered velvet of the seat. Stuffed cats, dogs and parrots with tow sticking out of their bellies, spy-glasses, a yard long, which fold up like an accordion, ships' compasses, weapons from the Philippines, old medals and crosses from some general's chest, books, papers, ink pots of stout glass or glazed pottery, and old iron. A great deal of old iron: twisted bars, of which nobody could guess the purpose, hoops, pipes, heavy pieces of machinery, monstrous cog-wheels which make you think with a shudder of hands crushed between their teeth, anvils with blunted noses, coils of wire covered in ochre rust, and tools. Outworn files with iron dust choking their ridges, fantastically shaped hammers, pincers with chipped jaws, tongs with a broken limb, beheaded chisels, gimlets, and angle irons. Then there are victuals: moldy peppered sausages, maggotty biscuits, raw ham, sweetish cheese, dried up like parchment but sweating honey in large drops like pus, tripe fried in tallow, stale crisps, squashed chocolate grown soft in the heat, shell-fish, river crayfish wriggling in dripping mud, buns with a shiny crust, apples dipped in blood-red caramel. There are hundreds of stalls and thousands of people, looking and buying. All Madrid walks about the Rastro on Sunday mornings.

Down in the Ronda, between the Americas and the New World, were the poorest stalls where the poorest people came to buy. One of the stalls called itself "The Flower of Cuba." In the center of its planks, two yards long and a yard wide, there was a pile of tobacco, black and evil-smelling, taken from the fag-ends of Madrid streets. To the right there were rows of packets of cigarettes, rolled in coarse paper and tied together with gaudy green ribbon. To the left, in neat, symmetrical files, were cigar-butts in dozens, sorted according to size and quality and with cigar bands to show it. Prices varied. A good stump of a Caruncho cigar, with its band to prove its authenticity, fetched as much as fifty centimos. The owner of the stalls was an eighty-year-old gypsy, with curving silver side-whiskers. Beside him squatted three women who rolled cigarettes with bewildering speed. The loose tobacco was sold by weight: fifty centimos the quarter pound. The establishment was always crowded, with buyers in front and sellers behind the counter. The sellers were street urchins who came with a tin or a sack full of cigarette stubs, already freed from paper, to offer them to the old gypsy. He weighed out quarter-pounds to those in front and those at the back, with hands the color of tobacco, and he took fifty centimos from the buyers and paid twenty-five centimos to the sellers for the same quantity. The tins were emptied on top of the tobacco pile, and the pile never diminished.

Among all that filth I felt happy, for the Junk Market was a huge museum of absurd things and absurd people. Little by little, my steam engine was born out of it.

On Thursday I went alone to the pictures, on Sundays I went with Rafael. Books, the cinema, the steam engine, Father Joaquín, and the classes at school made up my world. Sometimes I went for a walk with my aunt, and once a month she took me in a carriage to the cemetery to put fresh flowers on my uncle's grave and say a rosary. There were no more quarrels with my mother, but slowly my aunt began to lose her memory and her mind. She was becoming foolish.

I was going to enter the examinations for the Bank at the end of the summer. Don Julian came from time to time and explained things about which I would be asked. It turned out that what I learned in the school would not help me. At the Bank they had different, shorter methods of bookkeeping; everything was done with tricks and combinations of figures which had nothing to do with the rule-of-three and the rules of interest. Yet I found it easy and felt that if everything was of the same kind, they would pay me a good salary as soon as I was working in the Bank and they found out how good I was with figures. Then my mother would no longer go down to wash clothes by the river.

At half-past six I presented myself at the Bank. An old commissionaire who was sitting there went to fetch Don Julian. Behind him I walked up a stairway with a red carpet held in place by gilded rods. Upstairs was a passage covered with waxed linoleum on which one's shoes slipped, and stout wooden rails on both sides. Behind the rails were clerks such as I had not seen in my life. One of them was very fair, with almost ashen hair, a pipe hanging from his lips, which smelt of English tobacco, and a monocle screwed into his right eye so that the right brow was higher than the left. Another was short and grizzled, with a bald spot above his forehead, a black mustache which looked dyed, and a French goatee. There was a thin old lady with very slender wrists who used a typewriter at incredible speed. A spick-and-span orderly with the initials C.E. embroidered in gold on his blue uniform led us into one of the enclosures behind the wooden rails, which had six or seven tables, each with its typewriter.

Then came a gentleman in a coffee-brown frock coat, gold-rimmed spectacles hanging from a silk ribbon tied to his buttonhole, a gray French goatee and a long amber holder with a burning cigarette. Don Julian greeted him, and the two conversed in rapid French. The gentleman came up to me and asked me which of the typewriters in the place I knew best. I selected an Underwood. He seized the edge of the table, gave a tug, and the typewriter wheeled over, fell back and downwards. At the same time a slab was pushed forward and the desk was smooth and flat, the typewriter had disappeared as if by magic. Below the table was nothing but a sloping board, and the typewriter was invisible.

After this I came to learn my first word of French, destined to follow me throughout my life: *Dossier*. The man with the goatee and the gold-rimmed lenses took a yellow folder with a great number of sheets and said in bad Spanish:

"We shall now start your dossier."

Christian name, surnames, father, mother, studies, date of birth, and so forth. Then I was given sheets, with the problems I had to answer typed out on top, and space for the calculations left below. I stayed alone and worked out the figures. Don Julian and the Frenchman, whom I later learned to know as the Chief of the Personal Credits' Department, walked up and down in the linoleum-covered gangway. When I had finished, the Frenchman dictated a passage which I had to type, and another passage which I had to write out in longhand. Then they gave me a page of notes referring to the commercial report of a Lugos firm. From the notes I had to work out a complete report.

When the test was over, Don Julian accompanied me home. On the way he patted my shoulder.

"They liked you very much, only your handwriting is not so good. But that's something you can quickly improve."

In the Puerta del Sol we each drank a glass of vermouth. The seltzer-water tickled. I drank it greedily, for my mouth was dry and I still felt dazzled by those wide halls and globes of milky light. And I was going to work there? I was full of pride.

When we came home, Don Julian told my aunt that she could count on my having obtained the job.

Three days later I received a letter—the first letter of my life—in which the board of directors of the Crédit Etranger, 250,000,000 Frcs. Capital, informed me that Don Arturo Barea Ogazón would start in their service as from the 1st of August 1911.

I had still three months to go until I was fourteen years old, but I was already an employee of one of the biggest banks in the world.

3. Work

STANDING round the table, we were rapidly classifying the mail according to the initials in red ink with which each department marked the letters it had dealt with. Every now and again, Medrano went to the desk where the heads of the department sat, and brought back a new heap of letters in place of those we had already classified. Talking was forbidden, but the three of us, Gros, Medrano, and I, were talking in a whisper all the same. Nobody could tell whether we were speaking about our work or about something else.

"Who got you in here?" asked Medrano.

"The Head of the Stock Exchange Department."

"And me the Cashier, who's an old friend of our family's. What's your school?"

"The Escuela Pía—and yours?"

"The Salesians in the Ronda—more or less the same thing. Here we're at least not bothered with those eternal Masses and Rosaries. That's to say, Señor Zabala, the Head of Correspondence—the one who's sitting in the middle over there—is a Jesuit. He wears a scapulary under his shirt and goes every Sunday to hear Mass in the Calle de Cedaceros at the Jesuits' Residence. The one next to him—Señor Riñon, the little man to his right—is just the same. He's Head of Spanish Correspondence. The only one who's all right is the third one, the Head of Foreign Correspondence, Señor Berzotas. You see, he's done a lot of traveling and so he doesn't give a fig for priests and friars any more."

"What did you say his name was?"

"Berzotas.[1] He plays tennis. On Saturdays and Sundays he goes to play in the sports ground the English have got somewhere in town. And he wants to set up a sports club for our whole staff."

Just then, Señor Berzotas called me: "Hello, boy—the new one, I mean —come over here."

"At your service, Señor Berzotas," I said politely.

He flushed and gave me a very sour look. All the clerks sitting near by grinned, and I felt bewildered.

"So my name is Berzotas, is it? And pray who told you so?"

I had learned at school not to give anyone away, and answered quickly: "Nobody, I just thought I'd heard somebody saying it."

"We haven't got any fat cabbage-head here, because if there were one, we would throw him out into the street and that would be that. My name is Manuel Berzosa."

He had spoken severely, but when he saw that I was embarrassed to the verge of tears, he patted me on the shoulder.

"All right, never mind. There is something rather cauliflowery about the name of Berzosa. Look, the British gentleman over there, Mr. Clemans, has been calling me Birchosas ever since his first day here, and he won't change his ways for anything."

He gave me a bundle of letters to distribute and I went back to our table, furious with Medrano.

"Don't take it so seriously, we make jokes the whole day round here. You'll see. And if anyone gets sore about it, so much the worse for him."

[1] This name sounds ridiculous in Spanish, as it means Big Cabbages, from *berza*, cabbage.—*Translator's Note.*

The second practical joke came in the middle of the afternoon. Gros, who was manipulating a copying-press and a heap of damp cloths, said to me:

"Go to the w.c. and fetch two buckets full of water."

I came back with two buckets which were so heavy that they kept brimming over and splashing my trousers. Gros washed his hands with meticulous care in one of them, and Medrano in the other. Then Gros said:

"Now you can take them back." And they both spluttered with laughter. I swallowed the pill, took the two buckets and in passing Gros made one of them rock. The water wetted his trousers the whole way down from above his knees. He turned round in fury.

"Can't you look out?"

"Sorry, it was a joke. And if you get sore, so much the worse for you."

In the end the three of us were roaring with laughter, so that Señor Zabala, with his nasty beard fluttering, came up and scolded us in his womanish voice. After that they showed me how letters were to be copied. You first spread out a moistened sheet of thick, close-woven cloth, then you placed a sheet of copying tissue paper on it, and on top you put the letter which had to be copied. The moisture passed through the tissue paper under the pressure of the hand-press with gilt balls on its handle, and the letter was copied. Once you had mastered the technique it was easy. If the cloth was too moist, the print was turned into a single big blob, but if it was too dry, it did not copy at all. Moreover, typewritten letters had to be treated differently from handwritten ones.

And that was all I learned in the course of a fortnight: the correct degree of moisture required for copying a letter.

I was profoundly disappointed. The first day I came to work and was waiting for the Staff Manager to assign my duties to me, I believed that in a few minutes I would be sitting at one of those desks and using a typewriter or making calculations, those miraculous calculations which were being made in a bank. To be prepared for anything of the kind, I had brought along half a dozen of the nibs we called cock's spur nibs; I wrote best with them, although they sometimes spluttered. While I was waiting, Don Julian came and told me: "They're going to send you into Correspondence. It's a very useful section for you. Now do your work well and behave."

The Correspondence Section—writing letters for the Bank! They would surely give me a typewriter to handle. Most of those I saw in use were Underwoods or Yosts, and I had worked with both types. They would soon see what a good typist I was. I had won Yost's championship for speed on a typewriter with invisible writing and a double keyboard.

When the Staff Manager came, an imposing gentleman in a braided frock coat, white cloth spats, a graying beard and gold pince-nez, I followed him proudly. He introduced me to Señor Zabala. "Here's your new boy," he said. Señor Zabela called Gros: "You there, boy, show him things so that he can help you with your work."

Gros and Medrano took me between them, and there we stood armed with paperknives, at a deal table the black paint of which came off in flakes and which was covered with scratches and stains from ink or gum; we slit open envelopes, took out the letters and put them in a carrier which was sent over to Señor Zabala's desk.

"Take care you don't tear one of the letters while you slit an envelope," Gros warned me. "If you do, Whiskers gets simply livid."

"So you call him Whiskers?"

"Everybody does, and what's more, it annoys him more than if he were called a bastard."

After that I was always paired with either Gros or Medrano and spent my day running up and down stairs. We distributed the mail to various sections and collected letters which had already been answered. We ran up and down the stairs four steps at a time, because everything was urgent. In the evening we copied the hundreds of letters written by all the departments in the course of the day. After that we put the letters in their envelopes, closed them, sealed the registered letters and went to supper. By then it was a quarter to ten. I ate hardly anything and fell on my bed like a piece of lead. My aunt said:

"How tired you are, my poor little boy! Do go to bed quickly."

The fortnight that followed turned me into a past-master in copying, the cleverest copyist in the bank.

There were sixty boys like myself employed in the bank, who had no wages and were called learners. We were supposed to work a year without pay, after which we might be made employees. But to become an employee we had to collect good marks. No more than two or three vacancies a year turned up among a staff of three hundred employees. This meant that in the course of a year, fifty-seven of the learners were thrown out and replaced by new boys, while three stayed on and were given a permanent job.

The only way in which I could collect good marks was to be the quickest of the sixty learners, which was easy for me with my long legs, and to make myself liked by everybody. And besides, I copied letters particularly well. The three heads of the Correspondence Department noted it. Whenever there was an important letter to copy they called for me, because I did it without a blot and without the slightest stain from the damp cloth. The sheets came out of the hand-press as though they had been printed. It was a talent Gros and Medr'ano envied me.

Yet all the time it was impossible to let your mind stray for a single moment. Anybody, even simple employees of some standing, had the power to throw out a learner. As fifty-seven had to be weeded out in the course of the year, the Staff Manager, Señor Corachán, stalked the boys, as he did the other staff while they had a smoke in the lavatory. He haunted the place, he skulked behind corners, he hid in the w.c. and suddenly appeared to trap the employees. He used rubber-soled boots, and would come up silently behind you, listening. Suddenly he would put his hand on your shoulder and say:

"Please come upstairs to my office and report to me."

We called him *The Fly,* and when he turned up in one of the passages, the employees passed on the warning in a whisper:

" 'Ware The Fly!"

Those who were talking shut up and started writing at great speed. Those who were secretly reading a newspaper under the cover of a folder coughed, shut the folder with a casual gesture, pushed it into a drawer and began to write. As the sections were separated only by wooden rails some three feet high, and by glass panels, he could spy on people everywhere. Sometimes he came to the Correspondence Department which was on the first floor and had a rail directly overlooking the big central hall of the ground-floor departments, and from there he watched the employees one by one. Afterwards he went down, took the hidden newspapers out of the drawers and dealt out rows. While he was leaning over the balustrade, you felt like pushing him so that he would fall down, head first.

But there was one man whom he persecuted cruelly: poor Plá. As soon as he saw from the first floor that Plá's chair stood empty, he hurried downstairs, sat down on it, took out his gold watch and placed it on the desk. When Plá came back, he had to face Señor Corachán who said:

"Señor Plá"—and he said it in a ringing voice so that everybody should hear—"exactly twelve minutes by this watch I've been waiting for you in this chair. And you alone will know how long you have been absent from your post in all."

"But, sir, I only went for a moment to the w.c."

"Do you call this a moment? A quarter of an hour of your working hours wasted! Moreover, you are supposed to arrive at this place with your needs already attended to. But you use the lavatory as your pleasure ground. You simply stink of tobacco!" Then he rose, straightened his frock coat, shut the lid of the gold watch with a dry click and added: "Sit down, and don't let it happen another time. This is insufferable!"

Plá looked at him with his short-sighted little eyes glinting behind his
huge spectacles and stuttered something, because Plá was not only short-
sighted but also a bad stammerer as soon as he was angry or embarrassed.
His hands, which did not know what to do with themselves, but dangled
like round lumps of fat from the ends of his short arms, rested on his
paunch, for Plá was altogether a sweaty round ball, and his excuses
dripped spittle over the papers on his desk. When one of those raindrops
fell on a letter done in copying ink it made a purple blob.

Although Plá stayed every night until nine or ten, befogged with work
because it was his job to deal with people all over the world who wanted
to play in the Spanish Lottery, Señor Corachán specially checked his hour
of arrival in the morning, shoved his watch under Plá's nose and was rude
to him. Most of the other employees never took notice of Plá except to
crack jokes about his blindness and his stutter; but we boys were friends
with him. I had to hear the speech which he made to any new boy:

"You're new here, aren't you? What's your name?" (He did not wait
for an answer.) "Well, well, I hope you're going to learn something.
Your future is here in this place. Just think of it. A year without wages—
sixty boys like you—three vacancies a year, and after twelve years' work
in the place ninety pesetas a month, which is what I earn now."

At other times he made fantastic calculations.

"There are twenty banks in Madrid, with fifty learners each, which
makes a thousand altogether. In Spain there are—let's say—two hundred
banks with an average of twenty learners each, which makes four thousand boys. There are thousands of commercial firms which have learners
without wages, so there are thousands of boys who work for nothing,
but rob the grown-up men of their jobs."

"But, Plá," I told him, "it's apprenticeship."

"Apprenticeship? It's a systematic exploitation of young boys. It's very
cleverly worked out, mind you. When you have been here seven or eight
months, they chuck you out some fine day. If you then go to another bank
and tell them that you have been here eight months and been given the
sack, they won't take you. If you keep your mouth shut, you may be
taken on as a learner for another year, but then you run the risk of again
being dismissed after eight months. And you'll find yourself in the same
situation as now all over again. If you try to take a job in an office, they'll
tell you that their business is quite different from that of a bank, but that
you can join them as a learner so as to get acquainted with their special
requirements. The only chance to break out of this vicious circle is to
make use of the time you are still working in the bank to find another
job. In that way it's quite possible that you'll find a firm which will pay
you twenty-five to thirty pesetas a month."

"But I want to be a bank clerk."

"All right then, but you will have to be very patient."

We all cherished the hope of becoming members of the staff of the Bank and being promoted to a good post. After all, we saw something of the higher officials and knew their history. There was Don Julian, now Head of the Stock Exchange Department, with an income of a thousand pesetas a month. He had entered the Bank as a learner, like myself. The same applied to the cashier, who had been an employee for thirty years, and to some of the others. It was true that most of the officials with high salaries had never been learners, and had joined the Bank as employees, but they all had some kind of special knowledge. Some of them knew languages, and others were experts at investing the Bank's money so that it produced interest and profit. One of those was Señor Tejada. He had the Bank's Power of Attorney at the Stock Exchange and was above Don Julian; he was the only man who had the right to place orders at the Exchange, and Don Julian did nothing but carry them out and conduct the correspondence with the clients. Señor Tejada made millions for the Bank and was paid very well for it. He was one of the people with the highest income, almost as high as that of the directors. And I knew I might get where he was, because it was all rather simple; Don Julian once explained to me how Stock Exchange speculation worked.

The Bank could never lose. Those who lost were stock brokers with little capital, and the clients themselves. Moreover, the Bank got wind of things before anybody else knew about them, by means of code telegrams which Don Julian had to translate. Gambling on the Stock Exchange consisted in betting whether stocks and shares were going to rise or fall in value by the end of the month. If the Bank had many shares of a company in its safe, this was easy; then it was bound to gain either way. It accepted any offers, whether based on a rise or a fall, and at the end of the month it took stock of its purchases. If it found it more useful to raise the value, it offered to buy more of the shares at a higher price. Since the Bank already possessed the majority of the shares or else had bought them, there were few of them left on the market and the brokers themselves had to buy them so as to sell them back to the Bank. In this way the price was much higher by the end of the next month. But then the brokers who had sold shares to the Bank at the beginning of the month were forced to deliver them at a price much lower than the current one, or else to pay the difference. Later the value of the shares went down, but the Bank had sold them at the top price and cashed in on the difference. Thus many people were ruined, but the Bank made money.

There was another business which brought in still more. It was the great business of the Banco Urquijo, which belonged to the Jesuits, and of the Banco de Vizcaya, which was said to belong to them too. Suppose some industrialists wanted to establish a factory which would cost them five millions, but had not got the capital. In that case, and if the transaction sounded good to the Bank, it lent them the money, and issued shares, which it offered to the public. If the public bought all the shares of the issue, the Bank got its commission on the loan and on the handling of the shares. If the public did not absorb the entire issue the Bank kept the unsold shares and launched them on the market later on, when the factory was already working and the shares fetched a higher price; and then the people bought them. The Bank pocketed the difference. It happened frequently that the undertaking was not sound and collapsed after the Bank had sold out its shares; then the shareholders never saw a red cent, as all the Banks knew that it was better not to touch these shares. In a similar manner the Banco de Urquijo and the Banco de Vizcaya had made themselves masters of the Public Utilities of Madrid and of almost all the industries of Bilbao.

Another important branch of the business was the deposit accounts. Many people did not want to keep their money at home but took it to the Bank which kept it safe and paid a small annual rate of interest. This money, which did not belong to the Bank, was used for loans to business men who took all their drafts to the Bank. The Bank undertook to collect them and charged a commission for it. But as it did not pay them before it had collected the amount, and as the business man often needed the money at once, they asked for drafts to be discounted when they handed them in. The Bank charged the discount rate and brokerage commission. The discount rate was four per cent. The money advanced on the drafts belonged to the people who had deposit accounts and received an annual interest of three per cent for them. The Bank cashed in four pesetas on each draft of 100 pesetas it discounted—and it discounted many thousands a year.

For this purpose, they had a special reference department and knew exactly every customer's credit. In this department girls were typing out copies of all the information collected, and filing them by the hundred every day. The girls were paid two pesetas daily, and many days they had to work twelve hours without looking up from their typewriters. In the Securities Department there were girls too, but they were much worse off than those in Reference, although they had the same pay. I saw them every day, because I had to take round the correspondence to the various sections; sometimes the girls gave me sweets.

Down in the basement there were some rooms all in steel, roof, walls, and floor, tables, and chairs. The doors were steel grilles, and during the night the rooms were protected by another thick door of steel with many bolts and knobs bearing numbers which had to be arranged in certain combinations so as to open the door. There were no windows, and everything had to be done by artificial light. It was there that the girls worked. They had to file the bonds deposited by the clients of the Bank, to cut off the coupons of every bond due for payment, and to prepare the invoices for all coupons to be paid inside Spain. They spent the day, scissors in hand or counting packets of a hundred coupons each, and listing them one by one in the invoices for cashing. There was no ventilation and the air was suffocating. All the girls looked pale, and Señorita Magdalena, who was the senior in the service, had to be given three or four days' leave every month. The only man down there was the head of the department, Señor Perahita, a fat man, very fat and very jolly. He seemed not to be affected by working there, for he grew fatter and redder every day. Near the door of the section there was the engine of one of the lifts, and the smell of the grease came into the room and stuck in your throat.

Then there was the Safe Deposit, yet another steel room with a very stout steel door. It was entirely filled with safes like wardrobes with drawers inside, and every client had a key to one of the drawers. Most of them were jewelers of the district, for the Bank stood in the jewelers' quarter. In the evenings they would come with their cases full of jewelery and lock them up. Other clients, too, kept their jewels, bonds and cash in the safes. One of them had a lot of gold in bars and gold coins; when he opened his safe, it was all shining yellow. The coins and the bars were arranged in piles. One day he showed us a bar which had come from China and was covered with Chinese characters stamped in relief. It weighed at least half a pound.

There was an old lady who kept all her bank notes in the safe and used to come there every morning to take out the money she needed for the day's shopping. She opened her safe and looked round in all directions to make sure that nobody could see how much money she had. When another client was just opening another safe near by, she waited until he had gone. Once the cashier of the Bank asked her why she did not open a deposit account, so that she could draw whatever she needed each time, while saving the rent of the safe and receiving an annual interest on top of it. She replied that every bank went bankrupt sooner or later, and it was impossible to convince her. She always asked Antonio, the chief commissionaire, to accompany her down to the basement, because she was afraid of somebody hiding there to rob and kill her when she opened her safe.

This Antonio was worse than Señor Corachán. He was always spying on the messenger boys and on us, and reported us to Señor Corachán. Thus everybody loathed him, including those of the staff who had started as learners, because they knew he was a lick-spittle. Nobody spoke when he was near and he hated the whole clerical staff. Sometimes it happened that one of the commissionaires or one of the collectors passed his examination and became a clerk in the Bank. Then Antonio never spoke to him any more. He lived in the building itself and supervised the night watchmen until midnight or one o'clock, walking silently through the corridors on rubber soles like Señor Corachán. The night watchmen hated him so much that they played him a trick once which made him nearly die of fright.

One of the night watchmen, Señor Juan, hid in a corner and when Antonio had passed by, on tiptoe so that they should not hear him, he suddenly rang all the alarm bells and pointed his revolver at Antonio who was at the bottom of a dark passage. Señor Juan shouted: "Stop or I shoot—hands up!" Antonio was standing with his back to him and wanted to turn round, but the other said: "Don't turn round, or I shoot." "But, Juan," cried Antonio, very scared, "it's me—Antonio!" "Shut up or I'll put a bullet through you." As all the night watchmen were in the plot, they kept him for half an hour standing there, face to the wall and hands up, until some of them came back with the policeman posted in the Calle de Alcalá, who also carried their revolvers in their hands. We were watching, and had great fun seeing Antonio coming out with a frightened face in the midst of people pointing revolvers at him. Then Señor Juan said very seriously: "Well, it's a pure miracle you haven't been shot. I see a black shadow creeping about very softly, without making any noise, so I think it's a thief. If you'd started to run or to make any funny kind of movement, I can tell you, I'd have laid you out."

The next day the whole Bank had a laugh at him, even the directors. Señor Carreras, the assistant director, who liked a joke, cross-examined him in front of us all to get his laugh.

One after the other the boys who had entered at the same time as I had disappeared, until the three of us were left, Medrano, Gros, and I. It was peculiar that we were again three, just as in the Escuela Pía, and I had a hunch that we all would become regular employees. Christmas was drawing near, and then we would learn which way things were going. We were full of hope, because they attached two new boys to us so that we should train them. That meant that we were five and that two of us would be transferred to another section. If they had intended to throw us out they would have done so before and not kept us on to teach two newcomers. But on the other hand the fact that we had only two boys to train meant that one of us three was either to stay on in the section or was going to be dismissed, and so we were all afraid. Each one of us had gone to the person who had recommended him to the Bank, and each had been given good hopes, but you never knew what those people were going to do.

On Christmas Eve we were all waiting for the envelopes which had been put on the desk of the Heads of Departments. They were yellow envelopes which contained the Christmas bonus and the month's salary; in some cases the slip of paper that gave the two sums also carried a handwritten remark which could mean promotion, or else a warning that the directors were not satisfied with the employee's work. Thus everybody was impatient and nervous, waiting to know his fate.

Señor Zabala called the employees one by one in a loud, sharp voice. Some of them he congratulated even before they had had time to open the envelope. They all thanked him and wished him a Merry Christmas. Then they started to open their envelopes and stood around in groups talking them over, some happy because they had been given a fat Christmas bonus or a promotion, and others very annoyed.

Recalde was banging his fist on the table and cursing. Señor Zabala rose from his chair and called out:

"What's the matter, Señor Recalde? Come here."

Recalde came up, his hat pulled down over his forehead, and began to thump on Zabala's desk.

"It's a rotten trick! That's the third year they've done the same thing to me. I won't stand for it any more. The whole Bank and all those Jesuit swine like yourself can go to hell! I've been working here and nobody can say anything against my work, but of course, the Reverend Father Capuchin's made up his filthy mind that I mustn't have a mistress. I've got one because I damned well want one."

Señor Zabala, scarlet with fury and tugging at his beard, cried:

"Hold your tongue or it will be the worse for you. Hold your tongue, I'm telling you!"

"I don't want to. I'm shouting because it suits me and because I'm leaving this pigsty anyhow."

He strode out of the room and slammed all the doors along the corridor. A group of clerks clustered round Señor Zabala and consoled him with a lot of flatteries. But another group, those who were discontented, stood round another desk and said that Recalde was in the right.

We three boys were the last to be called. They had given each of us a bonus of twenty-five pesetas and the slip of paper said that Gros and I should transfer to the Records Department and that Medrano was to act as auxiliary correspondent. We were crazy with joy because these transfers meant that our promotion to real clerks was a certainty. We decided to have a glass of vermouth together at the bar of the Portuguese in the Calle de la Cruz.

There we found Plá, a Plá who was a stranger to us. He spluttered worse than ever and his little eyes were watering behind his lenses, he invited everybody to have a drink on him, and showed everybody his slip of paper and the banknotes he had received. It was a happy Plá, who hugged the three of us.

"Have whatever you like, it's on me. Boy"—he shouted at the lad behind the counter—"give those three a drink, and anybody else who wants one too."

Then he started once again on the story of his good fortune so that the three of us should know it.

"Granny will go crazy with joy." Granny was his mother, a tiny old lady, very kind, who sometimes came to fetch him. "You see, I was tearing the envelope open in a bad temper, as every year, and thinking it will be the same old story, they'll have forgotten me. And then there it was, I found a heap of banknotes and a note saying: 'As from January the 1st, Head of the Records Department with a monthly salary of 175 pesetas.' Double what I've been earning, less five pesetas."

"Then Gros and I'll be with you in Records," I said, and we showed him our slips.

He hugged us again and invited us to another round. Then we invited him to have drinks on us. More employees of our Bank came into the bar and a long row of glasses was lined up in front of Plá. Everybody invited him for a drink, and he invited everybody. He was going to be dead drunk in the end and out of pure joy. We went home. Plá had touched me. I too wanted to see the happiness in the face of my own "Granny" and of my aunt, when they heard the news.

All of us in Records had our hopes and illusions. Plá was happy. Gros and I were happy. Antonio Alvarez, the third boy in Records, was also happy, because they had given him 100 pesetas for a Christmas bonus and he was earning 75 pesetas. He had been no more than four years in the Bank. The future was ours. We worked like donkeys day and night.

The former head of the department had been dismissed because he had made "nests." That is to say, he took bundles of letters, and instead of classifying them and putting each letter in its file, he hid them away in corners. Then the letters were missing. One day they discovered one of those nests of his and gave him the sack on the spot. When we took over the work there were thousands of letters waiting to be classified. Every day we found a new nest. All this had to be cleared up even while the daily correspondence was being filed. We worked from seven in the morning to one at night. The Bank paid us a coffee every night. When we came home our fingers were rasped by paper dust and streaked with dry ink in microscopically small grains.

Who was it who had hit upon the idea of making Plá Head of the Records Department? It must have been Corachán. There the poor short-sighted man was, his thick slabs of lenses a-glitter with round specks of light from the lamp which burned day and night just above his head; he was crouched over the counter, his nose almost bumping against the heap of papers in his effort to decipher signatures and letterheads, for hours and hours. Afterwards he suffered from terrible headaches. At midnight they brought us the coffee and Plá drank it greedily. It was thick black coffee with a lot of chicory and gelatine in it, and it left black stains on the filing-counter. Plá took a small bottle filled with cheap brandy from his pocket; it cured his headache. Afterwards he could not sleep and in the mornings he ran round in circles, like a dazed owl, until the snack at eleven, fifteen centimos' worth of cheese sandwich and a drink of wine, brought him to life again.

We all worked ceaselessly, and Plá was fond of us as though we had been his sons. We had to take a bite of his cheese and a sip of his wine and a whiff from the cigarette he always kept lighted beneath the filing-counter. His little round body hid there; he took a long pull at his cigarette, flapped his hands to disperse the tobacco smoke and keep it from curling upwards, and then emerged with the grave face of a boy who has been naughty.

The counter ran the whole length of the records room, some thirty yards and the whole day long employees of other sections came there to find out about things in the old files. This meant that we had not only to do the filing, but also to answer the queries. When the directors or the Guarantees Department wanted information we had to take the files up to them, which we did for nobody else.

The Guarantees Department was the most aristocratic section of the Bank. It was the place dealing with all the rich foreigners who brought letters of credit, and with millionaires, who never had to stand in a queue to cash a check like tradesmen and other people with current accounts. The Department had a staircase of its own with a gilt railing and a thick carpet instead of the linoleum all the others had. All its employees wore frock coats. Its big waiting-room, with enormous leather armchairs and plenty of foreign magazines, was sometimes quite full of millionaires. One of the employees was an Englishman, with a monocle stuck in his eye, who always smoked a light brand of tobacco with a peculiar scent. For in that Department they allowed the employees to smoke; most of them were foreigners who would not have stayed on working in Madrid if they had been forbidden to smoke, but would have gone back to Paris or London.

Everything showed that there were different categories even among the people who had money. It was not as though none of the people with a current account had much money. It was simply because of their social standing. There was an ordinary Juan Perez who owned two million pesetas but had to wait in the queue downstairs in the central hall, and there was His Grace the Marquess of Something-or-other, with hardly 100,000 pesetas to his credit in the account, who dealt directly with the Guarantees Department and came with great airs to cash a check for 500 pesetas and to smoke the cigars supplied in the waiting-room. While everybody addressed him as Your Grace this and Your Grace that, Juan Perez was sitting on the wooden bench downstairs, waiting until the cashier sang out his number, No. 524.

But there were still more influential clients, the directors of the great industrial concerns in Spain and abroad. They were received in the boardroom by the director, Monsieur Michaud himself, or by Señor Carreras. One of those men, Don Carlos Mazorra, was one of the greatest men on the Spanish Stock Exchange. He always won. For a long time the Bank tried to fleece him like all the others, but when it was found that this was not only impossible, but that he sometimes tricked the Bank, they came to an agreement with him. After that the Bank informed him of good business in hand, and Don Carlos passed on information to the Bank. Sometimes Señor Tejada and he went in together for a deal worth millions and shared the profits.

They did so over the Banco Hispano deal. That bank captured within a short time a great part of all the other banks' customers. One day all the banks got together and agreed to wreck the Banco Hispano by making its shares fall and producing a run on the bank. They did create a panic; people stood in a queue all along the Calle de Sevilla to withdraw their money. When the Bank had no more ready cash to pay them, it applied to the other banks; they, however, refused to lend money on the securities the Banco Hispano had in its safes. Even the Bank of Spain refused to help, and on the following morning the Banco Hispano had to suspend payment. Most of the people who had been able to withdraw their money came to our Bank and opened an account with us. But in the end it turned out that the Banco Hispano had more than sufficient funds to continue payments and it did not go bankrupt. During the slump of the shares many people were ruined, but Don Carlos and our Bank made fat profits, because they had bought up shares when they were at their lowest.

On August the 1st, exactly a year after I had entered the Bank, they made me a paid employee, with a monthly salary of twenty-five pesetas. It was very little. But at least I was no longer afraid of being thrown out. At the same time I was transferred to the Coupons Section of the Securities Department, with Perahita as my chief. It was going to be all right. The Bank had just decided that it was impossible to go on working in the steel room, because everyone fell ill there; one of the inner courtyards was being covered with a glass roof and turned into a room. There the Coupons Section was going to work with all the girls, three clerks, and Perahita as the Head.

While the courtyard was being converted, I went to work in the steel room. The little staircase which led up from there ended just by the door of the courtyard where the builders were setting up the roof of steel and glass and painting the walls a cream color. When we came upstairs from that cold steel cellar which was always lighted by electric lamps, we looked at the new quarters which were our hope. With their roof and floor of glass, the light-colored walls, the sun shining down at noon, it made a violent contrast to our cellar and we were happy thinking that we would work there. We kept on asking the masons and painters:

"Will it be much longer?"

"Two or three days, and the time it takes for the paint to dry," they told us.

Everybody was content, but I wasn't. The two rooms had made me think. If they had sent me to the Coupons Section a year earlier, I should have passed that year between steel walls. I should not have stood it. Even in the few days I worked there I felt a pressure on my chest, and every time I came out into the Calle de Alcalá, the air seemed different; sometimes I was almost sick. Red sparks from the electric light seemed to stay before my eyes for a long time and I saw dancing spots when I came out into the daylight. If I had worked in the steel room for that year, I would not have been paid and if I had fallen ill they would have sacked me. Now, after a year as a learner, swallowing the dust of the files and running up and down stairs, I earned 25 pesetas a month, less than a peseta a day. This would go on for another year, and then I would follow the career of all the others. After the second year they would raise my salary to 37.50 pesetas a month, and after the third year to 50 pesetas. At twenty years I would earn 100 pesetas a month, if I was lucky, and then I would be called up for the Army. In the meantime my mother would have to go on washing clothes by the river to earn her living.

On one of the first days after my transfer to the new department a commissionaire came and told me:

"Señor Barea, you are to go up to the board-room. To Señor Corachán."
They all looked at me with scared faces and I, too, was scared. Such a
summons always boded ill. I climbed the stairs to the top floor with
hollow legs and a beating heart. The worst that could happen was that
they would dismiss me for some reason, but I could not imagine for
what. Still, I wouldn't lose so very much—twenty-five pesetas a month.

I went into the room with its deep leather chairs and conference tables,
with leather folders and agate inkstands. Señor Corachán was sitting
near one of the windows, reading some papers. He let me stand there in
front of him for a few minutes. I saw clearly that he was doing nothing,
not even reading; he was only showing off. In the end he raised his head,
looked me over, took a dossier, turned its leaves and asked me pompously:
"You're the employee Arturo Barea Ogazón of the Coupons Section?"
"Yes, sir."

"Good. Now look here (pause) the Management have agreed (pause)
in view of the positive reports in your dossier (pause) not-to-throw-you-
into-the-street." (He stressed each syllable, tapping the pencil on the palm
of his hand.)

"But why, sir?" I asked.

"You have——" and now he burst out in anger, "an infernal handwriting! This cannot be tolerated. Do you think you can work in a bank,
be employed by a bank, with a hand like yours which looks like spiders'
legs? You ought to be ashamed of yourself! The Management cannot
stand for this a single day longer. Take note of this: you are being given
a month's time—one month!—to improve your handwriting. If you don't,
you'll be dismissed. It is understood that in view of the fact that I am
giving you a month's warning the Bank is entitled to consider itself free
from any obligation to pay you the month's salary on dismissal, stipu-
lated by the law. You may go now."

"But Don Antonio——"

"Not a single word more! The Management cannot enter into discussion with you. Be quiet and go."

I should have liked to hit the whiskered beast in front of me, his chin
quivering with rage and his eyes protruding behind the gold-rimmed
lenses which danced on the bridge of his nose.

I told the story to my mother while she peeled the potatoes for supper
in the kitchen; my aunt had gone to church to say her Rosary. I cried
with rage.

Her gentle fingers stopped peeling potatoes and strayed through my hair.

4. The Will

DON PRIMO, the notary, had chambers paneled in carved wood, which impressed all the country relations as they sat down, one after the other, in a circle round the huge table. Many of them were sitting on the very edges of their chairs. The men held their round hats on their knees and fingered them, the women put both hands in their laps and kept plucking at the cloth. I had been so often in the room and had spoken so frequently to Don Primo that I was intimidated neither by the place nor by the severe figure of the notary with his black suit, gold-rimmed spectacles, and aristocratic head. When I arrived with my mother and Grandmother Inés, he patted me.

I did not know why all the people who had come to hear the reading of my aunt's will were looking at me with such resentment. They had split up into groups: Uncle Hilario with his wife and daughters—Uncle Basilio with his wife, sons, and daughters—Aunt Basilisa with Uncle Anastasio, who dared not smoke but was chewing a stinking cigarette stub, and Baldomera whose face was like a daft nun's—Aunt Eulogia with her Carmen—Uncle Julian, like myself a nephew once removed, with his wife and three small children clutching at her skirts. Why did they all bring their children?

While Don Primo read the will, they stretched out their necks better to listen. Every time a name occurred the named person's face changed and shone with pleasure at not having been forgotten, and all the others looked at him, annoyed that there was still another with whom to share.

I was the main target of their anger.

Apparently, my uncle and aunt had made their wills at the same time and in agreement. They left the fortune to whichever of them should survive, for free use during his or her lifetime, but whatever remained after the death was divided into two equal parts. Uncle and Aunt had disposed of one part each in favor of their own relations. I was the only one who figured in both wills and had a share in both parts. Otherwise my uncle's blood relatives inherited from his part, and my aunt's blood relatives from her part.

They all thought that they, who were either brothers or sisters or direct nephews or nieces of the deceased, had more rights than I, who was only a nephew once removed. When my name turned up in the second will, a

general murmur interrupted the reading. Don Primo stopped and looked
at them, questioning:

"Would you like to make any comment?"

Uncle Hilario stood up.

"If I've got it right, the kid inherits double."

"Just so," answered Don Primo, "once under José's will and once under
Baldomera's will."

"But that's all wrong, damn it all. Because I'm the brother of the
deceased, his own flesh and blood, and I say it's all wrong that a stranger
should just walk in and carry off the cash."

Uncle Anastasio, twisting his cigar stub between his lips, intervened:
"That's just it. And we won't stand for it. We shall go to law about it."

Don Primo smiled.

"I think Pepe knew you all very well indeed. When these two wills
were drafted, he asked me to add the clause which I'm now going to read
to you:

" 'It is our will that any of the heirs who may attempt to enter into
a lawsuit concerning our wills shall by this selfsame act lose any right to
his or her inheritance which shall thereupon be distributed among all the
other heirs in proportion to their inheritance.' "

Grandmother Inés rose gravely from her chair, turned to face the two
men and said:

"Well—are we going to law?"

"Nobody asked you to carry a candle in this procession," said Uncle
Anastasio severely.

"Of course not, my lad. But you see, the kid here has been given two
big candles to carry, and as I happen to be his grandmother, I'm here to
support his weak arms so that he doesn't drop them. Has anybody anything against it?"

All but myself were upset about the will. The only heirs were the
nearest relatives—brothers and sisters—and I. Beyond that, Uncle José
and Aunt Baldomera had left various legacies to all nephews and nieces,
which meant that those with the greatest number of children came off
best. Uncle Anastasio, who had only his Baldomera, and Aunt Eulogia,
with Carmen and Esperanza, were angry with Uncle Hilario who had
three children, and they were all angry with Uncle Julian who was no
heir but received legacies for himself, his wife, and his five children, so
that he got more than any of the heirs. When we left the notary's house
we were all enemies.

My mother had the keys of my aunt's flat, and out of fear that she might
take something, the others came after us so that in the end we were

all assembled in the flat. The door stayed open and they entered in small groups.

The room in which my aunt's body had been lying was empty, but it still smelled of flowers and of death, a faint, insidious, clammy smell. A few wax blobs were left on the tiles. It was as though at any moment her slight porcelain figure might come out of the bedroom with short little steps.

They all took seats round the table. All of them. As though anybody who had not taken his place there would forfeit his rights. Grandmother Inés squeezed herself into the rocking-chair below the clock. She had to force the two curved arm-rests apart to get room for her behind. When she had succeeded in sitting down on the plaited cane seat she heaved a sigh of contentment. My mother sat down beside her on the low stool on which my aunt used to sew beside the balcony until the daylight failed her. I threw myself on the floor, on the carpet. I could not have sat down at the table with the others. Stretched on the carpet and watching them all upside down, I felt better. Don Julian had spoken with Señor Corachán and I had been given ten days' leave from the Bank.

The Bank seemed no longer to exist. Lying there on the floor I was again a child, and in the end I rested my head on my mother's lap, between her knees. She had a black skirt which smelled of starch and new cloth and rustled at every movement of my head. One of the legal executors was speaking and explaining what had to be done. It was necessary to make an inventory of everything in the flat, to agree on the value of each item and then to make lots which would be distributed among the heirs. There were eleven lots: nine heirs with one lot each, and two lots for me. Now the disputes started. The lots had to be fixed by value in money, but it was difficult to agree on the big pieces of furniture. As nobody knew who would get each thing, the prices were fixed ridiculously low so as to pay as little as possible in death duties. But suddenly Fuencisla, one of Uncle Hilario's daughters, said:

"I've taken a fancy to the Virgin."

Carmen gave back at once: "And I too."

"There is no difficulty about that," said the Executor. "If all those present agree, we shall put a value to the Virgin and allot it to one of you, deducting the price from the corresponding lot."

The Virgin was placed on the dining-room table. The figure stood in a wooden case with glass in front and a door, with a little silver key, at the back. The statue was eighteen inches high. The Virgin held the Child Jesus in her arms and both had little gilt flames stuck into their hair. She had an embroidered mantle and the Child a little velvet cape flecked with gold.

"Well," said the Executor, "what value shall we put on this?"

Nobody spoke.

"Shall we say fifty pesetas?"

They all hesitated in giving their agreement, as though it were a serious problem. Uncle Anastasio, his cigar stub lighted at last, said nothing, went up to the statue, opened the door at the back of the case and touched the wooden face of the Virgin with one finger. He went on sucking at his cigar while he closed the door, and the others looked at him in astonishment. He addressed the Executor with gravity:

"You say, then, that the value of this Virgin will be deducted from the lot of one of those two girls?"

"Certainly. That is to say, if all those present are agreeable that one of them should get it."

"I've no objection to the Virgin's being allotted to one of them," said Uncle Anastasio in a throaty voice, "but I cannot permit a carving of the twelfth century—well, or whatever century it is," he added hastily when he saw the Executor's dumbfounded face, "to be given away for fifty pesetas. This Virgin is worth at least five hundred pesetas, and that's modest. Because you won't deny that it's carved wood!" He opened the little door once again and rapped a few times with his knuckles on the Virgin's face, which sounded like a block of wood.

"Wood, you see, gentlemen, authentic polychrome wood carving. It's rare nowadays to find one of these Virgins."

Grandmother Inés grunted from the depth of her rocking-chair:

"And of other virgins, too."

"I've no objection," said the Executor. "If you think that the Virgin should be put down at a value of 500 pesetas, or at 1,000 pesetas, it's all the same to me. Only, we'll have to establish first which of the two . . ." he stammered a little before he decided on his way of address, ". . . of the two young ladies is going to get it."

Both answered at the same time, each claiming the Virgin for herself, but protesting against the price. Five hundred pesetas were five hundred pesetas. For a while there was a medley of voices. In the end the Executor imposed silence and suggested a solution:

"Let us put the Virgin up to auction between these two young ladies." This time it came pat. "When the bidding is over, the winner will keep the Virgin, provided you all agree to that. If not, it will be added to one of the lots and whoever gets that lot will keep the Virgin."

"I'm willing to give fifty pesetas, as you said before, if only in memory of poor Aunt who was so fond of it," said Fuencisla.

"Of course, that's what you think, you'd get it for fifty pesetas," retorted Carmen. "I'd give one hundred pesetas, sir."

The two of them were hopping round the table like a pair of fighting cats, and between them stood the Virgin with her empty smile. They threw figures at each other as though they were chucking stones. Flushed red with rage, Carmen dealt the final blow:

"Eight hundred pesetas!" she bellowed.

Fuencisla burst into tears. Aunt Braulia angrily pinched her arm to stop her from bidding higher. Carmen looked at the lot of them arrogantly. "Yes, sir. Eight hundred pesetas—and I'm not going back on my word." She screamed it, arms akimbo, just like one of the shameless girls of El Avapies—which indeed she was.

Grandmother Inés broke out into loud laughter so that her breasts and her belly, which flowed over from the chair, shook and heaved. Carmen turned round and faced her:

"What's that? Do you mind? Because I can do with my own money what I damn' well please!"

Grandmother went off into gales of laughter, unable to speak. She coughed, sputtered, and her eyes ran over. When she calmed down, she said between chuckles:

"No, my dear girl, no, I'm not getting angry with you. You can take your Virgin away and read Masses to her. Anyhow, you'll spit on her more often than you pray to her. And as a consolation, I'm going to tell you that before you were born, Pepe bought it on the Junk Market for ten pesetas one Sunday, and they carried it home for him into the bargain."

Next day they began breaking up the flat. The relatives from Brunete turned up with their farm carts, the mules harnessed to a wooden yoke on their necks, with the pole sticking out between them. There were still bits of straw clinging to the bottom of the carts and in the esparto ropes which had been used to bundle up the straw. They moved down furniture and broke china in carting it down the stairs. Uncle Julian arrived with his children and two push-carts. When they had loaded them and dragged them away, the carts almost toppled over. We were the last. We had sold the big pieces of furniture which had fallen to our lot, because there was no room for them in the garret, but we had kept my bed, three wool mattresses, some cutlery, and all the clothes which had come to us. Beyond that there were a few banknotes which my mother had pushed into her black shopping bag. Uncle Anastasio had sold his whole lot. He kept the money and told his wife and Baldomerita: "Now let's go." But at the next corner he left them alone and the two came with us, trotting alongside the handcart which Señor Manuel was pushing for us. They lived close by in the Plaza del Angel.

Aunt Basilisa began to talk: "It's a burning shame, my dear, a burning shame, that's what it is. Those men! And there's nothing one can do. I would have loved to keep a few of my poor sister's things, but you see what happened. He put the money in his pocket and off he went. Later he'll tell us it's all in the way of business and we shan't even see a copper. The only good thing is that I was able to save a few things before Baldomera died, because if it hadn't been for that. . . . Of course, when we get the real money we've inherited it won't happen that way, it'll have to go into the bank for our girl when she marries, whether he wants it or not." She stopped for a time while we crossed the Plaza Mayor, walking round it the wrong way because they were repairing the asphalt.

Then she started again: "I tell you, my dear, life is hell. A good thing I've got that post as a concierge, it's a steady two hundred to two' hundred and fifty pesetas a month. But him—since they retired him with sixty pesetas a month he's made himself a very comfortable life. In the mornings he reads the paper and rolls his cigarettes. After dinner he goes to the café. In the evening he comes home for supper, and then he goes to the tavern and gambles away his cash. At the beginning of the month I've got to keep my eyes skinned to see that he doesn't get away with the rent the tenants pay. We wouldn't see the shadow of a copper otherwise. And it's no good protesting, because if I do he goes mad and starts knocking furniture about and shouting: 'After thirty years of honest toil those women won't let me have a glass of vermouth with my friends. But it's me who's master here!' Well, you know him, Leonor. And then he runs about with those servant wenches. He's an old man now, but he still goes to bed with any one he can get. It's a shame, my dear, it's a real shame, I tell you. He makes up to them on the stairs and then he takes them into the lift and stays with them, because he says they don't know how to work it. My foot . . . it's because he can squeeze them as much as he likes in there."

When we said good-by to her, she called out:

"Well, come and see me some time!" and walked away on Baldomerita's arm, limping because of her rheumatics.

Señor Manuel stacked up the pieces of the bedstead, the mattresses, the clothing, and the small bundles in the garret, and it was quite filled. Señora Pascuala had come up to see everything and pushed her fists into the wool filling of the mattresses, fingered the sheets, and weighed the silver cutlery. I started to set up my own bed. Its gilt rails mocked the two other beds with their green-painted iron bars and creaking springs. Then, only then, did I dismantle my little old bed and unscrew all its rusty screws. The pieces leaned like a green skeleton in a corner where the sloping roof and the floor met. We put the two big mattresses on my mother's, bed, her double bed with curved iron rails at the head and the foot and with two flat panels which had saints painted on them. My bed had its own mattress. And in the angle between roof and floor the two old flock mattresses were left lying, patched and faded.

"What are you going to do with them, Leonor?" asked Señora Pascuala.

"I don't know. We'll have to give them away to somebody."

Señor Manuel scratched his bald head and rolled one of his fat cigarettes made of stubs and twisted like a tree trunk.

"Are you going to give them away as a gift, Leonor?" he asked.

"Well, of course, they're not good enough to sell."

He scratched his head again and sucked his cigarette which he had lighted with his tinder rope.

"It's just . . . you see . . . it's like this. . . ." The words strangled him. "It's years since. . . . Well—you know I've got a landlady who lets me have a room. But for two and a half pesetas a month you can't ask for much. I've got a pallet, fixed it up myself, but it isn't like a mattress. Not to speak of a bed. I don't get a bed even when I go home to my village; there I've got a good-sized heap of maize straw and that's a fine thing to sleep on. But if you're going to chuck it away, well, give it away, then it's better I should get it. Don't you think that's right, Leonor? And then"—he had grown sure of himself in speaking—"let's make a bargain. You let me take the bed and the mattresses away, and I'll carry your washing up for you at half price for three weeks. I won't say that I'll do it for nothing, because if I lose that fixed amount I couldn't really manage. What do you think of it?"

He gazed anxiously at my mother and waited for her answer. My mother smiled as she sometimes knew how to smile. Then she turned to me.

"Here you've got the heir, he can do as he likes."

Señor Manuel looked at me with the eyes of a dog who fears that his master is going to abandon him. I was now a young gentleman employed in a bank. For months he had never dared to kiss me or to talk to me as he used to talk before. I filled him with awe and I knew that he talked about me to all the washerwomen as though I were a wonder: "Leonor's son, you know, he's working in a bank, he's become a real young gentleman!" Now he sucked at his foul cigarette and looked at me—looked at me—God, how he looked at me!

"Señor Manuel," I said gravely. "We're going to make a deal. I give you the bed and the mattresses, but on the condition that——"

He did not let me finish: "Whatever you like, master, anything you wish. I've been working with your mother fifteen years—as many years as you have, master—and she can tell you——"

"I'll give you the bed, but you must stop calling me master."

At first he seemed not to understand what I meant. Then he seized me, shook me with his big, strong hands, crushed me in his arms, kissed my face noisily, after flinging away the cigarette he had in his mouth, put his two hands on my shoulders, stood me in front of him, and began to cry.

We had to give him a glass of spirits. Afterwards he made two trips to carry home the old green-painted bed rails and the patched and re-patched flock mattresses. When my mother and I were left alone, we put the room in order; from time to time one of the neighboring women came in to see what was going on and to inspect the bed which shone like a jewel in the garret, with its gleaming bars and its heavy crocheted bedspread. At nightfall arrived Señora Segunda, the old beggar woman with her nose half destroyed by cancer.

My mother sorted out the clothes for which she had no use and gave them to her, one after another. Señora Segunda took them, held them to the light of the oil lamp and exclaimed with pleasure. There were my aunt's chemises, bodices, skirts, underskirts, and petticoats. My mother kept the best pieces for herself and gave her all the rest. She picked up a dark brown winter jacket of thick cloth with a huge tear right across the front.

"I can't imagine that this could be of any use to you, Segunda." She pushed her hand through the rent. "Aunt could never bring herself to throw anything away."

Señora Segunda held up the jacket and the light fell through the tear. "It'll do for Toby, my dear. The poor thing suffers so much from cold in the winter when we are out begging. I'm going to make a coat for him. Toby! Toby!"

Lazily, the dog got up from beside the brazier where he was lying, sniffed at the jacket and wagged his tail. Señora Segunda insisted on fitting it on Toby's back, while the sleeves dragged on the floor, and he stood quite still, wagging his tail under the folds. Then he licked her hands and went back to his place in the warmth under the table.

Our life in the garret settled down. My mother was still doing her washing on Mondays and Tuesdays. I went to the Bank. On Sundays, my brother and sister came to see us. On weekdays, I read in the evenings and my mother did her sewing by the light of the oil lamp. Sometimes we all went to the pictures on Sundays, in the afternoons, because Rafael had to be back in his shop, and Concha in the house where she was in service, by eight o'clock. I had become somebody. Señora Pascuala addressed me in the old familiar way but she looked at me with a respect mixed with a touch of envy, because her son Pepe was getting nowhere. Everybody else said "Sir" to me.

From time to time I drank a glass of vermouth and smoked a cigarette. Soon I would be getting a few thousand pesetas as the heir of my uncle and aunt. I was the master of the house and of my people and I knew it. We kept on hearing stories about the other heirs.

In Brunete, the two families, Uncle Hilario's and Uncle Basilio's, seemed to have quarreled. After my Uncle José's death, both had wanted to assume the command of the small community he had created, Uncle Hilario because he was older, Uncle Basilio because he was younger and had sons. Their quarrel started on account of the furniture they had taken out of the estate. Although everything had been distributed by lot, and they themselves had fixed the value of each piece, they were now throwing in each other's teeth that one piece of furniture was worth more than the other and that both of them had been cheated. The people of the village went to both their houses, and in each said that it had got the better furniture. In the end, they agreed no longer to work their land jointly. Yet when they came to divide the land they had bought under Uncle José's management, to distribute the mules, the farming implements, the crops stored in the barn, and even the pitchers which were used to bring drinking water to the farm hands, the row broke out in earnest. The women pulled each other's hair, and the men hit at each other with their sticks. In the end, they went to law to establish their claims to the land, and sought out Don Luis Bahía to advance them money on their inheritance from Uncle José, so that they could cover the expenses of the lawsuit.

Uncle Julian, too, was an odd case. His whole life he had worked as a wheelwright in a workshop, in the Ronda del Toledo. He had learned his craft from my grandfather, and had then come to Madrid as a master in partnership with the owner of the workshop. He and his five children lived in a tenement house in the Calle del Tribulete. When the furniture was allotted, he got the sideboard and the dining-room table. Both were big, heavy pieces of carved oak. He took them home to a flat which had only four small rooms—a dining room, two bedrooms, and a kitchen, while the lavatory was in the passage and used by all the tenants on the same floor—and naturally neither the sideboard nor the table fitted into the flat. But they pushed them in, and then had to squeeze themselves sideways between the table and the wall whenever they wanted to walk about the room. They took the sideboard to pieces. The lower part went into the parents' bedroom, and the upper part, where the glasses, cups, and platters had been, was hung on a few hooks in the kitchen. Uncle Julian had two grown-up daughters, one of them just about to marry. She asked for the two pieces for her new room. The other sister protested because she too was engaged, and in the end Uncle Julian had to box the ears of each and keep the furniture himself.

Uncle Anastasio's story was simple. He took the money from the sale of the furniture and went to gamble in El Bilbaino Club in the Calle de Peligros. And he won. He won a few thousand pesetas. He came home with presents for Aunt Basilísa and Baldomerita. For a month or so, they all lived in great luxury, and everything went well. They went to the theater and cinema, they had their fancies and bought cheap trinkets. After that, Uncle Anastasio began to be short of money. He pawned the jewelry he had given to the two women, then the jewelry my aunt had given to Baldomerita, then the Manila shawl, the mantillas and whatever there was. When everything else had given out, he began to pawn household goods, and in the end Aunt Basilísa came in tears to my mother to ask her for twenty-five pesetas.

Carmen's father, Aunt Eulogia's husband, had come from Galicia as a young boy. He was a giant. When he was young, he earned money which he used to establish himself as a coal vendor in the New World. He earned a lot, but then he began to drink. He was so strong that he never got really drunk, but as he was ashamed of not getting drunk like his friends, he tried to make himself drunk too, and drank whole bottles of spirits. He ruined himself and had to close down his shop. Then, when he was no longer young, he took on a job as a porter in the most expensive furniture shop in Madrid and carried furniture to the customers' houses. He had a mate who was as big as himself, and the shop had bought them a very showy livery. They carried the furniture in a kind of litter covered in red plush, with broad leather straps slung across their shoulders. People in the streets turned round and stared at the two enormous men who carried the heaviest furniture as though it were a feather. Once, they carried a piano in this way, and people stopped on the sidewalks. They walked in step, and the piano rocked in its litter like in a cradle. He had good wages and good tips, but he spent everything on drink. One day they carried him home with an attack of delirium tremens. He didn't die because he was so strong, but he had to stay in bed, a useless invalid, his hands trembling ceaselessly. The doctor let him drink three glasses of spirits a day, for he said that he was bound to die if his alcohol were suddenly cut off.

After he saw all the furniture and clothing which had come to his wife from the inheritance, he dragged himself out of bed one morning when Aunt Eulogia had left the house and he was alone. As he lived in the

Calle del Peñón, just behind the Junk Market, he called for a neighbor who was a dealer there and sold him all the inherited furniture and clothes, and some of the things from his own household as well. Then he called a boy and sent him for a two-liter bottle of spirits, got back into bed, and poured it all down. He went mad. The first person to come home was Carmen's younger sister, Esperancita. She found her father stark naked, smashing up furniture with a knob stick. He tried to kill her, and the girl ran shrieking through the corridors of the house. At that moment, Aunt Eulogia came home, and he struck her on the shoulder. He nearly broke her arm; if the blow had landed on her head, he would have killed her. All the neighbors had to come and truss him up between them with ropes, like a bundle. For three days he had to be kept in a strait jacket, tied to the bed and foaming at the mouth.

My mother went to see him the day before he died, and I went to the funeral. The room was smashed to pieces. The only thing that was left unharmed was the Virgin on top of the chest of drawers, with the little oil lamp inside, which filmed the glass and made soot stains on the top of the case.

It was a radiant Sunday, and I had gone to the Escuela Pía to see Father Joaquín. We had been chatting till lunch time, and I had my meal with the Father in the Refectory. In the afternoon, walking up the Calle de Mesón de Paredes, I went into the house where Señora Segunda lived.

Toby welcomed me in the doorway with his dirty paws, shedding white hairs off his gray, woolly fur all over my trousers. He looked very funny in his cloth coat edged with green braid, which was tied round his neck and under his belly. Señora Segunda was getting ready to go out begging and showed me with pride what she had done with the clothes.

From a short jacket of my aunt's she had taken off the jet spangles and turned it into a coat for herself. Where the small disks had been there were dark regular spots which looked like embroidery. She had put on an old silk skirt, bright flowers on a dull ground, all grayed over by age. She had made an old mantilla into a loose veil which fell over her forehead and hid part of her dreadful nose. She was about to take her folding stool and Toby in his coat, and go to her regular place in the Plaza del Progreso. In her new costume she looked like a lady who had come down in the world; surely, now that the gaping holes of her nose were hardly visible, people would give her far more alms than before! One by one she showed me her things and explained.

"Thanks to your mother, everybody looks at me in a different way now. With my veil and the silk dress, and my face hidden away, people are sorry for me, much more so than before, and I don't make them shudder

now. I've been teaching Toby to hold a plate between his teeth and to sit
on his hind legs. He does keep still for a while but then he gets tired,
poor darling. It's a pity. Now I always take my coffee without sugar at
the café and keep the lump so that I can give it to Toby in small bits to
make him stick it out longer. But he's old, poor thing, and gets tired of
holding the plate between his teeth. It's a pity, though, because while he
holds it people give us much more alms. Even men put a copper into the
plate and pat the dog."

She showed me four new sheets which she had made out of pieces of
linen my mother had given her. She had sewn them together with tiny
little stitches, and everything was white and well ironed.

"Just feel it," she said. "First I put them in lye for bleaching, because
some pieces were whiter than others. But now thanks to the bleaching
and the blueing they're all alike and so fine that it is a pleasure to sleep in
them."

Out of old stockings she had made new ones; she had cut out pieces
and knitted them together. Out of bits and snippets of material she had
made a blanket for the dog, sewing them on to a length of burlap like
loose flower petals.

And since it was necessary to brighten up her home, now that she had
new clothes and was earning more money, she had painted her room—
that little box shaped like a wedge of cheese—a chalky blue. It made stains
on my sleeves, to complete the work Toby had started with my trousers.

On Mondays and Tuesdays I took the tram just outside the Bank and
went down to the river to have my meal there. I was proud when the
washerwomen saw me, and my mother was glad and proud too. She
made me put on one of the white smocks of the Municipal Laboratory,
so that my suit should not get dirty. She did the washing for Dr. Chicote
and all the doctors of the Laboratory. So I could sit down on the grass,
with the washing-board upside down as a table, and feed worms to the
duck. I was no longer afraid of its bill; sometimes I caught it and held
it tight. Then the duck grunted like a pig and flapped its wings in rage.
It ran away, waddling and waggling its bottom like a fat woman with
bow legs.

Señor Manuel pressed me to visit him in his house. It was a wooden
shack which belonged to a widowed woman. She lived there, and he had
a small bedroom with walls made of planks. The chinks were pasted over
with paper. He had tacked up pictures of politicians, toreros, and dancers
cut out of magazines. The floor was beaten earth, but he had covered it
with bits of tiles he had found in rubbish heaps and laid out in a mosaic
of many colors. There were white lavatory tiles, blue tiles, black-and-white

marble tiles, and hydraulic cement tiles, red, or with little flowers, or with colored disks of all sizes.

"That's what made me sweat most," said Señor Manuel, "getting this floor even. Well, it looks all right now. The only thing that's still missing is two big bits of glass for my window."

The "window" was a rectangular opening in the boards of one of the walls, where he had put a gilt picture frame with discolored flowers and leaves. Half the frame was filled with two pieces of glass stuck together with putty, the other half was covered with greased paper. The frame was mounted on two hinges and closed by a hook. When it was open, the sunlight entered freely. When it was closed the light could only come in through the glazed half, and Señor Manuel wanted a pane for the second half so that he could have sun without having to open his window. He was very sensitive to cold.

"Look at the bed—your bed," he said.

I did not recognize my old bed. Señor Manuel had painted it yellow, a gaudy yellow with a greenish tinge; he had put on the color in thick blobs and it screamed against the background of the multi-colored tiles. On the head panel of the bed he had stuck a print of Our Lady of Perpetual Help, which was full of flames from which the damned souls stretched their arms towards the Virgin, imploring Her to rescue them from Hell. A packing case covered with white cloth was his night table; it had a door, which was really the lid of the case, swinging on two leather straps and fastened with a hook like the window. Inside was a huge chamber pot with a broken handle and in its bottom a painted eye and the misspelled words: "I see you."

On top of the bed he had put a thick mattress, two sheets, a patched-up blanket and a yellow bedspread.

"Don't you like it?" Señor Manuel asked me. "When I'm out, Señora Paca (she was the owner of the shack) comes in here and lies down on the bed for her siesta. The poor woman's got rheumatics, what with living here by the river twenty years and sleeping on a heap of sacking on the ground, and so she's quite envious of me. I told her she can have the bed when I die. But I'm sure she'll die before me, and then I'll be left with the shack. I'm still going strong, I am, apart from this accursed rupture. But I haven't the heart to let them operate on me. It's all very well if you die when your hour's come, but not in the hands of a sawbones."

He stooped and stroked the bedspread lovingly.

"Do you know, I've been doing more work since I've been sleeping in a gentlemen's bed. I've got something for you."

From the depth of a chest filled with rags, old newspapers, and books

without covers, with pages missing, picked up God knows where, he
fished out a white rag rolled up like a dirty bandage. He unrolled it on
the night table and from its last fold produced a minute gold coin. It
was a ten peseta piece from the time when the King was a little boy, a
centén, as small and bright as a new centimo.

"For your watch chain. It's the only thing I've got left from better times
when we earned a lot, and the money wasn't called pesetas. I've kept it
as a fancy, but after all, what good is it to me?"

I had to take it away with me, wrapped in a piece of the coarse paper
Señor Manuel used for his stick-like cigarettes. On the slope of the Paseo
de San Vicente I took the gold coin out of its wrappings and studied it. It
was so tiny that I would have to put it on a ring if I wanted to hang it on
my watch chain. And I thought that really the happiest among all the
people who had inherited were the poorest: we, Señora Segunda and
Señor Manuel. Those two had not inherited directly, but they had a share
in the inheritance.

The slope of San Vicente has nearly half a mile of iron railing set on
a granite base. It was the railing of the Campo del Moro, the garden of
the Royal Palace, where nobody was allowed to enter; the soldiers on
guard there would have shot anyone who tried to get in. When I was a
little boy and walked up the slope with my mother I used the railing to
make whistles out of apricot stones. It was easy. You took one of the
stones and rubbed it along the granite in walking; so it was whittled
down until a small hole with an even rim appeared at its end. You took
a pin and fished out the kernel so that the shell of the stone was left
empty and then, when you blew sharply on the edge of the hole, it made
a whistle which could be heard far away.

If I were to rub the edge of the coin along the granite now it would
also be whittled away.

I passed it gently over the stone for a few steps. The edge of the coin
was unchanged, but there was a very fine streak on the granite. A streak
of gold.

Now who would think of rubbing a gold coin on stone? Is it because
I'm still a child? A gold coin. There aren't any more left in Spain. People
used to carry them in their pockets as we carry pesetas. After that only
rich people kept them, and also the Bank of Spain, which stored them in
steel boxes underground. The Bank of Spain keeps the gold so that people should accept its banknotes. I've heard that through the foundations
of the Bank there flows a stream, the stream of San Lorenzo, and that the
boxes with the gold are kept below it. If there were a fire or a robbery in
the Bank, the watchmen would open the flood-gates and the whole river
would pour over the boxes. But all that doesn't really interest me. What

I would like to do is to take a hammer and beat out the *centén* to see whether it's true that you can make yards of sheet metal out of five grammes of gold simply by hammering it. Then I'd stick the gold sheet on the wall of our room, and our garret would have a golden wall. It must be true that I'm still a child.

In the Plaza de San Gil, which they now call the Plaza de España, they're spinning tops and people stand round in a circle to watch. The four who are playing are nearly men, they're older than I am; the youngest must be seventeen. They have drawn a big circle in the sand and each of the four throws a copper in the middle of the ring. Then one after the other spins the top and tries to make its point push the coppers out of the ring. The tops are spinning well and strongly, because the players are grown-ups. No, they're not grown-ups, they're tramps, because grown men don't play at tops and boys don't play for money. But then, they aren't tramps either, they've dumped a heap of books beside the ring. They're Law students from the college near by in the Calle Ancha. They're men, but because they're still students they have the right to be boys, to spin tops and to play hopscotch here in the square. They can run after each other, boys and girls, grown-up men and women, and they can play. People watch them and like it: "Oh well, they're students, it's all right for them." And the old men with white beards who sit in the sun of the square come up, stand round while the students are spinning their tops and applaud them when they do it well. I wonder what sort of face Corachán would pull if he came by and caught us spinning a top, Medrano, Gros, and me? He would sack us. He would tell us in his ringing voice that employees of the Crédit Etranger should not behave like children or tramps, and play at tops in public. But Corachán's son is studying law here at the university. He's twenty years old. I wonder if he comes here to spin a top?

After supper Concha and Rafael came to stay with us for an hour. Concha was in service in Dr. Chicote's house and Rafael worked as an apprentice in a shop in the Calle de Atocha. They brought their wages, as it was the second day of the month. I had got mine on the first. My mother put all the money on the table and began to make her calculations and separate it into little piles. There was not much money: five duros from me, six from Rafael, eight from Concha, ninety-five pesetas in all.

"Nine pesetas for the rent, two for Pascuala."

She put the eleven pesetas in a pile. This was the most sacred money for my mother: the money for the rent.

"Five pesetas for the Society."

Those monthly five pesetas meant that we all had a right to medical assistance, medicines, and burial.

"Ten pesetas for my washing things."

My mother stopped and counted her petty debts on her fingers. Then she made another pile of fourteen pesetas. The three of us were watching her in silence, hoping that the big heap would not be diminished much more. In the end she said:

"That's what we've got left to last us until the eighth, when I get my money from the Laboratory."

Thirty-one pesetas were left. Now our turn came. First Concha.

"I need underclothes—a corset, a chemise, and a pair of stockings."

"Well, you do look after yourself," Rafael grunted. "I need boots and a smock."

"And I need shoes," I said.

"Of course, the little gent needs shoes. He's got two pairs, but he needs a third."

"I've got two pairs, but they're brown and I can't wear them when I'm in mourning for Aunt."

"Dye them black."

"That's what you say—but you must show off your breasts with a corset!"

We wrangled, all three of us. My mother tried in vain to soothe us down. In the end she took a peseta out of her pocket, put it on the remaining heap of money and divided it into four piles of eight pesetas each. She kept one of them for herself.

Rafael pocketed his eight pesetas. Concha weighed hers in her hand and said: "What's the good of this to me?"

"Now, look here," said my mother. "Take a few pesetas out of your savings book and buy whatever you need."

Each of us had a savings book which caused eternal discussions. Rafael and I had had ours since the time when we were given prizes at school, but we could not withdraw any money while we were minors. Concha started a savings account when she went into service, and she was the only one among us who could take out money whenever she liked. My book showed a balance of over 1,000 pesetas thanks to the money Uncle José had put in for me in the course of the years. Rafael's had over 500 pesetas; and Concha had saved nearly 1,500 pesetas in her first years of service, while she had no need to spend her wages. But then the household had drawn on her savings every time there was a difficulty, and now they amounted to no more than 200 or 300 pesetas. And so she became as angry as a wild cat whenever there was talk of drawing on her account.

"So that's why I've got to spend my life working myself to the bone?

Only so as not to be able to buy myself what I need? Well, it's just not good enough that way. These two have got their cash safe while I've got to carry the whole load. Ever since the death of Uncle José you've always taken money out of my book so that the boy there can be a pen pusher and a young gentleman, while I can go on washing up dirty plates."

"You're jealous, that's all," I cried.

"Jealous? Of whom? But you'll be more unhappy than any of us. We're poor, and don't mind—the children of Señora Leonor, the washerwoman. But of course—you're a nice young gentleman who's afraid to say that his mother washes at the river and lives in a garret. I bet I'm right. I've brought along my friends and the other girls who serve with me, because I'm not ashamed to bring them to my home. But you—when have you ever brought any of your friends here? Well, there you are. A young gentleman who works in a bank, and then people might find out that you live in a garret and that your mother's a washerwoman? Oh no!"

Because she was right, I grew furious. Of course they didn't know at the Bank that I was the son of a washerwoman and lived in an attic. They might have given me the sack, they didn't like having poor people there. The bank clerk's relatives were people who wore hats and overcoats. It would not have been so good if Concha had turned up in her parlor maid's uniform, Rafael in his grocer's smock, and my mother in her apron, with the kerchief tied round her head. But Concha didn't understand. I talked to her and tried to make her see the future in store for me, when I would earn a lot of money as a bank clerk, and Mother would not have to go down to the river, and we would have a flat with electric light and a big lamp over the dining-room table; but she laughed in my face, shook me and screamed at me:

"You fool! What you'll be all your life is a miserable starveling—a pen pusher—a gentleman living on bread-and-water." She hooted with laughter, but then turned serious and burst out: "A starched-collar slave—that's what you're going to be!" And she turned her back on me, sat down in a chair and broke into tears.

Rafael and I went off, out into the street. We bought a packet of fifty, and lit a cigarette each. Then we had coffee with brandy. Then we took a tram and went to Cuatro Caminos where we had a meal of roast lamb and red wine. When we came back, we had spent our sixteen pesetas between us. Rafael said:

"It doesn't matter. I get my tips. But don't tell Mother."

The next morning, when I got up to go to work, my mother had already brushed my suit, as she did every day, and she gave me two pesetas. "Here, take it, you must have some money on you in case you need it."

She did not ask me what I had done with the eight pesetas of the day before. I felt ashamed as I walked down the stairs.

5. The Future

I FELT a longing, for what, I did not know. A longing to run, to jump, to throw stones, to climb trees, to sit in the shade and look. To look without thinking of anything, to look into the far distance. To fill my mind with the country; with those groups of trees, so deeply green that they seemed a black stain far away; with the yellow of the meadows in El Pardo which the King was said to use for agricultural experiments. There was an arid patch with an artesian well in the middle, from which the water leaped up thirty feet. To fill this head of mine with snow and stone, the snow and stone over there in the Sierra de Guadarrama. To shut myself up in the garret, alone, with my mother down at the river or wherever she wás. To turn the key in its lock so that Señora Pascuala should not come and see me doing nothing, filling my head with nothing at all.

I walked between the pine trees of the Moncloa. They grew on steep slopes and their needles had carpeted the ground. People preferred the Parque del Oeste, that English park with shorn lawns and fine sand on the paths. The grass looked as though it were tended by barbers with giant hair cutters, who scraped the ground and left it with nothing but side whiskers; they had made a parting in the middle, a runlet with a concrete bed and an edging of rocks full of holes, like petrified sponges, and cascades like the steps of a staircase. The stream bounded down the steps and laughed at the people who watched it foolishly from the height —seven feet high—of the rustic bridges. A mamma said to her child who went near the railing made of crossed branches: "Darling, don't lean over, you might fall in and drown." And there were four inches of water. The boy laughed at his mother, because he would have liked to wet his feet, and the stream laughed, and the fishes laughed. The boy saw the stream as a channel of water where he wanted to splash and tumble, and to snatch at the little sleeping fishes, those stupid little fishes they had transplanted there from the Retiro Park. They were so silly that they never dared to follow the current and swim downstream to the Manzanares, because they were afraid of the running water. They were so silly that they stayed in each of the levels of the cascade, swimming round and round in their concrete tub and swallowing the crumbs that fell down from the bridge. The mother saw the stream as a roaring Niagara: "Darling, you'll drown!" The boy and the stream laughed, but in the end they turned angry, for they wanted to play together.

I hated the Parque del Oeste. I hated it. I hated its symmetrical little lawns, I hated its narrow sand paths and little round pebbles with which the girls used to play. I hated the rustic huts, the faked rough-hewn bridges, the borders of rocks which looked cruel, but which I could have torn up and thrown into the stream. And I hated the stream itself, its belly and bottom slicked with smooth concrete, and its headspring, a cast-iron spout with an inscription in raised letters which said: "Isabella II Canal."

Moncloa was further away. It was open ground. There the grass grew high and stinging nettles sprouted in it. There were gullies and streams and springs with a hollow tile for a pipe, stuck into the soil by some old shepherd and lined by the years and the water with a thick, green, velvet cushion into which your lips sank when you drank from it. There were springs whose water gushed from the rock like bubbles from a boiling pot; you had to drink out of your scooped hand if you wanted to sip the froth from the cauldron of the earth. Some springs were crystal-smooth pools with sweat drops breaking out at the bottom of the hollows. The sweat of the earth filled the hole, flowed over and trickled away through the grass, unseen. When you drank from these pools the soil grew angry, its dregs rose and stained the clear glass with yellow mud clouds. When you stopped drinking it calmed down and in the end the glass emerged, clear once more.

Here and there in the grass stood trees, thousands of lone trees. Some, at the top of the hills, had bodies that were twisted from resisting the winds, and others were straight and strong. Some, at the bottom of the ravines, clutched at the slope with their roots so as not to fall and lifted their toes out of the ground to dig in their claws more safely. There were bushes, armfuls of spices, which scented the air. And there was a soft, slippery carpet of pine needles, on which it was pleasant to sit, to lie, to roll. I wore canvas shoes with hempen soles, and the pine needles polished the hemp. As though on skates, you could start on the top of the hill and glide down on the pine needles, until you lost your stance on the slope and sat down on the needles which pricked your buttocks. The pine trees chuckled and you laughed and rubbed your behind, and stayed on the spot where you had fallen, sitting among the pines with their checkered trunks.

When I left the house at six in the morning on Sundays, I took a black coffee in the Puerta del Sol, in a café which was open day and night. The strong, black coffe savored of night revels. The people who met there were different from the people you saw in Madrid in daytime. Firstly there were those who had been on a spree, some tipsy from a night of wine drinking, their mouths dry and their heads feverish from sleeplessness; they ordered black coffee without sugar. Others were sober, but in a hurry; they had spent the night with a woman and went home, bleary-eyed, to wash in haste, brush their clothes, re-tie their bows and go to their job in an office or workshop. Then there were those who had to be up at that hour because of their profession, night watchmen, telegraph messengers, waiters, newspaper sellers, street cleaners. They drank coffee with brandy or cheap spirits "to kill the worm." And then there were people like myself, who got up early on Sundays. Many had to catch a train and came with their suitcases, or left their cab in front of the door and came in to warm themselves. They often accompanied little old ladies who were frightened of the journey and of Madrid at dawn and who drank their scorching coffee in little sips, continually looking at their watches. Boys and girls of my age, or slightly older, came in parties on their way to the Retiro, the Moncloa or the Parque del Oeste, where they were going to spend the day. They were on the verge of becoming sweethearts, and while they drank their coffee they nudged each other, joked and laughed at the sleepy drunkards, while they came fresh from a long sleep, their faces scrubbed and clean. The boys pushed the girls against the counter and looked as though they would have liked to squeeze them then and there. Very few were alone like me, and they were only old people or boys close to manhood like me.

The old men, I knew it, would slowly walk up the Calle de Alcalá to the Retiro, sit down on a bench and watch the youngsters play like little animals let loose. They would speak with others of their age class and recall their young years, or they would converse with some lonely little old woman who had also come to see the young people having their fun, to enjoy it and to talk in a slow, slow voice.

We, half-men, half-children, we went further afield, to the pine woods of the Moncloa, with a packet for the mid-morning snack, a *tortilla* of two eggs between two slices of a loaf, or a cutlet fried in batter with breadcrumbs; with a small bottle in our breast pocket, just enough for a glass of wine after the meal, and a book in our other pocket to read under the pines. But we did not read. We looked. We looked at the bands of young people jumping, running, and chasing each other among the trees. We would have liked to be with them, to kiss and be kissed, but we were shy. And so we despised them from the height of our pine throne and our book. The society of young people did not yet admit us to its freedom. The old people gave us advice and patted our heads, but the young people—the young people laughed at us. The lads called us "shavers" and the girls did not want to have anything to do with us because we were "kids," or else they treated us maternally and kissed us all over like fake mothers, to get a thrill out of it, because no young man wanted them and they could not find anyone but us, half-men, half-children.

You couldn't read with all those disturbing images in your mind, so you had to think. On my Sundays in the Moncloa I did nothing but think. Sometimes I hated thinking so much that I did not go to the Moncloa on the following Sunday. Then I went down to my old school, looked for Father Joaquín, but did not know what to say to him. Little by little, I began to speak, and then I poured out all those Sundays full of thoughts and visions. Sometimes he laughed at the things I told him. Sometimes he told me to stop, and began to play his oboe. Then the pigeons from the courtyard and the birds from the roof of the school came to listen. He only told me to stop when I started talking of women; he played the oboe as though in anger, and calmed down with the cries of his oboe and the birds. When I spoke to him of my mother, he listened for hours. One day he took from his drawer a photograph, the portrait of his mother. A big-nosed Basque woman, straight backed and lean, with a handkerchief knotted on the top of her head; behind her his father, taller than she, big and equally lean, with little eyes, his right hand on a hoe. In the background a small house with a balcony running the whole length of its front.

"Now they've got a farmstead," he told me. Then he looked round his cell, at the books, the birds, the music stand like a bleak wooden skeleton in the sun. He looked as though he were missing something.

"They've got a farm. And a cow. Father is still working at seventy. The farm's down there, but you can't see it in the picture. There's a valley below the house, and the old man plants his maize there. And then Mother fries it for me when I go to stay with them." He paused and looked without seeing. "Each grain of maize bursts open with a crack, like a little white flower. When I go back to Madrid, Mother always puts some cobs in my suitcase. But where could I fry maize flowers here?" And he passed his glance round the cell.

Then he heaved his big, elephantine body out of the chair and went to the window, pushing me before him with a hand on my shoulder. He leaned out and looked into the huge school yard where the pigeons and chickens were bickering.

"But you will be a man," he said.

His words held something mysterious, I did not know what, something of soundless images, of a little house, of a father and mother, of children, of a wife. Something which was not this, not the cell with a number on its door and the courtyard for its horizon. Somebody who was not he in his priest's frock. I felt that he envied me something which I did not yet know. When I left the school, I was sad for him and for myself, and did not return there for many Sundays.

Once he told me:

"You don't know why I'm a priest? The parents"—the Basques always say *the* parents, not *my* parents—"the parents were poor. They had four girls already when I was born. It seems I was a great eater, worse than the father. At school I was fairly clever so that the parish priest noticed me. One day he said to the mother: 'Joaquín would make a fine canon.' I was a hefty lad. At eight years I chopped firewood with my father's axe, which must have weighed a good six pounds. I carried sackloads of chestnuts on my back, up to half a hundredweight. Every time the father took me out on the field, the priest wagged his head and said to him: 'Joaquín'—for the father is called Joaquín too—'let's make a little priest out of the boy.' And so they did. When I was eleven they sent me to Deusto. I left it at twenty-three to sing Mass in the village. The mother wept and the father fell round my neck when I'd taken off the chasuble. 'Now you're a man as I wanted you to be,' that's what he said. The Fathers in Deusto wanted me to stay with them as a teacher, but I couldn't stand their mangy frocks and heavy old shoes. I couldn't be a Jesuit. So I joined the Escolapians. Here one can live, one's free and can teach children."

I listened and saw him in my mind surrounded by children, but not as a priest. By children who were his own children, trampling the fields. I saw him with a hoe, like his father, in a fustian suit—why did I think of fustian?—which creaked on his strong, big body while he walked. I saw him putting an arm—why only one arm?—round a strong, high-colored woman with a red handkerchief tied on the top of her head. He slapped a little boy whose nose was running, and went off to dig. "Uuh— uuh!" Uncle Luis had shouted when I was riding on his shoulders. How Father Joaquín would shout it! If he were to lean out of the window now and shout: "Uuh uuh!" all the windows would be crammed with the heads of priests, and Father Vesga would complain to the Father Rector.

"And what if you had sons, Father Joaquín?"

I blurted it out and watched his face to see what it would say. He looked as though he had been struck by a blow. His mouth twisted down-wards, his heavy hands fell on to his frock. He looked at the music stand, the oboe, and the window. He looked outside, at the wall opposite. No, he looked further away. He looked into the far distance beyond the wall, beyond what was behind the wall.

"I can't have sons."

Sometimes men seem to speak inwards. The words do not come out of their mouth but sound inside, in the stomach, the chest, the flesh, the bones, and resound there. They speak for themselves alone, but they do not speak. Their whole body hears them. So spoke Uncle José when he told my mother that he was about to die. And so did Father Joaquín speak now. He went on:

"But I have one."

Then he woke up with a start.

"Don't take any notice of me. Sometimes one's so very much alone. I meant the Child Jesus. When I sang my first Mass I was in love with the Child Jesus. I saw Him even in my dreams. That's why I turned myself into a teacher."

He was lying; and as he did it badly, he saw that I understood his lie when I looked at him. He fell silent.

You can make canoes out of pine bark. You tear off a strip, one of those deeply lined strips which come off when you push your fingers deep into one of the furrows and pull. The wood is soft and porous, you can work it with a knife like a piece of cheese. First you cut it the shape of a cigar, broad in the middle, pointed towards the ends. Then you make the belly of the keel, either rounded or with two curved flanks meeting in a sharp central ridge. Then you scoop out the upper part. You leave two bits of wood in the middle, the rowing benches where the naked Redskins sit and handle their flat oars. And the puddle in which the canoe floats becomes a lake in the jungle of Brazil or the forests of Canada, with green banks full of snakes or with frozen edges where the wolves howl.

I made canoes on Sunday mornings and set them afloat on a pool at the Moncloa, or sent them to follow the current of a streamlet, four inches wide, and to jump the rapids formed by two stones. Always there was some small boy who would turn up from somewhere and watch the course of the boat in rapt silence.

"May I have it?"

"Take it."

He kept the canoe. He followed it downstream, he called to his parents and his friends to have a look at it. "A gentleman gave it me."

I would sit down with my back against a pine tree, angry with the boy. Why had he to come and claim his right as a child? Why did he come to make me ashamed of playing and to claim his right? "May I have it?" Of course I had to let him have it, for it was his by right. How could I go on playing with pine bark canoes when I was already the "gentleman who gave away boats"?

Boy or man? I liked so much to play with boats. I liked so much to look at the legs of the girls with their skipping ropes in front of me.

A man. Yes, I was a man. I had my standing. Employee of the Crédit Etranger. My mother worked down by the river. She must stop working there. I didn't want to watch her any more climbing the stairs on Mondays and Tuesdays and saying: "Run down and fetch the milk, will you, I'm tired." I didn't want any more to smell the dirty linen piling up in our room during the week, with its sour smell like moldy wine. I didn't want any more to see Señor Manuel leaning heavily against the wall by the garret door, with sweat bubbles on his forehead after the climb, easing down a six-foot stack of washing, gently, so that the bundle should not burst. I didn't want any more to count the sheets and the pants of Señor So-and-so and to make out the bills.

I didn't want to accompany her any more in the evenings, to deliver the bundles of clean linen and collect the dirty washing, and to wait in the house doors for her to come down and say: "They didn't pay me." When she came back to our street, my mother went to the baker. "Juanito, please give me a loaf . . . I'll pay you tomorrow." Then to the grocer. "Antonio, give me four pounds of potatoes and half a pound of dried cod. . . . I'll pay you tomorrow." And so we had our supper. The gentlefolk didn't pay her for washing their sweaty, mucky pants with buttons missing, and therefore the washerwoman couldn't pay for her supper. My mother was pleased because the tradesmen trusted her, I was furious because she had to beg favors and because her patrons hadn't paid. But I ate my supper. My mother was so glad that I had something for supper although the gentlefolk hadn't paid her, that I had to eat it.

Afterwards she made her coffee, her own private luxury. She made it in a pot blackened inside like an old Dutchman's pipe, in which the grounds piled up for days on end. My mother threw in a pinch of newly ground coffee and brought the water to boil; it turned black more from the old dregs than from the fresh coffee. She drank it scorching hot, in little sips. Sometimes she would say: "I couldn't live without my drop of coffee." She drank coffee down by the river, too. There was an old woman, a widow with children like my mother, who sold coffee and tea. She came down to the river at seven in the morning, winter and summer, and started up her coffee-urn and tea-urn. For a copper—five centimos—

she gave you a glass full of boiling coffee or of tea with a slice of lemon floating on top. Sometimes the washerwomen made room for her on the river bank and let her wash her clothes among them. Then she spread her washing out to dry in the sun and made her round of the other washing places, to come back at ten o'clock and collect her dried things. The washerwomen often told her: "I'll pay you tomorrow, Señora Luisa," and she did not mind. She went off, quite happy at having money owed her. Copper upon copper, it mounted until she sat down on a heap of dirty washing one day and said: "They owe me fifty pesetas by now."

I saw the whole tragedy of this woman who went down to the river at seven every morning, loaded with her urns the size of buckets, and to whom the others owed—copper upon copper—one thousand coppers. But because my mother hadn't been paid by Señor So-and-so herself, she, too, owed Señora Luisa the money for four cups of coffee. She had been twenty centimos—four coppers—short!

I did not yet earn more than twenty-five pesetas, but I was going to earn more. And Rafael and Concha would earn, too. Or rather, I didn't know about Rafael. But Concha would do it. She felt herself in duty bound as I did. She had resigned herself to being a servant girl, to washing up plates and sweeping floors. But still she wanted to become something better and worked frantically. Rafael, however, was a rebel against everything and everybody. He had walked out of his shop and when my mother wanted to get him a job in another firm he had walked out of the house and not come back. Only I knew at the time where he was; he slept in the street, on the benches of the Prado. Once a "pansy" gave him fifteen pesetas. Rafael took the money, hit the man in the face and ran away. That night, when I came to our meeting place he invited me to supper. We had two fillets of fried cod in a tavern on the Calle de la Libertad. "Come home," I said to him. "Mother cries the whole time." He said nothing, but munched his fried cod and bread, opening his mouth very wide to take big bites, because he was very hungry. Then he answered: "No. I don't want to be a grocer." He walked away, up the Calle de Alcalá, and I went home. After the cod I did not feel like having supper.

My mother ate her meal in silence. Between two sips of coffee she lifted her head—the paraffin lamp was on the table between us—and asked me: "Have you seen him?"

I ducked my head down to my cup. "Yes," I answered. I said no more and she asked no more. How could I tell her that he had eaten supper that evening because he had got money out of a "pansy"? How could I tell her that his white grocer's overall was torn and chocolate-brown?

"He says he doesn't come home because he doesn't want to be a grocer," I said.

She was silent. She looked into the flame of the lamp. She looked at her hands, those hands fretted by lye.

"Tell him to come home. If he doesn't want to be a grocer, he can do some other work. Anything but a street vagabond."

Again she took refuge in the flame of the lamp, white, yellow, red, and smoke-black.

"Tell him to come back. I forgive him. But don't tell him that. Let him come back as if nothing had happened."

When Rafael came back, because I made him come, he went to bed. By the time my mother came in, he was asleep. When he woke up supper was ready. My mother called gently: "Rafael—Rafael!" He opened his eyes which were drunk from sleeping in a soft bed. During the meal none of us spoke. When we had finished, Rafael said: "I'm going out."

"Don't be late," answered my mother, and gave me a wink.

"I'll come with you."

My mother gave me a five-peseta piece and the key to the flat. "Don't be late."

We drank coffee at a stall in the street. I had left a full cup behind at home because I had not wanted to let Rafael go alone. We went to the pictures and afterwards we had a few glasses of wine in the Calle de Preciados. On the way home Rafael walked slowly in my wake. In the Calle de Carretas I told him: "She'll be fast asleep by now."

And we both went to sleep in my big bed with the gilt bars.

Sometimes he went away and strolled about, alone, or lingered at the street corners as though he were looking for something. Then Dr. Chicote gave him a recommendation and he found work in the Aguila Brewery. As it was the summer season, he worked till midnight and earned as much as six pesetas a day. When he came home at half-past twelve he sometimes fell into bed without taking off his trousers and slept till six in the morning, heavily snoring. Some days I accompanied him to the brewery which was near the station of Las Delicias in the outskirts of the city. We watched the sun rising and took a cup of tea at a stall in the factory entrance. Then, when the whistle of the brewery sounded at seven, releasing a puff of white steam, he went inside together with two hundred other workers, and I walked slowly up the slope of the Paseo de Delicias, marking time until nine, when I had to start work at the Bank. Sometimes I went home and had breakfast there. My mother gave me coffee with milk and a little pat of butter swimming on top of it, and asked: "And Rafael?"

As though she had not seen him for days.

"He's at the brewery," I answered.
"It looks as if he was a bit quieter now. God grant it be so."

Since my aunt's death none of her acquaintances had kept in touch with us. Even Don Julian no longer treated me as the nephew of Doña Baldomera; I had simply become one of the staff to him, somewhat dangerous, since he felt himself responsible for my conduct. When I started work in the Coupons Section, I had gone to his room and told him: "Don Julian, they've transferred me to Coupons." He had looked at me from behind his spectacles and scratched his little mustache: "Good, good. Now see that you bear yourself well, Señor Barea. I hope you won't make me look ridiculous." It was the first time that he had addressed me in this way, and it was decisive. From then onwards I was Señor Barea to him.

I hated him. He was a bastard, a lick-spittle. After twenty years of service in the Bank he kowtowed to every head of department. He was ashamed of me. And what had he been? A poor fellow like me, a starved orphan whom his grandmother brought up between the canary, the parrot, and the tame priest who filled her house.

He still went to his grandmother's every day. He carried sweets for the parrot in his pocket, and his grandmother tittered when the bird picked them out; she kissed her grandson and sometimes gave him a banknote. Whenever the grandmother was not at home or the parrot was alone in the kitchen, Don Julian took a black pin out of his coat lapel, pricked the parrot through the bars of its cage and called it bastard. The parrot screeched, but it learned the word from Don Julian. When he came into the sitting room and the parrot was there, it began to shriek in a hoarse voice: "Bastard, bastard!"

The parrot was right. Bastard, cuckold, swine, dog, slave—he was all that—all that!

But it was not only Don Julian, it was the whole Bank. If the learner was afraid of being thrown out into the street before his year of unpaid work was over, the men who were already paid employees were even more afraid. That fear turned them into cowards. They told tales about the cigarettes the others smoked, about their girl friends, if they had one, about their going or not going to Mass, about the times they were late, the mistakes in their work, their visits to the bar of the Portuguese. They told those tales, the subordinate employee to his superior, the higher employee to the still higher one, the still higher one to the head of his department and the head of the department to the Staff Manager, Señor Corachán, all so as to get higher marks. Then Señor Corachán would send for a clerk. "We know that you make a habit of frequenting taverns," and the clerk would walk down the stairs with weak knees; that Christmas there would be no rise in his salary.

One day Corachán sent for Plá. "The management has learned that you frequent taverns." Plá stared at him with his short-sighted eyes and answered: "Of course. For two reasons."

"Two reasons for getting drunk? And pray, what are they?"

"Not for getting drunk, because I don't. Two reasons for the management to have learned that I frequent taverns. One is that there are plenty of toadies who like telling tales. The second is that with my salary, on which I have to keep my mother and myself, I can only afford wine at ten centimos a glass. I haven't gone up in the world far enough to drink *Manzanilla* in elegant establishments such as the Villa Rosa, following your example."

Corachán swallowed the hint. At Christmas they gave Plá a rise. I wondered whether it was so that he should be able to afford *Manzanilla* or so that he should keep his mouth shut.

And then there were the girls. In our section there were four women and two men. Three of the girls were old and ugly, and only Enriqueta was young. She was twenty. On some days it was hell. Antonio and I were the only men who counted, for Perahita was elderly and married. But we—there were days when the girls petted us as though we had been babies. Antonio touched their thighs and breasts and they only laughed. They came up to me and dictated figures, and while they did it they bent over the desk, their breasts pushed up on its surface, they leaned on my shoulder, they excited me, and when in the end I stretched out my hand, they squealed: "You naughty boy!"

Perahita laughed at them and at me and made peace. I had to make my excuses.

Enriqueta had a strong smell. Once she pushed the half-sleeve of her blouse up to her shoulder and asked me: "Does it smell? It's too bad, I wash and wash it every day, just look." She showed me her armpit, full of little black curls and a hot smell. I came very near it with my face and touched it with my fingertips. Later, when I came back from the lavatory she gave me a glance, her eyes smiled, and she blushed. I felt that I, too, was blushing and could not do my sums.

Once we both went down into the steel room where the section had worked before. We had to collect the coupons of the State Bonds and began to open drawers and take out bundles. She stood on one of the white steel benches, which looked like those in a clinic. I could smell her. Her stockings were stretched tight over her legs. I began to stroke softly along one of her calves and follow it upwards. We kissed, she bending down from the bench, I standing below her, with trembling legs and a *burning* face. We did not go upstairs together, we would have been too much ashamed. After that we used to caress each other even in front of the others. She would come and stand beside my high desk while I was sitting, and dictate to me. I plunged my left hand under her skirt, she went on dictating absurd figures to me, and my right hand went on scribbling.

These things pleased and repelled me. Once I asked her to come with me to the Moncloa. She said very seriously: "Now listen, I'm a decent girl." A decent girl—and once when we went to the pictures together she stroked my whole body with her fingers and never had her fill! Why was it necessary for women to be virgins when they married? She herself said it was so. She said that we could not be together without her losing her virginity, and she would have to marry sooner or later. What we were doing was just a childish game, it did not matter and was not dangerous. "But otherwise it might happen that I became pregnant," she said. "It's true that you're still a boy, but you can already have children."

What could I have answered? Nothing. The only thing I could do was to make good use of the dark corners where she sought me out. I wanted to stop that sort of thing, but she got so angry that it was impossible.

Perhaps Plá was right. There was no prospect for anyone in the Bank until many years had passed and they had found out, not that his work was good but that he was utterly docile. Work? Work at the Bank was so organized that anybody could be dismissed on the spot without the slightest disturbance to the whole machine. It was routine work: filling in blanks with stereotyped words, making deductions and sums, always the same, mechanically. Neither Antonio nor I knew French, German, or English, yet every day we credited clients in France, Germany, and England, with their coupons and filled in the printed forms in their own languages. Then the client was bound to acknowledge the great organization of a bank which wrote to him in English and kept a special employee, who knew English, to write to him. Medina spoke English, he had gone to school in England and lived there all his childhood. But he spent his time sitting on a very high stool and making entries in a copper-plate hand on the pages of one of the Bank's daybooks. It was nothing but idiotic copying, which took him endless hours. The only use he made of his English was to buy English magazines at the newspaper kiosk in the Puerta del Sol and to show them off to us, so that we should remember that he knew English. Once the Director himself passed by his desk and noticed one of the magazines. He had a look at it and asked Medina:

"Do you know English?"

"Yes, sir."

They launched forth on an English conversation. When the Director had gone, Medina was very pleased because he said: "Now they'll give me a transfer."

Three days later Señor Corachán sent for him. "The Management has learned that you waste your working hours reading English periodicals." Later he added: "We had intended to promote you in June, but it is obviously impossible in these circumstances." Medina came down in such a fury that his eyes brimmed over. The employees all started to pull his leg, asking him: "Do you speak English?" They repeated the English phrase so often that, the way they pronounced it, it became *Pickinglis* in a few weeks and stuck to Medina as his nickname. New boys, who entered as learners, called him Señor Pickinglis on their first day, and all the others roared with laughter.

He swallowed it, as all of us swallowed things. "If only I had the money to go to England," he said sometimes. Money—money—that was the key to everything. But I would not have to bother about it much longer. Don Primo was about to wind up my uncle's estate, and soon we would each be paid out our inheritance. I was to get about ten thousand pesetas. As soon as I had it, I would be able to do as I liked and send the Bank and Corachán, that swine, to hell without worrying. We ought to manage with that money. I spoke to my mother about it, because I wanted her to stop going down to the river, but she said that we would discuss all our plans when we had the pesetas in our hands. She was scared of the money. Once Don Primo, who knew how badly off we were, called her to his office and asked her whether she would like an advance, she should ask for whatever she needed. But she did not want it. The Brunete relatives came every other day to ask for advance money. Uncle Anastasio had come several times to ask for 500 pesetas, and had gambled the money away. All the others, too, had come to nibble at their account. But my mother flatly refused. Then she said to Don Primo that she wanted to talk with him and make an appointment for one of the mornings when I was at work. When I asked her why she had gone to see him, she said she had wanted to put a few questions to him, and gave me no further explanation.

I would convince her anyhow as soon as I was paid out the money. With ten thousand pesetas we would be able to live three years, while she would not have to work and I could study. Or, still better, we might buy out some tradesman and live on the shop. This meant risking the money, of course, but quite a number of shops were safe business. My brother and sister and I would work in the shop; I would finish my studies and become an engineer. Then the washerwoman would be Doña Leonor and keep a servant girl to do the housework.

On my way home I went into the Experimental Farm which the Institute of Agricultural Engineers kept in the Moncloa. It had rabbit hutches, chicken coops, cowsheds, and pigsties with every kind of breed, and it had beehives and a breeding station for silkworms. They let me have a packet of fresh mulberry leaves, and when I came home I spent my time watching the assault my silkworms made on them. Concha laughed at my worms and said they were a toy for children, but I was a man now. She made me feel ashamed of them and I almost gave them away. But then I found out at the Experimental Farm that she was quite wrong. They were by no means children's toys. The silk industry used to be one of the most important industries of Spain, but it had gone to rack and ruin. One of the professors showed me the various breeds of silkworms, their diseases and the cures for them, and the way to extract silk. He gave me a leaflet; I had the right to get free stock from the station and to sell all my cocoons to them, by weight, before they opened and the moths crept out. It might be a good business to breed silkworms. Then the laugh would be on Concha. We could go to Méntrida, where mulberry trees grew along the river, and breed silkworms and chickens. We could do it on the ten thousand pesetas and still have money left to live on for a year. Whenever we wanted to go to Madrid we could do it without difficulty, it was near enough.

One of the Sundays when I went to the station for my mulberry leaves I told the professor my plan. He listened to me very kindly, asked me details about my family, and, when I had explained everything, he said:

"My dear boy, that is all very nice, but you're still a minor and will have to do what your mother wishes. And she won't wish to plunge into this maze which needs a lot of experience and a lot of money."

So my mother can do whatever she likes with the money? I am a minor. Every time one has got something which belongs to one, one turns out to be a minor, but all the others are of age, always, and have the right to snatch away what belongs to one, just because one is a minor. But as far as working is concerned one is already of age. One is a minor when it comes to cashing in. One is paid as a minor. The family has the right to pocket what one has earned; so it happened to Gros, whose father came to the Bank and asked for his son's wages to be paid out to him, because young Gros had spent something out of his pay one month. Even when one wants to buy something people always take one's age into account. For years I've had my suits made by the same tailor. I didn't want him to make my last suit and asked my mother to give me the money to buy it for myself. I went to a tailor in the Calle de la Victoria. The good man looked me up and down, showed me his patterns, and when I told him to take my measurements, he said most politely that I should ask my papa or my mama to come with me to the shop. "You see, we're not allowed to serve minors."

I came back to him with my mother. The tailor was extremely polite to us, took out the cloth I had chosen and showed it to my mother. The two discussed the price between them as though I did not even exist. Then my mother asked: "Do you like it?" "Yes," I said. "All right, then, will you take his measurements?" The tailor armed himself with his tape: "Would you be so kind as to take off your coat?"

I burst out: "I don't want to! Put your old suit where there's a hole for it. That's the only right I've got as a minor, not to have the suit made and to tell you to go to hell."

My mother was frightfully upset and I was sorry for it afterwards. But I had to tell that fellow what I thought of him.

I went by myself to my old tailor and he made me a suit which I liked.

6. Capitalist

ONE of the most unforgivable things in a Bank is to stay away from work. I had told Perahita that I needed a day off to go to the Notary, who had summoned all the heirs for the liquidation of the estate left by my uncle and aunt. Next day Corachán had sent for me. "Your chief has informed me that you require a day's leave for personal reasons."

"Yes, sir."

He surveyed me, leisurely, as though he wanted to examine my person in every detail. If he was going to play me one of his tricks I would leave the Bank. I was fed up with this fellow. Then he began to speak, stressing every word.

"And may one know what sort of 'personal reasons' demand the young gentleman's neglect of his duties for a whole day?" He gave every syllable its full value, stroking his beard with his cupped hand and looking at me out of the corner of his little eyes.

"I am to receive an inheritance," I said, also careful to pronounce each syllable.

"Ah—an inheritance? Well, well . . . then you are about to leave us, I presume?"

"Leave you? Whom do you mean, sir? The Bank? No, I'll go on working."

"Oh, is that so? It is a small legacy, then. How much are you going to receive?"

"I don't know exactly how much it is, something like two—three—four—five thousand duros, sir."

"That's not so bad. That's not so bad." He stroked his beard again. "And in order to cash five thousand duros—provided that this is more than a fairy tale—you require a whole day off. Are they then going to pay it to you in coppers?"

I was dumbfounded. How was I to explain to this man, to a high official of a Bank accustomed to dealing in millions, that to receive a few thousand pesetas and to carry them to a washerwoman's attic was an event which forbade any work on the day it happened? In the Bank, thousand-peseta notes made no impression on me, but when I thought that next day a little bundle of them would be there in our attic and that we two, my mother and I, would have to stay at home to guard them until we had decided what to do with them—when I thought of this I was deeply shaken. Señora Pascuala would come and stare at the big banknotes in the glow of the lamp. "Señora Leonor, do let me look at one of them!" Then the neighboring women from the other attics would come, one after the other, to look at a banknote and to hold it between their fingertips, overawed.

I began to feel a resentment against this grumpy old man who was making a fool of me.

"I don't think they'll pay me out in coppers."

The rough edge to my words made him lift his head and look into my face. Pedantically and frigidly he said:

"And who is going to prove to me that all this is more than merely a tale intended to get you off tomorrow so that you can go on a spree with a friend—or a girl friend?"

I pulled out Don Primo's note. He read it slowly, folded it and gave it back to me.

"Very well, then. Tomorrow at ten o'clock in the Calle de Campomanes. Good. You will come here to sign on and then you may leave again. You will have the morning off. In the afternoon I myself will check on whether you turn up or not. You may go now."

I told Perahita about my interview, and he laughed at my indignation. He laughed so much that he had to clutch at the desk with his fat, short-fingered hands as though otherwise his rubber ball of a body would bounce up and down, and he dug his fingers into the desk until his flat nails went white with the pressure. Then he recovered and clapped me on the shoulder.

"Now, there, there, my boy, don't be upset. You won't come here tomorrow afternoon."

"Will you let me off yourself, then?"

"Not me, my boy, not me. You must find someone else to oppose Corachán! But you see, tomorow is Assumption Day and everything is closed."

We both burst out laughing, and the whole section with us. Enriqueta came up with a bundle of coupons and installed herself beside me. "Are you going to inherit a lot?" she whispered, and pinched me in the ribs. "You rascal, you do keep things quiet."

"Pooh, just some four or five thousand duros, or perhaps six thousand."

Magdalena who overheard the figure sighed and gave me an angry look, laden with the rage of an ugly, poor spinster. Calzada stopped writing out bills. "Six thousand duros—thirty thousand pesetas," he said. He and I shared a secret; he was the son of a concierge who repaired shoes in a hovel, below the staircase of a poor tenement house, and I was a washerwoman's son. He realized what thirty thousand pesetas meant to us, because he thought of what they would mean to him. Thirty thousand pesetas under the oil lamp where his father hammered at shoe soles, with his spectacles hanging on the tip of his nose. Surely his father would first wash the black dust of old shoe soles from his hands before touching a banknote.

Perahita said: "Well, six thousand duros isn't much, but it makes you independent. It's always useful to have something you can fall back on when you're out of a job or there's an illness at home. You never know. We'd saved one thousand duros, and thanks to them Eloisa was saved. The doctor asked three thousand pesetas for operating on her kidney. And she's quite well now, so I'm not sorry. Without those thousand duros I'd be a widower now."

What would the fat man do without his Eloisa who brushed his suits and ironed his trousers? He went on:

"So then we started putting something by again. During the last two years we've saved three thousand pesetas. It's hard work saving up a thousand duros. But never mind, it's something towards a rainy day when we have to pay for another operation. At least we haven't got to worry about it."

I began to laugh and all the others stared at me.

"I'm laughing because if that's how you go on saving, you and your wife won't have a kidney left in eight years, at this rate."

And the whole gang burst into laughter.

For the last time in our lives we met together, all of us who had inherited. Don Primo handed each of us a sheet with the statement of account for the final liquidation; we had to sign a receipt and then he paid out the money. No one went away; they all stayed to see how much each one was cashing in and to make sure that the Notary had not cheated. As they deciphered the accounts, rows broke out. The first to have an outburst was Aunt Braulia. She went up to the table clutching the sheet of paper and interrupted Don Primo who was just paying the money to Uncle Julian.

"Listen, mister, you read this out to me. Because I'm not learned enough."

"Just a moment, madam." Don Primo settled the account with Uncle Julian, took the paper from her and read aloud: "Paid to Don Hilario Gonzalez at his request: 500 pesetas. Paid to Don Hilario Gonzalez at his request: 750 pesetas. Paid . . ." There followed a series of six advance payments on request. The balance was 1,752 pesetas.

Aunt Braulia listened very attentively. When the Notary had ended, she said:

"So it comes to this: a bit of nothing on a salver. This man"—she shot out a swarthy finger at her husband—"has been eating up all the cash. And me in the dark all the while! So that's why you went up to town so often!"

She stood there, arms akimbo, her four or five skirts and petticoats spreading and swaying, and glared at Uncle Hilario in challenge.

"All right, woman, I'll explain it all to you, but don't make a row here."

"Of course I'm going to make a row here, and they're going to hear my say from here right to our village."

Their quarrel gave the signal to all the others. Every wife started to examine the balance sheet and every one of them found that her husband had been up to something. Uncle Anastasio went and signed the liquidation on behalf of his wife and his daughter Baldomerita. The Notary was counting the banknotes on to the table, when Uncle Anastasio stretched out his hand with great dignity: "Don't take the trouble to count them, it's not necessary."

He pulled the packet of notes out of Don Primo's hand and put it in his pocket together with the account. Aunt Basilisa protested: "Well, now, let's see."

Uncle Anastasio bridled:

"Let's see—let's see—what d'you mean? There's nothing to see here. We'll settle everything at home. Or d'you think I'm like the others and want to cause a scandal in this gentleman's house? Thank God I'm not a village boor. I've got my education, I know how to behave in public. Let us go home."

Aunt Braulia blocked his path.

"A boor you say—a boor? Proud to be it, you mucky squirt of a gentleman. You've done just the same as my man did, you've pinched all the cash and now you're cocky so that we shouldn't find you out. You're just as much of a shameless rascal as all the other men, so now you know."

Aunt Basilisa burst into tears and Aunt Braulia followed suit. They fell weeping round one another's neck. Uncle Hilario and Uncle Basilio glared at each other. Uncle Julian's children began to cry. Don Primo turned angry and banged his fist on the table.

"Damnation! You're in my house, remember!"

They all stopped and fell silent. Then Don Primo called my mother and me. We both signed the liquidation sheet. Don Primo put a hundred peseta note on the table, a second, a third, and so on up to ten notes. Everybody watched him to see what was going to happen, and I was dismayed when I saw that he put no more banknotes on the table. Then he brought out another sheet and another bundle of papers.

"This is the best thing we could purchase. Here are the certificates and here is the final account. You sign here; there is no need for the boy to sign because you are his guardian." My mother signed laboriously with her sprawling letters. Then Don Primo handed her a Bank of Spain receipt. I knew it well as I had to handle their bonds daily.

"Here you have the deposit receipt."

My mother put the banknotes into her purse, folded the receipt and stuck it into her bodice. Then she took my hand.

"Say good-by to Don Primo."

Just as when I was eight and she had led me by the hand, a child. Just the same. I felt like crying. Aunt Basilisa went up to my mother.

"What did you do, Leonor?"

"Nothing, only what Don Primo advised me to do. You see, I'm only the boy's guardian, so he bought State Loan Bonds for him. I took out a thousand pesetas so that we can settle a few things, and as to the rest, we'll leave it for the time when he's a man, then he can do with it whatever he wants to."

"Tell me, is it a lot?" asked Uncle Anastasio.

"At the present price of State Loan," Don Primo said, "we were able to purchase 12,500 pesetas nominal."

When Fuencisla heard the words "12,500 pesetas" she turned on Don Primo like a fury. "So you've played tricks, you robber!" she shrieked. We all gaped. Uncle Anastasio hit the table with his heavy hand and said: "This has got to be cleared up, eh?"

Don Primo, in his black suit, gold-rimmed spectacles, and little beard, looked at though he felt like slapping their faces for them.

"Señora," he said hoarsely, "I forgive you the insult because after all nobody can be forced to be knowledgeable. I spoke of 12,500 pesetas nominal, and you were aghast at the amount. The present quotation of State Loan is 69 per cent and people are selling out because the paper is not suitable for speculation."

The country cousins were clustering round the table and staring at him with wide-open eyes. "Quotation"—"State Loan"—"69 per cent"— what did the old man mean?

"Come now, let's have less fine words," said Uncle Hilario, "and let's rather get the facts clear. This young devil (may the wen on your head rot, you thief!) carries off more than two thousand duros and we get a pittance. Why?"

At three in the afternoon we left the Notary after a detailed explanation of the division of the estate, of State Loan Bonds and of the reasons why 69 per cent quotation price equaled 100 per cent nominal value. We said good-by at the corner of the street, and it was a very rancorous good-by. The relations from Brunete, the men in their corduroys, sashes and round hats, the women in their swaying skirts and colored kerchiefs, and the children stumbling over their heavy boots, walked on across the square, still carrying on the dispute at the top of their voices. People who passed them stopped and stared after them.

My mother and I went up the Calle del Arenal to the Puerta del Sol. I walked beside her, but not with her. I did not take her arm as I always had done when we went out together. I walked abreast of her, but at two feet's distance. Neither of us spoke. She went with short steps, the steps of a nervous little woman. I strode out with my long legs, one step for two of hers. I was full of resentment. I started by feeling resentment against some of the others and finished by feeling it against my mother. Nobody was excepted. I resented the relatives because of their suspicious, meticulous scrutiny of the accounts down to the last centimo, their adding up of all the sums, their asking ten times for an explanation of the difference between 69 and 100 per cent, their fingering of the receipts, the certificates, the Bank of Spain deposit receipt, with faces contracted by anger. I resented Don Primo because he acted in agreement with my

mother, because they both did as they liked without taking me into account, without even saying a word to me. I did not think it a bad thing
for the money to stay in the bank, but I thought it wrong of them to
have done it behind my back. "There is no need for the boy to sign."
Why should he? The boy is a boy, and they are grown people who can
do what they like with boys. They can make them work and cash in on
them, they can buy State Loan Bonds or a new suit, and that's all right
for them. In his time the boy will be a man, and when he is grown up
he can protest, if he still feels like it.

No, no, and no. As soon as we are at home there will be a row. I'm
going to speak my mind to my mother. If I'm a boy, then let them send
me to school, bring me up, and pay for my keep. If I'm grown up, let them
treat me as a grown-up. And if I'm neither, then let them go to hell,
all of them, but I won't be played with like a kitten!

I wanted to smoke a cigarette to get over my nervousness. I carried
cigarettes in my pocket, my mother knew that I smoked, but I had never
smoked in her presence so far, and I did not care to start it now. But so
much the better if she gets angry, so much the better. In the Puerta del
Sol I made up my mind, pulled out a cigarette and lighted it. My mother
looked at me and walked on with short even steps as though it were
nothing. I began to feel annoyed because she said nothing. If she had
scolded me, I could have exploded. I needed to shout, to quarrel, to get
rid of what I felt inside.

In the Calle de Carretas she asked me at long last:
"What are you thinking about?"
"Nothing."
"So much the better for you."
"Of course, if the other people do all the thinking for one, what should
one think about?"
"Why do you say that?"
"Why? You know as well as I do." I stopped and faced her. "Because
I'm fed up with being treated like a child and now you know it."

We fell back into a sulky silence, and so we came home.

Just as I had imagined, Señora Pascuala followed us along the corridor
and came with us into the attic when we opened the door.

"Well, is everything nicely settled, Leonor?"

My mother sighed, took the black handkerchief from her head and sat
down.

"Yes, it's all settled. I'm glad the whole thing is over and done with.
I must say, if it hadn't been for the boy. . . . People go crazy as soon as
they see a banknote. I almost thought they were coming to blows in the
Notary's office. And what for? Only to snatch at a pittance which isn't

even enough to lift you out of poverty. Now look here. José's brothers had been working together thirty years. José sold the grain for them, lent them money for mules and land, and made them the wealthiest people in the whole village. Well, because of the inheritance they've separated, they've gone to law against each other about the mules and the land. The brothers and their children look as if they wanted to knife one another. And they're all the same. Even he! (She pointed at me.) Here you've got him in a fury because I've done what I thought best for him. Even the children go crazy when they see money. I've been through a lot so that the four of them should get on in life—you know something about it, Pascuala—but for myself I prefer my stew and my warmed-up coffee. So I've lived all my life and so I want to die. I'll be content if they let me die in peace in my bed and not take me to hospital. And that's not asking for much, I think."

"I haven't said anything," I retorted peevishly.

"No, you haven't said anything, but don't you think I've got eyes in my head? You walked beside me the whole way like an altar-boy, a few steps apart. And then the young gentleman lights a cigarette for himself in the Puerta del Sol, quite brazenly. What did you expect—that I would make a row? No, my boy, no. You can smoke as much as you like. And now, let's have it out. What is the matter?"

"You ask what's the matter?—well, it's just that I—I'm fed up with being treated like a child or a little boy and having my belongings disposed of without any consideration for me. Who told you to buy State Bonds? You may have your views about the money, but so have I. And after all, it's my money and nobody else's."

"And what are your views about the money?"

"That doesn't concern anybody but me. You had to collect the money, because they wouldn't let me have it while I'm a minor, but afterwards we should have thought out together what to do with it. And you shouldn't have got together with the Notary and bought State Bonds. Do you know what State Bonds are? I'm working in a bank, precisely in that department which handles securities, and I must know about them. State Loan! If you'd bought Convertible Loan, then we would at least have a chance of getting a premium. But State Loan, which no one wants! But of course, you think I'm just a little boy who doesn't understand anything about anything."

"Of course I do, you silly." She stroked my tousled hair, her fingers twisted its strands and soothed my taut nerves. "Of course I think it. Listen. I'm your guardian until you stop being a minor. That doesn't mean that I can do what I like, it means that it's my responsibility to administer your money and that I must give you an account of what I've

done the day you come of age. We can't spend your money now just as
you like, because then you might come when you're a man and ask me:
'Where's my money?' If I then said 'You've spent it,' you might answer:
'I? But I couldn't have spent it, I was a child. You must have spent it
yourself, because you were the only person with a right to do so.' And
you could even send me to prison as a thief. No, your money is going
to stay in the bank until you can give the order to withdraw it—and then
you may spend it as you like, on business or on women, and may it bring
you joy. I don't need anything. I've been poor all my life and I'll die
poor. You have your life still before you, and I'm an old woman."

Her fingers in my hair and her last words dispelled all my anger, and
my eyes filled with water.

"Now, d'you see that you're a little boy and a silly?"

She wiped my face as she used to do when I was a child and kissed
me on the forehead. She took out a hundred peseta note and gave it to
me.

"Here, treat your friends and buy yourself something, but don't do
anything foolish."

Señora Pascuala sighed. "Goodness me, these children, Leonor, these
children! What they make us suffer! And what are you going to do
now?"

"Well, nothing. Just go on as always."

"I thought you were going to move out. I've been saying to myself, as
soon as Leonor's boy gets his money they'll move. I've been sorry, because
by now it's a good sixteen years that we've been living side by side, with
nothing but a partition between us."

"Of course we're going to move," I said. "I don't want to stay in the
attic."

"Now look here, my dear, let's be sensible. This money"—she took up
the deposit receipt—"doesn't make us rich. It gives you exactly one
peseta twenty-five centimos interest a day. Do you think that one twenty-
five more or less settles all our difficulties? No; here we pay nine pesetas
a month and don't get into debt. If we take a flat we only spend your
interest and a bit over. In the end we should be in debt, and then
what? When you earn more, and your brother and sister too, then we
can see what we can do about it. But, as things are now, you know
very well that all of us together just earn what we need to live as we do
live. The only thing I'd like to do is to take another attic room, like the
cigar-woman's or Señora Paca's, as soon as one of them gets empty. I'd
like it for your sake because you're getting older and if Concha comes
home to live with us one day we can't all sleep in one room. We could

do that, because the two rooms together would mean twenty pesetas rent a month, and that much we can manage."

"All right," I said, "but there's something I want, and it will be done."

"Tell me."

"I want to install electric light in our attic. I'm sick of having my eyebrows singed by the oil lamp every time I want to read for a while."

The electric light was granted and I promised to arrange with the company. It would have to be a lamp screwed on in the middle of the sloping ceiling, with a very long cord so that it would light the table, but could be hung on a hook over my head when I was in bed and wanted to read; and it would need a switch in the socket so that I could turn it off without having to get up.

Next day I had to invite all my colleagues at the Bank. The commissionaire secretly brought us two bottles of Manzanilla and some pastries. We shut the door of the department so that the others should not see us eating. But then the room smelled of wine and we had to open the door and the panel in the glass roof until the draft swept out the smell.

"How much did you get in the end?" asked Perahita.

"Not much, just a little."

"All right, keep it secret, we won't ask you for any of it. Anyhow, you wouldn't let us have it."

"Thirty thousand pesetas," I said.

"Good gracious, and you call that a little? Six thousand beautiful duros! Well, you must be happy! Wouldn't it be nice if a relative of that sort were to die every day?"

"It wouldn't be so bad."

But of course it would have been bad. If Uncle José had not died, I would not have inherited, but it would have been much better for me. I would not have stayed in the attic, I would not have worked in the Bank for a miserable salary. I would have been studying to be an engineer. But how could I explain all this? I had to show them that I was happy, very happy, and that I was wealthy, very wealthy indeed, and that as far as I was concerned all my relatives could die and leave me fat legacies.

Plá was the only one to whom I told the truth. We had a glass of sherry together in the bar of the Portuguese, all by ourselves.

"You were right," he said. "Only, you ought to have told them you'd inherited twenty thousand duros. Then the Director would have sent for you, tendered his congratulations and given you a rise in salary. They'll give you one in any case, you'll see. As soon as they find out that you've got money they'll give you a leg up."

Plá was not mistaken. They increased my salary to 72.50 pesetas. My colleagues were somewhat annoyed. Sadly—for his envelope brought no rise, only a small bonus—Antonio said to me:

"You see, it's always the same thing. You and I, we've done the same kind of work the whole year, I've been in the place longer and have a greater claim than you. Well—and they go and give you a rise—and you don't need it."

I went home, greatly pleased with my news. Now we would be able to move out of the attic.

My mother was alone, sewing by the light of the oil lamp which had only a few more hours to burn. I gave her the note which announced the rise, and kissed her on the nape of her neck where it tickled her. Then I pushed the low stool to her feet, sat down and put my head on her lap. Now at last things were beginning to go well.

"We can move now, Mother."

Her small, slender fingers were plaiting my hair.

"You know, Rafael's been given the sack today. But we shall manage. Dr. Chicote will let me do the whole washing for the Disinfection Service. Señora Paca'll help me, we'll do it between the two of us. You see, with Rafael out of work, that means six pesetas a day less. And God knows when he'll find another job. He hasn't learned any trade. . . ."

I heard her, watching her face from below, from her knees.

"Tomorrow at ten the electrician will call about the light, Mother."

He would fit the wooden plug from which the cord and the bulb were going to hang up there, just where the smoke from the oil lamp had made a round patch on the ceiling. The bulb was going to have a switch on its fitting, and when I stopped reading at night, I would turn off the light.

7. Proletarian

R A F A E L was working again. He had started with a regular profession at last, and was a clerk like myself. He had been taken on at the Head Office of the *Fenix Agrícola,* the insurance company which insured all horses, mules, and donkeys in Spain. The inheritance had helped to get him the job. With the thousand pesetas my mother had taken out in cash we had bought clothes and linen, the two things we needed most urgently. Rafael went to the Fenix in a new suit, armed with a recommendation, and was engaged.

They employed no learners there. Every clerk started with a monthly salary of six duros. One peseta per day. That was the invariable rate. The Fenix staff had made a joke of the facts that the salary was six duros—which is thirty pesetas—and that the offices closed at six-thirty; they called it the Six-thirty Company. The management was absolutely strict in both matters. Everybody was paid thirty pesetas, everybody left the office at six-thirty sharp. At that hour, four hundred employees streamed out into the street, and only some twenty of them had a salary over six duros. Always excepting the Directors, of course, who earned thousands.

The company used its clerks only for filling in forms: insurance policies, descriptions of the horses insured, receipts, premiums. All that was required of the employee was that he should be able to read and write and calculate the percentage of the premiums.

Hundreds of thousands of animals had the mark of the Fenix—a phoenix—branded on their necks. The gypsies called it the Dove Brand and whenever they discovered it on an animal they had meant to steal they kept off it. They knew that they would never get farther than ten miles along the road before meeting the Civil Guard, who would not fail to ask for the certificate as soon as they saw a horse with the Dove Brand led by two gypsies. And although it was easy enough to steal a horse, donkey, or mule, it was far less easy at the same time to steal the insurance certificate of that accursed company which had hit upon a trick to ruin poor gypsies trying to earn an honest living.

For it was a trick. The Company had invented the "Dove" and the "iron." When an owner insured an animal, the company's agent pressed a red-hot iron onto its neck, and it was branded with the Dove. Then he drew up a description which enumerated everything from the beast's height to its missing teeth, so that it could neither be bought nor sold without the change of ownership being entered in the certificate. You couldn't even ride on its back without risking the Civil Guard's demanding proof of your ownership, in the shape of the certificate.

The gypsies' hatred of the Civil Guard was ingrained, but their hatred for the Dove went even deeper. When you mentioned the Dove to a gypsy in the horse-breeding lands of Seville or Cordova, he touched wood or crossed himself. "Don't make bad jokes, mate."

Now, in order to fill in certificates, insurance policies, and receipts, the company which gave protection from robbery had set up a perfect administrative system manned by clerks paid at thirty pesetas a month. For its touts and agents it had found a different system; they kept the first premium paid as a bonus. And that was all. The high officials had only to dismiss employees who had had enough of earning thirty pesetas after two or three years' service, and to engage new ones in their place at the same rate of pay. True, anybody who was discharged received a month's salary in accordance with the Trade and Commerce Code, Paragraph four hundred-odd; it was a serious firm where work was restricted to exactly eight hours and where the Wages Code was rigorously observed. But it never paid more than thirty pesetas a month to its clerks.

One peseta from Rafael, two pesetas ten from me, one peseta twenty-five interest from the inheritance, and two pesetas fifteen which my mother earned with her washing, made up our daily income. Concha did not count because she earned just what she needed for herself.

When my mother went down to the river in the mornings she left the *cocido* simmering on the little earthenware stove. Señora Pascuala came from time to time to have a look at it. The chick-peas, the piece of meat, and the bacon, all colored yellow from the saffron, went on cooking under the joint supervision of Señora Pascuala and of Santa Maria de la Cabeza, the patroness of stewing pots. At midday Rafael and I ate the *cocido* all by ourselves.

For a few days Señora Segunda had looked after our meals, but then one day she failed to turn up. As she lived very near, we went to see her.

She was in bed, between snow-white sheets, the crimped collar of her nightdress—an inheritance from Aunt Baldomera—tied with a piece of ribbon and Toby lying at her feet on his patchwork blanket.

"What's the matter with you, Señora Segunda?"

Rafael and I hardly had room to stand up straight in her closet. Right over our heads sounded the footsteps of people going up and down the stairs.

"Nothing, my dear boys, it's just that I'm dying."

"But what's wrong with you?"

"Nothing, nothing at all."

"Has the doctor been to see you?"

"Yes. The doctor was here. He said they would take me to hospital. I said no. 'But you can't get well here,' he said to me. 'Not in the hospital either,' I answered. He shut up then, and later he said: 'That's true, too.' He wanted to come every day, but it's not necessary."

She spoke as calmly as though she were going to the theater that evening.

"I'm sorry for Toby. But there's a blind man in our café who's willing to take him as his guide, and he's a very good man. You know him, Arturo, it's Freckle-Face. He's an honest man even if he's poor. When I'm dead, you give him the dog."

Later in the evening we came back with our mother and stayed with her for a while, until Rafael and I went to the pictures. After midnight we went to fetch our mother. "Go home to sleep," she said, "I'll stay with her."

So we, too, stayed. We sat in the doorway, because the little hole was not big enough for the three of us. From time to time we walked out into the Calle de Mesón de Paredes and had a drink. She died at four in the morning.

We paid for the funeral because we did not want her to be taken away in a municipal van, wrapped in a sheet. It was a third-class funeral with two shabby black horses, and a coffin roughly painted with lamp black, and with cotton braid along the edges of the lid. Rafael and I were the only mourners. When we came back from the East Cemetery we had a quick lunch in Las Ventas, a cutlet and roast black pudding, and we kept Toby tied up beside us.

Toby would not take any food and died a few days later of sorrow. Freckle-Face was not able to make him eat, although he bought a whole fillet and fed it to him in the little café in front of all the beggars who never tasted meat themselves, but helped him in his vain attempts to persuade the dog to take it. In the end they fried the fillet in the frying pan used for making crisps, cut it into small bits and ate it between the lot of them.

"Silly dog," one of the beggars said to Toby. "Can't you see how nice it is?"

We had been out for a stroll along the Calle de Alcalá, looking at the girls, and when we came home, my mother was getting the supper ready. She had eaten *cocido* together with Señora Paca at midday. Señora Paca was having supper with us, as she often did lately, because she liked being in our room, where the four of us could sit round the table under the lamp.

"My dear, my room drives me mad. When I'm shut up there all by myself I've simply got to drink or I'd never go to sleep."

When she was with us she only drank a small glass of spirits after the coffee. My mother brewed fresh coffee every day since we had threatened to go out for ours if she went on boiling up the old grounds. We went to bed between eleven and twelve. Sometimes my mother and Señora Paca wanted me to read to them, and listened until Señora Paca began to nod. My mother never dozed. Sometimes when Rafael and I went to the pictures, the two women stayed behind and chatted; then Señora

Pascuala usually joined them and we would find them still at it when we came home at three in the morning.

In the afternoons, when Rafael had finished his work at the Fenix and I my work at the Bank, we met our friends. We had sorted them out with the course of time. From the Bank, there were Calzada, Medrano, and Plá left; from the Fenix came Julian, big, strong, and merry, and Alvarez, a little fellow who never kept still. In the back room of the bar we had two tables to ourselves. There we talked while we ate fried fish hot from the frying pan.

We thrashed out the staff policy at the Fenix and the learner system of the Banks. We dug out case histories.

Two steps further along the street lived a man who had made himself rich through child labor. He had set up a firm in the Calle de Alcalá, which he called *Continental Express*. It was a messenger service which delivered letters and urgent messages to people's houses. The whole business was built up on a few dozen boys in red jackets and caps, with satchels hanging from their shoulders, who ran round Madrid day and night. He paid them nothing, but they got tips. Some of them earned as much as ten or twelve pesetas a day. Even Ministers gave recommendations to boys who wanted to get into the Continental. Whoever joined the staff was fitted out with the jacket and cap of the boy who had left a vacancy, and off he went. After a time the business petered out, because most of the big stores copied the idea and employed a boy or two, paying him nothing if the store had many customers, or else fifty centimos a day. Now the whole of Madrid was full of young boys of that breed, with a satchel hanging from their shoulder, riding on the tramcar buffers or playing at pitch-and-toss with their tips in the middle of the pavement.

That man was not the only one. A solicitor established a commercial information agency and quickly acquired an impressive number of clients. He sent out hundreds of reports daily. He put advertisements in the newspapers: "Wanted, learners who can type." He had nearly fifty boys working for him ceaselessly. He walked up and down between the desks, his hands behind his back like a schoolmaster, and when he saw a boy not working at the speed he demanded, he boxed his ears. Later he improved on his business. When he accepted a boy as a learner, he demanded a deposit of five hundred pesetas in guarantee of his honesty. In the end the police were forced to intervene and closed down the firm.

Girls were no better off. Offices and shops had only just begun to employ women, but now they were doing so to an ever-increasing extent. They did not dare to take on girls as unpaid learners, but gave them an average salary of fifty pesetas a month. Yet the girls replaced male clerks and assistants with higher pay. It would not have been possible to man an office or shops with nothing but young boys, but it could be done with women and boys. The stores were sacking their male assistants; some of them had been thirty years with their firm and earned two hundred and fifty to three hundred and fifty pesetas a month, most of the others earned at least two hundred pesetas and were in a position to support a modest household. Now they were all replaced by young girls who looked very pretty in their black satin uniforms and white aprons, and who sold four times as much as the former shop assistants, but were paid at the most seventy-five pesetas. Hardly anyone was left of the old staff except here and there an old man who would amble through the rooms in a black cap and terrorize the girls by throwing them out on the slightest mistake, or else paw them while they were lifting down boxes in a corner, and they had no right to protest.

As this district was crammed with offices, the customers of the bar were nearly all employees and shop assistants. Day after day more of them came to tell their friends that they had been sacked. The young men had hopes, but those over thirty had to give up any idea of finding a job.

One of them told us his story in the back room:

"I found a good advertisement in the *Liberal* today. It said: 'Wanted an accountant. Steady job.' I knew that no office starts work before nine, but I went there at half-past eight all the same. There were five before me already. It was a store for surgical goods in the Calle de las Infantas, and the owner was a German. By ten o'clock there were at least two hundred queueing from the office door on the first floor down to the middle of the street. They let the first ten of us in, and we sat down on benches in the hall. On one side was a room with a counter, and the owner of the store took the first applicant in there. The owner had a round head, smooth as a baby's bottom. He began by asking the man's name, where he had worked before, and so on. The man answered in a low voice, but even so we all heard what he said. 'Speak up,' the old rascal said to him. Then he put him in front of a desk and started dictating calculations, entries in the day-book, problems of compound interest, foreign exchange rates—well, anything under the sun. The man worked well. You could see that he was a clerk who knew his job.

"The German looked over his shoulder while he was writing. After half an hour, when the man had finished his test, the German said: 'All right, I like you. We'll check your references and if they're good we'll engage you.' The man's eyes lit up. Then the German asked: 'What do you expect to earn?' 'Whatever the firm usually pays for the job.' 'Oh no, I wouldn't like to employ people who start by being dissatisfied. You tell me what you want.' 'Well, sir, for an accountant of a firm like this, as important as yours, seventy duros would be just about right, I think.'

'Three hundred pesetas? You're mad. Three hundred pesetas! No, my dear fellow, this is a modest firm, not a Bank which can afford to throw money out of the window. I'm sorry we can't come to an agreement. Let's see the next one.' 'But, sir, I could stay even if you paid a bit less.' 'No, no, I can't take you on any condition. You would be discontented from the first day, and I don't want discontented people among my staff. After three months I would have to give you a rise in salary or you would go. I'm a serious man in my dealings. This is a steady job, but there aren't any rises in salary to be had.'

"He turned to the next: 'What salary do you want?' 'Two hundred pesetas.' He simply turned to the third one with a sneer: 'And you, too, have got your ambitions, I suppose?' 'I could manage on a hundred and fifty pesetas. I've been out of work for the last three months.' Then the seventh in the row, an elegant youngster with gold-rimmed spectacles, got up and said: 'I'm an expert in commercial problems and I know both French and English, which may be of some interest to you. Thank goodness, I don't depend on a salary for my living. It would be quite enough for me to get the cash to cover my little vices.' The German made him pass through a lightning test. 'The vacancy is filled,' he told us. Then he said to the lad: 'You can start work tomorrow. I'll give you one hundred pesetas a month and later we shall see how you get on.'

"The man who had been out of work for three months came up to me and whispered in my ear: 'I'd like to bash in that damned swine's mug!' We walked down the stairs and out into the street together. There he saw the little commercial expert strutting along, and said to him: 'So you're a commercial expert, are you?' 'Yes, sir.' 'You're a son of a bitch, that's what you are.' And he lowered his head and ran it smack into the lad's face, right on his nose, so that his spectacles were smashed and he slumped down on the ground bleeding like a stuck pig. 'You won't start work tomorrow, I don't think,' the man said, and ran off like a hare, and the lad had to be taken to the first aid post. If the rest of us had had any guts, we'd have gone up to the store together and chucked that fat German out of his own window."

Opposite the Banco Hispano a house was being built: the workers came over to the tavern for their meals and for a glass of wine at the bar after working hours. One of them was there when the story was told and said in a very loud voice:

"That's right. Serves you right for being yellow bastards. I bet our boss wouldn't dare to take on a mason at four pesetas a day. And he wouldn't find a builder in the whole of Madrid willing to work at that wage, either. The trouble with you fellows is that you want to be gentlemen and don't want to be workers. You're ashamed of saying you're hungry, because you dress like the nobs. And then every blessed soul among you goes without food when he gets home rather than not wear a tie. Of course, it's true it cost us a lot of strikes and a hell of a lot of blows from the police and the Civil Guard before we got enough to eat. But how should gentlemen like you go on strike and how should they go to the Puerta del Sol in their starched collars to be beaten up by the police? Well, it serves you right for being a lot of cowardly bastards. And that's what I think."

"You're right, yes, sir," shouted Plá. "We're a lot of bastards and cowards." He thumped his chest. I thought he was a bit tipsy. "Cowards, that's what we are. But not me, mate, I've got my membership card of the Casa del Pueblo!"[1] He drew a little red book out of his pocket. "But a fat lot of good it does me! There's just a handful of us and as soon as our bosses find out that we belong to a union they'll chuck us out. We can't even form a union of our own. It's a disgrace, yes, sir. Here in Madrid where everybody is an employee, we've got to join the General Workers' Union because there aren't enough of us to form a Clerical Workers' Union! And let someone else make propaganda among that bunch of lick-spittles. Twenty-four hours, and then out with you into the street, and who's going to fight for you then? Your own union can't, and the other unions won't feed you."

Plá and the mason went on with their discussion and went on drinking wine. When we left the place they were still leaning on the bar with their elbows on the counter.

Next day Plá and I left the Bank together at meal time. He lived near our street in the Calle de Relatores and we often met on our way.

"Will you show me the card of the People's House?" I asked.

"You mustn't speak to anybody about it," he answered, and took from his wallet a little book of receipts for two pesetas weekly contributions. It had a rubber stamp which read: "U.G.T.[2] General Trades."

"Don't you think that it's only me. Quite a lot of us are members. As far as I know there are ten of us in the Bank. But of course we're very few, all the same. Not enough to organize a separate Union. So they put us into the General Workers' Union with all the workers who haven't got a craft or who work in a trade with very few members. Shop assistants are there, too. To tell you the truth, the only thing we get out of it is the Friendly Society."

[1] The *Casa del Pueblo*—the "People's House"—was the seat of Socialist Trade Unions and other Labor organizations.

[2] U.G.T.—*Unión General de Trabajadores*. The central organization for labor unions other than those under Anarchist influence, which were united in the C.N.T. The U.G.T. branches were mainly under Socialist influence.

He went on in answer to my unspoken question.

"Yes, that's our only benefit from it, and it's the only possible justification for our membership in the eyes of the employers. Sometimes they accept it and sometimes they don't. You see, we've got a medical assistance society which is called the Workers' Mutual Help Society, and it's the best of its kind in Spain. They give you everything, the best doctors, a dispensary and a clinic for operations. They even pay you benefit if you lose your wages through illness. But you must first be a member of the U.G.T. before you can become a member of the Society. So, if they find out that I belong to the U.G.T., I can always say that I had to do it because I wanted to have the right to a doctor and medicines through the Society. But we'll get further than that in time. Sooner or later we'll have our own union, and then we'll settle accounts with these rascally employers. And don't they know it! They wanted to steal a march on us and set up a Catholic Friendly Society, but nobody wants to be a member there. Quite a lot of people would join us if they weren't so frightened. Because, you see, if you're caught with the membership card in your pocket it may well be that they'll throw you out and you won't get any other job. When your former employers are asked for a reference, they'll say that you were a good worker, but a Red and a rebel who belongs to the People's House crowd. And that's quite enough for them to let you starve to death. I know a fellow who worked for Pallares, and he was sacked after fifteen years with the firm, for being a union member. When he applied for a job in another firm, the manager said: 'I hear you're a Socialist.' 'Oh no, sir.' 'Well, I hear from your former employers, Pallares, that you're a member of the People's House.' 'Well, yes, sir, I joined them because . . .' And he was going to tell the story about the Mutual Society. The manager wouldn't let him go on and said: 'Stop, stop, I don't need your explanations. D'you believe I want an employee in my firm who doesn't believe in God, and parades through the streets behind a red flag, shouting threats against the Government? My firm is no hotbed of Anarchists. You can turn yourself into a Freemason and spend your time planting bombs, but this is a respectable firm!' "

I pondered over these things for days. Of course I knew what the Socialists were. But I was not really interested in political questions. It was like this: every day they fought in the Cortes, Maura, Pablo Iglesias, and Lerroux.[1] People painted the words: "Maura—No!" in pitch upon the walls. Others sometimes scrawled in red ochre underneath: "Maura— Yes!" I knew that those who wrote No were workers, and those who

[1] *Antonio Maura,* conservative leader, repeatedly Premier; *Pablo Iglesias,* founder of the Socialist Party and leader of the Trade Unions; *Alejandro Lerroux,* at that time leader of the Radicals.

wrote Yes upper-class people. Sometimes the two groups met, each with their pot of paint; they would chuck the pots at each other and start a free fight. Sometimes a group of young gentlemen would appear in the Calle de Alcalá towards nightfall, when it was crowded with people, and shout: "Maura—Yes!" At once a group of students and workers would form and take up the cry: "Maura—No!" People would run away. Many took the cue and left the café terraces without settling their bills. The police charged, but they never touched the young gentlemen.

In the Calle de Relatores where Plá lived, Lerroux's crowd had one of their centers. They called themselves the *Young Barbarians* and it was they who made the greatest noise. The supporters of Maura used to come to their door and shout, and then there would be a row. Lerroux himself came and spoke at the Center; he said that priests should be castrated and nuns made pregnant. The crowd got excited by his speeches and formed to march to the Puerta del Sol. They never got there, though. At the Calle de Carretas the police waited for them and dispersed them with their sabers.

The Socialists started a new strike every day. Sometimes it was the bakers, another time the masons, still another time the printers. They were sent to prison and beaten up, but in the end they got what they wanted. They were the only ones who had an eight-hour day and the only ones who were paid the wages they demanded. In their workshops there were no learners, and boys like myself who had to work, earned two pesetas fifty a day from the start. Their leader was Pablo Iglesias, an old printer who said aloud in Parliament whatever he thought right. The workers called him Grand-dad. He had been to prison I don't know how many times, but he went on trying to turn all workers into Socialists.

I would have liked to be a Socialist. But it was a problem as to whether I was a worker or not. It sounded a simple question but it was difficult. Certainly I was paid for my work and therefore was a worker; but I was a worker only in that. The workers themselves called us *señoritos*, nobs, and did not want to have anything to do with us. And obviously we could not march through the streets with them, they in their blouses and rope-soled canvas shoes, and we in our suits made to measure, shining boots and hats.

I persuaded Plá to take me along to the People's House; one day, when he was going to pay his monthly contribution, I accompanied him. The building had innumerable small rooms for the various Secretariats. In each room were one or two fellow-workers behind a desk, and a treasurer with sheets of receipt stamps and a cash box. From everywhere came the clatter of money. The corridors were crowded with workers, in front of many doors there was a queue.

"Today's Saturday," said Plá. "You see, most of the organizations get their contributions weekly. Some unions are very strong. The builders' trade union, for example, must have millions, enough money to see their strikes through and to help out others when they go on strike. They pay their people unemployment relief, too, but there aren't ever many of them out of work. There's always work in the building trade."

He took me to the two meeting rooms, one big and one small. In the big hall, the printers of Rivadeneyra's had a meeting. Rivadeneyra's was a big publishing firm in the Paseo de San Vicente. There were over three hundred workers present. One of the men sitting on the platform stood up and came forward. The chairman rang a bell and everyone was silent.

"Fellow workers," said the speaker, "we will now take a vote for and against a strike. All those who are in favor of the strike, please stand up."

In a wave of noise from clattering benches and trampling feet many people got up. Others followed more slowly. In the end four or five were left sitting. The others stared at them, and one by one they rose. In the first row one man remained seated, alone.

"The vote is unanimous, in favor of the strike."

"I want to say something," said the man who had kept his seat.

He walked up to the rostrum and began to shout. He did not agree with the strike. Strikes were no good. Another kind of action was needed —direct action. Get rid of a number of bosses and set the workshops on fire. He was like a madman. The others kept silent, and when a murmur started, the chairman's bell cut it short. A group of people seemed swayed by the speaker. Finally, purple in the face, he said: "I've finished," and gulped down a big glass of water.

Another rose to reply.

"We're not Anarchists here, we're decent men who want to do a decent job of work. We've no need to kill anybody. What—smash up the machines? But the machines belong to the workers, they're sacred to us!" Suddenly he grew heated and shouted: "If I saw this comrade here, or any other comrade, lifting a hammer to smash up my Minerva, I'd smash his skull for him!"

The three hundred cheered him. The Anarchist crouched in his seat and grunted.

Then we went to the theater; for the People's House had a theater which was used for staging plays, showing films and holding meetings. Throughout the corridors we met nothing but men in blue or white blouses. When we opened the little door to the stage, a man waiting in a queue said: "Hullo, what's this? We've got tourists here!" All the others laughed and I felt ashamed of my suit, my boots, and my hat. So I turned to face the man who had spoken and cried:

"Tourists to hell! We're workers just like you, and perhaps more than you."

"Sorry, comrade," he said. "I've put my foot in it all right, but you see, we don't get many gents—I mean to say—comrades dressed like gents here . . ."

I let myself be carried away by a violent impulse.

"Well, then—in spite of our suits and our soft hands and anything you like, we're workers. And what sort of workers! One year as a learner, then five duros a month, with twelve or fourteen hours of work a day . . ." And I spoke on, pouring out all my resentment. When I finished another of the men in the queue said:

"Good for the kid!"

"What the devil d'you mean by kid? I'm as much of a man as you are, and maybe more."

An old man clapped me on the shoulder.

"Keep your shirt on, they didn't mean to hurt you. As soon as you start working you're a man!"

While we tried to find our way out of the maze of passages, I looked defiantly at all the blue and white blouses we met. I would have liked somebody else to call me a gent. I would have called them together in the big hall and shouted into their faces that we, the gentlemen employees, really were; for I saw clearly that they did not understand, that they despised us. They thought that to be a bank clerk meant sitting in a well-heated room in winter and near a ventilator in summer, reading a newspaper and drawing a salary at the end of the month.

Before we left the building, I joined the General Workers' Union.

8. Childhood Reviewed

THAT'S a fine woman! If I walk a little faster I can overtake her and see what her face is like. She might be ugly. But from behind she looks all right. Her bottom shows very clearly through her skirt. The backs of her thighs are a bit curved, you see it when she walks and one of her legs moves forward, while the other is left behind so that the skirt clings to it. How well she moves her hips. Of course, you fool! She's just like the other, exactly the same. And the woman in front of me too. People say young men like their women plump, and it must be true. I was right yesterday, anyhow. I liked that Maña better than the other girls, who were younger but thin. One of them was very pretty, with blue eyes and a face like the Virgin and she liked me too. But I preferred that Maña. She's a bit fat, it's true, but her flesh is firm and white. What would Aunt Baldomera say if she were alive? "Jesus! Jesus!" If anybody told her that her little Arturo had slept with a woman, with one of those bad women . . .

That Maña has a short little chemise, rose colored, which doesn't reach as far as her thighs. The embroidered hem rides up on her buttocks. They look just like the croup of a plump little nag.

Not to mention Father Vesga's face if he knew about it. "You have lost your purity," that's what he would say. What about his own? That obsession of his with the Sixth Commandment—thou shalt not fornicate. I believe that sometimes he just couldn't contain himself on those wooden boards he had for his bed. Now I realize why he always looked at females as he did.

There was a woman who kept a shop in the Calle de Mesón de Paredes, who had him for her Father Confessor. She was tall and big and had a splendid bosom. Father Vesga, tiny as he was, must have felt quite smothered by her in his confessional box. When confession was over, she always went to say her penitential prayers to the right of the altar beside the boys in rank and file. Father Vesga used to come out, red in the face from the heat in that narrow box, to stand behind her and stare at her hips and the little curls on the nape of her neck. He kept turning his four-cornered biretta round and round in his hands, and then he slapped it smack into some boy's face. "That's for talking." The woman turned her head, smiled, and said: "Don't be so hard!" The boy stood there, crying silently, and Father Vesga dished out slaps with his biretta all along the file.

In the end the woman rose and walked away slowly, swinging her hips. "Good-by, Father," she said softly as she passed him, and kissed his hand. "The Lord be with you, my daughter." He inspected the end of the file to see whether all the boys were listening to Mass, and not playing or squatting on their heels. But in reality he was looking after her, after the tall woman who swayed her hindquarters from one side to the other, like a mule. Afterwards he would kneel beside the altar, pray, and smite his breast. He unfastened his cassock and beat his flesh with his closed fist. I think he sometimes even clawed at it with his nails: once the chain of his small lady's watch was torn.

What would Father Vesga in his cassock have been like between the thighs of that Maña? The strong thighs of a woman from Aragon. She saw all right that it was the first time I was with a woman, and she made good use of me. Well, why not? But it would be funny to see Father Vesta, after always sleeping on his bare boards, between Maña's thighs on the soft, sprung bed, with her breasts rubbing against his face, because he is so small that he wouldn't reach higher. That Maña is very tall, taller than I, and I am taller than most of the men here.

If Uncle José knew it, he would say very seriously: "Well, my boy, I won't say that you shouldn't do those things. We've all done them. But take care where you go, and above all don't let your aunt know." He would give me a duro on Sunday, wink at me and chuckle.

When we were children—when I was a child, that is, because his hair and his mustache were already white—he used to come back from the office with the *Imparcial;* I threw myself down on the dining-room carpet to read and he would throw himself down beside me. At first he sat on the floor and then he stretched himself out on it. My aunt would cry: "Pepe, have you gone mad?" "Now you shut up, my dear." He taught me the letters from the headlines, the b's and the a's, and taught me to read "ba." At half-past three he said: "Now let's go to the pictures, the film starts at four." And I went out clutching his hand, still dressed in a smock, in my grand overcoat with many big, shimmering mother-of-pearl buttons. That's how I learned to read.

Uncle Luis wouldn't be angry either. He won't be angry—for he at least is still alive. As soon as he comes to Madrid I must tell him about it. Perhaps he'll burst out into one of his "Uuuh" cries. He'll say: "Make the most of it, boy, you'll get old anyhow. Now look at me. I've got rheumatics and can hardly move any more. But when I was your age— uuh—I knew what to do with the wenches!" He must have been a rascal. And Andrés too. His wife's eternally ill with her leg festering, and so he says to my mother every time he comes to Madrid: "Don't wait for me this evening, I'm going to sleep at the inn." At the inn, my foot! At the "Lovers' Inn." I must go and see the show called Lovers' Inn or something of the sort. It's on at the Eslava Theater and the women come on the stage quite naked, and everybody who goes to that inn wants to go to bed with them.

Look at those two sweethearts arm in arm. I'm sure that they want each other, both of them. And that whole story with Enriqueta is over and done with. If she wants to she can sleep with me, and if not we're through. I can get a woman for a duro. I don't want any more cuddling in the cinema.

Of course, now I know what it is all about. My cousin, too, made good use of me. I was eight or nine years old at that time. She was in service in the Calle de Vergara, and her masters used to go out for a walk after lunch so that she was left alone in the house. She always kept cakes and sweets for me. It was a place where there were a lot of sweets and cakes. But sometimes my cousin may have bought them to get me there. She also gave me oranges and bananas. I used to go there towards four in the afternoon, and when I came she was always in her chemise. "You woke me up," she would say. Then she would give me sweets and fruit and lie back on her bed again. "Sit down here beside me, I'm so tired. If you like, take off your things and rest a bit." Then we romped about on the bed and tickled each other. She became excited and rubbed her body against mine and then she threw herself down, stretched out on her back, quite exhausted. I liked the warmth of her body and its smell, I liked to pull the curly hairs in her armpits. Once I started pulling at the little curls in the other place. She said: "Put your hand here. You'll see how warm it is. We women aren't made like you men. Let's have a look at you," and kissed me all over so as to tickle me, and then she burst out laughing. "Now look at you," she said. After that day she amused herself by playing with me and rubbing her body against me.

That was people's secret, and now I knew what it was. I don't want to have anything to do with Enriqueta any more. And if my cousin were to come now and rub herself against me, I would teach her something, the dirty bitch! She took advantage of my being a child. But in a way she was right. She couldn't go to bed with a man without being a tart, and so she consoled herself some other way. Why can't everybody do as they want? I would like to go to bed with girls, and they would like to go to bed with me, but we can't. Men have whores for that; but women must wait until the priest marries them. Or they must become whores themselves. And of course, in the meantime, they get excited. If one of them gets too hot, she must become a tart. It would be much better if they could all go to bed with whomever they liked. And why not?

Of course, then I would not know who my father is, and my mother would have been a whore who slept with anyone. It's funny. I've never imagined my mother like that, as a woman who had slept with a man and done the same with him as that Maña with me. But there's no doubt that if she had not slept with my father, I should not have been born, nor Rafael, nor Concha, nor José.

José! He must be twenty-two now. I'm sure he's never yet slept with a woman. All those unmarried, bigoted girl cousins won't let him leave the house except to accompany them. He said in his last letter that cousin Elvira wanted to marry him. They're sure to cuddle without much on. Elvira saying that she isn't well, and José going up to her bedroom to visit her. "Come in, come in, it's all right for you to come in," she will say, and then the two of them will get all excited. And because it's getting too much for them, she wants to catch him for good. Perhaps she'll even get him, because he must be crazy to get a woman. And where else should he go? He hasn't got the courage to go to a brothel and to take a woman to bed with him. And besides, you can't do that sort of thing in Cordova as you can in Madrid. In Cordova everybody knows everybody else, and the next day all the world and his wife would know that José had been in such and such a house.

I seem to have turned philosopher. I talk about the facts of life. And why shouldn't I have the right to think about life? Perhaps because I'm not yet twenty-one and can't dispose freely of my belongings? Damn it all! What is life? The shutter of a camera. You press the bulb. Pff! A snap. You've seen nothing: just a little flash. Like the calves of the girl getting on to that tram. A flash! Are her legs ugly or pretty? I don't know; but today I like all legs. Oh well, let's leave the women out of it. What is life? That's more interesting.

From up here, from the highest spot of the slope of the Calle de Alcalá, I'm seeing life. Sunday morning. The Church of Calatravas, with its sellers of Catholic newspapers, its blind men, its old beggar women, its urchins on the lookout for carriages so that they can open doors and beg for a copper. With its rows of nice young ladies walking beside nice young gentlemen who bend over them and whisper into the curls behind their ears. When the girls hear something pleasant, they shake their earrings, which hang down like big drops, just as horses shake their ears when a motorcar passes. There are the tramcars with their clang-clang and their yellow-and-red bellies covered with advertisements. The solid stone houses, with their windows open or shuttered. The iron tram-rails between the square paving stones a-glitter with mica. The sidewalks of black asphalt, whitened by the dust of shoe soles and studded with cigarette ends. The round marble tables on the terraces, milk white or mottled black. The clock of the Bank of Spain, a grave gentleman who sings out the hours with a voice like an old copper cauldron: Boom, boom! The goddess Cybele with her serious face and her bored lions who spit water in all directions. Aquatic lions. Where is the Sahara for those lions? One night, Pedro de Répide wrapped the goddess Cybele in his cloth cape the color of well roasted coffee, and so the dawn found her. She had icicles hanging from her nostrils, but she was sweating under the cape. Pedro de Répide had to pay a fine. Who had asked him to cloak statues? And up there, in the Puerta de Alcalá, the gate with its three arches and the Latin inscription, *Carolus Rex* . . .

Is that life?

Of course, in Paris and London and Peking there are streets just like this, ant heaps where people take their walks or go to Mass. The stories tell that Chinese temples have a lot of pointed roofs, with a silver or even a golden bell on each point tinkling in the wind, and outside the gate, slung on three huge posts, an ancient bronze gong over a thousand years old. When Mass is going to be said—Chinese "Mass," of course—the oldest of the bonzes—their priests are called bonzes—comes out with a wooden mallet and strikes the gong. It sounds in the far distance like a cascade of quavering "ploms." The Chinese come with short little steps, bounding on their toes, their hands hidden in their sleeves and the knobs on their skullcaps dancing, and they climb the temple stairs in short little leaps. They kneel down and double up their bellies a thousand-and-one times in front of a grave Buddha with a polished navel. Then they burn strips of paper, which are their prayers. Rather like when Father Vesga told me to copy the Credo a hundred times. When the Chinese grow old, they have pigtails curved outwards and long mustaches that hang down in two lanky strands. But it's funny: in pictures and photographs I've seen a lot of Chinese with white mustaches and beards, but I've never seen a Chinese with a white pigtail, and I've never seen a Chinese woman with white hair.

But there are so many things in the world. Trains starting punctually, with their punctual passengers and their punctual engineers and station masters. The station master blows a whistle and the train starts. Harbors with ships riding close to the stone walls of the jetties, while people laden with luggage climb up a small wooden gangway and blow kisses to those who stay behind. A bell tolls and a gangway is withdrawn. A whistle blows and the ship begins to move. Some people stay quietly on land, waving their handkerchiefs, and others lean over the ship's railing. When a ship leaves, everybody has a clean handkerchief, a handkerchief without a snivel, because people would speak badly of anyone who used a dirty handkerchief to wave farewell.

Is that life?

To run up and down the Calle de Alcalá in Madrid, or some other street like it in Paris or London or China. To get on a train, to board a ship. To hear Mass or to burn strips of paper on an altar, before Our Lady or before Buddha's paunch. To ring great cathedral bells or to strike a bronze gong with a mallet or to let the wind sway little bells.

And that is life?

Old people, grown-up people, teach children what life is like. I am no longer a child. I am working, I am already sleeping with women. But the school still sticks to me as bits of egg shell stick to a chick's bottom. Let's sit down here on the bench in the Retiro Park. I'll review what the old people have taught me about life. Back—back—think. Look into the far distance.

What do you want, you sparrows? I haven't got any crumbs in my pockets. Don't flutter up and down in front of me. This is serious, and you're a lot of little rascals. Let me see whether I can remember the time when I was small, like you, and then I may discover what the grown-up people have taught me about life.

My grandmother told me—but no. Before they told you anything where were you then? Before you understood what they told you, where were you?

First was a morning. It snowed fat flakes, like big white flies tumbling down from high up in a daze. My mother dressed me up in petticoats and woolen stockings which she tied round my middle with white ribbons full of knots. She put on my boots, boots with plenty of buttons, and we went out into the streets. I in her arms, wrapped in a shaggy shawl like a sheepskin that hasn't been clipped. Beautifully warm, and my nose sticking out of the cowl of the big shawl. A column of steam rose into the air every time I breathed out of my open mouth. I had fun blowing, because it made a funnel of gray air which drifted away in the street like smoke from a cigarette. The trolley of the tram was covered with blobs of ice. In a big portal two soldiers were standing near a huge brazier filled with burning coal. One of the soldiers had his foot on the edge of a dark blanket, the other held its other end and waved it like a fan. The current of air hit the brazier and the coal burst into a shower of sparks which the wind carried down the street and smothered in the snow. They hissed, they squealed because the cold hurt them. Then I felt that my feet were cold. They were sticking out from under the shawl and snow had fallen on them. I laughed, because one of my boots was black and the other brown. My mother looked at my boots and laughed with me. We stayed for a while in the warmth of the brazier and we all laughed, the soldiers, my mother, and I, while the melting snow dripped from my boots. When they stopped dripping, my mother bundled me up, with my feet inside the shawl, and we walked down the street. The snow drifted against our faces.

That is my first clear childhood memory. Then came a black hole from which everything emerged by and by, I don't know when and how: uncle and aunt, brothers and sister, the attic, Señora Pascuala, . . . one day they came and put themselves into life, into my life. Then they began to fill life for me with "do's" and "don't's." "Don't do this"—"Do that." Sometimes they themselves didn't agree. "Do this," one said; "don't do it," said the other.

Once we were in a theater, I don't know which. I only remember the red velvet of the chair, just like the red velvet of the sofas in the Café Español, and the bright stage where men and women were singing. I wanted to make water. "Uncle, I want to pass water." He nodded. "All right, come with me." "What's the matter with the child?" asked my aunt. "He wants to do his little business." "He can wait." "But, my dear, he's a child." "He must wait. Arturito, be good." I wetted the red velvet seat and no one heard the small splash, because the music made so much noise. When the curtain had fallen, my uncle said: "Now come along." "I don't need to now," I answered. They both went on scolding me for days and days.

At that time they all started teaching me when it was right and when it was wrong to make water or the other, when it was right to speak and when it was right to be quiet. When I was crying, they told me: Men don't cry. Then, when somebody died, men and women came in tears to tell us about it. Don't scream! Children must not say blasphemies! And then grown-up people shouted at each other and most of them blasphemed against God and Our Lady. Uncle, too, swore and said dirty things at times. Even the Fathers at school. There was Father Fulgencio who played the organ and was our chemistry teacher. He used to scribble formulas all over the blackboard, take a few test tubes, mix salts and acids, explain their reactions and then say: "Have you got it?" Hardly any of us had understood it. Then he banged on the table: "You've damned well got to understand. What the hell is the use of my teaching you if you don't understand?" There was a daft boy in the class, another of those sons of rich fathers, I don't remember his name. One day Father Fulgencio fastened on him: "Have you got this?" "No, I can't understand the damned thing," he answered. Father Fulgencio boxed his ears for him. "What do you mean by using bad language? Who taught you such an ugly word? What a rotten life one has with these boys!" One day he sat down at the organ and pressed one of the keys, but the pipe gave no sound. He stopped playing and pushed away at the key. The organ sounded pffff, in a long wheeze, but no more. He got up and marched us off through the cloisters. There he met another of the priests who asked him: "What is it, Brother Fulgencio, why are you in a bad temper?" "Well," he said, "there's an *f*, a bitch of a key, that doesn't sound at all." With Chinese ink we painted its name, "Bitch," on the yellow key. Father Fulgencio went quite mad. "Who's done this? You shameless rascals!" And he struck the key hard. The organ pipe, thick as an arm, gave back: Pfff!

They taught us the Catechism and Biblical history before anything else. They taught me to read, and then they taught me to read nothing except what they permitted. They taught me to count, to add, to subtract, to shunt figures and letters, to use the signs of plus and minus, of minus-plus and plus-minus, roots, powers, logarithms. To draw beautiful letters of the kind called English writing, with fat strokes and thin strokes, which you had to write slowly with your hand placed right and your arm placed right and your body poised right and your bottom sitting right in its chair and the sheet of paper in its right place. Then the Bank: "This handwriting is no good—discount must be calculated like this—interest must be calculated like that—pounds sterling must be calculated in such-and-such a way." And the postures for the English script, and the rule-of-three are just good for nothing, and Biblical history too, and the Catechism even more so.

"Be good," they all said. "Don't fight with the other boys." Once I came home with a black eye. The whole family jumped on me: "You little runt, you cry baby, you let them beat you! You ought to have knocked his brains open with a stone, you ought to have kicked him in the belly!" I went away, out into the street, and looked for the boy who had hit me. I was sorry for him, because he was weak and small, and he had hit me in the eye without meaning to while we were playing. But I had a fight with him and hit him with my fists in his face, mainly the eyes, so that they should turn black like mine. A trickle of blood ran from his nose. I threw him on the ground and kicked him in the ribs and loins. He screamed. Then Pablito's father, the plasterer, came and separated us. First he boxed my ears, then he picked me up and carried me upstairs to our flat, the other boy in front of me, bleeding and with torn clothes. What a row they made! Uncle José slapped me, my aunt pinched me, my mother spanked me. They all shouted at me and called me a savage and I don't know what else; but they stuffed the other boy with sweets, biscuits, and coppers. He went off grinning and crying, and I would have liked to hit the whole lot of them. "It's he who gave me the black eye! I kicked him in the belly and smashed his face for him because you told me to. And now you thrash *me* and give *him* biscuits!" I cried, tumbled on the dining-room carpet. Uncle José said: "But, my goodness, if you beat somebody you must do it within bounds."

And so I learned to respect the grown-ups. Señor Corachán is a grown-up man, a "gentleman." One day he pulled my ears and called me a vagabond. I kept silent, but I would have liked to kick him in the belly, too.

They have all taught me how to live. And nothing they taught me is any good for living. Nothing, absolutely nothing. Not their figures and not their Biblical history. They've deceived me. Life is not what they teach it to be, it's different. They've deceived me, and so I must learn for myself about life. Plá has taught me more than all the others. And so has Uncle Luis with his rude words, and Señor Manuel with his innocent laborer's mind, and my cousin with her hot stuff, and that Maña in her short chemise. But the others who educate boys so as to turn them into "men"—what have they taught me? Only Father Joaquín once told me that I should believe what I felt to be good, and to say that cost him an effort as though he were betraying a secret.

Why rack one's brains about it?

But I would like to know what life is. I don't know what my mother was like as a little girl; when she was young she was in service, then she married and my father earned only just enough to keep them going, then he died and she was worse off than ever with her four children. Without my uncle and aunt the five of us might have starved to death. So off with her to wash clothes in the river, the mucky linen of rich people who can pay a washerwoman. The rich people. What are the rich?

Do you know who the rich people are, you sparrow? Of course you know, it must be those who throw you crumbs not of bread but of cake. Those are the rich ones for you. As soon as one of the women who sell buns passes, I shall buy one for you and throw you crumbs. Then you'll say I'm rich. The rich are people who throw cake crumbs to the birds and bread crumbs to the poor like my mother. You know—do listen, you little fool, don't fly away, the cake will come afterwards. You know, there's Señor Dotti, the millionaire for whom my mother does all the washing. He's married, and his wife once said to my mother: "Leonor, do you know how much we spent this year on toys for the children?" "No, madam," said my mother. "Twenty-four thousand pesetas, six thousand duros. And still they aren't content, just imagine, Leonor."

My mother said: "Madam, with that money we could have lived for a whole year, without my having to go to the river."

They gave me all the old toys of the year before, so many that I had to make three trips by tram to fetch the things home. There were enough toys for us all. I got an engine which could run by itself; it had a little spirit lamp in place of the boiler and when you poured water in it started running just like a real engine. There were hundreds of lead soldiers, and motorcars with doors which opened and shut, and dolls which could say "Mama" and "Papa." Concha came home after her washing-up and carried the dolls off. She was already in service, but she was still a little girl. In her spare time she knitted frocks for the dolls. Why did they ever buy dolls for their two boys? Señora Dotti told my mother: "They were keen on them—so what could I do about it?" Then the boys got tired of the dolls and threw them aside. Those old toys are still stowed in a corner of our attic, behind my books. But I don't feel like having them out. I'm no child any more. Sometimes it amuses me to play with a huge gyroscope, to let it gyrate on the rim of a glass or run along a string stretched across the attic.

Well, that is what being rich means. Señor Dotti has got a telephone in his house, and he has two houses, one in Madrid, one in Barcelona. When he stays in Madrid he rings up Barcelona every morning, and when he stays in Barcelona, he always rings up Madrid. When he's told that there's nothing new at the other end, he goes off to the Exchange. There he makes a few thousand pesetas, and goes home again. He puts on a frock coat or a cutaway and invites people home to tea. His boys wash and brush their hair and go in to kiss the hands of the lady visitors. Once one of the boys, Alejandro, was not allowed to sit at table during meals for a week, as a punishment. His father had come home from the Exchange, very pleased with himself because he had made a lot of money. He opened the door with his latchkey, took off his hat, and by chance went into the kitchen. There he found Alejandro sitting on the floor together with the dog, a very beautiful bitch, and the two of them eating the dog's *cocido.* For in Dotti's house a special stew for the dogs was cooked every day, with meat, sausage, and chick-peas; Alejandro used to come to the kitchen and share it with the bitch. When my mother heard the story and how they had punished him, she said to his mother: "Send him to our attic for a week and you'll see how quickly he gets tired of eating *cocido.*" That's how things go with the rich.

One day a few masons were sitting under the arches of the Plaza Mayor and eating saffron-yellow *cocido,* the kind my mother always cooks down by the river. An elegant carriage stopped in front of them, a gentleman and a lady got out, and he said to one of the workers: "Let me buy your *cocido* off you." The mason stared at him and said, "I don't want to." "Now look here," said the other, "my wife is expecting a baby and she wants to eat *cocido.*" The mason answered: "Well, she'll have to do without." But the mason's wife was there and made him give them the *cocido;* they carried the pots with the dish to the carriage and gave the worker fifty pesetas. He said to his wife: "I wouldn't have given it them—perhaps she would have produced a boy with the mark of a stew-pot on his belly."

And is this life, then? A rich man can afford to spend six thousand duros on toys, and to telephone to Barcelona just to know whether there's anything new at home, and to buy a mason's *cocido* off him?

Be quiet, you sparrow. Where did you get those grains from? Now look, there's a whole column of ants crawling backwards, each carrying a grain of wheat. Aren't you ashamed to eat the grain they carry with

so much labor, and perhaps to swallow the ant as well while it sticks
to its grain, clutching at it with its horny, black teeth? I wonder where
they get hold of corn here in the Park? Perhaps from the ducks. I don't
know whether I ought to make you drop the grain or not. Perhaps there's
a little sparrow in your nest, waiting to swallow the ant and the grain
you bring with you. I remember the swallows in the courtyard of the
Palace chasing flies and gnats with those shrill hunting cries of theirs,
carrying them off and dropping them into the square, wide-open, never-
filled beaks of their young. Perhaps you're right, sparrow, perhaps you
have a right to the ants' grain.

Is this life? To take away each other's food? To devour each other?
Watch out, sparrow, here's a little boy with a bun who wants to feed
you. Silly, why do you run away and fly off? Now then, do go and eat
—closer to him. Look how he smiles and holds out crumbs between his
fingertips. He wants you to come and peck at them. That fat crumb is
meant to tempt you. Is that life: to give for the pleasure of giving, to
take for the pleasure of taking?

People are taking their walks, nursemaids keeping the children in front
of them so that they shouldn't get lost, and screaming as soon as the
children go too far away. Lovers leaning against each other. Old women
sit there knitting socks on long steel needles, with quick, deft movements
and flashes as from sword blades. When they get up they limp from
rheumatics, but now while they're sitting their fingers fly like a conjurer's.
They call to their grandchildren who shovel sand into brightly painted
tin buckets. How sad the little boy it, the one over there in the perambulator with rubber tires, kicking his feet and waving his arms and wanting
to run about, instead of being stuck among the cushions that keep him
from crawling on the ground. Now he starts crying. You fool of a mother,
take him out of that black oilcloth box on wire-spoke wheels, put him
on the ground, tumbled on his back or his tummy, let him scratch about
in the sand or catch ants or splash in the mud and smear his face with
black streaks. Don't you see he's crying because that's what he wants?
The papa lights a cigar and goes on reading the paper: "Can't you keep
the boy quiet?" "But what shall I do with him?" "Give him the breast
and he'll shut up." The lady sits down on the fretted iron chair which
has produced coppers for so many years, and pulls out one of her
breasts. A flabby breast with a big, black nipple which looks as though
it were hairy. The kid doesn't take it. Of course he doesn't. He wants to
stick his fingers in the earth and make mud balls with the palm of his
hand. He goes on crying, and the mother doesn't understand him. You
silly goose, you animal, why do you slap and shake him and scream: "Be
quiet—be quiet!" Do you think he understands you? You nasty brute.

You lay him out in his perambulator as if he were a stuffed sack. I can see it in your face that, if you could, you would throw him away from you, like a dead frog—you would hold him by one leg and dash him on the ground so as not to hear him crying any more. "Now see what a silly fool you are," says the papa, and he's right. But he is as much of a silly fool as she is.

Is this life?

The path by the lake is deserted. The sunlight pours down, the sand is scorching hot. Why not bathe in the sun? Why not go where nobody else goes? In the big lake people are rowing boats, but the steam launch which takes children twice round the square basin is anchored. Anchored. No, it's tied to a rope, ridiculously anchored. There is no tide here. Just now the benches of the launch are clean. When it's full of children they can stretch out their hands and trail them in the water without fear of sharks biting them. The mammas imagine they are at sea and get sick behind their black mantillas. Then the boatman's lad, who always sings out the number of boats which have been out for the full half-hour of their hire, takes the ladies by the arm, gives them a cup of tea, gets a peseta's worth of a tip out of them, and shows off, standing up and walking about in the boats without falling, like a real sailor. "There you see, lady, it's quite easy, it's just practice."

But I'm grown-up now, and this is life. All this, all this together. So much the better. This is life, life is like this. One day I'll throw crumbs to the fishes or the sparrows, another I'll get sick in a boat, and still another I'll fish fishes or shoot birds. Yes, sir, it's necessary to scold little children when they cry. What, you've given him a perambulator and he cries? A perambulator with rubber tires? That couple must be rich. Some day I'm going to have a son, but my wife won't have black nipples like that woman's. How can a rich man marry a woman with black nipples? That's to say, she may be the rich one of the two, and then he's right, of course. What do black nipples matter if one's rich? For that is the only thing that counts: to be rich. That's living.

But perhaps not. We aren't rich in our attic, but we're happy.

Oh, there's Father Joaquín. He must have come here for a walk after Mass. Really, he's a fine man. I would like to look like that, tall, strong, broad-shouldered, as they say all Basques are. His cassock suits him well, because he's got no belly and a chest like a barrel. With most other priests the buttons on their cassocks—how many are there, thirty to forty?—mark a curve that sinks in under their chin and protrudes over their belly in a row of shiny dots. But not his. The buttons curve out on his chest and recede on his stomach and then go straight down to his legs, which seem to break out of the cassock as he walks.

I don't know the people with him. A lady leading a little boy by the hand. The boy is very serious for his age, but strong, much stronger than I had been.

Hat in hand, I walked at Father Joaquín's side. The woman and the boy came behind us.

"Are you out for a walk, Arturo?"

"Yes, I've got one of my attacks. I was thinking."

"What have you been thinking?"

"Well, I don't know, really. Stupid things. About life and death and animals. I've been laughing over a sparrow and a little boy in a perambulator with rubber wheels. What do I know? My mother says it's my growing up. I don't know what it is. And then .`. .`"

"Then, what?"

"Nothing . . . no . . . Nothing."

I had gone red, I felt it in my cheeks. But how could I have told him that I had slept with a woman for the first time in my life and that she wore a short pink chemise. . . .

Father Joaquín stroked my head as so often before and turned round to the others, to the woman and the boy who walked so gravely behind us.

"Do come here," he said.

He took the woman by the hand and drew her closer. He put his other hand, broad and strong, with fair fluff on the knuckles, on the boy's shoulder, and pulled him nearer. He placed them in front of me; and the three of us, the woman, the boy, and I, were waiting for something to happen, waiting for something very big.

He only said: "My wife and my son . . . Here you have Arturo."

We walked together on the sun-filled path along the lake, silent, without a word, and looked at the water in the square basin so that we should not catch each other's eyes. We walked slowly and the path had no end.

Then I left them with an awkward good-by, stumbling over my own feet. And I never dared to turn my head so as not to see the three of them looking at each other, looking at me.

9. Rebel

EVERYTHING was arranged. We four men would sleep in the old attic, Rafael and I once again together in my gilt bed, and Uncle Luis and Andrés in my mother's double bed with its green frame and the faded saints on sheet-iron panels fretted by the years and insecticides. The women, my mother and Concha, were going to sleep in the other attic which was formerly Señora Francisca's.

Señora Francisca had died and left behind nothing but a few blackened pots and pans and a basketful of monkeynuts, sweets, and squibs such as she used to sell to children in the Plaza del Progreso. We took over her attic room, as it was next door to ours, and inherited her belongings, the old clothes, cooking pots, goods for sale, and a truckle bed with a black wool mattress. Nobody claimed this inheritance, so we chopped up the bedstead for firewood, and shared the rest with the tenants of the other attics.

Rafael and I moved into the new room. In daytime it was used as the kitchen, because it had a little stove with a chimney pipe in a corner under the sloping roof, and as Concha's workshop. Concha had left Dr. Chicote's service and had learned the laundry trade, paying for the training herself, because she did not want to go on working as a housemaid. As my mother was a washerwoman, Concha easily found customers. She spent the days heating her irons in the corner under the roof and ironing clothes or linen on a deal table more than three yards square, which filled the middle of the attic. Now the two women slept by themselves, and so did Rafael and I; sometimes we stayed away for a night, thanks to our independence. Yet at the same time we were together. Besides the two big beds, the round table my father had made, our crockery and our linen were still in the old attic—all our wealth. That day we had to make room for four and needed the big beds, so we changed places with the women.

Uncle Luis and Andrés had arrived together, but each on a different errand. Andrés was on his way to Toledo where he meant to spend three days with his son Fidel, the seminarist; his wife Elvira had stayed behind in Méntrida, bedridden because of her festering leg. Uncle Luis had come, as he often did, to buy the iron for his horseshoes, iron in rods, soft and black, which had never been touched by fire since it left the crucible.

Every time I saw Uncle Luis buying iron I was reminded of the times

I had seen him tasting wine. He would make the round of the underground wine cellars of Méntrida with a dipper, and take a small quantity
out of each wine jar, just enough to fill half the glass which he had rinsed
most carefully. He would look at the wine against the light, take a sip "to
wash his mouth," roll it round his tongue, say nothing, rinse his glass,
and try another wine jar. Suddenly he would firmly grasp the glass, plunge
it into the jar as though it were the dipper, draw it out filled to the rim,
and pour it down his gullet. And so a second time, and a third. The
owner of the cellar would ask him: "What do you think of it, Luis?"
"This jar here is our Saviour's own blood, the rest can be poured away."

He did the same with the iron. He would enter the stores of the *Cava
Baja,* stooping his huge body, and ask for iron, just like that: "I want
iron." All the owners knew him and would get out rods two and four
yards long. He would weigh them, stroke them with the tip of a finger,
make them ring with his knuckles, and drop them back on the heap,
until he came to a heap where he would stop, holding the iron rod high,
and ask: "How much?" When he had made the deal, he would double
the finger-thick rods with his bare hands, tie them up in a bundle and
carry them away on his shoulder, as though he were going to march
straight from the Cava Baja to Méntrida and so start forging them then
and there. Sometimes he would pat the rods and say: "Pure gold!"

Rafael and I fixed the center leaf of the table so that six of us should
have room. My mother produced one of her white tablecloths and started
laying the table. At eight both of our guests were back from their business. Andrés arrived laden with parcels, good things to eat and clothing
for his boy. Uncle Luis carried a single parcel which he handled like a
club. He banged it on the table and guffawed: "It sounds hard, doesn't
it?" Then he unwrapped it and took out a smoke-cured ham, dry and
hard as wood. "Give me a knife, Leonor."

He cut it in the middle to show the almost purple meat, of which he
sliced off a strip for each of us. My mother protested:

"Now look, leave that to take home."

"Never mind, eat and shut up, you never know what will happen tomorrow."

He filled a glass to the brim with wine and tossed it off: "And now
let's have supper."

At the beginning of the meal we were all silent, for the slice of ham had
made us hungry and anyway we did not know what to say first. Uncle
Luis started the ball rolling. He addressed me:

"Well, and what about you?"

"I'm working."

"He's settled for life," said Andrés. "He's had better luck than my boy who'll have to stay nine years in that seminary."

Uncle Luis crunched a chop between his teeth, wiped his greasy lips with the back of his hand, and turned round to Andrés:

"Well, it'll be funny if in nine years' time the boy hangs his cassock on a nail and runs after some skirt or other!"

"If the boy does that to me, I'll kill him. Here I have been sacrificing myself for him all my life, and if he goes and chucks away the priest's habit and becomes a good-for-nothing I'll kill him!"

"T-t-t, what d'you call sacrifice? The seminary doesn't cost you a thing. They're letting him study free, because they need more silly little priests, and you've a mouth less to feed at home. You've even got savings by now."

"But you forget that it's a sacrifice to be separated from one's son for eleven years, only because one wants him to become a man."

"To become a man! Come now, d'you think I'm a silly fool? You may do it because you want him to become a priest, but not a man. Priests can be men, but they can't act as men. And that's your doing. When your boy's grown up he'll be either a man or a priest, but never both things at the same time."

"Let's leave it, Luis, there's no discussing things with you."

"Of course there isn't. I'm such a rough brute that I won't swallow anything which might hurt me inside. I call bread, bread and wine, wine." To stress his words he wiped his plate with a chunk of bread big enough to fill his mouth, and poured down another glass of wine. Then, when his plate was clean, he planted both elbows on the table and went on:

"Now listen. You're wrong, both of you. She here"—he nodded towards my mother—"and you. You've got the same bee in your bonnets as all the other starvelings, you want your boy to be a Prince of the Blood. Look at him"—he pointed at me—"so smart and fine, so nice to look at, with his white face, starched collar, silk tie, elegant suit—with two pesetas salary, living in a garret and his mother washing clothes. They've taught him to be ashamed of his mother being a washerwoman."

"I'm *not* ashamed because my mother's a washerwoman," I said.

"Oh no? And how many of your friends at the Bank come to visit you here?"

I flushed and gave no answer.

"D'you see it?" Uncle Luis said to Andrés. "Just like you. I bet your boy doesn't tell it to others in the seminary that he's a master mason's son, and I bet you don't have the guts to turn up at Toledo in your white overall. In Leonor's case one can still excuse it, because she's a woman, and because of a lot of other things as well. But what have you got to say? You're as well off as me. God won't forgive you—if there's such a thing as God anyhow. Every man to his trade. My boys are hammering iron now, and when they're men they can do what they feel like, but they'll always be able to earn their bread and they won't be ashamed of being blacksmiths like their father. And if it comes to being well off, you bet they won't be slow, they're going to be richer than you and your boy, even if he is made a canon."

"That's just what I don't want," said Andrés in a slightly hoarse voice. "I don't want my boy to have to carry pails, mix plaster, and whitewash walls in a blazing sun. What I'm doing is for his good, and one day he'll thank me for it."

"And when he sees a pretty girl passing and feels like having a woman, he'll call his father a bastard, cassock and all."

"Now come, come, the boy isn't quite a fool, and when he feels like being with a woman he'll take one to bed."

"That's just it. And you'll have turned him into a hypocrite or a poor wretch. My boy, Aquilino, already has an eye on the girls. Now he's hammering iron at the forge, and when a girl passes he tells her she's pretty. And if she lets him go on, the worst that happens is that the next day he finds the sledge hammer a little heavier than before. But he does his work with more pleasure than ever and eats like a devil and walks with his head high because he's got nothing to be ashamed of. The boy here's lucky in that it will be the same with him. But then all he'll ever be is a pen-pusher, a little gentleman who marries some consumptive girl in a hat, and afterwards the two of them will go crazy with hunger on thirty duros a month."

"So in your opinion one oughtn't to worry about one's children becoming something better?"

"Better than oneself, yes. But not something different. Now I've got everything. I've got my wife and my children and the smithy, and thank God we're all in good health. And then there's my bit of wheatland and my strip of orchard, and the pig and the wine, and the figs for dessert. Well, my boys have got all that too, and later on they can make it more by working hard, just as I did. In my house there's no God and no King and no nothing. I'm the master there, and nobody's my master. So why should I want to be richer if I'm my own master and have all I need?"

"What should I have done then?" asked my mother, who had listened to the men, silent and quiet.

"You? You've done quite enough by bringing them up and not turning them into priests. Now it's up to them to take care of you."

"Well, I work like a donkey," Concha said.

"What else did you imagine, my dear girl? I work like a horse. And

that's just our lot in this world, to work like beasts. But at least we must
have the right to kick now and then," said Uncle Luis.

Rafael lifted his head for the first time and said:

"All it comes to is that because we're poor we must put up with things.
You've got everything settled, and so you're happy. But I'd like to see
you in my office writing out invoices and getting thirty pesetas at the
end of the month."

"Well, d'you know what I'd do? I'd take my cap and shut the door
from the outside. The trouble with you is that you've got an easy life
in your office and you don't want to work. Come with me to Méntrida
to handle the sledge hammer, and I'll teach you the trade and keep you.
Of course you'll get black, and it won't wash off, and your hands will
get horny."

Until that moment I had kept out of the discussion because I knew I
was near bursting point. But when I found that all of them put things
in the wrong way, I cut in.

"I think you're all wrong. You're in love with your trade, Uncle, and
you've been happy at it. But your sons won't be able to live on your trade,
and you know it. Hand-forged horseshoes and wrought-iron grilles are
all over and done with. You and I, we've seen horseshoes of pressed steel
in all sizes, like boots, when we were in the stores of the Cava Baja. The
only customers you've got left are old friends of yours. Now ask Andrés,
who's a master builder and has built houses, how many orders for
wrought-iron grilles he's given you. He'll tell you that he buys them from
stock in Madrid, cheaper than the iron rods you buy for horeshoes."

"There's nothing like a forged horseshoe from the fire straight on to
a horse's hoof. It's like boots made to measure," shouted Uncle Luis, and
banged on the table.

"Just so," I answered. "When Uncle Sebastian was thirty he shod the
whole village. But today—today he's glad if he's given shoes to sole,
because sneakers are cheaper and last longer than half-soles on an old
shoe."

"That's just what I'm saying," cried Andrés.

"No, it isn't. I may be a pen-pusher, but after all I'm doing a job. But
your son is a budding priest, and that's no job. And then, there will
always be clerks, but very soon it will be all over with priests. People
are getting fed up with feeding loafers who bellow Latin."

"That's just being rude. But never mind. There will always be religion."

"Are you religious?" I asked Andrés.

"Well, to tell the truth, it's of no matter to me. If I feel like saying a
bad word I do it, because it's a relief."

"So why do you want your son to become a priest? You don't believe in God, or you don't care whether you do or don't. But you turn your son into a priest so that he can exploit the others with the help of a God you don't believe in. And the worst of it is that you leave him without having learned any trade or profession, and, as Uncle Luis says, you've prevented him from being a man."

"Now that's all nonsense. Everybody acts as he thinks best, and my boy will do what I want him to. That's my good right as his father."

"You've no right at all. Parents have no rights."

Andrés and Uncle Luis gaped at me. My mother looked at her hands. Rafael lifted his hanging head once again and gave me a sidewise look. Concha put her two fists on the table as though she were going to knock me down. I spoke on, looking round from one to the other.

"Yes, you needn't all stare at me like that. Parents have no rights. We children of theirs are here, because they brought us here for the sake of their own pleasure. And so they must put up with what had been their pleasure. I never asked my mother to bring me into the world, and so I can't allow her any right over me, such as you claim over your son. If I had a father and he said to me what you said just now, I'd tell him to go to hell."

Each of them reacted in his own manner. Andrés said. "You're a shameless rascal." Uncle Luis said: "If you were my son I'd break your leg to make you walk straight." Concha said: "Then Mother ought to have chucked us into the Foundlings' Home?" Rafael said: "Go on."

After all the others, my mother said slowly:

"Yes. Having children is a pleasure for which you pay dearly."

At that I saw tumbling visions of my uncle's house, of heaps of dirty linen, of her lye-bitten hands and her meek, silent forbearance, a smile forever on her lips. Kisses in the kitchen and behind the curtain of the Café Español. The struggle for centimos. Her falling into a chair, utterly worn out. Her fingers in my rumpled hair, my head on her lap. It all surged up in me and it put me in the wrong, but not the outcries and protests of the others who disputed and shouted.

"Let's go, Rafael."

We went downstairs, and out into the street. Rafael said: "You gave it to them."

I grew indignant and began to speak. I spoke without pause for streets on end, trying to convince him that I was wrong about our mother, that we three, he and I and Concha, had the obligation to take her away from her work by the river, from washing clothes, from breaking up the ice and being roasted by the sun and coming home worn out. That we had to get her away from all this if we had to smash the whole world for it.

Rafael let me speak and then said:

"All right, that's easy. Tomorrow we'll ask for a rise, you at the Bank
and I at the Fenix. We'll speak to our managers of our mamma the
washerwoman, and you may be sure they'll give us a good salary so we
can support her. . . ."

It's the easiest thing in arithmetic to add up sums, but it's also the most
difficult. To add up ten or twelve sheets of fifty lines with six or seven
figures in each is more difficult than to handle the rule-of-three or the table
of logarithms. At the end there is always a centimo too much or too little
—or a thousand—and you have to start again at the beginning.

I was adding up and never took in what the messenger said, but answered "Coming," automatically. After a short time he came back, touched
me on the shoulder, and said: "Señor Corachán's waiting for you. I told
you a while ago but you forgot."

I was startled and sprinted up the stairs, since the staff had no right to
use the lift which was reserved for customers and the high officials of the
Bank. What did that old fellow want of me? The commissionaire left
me for a long while cooling my heels in the management's reception
room. I used the breathing space to master my agitation and to wonder
what the man wanted. Surely nothing pleasant. Anyhow, I would soon
know, whatever it might be. I was sitting in a deep leather armchair the
seat of which tipped backwards and rocked. For a while I amused myself
swaying backwards and forwards, forwards and backwards in see-saw
movement. There was a silver box on the polished table in the middle of
the room. I opened it; it was filled with Virginia cigarettes. I wavered for
a moment, then I took out a fistful and put them away in my coat
pocket. The commissionaire opened the door to the office and announced
me.

Don Antonio was meticulously scanning a letter, as usual, and spent
long minutes over it. Finally he signed it, deigned to raise his head and
looked at me through his pince-nez.

"You're the employee of the Coupons Section who broke the plate
glass the day before yesterday?"

"Yes, sir."

"Well, well. This time no strong measures will be taken in view of
your past conduct. The Management has decided to deduct the cost of
the plate glass from your salary. It amounts to 37.50 pesetas. That is all.
You may go."

I walked slowly down the stairs and went to the washroom to smoke
one of the Virginia cigarettes and think the whole injustice over.

Less than a month ago every desk had been covered with a sheet of
plate glass. Most of the desks had a centerpiece lined with red or green

oilcloth, and a broad frame of varnished wood. They had laid the plate glass directly on the frame, which meant that a hollow space was left under the glass in the center. The backs of the coupons we sent out to the provinces or abroad had to be stamped with the initials of the branch office, to prevent their being stolen and circulated. We had to stamp thousands of coupons with a metal stamp, and there were days when the only noise in the department was that of the stamps hitting the ink pad and the coupons. When the desks were covered with the glass panels, I asked for a rubber sheet, because I foresaw that I would inevitably break the glass. I was told that no rubber sheet was necessary, and had to go on stamping coupons on the glass. The day before yesterday the glass was starred. They put a new one on and I gave it no further thought. And now that nasty old fellow said I had to pay for it. Well, I would pay, but I wouldn't stamp any more coupons as long as they didn't let me have a rubber sheet.

When I came down to our section they were all waiting to hear what had happened. The story of the plate glass went round the whole Bank immediately. Discontent was general, because the building was full of glass-covered desks and metal stamps; all the employees were afraid that the same thing would happen to them sooner or later. Plá sent for me to come to the lavatory—to our club—and there I found him in the midst of six or seven others, swathed in cigarette smoke. Somebody was keeping watch by the stairs against Corachán's coming.

"Now come along," said Plá, "and tell us what happened."

I reported my interview and told them that the price of the plate glass would be deducted from my salary.

Plá grew angry: "They're a set of robbers. All that glass is insured, and then they cash in on us when something gets broken. We must protest against it."

"Yes, but how?" said one of the others. "We can't just go up to the Management as a protest delegation, because if we do they'll give us the sack."

"Well, we must do something. If we let them get away with it we must expect to pay for all broken glass. And besides we must show that gang our teeth. Remember what happened on the First of May. They swallowed it and never said a word."

Years before, the First of May had been recognized by law as the Labor holiday. In the morning a procession crossed the city and went to the Premier's seat to present a paper with the demands of labor. Employers regarded the demonstration as an insult to themselves, and did what they could to make their men work the whole day. The Second of May was a National holiday, in commemoration of the Second of May 1808, when the War of Independence began with the rising of the people of Madrid against Napoleon's army of occupation. The employers used the second day to scotch the first. Only workshops shut down on the First of May, while the other trades, particularly commerce and the banks, treated it as a normal working day.

That year we had agreed that members of trade unions employed in banks would not go to work on the First of May, but take part in the procession, come what might. We felt certain that we should be sacked; but then *El Sociolista* would start an intense publicity campaign, because we were within our legal rights. There were about a hundred of us from the Madrid banks, who all tried to encourage one another and threatened with reprisals cowards who wanted to shirk. When the procession was marching through the Calle de Alcalá where all the banks have their head offices, the group of gentlemen in starched collars, so conspicuous before, dwindled away and disappeared down side streets. Only a few of us marched on, enough, however, to make the fact known. On the following day we went to work awaiting instant dismissal.

Nobody said anything. Cabanillas, who years later became chief editor of the *Heraldo de Madrid,* had no occasion to publish the article he had already prepared against the Crédit Etranger, an impassioned article describing the fury of French Capitalism which sacked employees for staying away from work, although they were acting within the law, but then shut up the Bank on the Second of May and decked the balconies of the building with banners and streamers, as a French firm's contribution to the celebration of Napoleon's defeat.

We were very proud of our success, and very much ashamed of the desertions in the Calle de Alcalá, and very much afraid of the reprisals which would later on hit us one by one. If they were going to dismiss us one after the other, taking their time over it, it would have been better if all of us had decided to march through the Calle de Alcalá among the workers, our heads high. Of course, if you asked each member of the group individually, it turned out that none of them had left the files even for a moment, except to take a quick glass of vermouth or to satisfy an urgent physical need.

That was the story of the First of May, of which Plá never ceased to remind us.

More employees joined us in the lavatory until the whole space between the basins and the cabins was crowded. Chubby little Plá was submerged in a mass of people, but his fury grew and he kept on shouting:

"We must do something! We must make a big row! If we don't we're a lousy lot of bastards!"

One of our more moderate colleagues found a solution.

"It's quite simple. If we pay for the plate glass between the lot of us, the whole thing is settled. Every time a glass cover is broken we'd solve the problem by paying ten centimos each, and so nobody will be ruined."

"Your big idea is to avoid any trouble."

"Of course it is, we've got trouble enough as it is. If they had sacked all of us, at one go, on the 3rd of May, the People's House would have supported us and in the end they would have had to take us back at the Bank. But now the first of us to open his mouth will find himself in the street—and can you tell me what he's going to live on?"

"The trouble with us is that we're a pack of cowards," said Plá. He thought a moment and then shouted: "I've got it."

He would not explain, but said: "Wait here a moment." He ran upstairs, and came back with a sheet of white paper at the top of which he had typed: "Since the Crédit Etranger, with 250,000,000 frcs. capital, lacks the means to pay for a glass pane, value thirty-eight pesetas, its staff have pleasure in paying for it."

Pressing the sheet against the wall, he put down his signature, all curves and scrolls. "And now—anyone who doesn't sign this is a yellow bastard!"

The sheet filled sluggishly with signatures. One of the men tried to sneak away, but Plá caught him by the coat tails.

"Now where are *you* going?"

"Upstairs."

"Have you signed?"

"No, I haven't."

"And you're a trade unionist? You sign. You sign, God's truth! The others who are not our comrades have no obligation to sign, but you will do it, or I'll take away your membership card and slap your face with it! You bastard!"

The timorous man put down a shaky signature. After that the paper was passed in secret from one department to the other. In the end, when it bore over a hundred signatures, one of the Heads of the Department got hold of it in the Deposit Section, and took it up to the Management. Now what? We tried to console each other: "They can't sack all of us!" Tense hours of waiting passed, while we all watched the big stairs every time a messenger came down. Towards the end of the evening Corachán sent for me. This time I did not have to wait in the anteroom. I went straight into his office. He was sitting under the lamp which made the plate glass on his conference table glitter, turning the pages of a dossier. My dossier, probably. He kept me standing in front of his table for a while, until he said:

"You are the employee of the Coupons Section who broke the plate glass?"

"Yes, sir."

He had the sheet of paper filled with signatures lying beside him. He spoke in a chilly voice, somewhat hoarsely.

"The Management of the Bank has decided not to deduct the price of the plate glass from your salary, because the Bank fortunately does not need the money. But since matters of this order cannot be left without appropriate punishment, an entry will be made in your dossier."

"What entry, sir?"

"What entry—a bad mark, of course. You won't persuade me that it is possible to smash a sheet of plate glass with a stamp. Plate glass the thickness of this!" He caught the rim of the glass panel on his table between his thumb and forefinger. "The only way to break this is by playing with it, as you did. After all, you're nothing but young cubs, you people. But I'm no fool."

"You're no fool," I burst out, "but you're an idiot. With this blotting paper weight, which is of wood"—I lifted the blotter and held it over the glass sheet—"I can smash your glass cover here, and your head, and the head of your bitch of a mother. You're just angry because of the subscription list. Yes, sir, it's a shame that the Bank should want to take away half my salary to pay for a glass pane which is insured anyhow. You're a pack of robbers and scoundrels." Gently, but firmly, Carreras, the Assistant Director, grasped my arm from behind.

"Are you mad, boy?"

"Yes, I'm mad with disgust and rage and contempt! This fellow here in his frock coat who hides in the lavatories to catch employees smoking, because that's how he shows he's worth his salary and his job in the Management—this fellow is a swine and the Bank is a pig sty!"

I went out, slamming the doors and going on shouting even when I was on the stairs.

At my desk I wrote out a receipt for my salary until that day and asked Perahita to get me a testimonial for my work.

"A clean testimonial, with no black marks, for my three years of hard labor. Tell Corachán that if he refuses I'll go straight from here to the People's House, because I'm a trade union member." I waved my membership card in his face.

The cashier took my receipt and said:

"I can't pay you out without the endorsement of the Manager."

"Go up and get it, then."

"You go yourself, or I can't pay you."

"Listen," I said to him in a low, tense voice, "I don't want to get you into trouble. Ring up Corachán, do whatever you like, but pay me out, or I'll make the biggest row there ever was in front of all the clients."

The man gave in and paid me half a month's salary, 37.50 pesetas.

Perahita came down on an errand of conciliation.

"I've spoken to Corachán, there's no need for you to leave. All you've got to do is to apologize, and you can stay on in the Bank without any bad mark in your dossier."

"D'you imagine I'll climb these stairs again to lick that man's bottom? And what for? So that my mother has to go washing clothes by the river? No, my dear friend, no. I'm too much of a man for that!"

I picked up the testimonial and walked to the entrance door. The huge hall of the Bank was studded with desks whose plate-glass covers shone like diamonds under the milky globes of electric light.

The Calle de Alcalá was full of noise. Newspaper vendors went by shouting, with enormous sheaves under their arms. People tore the papers out of their hands. The European War had begun.

At home my mother listened to me, sitting on her low chair, a piece of needlework had fallen from her hands, her hands on her lap. I told her what had happened, with a heavy heart. At the end I swallowed and said:

"So I've left the Bank."

We were both silent. Her fingers played with my hair, plaiting and un-plaiting it. After a short while she said:

"See what a child you still are!"

ARTURO BAREA

THE
TRACK

CONTENTS

PART I

PART II

AUTHOR'S FOREWORD

It does not seem easy to me, the author, to classify this book and *The Forge*, of which it is a kind of continuation. In *The Forge* I tried to show the world of my childhood in Madrid and Castile, and therefore it had to be called an autobiography. The present book describes the world of the Spanish Army, which I had known as a young man, and my own reactions to it, and therefore it also must be called an autobiography. But neither of these two books is meant to be auto-biographical in the strict sense of the term, for neither has been written with the intention of telling the public about the author's private life.

It is true—and this constitutes the autobiographical character of what I have written—that in *The Forge* and *The Track* I have tried to put down life as I have seen, lived, and imagined it at the time, as well as the history of my own adjustment to this life—to put down with as much sincerity, detachment, and ruthlessness towards myself and others as I could summon. Yet, in another sense, these two books are novels written in the first person : the child of *The Forge*, the young man of *The Track*, whom you may learn to know through my writing, no longer exist. A great deal of them may live on in me, transformed but still active; yet they are no longer " I ", not my self of to-day. I have tried to present them as they were, uncoloured by the glasses through which I see things to-day, as I might wish to write with truth about somebody other than myself. Neither of these two autobiographical books of mine embodies my present state of mind, imagination, and opinions otherwise than indirectly, through the pattern of what my memory has selected or rejected.

In attempting to resurrect myself as a child and a young man I had a very personal objective : I wanted to discover how and why I became what I am, to understand the forces and emotions behind my present reactions. I tried to find them, not through a psychological analysis, but by calling up the images and sensations I had once seen and felt, and later on absorbed and re-edited.

I also had a general objective. In taking and exploring my past self as a member of the Spanish generation which was the core of the Civil War, I hoped to expose some of the roots of that war. I wanted to describe the shocks which had scarred my mind, because I am convinced that these shocks, in different individual forms but from the same collective causes, scarred and shaped the minds of other Spaniards too. I wanted to expose my own reactions, because I believed that the others' reactions were determined by kindred forces, and that the world they saw was the same as mine, even though seen through different lenses.

What I have recorded in this book of the Spanish War in Morocco and the military dictatorship of the 'twenties, prelude to the fall of the Spanish Monarchy, is historically as strictly true as any individual experiences can be. I have checked the objective facts with my limited resources as a counter-check on my memory. It has become clear to me that what I witnessed was the embryonic stage in the development of military fascism in Spain, more particularly the beginnings of General Franco's political career. But I have constantly endeavoured not to let my present knowledge and conviction impinge upon the picture I formed at that time, because only the picture is historically relevant.

A very distinguished critic of *The Forge* pointed out that " the experiences chronicled by the author " are not " at all singular ", and that " the conversations . . ., the discoveries . . . and the disillusionments of experience are such as could be described by millions . . . ". This is perfectly true of the present book too, and it is as I think it should be. (It is, incidentally, also the reason why I cannot consider these books of mine as straight autobiographies.) The millions who shared the same experiences and disappointments do not usually write, but it is they who are the rank and file in wars, revolutions and " New Orders ", they who carry on in the Old Order, helpless, restless, and disillusioned. Some of them defended Madrid, some evacuated Dunkirk; others died for General Franco; some of them in this country wonder just what the war is about. They are usually called the common people or the " little men " or the " lower orders ". As I was one of them, I have attempted to be vocal on their behalf, not in the form of propaganda, but simply by giving my own truth.

There are stories, true stories, which I love to tell to my friends, but have not included in this book, such as " How I entered the Sacred City in Disguise together with the General ", or " How I leapt

Naked from a Bedroom into a Moorish Café ". These would have been suitable tales for an anecdotal autobiography which puts the highlights on the spectacular and amusing; but to me they carried no deeper association, either personal or general, and so I left them out. Yet the filth of the hospital, the gory nightmare of the massacres, the technique of petty graft, the boredom of endless marches, the boredom of night life, the noise of taverns, the unquestioning comradeship of the army, the smell of the sea at dawn, and the glare of the African sun—all this made us what we are, and this I have chronicled.

I am working on a third autobiographical book—autobiographical in the same sense as this and *The Forge*—in' which I deal with the crash towards which we travelled along this track : the Civil War. I could not have embarked on that third book without having laid bare the roots of the catastrophe, such as they existed in my own life. But I want to say frankly that I already mean the present book, *The Track*, just like *The Forge*, to illuminate to the public of this country the dark psychological and social under-currents of the Spanish War and its aftermath, which are so palpably still an integral part of this greater war.

And after all, the Spain which I would like to show to the British public must needs be a part of the greater peace.

It would be fatuous for me to give the usual thanks to the translator, because in this case the translator is my wife. But I want to acknowledge the great debt of gratitude we both owe to our friends Olive Corthorn Renier and Margaret Rink, who revised the English version of this book.

ARTURO BAREA

Fladbury, Worcestershire,
April 1943

1. Under Canvas

I AM sitting on a stone, polished by millions of raindrops, smooth like a bare skull. It is a whitish stone, full of pores. It burns in the sun and sweats in the dampness. Thirty yards from me stands the old fig tree, its roots twisted like the veins of a robust old man, its contorted branches hung with the trefoil of its fleshy leaves. On the other bank of the stream, beyond the ravine, the remains of the *kabila* straggle up the hillside.

A few months ago a group of huts stood there, built of straw and twigs. Inside, mats of plaited straw. One mat in the doorway, where you left your heelless slippers, the babouches, on entering; another inside, on which you squatted down round the tea cups. A few bigger ones lined up along the wall for sleeping. The *kabila* was nothing but straw huts and straw mats. Its bread was a kind of cake baked on hot stones and made of grain pounded between stones, a blackish cake bristling with bits of singed straw. The sharp hairs of the dry wheat ears stuck in your throat and bit you there with their hundreds of teeth.

The *kabila* would wake up in the morning and its men would come out of the huts, each beating his pitiful little donkey. Then he would mount it and his babouches would flap on the ground, so small was the donkey. Behind him came his wife, burdened, everlastingly burdened. The three would go to the flatter part of the hillside and the man would dismount. The woman would unstrap the wooden plow from her shoulders and harness it to the donkey. Then she would meekly yoke herself to the plow and the man would inspect the knots in the harness of donkey and woman. He would take hold of the plow, and the woman and the donkey would begin to walk, slowly, in step, the donkey pulling the ropes with his collar, the woman pulling the rope crossed over her flaccid breasts, both working slowly, planting their feet deep in the soil and sinking into their knees at each stop.

The lords of the *kabila* would begin their morning on horseback, on nervous little horses with thick manes. Their rifles slung on a bandolier, they would disappear into the hills. Nothing remained in the *ƙabila* but the chickens, the sheep, and the children, all playing about between the huts, pecking, browsing, tumbling in the dust; all smeared with dirt and slime, all toasted and bleached by the sun.

A few months ago the *ƙabila* was razed to the ground. It was done from so short a distance that the artillery had no need of range finders. The captain of the battery had said:

"What for? You simply fire, just as you throw a stone at a dog."

At the first shell, everything had come tumbling down. The straw of the huts burst into blazing chips. The children fled uphill among the rocks. The chickens and the sheep scattered as their instinct drove them. The women gave piercing shrieks which resounded throughout the valley. The lords of the *ƙabila* made their horses caracole, brandishing their rifles in the air. When a few shells had been fired, the infantry marched up the hill and occupied the hamlet. The soldiers rounded up the scattered chickens and sheep which returned to their homestead at sunset. They lit their campfires and ate their evening meal. The air was full of the breast feathers of chickens, which drifted slowly around, sometimes settling gently in a bowl. The operations had gone according to plan. At nightfall there was nothing but some heaps of smoking straw and two or three children mangled by the first shell, chicken feathers drifting in the air, and sheepskins, a banquet for flies, stuck on crossed poles. The place where the *ƙabila* had been smelled of jute from the thousand sandbags which formed the parapet; it smelled of roast meat, of horses, and of soldiers, of sweaty soldiers with lice in every fold of their uniforms.

The General who had conquered the *ƙabila* was sitting in his tent. On his table was a burning candle end, a tray, two bottles of wine, and several glasses. The officers of the units which had taken part in the conquest entered his tent one by one, each reporting his casualties in dead and wounded. Every officer had two or three dead, ten or twelve wounded to his credit. The General's adjutant noted them down. The General offered each officer a glass of wine. They went away dreaming of the decorations which the list of dead would bring them. During the night the General snored the snores of an old drunkard who sleeps with his mouth open and his teeth swimming in a glass of water.

The next morning the notables of the *ƙabila* arrived. They brought a bull and cut his throat before the General whose eyes were still puffed with sleep and wine. The bull bellowed to all the valleys and all the rocks on the hills. The General made a speech, though he wanted to go back to sleep. "Why must this rabble come so early in the morning?" he thought. Afterwards his adjutant gave the notables a bag of silver coins.

Months have gone by since this glorious battle in which a heroic army gained a great victory over the *kabila*. The *kabila* no longer exists except for a few smoke-blackened patches. Now I am here. The valley is like an ant heap. Hundreds of men are breaking up and leveling the ground for a broad track which is to lead past the foot of the hill and which will be very useful for the *kabila*. Well, the *kabila* will not be able to make use of it, because it exists no longer. But people say there is iron and coal in these hills. Perhaps a mining town will soon spring up where the *kabila* stood, or perhaps a blast furnace. Along the road, a train will run laden with ore and pit-coal. The Moors from the old *kabila* will come back; they will eat white bread without harsh straw. They will travel in the train, grimed with coal dust. They will go to the town and amuse themselves at the fair. They will ride on the merry-go-round and visit the booth with the Negro at whose face they can throw balls. They will shriek with laughter at the Negro's grimaces and will go back to the mines happy.

In the hills there will be a house built of cement, full of soldiers. When the Moors are no longer happy with the mine and with the bruised nigger, the soldiers will set up their machine guns.

But all this will come later, and perhaps I shall never see it. Yet the track for the road must pass here at the foot of the *kabila* and through the place where the old fig tree stands. As its roots go very deep we shall blow up the tree with half a dynamite charge tomorrow. Underneath the trunk we are boring a hole which will reach to its very heart.

And we have eaten its last figs. They were sweet as old honey.

Córcoles and I went right up to the Zoco del Arbaa in one of the four lorries which we had to take to Hamara Hill loaded with material. In the Zoco a group of soldiers was waiting for us under the command of Herrero, a re-enlisted sergeant, a veteran of Africa, dry and bony, with a good-natured face and sun-bitten but finely drawn features. We made friends on a few bottles of German beer, cheaper in Morocco than beer from Spain. The twenty soldiers of the group began to unload the lorry and to load the mule team which was to carry the material to the Hamara position. It was astonishing to see, as the pile on the ground mounted, what a load the four vehicles had contained: plaster and lime, cement and bricks, iron bars, wooden planks, and sandbags. The soldiers came and went. Those on the top of the lorries played at stoning the others, throwing the bricks from hand to hand in a chain. Time and again they furtively turned to take a look at me.

They wanted to look at the new sergeant with the silver stripes on his cuff, all new and shiny, sewn on a fortnight ago. "What will he be like?" they whispered to each other.

Córcoles and I left with the first convoy of mules which was loaded up, while Herrero stayed behind with two soldiers to see to the rest. Córcoles took the head of the column and asked me to bring up the rear so that nobody should straggle. Thus I went behind all the others, absolutely alone. I looked curiously at the landscape. The men in front talked about me. I felt it almost like a physical impact, but it produced no reaction in me. I looked at the landscape.

To the left there was the endless chain of bald granite mountains which follow the coast of Africa from Rio Martin to Alhucemas. To the right marched the distant green mountains of the Jebel Alam. We rode through a valley which was nothing but a wide, sand-filled bed into which the torrents poured from the mountains during the great rains. The gray-white granite and the yellow sand shimmered in the sun, glittering with sharp points of light, but the green mountains were soft and restful to the eye. Before us, tawny hills enclosed the bottom of the sandy waste. One of them was Hamara.

We reached its foot after two hours of march choked by the heat and the dust which the hoofs of the mules kicked up. A stream traced a semi-circle round the hill whose steep slope rose abruptly from the water. On the edge of the stream the bridle path was slushy where men's feet and horses' hoofs, wet from crossing the ford, had heaped up the mud. The crest of the hill was level as though its summit had been sliced off with a knife. Our position was there, on the round plateau: a circle of stone, three feet high, behind a circle of rusty wire bristling with spikes; inside, dirty canvas tents and two small wooden hutments. This was my first sight of Hamara.

Córcoles stayed with the soldiers who unloaded the mules, and I went to report to the Captain. As I did not know the ground I stumbled over tent ropes half hidden by the weeds and made two or three unnecessary detours. The soldiers behind my back tittered as they watched me, and I entered the Captain's tent in a state of irritation.

"All right," he said, "go to the sergeants' tent and rest until dinner time. Then I will introduce you to the company."

In the tent there was another sergeant.

"You're the new one, aren't you? . . . Manzanares, this is Sergeant Barea."

The orderly was a tiny little man with rapid movements, his features mobile as though his face were made of soft rubber. He spoke with the purest Madrid accent:

"Everything's in order. Here's your bed, good as a king's. And just let me know if you want anything."

"What about something to drink, then?"

"Poof! Heaps and heaps. Whatever you like: wine, beer, eau-de-vie, brandy, everything except water. Water gives you marsh-fever. Prohibited. The only thing it's any good for is washing."

"Bring me the coolest stuff you have."

He brought a bottle of wine which was instantly covered with a gray film of condensed moisture. The wine was almost ice cold.

"Have you got ice here?"

"No, indeed, sir, it's cooled by the sun."

I laughed in my ignorance. At five in the afternoon the sun was scorching hot and the tent like an oven. The sergeant asked me the obligatory questions and told me the obvious things. Anything new in Tetuan? I did not know, I had come fresh from Ceuta. He had not been to Ceuta for two years. There were four sergeants: Córcoles, and Herrero whom I had met, another one called Julian out on the track, and he himself, acting as orderly sergeant this week, besides being mess sergeant. His name was Castillo. Dinner time was at six in the afternoon. And then the orderly came to tell Castillo that the Captain wanted to see him. I was left alone and stared at the tent which was to be my home.

In the center, a pole about thirteen feet high supporting the canvas which stretched cone-shaped, with a diameter of twenty feet at the base. The rifles and knapsacks of the four sergeants leaning against the pole. The door, a gap in the canvas. Opposite the opening a folding-table and half a dozen seats hewn roughly out of branches. Seven beds, like the spokes of a wheel, head ends pressing against the sloping canvas wall of the tent, feet ends towards the center. Each bed made of six stout branches rammed into the ground, their upper ends in the shape of a fork, carrying a framework of four other branches to which a piece of wire netting had been nailed. Over the wire netting a mattress and bolster of sacking filled with straw, two sheets, and a blanket. Beside every bed a box or suitcase. But there were seven beds and we were five.

The bugle sounded for the meal parade. I buttoned up my coat and went out. Two enormous cauldrons were set up in the open space outside the encampment. A double file was slowly forming up, headed by the corporals. On the other side, beyond the file, was a huge wooden structure, obviously a storehouse, and a few straw huts no more than six feet high. Moors in filthy, tattered burnouses crawled through the low openings and clustered round the huts.

Herrero began the roll-call, standing in front of the double file formed by about one hundred men. When he had finished he waited until Captain Blanco, accompanied by a lieutenant and an ensign, came out of his tent. Herrero shouted:

"Atten-tion! Nothing to report, sir."

The Captain called me to his side in front of the double file.

"Sergeant Barea has been detailed to the Company and has joined us today." He turned to me: "Stand the company at ease."

"Company—stand at ease!"

I was presented. Afterwards, the Captain introduced me to Lieutenant Arriaga and Ensign Mayorga.

While the food was handed out, Córcoles introduced me to the last of the four sergeants, Julian. They made a good pair. Córcoles was tall, a gypsy type, with frizzy hair, nervy and lively; Julian was short and very plump, with the voice of a soubrette, smooth, apple-red cheeks and lanky hair.

The soldiers took their tins away and sat on the ground to eat. Then the Moors lined up, some carrying rusty, dented old mess bowls, others empty tin cans. The cook had doled out a ladle-full to each of them; the Moors went and squatted round their huts, most of them eating with their fingers, and a few with the short army spoons.

I looked at everyone and everyone looked at me. They whispered their impressions to each other, and I felt that some of them would have liked to come and finger me to find out more. The stare of the crowd annoyed me. It was a stare which hid distrust.

After the meal, the Captain sent for me to his tent.

"As from tomorrow you will be in charge of the works. These are the instructions I have received from Tetuan. Apparently you know topography. That's correct, isn't it?" He talked somewhat haughtily, squinting at me. The Captain was terribly cross-eyed.

"I know something of topography, sir."

"And of accountancy?"

"Yes, sir. More, really."

"All right. As from tomorrow you will take charge of the material and wages account and of the construction work. As my adjutant, of course."

"Of course, sir."

"You can go."

"But I would like to ... ."

"You can go."

"At your orders, sir."

When I left the tent I felt dazed. Ten months before I had been a civilian in Madrid. In the interval I had been a private and then a corporal; I had gone from a civilian to a military office, continuing to work among papers and figures. From one day to the next I found myself in the heart of the Lesser Atlas, in a front-line position, in charge of the construction of a road of which I did not even know the destination, and with the accountancy of works which I did not understand. Moreover, I was a sergeant, that is to say, a vertebra in the spine of the army, or rather—so much I did know—a member of the group which is kicked from above by the officers, and from below by the men.

In civilian life you weigh up difficulties and pit yourself against them, or else you avoid them. If you fail, it is bad luck; if you win, it is your merit; if you avoid the fight, you stay where you are and nothing happens. But in the army it is different. They confront you with the difficulties and you must tackle them. If you fail, they punish you; if you win, you have done your duty. In my civilian life I would never have dreamed of applying for the post of surveyor and accountant of road works. In the army the Captain had cut short my expostulations: "You can go." What the devil was I going to do next morning?

I went back to our tent. On one of the seven beds lay a civilian who raised himself on his elbow when I entered. A massive man, rather stout, his trousers unbuttoned, wearing only a singlet which showed the thick, dark mat of hair on his chest. Square hands folded over his paunch; sausage-like fingers with black tufts of hair on their backs; his shoe soles studded with thick, square nails; loosely hanging red socks. He pointed to a case of beer bottles at the foot of the bed: "Help yourself, but it isn't very cold." I poured out a glass of beer and gulped it down. Who was this fellow, this civilian in the sergeants' tent? He sat up on the bed, his belly folding in three rolls of fat.

"I believe we don't know each other yet. I'm José Suarez. Everybody calls me Señor Pepe. The stone contractor. I'm sure you and I will get on well together."

"I suppose so. Why not?" I introduced myself.

But the man was expansive. He got off the bed, holding up his trousers with both hands, and sat down opposite me at the folding table. He fumbled in an enormous cigar case and selected a cigar after crunching one or two between his fingers.

"Smoke this one. It's excellent."

"I'm sorry. I only smoke cigarettes."

"Me too. But these cigars are necessary for business." He grinned a knowing little grin.

We lit our cigarettes and fell silent, looking at each other. In the end he said:

"I suppose you know all about everything."

I started laughing, somewhat artificially. "Heavens, man, I don't know anything. As they say in Madrid, I've just come here from my village. The day before yesterday I was in Ceuta, today I'm here, without ever having served as a sergeant in a field company before, to say nothing of all this business of road making. To make things worse,. I don't know anyone here. So I just don't know anything about anything."

The orderly entered with a snack and another of his moisture-filmed bottles of wine. Behind the fat man's back he gave me a wink.

The other said: "That's what I thought. And that's why I'm glad we've met here alone. We don't need more than five minutes, and everything will be settled. I told you I'm the stone contractor. I've got a gang of Moors working, some quarrying and some crushing stone. The Company supplies the dynamite and I pay for it. And then the Company pays me the stone per cubic meter. You've got to book the dynamite I use and the cubic meters of stone I deliver. At the end of the month we clear accounts. Sometimes my Moors help your people to level the ground, and it's the same thing: so-and-so many cubic meters of earth, so-and-so many pesetas."

"It doesn't sound very difficult to me. I don't think we shall have any quarrel."

"Certainly not. There's enough for both. It's my custom to give a third of the benefits."

"To whom?"

He gave me a look of blank surprise: "To whom d'you think? To you in this case."

"You mean the accounts won't be straight?"

"The accounts will be as straight as anything. No one can find any fault in them. Of course, you must pass them. The Captain takes the other third."

"The Captain is in it, then?"

"We couldn't do anything without him. You go and ask him."

"I won't ask him. If he wants to tell me something he can come to me."

I must have answered rather sharply. Señor Pepe shut up. We talked about anything and nothing. After a short while he buttoned up his trousers and left. "I must see how the boy's getting on," he said. Who the devil was the boy? Ten minutes later the Captain sent for me.

"At your orders, sir."

"Shut the tent flap and sit down a moment." He looked at me with each of his eyes separately.

"I presume you've settled things with Pepe."

"He has spoken to me, sir. But I didn't really understand him. I don't know anything yet, as you will realize."

"All right, all right. That's why I sent for you. I'll explain. You know, the Spanish State carries out all its public works either by contract or by direct management. If it's contracts, tenders are invited and the contractor is paid the agreed sum. If it's direct management, the amount of costs is budgeted, the administration takes sole charge of the work, and pays for wages and materials. Now it is quite obvious that this road here cannot be given in contract since it leads through hostile territory. It is built under direct management. We pay the wages and buy the materials. We map out the project and we carry out the work. The Army Works Department in Tetuan is responsible for the technical and administrative sides. Everyone here gets paid for this work. The soldiers earn two and a half pesetas per day, the sergeants six, and we twelve. It means a great benefit for all. The soldiers get one and a half in cash and the rest goes to improve their food. So there is no need to pinch anything from their mess or equipment. It is easy."

He made a pause and took a bottle of brandy and two glasses from a box.

"I didn't want to call the orderly. To continue. I am going to speak very openly to you so that we really understand each other. The Company has a particular fund into which goes what we save on our budget. For instance: the Company has one hundred and eleven men but not all of them are working. Some are sick, others on leave, still others are detailed on this or that duty. But since the budget provides for one hundred and eleven men, we get the cash for their wages. Those who don't work don't get paid, and the wage surplus goes into the Company Fund. It's the same with the Moors. According to the budget, there are four hundred of them, but in fact they're never complete. We have about three hundred and fifty here. Now four hundred simply must be accounted for: we put approximately fifty Arab names on the list and everything is fine. Who's going to count them here? The Moors earn five pesetas a day, and they get as much bread on credit as they like. But that's your business. As regards Pepe, it is more or less the same story. He supplies stone to us and we pay for it. Every kilometer of the road requires so-and-so many cubic meters of stone. But if the road has five centimeters less in width, it means in stone . . . Well, work it out for yourself. Five centimeters less are two hundred cubic meters of stone per kilometer. As a matter of fact we put something more to account. In addition the Moors help us in leveling the ground and we pay them per cubic meter. It does not matter if we put some of the work done by our men to the account of the Moors."

He drank his glass of brandy.

"There are a great many more details which I'll teach you in due course. Now, we're agreed, aren't we?"

I found nothing to say, and I left.

After supper, Señor Pepe took a pack of cards from his pocket and started to deal for baccarat, putting two hundred and fifty pesetas in the bank. I refused to play and threw myself down on my bed.

"Here, all of us play," he said.

"All right. But I can't gamble with my first pay before I've even got it."

"Don't worry about money. How much do you need?"

"I? Nothing. I told you I don't play."

"I'll give you one hundred pesetas as a present. Sit down with us." I sat down. He dealt the cards, and I put the one hundred pesetas on the first cards he offered me.

"Now look here, that's no way to play. If you lose I'll have to give you another hundred pesetas."

I won the hundred pesetas and two thousand more. Señor Pepe stopped the game.

"Let's leave it for today. We must talk business." Pepe's son, Pepito, who occupied the seventh bed—a large-boned youth with the face of a stone mason in his Sunday best—applauded:

"Cheers, Father."

He looked the perfect idiot: he looked like a double-dyed rascal shamming the idiot.

Señor Pepe addressed my comrades:

"Barea has heard about our custom. And we agree. I think he's had a talk with the Captain, haven't you?"

"Yes, I've heard about everything. But I am not sure that we have agreed. Señor Pepe is to give me one-third of the price of the surplus stone I'm to put to account."

Córcoles exclaimed:

"One-half!"

"You agree, Don José?" I asked.

"Well, one-half for all of you, of course."

"Good. Now the Captain. He explained to me how it works with the wages and with Señor Pepe, but he didn't offer me anything. Apparently he gets it all."

Córcoles spoke up.

"The Captain won't offer you anything, of course. But it's all very simple. You can't ever pay wages to exactly four hundred Moors and one hundred and eleven men. The figures must always be less; if they were complete it would look funny. We keep, say, a day's wages of ten Moors, and it means fifty pesetas per day for the five of us. The same happens with Señor Pepe's stone and earth. That's where our profit comes in."

"And the Lieutenant and the Ensign?"

"The Lieutenant is a millionaire and has no idea of the whole game. Just imagine: he's a man who doesn't draw his pay and gives it to the soldiers' mess. The Ensign has a share of our part and a share of the Captain's too. He's a sharp one."

"So the Captain keeps all the savings of the Company for himself?"

"Don't be an ass. The company savings are what can be saved on the military budget of the Company. The savings from works and buildings are shared out between the Captain and the Works Department in Tetuan."

"Then the Major is in it too?"

"Now listen, without him we couldn't do a thing. Don't be stupid."

None of us spoke. It seemed to me that I was playing the fool. The cards were scattered on the table; I began to gather them mechanically.

"It seems robbery to me."

"So it is," said Córcoles. "We're robbing the State."

"And suppose I don't feel like stealing, what then?"

Córcoles looked at me, shrugged his shoulders and began to laugh. But my face was taut and serious. He stood up and took my arm.

"It's damned hot here. Come along, let's go outside for a bit."

We went out together and leaned against the stone parapet. It exuded moisture. The fields lay silent, furrowed by the moonlight.

"Did you seriously mean what you said?"

"Yes. This is a foul business. It's stealing."

"Listen. Stealing is when you take somebody's money. But this is quite different. It's the State. If we rob anybody it's the State—and the State is fleecing us anyhow. Do you think you can live on a sergeant's pay, ninety pesetas a month? Do you think you can live on the pay plus the war bonus in Africa, one hundred and forty pesetas? You've got the right to marry. But just you try marrying on a hundred and forty per month."

He looked at the distant hills and continued more softly:

"Come closer. Listen. There's something else, too. It's like when your hand gets caught in the cogs, and then your arm, and then the whole of you. You can't escape. And if you don't agree to steal for the others and for yourself, they'll take away your job and transfer you. They'll send you where you starve to death and where a bullet is waiting for you. If you want to talk and to protest there are simpler ways and means. They'll deprive you of your stripes for some blunder which can be made to look bad. And there's another thing too"—his voice was very low—"anyone can have an accident. There are snipers every day on the way to El Zoco. Now think it over. Maybe you haven't heard what they say: behind the door of every barracks is a nail; when we enter the service we've got to hang our manhood on that nail; afterwards, when we get out, we may collect what's left, if any."

We returned to the tent. Señor Pepe held the bank once more. We played until two in the morning. I lost everything. We went to sleep in our beds, the spokes of the wheel. The pole in the center, the rifles leaning against it. One after the other began to snore. Señor Pepe snored, it sounded like a pig guzzling watery potatoes in a trough. I thought of Córcoles and his advice, of the journey from Ceuta to Hamara, of the money I had lost.

That was in the first days of June 1920.

2. The Road

THE bugle sounded at six in the morning. The camp where nothing had been moving but the gray shapes of the night sentries burst into noisy life. Soldiers shouted at each other, their tin plates clattering against the tin mugs. They lined up beside the huge coffee cauldron and the basket heaped with bread and waited, shuffling their feet in the chill of the mountain morning, until the mess sergeant gave the signal for distributing the coffee. At seven, when the general clean-up of men, horses and tents was finished, the working gangs were formed. After the roll-call the men marched downhill, each armed with a spade and pickax. Then the Moors began to turn up, some drowsily leaving their huts, others coming from near-by settlements. Many of them preferred to sleep at the camp because their homes were far away or no longer existed, but also because they could count on the abundant left-overs from the mess for their food. Others lived somewhere in the neighborhood and arrived with their leather bags strapped on crosswise, stuffed with dried figs. These figs and the bread ration—about two pounds—which was given to every man who claimed it, constituted their meal for the day. They never returned to their tribe before nightfall.

The Moors were under the command of a headman, the *Capataz*, who passed orders on to them, saw to discipline during the work, held the roll-call and occasionally punished an offender or a recalcitrant sluggard with his stick. They feared the heavy hand of their *Capataz* and never stopped working, but each of their movements was so slow and measured that lifting and bringing down a pickax or shifting a shovelful of earth seemed a matter of minutes rather than of seconds.

Señor Pepe was in despair and would sometimes use his horsewhip on the ribs of one of his Moors to make him speed up. To us, and to me, the pace of the men hardly mattered. Nobody had an interest in the rapid progress of the work. The sooner it ended the sooner the pay would stop. The soldiers showed their resentment at being used as laborers with spade and pickax. The six hundred men scattered over four kilometers of track and over the granite cliffs of the quarry, a sluggish mass moving slowly under the African sun, did not look as though they were busy building a road.

The orderly sergeant never went down to the track. One of the other sergeants usually went "shopping" to the Zoco del Arbaa. The Captain slept off the brandy of the night before. The Lieutenant slept. The Ensign slept. At seven in the morning, only three sergeants marched downhill at the head of the soldiers and the Moors. Hours later the Captain or one of the two officers would come down on horseback and inspect the track. Afterwards they would go shooting. And frequently one of them would go to Tetuan or Tangier.

Thus the road building fell automatically to my share. I had to take charge not only of the accountancy but also of the topographical work. Major Castelo in Tetuan had sent an order that I should prepare a map of the terrain from Xarca-Xeruta to the Zoco del Arbaa and suggest the tracing of the road to the best of my knowledge. Previously, the men had worked in the plain and the level ground had ruled out the possibility of blunders. But from Hamara onwards the track had to skirt hills and to lead down into the vale of the river Lau. It was necessary to plan the track carefully. This took me about three weeks, during which I adapted myself to the daily routine without being aware of it. But after this period I found myself at leisure. There was nothing for me to do but to keep watch during the eight hours of work.

I would sit down on a smooth stone between the roots of an ancient fig tree, at the foot of Hamara Hill, from where I was able to survey the whole stretch under work. Sometimes the other two sergeants or the headman of the Moors joined me for a brief consultation, but for the greater part of the day I was alone, except for the little company bugler who sat near by. He had to accompany me wherever I went; he had to give the signal for the hours of rest, to blow the bugle for any general order and to carry messages to the men. If we were to escape boredom in those empty hours of watch, we could not help talking to each other.

I could tell from his age and his size that he had volunteered for our corps, because only tall men, and men with special qualifications, are officially selected for the Engineers. This one was a plump little fellow of about thirty-two years of age, with a grave and quiet countenance but with agile movements. And he was a past master in the rogue's wisdom of buglers and drummer boys. For buglers, drummer boys and batmen are in the army what the servants are in an aristocratic residential quarter: they have masonic signs and a secret language of their own. If one of them tells you that you'd better not speak to the Captain, the only thing to do is to follow his advice.

Our company bugler, Martin, was almost illiterate in so far as he was incapable of understanding anything he read, but he was full of what he called "African Science." This ranged from the ability to tie tent ropes in scientific knots to the knack of keeping a fire burning under the most violent torrential rain; it included an extraordinary skill in mending clothes and shoes and in manufacturing watch-chains, bracelets, and rings from horsehair which he would plait into minute ringlets and links and weave into fantastic patterns. But above all he knew every single piece of news, public or private, from the organization of the next military operations against the Raisuni to the hidden diseases of any private and any general.

From Tetuan, I had carried with me a great number of French novels, most of them with engravings; I usually took a couple or so down to the track to kill time. My first long talk with the bugler arose from this habit of mine. One day he approached me:

"Could you let me take a look at the saints, sir?"

He turned the pages eagerly. The illustrations of those novels mostly showed women who would necessarily seem seductive in the eyes of a primitive Spaniard. But by chance the novel I was reading just then was *Aphrodite* by Pierre Louys. The edition was sprinkled with steel engravings of Greek scenes showing nudes. At every new page the bugler exploded:

"What a wench! *Mi Madre!* What breasts, what thighs!"

Then he contemplated for a while the printed pages innocent of pictures, and said in the end:

"The things they must tell here . . . You understand them, sir?"

"What do you think they are?"

"Well now, you can see what it is. With these painted women here and in French—well, hot stuff. What they call pornography, about all the things they're doing in bed and about how to do them. Once I bought a book like this in Tetuan, it cost me ten pesetas, and it was stolen from me later on. But it explained all the postures. And there are post cards too, but they sell them for one peseta each. Now here am I telling you, sir, and you know much more about these things than me."

Abdella, the headman of the Moors, was coming towards us just at that moment. He was a strong man of Berber type, with a short black beard, wide open eyes, his very regular features disfigured by smallpox. He wore, not a burnous, but a uniform with the badge of the Engineers, a silver tower, on the collar. Before he could speak to me in his usual perfect Spanish, slowly choosing his words, the bugler called him:

"I say, you. A damn' fine woman!" He held one of the illustrations under the other's eyes. The Moor looked at the book and addressed me in French:

"You speak French, then, sir?"

"Where have you learned to speak it?"

"In Tangier, with the French. I served in the *Goumiers* and afterwards in the Spanish *Regulares* and now I have been with the Engineers for the last ten years. That's all."

Martin looked in surprise from one to the other.

"God save us! Do you speak Arabic, sir?"

"Don't be stupid. That was French, the same as the writing in those books."

This incident had various unexpected results. Martin spread the news that I spoke French among the soldiers, and their resentment against me—the natural resentment against the new sergeant—increased. Abdella made friends with me and came to seek me in the shade of the fig tree, with one excuse or the other. The bugler saw his opportunity for chats reduced and resented Abdella's intrusion; he made desperate efforts to capture my friendship and to turn me away from the Moor. My comrades, the sergeants, grew curious; their visits to the fig tree became more frequent. In the end a little circle met regularly under the fig tree. And from there I began to establish contact with the world which surrounded me. I began to see it.

Every four or five minutes I saw that Moor repeat the same procedure: he would drop his pickax and scratch all accessible parts of his body, furiously, with both hands. Then he would shake himself within the folds of his burnous like a dog coming out of the water. Sometimes he rubbed his back against the edge of the fresh cut in the earth, before he resumed work. I went to him.

"What's the matter with you?"

"I'm ill. The whole body itches. The whole body is very ill."

His hands were knotty, reddened, covered with dry scales—scab, but a horrible scab. I pointed to his hands:

"Is your whole body like this?"

"Yes, sir, and worse."

He was a pitiful figure: tall, bony, black, hairy, with the smell of a goat from the innumerable layers of sweat which had dried on his skin; bare-foot and bare-legged, with feet like an old hen, scaly, incrusted with filth, encased in a horny covering. His shaven head was jagged with scars from the scab and from the cuts which his savage barber must have bestowed on him. His eyes were bleary. This man was not ill. He was only dirty. He carried a horrible load of dirt, accumulated on his skin in the misery of all his miserable life.

I asked him: "Do you want me to cure you?"

He stared, aghast.

"Yes."

"I'll hurt you, I'll hurt you very much. But if you want me to, I'll cure you."

"Yes."

His "yes" sounded like the humble bark of a frightened dog.

We had in store great quantities of sulphur ointment and of what we called "dog soap." This was an English soap, red, with a penetrating smell of carbolic acid. I armed myself with ointment and soap, and that afternoon after work we went down to the stream, the Moor, two neighbors of his, and I.

I told him to strip. The two others then started to rub him down with soap and with sand from the stream. They rubbed him so brutally that blood gushed from his scab-corroded skin. Afterwards they smeared him from head to toe with the ointment. We buttoned him into an old pair of uniform trousers and a blouse. The old burnous was burned. Within two weeks he was cured.

One day he brought me a basketful of figs and two chickens. He seemed a different man; he had even put on fat. He dug the earth more quickly and whenever I looked at him he laughed like a child. Then other Moors began to turn up, timidly. They would show me the scab marks between their fingers and beg for a bit of ointment. Sometimes they would bring the best within their poor reach, and leave a few eggs or a chicken and always some dried figs between the roots of the fig tree. Sometimes one of them would stop working and come to the fig tree to talk to me in secret. He would stand before me, twisting the edge of his burnous between his fingers. And finally he would say:

"Sergeant, I'm going. I'll work no more. I've had enough."

"What are you going to do?"

Again he would twist the folds of his burnous in embarrassment.

"Listen, I'll tell the truth to you. I have thirty *duros*. I will buy a rifle. But I will never come here to kill the sergeant. None of us will kill the sergeant."

"Who's going to sell you the rifle?"

"The French. Don't you know? A good rifle, with bullets as thick as this." He would show the whole length of his thumb. "Good rifles. Then I shall get a horse and a woman."

They would go away, smiling happily like naughty children and assuring me that they would not kill me. But the rifle was the whole future to them: a rifle to kill Spanish soldiers. Their technique was simple. Towards dawn they used to hide in a gully with their rifles loaded, and wait for the first lonely soldier. They would kill him, rob him, and disappear. The old Remington rifles which the French Government was selling to unscrupulous contractors found their way here. The fat leaden bullet made a peculiar noise when it left the barrel, a noise which resounded in the hills: pa . . . cooo! For this reason the snipers were called the *Pacos*. Early in the morning, soldiers of the cavalry used to ride in pairs on reconnaissance between the positions; they were the most coveted prize for the *Pacos*. One lucky shot would win them a rifle and a horse.

One morning at the end of my first month in the position of Hamara, Major Castelo arrived at the foot of the hill. He came in a Ford, in one of those legendary old Ford cars which ran even better on a plowed field than on a road. Soon afterwards a soldier came for me to the fig tree.

"At your orders, sir. Order from the Major, you are to go to him."

The Major and the three officers of our company were standing beside the car. On its black roof they had spread out my plan of terrain. Major Castelo looked me up and down. We had never seen each other. He was a corpulent, stocky man, with the attractive child-like agility of some fat men who seem at each step to sit down on their bottoms. His small eyes were alive, his hands very fine, his feet tiny and his boots unbelievably shiny in all this dust.

He pointed to the plan:

"It's you who made this?"

"Yes, sir."

"Good. Come along with us."

I took the seat beside the driver, the Major and Don José, our Captain, sitting in the back. We crossed the plain and drove up to the Zoco. On the summit we left the car and went to the edge of the cliff. Castelo sent his driver to the Company of Engineers stationed in the Zoco to borrow the necessary topographical instruments and four soldiers with poles. We looked out over the plain and waited. In the distance the peak of Hamara burgeoned from the level ground like a woman's breast. Its green, fed by the stream, was sharply outlined on the yellow earth. Don José said:

"The sun's stinging. We ought to have taken some refreshment first."

Castelo gave no reply. He addressed me:

"You've traced the road in an almost straight line but it seems too much of a slope to me." He turned back to Don José. "I beg your pardon. You have traced the track in an almost straight line. But since it was Barea who made the sketch . . ."

"Yes, yes. It doesn't matter. Personally, I find it better like this. You know, Castelo, the shortest line between two points is a straight line."

He laughed a foolish little laugh which Castelo cut short with a look.

"Don't you think, Barea, that it would have been better to make it descend with an angle here, following the hillside?"

"Possibly, sir, but it was a problem of leveling. The trench I've sketched is about one hundred meters long, as you see. An angle would mean a track of more than four hundred meters to get to the same place. There would be more earth to clear away, more firm track to construct, and more wages to pay. By my calculations we would save approximately five thousand pesetas. . . ."

The car with the instruments had arrived. Castelo handed Don José the case with the theodolite:

"Set it up in station here and adjust the levels, please." He pointed to a spot at the edge of the cliff. A soldier set up the tripod. The Major explained to each of the men where he was to stay with the sights and the poles. Don José had taken the theodolite from the case and stood there holding it. One of the men took the instrument and screwed it on. The Captain made it gyrate and looked through the sight, curious. Castelo asked him. "Ready?"

"As soon as you wish, Major."

Castelo went to the instrument and then turned round:

"But I told you to adjust the levels, Captain Blanco."

"That's right. You can see Hamara perfectly."

Castelo asked me like an accomplice:

"Would you test it, Sergeant?"

I corrected levels and reticles. Castelo turned to me again:

"Take the clinometer."

We worked together the whole afternoon, the Major and I. Don José walked up and down beside us, smoking cigarettes. From time to time he asked: "How're things going? All right?"

We returned to our position. After dinner the Major sent for me. I went to the Captain's tent. They were in shirt sleeves, sitting opposite each other at the table, between them the plan, a case with bottles of beer at their feet.

"Help yourself to a bottle if you like," said the Major. "Let Barea sit there," he ordered the Captain.

I sat down opposite the Major. He began:
"There's a mistake here, but it is a small matter. . . ."
We entangled ourselves in a long discussion of the terrain. Don José
sat on his bed and contemplated us for a while with his cross-eyed stare.
Then he leaned his head on the pillow and fell asleep. He began to snore
gently, like a kettle about to boil.
Castelo was a most intelligent man. His explanations were clear and
plain. Time and again he easily settled my doubts. He knew every foot
of the ground. The lesson he gave me was admirable. We corrected the
plan in pencil. Finally he folded it up and took his coat from the back
of the chair.
"I'll send you a blueprint from Tetuan."
He glanced at Don José.
"I'm going." Outside the tent he jerked his head towards it: "For
God's sake, don't let that man put his fingers in it. If you meet with any
difficulty, ring me up. I'll fix it for you. Where is the telephonist?"
He gave orders to put the telephone at my disposal whenever I wanted
to speak to him. I accompanied him to his car and asked him half-way
down the slope:
"And, sir, what about the Lieutenant and the Ensign? It seems to me
that you have put me in a most awkward position."
"Don't worry. The Lieutenant is leaving the company in the course
of next month. He's joining the Air Force. The Ensign—poof! it took
him twenty years to become an ensign. What should he understand of
such matters?"
When Don José woke from his siesta he asked me:
"How did you like the Major?"
"Very much, sir."
"Good. I suppose you'll have got everything clear in your mind. Do
as you like. The plain truth is that I don't understand a word of it. I've
forgotten everything. And, anyhow, what's the good of it?" He made a
pause. "Tomorrow I'm going to Tangier."

Martin the bugler told me his story in instalments. When he was born
he was sent to the Orphanage in Madrid. A few days later he was handed
over to a foster mother in a little village somewhere in the mountains of Leon. He was lucky. Charity usually entrusted foundlings to
foster mothers in the country, who applied, tempted by the pittance
which in their villages represented wealth. They would stuff the children
with bread soaked in water and come back to fetch another baby if their
charge was carried off by dysentery. But Martin's foster mother was a
woman from the mountains who had had a miscarriage. The child died

and she was left unfit to bear any more children. She nursed the foundling at her own breast, and she and her husband loved him like a son. Their relatives hated the intruder and the whole village called him *El Hospiciano,* "The one from the Hospice." When he was fifteen years old, both his foster parents died within a few months of each other. The relatives took possession of the plot of ground, the two mules, and the old cottage where they had lived, and sent *El Hospiciano* to the Hospice. Nobody wanted him there, and he could not adapt himself to life behind closed gates. He applied for the post of bugler in a regiment, and there, a boy among the men of the barracks, he became once more the spoiled child. When he had reached the age of eighteen, he volunteered for Africa. He had never left it since. By now he had served in the regiment for almost twenty years. The things he had seen!

"And what are your plans? Are you going to stay here all your life?"

"Oh, no, sir. I've got the right to retire in three years. I'll have a pension of about five *reales* per day and that, together with my savings, well—it will be enough to set up a little tavern in Madrid. And I'll marry."

"Have you saved much?"

"Just imagine. All the bonuses for volunteering. When I leave the army it'll be more than six thousand pesetas in all. The only thing is, if I'd been able to read well they would have made me a corporal in the band, and by now I'd be a sergeant in the band and would not leave."

"Why didn't you learn to read?"

"I can't. The figures and the letters get all mixed up in my head, and I just can't. It's here. I've got a very hard head." And he knocked against his skull to convince me that nothing could penetrate there.

Each tent held twenty men. They slept on straw-filled sacks laid out on the bare soil like the spokes of a wheel. Sometimes they lighted a candle and put it in the center, stuck to the tent pole. Then they would take off their blouses and shirts and stay naked from the belt upwards. They would scan the folds of their clothes and pick out the lice one by one. The louse was lord and master of the camp. Nothing in Morocco was free from lice. There was a tale that on the day of the capture of Xauen, General Dámaso Berenguer had complained because there was no meat with the meal. General Castro Girona said: "Meat?" He stuck his hand in his armpit and when he took it out there were two or three lice between his fingers. "This is the only cattle hereabouts, if that's any help to you . . ."

It was as though the louse were a sacred animal among the Arabs of the hills. They dug their hands into the folds of their burnouses and extracted lice for hours, but let them fall to the ground without ever killing them. To sit down meant to incur the danger of being assailed by a swarm of voracious insects. A pool of the stream had been widened, and the men were made to take a bath there every Sunday. Afterwards they would wash their clothes which dried quickly in the sun. On Sunday mornings Hamara was inhabited by a tribe of naked savages. At meal time the soldiers put on their sun-warmed clothes. In the evening they were infested with lice. It was a silent battle in which there could be no victory.

One evening our orderly, Manzanares, got hold of me.

"You're from Madrid, aren't you?"

"Yes. Why?"

"Nothing. Just curiosity. Hot times I've had in Madrid!" He assumed a thoughtful pose which was comic because he was such an insignificant creature, and added: "Do you know who I am?"

"Who are you then?" I asked without showing my smile.

"First they called me the Manzanares but then they gave me the nickname 'Little Marquess.' Because I married three girls by telling them I was the son of a Marquess. Two in Barcelona and one in Madrid."

I looked at our orderly; either he had megalomania or he had drunk too much wine. "All right, go and leave me in peace."

When the other sergeants arrived I told them about it. Córcoles said: "I don't know whether the story about his marriages is true. But it is true that Manzanares was a famous pickpocket. It's funny how he came to be here. The Madrid police never caught him with the stuff and one of the inspectors decided he would put an end to his career in another way. One day they arrested Manzanares in the street and took him to the station. They asked for his name, age, residence, and so on, until they came to his profession. Manzanares had money, paid his rent punctually, spent much on women and wine, but he could not explain where the money came from. 'No profession, what?' said the Inspector. 'According to the Law of Vagrancy, fifteen days' arrest.' They could not give him more. Manzanares went to prison, was given one of the cells for those who pay, had his meals brought to him from outside and lived like a prince for a fortnight. One night they opened the gates and put him out into the street. Ten minutes later the police detained him and took him to the same station. Fifteen days again. And so on for months, until Manzanares got tired and asked the Inspector: 'Well now, what's the big idea?' 'To finish you off.' They sent him back to prison, and there he thought it out. He wrote a letter to the Inspector and offered to volunteer for Morocco if they would leave him in peace. And they brought him to us direct from the Model Prison."

"And here?" I asked.

"Pooh—apparently he has learned how to pick the pockets of the Moors on their market days. But he's making money with the cards now. He's wonderful with them."

"I don't understand why you've made him our orderly."

"Now look here, Manzanares has got his philosophy. He says that as he is the only accredited thief here he will be made responsible if anything's missing. And since he's been with the Company nobody has missed a button."

Julian told me about himself.

"You know my father?"

"I don't know. I don't suppose I do."

"No, boy, you must know him. He's Captain Beleno. Master in the Workshops at Ceuta."

I grinned. Of course I knew him. Who would not know him in Ceuta? Resentful of the grin, Julian said:

"Of course you know him. Everybody does. Well, I'm his son."

"I would never have guessed it. He's thin and bony and you are a round little ball. Don't be angry, but you really are fat."

"They call me Sergeant Dumpling, anyhow. I take after my mother who's like the plug of a barrel. Well, if I'm here it's because of my father."

Julian's father, Captain Beleno, had been a boat maker in Malaga when he was a strong young man of twenty. With a saw, an ax, and an adze, he built fishing boats with the same primitive craftsmanship and the same rules as the Greeks and the Phoenicians had used two thousand years ago. By reason of his craft he was put into the Pontoon Regiment of the Engineers after being called up. At the end of his military term, his Captain suggested that he should join the army as a craftsman. In the Spanish Army various artisans are attached to every regiment, such as blacksmiths, carpenters, and harness makers. They do not serve as soldiers in the ranks but are workers employed under contract by the State and subjected to military discipline. In their capacity of persons attached to the army they are given army promotion. Workers who have just joined have the rank of sergeant; in the course of the years they are promoted in pay and rank and finally made Captain. They have the right to wear a captain's uniform but in practice they dress as civilians and go to their work in the barracks at fixed hours.

However, Captain Beleno never took off his uniform unless his task in the workshops forced him to do so. He was famous for the military sternness which he, the honorary captain, showed towards soldiers. For more than twenty years he had lived in Ceuta. His dream was that his son should do what he himself had never achieved: command a company of real soldiers. Julian grew up in the discipline of the barracks. When he was taught how to spell, he was at the same time taught the first principles of military science, seen through the mind of his father. When he was seventeen years old, his father took him to the barracks, made him sign some papers in the office of the regiment, and then told him solemnly:

"My son: today your life has been decided. Work hard, and in thirty years' time you'll be a captain in the Spanish Army like your father. More than your father, because you'll be a real captain, not a poor worker such as I am."

The officers who respected the old man put the boy to office work and kept him there until he was made a sergeant.

"But now I'm a sergeant it's all come to an end. I'm studying for the Postal Service. I'll apply, and as soon as there are exams, I'll quit. To hell with my father and the captain's pips. I wish I'd seen the last of them."

Herrero protested angrily:

"You're an idiot. If it had cost you what it cost me to become a sergeant! But of course you've never gone hungry."

I said: "I think it's quite right that he wants to get a job and leave the barracks. When I've finished my three years, I'll leave too."

"Then why did you become a sergeant?"

"Why did you?"

"I? To get my food. When I entered the barracks twelve years ago I was starved and my back was beaten blue. When the sergeants in those days boxed your ears you saw stars; and I got plenty of knocks. I couldn't read or write anything. But they told me that by learning things I'd become a sergeant and wouldn't have to go back to digging and plowing behind the mules. Listen: it cost me twelve years, but I'm proud of it. And if God grants me the health, I'll have my pension when I'm old and I won't have to go to the Home."

Pepito, the son of Señor Pepe, looked on while I packed my suitcase to go to Tetuan. I had to clear the accounts of the month and to come back with the payroll.

"You'll paint the town red," he said.

"I don't think so. The whores of Tetuan don't interest me."

"You don't know them. With money there's something for every taste. Every kind of woman . . . You tell me when you come back. But while we're talking of Tetuan, my father asked me to give you this." He gave me an envelope. There were five hundred pesetas inside.

"What's this for?"

"Now what do you think? For you to enjoy yourself with."

Córcoles and I went together. On the way to the Zoco I told him of the incident. He waxed indignant.

"The old bastard. A lousy trick, five hundred pesetas. If he had given them to me. . . ."

We caught a lorry in the Zoco, which took us to Tetuan. Castelo received me with great kindness and glanced through the pile of papers bearing the Captain's signature.

"Everything in order?"

"Everything, sir."

He signed the pages quickly and handed them to me:

"Go and see the Paymaster, he'll pay you. Come back here before you go."

I took the money and returned to his room. The Major had spread the plan of the road on the table. He pointed to a spot at the foot of Hamara Hill, between the two parallel lines which indicated the track of the road.

"What's this here?"

"An old fig tree, sir. A wonderful tree. It would cost us hard work to get rid of it. It is at least five hundred years old."

"A borehole and a dynamite cartridge, that's all."

He lit a cigarette, put his hand in the drawer of the desk. He brought it out with a paper and an envelope.

"Now go and amuse yourself. You've got forty-eight hours free. Leave the money here with the cashier if you want to and go anywhere you like. I recommend Luisa's establishment. That's for yourself and your pleasure."

The envelope contained one thousand pesetas.

3. Tetuan

FOR the first twenty-five years of this century Morocco was a battle-field, a brothel, and an immense tavern.

Córcoles and I left the *Comandancia* together. I was to be introduced to life in Tetuan.

"Let's go to El Segoviano's," said Córcoles.

"What is it?"

"The first tavern of Tetuan. Later we'll go to the House of Luisa."

"And who is Luisa?"

"The owner of the most elegant brothel in Tetuan."

"And where are we going to eat?"

"Never mind, you can get good grub anywhere. The Calle de la Luneta is full of restaurants."

We entered the huge tap-room of El Segoviano's from the street. Opposite the open door was the zinc bar, water running from the open tap in its center. Three barmen handled hundreds of glasses which were being filled with wine, emptied, rinsed under the tap, lined up with noisy clatter and filled with wine again, ceaselessly. A long shelf spanned the wall behind the barmen. On its left it bore a row of square flagons filled with wine, a column whose head alternately retreated or advanced towards the barmen. On its right it carried an ever growing row of emptied flagons. At one end a boy put full flagons in the gap, ceaselessly. At the other end another boy cleared away empty flagons, ceaselessly.

Soldiers hustled each other along the bar. Their shouts were louder than the multiple noise of clattering glasses, splashing water, clink of flagons, and the scratching of coins on zinc. People yelled hoarsely at one another. Beyond the part of the room occupied by the bar and the customers there was a chaotic medley: barrels, cases of beer and wine bottles, demijohns of eau-de-vie, paunchy goatskins swollen with wine, three-legged stools painted red, open and half-open packing cases with straw straggling from them, tin mugs for measuring liquid, full and empty flagons and sausages of all sizes and shapes. Smoked and dried sausages and hams were hanging from the ceiling. The floor was slippery with froth kneaded into a thick paste by the dusty soles of hundreds of people. And everything was swarming with flies, with millions of flies whose drone fused into a single persistent, intense note as though everything were vibrating. The only clean thing in this infinite dirt were the glasses

emerging from the running water. The room smelled like breath from the
mouth of a hiccoughing drunkard.

Córcoles pushed me forward through the crowd. "We go inside." He
went through a little door into the second room.

The dark room, with its door to the street blocked by barrels, and its
stone flagged floor, was unbelievably cool. A few dozen people were scattered among the maze of boxes, cases, bottles, demijohns, barrels, and
goatskins. Each barrel served as a table, each box as a seat. One of the
barrels carried a big tray with glasses full of Manzanilla, and another a
bottle inside a circle of coarse beakers brimming over with red wine.

There was not a single private in the room. Nobody was allowed to
pass through the little door who was not at least a sergeant. The noisy
groups were composed of all ranks from sergeants to majors. Several boys
attended to the customers and carried their pewter trays with glasses and
bottles from one corner to the other in fantastic meanderings.

Carrasco, the Company Sergeant-Major, called us to one of the barrel-
tables. He was an Andalusian who had seen twenty years of service in
Africa, somewhat bald, somewhat paunchy, a tireless drinker. He was
with a Lieutenant of the *Regulares* and a sergeant of the Telegraph Company, and invited us to join them.

"Well, how are you getting on?" he asked me.

"Not too badly."

He gave me a friendly blow in the midriff.

"Not too badly, eh? You'll grow a belly like a prelate." He gave his
friends a short description of my career. The officer of the *Regulares*
maneuvered until he came to sit beside me.

"Your sort of work must be very interesting. What do you think of it?"

Without transition, without waiting for my reply, he continued: "The
thing for you is a watch like this one"—he produced from somewhere a
gold wrist watch.

Rather flustered and believing the Lieutenant to be drunk, I took the
watch and examined it. It must have been worth a good five hundred
pesetas.

"It's magnificent," I said when I gave it back.

"You like it?"

"Very much indeed."

"Then keep it."

"Who? Me?"

"Yes, yes. Keep it. Pay for it whenever and however you like."

"But I don't want to buy a gold watch," I exclaimed.

"What a pity. This is a watch for a man of taste, not for these yokels of the Infantry. It's a watch for an officer. Guaranteed for five years. But of course, if you don't want it, that's that."

From somewhere or other he produced a fountain pen.

"But you'll want this. It's made for you. Fifty pesetas. A real Waterman. You can pay for it now or in monthly instalments of five pesetas or as you like."

"Are you a living trinket store, or what?"

"Store for everything, for everything." He gave me a business card. Pablo Revuelta, Lt. in the *Regulares*. Fine jewelry of all kinds. Cash or instalment. "One has to make a living somehow. With this and the pay one can manage."

The fountain pen was good. I kept it for forty pesetas cash down, and Revuelta went on explaining.

"At home I've got everything, and it's all first class. Whatever you like: a gold watch and diamond earrings for your girl. Payment as it suits you. You sign a contract and the regiment deducts it from your pay in instalments."

"The regiment? But debts are prohibited. . . ."

"This is not a debt, it's a purchase. All regiments in the zone accept my receipts." When we left he whispered confidentially:

"If you are in a fix some day, come to see me at home, as a friend."

In the street I asked Córcoles: "What kind of a bird is that?"

"I really don't know how he came to be what he is. An officer in the *Regulares,* but never in the firing line. Officially he has a job in the regimental office but he never goes there. His house is a regular warehouse for jewelry and he sells by instalments to the whole garrison, sergeants and generals alike, anything from fountain pens to jewelry worth ten thousand pesetas. But that isn't his real profit. You go there and buy a trinket or whatever you like. But you don't take it with you, and he pays you what it's worth minus a discount of 20 per cent. That is to say, if you need money he gives you eight hundred pesetas and you sign a contract according to which you've bought a diamond ring for one thousand. You pay it back in instalments and you can't escape because the regiment accepts his receipts and also because you have the ring in trust as long as it isn't paid in full, and he has the right to prosecute you for theft if you try to get out of it."

"Still, I don't quite understand how the army can tolerate it."

"Ta ta ta. If that man opened his 'secret drawer,' as he calls it, not even the generals would escape a scandal. Eighty-five per cent of the garrison owe him money. And apart from that he's a necessary institution. Without him half of us would be in prison. Now look here. You know, we play our game of baccarat every night. One day Herrero played and lost.

Señor Pepe lent him five hundred pesetas. He lost them. Then he took
five hundred pesetas out of the mess fund, and lost them. Señor Pepe told
him that he would not give him a *céntimo* more. And Herrero had no
money to feed the soldiers. He asked for a permit to go to Tetuan, and
came back with one thousand pesetas. They deduct fifty pesetas from his
pay every month now."

We had reached the end of the Calle de la Luneta and Córcoles turned
round.

"Where are we going?" I asked.

"We are just taking a little walk."

"All right, but let's go over there. I'd like to see the town."

"There isn't any other walk here but this street. After supper we'll go
to the Alcazaba. But now there is nowhere to go. Here you see all the
people and here you can get a drink if you like."

In the Calle de la Luneta everybody was clearly doing what we were
doing: walking up and down the street from one end to the other, and
from time to time entering or leaving one of the taverns or bars. The
street was an ant heap, but you met the same faces over again the second
time you walked down it.

The entire trade, both of Europeans and of Europeanized Jews, is installed in the Calle de la Luneta. Away from it there are silent, solitary
alleys. The street itself begins at the railway station and ends in the
"Square of Spain," the Plaza de España. In a stretch of five hundred
yards the whole life of the town is concentrated. Off the sidewalk to the
left yawn the gates of the former ghetto and pour forth a flock of squalid
little children who, with equally squalid Christian and Moorish children,
indefatigably pursue the passers-by.

There is an odd mixture of colors in the street. The khaki of uniforms
is predominant, but it is spattered with the showy white capes, burnouses,
and puffed trousers of the Moorish units, the *Regulares* and the *Mehalla,*
with the red stripes of the General Staff and of a few generals, with the
gold braid of the aides-de-camp and with the blue of the Transport Corps.
Then there are Moors, dirty, barefoot, in gray woolen *chilabas,* and Moors
from Tetuan in burnouses of white and blue silk, in shining babouches
of plain or multi-colored leather. There are Jews in loose, dirty frock
coats, and Jews in kaftans of fine wool and silk, with snow-white shirts.
There are gypsies who sell everything under the sun, beggars of all three
races, bootblacks in hundreds who assail your feet even while you walk.
And there are few women.

When I saw it first, there were so few women in the Calle de la Luneta that the passing of every one of them, except for some old and obese
Jewess, raised a murmur along the entire length of the street. A fine

dust permeated the air, the dust of innumerable ceaseless steps. The whole street was thirsty and fed the open, ever-full taverns on both sides. At nightfall Córcoles took me to the Sergeants' Casino and entered me as a member. The casino consisted of a lounge with divans and chairs, a bar, and another room for games and gambling, with a few billiard tables, some tables for people who wanted to play cards in a foursome, and a big table for baccarat, trente-et-quarante or rouge-et-noir. A crowd of sergeants and sergeant-majors were playing; we looked on for a while, risked some money, lost a few pesetas, and then went to supper. After the meal Córcoles was planning to go to the House of Luisa.

"Don't you believe that just anybody can go there. They admit only those of us sergeants whom they know. But I am somebody there."

"To tell the truth, I ought to sleep," I said.

"You take a wench to bed there and sleep afterwards."

"I don't exactly like brothels."

"I tell you it's the best place for sleeping. All the inns here make you sick. You get full of bugs and can't sleep a wink. There you pay twenty-five pesetas, and get a woman and a clean bed."

"All right, let's go wherever you like."

We crossed the Plaza de España, entered the Moorish quarter, and went up a steep little street with low houses and a pavement of round pebbles, sloping from both sides towards the middle, so as to form a dirty and evil-smelling gutter.

"This is the Alcazaba," said Córcoles. "All the whores of Tetuan live here."

I saw nothing but miserable little houses and long whitewashed walls pierced by large iron-studded gates. Before one of these gates Córcoles stopped, and a grill was opened. Somebody scanned us; a door in the gate was unlatched. An old woman met us and took us to a lounge, brilliantly lighted, over-decorated with mirrors, a table in the center and a piano in the background. She clapped her hands and from behind us entered a group of women, most of them in dressing-gowns and almost naked beneath them.

Four sergeants were in the lounge, drinking and joking. The chilly repugnance of a brothel drove me to join the men and chat with them, avoiding the invitation of the women. We talked, we laughed, we sang, we made a bit of a row. And one after the other discreetly disappeared. Córcoles and I were left, he with a girl who claimed to be from Marseilles, with a strident voice and very guttural "r's," and who was fat and heavy like a cow. I was still the center of attention of three girls.

Córcoles was rather drunk by now. "If you don't know which one you want, I'll take this girl," he said, and smacked the massive naked shoulders of the French woman. They sounded spongy.

"I'll wait for you here, if you are not too long, and if you are I'll go away. I don't feel like sleeping with anyone."

I ordered a bottle of wine for my spell of waiting. The girls looked at me with contempt. Two drifted away, one stayed with me.

"You don't want to sleep with me?"

"No."

"Do I bore you?"

"No, do stay. Drink!"

She filled two glasses and gave me one. We both drank. She sat down meekly at my side.

"Let me stay here. One gets so tired, it's always the same—the whole day long. You know . . . this is a miserable life." And she started telling me the sentimental story which I had heard hundreds of times. I did not listen. I was bored, drinking the wine in little sips and lighting one cigarette after the other. She shut up in the end.

"I'm boring you. I'll leave you—I'm so sorry!"

Noiselessly she shut the door and I was left quite alone. I went to the piano and began to poke it with one finger. In the little street outside sounded the steps of a few passers-by, and sometimes the hoofs of a donkey or a horse clattered on the round pebbles. A voice behind me said:

"Poor boy. You've been deserted."

Another of them had entered, more elegant than the rest. She wore a cream-colored dress of heavy silk which fitted her body tightly. You could see that she was naked underneath and the dress seemed to make her more naked.

"They did not want me because I am too thin," I said.

"Poor boy," she repeated, sat down on the divan and looked at me. "Don't you like our girls?"

"No."

"Do you like me?"

"No."

She went stiff as though I had slapped her face. "There are many who like me."

"No doubt. Taste is free."

"Don't you like women?"

"Yes." And I added like an idiot: "But the others."

She laughed and said:

"Nonsense—we're all alike."

She left the divan, sat down at the piano and began to play. She played well, with a nervous touch. After a heavy chord she slammed down the lid. At that moment Córcoles came back, somewhat redder in the face than before. He filled a glass with wine and drank it down.

"You're in good company," he said.

"Not so bad. Shall we go?"

She intervened:

"What is the matter with your friend? He can't leave the house like this. Who would you like to sleep with?" She said it mockingly.

"I? Well—with Madame. Let her come."

The woman turned to Córcoles.

"This boy does not know me?"

"My dear girl, he's only just arrived in Tetuan."

She took me by the arm.

"Come. You shall sleep with Madame." And she laughed.

I was so tired in spirit that I did not resist. What did it matter? You must take a joke as it comes. Madame was sure to be a dropsical old woman, tied to an armchair, with a cat in her lap. We would have a good laugh. I followed her through the labyrinth of corridors and doors, rubbing elbows with girls and with homosexuals who turned round to stare at us.

We entered a bedroom, filled with cutglass and beautiful skins. She shut the door, I stood in the middle of the room and looked. I had never seen a room like this in a brothel. When I turned round, she had stripped off her dress and was naked.

"You know, here I am the mistress."

So she is the mistress. All my instincts rose. The mistress! She might be the mistress of this brothel. She would never be mistress over me, my mistress. She was nothing but a whore like the others with the privilege of being mistress over the other whores. But I had not gone there to sleep with anyone, even less to submit to anyone. If a woman had pleased me I would have accepted it and gone to bed with her. But how could I accept it as a foregone conclusion that if I pleased Madame I must go to bed with her?

Luisa was beautiful, and I slept with her. But I was actor and spectator at the same time. As a male I was completely delivered to the woman. With my brain I looked on, and made use of all my senses to check on my sensations. I watched the woman, I heard her, I felt her, I smelled her, I sampled her mouth, as one may sample a spectacle. She must have sensed it, for she tried to carry me down to the depths of lust and to make herself mistress of me. I came to understand the power of a pimp, the power of a mentally frigid male over a female.

In the small hours of the night we ate a cold supper, Luisa and I, in a little hall beside the bedroom. Many times she put her hand on one of my thighs, and many times my hand touched one of hers. Her skin burned. When we had finished, she sat down at the piano—how many pianos were there in·that house?—and I stood beside her watching her pointed fingers wandering lazily over the keys. She leaned her head against me and I looked down on the changing planes of her powerful chin, her long eyelashes and the waves in her hair.

There was a glittering emerald on her little finger. When she stopped playing the stone was quenched, almost dead, with a little subdued funereal glow. She had a blood red ruby hanging between her breasts and when she breathed, the stone sent a flash into my eyes, like a signal. She let her hands lie on the keys like two dead birds, turned her head and leaned more heavily against me.

"You know that I am a Jewess? My real name is Miriam. My father is a silversmith. He embosses silver with a little hammer. My grandfather was a silversmith, and his grandfather too. My fingers are the heritage of generations of men who handled gold and silver." She caressed the ruby and the emerald with the tips of her fingers, crossing her hands over her breast as though in a gesture of supplication or shame. "And stones. There is no gold now. In his house father keeps his old gold coins, very old ones, wrapped in a silken cloth together with a big rusty iron key. The forefather of my forefathers was thrown out of Spain, expelled from Imperial Toledo, and he came here with those coins and that key. When the key is returned to its old lock, the old coins will be exchanged for new money. Father dreams of returning to Toledo. They say it is a city with very narrow streets where we own a house built of stone. For they tell me that all the.houses which once belonged to the Jews still exist in Toledo. You've seen Toledo?"

She did not wait for my answer but went on:

"And meanwhile we were starving. Father hammered his silver and I went begging in the Luneta, here in Tetuan."

She stopped and stroked the keys. Then she threw her head back again and laughed the shrill, dry laugh of a drunk, hysterical woman.

"Gold! Do you know that I am perhaps the richest person in Tetuan? I've got thousands and thousands, perhaps a million. It all belongs to me. To Miriam the Jewess."

She rose and turned to me, full face.

"Do you want money? Much money?"

"No. What for?" I was tired and somnolent. "Does everybody think of nothing but money here in Africa?" I asked myself dully.

"You're right. What for?"

She dropped her hands on the keys and made them jingle.

"Ask for coffee, will you?" I said.

"Do you love me? Do I please you?" she asked, pushing her face close to mine.

"I don't love you. You please me."

Her face contracted in rage.

"Why do you say that you don't love me? They all say they love me. They all are willing to do what I tell them. All are my slaves and I am their mistress, and not you? Why?"

"Because it isn't so, quite simply."

"Don't you say that I please you?"

"Yes."

"Well then: wouldn't you fight for me? Would you not kill a man for my sake?"

"No. Why?"

Why should I kill anybody for the sake of this woman?

She laughed softly and watched me. After a long and painful pause she said: "How funny!" and left the room.

Shortly afterwards one of the homosexuals who acted as servants in the house came in with coffee and brandy. I let the sugar dissolve in my cup, with a feeling of unreality at the back of my mind as though I were reading a cheap French novel.

When Luisa returned, she was wearing once more the heavy cream-colored silk on her golden skin. Her eyes had an absent look. She walked rhythmically, like the Queen of Sheba, and her mouth was taut with arrogant disdain. Suddenly I saw her in a series of fugitive pictures, as a ragged little Jewish girl in the streets of Tetuan, brushing against the immaculate trousers of the officers, stepping on the silken burnouses of the Moorish notables, spitting at the silk kaftans of the rich Jewish bankers, deeply vindictive. I could sense her revengeful hatred now.

For a second I felt afraid and would have liked to go, but she said: "Give me the brandy. I think I want to get drunk tonight."

"You are feeling tragic?" I filled her glass.

She caught the glass and looked through it, holding it against the light. Slowly she lifted it to her mouth and stopped when it almost touched her lips.

"Tragic? I? Boy, you don't know what you're saying. Others make tragedy so that I may laugh."

It sounded like good acting. And then her face underwent a sudden madly violent change and she called out. At once the homosexual who had brought me the coffee appeared.

"Has he arrived?"

"No, Luisa, it's not his hour yet. You've got time."

"Time for what?"

The homosexual stammered: "For nothing. . . . For nothing . . ."

Luisa had sprung at him and shook him furiously. He trembled under her hands and looked as if he were about to break out into sobs like a frightened child.

"For what?" she screamed.

"I thought that you wanted to stay alone for a while . . . before he comes."

She pushed him through the door and shut the bolt.

"If he only could, he and the others would like to kill me. But they have not got the courage. They're all cowards. Those because they're pansies, and the others just the same. All men are cowards."

She stared into my face in naked insult. I took a cigarette out of my pocket, with deliberation, and lighted it while I watched her eyes. Weren't those eyes somewhat dilated? Was she mad?

"You're a coward too, like all the others!"

Quickly she lifted her hand to slap my face. I caught it in the air and twisted her fingers in a jiu-jitsu grip. She bit her lip so as not to cry out. But I increased the twist, coldly and intentionally, and felt a savage pleasure in hurting her. She fell on her knees and cried even while she attempted to bite me with her pointed teeth. I hit with her own hand against them. When I loosed her fingers, she stayed on the floor and bit her arm in fury. I drank some coffee, waiting for her next reaction. She rose, filled another glass with brandy, drank it and looked at me with deep, softened eyes from which the madness had gone. Then she said slowly:

"You're a brute. You've hurt me."

"I know it. I don't hit women, but I don't let a woman hit me either. You wanted to slap my face. It's better you shouldn't have done it."

She changed again.

"What would you have done? Tell me. Would you have dared to hit back?" She beat against her breast so that the ruby jumped.

"Hit you? No. I would have spat into your face and left."

"I would have killed you," she said after a silence. "It would have been better to beat me. Do you know that I'd enjoy being beaten?"

"Get a pimp to do it. I'm no good."

For the last few moments there had been an unusual commotion outside. Now somebody knocked at the door and Luisa opened. The homosexual stood there again, his eyes filled with fright. He whispered something and Luisa said:

"I'll come back in a minute."

How tired I was. My eyelids were heavy as lead after the supper. I drank another glass of brandy. I would have liked to leave but I was dominated by a lazy dislike of going back to the town, at this hour of the night, and looking for an inn. I would stay here in one of the bedrooms, alone, and I would sleep.

Luisa was back: "Come along, some friends have come and I want them to meet you."

She led me to the officers' lounge. The room was filled with women who laughed and made a noise, the table was burdened with bottles and glasses. When we entered, all fell silent. Luisa, still hanging on my arm, dragged me to the table. Officers and prostitutes gave way in silence. She stopped before the General.

"My boy friend," she said.

I stuttered under the glare, caught by surprise:

"At your orders, *mi general.*"

The General straightened himself, his face suddenly flushed.

"None of that, my boy. There are no generals here. In this house we are all equals as soon as the doors shut behind us. Take a drink with us." And he fell back on the seat, as though crumpling up.

In a very low voice he said to himself:

"That girl! That girl!"

An officer of the *Regulares* sought me out. Instinctively I stood to attention.

"So you're Luisa's boy friend?"

I must have laughed with a stupid grin:

"Just a joke of hers, *mi capitán.*" Was he Captain? The folds of his burnous covered the insignia.

He steered me away from the table and said softly:

"Do you know that this is an insult to the General?"

"An insult—why?"

"But don't you know? Where have you sprung from?"

"From out in the country. I've never been in Tetuan. I went straight there from Ceuta, and I don't know anybody here."

"But man alive . . . Luisa is the old man's whimsy, and he'll make you pay for it. Get away before anybody asks your name."

But the General had risen:

"Let us leave, gentlemen."

In passing he stroked Luisa's chin. The officers went with him as his escort. Most of the bottles were left on the table, full. While the patter of the group still sounded in the corridor, Luisa turned round and laughed. Rage choked me. I could have taken that woman by the throat which was swelling at each trill of laughter, and I could have knocked her head against the wall. I walked out into the street and nobody held

me back. Asking my way, I found the Sergeants' Casino. It was four
o'clock in the morning. Córcoles was playing baccarat. He rose when he
saw me.

"Is it true that you've slept with Luisa?"

The game was interrupted and all looked at me with curiosity.

"Yes. And what of it? Let's go to bed."

"Wait a moment, it's nearly finished."

I sat down on one of the divans and fell asleep. I woke there the next
day when the morning was well advanced. Soldiers were sweeping the
room. I went in search of coffee or something else to revive me. All the
sergeants I met on the way seemed to have known me all my life and all
asked me:

"Is it true that you've slept with Luisa?"

4. The Fig Tree

A BORE-HOLE is nothing but a hole in the rock, a tube hollowed
out by the three-cornered point of a steel bar driven in by hammer blows.
At the bottom of this tunnel in the stone you put a dynamite cartridge, a
percussion cap and a fuse. Then you block the tube with earth rammed
in tightly. You light the fuse, and the dynamite explodes. The stone opens
as an over-ripe fruit bursts open, spattering its juice.

"What's this spot?" the Major had asked. "An old fig tree," I had answered. "A bore-hole and a dynamite cartridge." And now Jimenez, an
Asturian miner, together with two soldiers, made a bore-hole into the
heart of the fig tree. Jimenez cursed and swore. At each blow the steel
bar caught in the wood and he had to twist it round, withdraw it and
insert it again. And again it would get stuck.

"It's easier to bore granite, God knows."

The soldiers laughed: "But this is butter!"

Their effort was small indeed. A single strong blow would have driven
the steel bar like a nail into the green wood. But Jimenez had to twist

the bar loose at each blow, and he sweated. The others waited for him, leaning on the shafts of their sledge hammers.

I was sitting on one of the roots of the fig tree. I was sorry for the tree; I would have liked to save it.

Further down the track a small crowd collected. Jimenez and the soldiers stopped and looked. "We've got visitors," they said.

A group was walking along the cut of the earth at a leisurely pace, stopping here and there.

"How is it going?" asked the Major when they had reached us.

"It's a very slow job, sir. It's difficult to bore the wood. The borer gets stuck."

The Major slapped his little whip against the tree trunk.

"A good tree. What a pity we have to get rid of it. . . . Come along with us. We'll see how we can set up the bridge."

I went uphill with them. Behind us sounded the intermittent blows, dully, as though the entrails of the earth were being beaten and not those of the tree.

It was in the Captain's tent, while I was studying the blueprint of the track, that I had an idea. We were just discussing how wide a curve eight-ton lorries would need. The fig tree was a speck on the paper, a cluster of tiny white lines on blue ground.

"I've got it," I said. "There is water here."

The Major gave me a highly surprised look.

"Caramba, what's the matter with you?"

"I beg your pardon, sir. I was thinking of the fig tree. There is no need to clear it away."

"How d'you propose to arrange it? With a bridge to pass over it?"

"No, sir. Something better. A spring."

"All right. Take some refreshment. Drink a glass of beer and let's continue."

"But I'm sure I'm right, sir, there is water here."

"Wine, wine—don't drink water or you'll get marsh fever." The Major lit a cigarette and looked me up and down. I must have been red in the face.

"All right, tell us your story about the spring and the fig tree."

The Captain laughed and winked with his squinting little eyes. I could have kicked him. Annoyed, I began to explain.

"I believe, sir, that here at the base of the slope there is water almost under the surface. There is a corner which is always damp and overgrown with grass and palmetto. If we found the source we could make a spring. And then we could make a watering-place for the horses and a little square with the fig tree in the middle. After all, between here and

Tetuan there is no drinking water anywhere; if you could give permission, we could bore for water. It would cost us no more than a few blows with the pickaxe."

The Major thought it over for a moment and said:

"All right, try it out. There's time enough to blow up the fig tree."

When I returned to the tree after the Major had left, Jimenez was swearing more violently than ever. The deeper the steel bar penetrated, the more sappy roots caught hold of its three-cornered point which by now shone like silver.

"Stop. We're not going to blow up the fig tree."

With childish pride I explained my idea to Jimenez and the two soldiers. At once we found a working gang of Moors and started to dig into the foot of the hillside. A short way below the surface, water gushed out, and we went on to search for the source. That afternoon we found a water vein. By the evening it was trickling gently over the slope, flooding the roots of the fig tree.

"And now, mother," I wrote in my letter to her, "we have got hold of an iron tube and made a spout thicker than my arm. We are going to make a trough where the horses will drink, and a little square round the tree."

The iron tube existed only in my imagination. But I could not tell my mother that the spring was there, spouting its water day and night, creating a marshy hollow in the ground and flooding it slowly while nobody cared.

For the story of the fig tree was to be the *leitmotif* of the letter to my mother. I had promised her a letter every week, but God alone knows what labor it cost me to write it: to find a subject. That day the subject was the fig tree, "my fig tree," and of course it had to have a happy ending. An iron spout and a watering trough. A multitude of horses drinking with all the thirst of Africa. We, too, would no longer suffer thirst.

For my mother was a simple woman with scanty book knowledge. She read but laboriously and wrote even more laboriously. She was sixty-four years old, and she was worn out by work and sorrow. Africa was to her a horrifying nightmare, a desert land with a few lonely palm trees where Spaniards were mercilessly slaughtered. My descriptions would never sound convincing to her. How could she believe that Ceuta was nothing but a little Andalusian town on the other side of the Straits? Her mind was crammed with a hotchpotch of memories and traditions: Berber pirates, captives redeemed by friars, captives aboard a galley, rowing under the cruel whip of a big Moor who went to and fro between the benches of slaves. Oh, she never said it, afraid that people would laugh at her. She only thought it. Her brain was full of stories from old books which had been read aloud before the fireplace in the big house of the village, when she was a little girl.

When I myself was a child I used on many evening to read to her out of *Uncle Tom's Cabin,* and she never tired of it. She herself had still known Negro slaves. She told me stories of the Cuban war. Terrible stories full of corpses of Spaniards who had been murdered with the *machete,* the huge knife used for cutting sugar cane, or killed by the Black Pest. She transplanted all these horrors into the African desert. The crossing from Algeciras to Ceuta meant to her sailing the ocean, braving the raging seas and risking shipwreck on the cliffs.

But that letter—I felt it then, and I learned it later—the letter with the story of the spring and the fig tree, my mother kept among her old papers. She read it again and again, her spectacles balanced on her short nose, and she bathed herself in the fresh coolness of the old tree and of the singing iron tube which poured its water into the deep trough where the horses drank greedily.

And we put a piece of zinc tubing to the source. We made a round trough from stones bound by cement. The Moors came there for their ablutions at sunset; they greeted me:

"Salaam aleicum."

"Aleicum salaam."

One day a soldier who was digging cried out: a scorpion had stung him in the sole of his foot through the rope-sole of his canvas shoe. There were many black scorpions in the region, about twelve centimeters long, which hid just under the surface of the soil and were furious at being disturbed. The soldier's foot began to swell almost immediately. We carried him in haste to the position and called for the medical orderly, a stone-deaf young man from Cáceres. I asked him for the surgical case. He gave me a box filled with rusty tools.

"What's this?" I asked.

"The surgical case. Nobody here uses the stuff. But it's all there."

I slashed the wound open with a razor and washed it thoroughly. Afterwards I took El Sordo—"The Deaf One" as everybody called him—aside and asked:

"Who made you the medical orderly?"

"Well, it's because I'm deaf, so they put me here and told me to be careful. Everything's there, sir."

"But don't you know that you must clean the instruments?"

"No, sir. Nobody uses them here. If anybody's got something wrong he gets iodine and that's that."

"But who made you medical orderly?"

"Eh?"

"Who made you medical orderly?"

"Well, the Captain, sir, because I was no good for anything else, being deaf."

"If you can't hear, why were you called up? Deaf people are unfit for service."

"Yes, sir. But they say I'm not deaf. The doctor in my village said so. Because of the proportion you know, sir."

"What do you mean?"

"Well, sir, it is like this. When a village is so small and has so few people that because of what they call the proportion they haven't got to send up a soldier, well, then the village is put together with another village and between the two of them they've always enough to give up a soldier for the army. Well, that's what happened to my place. In the nearest village the one who was due for the army was the son of the boss, and in my village it was me. We ought to have drawn lots, but because I was deaf the son of the boss would have had to go to the barracks anyhow. So then the doctor came and said I wasn't deaf and that the son of the boss had consumption. And so I had to go. Then out here they made me medical orderly, because I'm deaf, you see."

I took over the medicine chest. During my school days in Madrid I had picked up a few notions of medicine and surgery. I taught El Sordo how to keep the instruments polished. After some weeks there was a decrease in cases of sickness such as we used to have as a result of scratches and slight wounds, which in that climate became horribly infected within a few hours. Then one evening Manzanares entered our tent just as I had come back from the track.

"We've got visitors. An old man with a big beard and four fellows with rifles, and the old man is speaking to the Captain in his tent. He's the chieftain of the village on the other side of the ravine, and I don't like the look of him one bit."

Shortly afterwards the Captain sent for me. He had the indispensable bottle of brandy on his table but his face was darker than it used to get from alcohol.

"You've got us into a pretty mess. Now you can settle it yourself with that man there."

He pointed to an old Moor with a broad, white beard, straight and strong as a tower. The Moor began to speak, rhythmically, as if he were reciting a prayer.

"My son is ill. He is very ill. His belly is hard, very hard. He has great heat and great noise in his head. I want the Sergeant Doctor to come

with me. Nothing will happen to him. I leave four Moors with their
rifles here. If something happens to him, may they all be killed."

"Now, Mister Quack, it's up to you."

I argued with the Moor. I was not a physician and I could not make
myself responsible for the cure. He ought to go to El Zoco and fetch the
doctor of the hospital there. But monotonously the Moor insisted. To
refuse would have meant shooting that night, without fail.

"Look here," I said finally. "I'll come along and see your son, I'll do
what I can and tomorrow I'll send you the doctor from El Zoco." If he
wants to come, I thought.

"You come and you cure him. Nothing will happen to you. I promise!"

"And if he dies, what then?" I asked outright.

"The will of God is supreme."

"Do as you like," said the Captain, "but I wash my hands of it. If
anything happens to you, I know nothing about it. You've gone without
my knowledge."

I took Manzanares with me and various things from the medicine
chest. To judge from the old man's description, the son must have eaten
too many figs—or be suffering from an attack of malaria, or something
of that kind. Manzanares carefully loaded a pistol.

"I'm coming along, but the first disagreeable face I see will get it."

The village lay between the chain of hills along which we were building the track, and the granite mountains which extended towards the
coast. It was only one of the settlements of a large *kabila* which stretched
for about fifty kilometers across the mountains from the foothills of
Tetuan to those of Xauen. Theoretically, the *kabila* was friendly, but in
practice the friendship of its notables was in strict proportion to the
proximity of Spanish forces. Near Tetuan they were intimate friends and
received a subsidy from the Spanish Government. In the region of
Hamara they waged war not openly but singly, from ambushes. Near
Xauen they fought openly at the side of the mountain people.

The village consisted of a number of straw huts and a few clay-built
and whitewashed houses, in one of which we found the patient. He lay
on a straw mat, wrapped in old army blankets and surrounded by a
crowd of neighbors who were smoking *kiffi* and carrying on a shouted
discussion without heeding the sick man's eternal litany: "Ay . . . maa,
ay . . . maa!"

His stomach was taut like a drum, he had a high temperature and
complained of an intolerable headache, but I felt sure that he had nothing worse than violent indigestion from *kous-kous*. Yet I hardly dared
to give even the scanty advice I thought reasonable, and told the father
than I would send him the doctor on the following day.

"But what medicine will you give him now?" he asked, glancing at the surgical instruments and the medicine bottles Manzanares had spread out on a low table.

I had to do something. Quinine would not hurt—he had fever—and a glass of castor oil would help him. I decided in favor of both. The patient let me give him an injection in the arm, though he groaned pitifully. Then I gave him the castor oil. He sampled it and then sipped it slowly. I felt my own inside revolt at the spectacle and forced him to drink more quickly. When he returned the cup he asked for more. I refused it.

The father invited us to take tea with him. For the first time I partook of a Moroccan tea, mint leaves floating on top, offered with all the ceremonious ritual of a Moorish notable. And for the first time I smoked *kiffi*. When we wanted to leave, Manzanares went to fetch the medicine chest from the sick-room; he returned with a most bewildered face:

"He's drunk all the castor oil."

The patient had persuaded one of the small boys to bring him the bottle and both had drunk from it, though the child had not liked it much, to judge from its tear-stained and oil-smeared face. The quart bottle was emptied by half.

I made a row and told the father that whatever might happen would be his fault, but he did not believe in any danger, because of the ancient and primitive idea that you can't have enough of a good medicine.

On the following morning the old man arrived at our position before we went to work. I trembled when I saw him come. But he was more than content and gave me the exact details of the prodigious purge which had saved his son. Then he asked me for advice and help against the patient's extreme weakness. With great seriousness I told him that the young man should not be given any food during the whole day except for a cup of milk every two hours. And two days later the chieftain visited us again, followed by four women carrying baskets heaped with fruit and eggs, and four chickens tied by their legs. It seemed that the old Moor now considered me his friend and that not only I but the whole garrison would henceforward be held inviolable by the members of the *kabila*.

The old man himself, Sidi Jussef, would sometimes come to the fig tree and talk to me for hours; sometimes he would invite me to drink tea with him in his house. The Captain insisted once, when he was rather tight, on making the Moor drink brandy, thus putting us all in a difficult and ridiculous position. Sidi Jussef refused and I was afraid the Captain would be hit by a bullet from somewhere, in retribution for the religious insult. But he never strayed from the position alone; nothing happened to him except the final and complete loss of face among the Moorish work-men, the majority of whom belonged to Sidi Jussef's *kabila*.

In those days we were tracing the track which led down into the valley of Charca-Xeruta. I would leave with a dozen soldiers and three or four mules carrying materials and food, and we would go far down into ·the valley, unarmed, though it would have been very easy to kill us and to steal the precious mules. Sidi Jussef had asked us not to carry arms on those expeditions.

"Sometimes the Moors of the mountains come down here," he had said. "If they see you carrying arms they'll ambush you. But we have undertaken to see that nothing happens to you." And nothing happened except that we occasionally saw the silhouette of a Moor and his rifle on the crest of a hill.

In the asphyxiating heat of an afternoon, Sidi Jussef talked to me in the shade of the fig tree, and I do not remember how the conversation started.

"The Spaniards are bad conquerors," he said, "but they are good colonizers. The Spaniard has a very peculiar adaptability. He is able to adopt all the characteristics of the world which surrounds him and yet to preserve his personality. The result is that in the long run he absorbs the people he has invaded."

He paused and looked at me, at my surprised face. For though he and I had often discussed the divergences and affinities of Spaniards and Arabs, Sidi Jussef had never expressed his opinion of Spaniards in such dogmatic form.

"Look at the history of the conquest of America. The *conquistadores* were just like the soldiers who are in this country now: adventurers, desperadoes, thieves, drunkards, and women hunters. They conquer by killing and corruption. What else do they use but brute force, bribery, or political hypocrisy, the means used by Cortés and Pizarro who sought gold and nobility, money and fame. The military conquest of America is a disgrace to Spain. But its colonization is her glory. Those poor men who went there and clung to the soil and mixed with the Indians and had sons and re-populated the land, they were the real conquerors of America. It was not the Spanish colonies which rebelled against Spain, but the Spaniards in America rebelled against their old country. They were helped by the half-castes and the Indians, but every American revo-lution had a Spaniard at its head . . ."

I told Córcoles of this conversation because it had impressed me: that Moor knew Spanish history more profoundly than many Spaniards. Córcoles shrugged his shoulders.

"They say that Sidi Jussef is a Spaniard who escaped many years ago from the Penal Colony of Ceuta. It would not surprise me if it were true. My father was a warder there and he knew many prisoners who escaped or were released and afterwards joined the Moors. They usually became chieftains in their *kabilas*. But you're taking Morocco much too seriously."

"It interests me. I think we could do great work here. If we were less barbarian than we are . . ."

"Listen, you should not take it that way. It's just business."

"I agree. It's business. We kill Moors and the Moors kill us. Doesn't it matter to you?"

"No. If they shoot me, it's bad luck; if they don't get me, I'll be rich in a few years' time."

"Yes, with the fortune you're earning . . ."

"Why not? Sergeant-Major Pedrajas has just got his papers. After twenty years' service he gets 80 per cent of the pay as his pension. He's got three or four decorations which entail a pension, without ever having been at the front. He's got 150,000 pesetas in his bank, and a house, a very fine house, in his home town. And in the meantime he has refused himself nothing, neither wine, nor girls, nor a thousand pesetas' gamble at baccarat. You see, he was sergeant-major at Headquarters for eight years, and that did the trick."

"And how did he get rich?"

"By stealing. By stealing the grain from the horses, the clothes from the soldiers, the food, the electric lamps in the barracks, everything, including brooms."

"Oh yes, I can imagine how many soldiers have fallen ill because they had to go without the blanket he had filched. And it's all the same to you?"

"No, it isn't, my boy. I have been a soldier and slept under a blanket with more years of service than Sanjurjo. But I can't alter things. Here you must eat or be eaten, there's no third solution. Of course there have been men who tried to put things in order, but all of them have failed. The worst is that even if somebody has not stolen, they still put him down as having done it."

"But one day the soldiers will rebel as they did in Madrid in '09. Or the Moors."

"The soldiers? Nothing doing. One or the other may rebel, and then they execute him and that's that. The Moors? Their chieftains are bought, and we've got the guns and the MGs. Don't get all worked up about these problems—you won't solve them. And as to the Moors: don't get too friendly with them. There is only one way to treat the Moors if you want to get anywhere, and that's the stick. And again the stick. As soon as they see you're soft you're done. That's what they're used to. The best chief for them is the man who beats them hardest. They have to be treated rough. Come with me to El Zoco tomorrow, it's market day and I'm going shopping. You'll see how one has to treat that rabble. I was born in Ceuta and I've known the Moors ever since I could crawl on all fours. Come along tomorrow."

"All right. I'll tell Julian to deputize for me. Let's see your talents as a sergeant in this colonizing and appeasing army."

"Now then—did you ever think I was here as a missionary?"

5. The Blockhouse

ANYWHERE in Morocco, at least anywhere in the Morocco of the Moors, you find yourself in the vicinity of a *zoco*. A *zoco* is nothing but a free open-air market. It is usually called after the day of the week on which the actual marketing takes place, and after the name of the district; El Zoco el Jemis of Beni-Aros, El Zoco el Arbaa of Tlazta, and so on.

Before dawn they begin to arrive by all the mountain paths, the women carrying the burden, their lords and masters following them on their donkeys. Sometimes the donkey also carries a sheep or goat slung across its croup, or a string of chickens or rabbits, all tied by their legs and all alive, for the Moors never sell dead meat. At daybreak, the open space destined for the stalls is crowded with traders who are buyers as well.

Córcoles and I went to the Zoco del Arbaa, to give the name its Spanish form, accompanied by four soldiers and three mules. We had to buy fresh meat, eggs, and fruit for the whole Company. When we arrived at nine in the morning the market was in full swing.

"We'll buy meat last of all," said Córcoles. "Sometimes it turns high within half an hour. Anyhow, it's cheaper later on."

Aimlessly we wandered round and strayed into the crowd round one of the snake-charmers. We listened to his tale, which was as usual extremely long, but left when he began his operations, because it made us sick to see the man introducing the body of a reptile into his nostrils and expelling it through his mouth.

I have never been able to resist the lure of a junk-stall, and there was one of particular fascination. Kitchen papers in shrill reds and greens spread on the ground. Boxes with candles and Marseilles soap. A couple of burning oil lamps. Cartridges for hunting rifles of all calibers in a big heap. A basket of eggs. Five chickens tied to a pole. A rusty revolver with a broken hammer, six homeless cartridges beside it, their shells covered with verdigris, their leaden bullets dented and pounded out of shape. A heap of sheep's wool recently shorn and sticky with grease, and a heap of empty petrol drums. In the center, in the place of honor, a medley of pieces of metal: bits of spurs, cogwheels of watches, big needles for sewing straw mats, pincers with twisted jaws, and so on.

The owner was a Moor wrapped in a coffee-colored, ragged *chilaba*, who smoked his pipe of *kiffi* and did nothing else. He squatted behind his display, mute while all the others around him shouted their offers. For a moment he lifted his eyes to look at us and then sank back once more into the delights of his hemp seed. Córcoles pointed to the basket of eggs: "How much?"

"Fifty *céntimos* a dozen."

"Give me two dozen."

The Moor stretched out his hand to take the money, without changing his posture. Córcoles gave him a silver coin. The Moor did not take the money but corrected.

"Fifty Spanish *céntimos*."

Córcoles put the coin back into his pocket, took my arm and left the stall.

"What's the matter?" I asked.

"You know there are two currencies here, ours and what they call *assani*, that of the Sultan. What I gave him was a *duro*, worth half a *duro* of ours. But those beggars never want to take the Arabic currency. Well, he'll call us back, you'll see."

He did not call us. We walked slowly away but the Moor stayed there motionless, blowing smoke rings. Córcoles murmured:

"Let's go back. The eggs are cheap." He said to the Moor: "Give me six dozen eggs."

"Six dozen?"

"Yes, six."

"Six dozen are a Spanish *duro*—five pesetas."

"But look here, just now you wanted fifty *céntimos* per dozen . . .?"

"That was then." He went on smoking his pipe.

Córcoles took a cartridge case from his pocket. The Moor put down his pipe and looked at it.

"You sell it?" he brought himself to ask.

"No," said Córcoles. And we turned disdainfully away. The Moor rose and came after us. He plucked Córcoles by the sleeve.

"I buy the cartridges."

"How many eggs are there in the basket?"

"Nine dozen."

"How much?"

"Fifty *céntimos* the dozen."

"*Assani céntimos?*"

The Moor swallowed his saliva. "*Assani,* yes."

"How many cartridges do you want?"

The Moor became obsequious.

"All you want to give me. Hundred, thousand, I buy."

"They're expensive, you know."

We went back to the stall. Córcoles took the egg-basket and hung it over my arm. "Here, give it to the boys; they'll pack the mule," he winked and I went away.

When I returned Córcoles had a Moor of the Mehalla, the native police, at his side. The three were in a heated discussion. After a short while Córcoles left the two others standing and joined me. "What was that?" I asked.

"Nothing. We've got the eggs cheap, at twenty *céntimos* a dozen, and it's given that little Moor a scare he won't get out of his system in three months."

"What have you done to him?"

"Nothing. I simply promised to supply one thousand cartridges at twenty-five *céntimos* apiece. When he accepted the price I called the Mehalla guard. And of course, with the police there, the fellow turned repentant, and—nothing happened at all. Those people are worse than the gypsies. You'll see. Now let's buy a goat."

The butcher's stall consisted of rows of poles with hooks, from some of which hung the skins of animals already sold. In the background was a pen crowded with sheep, lambs, and goats. Córcoles chose a goat.

"How much?"

"Seven *duros,* Sergeant?"

"Five."

"Six and a half."

After the interminable bargaining they agreed on five *duros,* the skin to remain with the butcher. "Now you'll see," Córcoles whispered.

The butcher killed the goat on the ground and hung it on a hook.

He made a triangular cut in one of its legs, lifted the flap of skin, put his lips to the slit and began to blow. Slowly the skin lifted from the flesh and the goat swelled up to a monstrous shape. Finally he cut a long slit in the belly and stripped off the skin as though it were a coat. He laid the naked animal on the table which was covered with a yellow oilcloth crawling with flies. Córcoles put five *assani duros* beside it. The vendor broke out into violent protest: No *assanis!*

Córcoles left the carcass lying on the table and dragged me away. "You'll see, the goat is ours."

The butcher followed us. He shouted, remonstrated and implored. We paid no attention. Finally he accepted four Spanish *duros,* twenty pesetas, for the goat and we took it away, with all the curses of Allah following us.

"It's very simple," said Córcoles. "He couldn't have sold this goat. The Moors don't buy meat when they haven't been present at the killing. After an hour in this July sun the goat will no longer be salable. No Spaniard would give him as much as ten pesetas for it then. Except perhaps a sergeant of the infantry."

"Why should he do it?"

"Because that's where their graft comes in, my boy. They pay five or ten pesetas for a goat or a sheep which is half rotten. They use it in the soldiers' mess, and in their account it is put down at thirty pesetas. That's their profit. You see, they haven't got extra pay like we have and they can't grow fat on road gravel like we do."

"But it's a beastly thing to do. What about the men?"

"The men? Why, they get dysentery and fever and typhus. But soldiers are cheap."

"Really, there are not so many epidemics among us."

"We're well off. You're all right out here, if you've got money. Have you ever met a general with malaria? But just take a look at the infantry, especially the Chasseurs, and you'll see."

The butcher turned up again, this time leading a goat with milk dripping from the udders.

"I've sold the kids. I'll sell her to you."

"What do you think," Córcoles asked me.

"It would be nice to have milk."

"How much?"

"Ten *duros*. Spanish."

"Five."

We got the goat for five *duros* and took her away tied to the tail of one of the mules. I resumed the discussion.

"Then you think there would be less sickness if the men had better food?"

"Of course. Well, you don't know these things yet, but I'll tell you. Nearly all the officers come here to get rich. As a matter of fact they spend all their money and never get rich—but that's by the way. It's different with the warrant officers and the sergeants. They come here as privates, directly from their villages where they've gone hungry. And one fine day they find themselves with pay they could not have dreamed of while they were laborers, and with a uniform and a rank which gives them a chance for graft. Now these are the men who get rich out here. It's time you got wise to things. Tomorrow I'll take you to the blockhouse."

Blockhouses, as we knew them, were wooden huts, six to four meters wide, protected up to a height of one and a half meters by sandbags or, very occasionally, by armor plates, and surrounded by barbed wire. In this small space a platoon under the command of a sergeant would be stationed: twenty-one men, isolated from the world. In exceptional cases a signaller from the Engineers would be detailed off with a heliograph and signal lamps to keep in day and night communication with the nearest blockhouse, and through it and a chain of others with the base. But mostly there was no such means of contact.

On a hill overlooking ours, on the other side of the stream of Hamara, was a blockhouse. Day and night we could hear the sound of stray shots over there. It was an outpost facing the valley of Beni-Aros, and the Moors were forever lying in ambush to fire at the outline of a figure or the light of a cigarette. The post was garrisoned by Chasseurs.

When I arrived with Córcoles we were welcomed by a lean and bearded sergeant, his ash-colored face marked by fever. Our horses carried a few bottles of beer, a string of sausages, and two bottles of brandy, and a dirty little man in a tattered uniform was told to cook rice in our honor. Another little man was walking up and down, a rifle on his shoulder, behind the parapet of sandbags which covered the opening in the barbed wire. The fields below us were infinitely peaceful.

"We'd better go inside," said our host. "Here you're never safe, and even less so a group of people as we are now. Those bastards are good shots."

We went inside. In the right-hand corner beside the door the sergeant had put up boards to make himself a bedroom. Otherwise the hut was a single room with bare soil for its floor. The beds of the men stood in two rows along the side walls, with a narrow passage in the middle. On each bed was a knapsack and a wooden box. Most of the men were lying there smoking. A little group clustered round one of the beds in the background gambling. At head level, the walls were pierced by loop-holes. The sun fell through them in jets of light which threw dazzling rectangles on the floor, dipping everything else in darkness until your eyes were accustomed to the twilight. There was a smell which not only assailed you through the nostrils but seemed to stick to your skin and clothes and deposit layers on them. It was like the stench of dirty linen left for months in a damp corner; only much worse.

We chatted of this and that until I said that I would like to know the details of their existence.

"He's new here," Córcoles explained. "And what's more, he's got socialist ideas, or something. He's not one of us, anyhow."

He grinned the grin of a man in the know, and the bearded sergeant looked at me pityingly.

"He'll change," he said. "As for me, you can do what you like. I'll stay here with this beauty." He patted the neck of one of the beer bottles.

I left the sergeant's bedroom and went into the common room. While I was walking along the beds the men watched me with the eyes of curious dogs. A few got up from their camp beds halfway to salute me. Further down, someone rose obsequiously:

"If you want to make water, Sergeant, the tin is over there." In a corner at the back there was an oil-drum. Later I was to hear all about it. The men used it for urinating because otherwise they would have to go outside. While enemy attacks were particularly frequent, they used it for all their needs. When the drum was full, the orderly on duty had to empty it outside the barbed wire. This feat usually provoked a shot; sometimes there would be a casualty, and the tin would be lost. The first to feel an urgent need then had the choice between fetching back the tin which was certain to be covered by an enemy marksman, or relieving himself somewhere else outside the barbed wire at his own risk. In a place where only a very few disciplinary measures could be taken, offenders were punished by double time on watch, by having to fetch water or by having to empty the tin for a certain number of days. Thus the oil-drum had become a symbol of life and death, and the main topic of conversation and commentary.

When I reached the camp bed where a game of cards was in progress, the men stopped and kept silent in embarrassment. I produced a packet of tobacco and they rolled their cigarettes, parsimoniously.

"How are things?" I asked.

"All right," one of them replied after a long pause. "If they don't hit you and if you don't get fever."

I sat down on the bed, a piece of sacking stuffed with straw, laid on the naked floor and covered with two ragged blankets.

"But what do you do with yourselves here?" I tried to make them talk. "Over there in Hamara we are building a track for the road, and we can see you from there. And sometimes we hear the *pacos*."

"Well, we don't do anything at all," said the one who had spoken before. "I've still got three months to go——"

"Then you're a veteran, really."

"Thirty-three months. I'm the oldest here. All those are just green. The number of lice I've caught! Never since I was a boy (you see, sir, when we were children we all had lice) have I had lice like in this place. They've got their nests in the boards, you know."

"What will you do when they sign you off?"

"What can one do? Work."

"Then what's your profession?"

"My profession—digging and plowing with the mules. What profession can you have in a village, if you're not a priest? And the priest has to dig sometimes, too. So it means everybody to the land!"

"Now look here, there must be some shops in your village, and a doctor and a chemist. And a cobbler. They can't all be laborers."

"Oh, yes, sir. I'm from a little place in the Sierra called Maya, in the province of Salamanca. And there's nothing like what you say. A sort of inn, that's all. If anybody falls ill you've got to call the doctor from Bejar. But we have a healer, an old woman who knows more than a doctor. As soon as the doctor comes somebody dies, that's sure."

"Have you got a girl?"

"Oh, yes."

"Do you write to her?"

"I can't write. The only one here who can write is Matías over there." He pointed to a soldier with the face of a poor brute who began to laugh foolishly.

"And I write her things," said the scribe.

"What things?"

"What things do I write? Well, the things like he says: 'I want to give you a good squeeze.' One day he said a good thing and I wrote it to her just like he said it. And then I wrote the same to the girls of all the other boys, and to my girl too: 'When we are married, I'll put my snout between your breasts and I'll burrow there like a pig until I choke.'"

The inventor of the phrase went red, more with pride than with modesty, and explained:

"You know, sir, if you're doing nothing all day long, you think and you think and then you get ideas. And then this chap, who's slept with lots of women, tells us things and—well, you know what I mean." He paused. "Not that I'm ashamed, because men are made that way, but then, you see, well, you can't sleep afterwards."

"So you've had your experiences?" I said to the boy who knew about women, a little town rat in an over-large uniform.

"Just imagine, sir, I was a bootblack in Salamanca, and that's something: The City of Syphilis. You've been there?"

"Oh, yes."

"Then you'll know how it is. In daytime in the cafés and in the doorways of the Square and at night in the houses. The tarts are good girls and you clean their shoes and the suckers pay. And then you've always a girl of your own. These boys here don't know anything about life."

"But I slept with my best girl before I came here," said one of them.

"You say you've slept with her? You're sissies, all of you. When you go to Tetuan you're afraid of taking a woman to bed."

"Because they're sows. You give me one of the sergeants' tarts and I'll show you. Listen, sir, in Tetuan there are women for fifty *céntimos* but they've got more lice than we have here. The only thing they're good for is when there is an operation on."

"An operation?"

"Yes, sir. When there's going to be fighting. If you're lucky you get leave to go to Tetuan and you find a bitch who's sick and you sleep with her. Then they send you to hospital for three or four months and you don't have to run about when it's raining bullets. But those lousy bitches know it and ask for double the price."

We were interrupted by dinner, a huge bucket of beans swimming in a brick-red gritty soup, followed by coffee, faintly tinted water into which the men threw chunks of bread. One of them produced a tin of condensed milk and poured a fine trickle into his coffee.

"*Caramba,* what a luxury!"

"Oh, no, sir. It's only because I've got the tertian ague and they give me a tin of milk every three days."

"But if you've got tertian fever you ought to be in hospital."

"Oh, well, that's if you've the ague all day long. But with a little bout of fever every third day you get quinine and milk and you stay on duty. Of course I'm off the day the fever comes."

We ate with the sergeant, rice enriched by the sausages we had brought along, and drank coffee which was certainly better than that of the soldiers, though it was still infernally bad. Then we chatted, the brandy bottle between us.

"How do you get along?"

"Not too badly. The kitchen yields me about ten pesetas a day. And there's always something to be got out of the clothing, even if I must leave the quartermaster-sergeant his portion. And my food is thrown in gratis: where sixteen eat, seventeen can be fed."

"It must take a bit of figuring to keep ten pesetas daily and to feed seventeen."

"Not as much as you think. Beans, chick-peas, potatoes, rice, and dried cod; oil, salt, and pepper. All from the Commissariat and all cheap. I don't spend more than seventy-five *céntimos* per head and sometimes I get a barrel of wine for them at that. I don't like exploiting the poor devils. They know I'm robbing them, but others are worse than me, and they know that too. In Miscrela they had a sergeant who fed them for two months on nothing but beans boiled with water and red pepper. My men look after themselves as much as they can. If one of the Moors in the district is careless they steal some chickens or lambs. They set traps for rabbits and when they get a chance, they shoot birds." He stopped and thought. "One earns more money, though, when there is an operation on or when we go on convoy duty. Then every man gets a tin of sardines and biscuits, and that's all for the day."

"No wonder they crack up and land in hospital."

"Those who crack up aren't any good. I've been in Africa for twenty years, and nowadays it's fine. You ought to have seen the food when I came here. Biscuits at every meal. Biscuits from the time of the Cuban war, so hard that we had to pound them on a stone with our *machetes* and soak them in water if we wanted to eat them. There are still some left, but they can't risk distributing them because they're full of maggots."

"How long do you stay in the blockhouse?"

"The rule is a month, but I stay on here. If you go to Tetuan you just spend your money. Here you earn money, and that's the only way to live. I've saved more than ten thousand pesetas already. And apart from that, one's better off in the blockhouse than at the front; it's quieter. But you, you're lucky. If I served in the Engineers, I would be rich."

Towards evening, Córcoles and I went down the hill from the blockhouse. The fields were still absurdly peaceful. A Moor rode along a field-path on his little donkey, a small dog trotted behind him. From the track, a milling ant-heap in the distance, there came the notes of the bugle calling the cease-work.

"But those men live worse than the Moors in their straw huts," I said to Córcoles.

"Never mind. Muck that doesn't choke you makes you fat," he replied.

6. Eve of Battle

I T is frighteningly easy for a man to slide back into an animal state. In the monotony of unvarying days, confined to the narrow circle of the position which was my city and to the even narrower circle of the cone-shaped tent which was my house, I slowly went under in the daily routine and abandoned any effort to break with it. Breakfast, sit in the shade of the fig tree, lunch, sit in the shade of the fig tree, dine, sleep and wake up with the same prospect before you.

At first, I used to read; by and by I forgot to open a book.

At first, I liked to go shooting rabbits and partridges; then I left my rifle leaning against the fig tree for hours; finally it stayed in the tent for days on end.

I had finished the topographical work and had nothing to do but to muster the Moors and to sit and keep watch. Keep watch for what? I let the slow hours pass by, like a ruminant beast, with a sluggish nodding of the head, in a doze, telling myself at times that I was thinking, but in truth thinking of nothing, submerged in a lazy mist.

I remember making only a single observation during that time, the observation that what happened to me was happening to all the others. The soldiers, in civilian life simple workers or laborers, were rapidly stultified and turned into eating and digesting machines, possessed by the one thought that work was something to be avoided at all costs. Everybody was degenerating in this existence without action, in the orbit of a radius of one kilometer. We all forgot what day of the week and month it was. We slept, we ate, and we digested.

When I received a telegram ordering me to Tetuan it came as a relief and as a worry. I did not feel like going to Tetuan; I wanted to go. The drowsiness was there, and the desire to break away from it as well.

In the army an order is an order. I left the following day.

Major Castelo said:

"Until the army has crossed the river Lau, we can't do anything. H.Q. need somebody who knows topography. Report to Major Santiago of the General Staff. I think you'll be all right."

Major Santiago was a halfbreed. The soldiers called him "The Chink" because he had slanting eyes and a greenish-yellow skin. Apparently he was the son of one of those Spanish officers who had been stationed in the Philippines and married a native girl. His color and his almond eyes had given him a very bad inferiority complex; he was in a state of perpetual irritation. But he was a clever man of exceptional mental agility.

He told me to sit down at a draftsman's table.

"Copy this." He gave me a topographical sketch of the bay of Rio Martin. When I had finished he examined my work carefully.

"You'll stay here. We have to make a map of the whole region of Beni-Aros."

"At your orders, sir."

"My orders! Making a map of Beni-Aros! Do you know how to do it? No? Neither do I. But we haven't any map at all and the French maps of the region are rubbish. They've drawn the line of the frontier and then a few little strokes, and that's all there is. All right, my boy, we have to make a map of Beni-Aros."

He went out of the room and left me alone with a Chasseur who was bending busily over some tracing paper. After a short silence I asked him:

"The Major doesn't seem to be in a very good temper?"

"How could he be? Berenguer says: 'Make me a map of Beni-Aros,' when nobody knows Beni-Aros, with the exception of Castro Girona who went there once to a wedding in the Raisuni's family. And there are no maps, no sketches, nothing. Make me a map of Beni-Aros. He might as well tell us to make a map of the North Pole. . . . You've come here as a draftsman?"

"Yes, I suppose so."

"Good, then there will be two of us. We'll share our furies fifty-fifty. You don't know this job yet."

He stood up and I saw that he was a corporal. Finely drawn features, spectacles for nearsightedness, tapering hands.

"Come and have a look."

The sketch on the transparent paper before him showed part of the Spanish zone of Morocco, with a blank space in the middle.

"This is Tangier, here are Tetuan, Ben-Karrick, El Zoco el Arbaa, Xauen, and here the French frontier passing by Larache. Here's Larache, Alcazarquivir, Arcila. So far, so good. But the whole white space here is Beni-Aros. And we must fill it in. Operations will start in the spring, and the plans are needed."

"How can we fill it in?"

"That's precisely the question. You'll see. They'll drop in soon."

The Major came back. "Well, Montillo, are you explaining the problem?"

"Yes, sir."

"When the people arrive, give him the necessary instructions. Barea, this is Montillo, topographer at H.Q. The two of you will have to work together, and you'll have to follow his orders though he is only a corporal."

"Very good, sir."

For a while Montillo showed me maps and more maps. He explained their method of working; they drew on tracing paper and made blueprints. There was a stupefying lack of maps. Not even a complete plan of Tetuan existed.

An hour later a native soldier of the *Regulares* arrived, together with a Moor. "Where do you come from?" Montillo asked.

"From Tlazta. This man here knows the district."

Tlazta was an advance post, a speck on the map. Montillo, the soldier and the Moor immersed themselves in a series of questions. "Here is Tlazta. From here towards Beni-Aros, how would you go?"

"Well, you go down a path and then you turn to the left and then . . ."

Montillo extracted every imaginable piece of information from the Moor. Here a tree, there a stone, a field-path, a stream, a ravine, and so forth.

After the two had gone Montillo exclaimed: "How easy it could be! An airplane and a few photos. Do you know that we have a captain here, Captain Iglesias, who wants to do it and they won't let him? There is a new system, they call it the photogrammetric system. You simply take some pictures with a new German apparatus, and from them you can make a sketch of the ground and get the altitude of all the points."

"I've never heard of it."

"Still, it exists. But Iglesias demands I don't know how many thousands of pesetas to carry it out. As he's a decent chap they won't give him the money, and we here must cudgel our brains. What a bloody mess!"

During the morning we did no work at all. We took our meal together and walked up and down the Calle de la Luneta. Late in the evening Montillo said:

"Let's go to the House of Luisa."

"You go if you like. I'd prefer not to go myself." Suddenly I asked: "Do you know that I have slept with Luisa?"

"The devil you have." He stared at me and added: "But we've got to go, you'll see why."

While we were walking up the Alcazaba he explained.

"We must have agents for all kinds of information. But most of them would not be seen entering H.Q. for anything in the world. Now, everybody can go into the House of Luisa and nobody cares. Why do you go there? To sleep with a woman. It's the best place for a talk."

The House of Luisa was a center of Military Intelligence. They led us into a little hall where we were visited by a motley crowd of people entering one by one, at short intervals: Moors from the mountains, sutlers, itinerant tea vendors, a storyteller of the *zocos*. Montillo interrogated and made sketches and entries. Then he shut his note-book. "Enough for today. Let's get a bottle of wine."

Luisa entered. When she recognized me, she openly showed her surprise at seeing me involved in such activities: "How well you've kept it secret. . . . I'm glad you've come. Tonight I shall enjoy myself, I can feel it in my bones."

"But I can't."

We emptied the bottle between us and then Montillo left. Luisa and I were alone. She was cajolingly affectionate, like a cat.

"And you'll take part in the operations?"

"I don't know."

"They'll start in April."

"So they say. Spring is the best season."

"Some people say they'll begin from Ben-Karrick and others say from Xauen. Of course you know it better than I . . ."

"Of course."

I had not an inkling of the plans, but I could not resist the desire to show myself well informed.

"Tell me about it. I bet you're going by Xauen."

"Of course. Look, the valley of Beni-Aros is shut off by Xauen and by Larache at both ends, and by the French positions and ours on the two sides. We're going to send a column down from Larache and another from Xauen, and the Raisuni will be caught in the middle, without an escape."

But Luisa wanted to know more. Like a perfect armchair strategist I expounded all the operations. And then we went to bed. That night she did not expect the General. But on the following day I told Montillo of Luisa's curious interest in the operational plans.

"You were right to tell her a tale. The bitch is trading with both sides, or rather with three, I think, for it seems to me that she's passing on information to the Moors, and to the French in Tangier. In any case we'll tell the Major."

The result was that I was asked to cultivate the friendship with Luisa and to give her increasingly detailed information about the operations which were to start via Xauen. I had no more idea of the plans than before. My work was to cull information from agents, to collect notes and to trace a more or less rudimentary map of the valley of Beni-Aros and its communication lines.

Slowly I came to know the commanding officers of the operating forces: General Dámaso Berenguer, High Commissioner of Morocco, fat and heavy, with an unctuous voice; General Marzo, also of the tribe of fat generals, with a corset beneath his uniform, sanguine and apoplectic, prone to anger; Colonel Serrano, a stout, resolute, fatherly man, adored by his soldiers for his good-natured humor and his absolute fearlessness; Lt. Col. Gonzalez Tablas, tall, energetic, an authority to the Moors of the *Regulares* whom he commanded, very much the aristocrat among the high officers who mostly looked like wealthy farmers and who hated him cordially—or so I believed. And finally, there was General Castro Girona, very affable, but outlandish with his deep tan, his clean-shaven head, and his genuine interest in the Moors.

This General, who seemed cast for the Man of Morocco, enjoyed an immense prestige among the Moors, many of whose dialects he spoke very well. An astute politician, he made it possible for us to occupy Xauen without bloodshed, at the cost of a few stray shots; weeks before the action he entered the town disguised as a Moorish charcoal-burner and negotiated the surrender of the city with the notables, threatening them with a bombardment of the town and promising them financial benefit at the same time.

This feat had doubless saved hundreds of Spanish families from bereavement, for Xauen lies hidden between mountains in an almost unassailable position. But it had earned him the enmity of the Generals who dreamed of a "conquest" of Xauen, the Sacred City, and of a "glorious page in history." In the actions to come, Catro Girona was not given any operational command. Decorations and promotion were to be reserved for the others.

What I saw of the Spanish General Staff at that time makes me wish to do it justice. I saw men who represented what there was of military culture, studious, self-denying, eternally struggling against the envy of their brother officials in other corps and against the antagonism of the Generals, many of whom were unable to read an army map and, being dependent on the General Staff, hated or disparaged its members. The officers of the General Staff were on the whole powerless; whenever a General had an idea, their task was to find the least dangerous way of putting it into practice, since they were unable to quash it. The ideas of the Generals were almost without exception based on what they were pleased to call guts, though they used a cruder word.

Towards the end of March 1921, the preparations at H.Q. for the impending operations were finished. I went back to my Company at Hamara. They had orders to cease work on the road and to join one of the columns, leaving behind a platoon under Ensign Mayorga, and Señor Pepe with his Moors.

I was to go to war for the first time.

Every soldier who is caught in the machinery of an army asks himself on the eve of going to the front: "Why?"

The Spanish soldiers in Morocco asked themselves the same question. They could not help trying to understand why they found themselves in Africa and why they were to risk their lives. They had been made soldiers when they were about twenty years old, because they were twenty years old; they had been put into a regiment and sent to Africa to kill Moors. So far theirs was the story of all conscript soldiers who are mobilized by a decree and sent to the battle front. But at this point began their Spanish story.

"Why have we to fight against the Moors? Why must we 'civilize' them if they do not want to be civilized? Civilize them—we? We from Castile, from Andalusia, from the mountains of Gerona, who cannot read or write? Nonsense. Who is going to civilize us? Our village has no school, its houses are of clay, we sleep in our clothes on a pallet in the stable beside the mules, to keep warm. We eat an onion and a chunk of bread in the morning and go to work on the fields from sunrise to sunset. At noon we eat the *gazpacho,* a mess of oil, vinegar, salt, water, and bread. At night we eat chick-peas or potatoes with dried cod. We crack up with hunger and misery. The boss robs us, and if we complain we are beaten by the Civil Guard. If I had not reported at the barracks the Civil Guard would have beaten me. They would have carried me off and I would have to be here for three years. And tomorrow they're going to kill me. Or will I do the killing?"

The Spanish soldier accepted Morocco as he accepted inevitable things, with the racial fatalism in face of the inevitable. "Be it as God wills"— which is not Christian resignation, but subconscious blasphemy. Said like this, it means that you feel powerless in front of reality and must resign yourself to God's will, just as you might have to resign yourself to the will of the usurer when he takes away your land, even though you have paid up three times its value, on the ground that the total sum of the debt was never once in your hands.

This Spanish "Be it as God wills" does not signify hope in God's kindness but rather the end of any hope, the expectance of worse things to come.

The Spanish soldiers in Morocco had every cause to feel it.

On the eve of our departure three soldiers were on the sick list. One had a high temperature and had to stay in the tent. Another, who had slightly hurt a finger on barbed wire, had his hand badly inflamed. A third had gonorrhea. They were to stay in Hamara until they could be sent to the hospital in the Zoco del Arbaa. The rest of the Company started the march towards Ben-Karrick.

The bugler Martin walked beside my horse. Not only was he thus resuming the intimacy of our conversations beneath the fig tree, but he could also rest part of his equipment against the horse and catch hold of its tail when we had to climb a hill.

"Martinez has a violent temperature," I said.

"All he has is a dodge."

"A dodge?"

"It's clear that you don't yet know these people, sir. There's nothing the matter with him. Nor with the other two."

. "Don't tell me that I'm blind and dumb. Martinez had fever. Sotero's hand was as big as my boot. And Mencheta is dripping pus all the time."

"Yes, yes. And none of them wanted to go where we're going now. Martinez put a head of garlic in his armpit during the night. Sotero put pounded stinging-nettles into his wound. And Mencheta used a poultice."

"A poultice?"

"Yes, sir. One of those mustard papers you buy at the chemist's. You make a little roll and put it in the urinary passage, and on the following day you've got something awful. Now the three will go to hospital, and when their tricks no longer work the operations will be over. I've done it many times. There are plenty of other things you can do. You eat tobacco, and turn yellow as if you had jaundice. You heat a copper, and get an ulcer on the leg. Now we're here in the country. But I'm sure in Tetuan there were queues before the houses where there are sick women last night. In a fortnight's time dozens of the men will be in the hospitals."

"You know what it means, though."

"Yes. But a bullet in the stomach is worse. If you get it in the stomach you're finished. You get peritonitis and you die. For the doctors stay in the rear. You'll see. All these fellows here come along because they're dumb, most of them, and because they can't do what they would do in Tetuan. Sometimes there are as many as twenty on the sick list the day before an operation, and after the first few days a dozen more."

"And you, why do you come? You could have used one of those tricks."

"I can't do it any longer. Sooner or later they spot you, and then they send you to jug. Nowadays when an operation is on, I tell myself: 'Be it as God wills,' and start marching."

Early in the afternoon we reached Ben-Karrick. At that time it was a base. The place was a small settlement with a barracks of the *Regulares*, Infantry and Commissariat units and supply dumps of the army contractors. Various canteens had been set up by sutlers, well stocked with wine, spirits and tinned or pickled food. From time to time two or three women would come from Tetuan and stay for a week.

We pitched our tents outside the position. A column of eight thousand men was being formed under the command of General Marzo. We would have to wait a couple of days until we left, and in the meantime Ben-Karrick became a *fiesta*. It offered nothing except food and drinks, but how we ate and drank!

In the Spanish code of personal relations, drunkenness is considered not only disgusting but also as proving a lack of virility. A group of friends will relentlessly exclude a man who cannot carry his drink or at least restrain himself in accordance with his powers of resistance. They will expel him because he showed himself wanting in manhood. But on certain occasions there is an exception to the rule, as for instance on Christmas Eve and New Year's Eve. And it was the same in Ben-Karrick. The men drank in order to get drunk.

The cabin of El Malagueño was the favorite meeting place of the sergeants, and the owner, proud of his clientèle, drove away any soldier who dared to enter. El Malagueño had begun as a peddler who followed marching columns with a little donkey and four pitchers filled with water. The water pitchers became goat-skins full of wine. Then he set up a little wooden structure in an encampment at Regaia. Now he had a big store in Ben-Karrick, complete with hams, sausages, tins of sardines, German beer, Dutch tinned milk, spirits from everywhere, fine Andalusian wines, and a kitchen which could produce a meal within ten minutes. Close to the stores he had built a hut where he killed lambs and occasionally a cow, and from where he supplied the kitchens of all officers and sergeants in the position with fresh meat.

Julian was in the same situation as I was: he was going into action for the first time. His natural gaiety of a fat young man was clouded by his feelings. He who used to drink wine mixed with water at meals poured down big glasses of Manzanilla.

"You'll get tight," I told him.

"The more the better. I want to get tight. It's my father's fault: if they hit me tomorrow, what then?"

"We'll bury you, don't worry."

"Poor fellow, he's so fat that he'd make a good target," said Herrero. "They'll hit you right in your tummy."

"Don't be afraid, just hide behind me," Córcoles wound up, showing off his slimness.

But Julian was not susceptible to jokes. He became increasingly sulky, and he drank and drank. Suddenly he smashed his glass on the floor and shouted:

"I spit on my father!"

El Malagueño knew Julian and his father and the story of both of them. He opened the flap of the bar, crossed over to us and patted Julian on the back.

"Yes, I spit on my father!"

"Well done. If I were you, I'd do the same. And I'd play him a dirty trick. You know what I would do if I were you?"

"What?"

"Well then, tomorrow or the day after, when you're in front of the Moors, if I were you, I should go ahead and let them hit me. And my father would tear out his hair."

We shouted with laughter, but Julian turned livid and hit El Malagueño in the face. The other screamed hair-raising blasphemies, then caught up the knife for cutting ham and shouted:

"I'll kill him! Let me kill him! Not even the Almighty may lay hands on me. I'll slit his guts open like a pig's!"

Herrero cut him short:

"First bring us some glasses of Manzanilla. Then you can kill him if you like. But the best thing to do is to give him a double brandy."

"That's an idea, old man!"

El Malagueño filled our wine cups and then poured eau-de-vie into a glass which he handed to Julian:

"Drink, son, drink this, to get rid of your blues."

Julian drank the stuff at one gulp. Three seconds later he was lying on the floor like a stuffed sack. El Malagueño lifted him tenderly and laid him on some bales in the warehouse. We drifted into a group of infantry sergeants, all mature men of long service in Africa. One of them, a tiny yellowish fellow, seemed to take a liking to me.

"I've been waiting for operations to begin," he said.

"So you like a fight?"

"Oh, well, I don't exactly like it, but it's the only chance for a bit of luck."

"For what did you say?"

"For promotion, I meant. With us it isn't like with you Engineers. It takes us a good ten to twelve years to become a quartermaster sergeant. The only stroke of luck one of us can have is to get the right sort of wound or to have one's platoon bumped off. It's easier to be promoted for merit in action than for seniority."

"But how much would you gain? Ten *duros* per month."

"How much would I gain? Just a little more. As a sergeant you get your fingers in the pie only when you're mess sergeant or when they send you to a blockhouse. But as a quartermaster sergeant, who dresses the whole company, you're on top. At the least a thousand pesetas per month, I bet you. And with a bit of luck during operations . . ."

"What do you mean by luck?"

"You're a fool, my boy. If I'm quartermaster sergeant and I take part in one of those operations where they make it hot for us and half the men get killed, then it's simple. Next day I report the Company's equipment as lost. Just imagine. Two hundred blankets, two hundred pairs of boots, two hundred shirts, two hundred coats, and so on . . ."

7. The Legion

W E were among the first to arrive. Only the artillery and the commissariat had come before us. On the crest of the hill we saw the outline of eight guns pointing towards the valley. At the foot of the hill the commissariat had pitched their tents; there rose a strong smell of straw and horses. We had been allotted the slope by the Captain of the General Staff who organized the encampment. Within half an hour our tents were set up and the kitchen fires burning.

The hill rose from a stubble-covered plain. The barley had just been cut. Far back in the rear we could see the huts of a Moorish village which had surrendered a few weeks before. At this distance the ugliness of its hovels was softened and it looked a homely enough place in the middle of the harvested fields. Our cone-shaped tents, scattered over the hillside, looked as though the village were preparing for a fair.

Our Captain had suggested to the Captain of the General Staff that we should be given the open field for our camping ground. The answer had been: "It is reserved for the Legion." Our Captain had pulled a wry face.

The Legion arrived in the afternoon, a whole battalion—they call it *bandera*, Standard—which was to go into action for the first time. Their tents were quickly pitched. At the far end of the camp barrels of wine were lined up beside two square tents; the canteen and the brothel. The soldiers of the Legion began to crowd round the casks and the tents; they started drinking and "making love."

Together with the other sergeants I watched the bivouac of the Legion growing below us.

"Those are the new Americans," said Julian. "I suppose most of them are here because they've been duped."

"Duped? Don't tell us that anybody comes here by mistake."

Córcoles said: "There are still some saps left in the world. They'll have heard fine words about the Mother Country and her daughter nations in America, and so the grandchildren have come here. Well, they won't find these four years much fun."

A legionary was coming up the hill towards us. Córcoles pointed to him:

"Where's he going? I think he's got on the wrong floor."

In those days it was the rule for legionaries and ordinary Spanish soldiers never to mix.

When the man came nearer I recognized him. It was Sanchiz. We waved to each other. Córcoles turned to me:

"So you know him?"

"Yes, he's an old friend of mine."

"Nice friends you've got."

Meanwhile, Sanchiz had arrived.

"Hallo, how are things? I've come to fetch you. We've got some first-class wine down there. They told me your company was here, so if you're free, come along with me."

We went down the hill together; Sanchiz had taken my arm. The legionaries looked at me askance. We met a sergeant with the face of an old jailbird, and he asked Sanchiz threateningly:

"Where are you off to with that fellow?"

"He's an old friend of mine. Come on and have a glass," said Sanchiz.

"No, I'm on guard tonight, and if I start drinking, I'm lost."

The caterer was a thin, yellow-skinned old man with transparent ears and a nose like a beetroot. He was so deaf that we had to shout our orders and point with our fingers at what we wanted. As a rule, the wine which was sold to the forces in Africa contained a shameless dose of water and half a dozen chemicals to prevent quick fermentation. But this wine was excellent, dry and strong, so that you had to smack your tongue against your palate.

"What do you do to stop them putting water in your wine?"

"*El Sordo* takes jolly good care not to play tricks. Otherwise he wouldn't have a sound bone left in his body—to say the least."

"But how is it you're here? I thought you were doing office work in Ceuta and living like a prince."

"Wine's to blame for that. I got tight, and the Captain sent me along with these fellows for two months. I've got to teach them. They're a lousy crowd. Sons of niggers, and Chinks, and Red Indians. To hell with them. They talk to you, all sweetness, and as soon as you turn your back they stick a knife between your ribs. A rotten lot. Just look at their faces. . . . I wonder what Millán Astray will say to them tomorrow."

"Has he come here, too?"

"Yes, and tomorrow at ten he's going to address them. Come and listen. He's terrific. I'll come and fetch you at your tent."

The abstemious sergeant joined us: "You've made me envious. Will you stand me a glass?"

He drank in slow sips, staring at me.

"Is he really a friend of yours, Sanchiz?"

"Yes, he's like a brother to me. Or rather, like a son, for I could be his father."

The sergeant offered me a huge calloused hand:

"If that's so, I'm glad to meet you." He took another sip. "And if you are his friend, why don't you come with us? If I were in his skin," he said to Sanchiz, "you'd see—I'd be a lieutenant tomorrow."

"Don't be a fool. A sergeant-major at the most. But he's no good for us. We scared him stiff in the tavern of *El Licenciado.*"

The din round the wine casks was infernal, it was impossible to understand one another. Sanchiz and I parted at the boundary of the Legion's camp. Walking up the slope, I wrestled with the problem of my old repugnance against the *Tercio,* and remembered the tavern of *El Licenciado* in Ceuta.

Spanish taverns usually paint their doors red. That one in the little square behind the church of Our Lady of Africa had been lavish with red paint. The harsh vermilion of red lead had been daubed on doors, tables, three-legged stools, the bar and the shelves, laden with bottles. The tavern was like a bleeding gash in the whitewashed front wall. Outside the sun had bleached the red color to a dirty pink. Inside, smoke had blackened it to the shade of dried blood. The landlord was an old convict from the penal colony on Monte Hacho; he went about in a dirty sleeveless vest, with the hairs of his chest sticking through the mesh. His customers were legionaries and whores. His nickname—"The Licenciate" —was a reference to his convict past and a cheap joke at the same time. The wine was greenish-red and tasted of copper sulphate. To drink it, you had to have a thirst such as *El Licenciado* produced by serving chunks of sun-dried tunny along with the glasses of wine. The fish

hung in a row from a beam above the long bar. Slit open from head to
tail and spread-eagled on bamboo frames, they looked like small kites.
The same beam carried two hooks from which two oil lamps hung suspended on twisted bits of wire. At night, *El Licenciado* lighted the lamps,
and their smoke licked slowly at the dried fish until they were dyed
black and tasted of oily soot.

At noon the tavern was empty. A woman or a legionary would come
in for an instant and take away a bottle of wine. Towards nightfall the
customers drifted in. I went there some evenings while the bar was still
deserted, to wait for Sanchiz. The first to come would be a lonely legionary who sat down near the light, and wrote, nobody ever knew what.
Then came an avalanche of men who had finished their duty at the office
of the Ceuta delegation of the *Tercio*. They leaned against the bar in a
row and argued about who was to stand whom drinks. After a time some
started a game of cards, others sat down in small groups round a square
flagon of wine, and a few went away. The women came only with the
darkness. Their coming coincided with the lighting of the lamps. Mostly,
they were accompanied by a casual bed-fellow of theirs who had invited
them to a drink afterwards. Others came to look for someone and asked
for him from the doorstep. Then they were invited to sit down, and
entered. A few regular customers came simply to drink and to find somebody who would pay for their drinks.

The cross-fire of blasphemies, the barbarous language, the smoky light,
the red paint, and the metallic wine filled the tavern with a naked brutality which was scarcely disguised—was indeed rather heightened—by the
uniforms. The women added the high lights: they were old, corroded by
disease, in rags of glaring colors, hoarse from syphilis and alcohol, their
eyes red-rimmed. When the women came, the blasphemies tore through
the room like the lashing of whips, in a sexual battle between males and
females. Sometimes a man slapped the wrinkled cheek of a woman, sometimes someone caught a trestle in his fury and lifted it above another's
head.

When the quarrels went beyond the limits of the Licentiate's code, he
slowly left his place behind the counter, moving like a boar, and put the
adversaries outside into the little square without saying a word. Then he
turned and slowly fastened the latch of the door. The door had no bolt
and was a simple glass pane with short red muslin curtains. Yet I never
saw anybody attempt to force the entry. The tavern keeper was taboo
through a mixture of physical fear of his murderous past, and of instinctive dread that the tavern might be closed, since it was one of the few
which belonged to the Legion.

That tavern had for me the same fascination which the first visit to a lunatic asylum has for a normal person: repulsion, fear, and the attraction of the unknown horror of madness. Through the peculiar code of the lawless, I was a sacrosanct person there, for I did not belong to them and yet was the friend of one of them. But this contact imbued me with a fear, almost a terror, of the *Tercio,* which has lasted all my life.

On the eve of a battle there is always the nervous tension born of the risks to be run. That night I found it difficult to sleep, but my nervous tension, my fear, rose from the stubble field where the barley had been cut, and not from the other side of the hills, where the advance guards were firing at each other in the darkness.

Lieut.-Colonel Millán Astray came out of the tent, followed by a couple of officers. The crowd fell silent. The Commander stretched his bony frame, while his hands mangled a glove until it showed the hairs of the fur lining. The whole might of his stentorian voice filled the encampment, and the noises from the bivouacs of the other units died down. Eight thousand men tried to hear him, and they listened.

"*Caballeros legionarios!*"

"Gentlemen of the Legion . . . yes, gentlemen! Gentlemen of the *Tercio* of Spain, offspring of the Flanders *Tercios* of old. Gentlemen! Some people say that before coming here you were I know not what! but anything rather than gentlemen: some murderers, others thieves, and all with your lives finished—dead! And it is true what they say. But here, since you are here, you are gentlemen. You have risen from the dead—for don't forget that you have been dead, that your lives were finished. You have come here to live a new life for which you must pay with death. You have come here to die. It is to die that one joins the Legion.

"What are you? The Betrothed of Death. You are the gentlemen of the Legion. You have washed yourselves clean, for you have come here to die. There is no other life for you than in this Legion. But you must understand that you are Spanish gentlemen, all of you, knights like those other legionaries who, conquering America, begat you. In your veins there are some drops of the blood of Pizarro and Cortés. There are drops of the blood of those adventurers who conquered a world and who, like you, were gentlemen—the Betrothed of Death. Long live Death! . . ."

"*Viva la Muerte!*"

Milán Astray's whole body underwent an hysterical transfiguration. His voice thundered and sobbed and shrieked. Into the faces of these men he spat all their misery, their shame, their ugliness, their crimes, and then he swept them along in fanatical fury to a feeling of chivalry, to a readiness to renounce all hope, beyond that of dying a death which would wash away their stains of cowardice in the splendor of courage.

When the Standard shouted in wild enthusiasm, I shouted with them.
Sanchiz pressed my arm:

"He's a grand fellow, isn't he?"

Millán went round the circle of legionaries, stopping here or there before the most exotic or the most bestial faces. He stopped in front of a mulatto with thick lips, the liverish yellow-white of his rounded eyeballs shot with blood.

"Where do you come from, my lad?"

"What the devil's that to you?" the man answered.

Millán Astray stared straight into the other's eyes.

"You think you're brave, don't you? Listen. Here, I am the Chief. If anyone like you speaks to me he stands to attention and says: 'At your orders, sir. I don't want to say where I come from.' And that's as it should be. You've a perfect right not to name your country, but you have no right to speak to me as if I were the likes of you."

"And in what are you more than I am?" The man spat it from lips wet with saliva as if they were on heat.

At times men can roar. At times men can pounce as though their muscles were of rubber and their bones steel rods.

"I . . .?" roared the commander. "I am more than you, more of a man than you!" He sprang at the other and caught him by the shirt collar. He lifted him almost off the ground, hurled him into the center of the circle and smacked his face horribly with both hands. It lasted two or three seconds. Then the mulatto recovered from the unexpected assault and jumped. They hit each other as men in the primeval forest must have done before the first stone ax was made. The mulatto was left on the ground nearly unconscious, bleeding.

Millán Astray, more erect, more terrifying than ever, rigid with a furious homicidal madness, burst into the shout:

"Attention!"

The eight hundred legionaries—and I—snapped into it like automatons. The mulatto rose, scraping the earth with his hands and knees. He straightened himself. His nose poured blood mixed with dirt like a child's mucus. The torn lip was more bloated than ever. He brought his heels together and saluted. Millán Astray clapped him on his powerful back:

"I need brave men at my side tomorrow. I suppose I'll see you near me."

"At your orders, sir." Those eyes, more bloodshot than ever, more yellow with jaundice, held a fanatical flame.

Dawn was breaking. At the bottom of the vale, where the river ran the light was pushing against the blue-black of the sky. Suddenly the flame of the sun rose, and its red disk showered crimson stains on the waters. From the height where we were posted, the light seemed to creep up the mountain slopes, and the shadows stretched across the valley, immense and shapeless. The crests were illuminated by the light coming from below, and the tree tops glowed as though the trunks were on fire. The smoke columns from the shelled *kabila* were tainted red as though the flames had flickered up once more.

Our artillery protected the advance. We saw the fast Moorish cavalry riding uphill and the infantry of the *Regulares* running between the shrubs and the dwarf palms. Little white puffs dotted the ground, transient as a photographer's magnesium flare. The shots merged into a continuous crackling noise which grew steadily. The *Tercio,* in the center, carried the assault against the summit where, in the middle of a bare, stony clearing, stood the *kabila,* surrounded by a stone wall. Once more shells fell within the enclosure. The machine guns sounded like motorcycles accelerating on many distant roads.

At ten o'clock we sappers were given the order to advance. We were to fortify the hill which the Legion had just stormed. It was to be a position big enough to hold a whole company as well as a battery of field guns, protected by a circle of ten thousand sandbags. When we reached the edge of the summit, we were ordered to lie flat on the ground, load our rifles and scatter. A staff captain came and went. He held a whispered conversation with our commander and galloped away to the hilltop, only to reappear shortly afterwards. Then we were ordered to advance again. And we advanced, slowly; we reached the edge of the clearing and cautiously raised our heads. Behind every stone, every ripple on the bare ground there was a legionary, firing his rifle. Now and then one of them started to rise and collapsed. A few tried to find better shelter by going backwards. It was a slow, individual retreat, but the legionaries were retreating. Again and again, another of them came closer to us as we crouched motionless, fascinated, behind the evergreen oaks. The stone parapet of the *kabila* was ablaze, a single firing-line. The bullets whistled over our heads while we clung to the ground, straining to see.

In the middle of the clearing was a rider on horseback, dashing to and fro; at his side ran a tiny figure: Millán Astray with his bugler. There was a momentary lull in the fighting. The horse stopped, the horseman stood upright in his stirrups:

"To me the Legion! Fix bayonets!"

He raised an arm stained with blood.

The men jumped the stone parapet in clusters.

The handling of explosives was one of my specialties. That afternoon they came to fetch me. A sergeant of the Legion came together with one of our officers. They explained the case to me. They were just burying the dead. A legionary had bayoneted a Moor and stabbed him through the chest, but with such barbaric force that the rifle had penetrated up to the bolt. It was impossible to pull out the weapon except by sawing the corpse in two. But the rifle was still fit for use. So they had thought of introducing explosive into the rifle and blowing it up.

I organized the explosion as best I could. I poured a few percussion caps of mercury fulminate, such as we used for blowing up bore-holes in the quarry, down the rifle barrel which stuck out from the Moor's back. His was a skeleton-like body, wrapped in a torn gray burnous soaked with blood.

The mulatto, his lips still inflamed, his hands idle, watched me with curiosity while I dropped the golden little percussion caps with much care into the barrel. He stood back when I gave the order. I set fire to the fuse in the rifle mouth and ran away. The Moor's stomach burst open.

The mulatto laughed like an animal, with a twist to the lip that still smarted.

Back in my tent, I drank a large glass of brandy and stopped myself from being sick.

Dusk came. On the far side of the mountain, at the bottom of a ravine, the Moors had ceased firing. There was a great silence in the fields. Only in our position the fire crackled on through the din of the victors as they pitched their tents, tied up their horses, sang, complained of their wounds, and shouted orders at each other.

A voice rose from the depth of the ravine, intoning the evening prayer. I saw the distant, earth-colored figures of the Moors making their salaams to the sound of the savage, wailing psalmody, their rifles at their sides. At the foot of the shadowy mountains the mist began to rise, enveloping the praying figures. Only the chant rose above the swirl of the fog, as though the fog itself were singing. Outside the parapet, on the stony clearing, lay a dead Moor who had fallen face downwards, black arms flung wide, hands clenched, black desiccated legs apart. The big tuft of hair on his shaven head fluttered in the blue night wind.

8. Disaster

I T is three o'clock in the afternoon, and we are still waiting for the order to advance and to start with the fortification work.

At dawn the Spanish columns poured into the valley of Beni-Aros like armies of migrant ants; we, the Ben-Karrick column, from the north, the Larache column from the west. The two groups are now converging towards the center where we can see the huts of the Zoco el Jemis of Beni-Aros, one of the most important markets of the whole region. The French frontier positions close the valley to the south, the hills of the Jebel Alam and a supporting column gathering in Xauen close it to the east. The forces of the Raisuni are shut in from all four sides, and their only way out is to cross the French frontier, or else to flee to the mountains of the Jebel Alam.

The Moors defend themselves furiously behind every stone and every shrub. The attacks of our advance troops, the *Regulares* and the *Tercio,* batter against an impalpable enemy who is everywhere. Now the rebel cavalry is challenging ours. We see the charge of the Spanish cavalry against the Moorish horsemen who gallop away across the green lawn of the *zoco,* leading their pursuers on to where riflemen are lying in ambush between the stones.

We see our cavalry close its broken ranks and withdraw. Somebody must have given the order to shell the enemy guerrillas, for the shells are falling just where our riders are. Heliographs throw sun-sparks in every direction. In front of us, at six miles' distance, the French are sure to be following the spectacle at our feet, just as we do.

The day is so beautiful, the light so violent in a cloudless sky, the land so rich with trees and grass, with rocks and harvested fields, yellow squares in the green, and the men in the battle are so very small, that you lose every thought of the military operation and seem to be looking at a great play performed in a gigantic setting. The crackling of the machine guns and the detonations of the guns, the single aircraft which has dropped three bombs on what from here looks like a white house, wrapping it in smoke, the tiny figures which run about and sometimes fall, all of it is false and artificial against the background of these fields and under this sun.

It is a long time since we have eaten our cold meal. For hours we have been waiting in the shelter of the hill for our turn. The men are nodding with sleep, many have thrown themselves on the ground and are now dozing, bored with the spectacle of a fight which is still undefined and which consists of the same scenes played over and over again for hours.

At long last a captain of the General Staff arrives at a gallop. And we begin our march, suddenly in a great hurry, climbing up and down slopes. Sometimes the mules stumble and their drivers swear, but more to keep themselves awake by the sound of their own voices than to curse the girth which has worked itself loose or the pack-saddle which is knocking against the mule's legs.

It takes us an hour to reach our destination, a hill jutting out over the valley, on which we have to set up a blockhouse. The *Tercio* is still fighting on the very hill top, but this makes no difference. We must clear out before nightfall, and the blockhouse must be set up at any price.

On the sheltered side of the hill, our men hastily dig earth and fill sandbags. The wooden parts of the blockhouse frame are laid out on the ground so that the jig-saw puzzle can be fitted together. The rolls of barbed wire are untied and their ends straggle, sharp-clawed whips.

The first thing to do is to build a parapet facing the enemy. Otherwise we cannot work at all. The men crawl up the hill, pushing the sandbags in front of their heads; but once they reach the top they lose their cover. They put the bags into line and crawl back, swifter than any reptile, while the bullets whistle overhead and hit the earth or the bags with a dull thud. The enemy is concentrating his fire on the crest of the hill, and the scattered legionaries, who bump against our legs and our sandbags, curse us in protest. But when the parapet is finished, the legionaries use it as their cover. The thuds on the earth wall sound like the fat rain drops of a thunderstorm falling on the stone flags of a cloister; but the bullets over our heads hum like bees in mad flight. The wooden frame is rising skeleton-like and the sun draws out the scent of freshly sawed pine wood.

There is a lull. The Moors know what is to come, and they wait for it. We know, too. We know that they are taking aim most carefully, waiting until we emerge up there with the zinc sheets of the roof, clearly outlined against the hill, the wooden frame and the shining metal.

These sheets are now lying at our feet like a monstrous book with corrugated pages. We are afraid of opening it, for fear that we might find our fate written on one of its pages, in undulating writing, like a snake stretched across the folds.

History tells a thousand times of heroism in the heat of battle. A warrior or a soldier cuts, hacks, thrusts, smashes skulls with his battle club or rifle butt, and enters the pages of history. There is nothing of this kind here.

We do not fight, we do not even see the enemy. We take a metal sheet, half a meter by two meters in size; we climb a ladder, laboriously; we place the sheet at an angle of forty-five degrees while the sun shines in our eyes; we drive nails one by one into its four edges, taking care not to crush a finger with our hammers. Meanwhile, ten or twenty or a hundred eyes behind rifle sights take aim at the little doll posturing before the sheet mirror. Bullets tear sharp-edged holes into the zinc and sometimes into the flesh. The hole where a bullet entered a man's back is small and neat. The hole on the other side is wide, with bleeding rims lacerated by the metal, plastered with shreds of flesh and cloth.

The blockhouse stands, but we must still set up the barbed wire entanglement. In groups of five our men have to jump over the parapet. One holds the wooden stakes while another hammers them rapidly into the ground. A third unwinds the barbed wire, which bites into his hands, from a reel guided by a fourth. The fifth fastens the wire to the stakes with steel staples. They work under fire.

By seven o'clock we had finished our work. Our casualties were three dead and nine wounded. One more blockhouse rose over the valley of Beni-Aros. We received the order to withdraw; night was beginning to fall, and we had thirteen miles to go back to our base. Two hours later the Company of Engineers was still marching through the darkened fields. The battle noises behind us had long ceased.

Of what did we think? In a war men are saved by the fact they cannot think. In the struggle man reverts to his origins and becomes an animal in a herd, his only instinct that of self-preservation. Muscles which had not been used for centuries come alive. Ears stiffen at the whistle of a bullet close by; the little hairs on the skin bristle in a critical moment. You jump sideways like a monkey or you throw yourself down behind the only wrinkle in the ground, just in time to avoid a projectile you have neither seen nor heard. But think? You do not think.

During those withdrawals in which one man marches behind the other like a sleep-walker your nerves grow calm at last. Nothing is then left but the rhythm of heavy feet—and how heavy they are!—of hands hanging down and swinging like automatons in line with your legs, and of a beating heart that you hear inside yourself, marching, sleep-walking, in step with the heart of the man in front of you, which you cannot hear because your own heart makes too much noise. Drink and sleep. Drink and sleep. Your brain is filled with a longing for drink and a longing for sleep. In the darkness, thirst and sleep ride on the neck of a hundred soldiers on the march, a hundred empty brains.

By midnight it was obvious that we had lost our way. We found our-

selves at the foot of hills which were immense shadows under a starry
sky. Where were we? We called a halt, and the Captain consulted the
sergeants. We had not a single lamp and not a single compass. Before us,
the stone wall of the mountain; behind us, the shadowy fields with dogs
or hyenas howling in the distance. We decided to climb the mountain.
We might see something from the top, a light, a point which could guide
us. And we began the ascent, stumbling in the darkness, bent like pilgrims
but muttering blasphemies.

From the top we saw one light, two lights, and very far away a tiny
white speck of light blinking rhythmically. The mountain dipped down
in a precipitous slope before us. To go down there might mean crashing
on the rocks. It was decided to camp on the spot and to wait for the day
which would come in two hours. We improvised a parapet, using the material carried by the mules and the mules themselves. In its shelter we
lit fires and set out sentries, and within its narrow circle we all slept,
men and beasts, wedged against each other, frightened like children.

At dawn we saw before us the sea. The sun rode on ripples of glittering,
silvery gold on a ground of green waves tipped with white crescents of
foam. Down there to our left was Rio Martin.

We never knew how many miles we had marched that night. Our feet
were swollen, all our limbs numb. We had to rest until noon before we
were able to start on the slow descent to Rio Martin.

It was there, while the Captain was waiting for his call to Headquarters
to come through, that I had the first conscious thought—it had stirred in
my brain ever since the night before: not a compass, not a light, not a
map! The units of the Spanish Army in Morocco went into action without
any means of finding their bearings. Men were sent out, and it was left
to their instinct where to advance and, above all, how to return to their
bases; unit after unit was lost in the night. Suddenly I understood those
tragic Moroccan withdrawals in which, after a victorious operation, hundreds of men perished in ambushes.

Two days later we received orders to march to Xauen, fifty miles to
the east. We were to join the column which covered the exit from the
valley of Beni-Aros and the slopes of the Jebel-Alam.

Xauen is an infinitely old city in a gorge hemmed in by mountains.
You only see it when you enter the gorge itself. The town comes as a
surprise. It is not an Arab city, but a town of the Spanish Sierras with
the pointed, red-slated roofs on its whitewashed houses, roofs from which
the snow slides off in the winter. The Moors call Xauen the "Sacred" and
the "Mysterious." When you see the city nestling behind its granite walls,
you understand why it was unconquerable for centuries. A small number

of men distributed on the surrounding peaks, invisible marksmen hurtling stones, could close the path to any invader.

Xauen's narrow, steep, and twisted streets were a maze. Early during our occupation, it happened not infrequently that a Spanish soldier was pierced by a poignard without ever knowing from where it had struck. The Hebrew quarter was a fortress shut in by iron gates which opened for the first time in centuries when the Spaniards occupied the town. Within its precincts—thick walls, tiny doorways, mere holes for windows —they still spoke Spanish, an archaic Spanish of the sixteenth century. And a few of the Jews still wrote that dusty Castilian in antiquated letters, all curves and arabesques, which made a sheet of paper look like a parchment.

I loved Xauen. Not the Xauen of the military, with its Plaza de España and its General Encampment, with its canteens and brothels, its eternal drunkenness, its pretentious officers and obsequious, false Moors. I loved the other Xauen, Xauen the Mysterious: its tranquil streets, in which echoed the hoofs of the little donkeys; its muezzin intoning his prayers high from the minaret; its white-veiled women with nothing but the sparkle of their eyes alive in their phantom robes; its Moors from the mountains, in rags and tatters or resplendent in milk-white wool, but always haughty. Its silent Jews gliding along the walls, so close that they seemed disembodied shadows, forever running in short, rapid, timorous steps.

On moonlit nights Xauen always evoked Toledo for me with its solitary, crooked little streets. And Toledo on moonlit nights always evoked for me Xauen. They have the same background of sound, the river running swiftly and tumultuously, the wind entangled in the trees and in the crags of the mountains and growling in the depths of the gullies.

Xauen was an industrial town. They washed their wool in the torrents, bleached it in the sun and tinted it with ingenuous reds, blues, and yellows, made from the juice of trees and from pounded stone, following prescriptions handed down from father to son. They tooled their leather with the lost art of Cordova, City of the Caliphs. They ground their grain between pear-shaped stones which the water had made to go round for five hundred years; they were smooth, covered with minute pores, and they turned slowly like the breasts of a woman turning in her sleep. They hammered their iron and tempered it over charcoal made from old oak; they dipped it hissing into the water of their river, and it emerged blue as steel or yellow as sun-toasted straw. The Jews embossed silver with rapid little hammer blows, on pitch plaques which made a soft bed for the figures their tools raised on the metal. They had lime-kilns and potters' wheels for primitive pottery with simple lines and graceful proportions. And they had the Legend of the Burning Stones.

A holy man from one of the great tribes which live in the southern desert went with his disciples on a pilgrimage to the Prophet's Tomb. They marched day and night, for months and months, until they came to the big mountains which shut in Xauen. In winter the nights are cold and snow sleeps on the summits; the men from the desert thought they would have to die in the snow. The holy man withdrew in prayer. They could not light a fire where there were only stones, and the hour had come to die. Then Allah bade him take the black stones which hurt his knees when he prayed, and light a fire. This fire burned with a brighter flame than any wood could kindle. And the pilgrims were saved. At daybreak they wished to extinguish the fire and poured onto it water from a source which gushed forth among the stones. And the fire was so powerful that the water burned in flames higher than a man.

In a hidden corner of the mountains, the legend said, the stones and the water are still burning in honor of Allah. And many eyes look out at night to see the flame which burns, nobody knows where.

The Arabs scanned the night for the miraculous flame. Prospectors from all parts of the world have searched, and are still patiently searching those mountains with their hammers, to find the coal and the petroleum which doubtless gave rise to the legend.

But nobody will find those visions in Xauen now. They were lost many years ago. The Spanish invasion drove out the magic of the old city. Nowadays its wools are dyed with the aniline dyes of the I.G. Farbenindustrie and mixed with cotton. The few looms left are not worked with hands and feet but with engines. The silversmiths closed down their workshops years ago, and stamped plate from Marrakesh and from Pforzheim is shamelessly exhibited in Europeanized shops. Leather is no longer tanned with bark and laboriously fined down by handicraft, its pattern is no longer tooled with hammers and heated irons; it is tanned by a chemical process, cut by machines, stamped in relief with steel plates produced in Paris or God knows where. The Fondak, the old Arab inn for travelers, no longer exists, but there are hotels with French cooking. Xauen is neither mysterious nor sacred any more. There are taverns and brothels. In 1931 it was a show place for tourist traffic, with posters on the walls and a wide road which rich Americans and Englishmen could travel to make the trade in printed silks from Lyons prosper.

But I knew Xauen when it was not yet cheapened and when it meant adventure to walk through its streets. A Moor would look at your silver stripes and salute you: "Salaam aleicum." A Jew would stutter the old Romance greeting: "Dios os guarde"—God guard you. A mountaineer

would give you a hate-filled glance and clutch the horn handle of the
dagger in his belt; he would spit ostentatiously in the middle of the street.
The eyes of Moorish women would look at you from the depth of their
veils, and you would never be able to guess the age and the thoughts of
their owner. The Hebrew girls would lower their eyes and blush. Your
feet would slip on the smooth round pebbles on which horses and donkeys would walk at ease.

When we were there, in the midst of that medley of races and hates,
old and new, of rival religious communities enclosed within four city
walls—our field in the General Encampment, the muezzin chanting the
wonders of Allah and the Jews silently seeking their synagogue, their
hands crossed and hidden in their kaftan sleeves—it was as though I saw
medieval Spain come alive. If I was not astonished to see an Arab warrior astride his horse, with a silken horse-cloth and silver stirrups, then
neither would I have been astonished to see a warrior encased in iron, the
double cross of the Crusaders in enamel on his shield.

We were resting in the General Encampment, reorganizing for the
coming operations. As usual, conjectures and comments were carried
from tent to tent, from canteen to canteen. Manzanares came to me
with an air of mystery:

"There's something big on."

"What is it?"

"I don't know. But all the senior officers are running about from the
tent of the General to the tent of all the corps commanders, and all the
time they're in conference with Ceuta and Tetuan. One of Colonel Serrano's orderlies says the Moors have taken Ceuta and cut us off, and that
they'll hack us all to pieces."

At nightfall that day—it was the 11th or 12th of July 1921—the bugles
sounded the officers' call and the commanders of all the units gathered
before the tent of the C.-i-C. At daybreak we all began the march towards
Tetuan, with the exception of a small garrison which was left behind in
Xauen.

The miles piled up. The march and the July sun choked our need
for comment. But at noon the halt which we so eagerly expected was not
called. We went on without rest in a forced march. Some of the men were
unable to go on and began to lag. When the first of our Company fell out
the Captain gave me the dry order: "If he cannot go on, let him stay and
look after himself."

At ten o'clock at night we entered Tetuan. We slept on the stone floor
of the barracks without time to take off our leather straps. At dawn we

left for Ceuta. In Ceuta we went on board a steamer; in Ceuta we learned the news.

The Moors had killed the whole garrison of Melilla and were standing at the gates of the city.

History books call it the Disaster of Melilla, or the Spanish Defeat in Morocco in 1921; they give what is called the historical facts. I do not know them except from those books. What I know is part of the unwritten history which created a tradition in the masses of the people, more powerful than the official tradition. The newspapers I read later spoke of a relief column which had embarked in the port of Ceuta, filled with patriotic fervor to liberate Melilla.

All I know is that a few thousand exhausted men embarked in Ceuta for an unknown destination, worn to the limit of their endurance after a sixty miles' march through Morocco in the glare of the sun, badly clad, badly equipped, badly fed. They left port and at once began to be sea sick and to sully the decks of the ship. They began to swear and to take whatever liberties they could: drinking, gambling, getting drunk and coming to blows over gambling losses, singing and brawling, mocking those who were vomiting, laughing at the pot-bellied colonel with the greenish face and•the uniform spattered with half-digested food. The ship was hell.

And Melilla was a besieged town.

Many years afterwards I learned what life means in a besieged town, under the constant threat of entry of an enemy who has promised himself loot, lives, and fresh women. People in the streets walk rapidly, because nobody goes out except for an urgent reason. All public services are stricken; the telephone does not function, the water taps are leaking, there is no coal, the light suddenly fails, shoes are worn through but the shoe shops are shut, men who had not been ill for ten years fall sick, and the doctor must be fetched while the guns are firing; the streets are dark and there is danger at every corner.

Into besieged Melilla a big steamer poured those thousands of sick, drunken, over-tired men who were to be its liberators. We set up camp, I don't know where. We heard guns, machine guns, and rifles firing. somewhere outside the town. We invaded the cafés and taverns, we got drunk and rioted in the brothels. We challenged the frightened inhabitants: "Now you'll see! Now we're here and that's that. Tomorrow not a Moor will be left alive." The Moors had disappeared from the streets of Melilla; after the ship had anchored alongside the jetty, a legionary had cut off the ears of one of them and the authorities had ordered all Moors to stay indoors. On the following morning we marched to the outskirts of the town; we were to break through the encirclement and to begin the re-conquest of the zone.

During the first few days we Engineers built new positions but returned each time to the camp within the town. The newspaper headlines screamed of horrors which we had not yet seen. Then we went farther afield, away from the city, and we saw horror.

A big house pitted by bullets. The white chalk scooped away from its walls so that the bricks showed like flecks of dry blood. In the courtyard a dead horse, its belly slit open as though gored by a mad bull, the blue entrails clustered with flies, and one of its legs cut away. In the windows of the first floor one, two, three, five dead men, a dead man in every window, some with a neat hole in their foreheads, crumpled up like dolls with the sawdust stuffing gone, some lying in the pool of their own blood. Empty cartridge shells rolling on the floor, sounding like broken rattles, making us stumble comically in face of the dead. In the ground-floor rooms bloody tracks, traces of men dragged away by the shoulder with blood streaming down their boots and tracing two wavering lines as of red chalk on the stone flags.

And then the back room.

A little boy has got hold of a jug of chocolate sauce in his mother's absence. He has painted his face and hands, his legs and his clothes, the table and the chair. He has climbed down from the chair and poured a big blob of chocolate on the floor. He has passed his fingers across the walls and left the print of his hand in every corner, on every piece of furniture, in lines, hooks and hieroglyphs. Jumping up and down in his joy at seeing dark stripes on all the clean things, he has put his foot in the jug and splashed the chocolate on the walls, right up high. It was so beautiful that he has plunged both hands into the jug and spattered big drops and little drops everywhere, even on the ceiling. Right in the middle a big blob has stuck half-dry.

In the back room were five dead men. They were smeared with their own blood, face, hands, uniforms, hair, and boots. The blood had made pools on the floor, stripes on the walls, blobs on the ceiling, sprawling splashes in all the corners. On every clean, white place it had painted hands with five or two or one finger, fingerless palms and shapeless thumbs. A table and a few chairs were turned into scattered kindling wood. Countless flies, droning incessantly, were sucking blood from the thumb printed on the wall and from the lips of the corpse in the left hand corner.

But I cannot describe the smell. We went into it as we might have gone into the water of a river. We went down in it. There was no bottom, no surface, and no escape. It saturated clothes and skin, it filtered through the nose into throat and lungs, and made us sneeze, cough, and vomit. The smell dissolved our human substance. It tainted it instantaneously and turned it into a viscous mass. To rub one's hands was to rub two hands which did not belong to one, which seemed to be those of a rotting corpse, sticky and impregnated with the smell.

We heaped the dead in the courtyard on top of the horse, poured petrol over them and set fire to the pyre. It stank of roasted flesh, and we vomited. That day we began to vomit and we went on vomiting for days on end.

For the fighting itself was the least of it. The marches through the sandy waste land of Melilla, the outpost of the desert, did not really matter, nor the thirst and the dirty, salty, scanty water, nor the shots and our own dead, warm and flexible, whom we could put on a stretcher and cover with a blanket; nor the wounded who groaned monotonously or screamed shrilly. All that was not important, it lost its force and proportion. But the other dead: those dead we were finding when they had lain for days under the African sun which turned fresh meat putrid within two hours; those mummified dead whose bodies had burst; those mutilated bodies, without eyes and tongues, their genitals defiled, violated with the stakes from the barbed wire, their hands tied up with their bowels, beheaded, armless, legless, sawed in two—oh those dead!

We went on burning the dead in piles sprayed with petrol. We fought on hill tops and in ravines, went hither and thither, slept on the ground, were devoured by lice and tortured by thirst. We constructed new blockhouses, filled thousands of sandbags and lined them up. We did not sleep; we died each day, only to wake the following morning, and in the interval we lived through horrible nightmares. And always we felt the smell. We smelled each other. We smelled of death, of rotting corpses.

I cannot tell the story of Melilla in July 1921. I was there, but I do not know where: somewhere in the midst of shots, shells, and machine-gun rattle, sweating, shouting, running, sleeping on stone and on sand, but above all ceaselessly vomiting, smelling of corpses, finding at every step another dead body, more horrible than any I had known a moment before.

One day at dawn we came back to the city. It was filled with soldiers and with people who were no longer besieged. They lived and laughed. They stopped to speak to each other in the streets and sat down in the shade to take their vermouth. The bootblacks worked their way through the crowds in the cafés. A silvery airplane traced circles overhead. A band was playing in the park. That afternoon we embarked.

We went back to Tetuan. After passing through two days, maddened by images and suffering torture from my disordered stomach, I fell in a

dead faint on the table of the sergeant on guard in the barracks of Alcazaba.

9. The Aftermath

SOMEBODY pulled me by the arm. I had been asleep. It must have
got very late. In front of me I saw a sun-filled window.

"Yes, yes, coming." But I could not speak. The tongue inside my mouth
was a shapeless chunk of flesh. My jaws ached.

"The doctor," said somebody beside me.

"The doctor?" I answered, but again without speaking. My mouth
refused to speak.

At the foot of the bed were an army doctor and a soldier, two blurred
figures with the white cross on their collars.

"How do you feel, my boy?" the doctor asked.

"I? What? Well." But without speaking.

The soldier said something: "It looks as if he understood. I believe
we've pulled him through, sir."

"All right. Go on with the treatment."

The two disappeared from the foot of the bed. Slowly I began to take
in the details of my surroundings. I was in a bed; opposite there was a
row of beds; on my right and on my left there were rows of beds. I felt
a nauseous smell rising from my sheets, that is to say, from me. But it
was different from the smell of the room. The room? It was a huge
wooden hut with a pointed roof on cross beams, a row of windows on
each side, and the sun streaming through those in front of me. There
was a sticky smell of fever and a ceaseless drone overlaid with panting
breath and dull groans. Flies and dying men.

By the side of the bed stood a glazed white jar and a round box of
pills. There was milk in the jar and dozens of flies paddled in it. I felt a
torturing thirst, with that piece of flesh which was my own tongue between my teeth. I turned away from the fly-pool and saw a livid, emaci-
ated face, laboriously breathing as though at any moment the breath
might stop.

I knew where I was: in the hospital in Tetuan, in the ward for infectious diseases. They used to call it the mortuary, for patients would leave it through a back door on a trolley with rubber tires, wrapped in a sheet. And they would never come back.

Only the sick were in the room, but no nurses or medical orderlies. Nobody. My clothes hung over the foot of my bed. The silver stripes on one of the empty sleeves shone. I thought that another "I" was waiting there at the foot of the bed. There was tobacco in my coat! An irresistible longing to smoke took hold of me. I crawled over the bed, snatched my uniform from the iron bar and took out my cigarettes and matches. An hour passed before my heart calmed down and the sweat ceased pouring from me. Only then did I light a cigarette. It tasted of nothing and it hurt to suck it; my lips must have been terribly swollen.

A medical orderly came in and went from bed to bed. He put a thermometer into one man's mouth, left it there, took it out, rubbed it with a rag and put it into the next man's mouth. He chalked something up over the head of each bed. Another orderly followed him with one empty and one full pail. He emptied the glazed jars on each night table into one pail and filled them from the other.

The man with the thermometer came to me.

"Are you better?"

"Yes," I told him by nodding my head.

"Open your mouth."

"No." I pointed with the right hand to my left armpit.

"No, it has to go into the mouth."

"No."

He put the thermometer into my armpit and bent my arm to cover it. "Stay quiet now. Do you want milk?"

"No. Water." But I could not speak and made an effort to show him by gestures what I wanted. He understood in the end.

"Water?"

"Yes."

"No, milk; only milk. Water is prohibited." He wanted to give me the jar which was still dripping from having been dipped into the pail.

"No."

He left the milk on the night table, and flies dived humming down into it. The medical orderly gave me one of the pills from the box. It stuck to my palate until the wafer dissolved and my mouth was filled with a bitter taste. Quinine. Was I down with malaria, then?

When the two men had left I turned round, very painfully, to read the slip at the upper end of my bed. It said "Typh. Ex." below my name and a date and above a fever curve traced over four squares. Had I been here four days? And—"Typh. Ex."? Exanthematic Typhus..

But I had been inoculated against typhus!

The mind of the very ill is like the mind of a child. It clutches at hope with a faith, or sinks into a despair, which hardly ever has any foundation. I was inoculated against typhus, therefore I would not die of typhus. I could not die. All the medical treatises in the world affirmed it: I would not die. Of course, if I had not been inoculated. . . . An infinite calm pervaded me. I would be ill for a week, or two, or three, but I would not die.

"Give me a cigarette," said a very weak voice, "and light it for me." A skeleton-like hand appeared from under the sheet.

I lit the cigarette and gave it to him. "What is the matter with you?" I was astonished to hear a hoarse voice, coming out of me, speaking with a swollen tongue.

"Consumption."

"Then don't smoke. Throw it away."

"What does it matter? I'll die today." He said it so flatly that he convinced me he was going to die. At dusk he moved a hand and said something.

"Eh?" I tried to ask him.

"A-d-i-o-s," he pronounced distinctly and very slowly.

Shortly afterwards the two medical orderlies returned, the one with the thermometer, the other with the pails. They pulled the sheet on my neighbor's bed up to the iron head rest, covering him completely. When they had finished their tasks, they came back pushing one of those high hospital trolleys. One man took him by the feet, the other by the shoulders, without turning back the sheet, but gathering the drooping folds under him, and put him on the trolley. They wheeled him out through the back door.

That night I could not sleep. Drowsy flies kept falling on the whiteness of the sheets and on my face and hands. The heat was suffocating. Electric lamps on the beams shone with a reddish light through their film of dust. Someone at the end of the room began to scream, or rather to howl. He threw himself out of his bed and crawled down between the two rows of beds. But just before he reached me he gripped the iron posts at the foot of a bed, drew himself up, vomited, and crumpled up. Not a single orderly, not a single bell. He stayed there the whole night long on the beaten earth of the floor. In the morning they wrapped him in a sheet and took him away on the trolley.

Then came the doctor. He passed quickly from one bed to the other. "How are you, my boy?" he asked me.

"Better, sir."

"By Jove, it's true." He turned to the next bed. "And this one?"

"He died yesterday."

"All right. Well, go on giving the sergeant quinine. Buck up, my boy, that's nothing."

That day two died. The next night five died. One of them died of smallpox in the first hours of the night. By daybreak he was in full decomposition. Nausea, fear and horror were choking me. In the morning I asked the doctor:

"*Mi capitán,* could I be evacuated to Ceuta?"

"Why, aren't you all right here?"

"Yes, sir. But I've got my family in Ceuta."

"That's a different matter. All right. This afternoon I'll give you an injection and we'll send you there. I quite understand."

They gave me an injection in the arm, wrapped me in blankets, and took me on a stretcher to an ambulance car. There were six of us, three on each side. They must have given me morphine. I went under. When the car began to move, it sickened me and I lost consciousness altogether.

I woke up in another bed beside a wide-open window. There were trees nearby, with many noisy birds. I was on the top of a hill and there, in the distance, was the sea. The small hut held six beds, five of them empty. There were three more windows and the sun flooded the hut. "Morphine is a good thing," I thought. But it was not the effect of morphine.

I was in Ceuta, in the Docker Hospital for infectious diseases, two miles from the city on a hill overlooking the Straits of Gibraltar. An old man in civilian clothes was sitting near the door reading a newspaper. He turned his head, glanced at me and came limping up:

"Now, my boy, are you better? Do you want a drop of milk?"

He went into a little room beside the door and came back with a glass of cold milk. I drank it greedily.

"All right, stay quiet. The Major will come soon."

I have forgotten the Major's name, as we are apt to forget those who have helped us, while we remember enemies. He was a tall, slim man with gray hair, a young and sensitive face, and the hands of a conjuror; he was a most able surgeon and a great psychologist.

He sat down at the upper end of my bed, took out his watch and felt my pulse. He auscultated my chest. He turned down the sheet and examined my abdomen with his clever fingers. I felt as though he were singling out each of my entrails and testing it. Then he covered me up and said:

"Where are you from, my boy?"

"From Madrid, sir."

"Right. Do you smoke?"

"Yes, sir."

He took out his cigarette case, gave me one, and lit another for himself.

"You like girls, don't you?"

"Rather."

"All right. I suppose you've been gadding about like everybody else. Have you had any venereal diseases?"

"No, sir."

"That's good. And what did you have as a child, tell me."

Within a quarter of an hour he had drawn out a general confession of my sins and of my whole life. In the end he said:

"Do you know what you've got?"

"Typhus, I think. But I've been inoculated."

"Yes, typhus. And you're very weak. But never mind, we'll pull you through."

At noon the old man put a bucket of water at the foot of my bed. The Major came back, took my pulse, and told the old man: "Let's get on with it."

He soaked a sheet in the water and between the two of them they wrapped me in the wet sheet and several blankets. The chill moisture on my feverish skin hurt; it dried within a few minutes. They took off the steaming wrappings and put me into another cold, wet sheet, gave me a glass of milk and a pill. I fell asleep. In this way a few days passed. The Major came each time to help the old man. My hands on the sheet grew transparent. I had lost all notion of time.

One day the old man wrapped me in a blanket, lifted me and carried me to a chair by the window. There he left me for an hour to look at the sea and the trees and to listen to the birds. I had forgotten how to walk. The old man taught me each day for a short while. Then I went out and sat down under a tree on the hill top breathing deeply. But I was so weak that the fifty steps from the hut to the tree cost me a river of sweat. I weighed thirty-seven and a half kilograms, about eighty-three pounds.

Then one day they put me into an ambulance and took me to the Central Hospital of Ceuta. There was a panel of five doctors; they read out my name and the Major gave the necessary explanations; the five whispered among themselves and one of them said:

"Two months."

A sergeant came to ask: "Where do you want to go? You have got two months' leave."

One morning I went to the barracks, packed my suitcase, and embarked for Spain. Before I went Major Tabasco, the chief of the regimental office, told me:

"When you come back I shall have a surprise for you."

One day when I was seventeen, I took a bad fall while doing gymnastics, and lost consciousness. They carried me to the first-aid station and from there home. I came to in my bed, wrapped in bandages and feeling a sharp pain. It had been a nasty knock which might have cost me my life, but a week later I was already able to leave the house. The gravest scar the accident left me was the shock I had received when I woke up in bed without having consciously gone there, surrounded by the frightened faces of my people—a shock which was repeated when all persons and things looked so utterly different the first time I went out into the streets again.

I had a similar feeling when I arrived in Madrid. I had carried a very clear and well-defined picture of Madrid and of my people in my mind. But when I was welcomed at the station by my mother, sister, and brother, and when beyond the station gates I met Madrid, my Madrid, everything was changed. There was a vacuum of two years between my family and myself, between Madrid and myself. We had broken the threads of daily contact. If we wanted to join our lives together once more, we would have to tie the broken ends into a knot. But a knot is not a continuity, it is the joining of two separate bits with a break between them.

"How are you, son, how are you?"

"Well, Mother. Quite well."

"Very thin . . . just bones."

"Yes, I know. But never mind. I'm alive. Others have stayed there."

"Yes, yes, I know. Many have stayed there."

"And how are you, Mother?"

"Well."

"And all the others?"

"We manage. Don't worry. We'll fatten you up here in a couple of weeks."

We linked arms and left the station, Rafael carrying my luggage.

"Have you brought tobacco?" he asked.

"Yes."

"And for me, what have you brought for me?" asked my sister.

"A piece of silk. But I've brought nothing for Mother."

"You've come back."

"Ah, but I have brought you something, old lady, old granny—I have brought you something!"

She laughed that little, restrained laugh of hers.

The Plaza de Atocha was filled with early morning noises. People were storming the trams. The taxis waiting at the station and the lorries going to market fought each other for their right of way, and the carts laden with vegetables and fruit tried to filter through, their drivers swearing at the tops of their voices. The street was swept by the sound of tramway bells, motor horns and shouts. For two years I had not heard city noise; I felt weak, weaker than I had been at any time since I left hospital.

"Let's take a cup of coffee or something. I slept badly on the train."

We took coffee, and I drank a small brandy to revive me; but in the end we took a taxi. As soon as we arrived home I went to bed, pausing only to take out the tobacco for Rafael, the silk for Concha and the scarf for my mother. They had prepared my bed for me, my old gilt bed with fine white sheets, and the room smelled of fresh paint.

In the afternoon I reported to the military authorities to get my papers in order, then went home and dressed in mufti. My uniform was left hanging on the clothes-peg of my bedroom, and Rafael and I went out for a walk. When we were already in the doorway my mother pleaded:

"Do go and see So-and-so and So-and-so. They've kept on asking about you."

"Mother, I won't go and see anybody."

"Do as you like, my boy."

But Madrid was still too much for me. My ears could not bear the Puerta de Sol. We took refuge in the silent little streets round the Calle de Segovia, walked round a bit and returned home. We had not spoken much; we did not know how to begin. We commented on street incidents and fell back into silence. At home, mother laid the table for supper. She had prepared steaks and fried potatoes and put them on the table proudly and gaily.

None of us had spoken a word about Morocco yet. I would have wished to spare my mother the pain, I would have liked to be able to eat that meat with an appetite and a happy face. But since those dead of Melilla I could not touch meat. The sight and the smell of it invariably made me see and smell corpses, rotting or burning on a petrol-soaked pyre, and made me vomit. It produced an immediate mental association and reaction against which I was powerless.

I wanted to master myself, and began cutting the meat on my plate. Rosy juice trickled out. I was sick.

The others were alarmed, and I had to explain.

"It's nothing. I'm not ill. It's only nausea."

In order to escape from myself, I began to speak. I told them what I had seen, in all its details. I told them of the dead of Melilla, of the dying in the hospital of Tetuan, of hunger and lice, of moldy beans boiled with red pepper, of the miserable life of Spain's soldiers and of the shamelessness and corruption of their commanders. And I began to cry like a small boy, unhappier than ever because of the pain I was causing, because of the pain I had seen.

"How you've deceived me!" said my mother.

"I?"

"Yes, you with your letters. I knew things were not going well. They never go well for soldiers. But lately I'd been content. You were a sergeant. And I believed many things, very many, you told me in your letters."

"But, Mother, they were all true."

"Yes, to be sure, they were true. But you always wrote about things and never about yourself. Now I see what it meant. A curse on the war and whoever invented it!"

"But, Mother, we can't do anything about it."

"I don't know—I don't know."

On the following morning I felt unable to get out of bed. My mother sent for the doctor, a kindly old man who examined me from head to foot. There was nothing the matter with me, I was just extremely weak and suffering from the sudden change of climate and altitude. I should gradually accustom myself to the city, go to a park and sit there in the open, simply breathing. As soon as I felt stronger I should begin to walk about.

In the meantime I was left alone. My brother went to work. My sister was in the little fruit shop the family had set up in the Calle Ancha. My mother pottered about in the flat. I got up and searched for something to read.

In an odd corner I found a heap of old newspapers, over a hundred of them, an odd assortment of dates and types; there were morning and evening papers, illustrated weeklies and literary reviews. The main theme of their headlines was Morocco. I read them all.

What a soldier sees of a war can be compared with what an actor sees of a film in which he has a part. The director tells him to stand in a certain spot, make certain gestures, and say certain words. He puts him in a field and makes him repeat a sequence of phrases and a sequence of gestures; ten times he makes him open the door of a drawing room which has only three walls, and kiss the hand of a lady. When the actor goes to see the finished film, he hardly recognizes himself, and is forced to reconstruct scenes which he had repeated a number of times. Thus the actor has two sets of impressions. The first is part of his own life and consists of a series of postures, make-ups, lighting effects, rehearsals, decorations and instructions from the stage manager. The other set of impressions comes when he sees the finished picture in which he is no longer himself but quite a different personality, part of a plot, a person with an artificial life which depends on the way in which scenes acted by him are linked up with the scenes of the other actors.

I found myself passing through a similar experience when I read that heap of out-of-date newspapers.

"The vanguard advanced amid a hail of bullets, the soldiers singing patriotic songs. 'Give it to them, boys,' shouted the Colonel at their head. Ferocious Riff warriors were lurking behind every shrub and stone. The gallant Major X led his *Regulares* in a bayonet attack. A cavalry squadron pursued the fleeing Moors with drawn swords. At the same time the Larache column scattered into small groups on the left flank, over a front more than two kilometers long, and began an enveloping movement." And so on and so forth.

I had seen the Spanish war correspondents in Morocco, attached to the Staff of a column, clad half in uniform, half in sports clothes, field glasses over their shoulders, observing the front at a distance of five kilometers, taking notes and asking the staff captains to explain things to them. Occasionally one of them would risk his life by joining advanced troops during an operation. In neither case did they see the war as a whole, but they were forced to tell about it as though they did; therefore they created for the benefit of their readers a war as artificial as the plot of a film, and described it as though they had been magically floating in the clouds, taking in the battlefield as a whole and with every minute detail at a single glance.

The war—my war—and the Disaster of Melilla—my disaster—bore no resemblance to the war and to the disaster which those Spanish newspapers unfolded before their public.

One photograph showed "General X addressing the heroic forces of the Ceuta Relief Column before their embarkation for Melilla."

There I was, somewhere among the "heroes." The report which accompanied the photograph stated that the General's address had been listened to with reverence and received with acclamations. As though we were in a state to acclaim anything after our march through Morocco! They had lined us up on parade to be inspected by the General and his Staff. A few soldiers at the back lay down and immediately fell asleep. A few fainted while they were standing at attention after that day of ceaseless marching. The only acclamations I remember were muttered curses. While the old man with the beard was walking up and down the rows we called him "son of a bitch" and "bastard"; our feet were swollen, our throats parched, and he forced us to stand at attention with every bone in our bodies aching.

"A fifteen-centimeter howitzer shelling the enemy."

The photograph showed an enormous gun with smoke pouring from its mouth. Perhaps it was one of those ill-famed batteries sent over from the Canary Islands, which showered shrapnel on our own troops and made us scatter like rabbits.

The descriptions of the Disaster of Melilla were full of the horrible sights in the reconquered positions, sights which enabled the garrison's last hours to be reconstructed. Occasionally the "sole survivor" was quoted on the tragedy. All accounts agreed on the matchless valor of the officers, which had sustained the morale of the men.

I had met survivors whose officers had torn off their insignia or simply changed uniforms with a soldier, because it gave them a better chance of being spared by the Moors, and had run away from their posts, pursued by the bullets of their own men. And I had known at least one surviving officer who had earned his laurels by wenching in Melilla town during the night of the Disaster, after which there was no one left at his post to testify against him. His superiors were faced with the alternative of decorating him for bravery or court-martialing him for desertion from a front-line post. They had decorated him. He might have been one of the men quoted in the press. .

I vented my bitterness to Rafael. "You don't know any more about Morocco here than about the moon," I said.

"Don't you believe it," he answered. "You've been reading the front pages, but in reality things are far more serious. I believe they'll cost the King his crown. People are demanding an investigation into what happened, and of course the whole Opposition has made use of the opportunity to air the Moroccan problem in the Cortes. It has been said publicly that the King himself gave the order to General Silvestre [1] to advance, even against Berenguer's instructions. And they say that an inquiry will be held."

"An inquiry? Do you mean a military inquiry directed against the

[1] Silvestre was the commanding general of the zone of Melilla, one of the three military zones into which Spanish Morocco was divided. He launched a series of operations against the *kabilas* of the Riff, at a time when operations against the Moorish leader Raisuni were in full swing in the zones of Ceuta and Larache. Silvestre advanced in a straight line from Melilla to Annual, leaving nothing but a thin chain of strong points behind to cover his offensive. Abd-el-Krim roused the Moors in the rear, and Silvestre with his force, as well as the garrisons of all his outposts, were massacred.

Army and the King? Who is supposed to conduct it? You're all crazy. The first Parliamentary Commission to go to Africa and investigate what those fine gentlemen have been and are doing there would be chucked out, or driven out by bullets."

"I tell you things are getting serious. There is a very important factor in public opinion now, I mean the expeditionary corps. The people who paid up their 'quotas' for others to go to Morocco instead of them must now go themselves. All those fathers who've paid cash to keep their sons out of Africa now find that the boys are being sent there all the same, and that they must pay for the equipment on top of everything, and they feel they've been swindled. Oh yes, if it was only the poor people who were affected you would be right. But now the others feel it where it hurts most. Things are moving."

Slowly I was absorbed into the atmosphere that reigned in Madrid. My ignorance of past events made things difficult for me. Very few Spanish newspapers, if any, had reached the Moroccan camps. In Ceuta a few Madrid dailies and the local paper, *El Defensor de Ceuta,* were on sale. But everywhere in Morocco, in Ceuta as well as in the outposts, only the most reactionary press had been admitted. A soldier who read *El Liberal* was at once marked as a "revolutionary." In the barracks, papers like *El Socialista* were strictly prohibited; to be found in possession of a copy meant immediate arrest and ceaseless persecution. Theoretically, everyone was free to buy whatever periodical he wanted. But in practice the owners of the few newspaper kiosks knew the tricks of the game; when anybody asked for a leftish paper he was told that it had just sold out or that it had not arrived that day—and he was offered *ABC* or *El Debate.* The civilian population kept up the boycott. The majority depended on the army for their living, directly or indirectly; as there was no industry, there were no skilled workers apart from those attached to the army, and the few fishermen and laborers were nearly all illiterate, and all subservient.

When I had first come to Africa I had tried to keep up my daily reading of the Madrid press. I had been told gently that if I wanted to stay in the Regimental Office (where I was a corporal) and not to go to the front line, I would have to become a reader of *ABC* or *El Debate.* For a time I had read nothing but *El Defensor de Ceuta;* I had even sent in a few sentimental poems under a pen name. They were printed, paid for at a rate of five pesetas each and served me as a half-conscious vengeance. Later I had stopped reading newspapers altogether and confined myself to books of which I soon had a small library. But one day, when I was reading in the office, the senior major had happened to see me and asked me the title of the book. It was a cheap and bad edition of Bertha von Suttner's *Lay Down Arms!*

"*Caramba,* you certainly bring a nice kind of book into barracks!"
I had not read more than a few pages, and said ingenuously: "They've
sent me some books from home, including this one. As you see, sir, I've
only just started it, and can't say anything about it, but since the author
is an Austrian aristocrat"—I had read the introduction—"it won't be very
revolutionary, I imagine."

"All right. . . . So they've sent you more books, have they? Let's have
a look at them." He said it, not severely, but paternally. He was a very
kind and good man, was Don José Tabasco, but very much the Catholic
army officer. He was convinced of the infallibility of all the laws and
rulings of the Roman Catholic Church, and of their good effect when put
into practice. Thus I lost a number of books by Victor Hugo, Anatole
France, Miomandre, and Blasco Ibañez, and of course *Lay Down Arms!*

He had not confiscated the books because he was incapable of violating
the letter of the law which entitled me to read all books published in
Spain. But he patted me on the back: "My boy, I'm going to speak to you
as if I were your father. We're in barracks here. I know you for a good
lad, and I've nothing against your reading these books. But I know how
things happen in barracks. Your comrades will want to borrow the books,
and you won't say no, of course. Now, once put these books into the hands
of poor devils who can hardly read or write, and they act as explosives.
Look here, do as I tell you and burn them."

The Major was my direct superior. I had years in barracks before me.
The Major was pleased when I burned those books in the fire of the
regimental kitchen. Yet I knew that the clandestine sale and purchase of
pornographic books was viewed with more than tolerance by the officers
in general, both in barracks and in front-line positions. Whenever one
of the captains began a campaign to rid his company of filth, his fellow
officers would say to him: "Look here, you fool, you must leave the men
something to amuse themselves with. After all, we all like to see a fine
woman without her clothes on. You won't change things. You can't
search their pockets every day, and anyhow it's better they should read
that sort of stuff than *El Socialista.*"

After these experiences in Ceuta I had clung to my reading of French
books while we built the road at Hamara; and I had wearied of it. I had
not seen any newspapers there. In Tetuan I did not even try to break
through the laws of military life. And then came the campaigns in Beni-
Aros, and Xauen, and Melilla, and the hospital: when I found myself in
Madrid I had to begin all over again, to pick up threads, to understand
what was going on.

The bar of the "Portuguese" still existed at the corner of the Calle de la Paz. The clerks from the banks and the insurance companies in the neighborhood continued to meet there as they had done when I was serving my apprenticeship in the bank. At seven o'clock in the evening the bar was overcrowded, but I knew that my old colleague Plá would be in his customary place. I saw him at once when I entered, at the second table to the left in the back room. He was fatter and more short-sighted than ever. It seemed as though his eyeglasses had become bigger, and his nose was glued more closely to the newspaper. He wore his hair cropped, and as it was of the stiff, black variety, his head looked like the back of a worn-down nail brush.

I tapped him on the shoulder: "Hullo, Plá!"

He raised his little pig-eyes, made still smaller by the lenses. Either he could not see me well enough, or he did not recognize me; but it must have been due to his eyesight, for my face had hardly changed since I was sixteen, except for the beard which had begun to sprout in odd places.

"Eh? Hullo. Have a drink and sit down."

"So we don't remember our friends any more?"

His small eyes seemed to sniff me; for when he tried to see you, moving his head from side to side to find the right focus, his protruding eyes appeared not so much to look at as to scent you. When his face was only a foot from mine he recognized me. He stood up, his short legs shuffling, and embraced me with excited ejaculations.

First I told him about myself, then he poured out his lamentations about the work in the bank, and finally we began to talk about the political situation.

"What do you think of it, Luis?" I asked him.

"I think things are coming to a head now. The racket has just about finished for 'Narizotas.'" (Narizotas, Long Nose, was the name by which the King of Spain was known among the people during the last years of his reign, the same name which had been given to his great-grandfather Ferdinand VII before him.) "In a year at the outside we'll have our Republic."

"You're an optimist, Luis."

"But it's bound to come." He waxed confidential. "All kinds of dirty stories are coming out now about Narizotas. Marquet paid him millions to get a license to open his gambling houses, the Ice Palace, you know, and the Casino of San Sebastian. People say Narizotas has got his fingers in the *Circulo de Bellas Artes,* too. He's in the Riff Mines together with Romanones, and in the supply business of motor vehicles for the army with Mateu. And now there is the Morocco business on top of it."

"The Morocco business—and what is the Morocco business?"

"Pooh, a nasty story! Because it's he that's responsible for the Disaster.

He wrote to Silvestre behind Berenguer's back and told him to carry on.
They say he even sent a telegram to Silvestre after Annual had been
taken, in which he said: 'Long live your guts!' And when he was told
about the catastrophe and that there were thousands of dead, he is supposed to have said: 'Chicken-meat is cheap!' Of course, all the reactionaries
are defending him in the Cortes, but the Republicans and Socialists are
getting very strong. And then there's another thing. Now that the expeditionary forces are sent over and all those fellows who had bought their
exemption have got to go too, many of the Liberals want to get to the
bottom of things. It smarts when they've got to lose their sons after paying the money. One thing is certain: there will be legal proceedings."

"Proceedings?" I exclaimed.

"Yes. Proceedings to establish the responsibility for what happened in
Africa. The generals themselves are seething with rage. They have
threatened to demonstrate in the streets as in the times of Isabella II. But
things are different now. Just let them come out! They'll see fireworks all
right."

"And what about Barcelona?"

"Oh, nothing. Only that people in Barcelona go for a walk, and someone comes up and pumps them full of lead. And the other people don't
even turn their heads. Sometimes the gunmen are Anarchists and sometimes they are paid by the Government. But the Catalans don't interest
me. They can all get killed, for all I care. Mind you, all these things
help, of course. The greater the row, the better. Then we'll have a new
government every fortnight, and then d'you think the Ministers will even
have time to sort themselves out?"

He paused, drank his glass of wine, called for the waiter, and ordered
more drinks.

"But it's all because of the European war. It's a question of economics,
d'you see?"

"Not quite."

"But it's very simple. Look, during the war our people got sick of
earning money. Men who had been going round with their trousers torn
suddenly opened fantastic bank accounts; newspapers with no sale at all
got paid by some embassy and bought a rotary press over night; Ministers
got million-peseta tips; old mules, for which a gypsy wouldn't have given
fifty pesetas, fetched five thousand; the Catalans manufactured millions
of blankets; people in Valencia sold their fruit before the crops were ripe;
wheat brought in a double price; sailing boats got a thousand *duros* to
sail from Bilbao to St. Jean de Luz; they were torpedoed as soon as they
left harbor, and got ten thousand *duros* insurance money. And then the
war was over, and everything came to an end. The new factories have

all been closed and the workers have been turned out in the streets. The railways are ruined, or at least they say they are. While everybody had money Madrid was invaded by taxis; and now the taxi owners are starving. And the banks established during the war have suspended payments. . . . From the King down to the last Spaniard everybody needs money now. The King sells a license to open a casino, or eggs on Silvestre to conquer the Riff so that he can sell a few more mines to Romanones. The railway companies demand State subsidies and threaten to suspend traffic without them. Then they get their subsidies, and the Ministers get their commissions. You can go to any Ministry with fifty pesetas in your hand, and they'll give you what you ask for. If you have a million they'll give you the whole Ministry with all the Civil Servants and their desks thrown in. And because somebody has to pay for it all, they get rid of workers or reduce their wages. And so we have a strike every ten days. Believe me, it'll all come to a bad end."

Rafael brought me an invitation to see his boss. Don Manuel Guerrero was at that time Managing Director of the Madrid Bakeries (in liquidation), but he had been a major in the Engineers and had left the army, as had many of the more cultured and socially more independent officers of the Engineers and Artillery corps, because they found themselves involved in ugly conflicts with the other type of officer, those who were only interested in making a rapid career and doing business in the Moroccan War.

Don Manuel was some fifty years old, gray-haired, short and squarely built, with deep-set eyes, a powerful forehead and a somewhat aggressive jaw. He spoke brusquely, but after a few minutes of conversation all his stiffness vanished, and he took me over his closed factory, telling me his story, which was filling his whole mind.

He had set up a big, modern bread factory in the outskirts of Madrid, near a railway junction, apparently with every prospect of revolutionizing the bread supply of the capital. His organization and the site of his plant permitted him to buy and transport the wheat direct from the Spanish producer or from the ports. He was able to produce bread more cheaply and under far more hygienic conditions than small bakers, many of whom still kneaded the dough with their feet and undercut each other by adulterating the flour and cheating over the weights. There was a single other modern bakery, belonging to Count Romanones. The enterprise was launched as a limited company, financed by the banks. But soon he had found himself pitted against the vested interests of two powerful groups, both profiting from the high price of wheat: the landowners and traders in control of Spanish wheat and the businessmen controlling the wheat imports. He had had to obtain special permits for importing his own cheap wheat, but he was unable to pay the customs duties which were raised as soon as his grain cargoes had arrived. He had tried to fight. And then he had come up against the banks which preferred their bigger and more profitable customers, his adversaries. Now he was ruined.

"My last hope," he said, "was to get a supply contract with the army; but to come to an agreement with the Commissariat, I should have had to stop being honest. And I've always been honest."

Between the huge trays of the ovens, the shovels of the kneading gear, the beams of the roofs and the conveyor belts hung spiders' webs.

"Do you realize that this is an object lesson—a very grave symptom of the catastrophe which is overtaking Spain? If God does not avert it. But it does not look as though He would avert it! You see, we are an exporting country, and if we don't import the grain and the raw materials we need, the other countries won't buy our oil and fruit and textiles. I can't import wheat, but the textile plants of Catalonia are lying idle because the Argentine no longer buys cloth in exchange. Then the workers there demonstrate, and it all ends in man-hunts in the streets. And now, to crown it all, Morocco: tell me about it."

I told him I knew nothing of Morocco but what I had seen; I spoke of the track of Hamara and the expedition to Melilla. He listened, nodding his head sharply from time to time. Then he said:

"It would be best to clear out of Morocco. Let the Powers of the Algeciras Treaty see how they can clear up the mess. But the trouble is that anyone who tries to follow such a course will provoke a revolution from above. Where and on what are all those people to live? They cannot live without their profits. And they are too powerful."

He stopped, thought it over and fell back, inevitably, into his own story:

"Even this poor factory of mine would have worked if I had liked to take part in shabby deals, or if I had listened to the good advice of the biggest baker of Madrid, Count Romanones."

But I hardly followed his argument any longer. The name of Romanones sounding through the dusty, deserted hall made me think of another plant in which I had worked years before, as secretary to its Managing Director: Spanish Motors, Ltd., the great factory whose aircraft were to transform Spain's aviation.

I had been a lad of nineteen then. I had seen and taken in things as they came, without understanding them. I had an important and enviable job; the prettiest girls of the small town of Guadalajara were interested in me because I was the secretary of Don Juan de Zaracondegui, and because the thousands of pesetas on the pay roll went through my hands, and because I had to interview and engage workers. I had my adventure and liked it, enjoying myself hugely when I deceived the watchfulness of the girl's parents and the blackmailing brutality of her brothers.

Guadalajara had been the seat of the administration of a small province, a tiny, miserly town under the iron rule of its greatest land-owner, political boss and permanent deputy to the Cortes, Count Romanones. It consisted of farmers, tavern keepers, and a Military Academy for Engineers. The girls became engaged to the cadets but married farmers, with the result that at night the students from the Academy and the farmers' sons went in separate groups to play the guitar under the windows of pretty girls and to end up in free fights. Occasionally a captain of the Engineers would come back to Guadalajara and marry one of the girls; this fact kept alive the hopes of the unmarried ones.

When the plant of Spanish Motors had been installed in Guadalajara, it had caused an upheaval. A host of draftsmen, employees, and mechanics invaded the taverns of the cadets. Farmhands who had earned two or three pesetas a day became workers in Spanish Motors and earned double. Parents and daughters saw unhoped-for vistas beckoning. Their life was changed and to me it had seemed fun to be part of it.

Now, four years later, I saw the other side of the story; I saw the pieces falling into place.

During the Great War, Spanish Motor Engines of Barcelona had produced engines for the Allies in co-operation with French factories, and as a side-line for the Spanish Army which was then going through the first stages of mechanization. Later, the new Service Corps were placed under a separate military department called the Electro-Technical Center, with a captain of the Engineers, Don Ricardo Goytre, at its head. Perhaps because there were so many commissions to pay, Spanish Motor Engines, Ltd. began to supply the Spanish Army with material which failed in the hard test it had to undergo in Morocco from 1918 onwards.

Soon, extraordinary budgets had to be granted to the army to buy new and better cars. Finally the Cortes decided that a big national competition was to be held for motorcars and aircraft. The successful types were to be adopted by the army, but only Spanish factories were admitted.

The only national plant of any importance was Spanish Motor Engines; but too many of its motorcars and lorries were lying dismantled, as scrap-iron, in the military car parks of Spain and Africa. It would not have been popular for Spanish Motor Engines to emerge as the winner in the competition. So Spanish Motors, Ltd. was created.

Count Romanones supplied a large site near the railway station of Guadalajara, where workshops were constructed as soon as shares had been issued to a value of five million pesetas. Ample room was left for

an airdrome which, by its strategic situation, seemed destined to become
the most important in Spain, and indeed, one of the most important in
Europe. Don Miguel Mateu became Chairman of the Board of Directors;
he happened to be the Managing Director of Spanish Motor Engines, Ltd.
in Barcelona. Don Ricardo Goytre resigned from his post as Director of
the Army Electro-Technical Center and became Technical Director of
Spanish Motors; Captain Barrón, the designer of one of the two plane
types which were to be entered for the competition, became Chief Engineer. Don Juan de Zaracondegui, a Basque aristocrat who had been a
highly placed official of Spanish Motor Engines, became Managing Director. And finally, the Director of the Madrid branch of Spanish Motor
Engines, Don Francisco Aritio, became Business Manager of Spanish
Motors.

"Rich people get everything for nothing," is a saying of the Spanish
poor.

Don Miguel Mateu owned one of the biggest iron and machine-tool
stores of Spain in Barcelona; he was also the agent of the biggest North
American and German tool factories. He supplied all the machine tools
to Spanish Motors.

Count Romanones owned extensive waste lands in Guadalajara. He
supplied the site for the factory.

Neither of them accepted any money for this. Spanish Motors was a
patriotic enterprise which would free Spain from her dependence on foreign countries, and give her her own aviation.

Five million Free Shares, or rather, Shares allocated for a Consideration
other than Cash, were issued. I was ordered to begin the Account Books
of Spanish Motors by entering the following accounts in my best copper-
plate letters:

S.M. Don Alfonso XIII	1,000,000
Don Miguel Mateu	2,000,000
El Conde de Romanones	1,000,000
Don Francisco Aritio	500,000

The rest of these Shares were entered in the name of the inventor of the
engines of Spanish Motor Engines. They were the payment for his patent
rights on those very engines which were now to be produced under the
name of Spanish Motors, Ltd. But I forgot what name I wrote.

The competition was duly held. The contracts for the army were given
to Spanish Motors, Ltd., while the engineer Lacierva, with his first auto-
gyro models, was ridiculed. The new plant of Spanish Motors was inspected by His Majesty the King. Don Miguel Mateu sent machinery
from his stocks in Barcelona, provided by the Allied Machinery Company

of Chicago. The Shares rose on the Stock Exchange. Green-painted lorries arrived from Barcelona in Guadalajara and were handed over to the army. The Board of Directors of Spanish Motors arranged for an English firm to construct aircraft for them.

At that stage I left my job because my amorous adventure had led me into deep waters. Since then I had forgotten about the books I had kept there.

Now, with the typhus of Africa still in my bones, in the storm-laden atmosphere of Madrid, I saw that the track from that deal in Guadalajara had led to Africa.

I went back to Africa after two months' leave, deeply afraid for Spain.

Part II

1. The New Game

THERE was a rough sea in the Straits. The little old steamer rose and sank, pitched and lurched. Hills and houses were swaying drunkenly as we entered the port of Ceuta.

I found the town utterly changed.

When you live in a place you build up a mental picture of your surroundings. It sleeps at the back of your brain while you are there in the flesh, but when you go away it comes alive and takes the place of the lost direct vision. Then you return one day, expecting to find places, things, and people as you have carried them in your mind, as you have come to believe them to be. But your mental picture and reality clash, and the shock goes right through you.

The cool silent little street is now filled with people, noise, and glaring light. The crowded café, where your friends had sat in heated discussions, is half empty and the friendly waiter cannot remember what you used to order. It is as though an actor were to go to the theater at ten in the morning, convinced that he would have to appear on the scene, only to find charwomen dusting the plush seats in front of an empty stage strewn with props and flooded with gray daylight.

Often have I suffered this jarring shock, but when I came to Ceuta from Madrid, I was conscious of it for the first time. I had known every corner of Ceuta, each corner in its own moment. Now, time and place failed to synchronize, and I found myself on strange ground.

I wanted to breakfast before reporting to barracks, and I went to my café, that is to say, to the café I had frequented as a corporal. But in the doorway I realized with a jolt that I was now a sergeant. This was not the right place for me. I would have to go to the sergeants' café. So I went to the "Perla." A few other sergeants were breakfasting on coffee and buns; I sat down and ordered coffee. The waiter did not know me, I did not know the place, and everyone looked at me because I was a stranger to them. I gulped down my coffee and left, bitterly resenting that I had not been able to feel the welcoming warmth of my soldiers' café where the waiter had been a friend and the room had been dirtier and less pretentious, but more human.

To be a sergeant in Ceuta meant to have social standing. There were three castes in the small town, neatly separated into water-tight compartments. The privates and the corporals, together with the simple workers, dockers, masons, street sweepers, and so on, were the proletariat. The non-commissioned officers, sergeants and sergeant-majors, the few skilled workers and minor tradesmen, the lesser clerks and employees, were the middle class. The upper class, or aristocracy, consisted of the officers, businessmen, civil servants, judiciary and clergy. The whole social life of the town was so regulated that these groups could not mix. There were cafés for soldiers, for N.C.O.s, and for officers. There were brothels for each of the three castes. Certain streets and even certain parts of the same street were practically reserved for one or the other group. In the Calle Real, which runs straight through the town from north to south, the soldiers would keep to the middle of the street. On the pavement they would have to make room for women and for all their superiors; and as they could not fail to meet a woman or an officer at every five steps, they preferred not to leap continually from the pavement to the street. On the whole the soldiers fled the streets in the center of the town where they had eternally to salute; the officers avoided the side streets where they could not exhibit themselves to the public that counted.

As in other Spanish towns, people in Ceuta used to promenade from sunset to dinner time, walking up and down a length of pavement, greeting friends and flirting. Each caste had its own length of street. In one, the soldiers walked out with the servant girls. In another, the officers walked out with young ladies who were accompanied by their mammas and watched over by grave-faced papas. And the sergeants had a promenade of their own, where they courted girls pretending to be well-to-do young ladies, with papas pretending to occupy important posts.

I could no longer go to the soldiers' café.

I would no longer be able to enter the familiar tavern, I would not be able to promenade on that length of pavement, and so on and so forth.

In this frame of mind I reported to barracks; they told me to present myself to the Major who would come at eleven o'clock. For more than an hour I wandered round the Engineers' barracks. A building with two terraces, an enormous wooden hut, outhouses for kitchens, stables, workshops, infirmary, flanking big courtyards and small courtyards, all whitewashed and very clean. Every day a soldier was detailed off to put another layer of whitewash on some of the walls, so that every few days the cycle would begin again.

I was bored with waiting and I was bored with the endless white glare of the barracks, almost deserted at that hour. Well, next morning I would go to Tetuan and from there to the front; there I would be less bored. I would at least know people and find company. In Ceuta I knew hardly anybody. My contact with the soldiers was severed, my contact with the sergeants stationed in the place not yet established on the new level of equality. I felt an outsider with both.

At eleven the Major entered the regimental office. I let a short time go by, and went into his room. "At your orders, sir."

"Hullo, Barea—back already? You're still pretty thin. Take care of yourself. Now, Sergeant Cárdenas has been promoted to quartermaster sergeant. I thought that you might take over the office work. Let me know whether you would rather go to the front. Not that I imagine you would."

I thanked him.

"Take it easy for a few days and get into touch with Cárdenas, to learn about things. But no fooling about, eh?"

You entered the Regimental Office through a small anteroom furnished with two tables and a monkish bench of hard wood, just wide enough for six persons. The two orderlies were forever sitting on that bench, zealously preventing anybody else from occupying their territory. Behind the table sat two scribes, who interrogated arrivals and made everybody fill in a form. Then there was a wooden partition topped by wire netting, and behind it two cubicles separated by a wire screen and joined by a small opening in the wire. The left-hand cubicle was that of Corporal Surribas, the right-hand one that of Sergeant Cárdenas. Surribas was a kind of secretary to Cárdenas, from whom he received orders through the little window. Cárdenas was a kind of secretary to the C.O. and had not only a desk of his own but also a smaller desk in front, so that he could dictate to somebody else if he wished.

There was a bigger room at the back, with five desks and four clerks. The shelves that ran along its wall were stacked with paper bundles tied with red tape. These bundles contained the history of all the soldiers who had passed through the regiment within the last twenty years. One book-shelf was bulging with larger folio files which held the history of all the officers throughout the same years.

The room smelled of worm-eaten paper and of insects. For there is an insect smell; it is sweetish and sticks in your nose and throat, inseparably mixed with the finest dust. If you lift a stack of very old papers or a worm-eaten book from its place, there rises a little cloud of dust and

powder, and the smell is so strong that even the oldest clerk cannot help
sneezing.

And the room was filled with insect sound. In my days as a corporal
I worked there and came to know it. While the four of us were busy
writing or typing, and chatting in low voices so as not to incense the
sergeant, we would not hear the sound. But whenever I sought refuge
there on hot African nights, I heard the ceaseless toil of the demolition
squad attacking bureaucracy. They were gnawing the paper, boring
through it, nesting in it, making love. There were centipedes with a nib-
like claw like crayfish, which dug through whole bundles from cover
to cover. There were crunching cockroaches which slowly ate away the
edge of the pages. There were caterpillars spinning their cocoons underneath a file, to leave them as butterfly-moths in May. On the highest
shelves with the oldest stacks of paper monstrous spiders, wasps, and
horseflies had their nests where they slept through the winter. In the lowest files, near the floor, mice were padding their holes with fibers taken
from the red tape. Time and again, ants would invade the place, as
though they wanted to carry printed and written letters away to their ant-
heaps, like grains of wheat.

While I had worked in the office I had nicknamed Sergeant Cárdenas
"The Parrot," partly on account of his wire cage and partly on account
of his shrill voice which would cut through the silence, always rasping,
always angry. Otherwise I knew nothing about him but the outside: a
well-built, dark man, meticulously shaved, exceedingly grave and exceedingly irritable, his peasant origin visible only in the uneasiness with
which he wore his expensive, correct uniform, as though it belonged to
somebody else.

Now I found myself in the parrot's cage, sitting at the desk in front of
him and waiting. He wore a brand new uniform of quartermaster sergeant; after his promotion he had not sewed on the new stripes, but
simply bought a new outfit.

"Well now, you're going to be my successor. It ought to have been
Surribas by the right of seniority, but the poor fellow is quite mad. One
couldn't rely on him. This is a post which needs a lot of tact. The work
isn't difficult but you must always know where you're treading, and who's
who. Keep your eyes skinned, because if they can, they'll try and put a
fast one over on you. I'll explain to you how it works, in general terms.
You'll grasp the details in time, and anyhow you'll be staying in contact
with me because I'll be on H.Q. duty."

He made a pause. We lighted cigarettes, and he went on.

"I've been looking after the accounts myself. You'll have to do the same
if you want to get on. Surribas keeps the books and will help you in

all the auxiliary work, but the accounts are your job. Surribas may write the figures into the ledger and add them up, but it's you who give him the figures and you alone know why they are given. Sometimes you won't know either; for instance, if the Major comes and tells you to enter something or other. Then you put it down and that's that. You may guess at the reason, but keep your mouth shut and don't ask questions. In such cases you're to the Major what Surribas is to you. But those are exceptions. Normally you simply keep the regimental accounts.

"As you know the State allots a certain sum to every man in the army, from private to colonel. On the basis of this budget, each Company makes out its accounts and presents them to you at the end of each month. You examine them, pass them, and the Company gets the money due to it from the Cashier."

"It doesn't sound very difficult."

"No. That isn't difficult. A statement of accounts is sent to the *Tribunal de Cuentas* where they're passed and filed. Now the point is that no statement of account must ever be rejected as inaccurate. Therefore each entry must have its voucher. And here you have the key to our accountancy: The Voucher. No voucher, no money is our rule."

"That's not difficult either, it seems to me."

"But it is difficult. The voucher question is the most difficult of all. I'll give you an example, and you'll see why.

Then, using as his example the issuing and accounting for rope-soled canvas shoes, he explained the complicated machinery by which the privates were made to pay for thousands of pairs of those *alpargatas* which were officially a part of their free equipment. The swindle went all the way up the line to the manufacturer who supplied the *alpargatas*. The privates knew, of course, that they were being cheated, and that the thievery began with their quartermaster sergeants, but they didn't dare to make a formal complaint about them. Having explained in detail the *alpargatas* fraud, all covered up with vouchers, "The Parrot" said: "And now do you see?"

"Yes, I see more or less. No wonder you've got as nervous as you are with all these complications."

"Yes. Imagine that it is the same with every scrap of equipment and even armament. And all the accounts with their vouchers go through your hands. The only thing you've got to do is to see that every item in every account has its voucher, never mind about the other things. Now I'll tell you what to do. Take the latest statement of account, go and see Romero, the sergeant of our depot, and meet the various quartermaster sergeants of the companies. I won't give you any work to do until Monday at the horse auction. You'll have to act as secretary there, but since it is the first time I'll help you."

In the courtyard flanked by the stables stood a big table, a comfortable armchair, and on both sides of it a row of chairs. The papers for the twelve animals to be auctioned were on the table. Civilians, who were allowed to come to the barracks on this occasion, were milling around in the canteen. The sunlight thrown back from the lime-washed walls was blindingly white. In this crude light the gypsies stood out like statuary, their short white jackets showing off wide shoulders and narrow waists, their dark corduroy trousers tight across the hips and widening around the knees. They beat a tattoo on the paving stones with their sticks, the kind of stick all cattle dealers carry, they whispered in the fashion of conspirators among each other and counted their money and shouted for wine. Horses and mules were tied up along the watering trough, plunging their noses into the water now and again more to cool off than to drink. The whole courtyard smelled of the sweat of men and horses.

People had been waiting since ten o'clock in the morning. The auction was supposed to start at eleven. At half-past eleven the Colonel of the Army Service Corps arrived; he was to preside over the auction board. I felt uneasy. I was to be auctioneer and secretary; I was to take down the prices fetched, to receive the cash, to write receipts, to issue the papers for each animal to each buyer and to get his signature for them.

At last the board was assembled at the table: the Colonel of the Army Service Corps, a slow-moving, rheumy old man with a weak, shrill voice in the armchair, to his right and left the Colonel—our C.O.—the Major, the Veterinary Captain, the Adjutant, and two officers I did not know.

The gypsies ranged themselves in a circle round the table. The Veterinary Captain, standing in the center, gave the order to lead in the first horse. I rose and read out:

"Fundador. Three years old. Sixteen hands. Bay with white markings on the haunches. Tuberculosis of the lungs. Fifty-five pesetas."

Every six months the horses and mules unfit for army service were sold by public auction. The tubercular horse was a beautiful creature on fine legs, twitching nervously in the middle of the crowd. An old gypsy, hat slant-wise on his head, came forward, pulled the horse's nether lip away from the teeth and examined the gums. He patted it on the back and said, slowly:

"Seventy-five pesetas."

A voice in the ring shouted:

"One hundred."

The old gypsy dug his hands into the horse's flanks and waited, listen-

ing to its excited breathing. After a while he stood aside, paused, walked
back into the ring and said to the second bidder:

"Yours, kid."

"Nobody offering more?" I said.

Silence.

"Gone."

A young gypsy stepped forward, carefully untied the string wound
round his pocketbook, and put a one hundred peseta note on the table.
I took it, noted his name and address, and wrote a receipt.

"You can come this afternoon at three and fetch the horse."

The auction went on. The old gypsy bought a horse and a mule. The
twelve animals sold at an average of fifty pesetas. In the end the two
colonels took the officers upstairs for a drink before they went to lunch.
Cárdenas and I did the same; we were back in the office at three o'clock
to deal with the gypsies. It was the hour of the siesta, stifling, sultry, heavy
with vapor. One of the orderlies fetched us beer from the canteen.

The first gypsy entered. Cárdenas turned round to the orderly: "You,
there, Jimenez, stand outside the door and tell the next one to come that
he will have to wait until this gentleman leaves."

This gentleman, a gypsy as greasy as though he had just handled a
spluttering frying pan, pulled off his hat with a flourish, sat down on the
chair waiting for him, planted his stick between his thighs and offered us
fat cigars with gold bands.

"Have a smoke."

"Let's leave them for later," said Cárdenas; we were smoking. He
pulled out a drawer and put the cigars inside.

"Well, now, I've come to settle the bill."

The gypsy opened a pocketbook bulging with banknotes and began to
count, wetting his fingers and crunching each note between them. "Because one day, you know, it happened to me that two big notes were
stuck together, and I got one back only because I was among honest folk.
But you can't count on that—I beg your pardon."

He spread notes to an amount of one thousand five hundred pesetas on
the table.

"Now you sign here," Cárdenas said.

The gypsy scratched his signature and Cárdenas handed him the papers
for the horse.

"Go down to the stable and they will give you the horse."

When all the callers had gone, there were more than eight thousand
pesetas in our drawer. Cárdenas took them and locked them up in the
strong box.

"Let's go for a walk," he said to me.

Outside the barrack gates I asked him:

"But tell me now, what exactly is the game?"

"The voucher, my boy, the voucher. Everything is checked and found in order. Tuberculosis of the lungs, according to the chit of a veterinary and the certificate of a veterinary inspector. Worth a hundred pesetas. This African climate is very bad for horses, they just die from one day to the next, of a hundred and one illnesses."

"But nobody would pay one thousand five hundred pesetas for a tubercular horse."

"Of course not. The tubercular horse is over there in the stables and will die within the next few days. We've sold a healthy brute. But in our files we've got the certificate that he was tubercular and the receipts vouching for the fact that a gypsy has paid one hundred pesetas to take him to the only place where they have any use for a tubercular horse, to the bull ring."

Next morning, when the Major arrived, Cárdenas fetched the bundle of notes from the strong box and took it to the Major's room. He did not say a word to me when he came back.

I took charge of the Regimental Office. Those who had been clerks with me when I was a corporal were still there, still soldiers, and still scribes. They were no longer my friends. They called me "sir" and lived their lives apart. The two orderlies were still the same; they showed me increased respect. Cárdenas was now H.Q. quartermaster sergeant. He treated me paternally and tried to endow me with his vast store of experience.

Again, I found myself isolated from all of them.

On many afternoons we did not work, not only because of the heat, but also because there was little to do except towards the end of each month, or when a class was discharged, or when a shipment of recruits arrived. A few steps from the barracks was the sea. I bought tackle and went fishing.

2. Face to the Sea

FISHING gave me an excuse to escape from the orbit of the barracks. The diversions Ceuta offered were taverns, brothels, and gambling tables in a casino. If I went about with my own set, the other sergeants, I could be certain of landing every single evening in at least one, possibly in three of those kinds of establishment. I was by no means a puritan, but I found myself incapable of organizing my daily life after the patterns of the others.

I liked wine, women, and an occasional game of cards, but not for seven days a week in monotonous repetition. All my life I have enjoyed drinking a few glasses of wine with friends in the evenings, chatting for an hour about a hundred and one personal and impersonal matters, and then going home. I disliked having to sit before a bottle with the people whom I had seen all day long, having to empty a second bottle, and a third, and let the hours go by until we were all more or less tight. I disliked being a regular customer of a brothel, going there every day with the same people, hearing and repeating the same phrases and the same jokes. I disliked sitting down at the same gambling table every night and passing the thirty days of the month in a chain of good or bad streaks of luck, borrowing money from one or the other of my inseparable partners.

Four sergeants, one from the depot, one from the Colonel's office, one from the pay office and I, lived in a room behind the offices. There we had our beds, a table, half a dozen chairs, and our trunks. We had an orderly who cooked for us and served our meals in the sergeants' mess-room. Through our work we were in continuous contact with each other. At meal times we ate at the same table. We slept in beds six feet apart from each other. We knew one another's intimate affairs and most intimate habits. As the heat compelled us to sleep naked on top of our beds, we knew each other's skin and movements. It was an astonishing fact that the friendliness of our communal life was never shattered. Yet a link was lacking.

Romero, the sergeant of the depot, was thirty-eight years old, a merry, expansive, agile Andalusian. He came from a little village in the province of Cordova, where his parents had been small holders with a flock of children, eking out a meager existence. It was to escape from the petty misery at home that he had stayed on in the army.

Oliver, the sergeant of the pay office, was a tall Castilian of thirty-odd years, the son of an underpaid civil servant. After the death of both his parents, the boy had been taken on by an uncle in what is called reduced circumstances. At eighteen, Oliver failed in the examination for the postal service. His uncle suggested the army as the only road to a career. He joined as a volunteer, intending to enter the Officers' Training School in Cordova as soon as he became a sergeant. But he was made assistant to the Paymaster. And the atmosphere of Ceuta, combined with his strongly sensuous temperament, smothered his plans, leaving the empty shell of an ever remote project.

Fernandez, the sergeant in the Colonel's office, was only twenty-two years old, but he had lived in barracks for almost six years. He was the son of a colonel on the active list. Born and bred in Madrid, he began to study law at the university, but his pranks were so wild that his father sent him straight to the barracks "to drive the nonsense out of his head." First he rebelled and stayed away from barracks for a whole week; he was sentenced to two additional years of army service and sent to Africa for the period. There he was used for office work; later his sentence was lifted and in the end he was made a sergeant, thanks partly to his father's influence and partly to his education and intelligence. He had learned to work well by now, but he still remained the Madrid ne'er-do-well, always wanting to paint the town red. His only worries were how to cope with his deficit at the end of each month and how to preserve his standing as the Don Juan of all the brothels in Ceuta. He was a dapper young man, exquisitely dressed. He had special protégées in three or four brothels and let them give him presents, although he was not out to exploit them, but was simply the type of man with whom prostitutes get infatuated.

Those three were my companions. I lived together with them and we got on well, but that was all. The company of ordinary rankers was prohibited to me; the Spanish Army frowned upon intimacy between sergeants and privates or even corporals. Equally, officers were not allowed to make friends with N.C.O.s. They might favor one of them with their particular esteem, but they had to respect the class barrier.

So I went fishing to be free.

At the edge of the sea there is a fringe of rocks. The high tide covers them and at low tide they are dry. They are carpeted with a thick moss which is harsh to the touch and pale green in color, as if bleached by the salt water. Crabs nibble at it and fish burrow in its pile for worms hidden among the roots.

You pour a few drops of vinegar on the moss, and the worms appear in legions, madly wriggling their frail bodies and craning their heads as though they were choking and fighting for a last breath of air. You pass your hand over the moss and gather them in hundreds; you put them in an old tin can half filled with mud, and they dig themselves in at once. There you have your bait. You put a worm on your hook, taking care not to squash it and to leave the tail free so that it can wriggle in the tranquil water. Sardines, cackerel and gilt-head pounce on it voraciously, and an infinite number of other fish hover near, dappling the water with blue, black, russet, silver and gold.

The ledges of the huge concrete blocks of the mole were teeming with anglers who hung out their rods between the wall of the quay and the bellies of the moored ships. I was not interested in fishing there. I explored the rocks fringing the Monte Hacho and found a stone balcony overhanging the sea.

There were three boulders: two smaller ones in front, in the form of a V, a bigger one topping them, shaped like an armchair, its seat polished, the back seamed and wrinkled. Below the V, the bottom of the sea dropped sheer to a depth of six or eight yards, forming a wide, deep, well-like pool. Farther out, a row of rocks, hardly visible above the water, acted as a breakwater so that the pool was always calm. Only during a storm were the three boulders drowned in a fountain of spray.

I would collect worms among the rocks, catch sardines or small cackerels in the deep well and use them as live bait for my lines. A line consists of fifty meters of silk cord with a leaden sinker at one end. You slip a cast carrying a large baited hook on to the cord with a running knot. You swing the lead in the air and cast the line. The sardine swims and moves freely, though held by the cast, all along your line from the pool to the open sea. Big fish which would not come near the rocks go for the bait, and your catch is a matter of luck.

Every day I laid out four lines, each tied to a solid rock, and sat down in the stone armchair to read, to write, or to think. If a fish was biting, the little bell fastened to the line gave the alarm.

It was a day of calm. The waters in the Straits were tranquil as a garden pool. They mirrored the blue sky and were themselves a limpid blue filled with glitter. On this mirror small streams were running in milky little ripples. Faint outward traces of the deep currents of the two seas which met there, they gathered in a wide band, a bigger stream, which entered the port of Ceuta from the west and swept out again towards the east. At times this stream and its tiny rivulets changed direction; sometimes the Mediterranean pours its waters into the Atlantic, at others the Atlantic sends them back.

I dropped my book and submerged myself in this tide of perfect peace. I saw the coast of Spain in the far distance, and the outline of the Rock, and all was full of light and calm as though the sky were an immense glass dome with a reflector in the apex, and there were no world outside. I had come to a crossroads in my life. I was twenty-four, I had no fortune, and I was still the son of Señora Leonor, the washerwoman, although my mother had long since ceased to break the ice of the river with her wooden beater in the gray winter dawns, or to be scorched by the noonday sun of July. In less than a year I would have finished my subjection to barracks life. I had to plan my future.

I was a sergeant in the army. If I were to re-enlist instead of taking my discharge I would have a fixed pay of 250 pesetas per month, stay on in Africa and never have my hands clean. I had come to be the office sergeant at headquarters, an enviable and envied post; I could live in peace and make money for eight or ten years, at the end of which I would become a warrant officer. I could also enter the Officers' Training School at Cordova, study for three years, and become an officer.

If I took my discharge at the end of my military term, I would have to return to civilian life and at once seek a job. There were thousands of unemployed clerical workers in Madrid. After my three years in the army, out of contact with the business world, with old testimonials, I would in all probability become just one more unemployed clerk. And even were I to find work immediately, my salary would be 150 pesetas a month at best.

And yet those were the only two practical solutions open to me, one of them—the army—certain, the other problematic. Who would support me if I were to stay in Madrid without work for six months or more?

There were two other potential careers, more in keeping with my wishes; both of them seemed so difficult to realize that they became practically impossible. And yet I would have liked to be a mechanical engineer, or I would have liked to be a writer.

My wish to be an engineer was as old as I myself. When my uncle's death had cut short my prospects and forced me to turn myself into a clerk to earn a living, I had not given up hope. The Jesuits had established a Polytechnic in Madrid which was infinitely better than the State School. The sons of the wealthiest families studied engineering there; at the end of their courses they paid matriculation fees to the State, passed the official examinations and became professional engineers by title. At the same time the Jesuits' school offered free instruction to the sons of poor families who were guaranteed to be safe Catholics. My Cordovan relatives, knowing my ambitions, had sent me an introduction to the Head of the Polytechnic when I was seventeen. I went there.

We had an endless conversation. He showed me all over the school, at that time a marvel of technical organization, and in the end put the whole issue before me with complete frankness. An intelligent youth like myself would be able to complete all the studies for an engineering career in their school. When I had finished, the Polytechnic would give me a certificate which meant the certainty of employment in Spanish industry. Of course this certificate was not an official title, for which I would have to pay the State a matriculation fee of several thousand pesetas. It would simply be the certificate of a school testifying that its holder possessed the same knowledge as an official Engineer—or even more. Spanish industrialists accepted this certificate because they knew to what degree the School vouched for its pupils. I would not find it difficult to get a job. There were ample possibilities.

I had learned enough in my years of apprenticeship in the bank to realize the power of the Society of Jesus in Spain. I knew that the Sacred Heart had been enthroned in the factory plants of the north, and that the big shipowners had Jesuits for their father confessors, and that big banks were so intimately bound to the Order that some of them were assumed to be its financial figureheads. I had seen that a letter of recommendation from a Jesuit opened all doors in Spanish industry and that a discreet hint from the same quarters had the power to shut those doors for good.

I would be able to work in any factory in Spain as a mechanical engineer without the legal title, but it would be tacitly understood that I was to remain in contact with the Order, confess my sins to a Jesuit, and obey his instructions unless I wanted to lose my job from one day to the next. And where would I go then with a certificate which was nothing but a scrap of paper when the *placet* of the Society of Jesus backed it no longer?

Under such conditions I did not accept the invitation to become a student in the Polytechnic of Areneros. I went back to the bank, to the figures in the ledger, and shelved my ambitions.

Later, when I was secretary to Don Ricardo Goytre in Spanish Motors at Guadalajara, he found that I could help him with the sketches of engine projects. He sent me to the evening classes the Augustines had started in the little town.

The Order had seen an opportunity for influencing the workers as soon as the big new plant was established, and had opened a technical school with classes for drawing and mathematics. I went there. A priest needed no certificate in Spain in order to conduct a school or to act as a teacher; the good Brothers of Guadalajara had embarked upon technical tuition without further preparation. After a week I saw clearly that I was only a disturbing element. With my scanty knowledge I knew more about technical drawing and mathematics than the masters. The Head sent for me:

"Would you like to help us, my son? As part of our endeavors on behalf of the poor we have opened this institute which is only an elementary school of its kind. You would need more advanced tuition than we are able to give you. Yet I do not want to tell you not to come; on the contrary, come and help us. Your assistance would be very valuable to us." For a time I gave lessons in elementary French and in instrumental drawing. But the only advantages for me were that I had to attend all religious functions, to dine late, and to incur the hostility of the workers. After a few weeks I deserted from the Augustines and tried to learn integral calculus from a colleague.

When I was called up for military service I signed on for the Second Railway Regiment. They accepted me as draftsman; I hoped to receive some training there. Then the lots were drawn for Africa, and I was sent to Morocco. I served with the Engineers, but my technical qualifications had only succeeded in turning me into a clerk.

I still had the possibility of starting as a simple mechanic after my discharge. I would have to enter a workshop as an apprentice—but could I do it? The workers' organizations did not tolerate apprentices of twenty-five years of age, and even less, apprentices who paid for their training. Adult apprentices would have meant that in times of industrial crisis workers would be taken on at low wages in the guise of apprentices; apprentices paying for their training would have robbed a worker of his job. I knew I would have been an excellent mechanic. And yet in the order of things there was no room for me either as a mechanic or a mechanical engineer. That road was closed, and I might as well accept it.

I might be a writer.

It had been the second ambition of my childhood. My school, the Escuela Pía, had published a children's magazine under the title *Madrileñitos*. When I was ten years old I was a contributor to every issue. They published my ingenuous stories and verses, all profoundly religious and moral. I had forgotten all but the two most important contributions: a biography of Saint Joseph of Calasanz, founder of the Order of the Escolapians, and a biography of Paul of Tarsus, which earned me an edition of the Epistles to the Corinthians. I still had it at home.

When I was a clerk in the bank, at sixteen, I wanted to gatecrash the literary world. My colleague Alfredo Cabanillas and I encouraged each other to send our work, he his verses, I my prose, to every single literary competition organized by a number of weeklies. Neither of us ever won a prize, but they published some of his poems and two of my stories, naturally without payment. When the second of my short stories had appeared in the press, my neighbor in the old tenement house, Rafael, son of the cigarette maker, took me along to the Ateneo to introduce me to the great men of Spanish literature. Rafael was the barber of the Ateneo.

"If you've got your wits about you, you'll make your career here," he said.

I found myself near the circle of the great intellectuals of the country, intimidated and shaken in my self-confidence in that atmosphere of ardent discussion. Somehow I was singled out by the man who bore with a swagger his self-chosen title of "The Last Bohemian": Pedro de Répide. He was round-faced, with a big mane, a wide-brimmed soft hat, a thick scarf knotted round his neck, and the body of a farmer turned man-about-town, incessantly sucking his pipe which, at times, he filled with cigarette stubs. I felt it was an honor when he deigned to let me invite him to a glass of beer. One evening when I was in cash I suggested that we might go to Alvarez' at the corner of the Plaza de Santa Ana, a bar famous for its beer and its shellfish. He began to talk to me:

"So you want to become a writer? I'll give you a few tips. In Spain being a writer means to court starvation. The only way to earn money as a writer is to become a playwright or to produce pornography. Or rather, there is only one way to become a writer. Who's your favorite living author?"

"I don't really know. Benavente—Valle-Inclán—and a good many others too."

"Never mind, you just choose the one you like best. Then you stick to him, flatter him, find a way of paying for a cup of coffee for him, but so that he is aware of it, and one fine day, when he's in good humor you read one of your things to him. But take care to wait until he knows who you are and that you always applaud whatever he says, even the most arrant nonsense. Then he'll give you an introduction to a newspaper and they'll print your stuff, without paying for it, of course. If you're lucky and if you really can write, you may get fifty pesetas for an article or a story in, let us say, ten or twelve years' time. It's more difficult to get a play accepted, but the technique is the same. At any rate, once you have selected your master you belong to him, unconditionally. If he's of the Right, you belong to the Right. If he's of the Left, you belong to the Left. It doesn't matter what you write. In this country you have to belong to one side or the other, right or wrong."

He spoke well, but I resented his advice, just as I used to react against his work. Pedro de Répide had made his way in Spanish letters by specializing in the cynical short story. His tales of beggars, prostitutes, drunkards and débauchés were always built round himself as the hero who showed in his narrative that he could not only acclimatize himself to any surroundings, but also surpass them. I thought his explanation was malicious and libelous, and decided to acquire my own experiences.

In the lounge of the Ateneo grave gentlemen were discussing politics, science, and letters, but I quickly tired of playing the role of audience to discussions about Plato's political theory or the esoteric significance of Don Quixote. I possessed neither the necessary knowledge nor interest. The many literary groups gathering evening after evening in the cafés of Madrid attracted me more, and I started to explore them.

The most aristocratic circle was that of the Café de Castilla, presided over by Don Jacinto Benavente who was then at the pinnacle of his fame as a playwright. The Café de Castilla was a single room with cast-iron columns, red divans, and walls covered by mirrors and caricatures, in which no one could hide from anyone's sight, but had to see himself and others from innumerable angles through the manifold reflection of the mirrors.

One evening I went in, hesitating, clutching the red door curtain while I looked round the small room which seemed enormous to me .in its reflected multiplication. Somebody waved to me from one of the tables: a young man whom I had met in the Ateneo. I joined him with all my aplomb recovered. Then I recognized Don Jacinto in the midst of a large party two tables away. He was half-reclining on the divan and looked smaller than ever; all I saw of his face was a cigar between a gray goatee and a huge bald forehead.

Don Jacinto was listening to the arguments of one of his circle who was expounding the weaknesses of an extremely successful comedy then on the Madrid stage. In support of each of his critical points he quoted a scene or a passage from one of Benavente's plays. As soon as the man had finished amid murmurs of assent from the whole table, another started dissecting a second play, drawing a new set of comparisons with Benavente plays. Don Jacinto stroked his little beard and listened. He looked profoundly bored. In the end he took his cigar from his mouth and said in a mellifluous voice:

"Quite so; we are all agreed, gentlemen, that I am a genius. But who is cashing in? All those others whom you have mentioned!"

"Ah, but Art . . ." somebody exclaimed, "Art, sir, is a truly great thing. Money, on the other hand . . ."

"You have no reason to complain, Don Jacinto," interrupted another. "You always fill the theater."

"Oh, yes, I fill the theater all right, but the theater doesn't fill my pockets."

And the conversation returned to the subject of Benavente's superlative prose. Don Jacinto listened and sucked his cigar.

The young man from the Ateneo nudged me and we left.

"You know," he said, "it's always the same story in there. The only thing you hear is frankincense for Don Jacinto. Of course, it's necessary to go there so that they get to know you, but if you want to learn something you must go to another place. Let's go to the Granja, Don Ramón is sure to be there."

The Granja, a café with a low ceiling, its paneled walls and stout wooden pillars painted a light ochre, was overcrowded and its air fetid. Don Ramón del Valle-Inclán sat there as the center of a gathering, to make room for which tables and chairs had been joined together so as to form a solid mass of marble, wood and people. When we entered Don Ramón was on his feet, leaning over the table, his big rabbinical beard fluttering like a pennant, his tortoise-shell glasses ceaselessly turning from one face to the other, to see whether anybody would dare to contradict him.

Nobody did dare to contradict Valle-Inclán. He waited for it when he had finished his peroration, but his whole circle broke into applause, seconded by many other people in the café. When they ceased Don Ramón banged his fist on the table:

"You're a pack of idiots!" and he sat down.

The public laughed heartily, as though the invective had been a stroke of genius. My companion said:

"That is Don Ramón's way. He would insult anybody, but always with so much charm . . ."

I felt, on the contrary, that he had done it in an overbearing and crude manner. But I went back to the Granja, fascinated, and took my place at the edge of Don Ramón's circle.

One evening I took the liberty of disagreeing with one of his statements which, like many he made, was a patent absurdity, only proffered to humiliate his hearers.

Don Ramón pounced on me, irate:

"So the young man thinks I am wrong?"

"I do not only believe you are wrong, sir, but also that you know it and that all these gentlemen here know it too."

A murmur of disapproval rose around me. Don Ramón called for silence with a haughty gesture:

"Be quiet! Nobody asked your opinion."

He began a dispute with me and I answered back, resentful of the disdain he showed towards all of us. But Don Ramón cut the discussion short:

"Well, now, young man, what's your profession? Do you write?"

"I would like to write."

"Then why are you here? To learn how to write?"

"I might say, yes."

"Then don't say it, and you'll avoid saying something idiotic. You may come here to drink coffee, preferably at the expense of somebody else, to speak evil of all the others and to ask for an introduction. But if you want to learn how to write, stay at home and study. And then you may begin to write—perhaps . . .

"Now you think I'm offending you, but you're wrong. I don't know you, but I have a better opinion of you than of many of those who are sitting here. And therefore I tell you, don't come to this kind of gathering. Stick to your work, and if you wish to write, write. Here you won't reap any profit except perhaps a petty job in a newspaper office and the habit of swallowing insults."

Alfredo Cabanillas took me to the old Fornos, a café frequented by toreros and by several sets of budding writers and artists. I thought they were behaving like irritated madmen. Many of them wore the traditional long hair, knotted scarf and broad brimmed hat. They used to discuss the most recent movements in art and literature, at that time Dadaism, Futurism and Expressionism, and they recited pieces of verse and prose to each other, which I found impossible to follow.

Cabanillas played quite a role in these gatherings because he had just published a book of verse and had moreover paid for its publication himself, a unique event in this circle of hungry bohemians. His friends praised the book beyond measure, asked him for free copies and let him pay for their coffee. They all grew heated on hearing Cabanillas tell and re-tell his experiences.

First, he had sent his manuscript to one publisher after the other, only to get it back unread. He knew this for a fact because he had glued several pages together and they had come back as they had left him. When he had finished with the whole list of publishing firms, he decided to have the book printed at his own expense, that is to say, at the expense of his family. He had gone to one of the best printing and publishing firms, and the manager had given him a polite hearing.

"All right, we have no reason not to publish your book if you bear the expenses. Poetry, you say? What kind of poetry?"

"Modern poetry, of course."

Cabanillas had launched forth with all the enthusiasm of his eighteen years: modern poetry, a revolution of poetic art, kindred to the new currents in French poetry, but in a purely Spanish sense.

"Well, then, it's revolutionary poetry, isn't it?"

"In a poetical sense, yes. As to revolutionary, I'm not an Anarchist, of course. It is romantic poetry in a modern form."

"Well, well—and what are you?"

"I—I'm a bank clerk."

"No, no. I don't mean that. I mean, what are your political ideas? You sound like one of those modern, advanced young men. That is so, isn't it?"

"Naturally, we must bring about a revolution in art and . . ."

"Yes, yes, I quite understand. I'm sorry, but ours is a serious firm. You are a new author. I quite understand that you want to pay for having our name on the title page when you publish your book, because the public know that we only touch serious stuff. I'm so sorry, but I'm afraid we cannot publish your work."

Cabanillas visited other publishers. One of them was of the Left. Over his desk hung an engraving of an impressive woman with a Phrygian cap, symbolizing the Republic. But Cabanillas did not belong to the political Left; his poetry was not republican, nor even revolutionary, but simply lyrical with a slight modernistic flavor. The publisher was so sorry. He turned the book down, without even looking at it.

In the end Cabanillas had settled with a little firm which printed mainly handbills. He gained by the process, because he had to pay very little for the whole edition. Nobody bought the book, but he did not lose much money by it either. The critics took no notice of him; after all, the book had not even been printed by a serious firm and he did not belong to any of the political groups.

I began to think that Pedro de Répide had been right after all. Yet I was unable to practice wholesale adulation, and I had neither the time nor the money nor the temper to become one of the regular members of a literary set.

There existed a progressive cultural center in Madrid, Giner de los Rios' *Institución Libre de Enseñanza*. From there and from his *Residencia de Estudiantes* issued a new generation of writers and artists: my own way of thinking might have fitted in there. But when I probed the chances of entry I was confronted with a new aristocracy hitherto unknown to me, an aristocracy of the Left. It was as expensive to get into those Institutes as to enter one of the luxury colleges of the Jesuits. There were free courses and lectures, but to follow them would have meant giving up the work I had to do for my living. I came to feel that the marvelous achievements of Giner de los Rios had a very serious defect, the basic defect of all Spanish education: the doors were closed to working people. Intellectuals of the highest standard might issue from there, as in fact they did, but all of them came from well-to-do families which could afford not only to give their sons a professional career, but also to let them study for this career in open challenge to the formidable organization of religious schooling.

There was no road for me there. I gave up writing for the time being. And now the old problem had to be tackled anew. In the barracks I had started to write again. I felt both the urgent need and the gift of expression.

But could it give me a living? Perhaps, after years of hard work and submission to the rules of the game. Yet, it could not be a solution to the problem I would have to meet on my discharge.

Life does not consist of earning or not earning money; but I had to earn money in order to live. I would not be able to take up the fight against the hundred closed literary circles; I would not have money to invite people to have a drink on me, nor would I have time to follow café debates for nights on end. One of the things one can neither buy nor sell is one's self-esteem. But to stay on in the army would mean that I would lose my self-esteem for good. On the other hand, to take my discharge would mean misery . . .

Above all, I had to think of my mother. I was responsible for her as long as she lived. It was my responsibility to make sure that she should not have to work any more, neither washing in the river, nor washing dishes as a charwoman. And then I wanted to have a home and a family one day, to become a complete being through my wife. But to have this complement it was necessary to earn money; if you want a wife, a home and children, you must pay for them.

The barracks offered me the certainty of all that as long as I lived and even after my death. If I died, my mother, or my wife and children, would be saved from sheer poverty. The wife of a bank clerk has to face poverty the week after she has buried her husband.

But was it true that the barracks offered that security? Was it true that, come what might, I would always have my post and my pay and my family's daily bread assured?

The line you cast into the sea is never quite taut. You roll up its slack end and drop the little coiled heap beside you on the rocks.

One of my coils unfurled and the cord shot away, a snake striking to attack. The bell tied to its end tinkled madly. The line tautened and moaned, like the thick string of a violoncello, which rumbles and quivers plaintively when you pass a finger across it. An angry furrow crested with froth was tracing an arc in the quiet pool of the sea. A red-hot iron seemed to have plunged into the water.

I grasped the line and gave it a tug. A fierce tug answered from the other end, as though a runaway horse were tearing at the reins. The cord slipped from my hand and pulled furiously at the rock to which it was tied, tense and vibrating, trying to escape into the sea. I caught the line with both hands, squared myself against a boulder and hauled. The fish suddenly stopped tugging, the line went slack and I stumbled. Before I had regained my stance, the live thing on the hook out there had turned towards the open sea. The running cord scorched my hands and tore itself free once more, the angry whirlpool in the sea grew enormous. Better leave it. Better wait until the fish becomes tired, or the line breaks, or a bleeding piece of gum is left behind on the hook, or the rock topples and rolls into the water. I stood there watching the foaming trail, the quiver of the cord, and the jig of the little bell.

A fish fighting for its liberty is surely one of the most splendid beings in creation, yet no one of us is quite able to gauge its valor. There it is, a single smooth muscle gathering strength from the resistance of the water where the hardest blow of a man's fist comes to nothing, laden with the furious energy of a cornered wild boar or a cat attacked by a pack of dogs. A steel hook had dug itself deep into the curved jawbone. It would bring relief from that savage pain clawed into splitting flesh and crunching bone to slacken the cord, to cease struggling. Yet even the smallest fish twists and jumps, leaps out of the water or down into the deep, always pulling, ceaselessly pulling, at the price of maddening pain, only to get free.

I tried once more to haul in the line. The ferocious brain which animated the powerful muscle felt every movement of my hands through the wound in its flesh and rebelled against it in tireless fury. Time and again the line was torn out of my grip, leaving a damp, searing trail on my palms. At one of the pulls I managed to loop the cord once round the rock, shortening its length by something like two feet. For minutes the fish tugged at it in tearing rage; the line groaned so that I expected to see it snap at any moment. The fish seemed to be aware that it had been robbed of a few inches of freedom.

After more than an hour's battle I saw that I would never be able to overpower the beast. Two workers were just passing on the road behind me, with lunch packets in their hands and white blouses slung across their shoulders. They threw their blouses on the rocks and watched me with a supercilious air, slightly contemptuous of the lanky sergeant who wanted to fish and could not manage it. One of them started hauling in the line, then both of them, then I joined them and the three of us pulled together, panting and sweating, our arms and legs propped against the boulders. And thus we wound the line round the jutting rock in slowly growing loops.

"Whatever sort of a beast is this, in the Devil's name?" growled one of the men. The three of us rested for a while, staring at the churn of water and foam, now only some twenty meters from us. A sharp flick of the tail showed a long, blackish back mottled with silver.

The worker shouted "A moray—we'll never catch it!"

The moray is a kind of sea-eel, usually not more than a meter long and ten centimeters broad, with a squat head and powerful jaws bristling with triangular teeth. It fights and devours fish far bigger than itself, destroys fishing-nets and tackle and even attacks people, inflicting bites like the clean cut of an amputation. A moray's tail can break a man's arm hours after the head has been cut off. People on the coast are often reluctant to eat it, for it might have feasted on human flesh.

The moray on my hook looked about two meters long and as thick as a thigh.

One of the men went to a roadside tavern and came back with a boat-hook, accompanied by a couple of curious spectators. Between the lot of us we hauled in the cable until the moray was inside the well-like pool in front of the rocks. Incredibly enough it did not dash itself to pieces against the cliff walls. Even when we had it there at our feet we felt sure that the line would snap and the beast escape in the end. The man with the boat-hook tried to grapple the head, while we held him in a safe grip on the ledge of the cliff. Furiously the fish turned against the new weapon and slashed at it. Then we saw that it could not close its jaws. The line passed freely from the red, bleeding hole of the throat through between the rows of teeth which tried in vain to shut on it.

The man finally pinned the hook into one of the eyes, and a stain like a swirl of mist floated on the water. The fish was now moving in spasmodic ripples. We all pulled. It fell onto the rock, contracting in mad rage, smearing the stone with viscous froth, staring at us out of its single eye, twisting on its whitish belly in search of a prey. We took cover behind boulders and stoned it from there. We threw our stones so as to crush the hideous squat head, to kill it and to free ourselves from the sight of that hate-filled mask. A huge stone hit the head and turned it into a gray-white mass flecked with slime. The body jerked and then straightened.

Three of us carried it away. The two workers eagerly offered to go with me and my catch to the barracks. We would drink a bottle of wine there. Antonio, the canteen-keeper, would cut the fish into slices and fry them for us.

It weighed quite a hundred pounds and we had to walk at a slow pace, followed by a small crowd of lookers-on and urchins who touched the body of the moray with their fingers, as a daring deed. Something like a filthy rag hung where the head had been.

The body contracted in a spasm and jumped out of our hands, leaping in the road dust, a live mass of slime and mud. The man who had carried the tail end shouted a curse and doubled up. The tail had hit him in the ribs. He kicked the mass which was rolling in the dust, and the headless body twisted and then stretched, suddenly motionless. We caught it up and walked on, smirched with sticky mud. It escaped us twice more. The boys shrieked and laughed. We must have been a dire sight, with mud dripping from our faces and hands, clutching at that mass of dirty slime which shuddered in spasms and made us stop at intervals.

When we reached the barracks we threw it into the horses' watering-trough, and it whipped the water as though in an electric discharge. The blind body hurled itself against the cement walls with all its undying strength.

Soldiers came running through the courtyard; Antonio, the canteen-keeper, came, looked and walked away to his canteen. He returned with a big knife for cutting ham. "Catch hold of it, some of you, and put it here on the edge," he said.

Twenty hands held the body, now clean and shining, against the edge of the trough. Antonio began to cut it into slices which slipped back into the water, each with a drop of red blood in the center, which slowly dissolved.

Antonio paid me thirty pesetas for it.

3. The Barracks

I LEARNED about the races of Spain by dealing with the shipments of recruits.

It was our busiest time at H.Q. First we would receive a list of the raw recruits detailed to the Engineers in Africa from all the recruitment centers in the country. Then the ships with what, in the language of the barracks, were called "the sheep," began to arrive. The recruits came in groups of five hundred to a thousand, guided by a sergeant and a few corporals from the Military Region which sent them. The moment they reached port they were taken over by sergeants of the various units and sorted out according to their destination.

The ship moored, the gangplank was fixed, and they began to stream out of the boat, mostly land workers and laborers from all parts of Spain.

There were the Andalusians in their short, light jackets, white or khaki, often in shirt sleeves, their trousers held in place by string or a sash. Most of them were slim and straight, dark, sallow, gypsy-like, with black eyes opening in mingled apprehension and curiosity, talking quickly in a torrent of obscene swear words.

There were the men from the Castilian plains and sierras, taciturn, small, bony, tanned by sun, wind, frost and snow, the legs of their corduroy trousers fastened with twine over their bulging pants which in their turn were tied with tape over thick, blue or red, home-knitted socks. Every now and again the whole formation would be upset because a man's tape ends had come untied.

Basques, Gallegos and Asturians usually came in a mixed lot on the same ship, and their discrepancies were astounding. The huge Basques, in blue blouses, with the inevitable beret on the crown of their small heads, were serious and silent, and if they spoke in that incomprehensible language of theirs, they measured their words. You felt the strength of their individual being and of their self-contained culture. The Gallegos came mostly from poor, forlorn villages; they used to be incredibly dirty, often barefoot, and they faced this new affliction, worse than the familiar penury at home, with a bovine resignation. The Asturians from the mountains were strong and agile, great gluttons and bawdy merrymakers, and they mocked at the wretchedness of the people from Galicia, as well as at the gravity of the Basques.

Then there arrived pot-bellied, black, old transatlantic steamers with a load of recruits from the Mediterranean provinces, from Catalonia, parts of Aragon, Valencia and Alicante. The mountain people from Aragon and northern Catalonia differed in language, but they were much alike, primitive, harsh, and almost savage. The Catalans from the ports, in contact with all the Mediterranean civilization, were a world apart from their own countrymen of the mountains. The people of the Levante, in black blouses and laced *alpargatas,* rather handsome, but lymphatic and flabby with promise of an early paunch, were a group by themselves.

And it seemed to me that a Madrileño is less of a stranger to the New Yorker than a Basque is to a Gallego, with their villages a bare hundred miles apart.

Along the motley stream of recruits the sergeants began to shout: "Regiment of Ceuta! Regiment of Africa! Chasseurs! Commissariat! Engineers! ..."

Some of the newcomers would catch the meaning of the shouts at once and range themselves in a double file beside their sergeant. Yet the great majority were thoroughly confused, after having seen strange cities and made their first sea journey, shaken by seasickness and with the fear of

the army in their bones. They drifted hither and thither, helpless and
bewildered, so that we had to pull them by their sleeve and round them
up, one by one, like frightened sheep.

"Hallo, lad, where do you belong?"

The doltish eyes looked at you filled with fear.

"I don't know."

"What are you, infantry—or cavalry—or what?"

"I don't know. They told me I'd be artillery. I don't know."

You shouted for the artillery sergeant: "You there, here's another one
of yours."

Thus we went on shunting the men about until nobody was left on
the mole but the three or four dumbest, out of whom we had patiently to
drag their own name and the name of their village, so as to be able to
find them in our lists. In the end, one or two would always be missing.
We would find them in a dark corner of the ship, dozing or monotonously moaning, tumbled in their own filth.

The Commandant of Ceuta, General Alvarez del Manzano, used to
come down to the mole whenever big troopships from Catalonia or the
North arrived. Heavy and paternal, he liked to speak to the most scared-
looking recruits and to give them gentle little pats on the back. One day
he tackled a peasant from Galicia, whom we had had to track down in
the remotest corner of the ship and to drag out, frightened, like a whipped
dog.

"What's your name, my boy?"

"Juan—Juan."

"All right. And where do you come from?" And the General patted
his shoulder.

The peasant swung round like a startled beast:

"Don't touch me, God damn you!"

"Why, what's the matter with you, my boy?"

"You won't touch me. I've sworn by this"—he kissed his crossed thumbs
—"to bash in the head of the first whoreson sergeant who lays hands on
me!"

"But, my man, this isn't hitting you. Nobody will hit you here."

"Nobody, huh? And all the kicks they gave my father and grandfather?
I told them. I said if they lay hands on me I'll kill someone."

"Well, listen: I'm the General here. If anyone hits you, just come and
tell me about it."

"Pooh—the General! That's a good joke, that is. D'you think I'm one
of those silly sheep?"

When we had taken them to the barracks, we let them come into the
office one by one to make the entries in our files.

"What's your name?"

"My name? The Rabbit."

"Yes, that's all right for your village. They call you the Rabbit there, don't they?"

"Of course. Everyone's got a name. My grandmother had twenty children and they called her the Doe, and then they called our whole family the Rabbits. And that's our name now."

"All right, but you've got a Christian name as well, haven't you? Antonio, or Juan, or Pedro?"

"Yes, sir, Antonio."

"And then you'll have a surname as well, Perez or Fernandez?"

"Yes, sir, Martinez."

"There, we've got it. Nobody will call you the Rabbit here. Here you're Antonio Martinez, and when they sing out 'Antonio Martinez' at roll call, you must answer, 'Present.' Do you understand? You're called Antonio Martinez. And your father and mother?"

"They're all right, thank you, sir. And how's your family?"

When they had been listed they were given their first meal in barracks. The Engineers were privileged; our kitchen provided copious and substantial meals. Many of the recruits had never eaten so well in their lives.

One day a recruit who came straight from one of the poorest districts in the province of Cáceres refused to eat.

"Why don't you eat?" I asked him.

"I won't touch mess food."

"Why not?" I knew well that deep-rooted resistance which had its origins in the stories the men had heard about the food in Spanish barracks, food which until the year after the Great War had indeed been sickening refuse.

"Because it's filthy."

"Now, look here, you must eat something. Take the stuff and try it. If you don't like it you can always throw it away. But you must take your share and eat at least something of it. In barracks you can't just say: 'I don't want to.'"

The recruit filled his mess tin. That day the soldiers had rice boiled with scraps of mutton. He tasted it, and his face was transfigured.

"You like it?"

"Do I! I've never eaten anything like it before."

"All right, if you want more, go to the cauldron there, and they'll fill your tin. Eat as much as you like."

After the meal the recruits walked about the courtyard waiting to be called to the depot to be given their clothing and equipment. My recruit drifted nearer to me, timid but determined. It was so obvious that he wanted to speak to me that I called him:

"Do you want anything?"

He whipped his greasy cap from his head and twisted it round and round in his hands.

"Yes, sir . . . I wanted to ask whether we'll always get a meal like that here."

"Yes, you will, and sometimes better meals than today. On Sundays they often give you cutlets and fried potatoes. In the evenings, beans cooked with pigs' trotters. And at dinner, mostly a *cocido* with meat and sausage and soup paste. You'll see."

"You're pulling my leg, sir."

"Oh, no, my boy, you'll see for yourself."

The cap was gyrating more quickly in his hands. He stood there, chin on his chest, thinking strenuously. Suddenly he straightened himself and said:

"Well, if we get meals like that I won't ever leave."

"What kind of meals did you have in your village?"

"Well, it was all right in the summer because we had tomatoes and lettuce and onions. The autumn was best, then we had work in the oak woods knocking down the acorns for the pigs; they let us eat as many of them as we wanted to. But in the winter we hadn't anything, you see. Just a piece of hard bread with garlic or a dry onion."

"But didn't you get any *cocido?*"

"No, sir, never. When we'd earned something picking acorns, mother cooked stew for supper with a piece of bacon in it. But when we were out of work. . . . Well, I'll tell you the truth, we *did* lay snares for rabbits and sometimes we caught one, and we stole acorns from the pigs. But it was risky. If the Civil Guard caught you they beat you up. They beat me up twice, but they didn't mark me. The son of Mother Curra was crippled for life. The doctor in Cáceres said they'd broken one of his ribs and it got stuck to another rib and now he can't get straightened out ever. He's lucky, though. They haven't called him up. Well—perhaps not so lucky. If he knew how they fed us here, as you say, he would join up like a streak, crooked back and all."

The hunger of so many of the recruits was what impressed me most deeply, but next to it their illiteracy. Among the men of some regions over 80 per cent were completely illiterate. Of the remaining 20 per cent, some were able to read and write—badly though—but many more just managed to decipher print letter by letter and to draw the letters of their own signature. The completely illiterate men were usually sent to the Chasseurs and the remainder carefully sifted to find men for special duties. We were lucky if, in a group of four hundred recruits sent in replacement of discharged soldiers, we found twenty who could enter the signaling school at once to be taught morse, and fifty more who could be trained for signaling after an intensive course in reading and writing. We would hardly ever discover more than two or three men qualified for office work, but we usually found a certain number of skilled workers who could be detailed to the various units as barbers, shoemakers, masons, carpenters and blacksmiths. There was always an acute shortage of personnel for any service requiring more than the most elementary schooling.

This state of affairs involved me in difficulties not very long after my appointment to the regimental office.

In 1922 radiotelegraphy was still in its heroic stage. In a small room of the pavilion opposite our barracks there was a Marconi transmitter of the early type, with an oscillator between points, a helmet with earphones for reception by sound, and a carbon filament lamp for reception by sight. Listening, you would occasionally receive an electric shock in your ear. This station was run by a sergeant, two corporals, and a number of soldiers who had been trained in transmitting and receiving morse by ear. The only person, however, who understood anything of the installation was the Captain of the Telecommunications Company.

During Captain Sancho's brief visits to our office and in our occasional conversations, I had become aware of a current of mutual sympathy. Once he came to Ceuta to carry out repairs in the radio station, and I hinted that I would like to see it. He invited me to go with him. We began to discuss the installation, but as soon as he saw that I was not completely ignorant of its problems, he plied me with questions. We were soon enmeshed in a technical conversation. In the end he asked:

"Do you know morse?"

"No, sir."

"What a pity. But after all, you would learn it in a fortnight. I'll speak to Don José. I want to have you here with me."

"I don't think the transfer would be at all easy."

"We'll see. I need people who understand about these things, and they simply don't exist. But clerks for office work are found quite easily."

Captain Sancho spoke to Don José. He met with a blank refusal. Shortly afterwards the Captain took me along to the Colonel's office. The Colonel was a kindly old man who had attained his post exclusively through the merits of seniority.

Captain Sancho plunged straight into the question. "Sir, this is the sergeant I spoke to you about. You realize the importance of the station. I've a few men under my command who can transmit morse, but they don't understand the least thing about the set. You know yourself that every time something goes wrong I'm forced to come down to Ceuta, which means leaving the Company and the field stations alone. And while we're engaged in operations this station here is out of order for days the moment anything happens to the apparatus."

"*Caramba*—you didn't tell me it was Barea you were thinking of! Have you spoken to Major Tabasco?"

"Why yes, sir, but he doesn't agree, otherwise I wouldn't have bothered you."

The old man turned livid:

"That's to say, if the Major had agreed to your suggestion, it would not have been necessary to tell me anything? You gentlemen have got into the habit of doing whatever pleases you, without reckoning with the C.O. That has got to end."

"Sir . . .?"

"I beg your pardon. I've not yet finished my say and I don't like being interrupted."

He pushed the bell button and told the orderly to call in the Major. "I believe you know what the Captain wants. What is your opinion?"

The Major hedged: "My opinion? It's up to Barea. If he wants to leave . . ."

And so I found myself between the three of them. Captain Sancho gave me a look and said, smiling:

"What do you say about it, Barea?"

"I—I'll stay in this office, sir."

Captain Sancho walked up to me, took my hand and shook it:

"I understand. You're clever. I assume you won't be so dumb as to stay on in barracks when your term is over." He stood at rigid attention in front of the Colonel: "Any orders, sir?" He swung round and stood at attention in front of the Major: "Any orders for me, sir?"

The Colonel stiffened behind his desk and his face grew apoplectic. "What does this attitude of yours imply?"

"Nothing, sir. We carry the insignia of rank on our sleeves, but we carry the insignia of talent somewhere else. The former are visible and command respect by compulsion, the latter are invisible and earn respect by conviction alone."

"I don't understand all this rhetoric."

"Quite so, sir, and I hardly think I ought to make it any clearer. You place before the sergeant the alternative of making enemies either of you both or of me, but you don't give him a chance to choose what he thinks best. He's intelligent, but after all he is only a sergeant and naturally he prefers making an enemy of me. Only, I don't take it amiss. I shook his hand because I understand his position, and for the same reason I told him that I hoped he would continue to be intelligent and not stay in this place for good."

"You'll oblige me by withdrawing. This is an impertinence."

The Captain [1] left the room and I was left there, face to face with the two lords and masters of the regiment. The Colonel scratched his white beard:

"So, so. A nice scene. Very nice indeed. How is it that you've applied for a transfer?"

"I haven't applied for any transfer, sir." I explained how events had developed. The Colonel said to the Major:

"It's always the same story. That man steals the best boys from us because Telecommunications is a technical unit."

"I can understand that he wants to get the men with the best education, but the devil take it, in this case it was the Sergeant of the Regimental Office!"

"Quite my own opinion! Never mind, the affair is closed now."

The Major beat a retreat and I followed. Suddenly the Colonel called out:

"Just wait a moment, Sergeant."

When he was alone with me the Colonel dropped his stern rigidity.

"So you know something about radiotelegraphy?"

"Not much, sir, but something."

"And so you would have liked to be on duty at the station, eh?"

He said it with so fatherly a smile that I felt I had to tell the truth.

"Well, yes, sir—frankly I'd prefer it to the office."

He changed at once to fury:

"You're a disgraceful lot, all of you. Here we pull you out of the front line, offer you a post which means safety for your whole future, and this is how you reward us! Out of my sight—quick!"

When the recruits were fully equipped, they were distributed among the companies attached to Ceuta or Tetuan, for a few months' training. The clash between the veteran soldiers and the newcomers was always violent, all the more so since the veterans had the same background as the newcomers. Their barrack life of one, two, or three years had not made them less primitive, but only helped to build up their defenses against their surroundings and often to bring out their worst qualities.

There were the brutal but ageless jokes of initiation. During one of

[1] Years after this scene, Captain Sancho became one of the victims of the fascist-reactionary movement in Spain. His name belongs to the history of the Spanish Republic, as one of its heroes.—Author's note.

the first nights in our barracks the inspecting corporal would wake each
of the recruits, with a list in his hand.

"You there—get up."

The recruit, in his first sleep of exhaustion after the drill under the
African sun, would open bewildered eyes.

"What's your name?"

"Juan Perez."

The corporal would search the list.

"You've forgotten to make water before going to bed. Quick, get out
and make water!"

He would force fifty recruits to go down to the other end of the courtyard in their pants. A corporal of the First Company of Sappers had invented the procedure and it had become a tradition. So was the schoolboy
practice of putting a pail of water on the equipment chest at the head of
the bed, placed so that the man would bring the water down on himself
as soon as he lay down. Inevitably, he would play the same trick on the
dumbest among the next batch of newcomers. But these were the innocent jokes.

Normally, the training period lasted four or five months. Yet in that
particular year men were needed in the front line. The recruits were
given a summary training and sent out to the field, wedged in between
the experienced soldiers. And that mass of illiterate peasants commanded
by irresponsible officers was the backbone of Spain's Moroccan field
armies. So-called expeditionary regiments had been sent over from the
Peninsula, seen off with patriotic speeches and music, and landed in the
three zones of Morocco to the accompaniment of the same speeches and
the same music. They had filled the front pages and the society columns
of all the papers; sons of good families were among the ordinary rankers,
and sons of the noblest families of the realm among the "auxiliary officers." Yet those units were nothing but a liability; the stories about them
which reached H.Q. were legion.

An artillery regiment sent over from the Canary Islands became famous
for its marksmanship: whenever our advanced posts set up their signals
to inform the range finders of their position, the batteries from the Canaries showered their shells on the signals with unfailing mastery. An
infantry regiment from Madrid had scattered in wild disorder in the middle of an operation, leaving a company of the *Tercio* exposed; that night
men of the *Tercio* and of the Madrid regiment fought with daggers
against each other in a canteen on the beach of Tiguisas.

The soldiers who had bought themselves out originally and now had
been called up demanded privileges over the ordinary soldiers of the line.
This led to general discontent, not only among the men, but also among

the officers. Among the arrivals were young men with letters of recommendation from deputies, bishops, or even cardinals. In the rooms where the regimental colors were kept officers competed in feasting the son of some grandee or other, who, in acknowledgment of favors received—they let him pay for the champagne but saved him from going to the front—would send his father a list of candidates for promotion for merit in battle, or at least for a decoration.

The old African campaigners had the worst of it. They felt it, and resented it. They knew that, since the arrival of the reinforcements, their own share of work, of forced marches and dangerous operations had increased. Even the *Tercio* showed signs of insubordination.

One day a company of the *Tercio* refused to eat the rotten food of their mess. The first man in the queue shouted something like:

"Those sons of bitches of the Expeditionary get chicken and champagne in the officers' mess, while we have to eat stinking muck."

He took the mess tin and shoved it back. The officer on duty shot him clean through the head. The next man refused the filled tin. The officer shot him. The third wavered, carried his mess tin away from the field kitchen and smashed it on the ground. The officer shot him. The others ate their portions.

A few days later three officers of that Company were killed in action at Akarrat, shot in the back.

Yet this kind of violent reaction was rare. Generally, the men adopted an attitude of passive resistance, evasion and listlessness, which made the handling of the forces in the field most difficult. When the officers tried to tighten up the discipline, matters only grew worse. The recruits suffered more than all the others through the violence from above and through the violence of their own comrades, which cowed them for good or else turned them into undisciplined, restless soldiers prone to any kind of rebellion.

These soldiers, the class of 1900, the echo of whose training I heard in Ceuta at that time, were to bear the whole brunt of the withdrawal of 1924, a disaster infinitely greater than the disaster of Melilla in 1921.

The attacks of the rebel Moors were growing in intensity. This was the period of Abd-el-Krim's victories; even the zone of Ceuta was under the shadow of his threat. All men fit for field service were at the front, with the exception of the "indispensable services." Not more than thirty of us remained stationed in Ceuta. At night the Engineers' barracks were almost empty. During the day a corporal mounted guard with four men; by night, one of the four sergeants took over the command of the guard and slept in the guardroom. The Major lived in a little house a hundred yards from the barracks, so that it was easy to call him in when necessity

arose. All those not on guard duty had passes which allowed them to be
out at night or even to sleep elsewhere. Other regiments had similar
arrangements. Thus we all knew each other and each other's whereabouts. The barracks with their regular inmates formed a single clan with
set sympathies and antipathies. When a company came from field operations to rest for a week in the garrison, we saw little of them. The unit
was then lodged in one of the big halls, the officers disappeared immediately, the sergeants followed suit, and we closed both our eyes to the
doings of the men. They wallowed for a week in their short-lived freedom
and sought amusement as best they could. This little world of ours seemed
settled in its grooves, even while the fighting was going on not too far
from us.

It was an upheaval when our Colonel reached the age limit and was
pensioned off. The new Colonel came from the 30th Sappers' Regiment
of Valencia. Immediately on setting foot on land, he turned up at the
barracks, at the unusual hour of half-past nine in the morning.

At the gate he was met by the corporal on mess duty, a short fat young
man, his uniform greasy from kitchen work, and by two equally untidy
soldiers.

"Where is the officer on guard?" bellowed the new Colonel.

"There is no officer on guard, sir."

"What, no officer? Fetch him at once. How is it that you're all so dirty?
And why are there only two men? Where are the other men on guard?
In the canteen, I suppose, what!"

"Sir, we're alone . . ."

"Shut up. You're all under arrest. Wait, one of you will come with me."

The corporal took him to the office. There I was, alone, working at
some accounts.

"You, what are you doing here?"

"I'm the sergeant in the regimental office, sir."

"I suppose you're something because otherwise you wouldn't be here.
I'm not a fool. Where is the senior Major?"

"I think in his house, sir. He usually comes at eleven."

"And there's no officer here?"

"No, sir."

"When the Major arrives send him to me immediately. How does your
coat come to be unbuttoned?"

"Because I was alone here, sir. And it is so hot here that most of us
work in shirt sleeves."

"Well, that won't happen again. You're under arrest. That will teach
you how to present yourself to your superior."

When the Major came he had an interview with the new Colonel behind closed doors, but all of us, down to the office orderlies, found a strategical position for eavesdropping. The site of the Colonel's room made it easy. And the Colonel roared:

"This is a disgrace! No officer on guard, a filthy-looking corporal and two even filthier soldiers at the gate! Not a single officer on the premises! And you asleep, what! All this must finish. Do you understand?"

There was a pause; it was impossible to catch the Major's reply. Then came another bellow:

"I see. Here you're all accustomed to grab as much as you can, what! That's got to end. From today onwards all accounts will go through my hands. And I don't want to see any more dirty soldiers!"

The Major came out of the room with purple ears. By afternoon, nearly everybody in the barracks was under arrest.

That night the First Sappers Company arrived, sent to garrison after a year in the field. Probably not one of the men realized that there was a new C.O., for an hour after their arrival they were scattered all over the taverns and brothels of the town. I went to town for supper and returned to the barracks at eleven, to take over the night guard. But I arrived at five minutes past eleven. The corporal on stable duty met me:

"Nothing to report. The only thing is that Captain Jimenez"—the officer in command of the First Company of Sappers—"is in the officers' room and you have to present yourself to him."

There was nothing unusual in the fact that the Captain was in the officers' room; it often served as headquarters for officers passing through Ceuta, since there were three dormitories and a bathroom behind it. It was also quite normal for a strange officer to call in the sergeant on guard and ask him about something or other. I knocked and entered.

"At your orders, sir."

"Do you know the time?"

"Five minutes past eleven, sir."

"Be quiet. If a superior speaks to you, you have to keep quiet. What time of day is this for a sergeant to come in? The sergeants must be here at eleven sharp. You're under arrest."

"But . . ."

"Shut up, I told you. And be off with you."

"Sir . . ."

"Shut up!" He jumped up from his chair like a man possessed and seemed about to pounce on me. I lost my self-control.

"You shut up. Here it's I who am in command of the guard. And while I'm in command I won't allow such treatment."

The absurdity of the situation must have paralyzed him. He sat down again.

"So you're in command of the guard? Let's sort that out. Then you're in command of the guard like myself, without knowing it. Where have you come from just now?"

"From my supper. I've a pass for sleeping out of barracks—all of us sergeants in barracks take turns at guard duty on certain nights, from eleven onwards."

"I understand less and less . . . All right. You're under arrest. Take over the guard and tomorrow we'll clear up the muddle. By the way, I'd forgotten to tell you: I'm Captain in command of the guard."

That night all four of us sergeants were put under arrest; there followed all the men of the First Sappers Company with the exception of about a dozen, each being put under arrest on his belated arrival in barracks; and finally all those on special duty in barracks. Reveille was sounded at seven in the morning. At five minutes to seven the Colonel appeared. Fortunately I was awake, because the sergeant on guard had to supervise the distribution of the morning coffee and to prepare the report for the Command to be submitted at eight. Captain Jimenez was lying fast asleep on his bed, stark naked, having forgotten all about the guard duty. To sleep in a real bed with a real mattress after a year in the front line must have been irresistible. I had no time to wake him, and thus had to report to the Colonel myself.

"Where is the Captain on guard?"

"I think he's asleep, sir."

The Colonel hurtled himself into the officers' room. Five minutes later he came out with the Captain whose face was red from sleep and who was fumbling at his buttons. The signal for breakfast sounded, but the only persons to appear were a dozen soldiers. The Colonel emitted another of his roars:

"Where are all those rascals? Asleep, what! That's why I've come. This is a disgrace." He marched towards one of the dormitories, the Captain behind him, and I following them. It was empty. The Colonel stood there in the middle of the huge room, staring bewildered at the heaps of equipment on the beds.

"Where are all those men?"

The Captain swallowed.

"Under arrest, sir. In quod."

The explanation followed. When the Captain was finished, the Colonel put him under arrest as well. We sergeants decided to stay in our room under arrest and not to go to our various offices, where work was waiting. They came to fetch us later in the morning. Our arrest was called off. Yet from that morning there was open war between the Colonel and the Regiment. The most important share in the battle fell upon the senior

Major and myself. The rigor of military discipline may make a subaltern's life unbearable, but the same rigor, applied by a whole regiment, can make the Colonel's life a misery. Occasionally I enjoyed that warfare.

But I had learned another lesson. I knew the limits of security in barracks. A sergeant was just a sergeant. The troubled liver of any officer might turn him into an ordinary ranker from one day to the next, after three or after twenty years of service.

4. Dictator in the Making

MY friend Sanchiz had come back to the Ceuta office of the Legion and took me once again to the tavern of the Licentiate. I went along with him, struggling against my ingrown aversion, but my nightmare was laid. The entrance had lost its color of a bleeding gash and was painted a clear pink. Instead of the oil lamps hanging from their hooks there was plain electric light; the red walls were now a deep cream and the bar table was just like that of thousands of taverns in Spain, an oak slab with taps and a zinc running board. The Licentiate himself looked a prosperous tradesman in his green-and-black striped apron.

The main customers were still soldiers of the *Tercio* and prostitutes, but the gallows-birds and the old hags with the markings of syphilis and scab in their faces had disappeared. Men from other units entered freely to drink a bottle of wine and to eat dried tunny. The fish were still hanging from the big cross beam over the bar table, but now the beam was clean, the tunny no longer tasted of oily soot.

"My word, it has changed," I said to Sanchiz.

"Nothing changes things so much as having money. When *El Licenciado* started here with his few old packing cases and his vitriolic wine, he hadn't a bean. The only thing he had was the courage to set up a tavern for the *Tercio*, when no one in Ceuta wanted to sell us so much as a glass of wine. He's made a lot of money by now, and he picks his customers. Just wait, in a couple of years he'll set up a modern bar in this place and stand as town councillor."

Sanchiz paused and looked moody.

"Do you know that of all of us who formed the First Standard of the *Tercio* there's almost nobody left? The Betrothed of Death—do you remember?—have married. I'm one of the very few who have not yet met the Bride, and it seems to me that I'll have to wait a long time yet. It's a pity."

"Don't think about it. You'll die like all of us when your hour has come, and you won't change it, even if you have got it into your obstinate head that you want to kill yourself or to get somebody to kill you. Do tell me instead what you've been doing with yourself all the time."

"I've changed a lot, my boy. D'you know that it's a year since we met in Beni-Aros? In that year I've seen more than in all the thirty-eight years of my life. I've gone white." He pulled off his cap, and I saw that his fair hair had turned silver.

"All right then, tell me about it."

But on that day Sanchiz did not feel like talking of the war and the *Tercio*. He talked ramblingly of the events which had driven him to Morocco when he was thirty-six years old, a man who had never been a soldier and who seemed predestined to work in an office all his life.

Sanchiz came of a wealthy middle-class family. His parents had given him a solid education; he had studied for a commercial career at a time when such studies seemed a novel and preposterous thing in Spain, and he had also obtained the title of lawyer. Before he was thirty he had become the manager of the Spanish branch of a big American manufacturing firm. Then he married. It was a perfect marriage. After a year the woman expected a child, but it was never born. She had to be operated on and became unfit to conceive any more children. Sanchiz resigned himself to their childlessness and devoted his whole energy to making his wife happy. He loved her blindly. After a few years she began to languish. The physical sensitiveness caused by the operation sharpened. It was at that stage that I came to know Sanchiz. He was taking her from one specialist to the other, but she was only getting worse. Then the doctors passed sentence: they could no longer live together as man and wife. She had cancer in the matrix. An operation was possible, but the doctors were extremely pessimistic about it. The invalid refused to be operated on.

I saw something of what happened to Sanchiz then. For months the physical contact which to him was both need and happiness had hurt the woman he loved and had thus turned into intimate torture for him. And then even that was past. He, who was a healthy, normal male, lived close to his wife whom he desired ceaselessly and hopelessly. He tried to escape from the bodily strain by going with other women, but it was impossible for him. He loved her. Then he started to drink. Her illness ate up his savings. His drunkenness lost him his job. After a period of acute poverty Sanchiz found employment in an office as an accountant at two hundred pesetas a month. What were two hundred pesetas to him who had a sick wife in need of daily morphine injections?

When his wife died I went to see Sanchiz in his flat. She had died wrapped in an old blanket, on a spring mattress barely covered with straw-filled sacking. He had neither furniture nor clothes. All had gone to the pawnshops.

After they had carried away the dead body Sanchiz locked the door of his flat and gave the key to the concierge. He never came back. The few who knew him at all thought he had committed suicide. Yet he had not been able to bring himself to it. He wandered round Madrid, begging for a pittance, and slept on the benches in the avenues. When the Foreign Legion was formed he enlisted at once.

The age limit set by the *Tercio* was far too low for Sanchiz, but he passed for younger. He was fair, with milk-white skin, fresh, rosy cheeks and a scanty beard, a type rarely found in Spain. He met with no difficulty in joining. The Legion did not insist on papers or even on the names of its recruits.

He joined so as to be killed. But when the Legion's offices were set up he was picked out from the ranks and sent there. The risk of the front line had eluded him. He got drunk and disorderly, in an effort to be kicked out of the office. But his superiors had grown fond of him, and all they did was to put him under arrest in barracks for days on end.

He tried to provoke the violence of the worst gangsters of the First Standard. But in a place where brawls were often decided by a bullet or the knife, the men simply grinned at Sanchiz and bought him a bottle of wine to get rid of his blues.

Finally, he succeeded in being sent to the front for two months as instructor to the South American Standard. That was meant as a punishment. After the first engagements, the disaster of Melilla intervened. Sanchiz was sent to Melilla. There were companies of the *Tercio* of which not a single man escaped unscathed. More than half their number were killed. Sanchiz did not receive a scratch.

And then he was called back to office work.

We saw much of each other. Whenever Sanchiz came to think of his own history he would drink himself unconscious. When he came out of his drunken fit he was repentant. Then he used to send for me, or come and fetch me for a walk. We would stroll along the West Mole to its farthest end, two miles away from the town, and sit down among the rocks facing the sea.

"We got fifty new recruits today," he said one evening. "They've no idea what they've bargained for. These people don't come for the same reasons as the old gang. They just come because they want to show off." He threw flat stones into the sea and watched them ricocheting.

"You know, barbarism is surely one of the most contagious things in life. When the First Standard went to Melilla, we attuned ourselves to the bestiality of the Moors. They cut off the genitals of Spanish soldiers and stuffed them into their dead mouths and left the corpses rotting in the sun. You've seen it yourself. Then we cut off the heads of the Moors and put them on the parapet of our position in the mornings. Well, you've seen that too. Anyhow, that's what the *Tercio* was like from the beginning. And there is no remedy. But I don't know whether you've seen that we've got a new form of enlistment for the Legion now. People sign on just for the period of the reconquest of Morocco. They're different from us. Hundreds of them have come already, many of them from good families, educated men with university degrees. There was a big clash between them and us old campaigners, and some couldn't stick it out. But most of them are staying on, and do you know, they're more savage than any of us."

"I believe it depends mostly on the officers."

"Yes, of course, it all depends on the officers. But don't you see, the same thing happened to the officers as happened to us. I remember perfectly well that when the *Tercio* was organized, our officers were just like any other officers, with the only difference that they'd gambled away the funds of their company and had no choice but to join the *Tercio,* or else that they were really brave and wanted to get promotion by risking their skins. But then they had to tackle the First Standard—you remember, the first thing we did in Ceuta was to bump off three or four people, and then they had to send us post-haste to Riffien!—and the officers changed at once.

"I believe that at bottom it was only fear. They were afraid of us. But they were in command, and most of us hadn't even a name to ourselves. They imposed the brutal discipline we've got now. If a man refused to obey an order he got two bullets in his head. If a man overstepped his rights—a knapsack filled with sand and two hours' running in the noon sun. What I mean to say is, we infected one another, and by now the officers have become savage barbarians, not only against us, but against everything and everybody. Of the First Standard there's not a single officer left unhurt. At least, Major Franco is the only one who got through it without a hole in his skin."

"Tell me about him. I've heard a lot of stories. For instance, is it true that Millán Astray hates him?"

"Of course. Listen, Millán Astray is a braggart. I've seen it for myself by now. When he starts shouting, 'To me, my brave lions!' or something of that kind, we can be sure that we'll soon be in the thick of a fight. We march forward in an avalanche while he makes his horse caracole and turns round to the General Staff: 'How do you like my boys?' Of course, the General Staff and the Generals are never at the head of the troops when we make a real attack. And so nobody sees through his tricks. He's got the fame of a hero and no one will take it away from him. The only man who could do it is Franco. Only that's a bit difficult to explain."

He began to throw stones into the sea again, and became engrossed in the game until I urged him:

"Leave that and go on with your story."

"You see, Franco . . . No, look. The *Tercio's* rather like being in a penitentiary. The most courageous brute is the master of the jail. And something of this sort has happened to that man. He's hated, just as the convicts hate the bravest killer in their jail, and he's obeyed and respected —he imposes himself on all the others—just as the big killer imposes himself on the whole jail. You know how many officers of the Legion have been killed by a shot in the back during an attack. Now, there are many who would wish to shoot Franco in the back, but not one of them has the courage to do it. They're afraid that he might turn his head and see them just when they have taken aim at him."

"But surely it is the same story with Millán Astray."

"Oh, no. One couldn't take a pot-shot at Millán Astray, he takes too good care of himself. But it wouldn't be difficult to fire at Franco. He takes the lead in an advance, and—well, if somebody's got guts, you just have to admit it. I've seen him walk upright in front of all the others, while they hardly dared to lift their heads from the ground, the bullets fell so thick. And who would shoot him in the back then? You just stay there with your mouth open, half-hoping that the Moors'll get him at any moment, and half-afraid of it, because if they did, you would run away. There's another thing too: he's much more intelligent than Millán Astray. He knows what he's after. And that's another reason why Millán Astray can't stand him."

"And how did he behave in Melilla?"

"Franco? Believe me, it's sticky going with Franco. You'll get whatever's due to you, and he knows where he's taking you, but as to the treatment you get . . . He simply looks blankly at a fellow, with very big and very serious eyes, and says: 'Execute him,' and walks away, just like that. I've seen murderers go white in the face because Franco had looked at them out of the corner of his eye. And he's fussy! God save you if anything's missing from your equipment, or if your rifle isn't clean, or you've been lazy. You know, that man's not quite human and he hasn't got any nerves. And then, he's quite isolated. I believe all the officers detest him because he treats them just as he treats us and isn't friends with any of them. They go on the loose and get drunk—I ask you, what else should they do after two months in the firing line?—and he stays alone in the tent or in barracks, just like one of those old clerks who simply must go to the office, even on Sundays. It's difficult to make him out and it's funny because he's still so young."

In the year 1922, events developed quickly in Morocco and in Spain. More than 60,000 men had been sent over from the Peninsula under the title of reinforcements, but the disorder and disorganization among these troops was such that commanding officers with any experience in the African campaign refused to employ them anywhere but in the rear. The discontent spread. In Spain the public protest against the disaster of Annual and the demand for an investigation into the responsibility for it had first been centered on the King and on the dead General Silvestre; now they became focused on the High Commissioner for Morocco, General Berenguer. In the zone of Melilla, nearly all the territory lost to the Moors in the catastrophe of the previous year had been taken back in a spectacular reconquest. Yet the situation remained critical. Abd-el-Krim had made contact with different political groups in various countries of Europe and his forces under the command of his brother had filtered into the zone of Ceuta, menacing Xauen. The Raisuni had allied himself with Abd-el-Krim whose thrust towards Xauen promised to smash the ring of encirclement in which the Raisuni's men were still held. It also threatened to provoke a rising in the zone of Ceuta.

The number of casualties grew incessantly. General Berenguer began to speak of resigning as soon as the Raisuni was overcome. It was a matter of public gossip that General Sanjurjo, in command of the zone of Melilla, was the real High Commissioner. In Madrid Governments succeeded each other after holding office a few weeks; each one left the problem of Morocco to the next as a dire legacy.

The Chancelleries of Europe envisaged the possibility of Spain having to resign from the Moroccan Protectorate and France taking over the heritage. No one doubted the fact that Abd-el-Krim was receiving war material and technical support from across the French frontier.

We were all aware of cross currents which affected us, but which we could not gauge. The only things we knew for certain were the changes in personnel. Thus, Lieut.-Col. Millán Astray had been made Colonel and had resigned from the command of the Legion on the plea of physical incapacity, owing to his many and terrible wounds.

I asked Sanchiz one day:

"Who's going to succeed Millán Astray? Franco?"

"Pooh, Franco—this time they've pulled one on him. They're going to appoint Lieut-Col. Valenzuela. You see, there are only three possible successors among our officers here: Gonzalez Tablas, Valenzuela, and Franco. But Franco is only a Major and the other two are Lieutenant-Colonels. Before making Franco Chief of the Legion, they would have to make him a Lieutenant-Colonel too. Apparently Sanjurjo has put him forward for promotion twice, but all the graybeards say that it would be too much to promote him and to give him the command of the *Tercio* into the bargain. So they're going to give it to Valenzuela. But Franco has been given a medal."

In the spring of 1923 General Berenguer launched the operations against the Raisuni's last place of refuge, Tazarut. Towards the end of May the troops entered there. Lieut.-Col. Gonzalez Tablas was killed during this action. Berenguer handed in his resignation; the Government in Madrid decreed that operations were to be suspended and a great number of troops discharged. For a few days it looked as though the war in Morocco was coming to an end. Negotiations with Abd-el-Krim had been started, in an effort to make peace with the tribes of the Riff. In the zone of Melilla the Spanish Army had stopped its advance and lay in front of Beni-Urraguiel, waiting for the result of the negotiations. Yet Abd-el-Krim wanted the recognition of the Riff as an autonomous State, as the Republic of the Riff; to give weight to his pressure, his troops continued attacking the Spanish outposts by day and night.

Early one morning the rumor spread all over Ceuta that a second disaster had occurred in the zone of Melilla. The Legionaries stationed in Larache had been sent over to Melilla at breakneck speed. There was no reference to it in the press, and the officers who were informed of the happenings kept silent.

Major Tabasco was rung up from the General Command in Tetuan every half hour. He had a conference with the Colonel and when he left the room his face was very grave. In the end he told me:

"Things are going badly again, Barea."

"Something's happening in Melilla, sir, isn't it?"

"Yes. Apparently, the Moors have surrounded Tizzi-Azza, and if they take it there will be a second Annual. Don't go out for a walk this afternoon, because we may have to organize a relief column in Ceuta."

I had often heard about the fortified position of Tizzi-Azza. It lay on the top of a hill and had to be supplied periodically with water, food and ammunition. The supply convoy had to pass through a narrow defile, and every passage had to be forced by fighting. Now the Moors had cut the road. The last convoy had entered, but not left, and the outpost was encircled.

A huge relief column was organized and the ring round Tizzi-Azza was shattered. But during the attack the new commander of the *Tercio*, Lieut.-Col. Valenzuela, was killed.

"Now Franco is the Chief of the Legion," said Sanchiz, when he heard the news.

"But they haven't made him a Lieutenant-Colonel yet," I quoted back at him.

"They'll promote him now, whether Millán Astray likes it or not. Whom else should they put there? Of all the officers we've not got one who would take the post, even if they gave it him on a platter. They're all afraid of it."

Sanchiz was right. In the Cortes Franco's promotion was passed. He was made Chief of the Legion.

Major Tabasco's only comment was: "Well, it's his funeral."

At the beginning of July, General Berenguer ceased to be High Commissioner in Morocco; he was succeeded by General Burguete. Ceuta prepared a parade for his reception. On the day before his arrival the Major sent for me:

"There will be a review tomorrow in honor of General Burguete. I'm sorry, but we haven't anybody but yourself to lead the *gastadores*."

In the Spanish Army, in front of any regiment in full formation there marches a so-called squadron of *gastadores*—eight soldiers, chosen for their height and bearing, in two files of four each, and at their head a corporal who acts as the guide of the regiment and executes all the motions to be followed by the rank and file.

We had no corporal who could have gone through the intricate movements without disgracing the unit. I had to take off my sergeant's stripes for a day, to sew on the insignia of a corporal and to select the best-looking eight soldiers in barracks. By dint of a series of manipulations we were able to muster something like two companies, with our senior Major on horseback as Chief of the force. Luckily, the Colonel happened to be away in Tetuan. The other units in Ceuta were equally short of ordinary rankers and consisted mainly of men on special duties; they all had to make shift in a similar manner. There were quite a number of sergeants converted into corporals and quartermaster sergeants converted into lieutenants.

We had to dress in our "semi-gala" uniform, dark-blue cloth, unbearably hot in a Moroccan July. But we were confident that the review would not last more than half an hour and consoled ourselves with the thought that the ship was due at half-past nine in the morning.

As the Engineers are considered an *élite* corps, we were detailed to the quay where the ships was to be moored. We were lined up at eight o'clock. It was a radiant day and the sea was perfectly smooth. For an hour we waited, smoking cigarettes and drinking the refreshments offered by the street vendors. Shortly after nine the ship moored and the regimental bands began to play. The High Commissioner received the same honors as the King—in the King's absence. All the officers had to present themselves to pay homage. Afterwards the General reviewed the troops.

General Burguete was a tall, slightly pot-bellied man, with an enormous black Kaiser moustache. He showed at once that his inclination towards Prussianism was not confined to his style of whiskers and kept us there in the broiling sun, motionless, while he scrutinized the exterior of every single private.

The dark-blue cloth uniform was hardly ever used in Morocco; most of the men had been given theirs in the various depots at the very last moment before the parade. Thus, the General had occasion to find fault with every detail of every part of the uniforms. Soon he was indignantly shouting; the commanding officers of each unit shouted at their subalterns with equal indignation, and so on down to the men in the ranks. Eighty to a hundred men were put under arrest then and there on the mole. The review lasted until eleven o'clock. When it seemed impossible to prolong it any more and we began to hope that our sweat and toil would soon be over, the General decided that the troops had to render the traditional homage to the statue of Our Lady of Africa, to whom he was to offer his baton of command.

We stood lined up in front of the church for another hour. Then the General went to the *Comandancia General* and from the balcony of the building reviewed the troops marching past. We were back in barracks at two o'clock. We had two cases of sunstroke and five of illness. It was the same with other regiments. The new High Commissioner had started his career well.

Yet General Burguete had come to put Morocco in order. That same afternoon he walked round the streets and put soldiers under arrest. They arrived in droves to report for arrest in the barracks. Officers followed suit. The Colonial Army had created its own code for dressing and behaving in the streets, which was obviously different from the military rules applied in the Capital. But General Burguete intended that the soldiers of Morocco, with their uniforms bleached by the sun and marked by campaign life, should look like soldiers of the Madrid garrison on a Sunday afternoon.

One of the men answered him back sharply:

"I've no other clothing, sir. I've got these rags—and they're full of lice!
—because they don't give me any others."

"Any man who's without a decent uniform will have to stay in barracks. You'll present yourself to the officer on guard in your regiment."

"Now, Franco could be his brother," said Sanchiz to me when I told
him the story. "You'll see when he comes to Ceuta."

Burguete at once opened peace talks with the Raisuni. From one day to
the other, the Raisuni, who had been encircled in Tazarut and at the
mercy of the Spanish Government, became an important personage; his
princely honors were restored to him, he received a large amount in cash
and our troops were withdrawn from the Jebel-Alam. Then he made
suggestions as to which officers, native or Spanish, should be discharged
because he disapproved of them. The Engineers were not affected by
these intrigues, but the repercussions on other units were very grave.

"Things are getting serious, my boy," said Sanchiz to me one day. He
heard more than I did, through his post in the Central Office of the
Tercio.

"You know that our officers are very friendly with the officers of the
Regulares. After all, many of them served with the Moorish troops before
they joined with us. Like Franco himself. Now Burguete is discharging
people, and they say that he does it according to a list he's got from the
Raisuni. And some of our people want to organize a rising. You know,
I think it's a dirty trick myself, to put that old rascal, the Raisuni, in cot-
ton wool, after the thousands of dead he's cost us. I don't know what
Franco is going to do. They say he's very angry and has made a protest.
But I can tell you one thing: if he decides to raise the Legion in rebellion,
we'll all go with him. And there'll be hell to pay."

Yet what was happening was not Burguete's personal policy, it was the
policy of the Government. They wanted to get rid of the Raisuni so as to
have their hands free against Abd-el-Krim and to put an end to the conflict in one way or the other. Peace negotiations with Abd-el-Krim were
still going on, and so were negotiations for the release of the prisoners in
his hands.

It was a renewal of the old Spanish policy in Morocco, the policy of
suborning those tribal chiefs who were powerful enough to stand up
against the army. The Raisuni was being bribed, and there were hopes
of doing the same with Abd-el-Krim. The expeditionary forces were being sent home. The country was left in the dark about all the moves; yet
we in Morocco sensed them, and among the troops factions began to form.

There were three big parties within the army. Leaving aside the few
who were against the Moroccan venture by reason of their general out-
look, the Government's part was taken openly by all those who were

pining for the ease and tranquillity of their provincial garrison. Then there were the old "Moroccans," interested only in the return of the times when profiteering and racketeering were possible without much risk. And thirdly there were the "warriors" who spoke of the honor of the Spanish Army and the honor of the Monarchy and the honor of the country, and who demanded war at any price.

Among the "warrior" party was the new Chief of the Foreign Legion. And the Legion grew quickly into a State within the State, a cancer within the army. Franco was not content with his promotion and his brilliant career. He needed war. Now he held the *Tercio* in his hands, as an instrument for war.

Even the last soldiers in the ranks of the *Tercio* had their share in it and felt independent from the remainder of the Spanish Army, as though set apart. They would draw themselves up, recall their deeds and express their contempt of the others.

"We saved Melilla," they said. And it was true.

But from being a hero of this kind to being a rebel—and a Fascist— there is only one step.

5. Farewell

MAJOR TABASCO called me to his room and gave me a batch of handwritten pages.

"Will you please type this for me, with as many copies as possible? It's confidential stuff. The best thing would be to do it in the evenings."

I copied long lists of "members" and "proposed members," of motions and resolutions. It took me some time until I realized that Don José was something like the Secretary General of the Officers' Juntas in Ceuta. A big meeting of all the Military Juntas of Spain was apparently planned for the second half of the year 1923 in Madrid, "pending unforseen events," and Don José was to go there as a delegate. It would be easy to organize the conference during the summer leave period, and representatives of all arms, units, and military zones would meet:

"We cannot shut our eyes to the course events are taking in the coun-

try. We of the Armed Forces have the obligation to serve the Nation.
The country must not go further along the present disastrous road. We
are in the hands of revolutionaries. How else could it happen that a Parliament should attack the Supreme Chief of the Nation, or that one part
of the country should intend to declare itself independent? It is our clear
duty to cut short these developments." And so on.

I had heard of the Juntas—what Spaniard could have failed to hear of
them?—but I had never to my knowledge met any of their members.
Eager to find out more, I asked the Major as ingenuously as I could:
"Are the Juntas run by the Government, then, Don José?"

"That would just about suit the Government! No, the Juntas are independent. They are the bedrock of the nation."

I made a vacant, foolish face, and Don José laughed.

"You don't know anything about what's happening round you, I can
see that. Now listen, my boy. Spain was on the brink of perdition once
before, in 1917, during the Great War. The French and the English
weren't pleased with our neutrality and tried to embroil us in the war,
by making friends with all the enemies of the country, the Anarchists, the
Socialists, and the Republicans, and even with the Liberals. They managed to win over Romanones who was Premier then. The Socialists and
the Anarchists organized a strike—but you must remember it, you weren't
as young as all that."

"Of course I remember, sir. But the General Strike started because of
the increase in prices, and because the people said that all the commodities were being sent abroad. The workers demanded a reduction in the
price of bread, or an increase in their wages."

"Pooh, that was only the pretext. The truth was that they wanted to
make a revolution like the one that was just beginning in Russia then."

"But—the Allies were against the Russian Revolution, sir!"

"You just don't understand the whole story. The Allies turned against
the Russian Revolution later, when the Russians refused to go on fighting
for them. It served them right, too, because the revolution was manufactured by the English and the French themselves. What happened was
simply that their child turned out to be a changeling. Remember how
the Allies fomented the revolution in Germany."

"So you think the Allies made the German Revolution?"

"Of course, my boy. Who else? Certainly not the Germans. They were
too wretched, poor devils, to involve themselves in new complications.
The Allies did it because they wanted to destroy Germany for good.
But never mind, that's another story. Anyhow, in Spain, Romanones
wanted to drag us into the war, and because he alone was too weak, he
and his friends incited the Republicans and the workers so that they could

pretend that the whole country wanted to help to defend the Allies. One had to show the rabble they had reckoned without their host. A great patriot called together all the officers with a sense of honor, and the Government got some plain speaking: 'Either you break with the mob, or the army will march!' Fortunately, it wasn't necessary. But the Juntas continued functioning. After all, we had had a sample of the sort of things bad Spaniards are capable of, and we didn't want to be caught unprepared the next time."

"I seemed to remember that in 1917 the army was not all united. Millán Astray set himself against the Juntas, didn't he, sir?"

"Oh, yes, and he even wanted to shoot us all! But Millán Astray isn't a military man, he's a maniac. Do you know his history?"

"No, sir."

"Well, some time in the 'nineties, his father was the Director of the Model Prison in Madrid. When the prisoners wanted to go on a spree, they tipped the Director and he let them gad about in Madrid all night long. It so happened that a prisoner by the name of Varela went out one night and bashed in his mother's head and stole her belongings in complicity with a servant girl. When the police found out how the crime had happened, they sent Millán Astray, father, to jail himself. And the son, who was only a child then, went quite mad. He said his father was innocent, and that he himself would have to restore the family's honor. Then in the Philippine Wars he became famous. He was promoted and his father was set free, but it didn't cure the son. In 1917 he machine-gunned the strikers, and he would have liked to machine-gun us as well."

"And now the Juntas want to prevent a rising of Millán Astray's?"

"No, the Juntas don't deal with small matters. What we want to prevent is things going on as they are at present. We are on the brink of a revolution. The rabble has managed to make the King responsible for every muddle in Morocco. They intend to proclaim the Republic and to make us leave the Protectorate. The English would like that very much indeed. Then they would establish themselves here in Ceuta and be able to wave across the Straits to their people there. But they won't get it all their own way."

"Then you believe, sir, that General Picasso [1] is in league with all those people?"

"General Picasso is a poor old fool who can't see beyond the tip of his own nose. They've pulled wool over his eyes, and he believes that everything he's been told is gospel truth. As if the kind of papers he's

[1] The Judge Advocate who was entrusted with the investigation into the causes of the disaster of Melilla, and who in 1922-3 was preparing the so-called *Expediente Picasso*, a documented account inculpating the King.

supposed to have found in Silvestre's desk would have been left lying
about for everybody to see! Never mind, all those tricks won't get them
anywhere, because we're here. And if a rising is necessary, we shall rise."
I found that difficult to understand. A military rising? Against whom?
For what? For a return of the times of Ferdinand VII or Isabella II, when
Generals ruled the country?

I talked to Sanchiz about it, and he grinned.

"It's all very well for those people to talk, but they haven't counted with
Franco—nor with us. Everything will happen just as the Legion wants it
to, you'll see."

I felt muddled and uneasy. A few days later I spoke to Captain Barberan, our paymaster, whom I knew to be different from the others.

There was an odd kind of fellowship between the Captain and myself,
ever since he had found me trying to draw a map of Morocco, in my early
days as a corporal on office duty. Captain Barberan used to shut himself
into his room every evening to study, to make notes and calculations.
Once he came to my desk, looked at my sketch, criticized it and then
proceeded to teach me topography. Occasionally he took me to the quar-
ries at Benzu for surveying practice and carried on his own experiments
with strange electrical apparatus, while I sketched away under his guid-
ance. After a time he explained to me what he was doing. He was a pilot
and he was doing research. There was a new method of taking one's
bearings in the air, which was known to not more than half a dozen
people in Spain; it was too complicated to explain, but roughly speaking
it meant steering by radio-telegraphic waves. And now he was working
at it: "A few friends and I, we have a project, we want to fly to America."

He was obsessed with flying: I presume that he talked to me simply
because I never tired of listening to his technical dissertations. Captain
Barberan was a small, nervous man with feverish eyes behind his glasses,
prematurely bald, silent and self-contained. His relations with the other
officers were scanty; he never took part in their amusements, but lived
the life of a single-minded recluse. He looked like an ascetic monk in
uniform.

I would hardly have dared to speak to Captain Barberan about political
problems. But a few days after I had come across the Juntas within the
narrow circle of our garrison life, he gave me the chance, beginning as
always with his obsession:

"Of course you risk your life, flying. But at least you risk it for something great." He laughed a nervous little laugh. "I'm an ambitious man,
really. There have been Transatlantic flights already, but we as Spaniards
have the obligation to fly to South America. We have many obliga-
tions . . ."

We were standing on the terrace of the barracks, which dominates the whole Straits of Gibraltar. Captain Barberan went to the telemeter and adjusted the screws. There he remained for a while, stooping, looking through the lenses. When he straightened up, he said:

"That is another of the things we must do. The Rock is a bit of Spanish soil which we must redeem . . . What do you think of this war?"

"It's not for me to have an opinion, sir."

"Everybody has an opinion. Forget for a moment that I'm your Captain."

"Well—Morocco is quite simply a despicable affair, in my opinion."

"*Caramba*—despicable—you're very outspoken. And whose fault do you think it is?"

"The fault of very many people. Firstly, of those who made the Treaty of Algeciras. On one side the Spanish leaders wanted something which would permit the army to wipe out its defeats in Cuba and the Philippines, and give our generals a living. On the other side there was England, interested in having no other power facing Gibraltar, not even France. And Germany, too, not wanting France either. Between them they've brought it on us. While we were wrestling with this damnable problem of Morocco, we had no chance to become a power in Europe. Perhaps it saved us from the Great War, but certainly it has ruined us as a nation."

"Hm—you've got hold of a nice set of theories. There's a grain of truth in them, though. Do you know that England won't allow us to fortify Ceuta or the Sierra Carbonera? We've still got our old batteries from the year 1868, and in a few places even bronze guns."

"But who has been keeping the Moors supplied with munitions ever since the attack began in Melilla, twenty years ago? The rifles are French and the cartridges too. But this trafficking suited many of our own people down to the ground, sir. Why not admit it? They didn't want things to be settled. Once, in Kudia Tahar, I overheard a telephone conversation between General Berenguer and General Marzo. Marzo had carried through an operation with the aim of setting up a few blockhouses and a fortified position. I happened to be with the soldier on telephone duty who made connection with H.Q. General Berenguer asked: 'Well, what was it like?' 'Very bad, old man,' said Marzo. 'Why, what happened? Did you run into heavy fire?' 'No, what happened was that those sons of bitches did not fire a single shot against us—you can't get anywhere that way!'

"And now we've made a pact with the Raisuni, given him every honor and a peace treaty, and are trying to do the same with Abd-el-Krim, simply because things are getting too hot. A real war doesn't suit certain

people, because it could only end with a complete conquest and a final
settlement with the chieftains. And then the goose which laid the golden
eggs would be dead."

"Then in your opinion we should either conquer or evacuate Morocco?"

"Yes, evacuate it. I think we ought to address ourselves to the Powers
who gave us the task to tackle, and say to them: 'Gentlemen, here you
have it back; settle it between yourselves as you like.' And I believe that
three-quarters of the Spanish people think the same. Except the professional soldiers, of course."

"Well, quite a few men in the army would agree with you. We shall
see how things work out."

Suddenly, a new personage was featured on the front pages of the
Spanish press: Horacio Echevarrieta, one of the Spanish mining mag-
nates. He was a friend of Abd-el-Krim's and offered to seek him out in
the heart of the Riff to negotiate the release of Spanish prisoners. The
public enthusiastically acclaimed the idea. Echevarrieta appeared as a
savior. The officers of the Moroccan Army protested: It would be an
intolerable disgrace—the prisoners had to be freed at the point of the
bayonet. But the Government backed the undertaking and Echevarrieta
obtained the release of the prisoners, at the price of some four million
pesetas.

Major Tabasco raged up and down in our office.

"It's a dirty shame! They didn't even let the army intervene. The army
counts for nothing. Of course, Echevarrieta is a good friend of the Man-
nesmanns, and wolves always understand one another."

I was honestly puzzled by Tabasco's outbreak. To me it seemed an
excellent thing that somebody had ransomed hundreds of Spaniards from
a slavery worthy of the Middle Ages. I knew, however, that I could not
discuss this problem with my chief and that it would be best to pretend
to be deaf and dumb. But Tabasco needed a responsive audience:

"Why are you making faces? Perhaps you don't even know who
Echevarrieta is?"

"I know just as much as everybody knows, sir, that he's a wealthy
man from Bilbao who knows Abd-el-Krim from the time when they
studied together at the school for mining engineers."

"Yes, yes, very nice. He's a trickster and a rogue. A friend of Prieto's,
the socialist millionaire, you know. A rogue, that's what he is. Don't you
realize that Abd-el-Krim has some extremely rich mines in the Riff, and
that those mines really belong to Echevarrieta? Here you have the reason
for their so-called friendship."

"That's the first I've heard of it, sir."

"It doesn't surprise me. These are things the people who want to get rid of Morocco won't tell you—those people who want us to make Abd-el-Krim Sultan of the Riff Republic! Now listen. A couple of Germans, the brothers Mannesmann, found out that there are iron ore mines in the Riff and something else, manganese, or whatever it is. And when Abd-el-Krim's father was chief of Beni-Urraguiel they talked him round and got a concession from him. That happened twenty years ago. Of course, we couldn't agree to this kind of plunder. Then the brothers Mannesmann engineered the war of 1909 against us, and Abd-el-Krim, the father, wanted to destroy our mines. We had to let them all feel a heavy hand. We even had to put one of Abd-el-Krim's own sons in jail—a good-for-nothing who had established himself in Melilla and was editing a newspaper. When the Germans saw that their business was coming to nothing, they arranged things with Echevarrieta. He bought up their concession for a pittance and then he made a deal with his little friend Abd-el-Krim, the son. Together, they demanded from the Sultan his official signature for this concession. Yes, my boy, people say that we in the army are responsible for everything that happened. But nobody tells you that in 1920 the Sultan decided the concession was not valid—and that that is what we're paying for now. It's the height of impudence that one of those men who provoked the whole thing should now visit his accomplice and bring him four millions, paid by the Spanish people, as a gift! I can well imagine how the two rascals enjoyed sharing the money. Quite a rich mine they've struck there! Well, it won't last them long."

When I told Sanchiz about this explosion he said:

"He's only forgotten to tell you that the man who's after the mines now is Count Romanones. He's the owner of all the Riff mines."

"So the papers say."

"And I believe it. The generals and the millionaires always come to an agreement. The generals because they don't want to lose their revenues, and the millionaires because they want to increase theirs. It's all the same to me. A clean bullet for me—and all the politicians can go to hell."

"It may be all the same to you, but it isn't to me," I told him. "I believe we ought to finish with Morocco one way or the other. Then at least they won't kill those people who don't want to die. If you like, they can leave you and your *Tercio* here all by yourselves."

"Well, that wouldn't be such a bad idea, either! But what would all the generals do then, and all the people who get their graft out here? Would you put them into the Legion with us? Don't be a fool. The day the Moroccan business is over, you'll have to find another war for our generals or they'll make one. If the worst comes to the worst, they can always make war among themselves, as they did for a hundred years."

In the meantime the day drew near when my term of service was coming to an end and I would have the right to ask for my discharge. Financially, my family's situation had become more troublesome. My brother Rafael was out of work, the liquidation of the bread factory being completed. His letters spoke of the impossibility of finding a job; not only were there few vacancies, but the mass of unemployed office workers had lowered the level of salaries. The best-paid clerks earned no more than 125 pesetas monthly. My mother, my sister and he were living on a few savings and the earnings from the fruiterer's shop. Yet if things went on as they were, he wrote, the shop would have to close down.

Obviously I had not the right to come home as an additional burden on them.

And yet I felt that I had to leave the army. The decision had grown in me, or else it had been there all the time. I found the atmosphere of the barracks unbearable, even more so now when it was charged with tension. I felt that I could not keep up my equivocal position much longer. It had become too much like tight-rope walking. So far, I had been able to avoid being enmeshed in any deals, without antagonizing the others, because Cárdenas had continued to liquidate the monthly accounts. He had found it irksome to lose his extra income from the Regimental Office all at once and had signed vouchers and papers as before, first with the excuse that he had to keep things going until I was run in, and later on the plea that the new Colonel with his interfering, fussy and grabbing ways created difficulties with which only an old hand could deal.

But now he began to think that it was time for me to become part of the system, and repeatedly said:

"I'll leave the whole thing to you in future, because the truth is that I'm not letting you profit from the opportunity."

"Don't worry," I would tell him. "I've got plenty of time. I should hate to mess things up and come a cropper, just for the sake of earning a little more."

So far, Cárdenas had paid me five hundred pesetas a month out of his pocket. I never knew how much he kept for himself, nor did I find out the secrets of the accountancy which he and the Major managed between themselves. Yet even though the Major was patently loath to lose the man who had been his partner for eight years, Cárdenas could not go on forever. I knew that sooner or later I would have to sign an account or a receipt with an obscure history behind it. Both the Major and Cárdenas were confident that I would re-enlist and stay in the profitable job, otherwise they would never have taken me on, and I had said nothing to cause them qualms. But now I was trapped in a blind alley. There were only the two clear alternatives which had worried me all along: either I could take my discharge and risk starvation, or I could stay and say good-by to any life of my own.

I started writing letters to almost everybody I knew in Spain. The answers were most discouraging; relatives and friends told me I should not be a fool, but should stay on in the army. There I had my future career assured—what more did I want?

I wrote to my mother, explained my situation and asked for her advice. "Do what you like," she wrote back. "Things are going badly here, but where three cat, four can eat as well. I would be glad to see you rid of the barracks. And I feel sure you will get on, even if the beginning is hard."

So I made up my mind. After my discharge I would have money enough to carry me through three or four months, and in that time many things might happen. I racked my brains to find the least offensive form in which I could tell the Major of my intentions, but my difficulty was settled by pure chance, as so often happens.

I fell ill of acute rheumatic fever. My experience in Tetuan had made me fight shy of military hospitals and I persuaded the Medical Officer to let me stay in barracks. He was a young captain, friendly and loquacious, but not very much interested in his profession, and he filled my body with salicylate and morphine. One day he sat down at the head of my bed.

"Well now, you're getting on much better. Still a bit weak, aren't you? You're not strong anyhow. It's the fault of the climate. This hot, damp climate doesn't suit you. You ought to go back to Spain and live in a high, dry place."

I seized my opportunity.

"To tell you the truth, it's given me a scare. In a month's time I'll have to decide whether I'm going to take my discharge or re-enlist. Naturally I thought of re-enlisting, because I've got my living assured here, but I must say, I'm even more interested in my skin. Only, I wonder what the Major would say."

"Think it over and don't worry about the Major. I advise you to take your discharge. Your heart isn't strong, and these attacks always lead to complications of that kind. It's quite possible that you won't be fit for service. I'll speak to the Major about it."

He did speak to him. Tabasco came to see me:

"How are you getting on?"

"Much better, sir. I hope to get out of bed in two or three days."

"Fine. But don't hurry. The doctor told me that you're not really strong enough for this climate. What do you intend to do about it?"

"To tell you the truth, sir, I'm thinking of getting my discharge now, because it wouldn't suit me to ask for a transfer to a unit in the Peninsula. You know, sir, that I've no real vocation for the army, and a sergeant's pay over there is less than I could earn on my own. . . . Of course, I would stay here as long as you needed me, until you'd found somebody else."

"I don't like to lose you, personally, but I can see that there's no other way out. It won't be necessary for you to stay beyond your time, we've got Surribas who knows all the ropes."

And that was all. It was astonishingly easy.

6. Coup d'Etat

I HAD been to my old tailor, I had selected some dark cloth and had my measure taken for a new suit. Before I could wear this civilian uniform in place of my army uniform there was nothing for me to do. I went to the Puerta del Sol, for no other reason than to have a look at it and see whether I would not meet someone I knew. Everybody in Madrid sooner or later passes through the Puerta del Sol.

"*Caramba*, Barea, back in Madrid? I thought you were in Morocco?"

"I came back from there today, Don Agustín."

"I'm glad to hear it. Are you on leave?"

"No, my term is over."

"So much the better. And what are you going to do now?"

"Office work, I suppose. That's to say, if I find a job, which seems to be difficult."

"Yes, rather. . . . I tell you what, look me up in my office. I can't offer you much, but there's always room for you."

Thus I entered the firm of Don Agustín Ungría as a clerk on the very day I arrived in Madrid.

In the Plaza de Encarnación, Don Agustín had an office with fifty-odd employees, housed in two huge rooms with iron pillars and a maze of tables of every description. There were tall old writing desks with sloping flaps, ministerial tables which had lost their varnish, two or three roll top desks, each of a different color, and a host of big, small, square, round, polygonal and oval tables. There were chairs with seats of plaited straw and curved legs, chairs with square, massive oak seats, wooden armchairs of monkish aspect, round stools, square stools and even benches. The firm had been in these rooms for thirty years, and it had started with six clerks. For every new employee up to the fifty who made up the full strength, a new table and a new chair had been bought in a secondhand furniture shop.

The staff was like the furniture, all secondhand. Only four of the employees were expected to know more than is necessary to fill in forms and to add up figures. The salaries were miserably small. There was a core of ancient clerks who had nowhere to go and clung, rheumy and coughing, to their old table and chair. Then there was a group of young people who were noisy and troublesome and disappeared from one day to the next, to be replaced by others of their ilk. Jobs in this firm were only taken to fill in the gap before a better job came along.

The business activities of the firm were as checkered as its furniture and its staff. Don Agustín Ungría was a business agent. He provided commercial information, collected debts for private individuals and for the State, registered patents, conducted proceedings, and altogether undertook everything which meant coping with papers and forms in the hundreds of official departments.

Don Agustín himself, the head of the firm, was sixty-five and looked like a portrait by El Greco. His hair, purest white, swept back in long, curly waves from a high, open forehead; his long face with fine, waxy skin was made longer by a small pointed beard, as white as his hair and his moustache. But the arch of his eyebrows over the very bright eyes was heavy and hard, his wide mouth sensuous, and his nose strong and arrogantly curved. His body seemed to belong to another person, a man of mighty bone without an ounce of fat. It was the body of a peasant from Aragon. He was still able to work for thirty hours on end, to eat a fried chicken after a three-course meal and to empty half a dozen bottles of wine. No one knew the exact number of his illegitimate children.

He came to Valencia from an Aragonese village when he was twenty years old. Until then he had worked on the land. In the city he learned to read and to write. He worked as a laborer and lived among the people of the port. The story was that he earned his first little capital by deals in smuggled silk and tobacco. Anyhow, he invested his savings in the orange trade, lending money to small growers to whom the customary delay in payments caused great trouble. He established a little office in Valencia. In his dealings with the orange merchants he had noticed that foreign exporters were eager to get commercial information; he turned his office into an information agency, exploiting his intimate knowledge of all the local people. Later he paid the deposit required to become a full-fledged business agent. There were few competitors. Don Agustín prospered and transferred his business to Madrid.

He treated his family and his staff in the manner of a patriarchal despot, and with all his worldly success he never lost the standards of his youth in the village near Saragossa, where a silver coin meant wealth. Honors and decorations had an irresistible attraction for him. For some service to the State during the reign of Alfonso XII he had been granted the Order of Isabella the Catholic, and it was his greatest pleasure to go to every banquet clad according to the most rigorous etiquette, with his Order pinned to his frock coat. It was of enamel ringed with small diamonds and his staff used to call it the "Fried Egg."

He was not miserly. If he paid miserable salaries, he did it because his instincts were still those of a poor peasant to whom one hundred pesetas are an exorbitant sum. "When I was your age," he shouted at one of the clerks, "I earned three pesetas a day, had a wife and children and a mistress on top of it, and I was putting money by!" But then he loaned a hundred pesetas to the man to get him out of a tight spot, and never collected the debt. Once he showed me a thick old ledger: "Do you know how much my employees owe me in debts they've never paid back, ever since I started having clerks forty years ago? Over one hundred thousand pesetas. It's all entered in this book. And yet they're not satisfied! Every day I see new faces in the office. The only people who stay on are the old clerks who are no good for anything any more. But still, I can't throw them out into the street."

I myself had passed through the office for a few months years before and got on well with the old man. Now he offered me a position of trust. I was to work with his son Alfonso who "had ideas in his head," as the father put it, and wanted to build up a patent agency business with foreign firms. He already had an English secretary and wanted me because I knew some French and would be able to deal with Spanish customers in technical matters. Don Alfonso himself had an oddly limited mind. He learned with great ease and remembered everything, but was incapable of the smallest creative effort. He was a lawyer and quoted from memory intricate paragraphs out of any legal code, but he was not able to give a legal opinion based on those same paragraphs; his French was perfect and his translations from Spanish into French excellent, but he could neither dictate an ordinary business letter, nor keep up a normal conversation in that language. He was deeply interested in industrial organization and knew Ford's system in all its details, but he was unable to organize his own office.

This gave me my chance. I had accepted the job as a stop-gap, but very soon I became absorbed in the problems of industrial patents. They led me back to mechanics. The Spanish patent laws require no more than a simple registration, but the firm began to deal with countries abroad where patents involve a meticulous technical and legal preparation. No one in Ungría's office was qualified for this kind of work. For my private satisfaction I started studying the technical and theoretical side of every patent which came our way. Soon I specialized on this. My salary was small—150 pesetas a month—but patent translations were paid according to the number of words and thus there were months when I doubled and tripled my salary, though at the price of working fifteen hours or more.

This gave me financial independence as well as independence in my work, and it earned me the confidence of even the oldest clerks.

Señor Laguna—old, or rather aged, thin, his trousers hanging loose on his shins, his cheek bones protruding and his hair lank, earning seventy pesetas a month for eight daily hours of silent, humble work—accosted me when we left the office:

"Could you spare a little time for me?"

We went out together and for a long while he said nothing. Suddenly he stopped walking:

"Do you think that Don Agustín would lend me a hundred pesetas?"

"Well, it all depends on his mood. Probably it will be no at first, but if you're insistent, it'll be yes in the end."

After another long silence he stopped again:

"Do you think he would take my boy into the office? It would be our salvation."

"It's the same thing again. First he'll say no and in the end he'll say yes. Especially if you speak of his kindness. Are things going so badly, then, Laguna?"

He gave a deep sigh and walked on. I began to get tired of his spells of silence, of his slow pace and of his wistful countenance.

"Let's have a drink. Come with me."

We entered a bar and they served us with two pints of beer and potato crisps. When Laguna put the first chip into his mouth I saw that he was hungry. A second glass of beer and a ham sandwich broke through his shyness.

"You wouldn't know," he said, "but we're five at home, my wife, the two girls, the boy and myself. And I'm the only wage earner. Just imagine."

"Your girls are still very young?"

"No, but they're so delicate, poor kids. Our room is very damp. Of

course it's cheap. Fifteen pesetas per month. But it's six feet below
street level. . . and we can't give them much to eat, they're still growing . . ."

He was so pitiful that I spoke to Don Agustín the following day. He
took the boy in as clerk and raised the father's salary to one hundred
pesetas, for it would not have been right for the son to earn almost as
much as the father. The lowest salary was fifty pesetas. Between the two
of them they were earning 150 pesetas now. Laguna brought me the fattest and biggest cigar he could find in the tobacco shops of Madrid.

Within twenty-four hours after Pepito Laguna started working he had
a nickname: Charlie.

He had huge, feverish eyes in a small, pale, pinched face, curly hair,
and a thin neck which emerged from an outsize shirt and padded shoulders as the hook of a clothes hanger emerges from a heavy tweed coat.
His too big and too long trousers fell over boots in which his small feet
must have had room to dance.

Marquez, the accountant, looked at the boy, produced a small bamboo
walking stick from somewhere and presented it to him:

"Here's your stick, Charlie."

The lad blushed violently and his eyes filled with water. There he
stood, amid general laughter, with the little stick balancing in his fingers.
Marquez snickered and tried to cap his own triumph:

"Just look at him, boys. Charlie Chaplin in person!"

Laguna invited me to lunch one Sunday. They lived in the Calle de
Embajadores in a big stone building, three centuries old. From the flagged
doorway I had to feel my way down a small, dark staircase, as to a
medieval dungeon. There in the basement was a square room with cemented walls: two iron bedsteads behind a curtain of bleached flowers
on a yellowed ground; a table with a frayed oilcloth, surrounded by half
a dozen battered chairs; an old chest of drawers, and a leather covered,
worm eaten trunk; a plaster Virgin and a bunch of paper flowers on the
chest of drawers. The room smelled of sour milk.

"Fortunately we can cook outside in the courtyard," Laguna said.
"There's a little room with a cooking stove. Only it has no door and in
the winter my wife gets simply frozen."

Steps sounded overhead. Through the iron bars of the window, which
was one foot high and three feet wide, just overlooking the pavement
stones, we saw the shadows of the passers-by and half their legs.

It hurt to be in that room.

Charlie lasted no more than a couple of months. He caught a cold and
died. Laguna became a little more wistful and silent. Sometimes he said

to me: "Just now, when we could afford a meal every day . . ." and stopped. Charlie had died of hunger.

I hated that terrible, hidden, shame-faced hunger of the office workers, which then ruled so many hundreds of homes in Madrid.

One day I met my old companion Antonio Calzada. He was gaunt and sallow, his suit had carefully mended cuffs. He was out of work. What he told me about himself was the old story of war prosperity and post-war crisis. During the Great War he had been given a promising job as manager of the newly founded Puente de Vallecas branch of the Banco Hispano. His salary was only 250 pesetas, but he had a flat on the floor above the office premises free of rent and including lighting and heating. He married and had three children. The branch flourished; he soon had an accountant, two clerks and an office boy, a steel safe, and the right to sign. If his business continued to prosper, he could count on promotion to a bigger and more important branch in the city. Then the War came to an end and the bank began to dismiss its staff. His branch was left with only the office boy, and then even he disappeared. Calzada remained as manager, clerk, and errand boy in one, living in constant dread of a sudden dismissal.

All the bank clerks, he said, seemed to feel the same dread and they tried to get together so as to be strong enough for collective resistance. First, the banks gave all those the sack who were known to belong to a trade union. Then the "Free Syndicate of Banking and the Stock Exchange" appeared on the scene. Its organizers came from Barcelona with the reputation of settling all social questions by direct action; they would solve the problems of the employees, if necessary by machine-gunning the directors. "I thought they were different fellows from your old fuss-pots of the U.G.T., and I didn't believe, then, that Martinez Anido and his gunmen and the banks themselves were behind them. I joined too," said Calzada. Thousands of bank clerks had joined the organization, which then demanded the cessation of dismissals and the fixing of minimum salaries They started a strike and the strike was lost. The organizers of the "Free Syndicate" left the strikers in the lurch; many hundreds got the sack. Calzada went on strike and lost his job. "Up till now I've managed on our savings, what there was of them, and by pawning everything of any value at home. Now I'm at my wits' end. I've just got what I'm wearing now, I owe two months' rent—and God knows how we're getting our meals."

Don Agustín took him on at 100 pesetas per month, and he was privileged among the thousands of poor wretches looking for jobs in that summer of 1923. At the time, assaults, robberies, and murders began to occur in Madrid, such as Barcelona had known on a much larger scale.

Governments came and went, and the chaos only seemed to grow worse. I met Major Tabasco in the streets one evening. He greeted me affectionately and wanted to hear all about my way of life. I knew why he had come to town, but it would have been an impertinence to make a direct allusion.

"Are you here on holiday, Don José?" I asked.

"Quite, on holiday—you're as sly as ever! A pity you didn't stay in the army, you would have been useful to us. You know quite well why I've come here. If you'd been in Ceuta now I would have brought you with me. I'm dead-tired and could do with a secretary."

"But things are going well, aren't they?"

"Oh, yes, everything's settled. Within two or three months there will be a complete upheaval. They've come to a dead end with all their intrigues. We must show the rabble that there exists a Fatherland and that Spain is not just a foreign colony. Look what happened in Italy"—in Italy Mussolini had snatched the political power—"and then think: we're in just the same situation. Either there will be a Russian Revolution here, or the Spaniards, the real Spaniards, must take matters in hand. It's high time."

"Frankly, I can't make out what's happening in politics. In the few months since I've left Morocco I've worked and worked, and nothing else. And then, life here is so different from the barracks, I can't say I've disentangled all the problems. Nobody agrees with anybody else here. And it seems to me that things in Morocco aren't going well."

Don José grew excited: "How can things go well, the devil take it, when they don't let the army settle them? There they are, sending us civilians to negotiate with Abd-el-Krim—what do they know of Morocco? That scoundrel wants an independent Republic, supported by the French Bolshies and our own Reds of the 'People's House.' What we need is to shoot a few hundred of them and to raze the Riff to the ground. Oh well, it will all come in due course, and sooner than people think!"

That night I wanted to be among people and to talk. I went to the little tavern in the Calle de Preciados (a German bomb wiped it out in November 1936), where clerks from the innumerable offices round the Puerta del Sol met after work. I joined some of my cronies and told them the gist of my conversation with the Major.

"What we need is a Republic," exploded Antonio, a small sickly youth whose pockets were always bulging with Anarchist and Socialist pamphlets.

"No, what's needed here is a man with guts to teach all those people discipline," retorted Señor Pradas, a short-sighted accountant with thick-lensed glasses balancing on the bridge of his nose.

"That's it," applauded Manuel, prosperous first salesman of a big shop.
"I have nothing against it," said Antonio, "as long as the man really has guts and is a Socialist—a real Socialist—a Lenin. Yes, that's what we need, a Lenin and a revolution."

Señor Pradas put both his elbows on the table: "Look here, you're just crazy. Well, now, not crazy, but just a raw boy. The misfortune of this country is that we haven't got another Espartero—a general who's as great a fighter as he was and wipes the floor with all the politicians. We need a grand fellow who will go into the Cortes, bang his fist on the table and chuck them all out into the street. I'm not in favor of killing, but I can tell you, a few dozen executions, and everything would be settled. And about your Socialists—a bullet for Prieto and Besteiro and company, that's what they need."

Antonio rose, white in the face:
"You're a dirty swine and the son of a bitch!"

In the little tavern no conversation was ever private. Half a minute later a hundred people, crowded together in a room of thirty square yards, were shouting and shaking their fists. Five minutes later the first blow sounded, and shortly afterwards Antonio and four others were taken to the police station between a pair of policemen. There was broken glass and spilt wine on the floor, and Miguelillo, the brightest of the tavern boys, was bathing the bruise on the forehead of an old customer with eau-de-vie. Señor Pradas, red in the face and his eyes unseeing behind their lenses, perorated:

"Anarchists, gentlemen, anarchists, that's what they are! And all this because somebody dares to tell the truth as an honest man. I'm an honest man. Forty years I've been working like a beaver, and now that young boy wants to lecture me! What we need here is a man like General Espartero, a man with guts to teach everybody discipline. Long live Spain!"

A second incipient row was drowned in wine. The tavern keeper, an energetic man with the philosophy of his profession, cut it short:

"All right, gentlemen, that's that. No more politics. If anybody wants to talk politics he can do it outside in the street. Here, people come to drink and to have a good time. Miguelillo, bring these gentlemen a glass of wine each, on the house."

I did not feel like talking any more.

General Picasso had finished his investigation into the Disaster of Melilla in 1921. His report was in the hands of the Parliamentary Committee: the announcement of the date for the debate in the Cortes was expected any day. The Socialist minority had copied and printed the report; a few copies were already circulating in Madrid. Among the papers left in General Silvestre's headquarters, General Picasso had found a number of documents which revealed Alfonso XIII's personal interference in the course of military operations. But none of the short-lived Governments of those days dared to tackle the question in the Cortes. The Opposition formed a bloc and demanded with increasing energy a public inquiry into the responsibility for the Moroccan catastrophe. Something was going to happen.

If you want to hypnotize a hen put her on a table covered with a black cloth and force her beak down until it touches the dark surface. Then place a piece of white chalk just in front of the hen's beak, close to her eyes. At the psychological moment you move the chalk slowly away, drawing a white line on the black cloth. Then you loosen your grasp. And the bird will stay there motionless in its precarious equilibrium on two legs and the beak, following the growth of the white line with staring eyes.

It seems to me now that something very similar happened to us in those days of September 1923, when General Primo de Rivera made himself the Dictator of Spain by a *coup d'état.*

We were all waiting for something to happen, something very grave and very violent: the overthrow of the King—an Army insurrection—a rising of the Socialists or the Anarchists—somebody's revolution. Something had to happen, for the life of the nation had come to an impasse.

I was in the Café Negresco in the night from the 12th to the 13th September. My old friend Cabanillas used to come there when his work on the editorial staff of *El Liberal* was over. I had joined his circle of journalists and half-baked writers because I wanted to hear the stop-press news from him. He arrived at two in the morning, excited and pale, his hair in wild disorder.

"Have you been to the première—what's the matter with you?" I asked.

"Nothing's the matter with me. But do you know the latest?"

"What?"

"The garrison in Barcelona has revolted, with Miguel Primo de Rivera at their head."

"Alfredito, you're not quite all there," someone shouted. "Have a brandy."

"But look here, it's true. Primo has proclaimed a state of siege in Barcelona and has assumed all power in the city. Now they say he's put an ultimatum to the Government."

The news spread through the café, as it must have spread through all the crowded cafés of Madrid at the same time. When we left, the Puerta

del Sol was a milling ant heap. People asked each other: "What's going
to happen here?"

Nothing happened. My brother and I stayed in the Puerta del Sol taking part in the shouted disputes until the first tram with early workers
arrived from the outskirts of the city and the street cleaners began to
sweep and spray the square. When the newspapers came out with huge
headlines above the General's proclamation and the announcement that
the King had sent for him, nothing happened. Most of the papers unconditionally welcomed the military dictatorship, a few reserved their
judgment. The two most important dailies of the Left, *El Sol* and *El
Liberal*, maneuvered skillfully, neither criticizing the jump to power nor
offering full support. The man in the street stared at the facts, as the
hypnotized hen stares at the piece of chalk, and when he tried to recover
his stance events had forestalled him.

The Government had resigned, some of its members fled abroad, the
King had given his approval to the accomplished fact and Spain had a
new Government called the Directorium which suspended all constitutional rights.

"Hullo, Luis, how are things?" I said.

Plá's pig-like eyes tried to place me somewhere in the direction of my
voice.

"Sit down, have something with me."

"Are you still in the bank? How have you survived the strike?"

"I was lucky, my boy. Two weeks before the strike started I caught
pneumonia, and when I went back to work everything was over. Otherwise I would have got the sack, I'm sure I'm not in favor of those rascals
of the 'Free Syndicate,' but I would have gone on strike with the others.
As it is, they've raised my salary. I got 250 pesetas now. It's true that I've
been in the bank for nearly twenty-five years . . ."

"Don't exaggerate."

"Well, since 1906, that's seventeen. Anyhow, all my life."

"Tell me, what do you think of Primo?"

"To tell you the truth, I like him. He's got guts. And he's got a sense
of humor. Have you read his latest manifesto? It's very Spanish to tell
people that he is where he is through his 'attributes of masculinity.' I
like him. Of course, I can't quite imagine how it will all develop. Apparently he wants to collaborate with everybody, even with the Socialists.
He's invited Largo Caballero and a few others to settle labor problems.
And the gunmen in Barcelona are piping a different tune now. He has
declared that he'll shoot the first of them who gets caught, even if he's
one of Martinez Anido's own gang."

A flock of newspaper boys came running down the street with shrill cries. Two of them entered the tavern, shouting:

"Mail crime in Andalusia!"

Every customer bought a copy. Giant letters announced the latest murder and robbery: a mail coach of the Madrid-Seville line had been assaulted, the postal official murdered, and the post bags robbed.

"Primo won't have an easy time after all. Here they are, the gunmen, alive and kicking, and he thought he'd finished with them!"

"It's the Anarchists," said somebody.

"You'll see, those fellows won't ever get caught," grumbled Plá.

This crime was a serious test for General Primo de Rivera. The Spanish public is inclined to feel entertained by any attack against a ruling power and to look on at the spectacle, with a certain bias in favor of the rebel against authority. Robbery by armed violence had almost disappeared at the time, and the feeling of general danger and uneasiness resulting from the wave of crime had subsided. Now this new assault, though it provoked the natural recoil from brutal murder, also held the thrill of a challenge to the new Dictator.

The press of the Right exploited this opportunity for a violent, indiscriminate campaign against the "unleashed forces of Freemasonry, Bolshevism, Socialism, Anarchism, and so forth, still rampant in a most Catholic country ruled by a patriotic general." Now was the time to set a stern example and to give short shrift to all the guilty men, so as to save law and order in the country.

The mail robbers were caught. The assassins were two young men from wealthy middle-class families, vicious degenerates, with a homosexual of the effeminate kind as their accomplice. The two murderers were hanged and their associate sentenced to hard labor for life. It would have been impossible to let them escape capital punishment after the intense campaign carried on while the criminals were assumed to belong to a political group. Yet even though that myth was exploded, the full rigor of the dictatorship hit all Left-wing associations. Some were dissolved, others subjected to close control and curtailment; the workers' right to strike was suppressed. At the same time, special tribunals were set up to decide on social matters. The Directorium launched large-scale public works. Unemployment figures sank rapidly. The new régime seemed to be consolidating itself on the home front.

But there was still the struggle in Morocco.

The Duke of Hornachuelos came to the office one day and wished to register a number of patents for cigarette cartons. Told that this was not a matter for patents, he said: "You just apply for the patents and the

Patent Office will grant them." The Head of the Patent Office refused to accept the registration because these were not inventions of any kind, but a friendly letter from the new lord and master of Spain made him change his mind. Our office carried through the proceedings, which brought me into frequent contact with the Duke.

I was interested in him and he seemed interested in me. On my side this interest went back to a childhood memory. On one of my holidays in Cordova I had heard a tale about the young heir of the avaricious old Duke of Hornachuelos. At a carnival he had been exposed to ridicule because his father gave him no more than fifty *céntimos* a week as pocket money, and had exclaimed furiously: "How I wish that my papa would die, so that I could spend five pesetas!" When I came to know him, he had kept his word. He had spent the family fortune and was over his ears in debt, but as one of the boon-companions of Alfonso XIII he was a privileged person. Now, under the Dictatorship, he counted on getting the monopoly for cigarette and match packings, protected by his worthless patents. It would be easy for him to find somebody to finance him. And he spoke about Morocco:

"I was there as a lieutenant, and I know the country. That's where Spain's future lies. But now Primo's talking of abandoning Morocco—it's intolerable cowardice, and so I told him to his face. Morocco is Spanish by right, it is our inheritance from the Catholic kings, it is our sacred duty. The last thing we want is for old Miguel to kick over the traces and play the fool about Morocco. It would mean that the English would establish themselves there within a fortnight, and then the fishermen from Malaga would have to ask permission to go fishing in the waters of Cadiz. It would cut Spain in two. No, if Primo seriously intends to abandon Morocco we would have to kick him out."

The second of our clients who spoke to me about Morocco at that time was Major Marín, a swarthy, cynical, easygoing little man. He worked for a condensed milk company and acted as its go-between in matters referring to army contracts for Morocco. Now, some of the Dictator's protégés had set up a factory for condensed milk, counting on orders for the army in Morocco as the mainstay of their business. They had registered a series of trade marks which encroached on the trade marks of Marín's firm. The Agency Ungría was to conduct legal proceedings in the case, and Marín frequently visited us to discuss matters. Thus he came to tell me one day:

"What a business! That man Primo will drive us all crazy. There he is dishing out favors to his friends and giving away monopolies right and left, and in the meantime he has quite forgotten that Morocco is the only place where we can keep our army fed. There are more than a hun-

dred thousand men in Africa at present. So now is the time of the fat
kine. Those rogues who've set up the milk factory know it only too well.
If we give them time to do it, they'll sell more condensed milk in a year
than we've sold in ten years. And that man has got it into his thick skull
that the country wants him to clear out of Morocco, and that he only
wants to serve the country! I tell you, the old fellow may be honest, but
he's a fool, nothing but a poor fool. He hasn't the faintest idea of how to
govern the country."

My brother and I were living alone with our mother since my sister
had married and set up her own home. Whenever Rafael and I hotly
discussed the present and future of the country, my mother showed
neither excitement nor apprehension. She had shown none when she had
heard of Primo de Rivera's *coup d'état.*

"It was bound to come to this," she said. "It's just as it was in my childhood and later, when I was a young girl and served as a maid in the house
of the Duke of Montpensier. There were people who wanted to make the
Duke King of Spain instead of Isabella II. That was all before the Republic, and General Prim himself came to Cadiz all the way from England to take the Duke's part. I was a child then, but I remember that
there were mutinies every day until the Queen was dethroned and the
Republic came. But then the Generals had nothing to do, and they began to seek for a king everywhere. Some wanted to make the Duke king
again. In those days, some General or other was always making an insurrection with two or three regiments, and either he was shot or he became the Leader of the Nation. When I was there, the Duke's palace was
always full of Generals, and one of them was the father of this Primo
de Rivera—a man who at times was fighting the Carlists and at others
trying to find a king to get rid of the Republicans. In the end they got
hold of Alfonso XII, and he married the Duke's daughter. A pity she
died that summer. And from then onwards till now there has always been
a General to make a rising in protest against something, but none of them
ever put the country in order. This one won't do it either."

"What do you think would put Spain in order, then?" I asked her.

"What do you expect me to say? I don't know. If your father were
alive, he could explain it to you better than I. He was a Republican all
his life and I think he was right."

I knew my mother's secret weakness for the one historic incident in my
father's life. "Come on, tell us the story again," I said.

"Well, it happened in '83 when they wanted to get the Republic back, a
short time after Alfonso XII became King. And your father saved his
skin only because he always slept like a log. In Badajoz the sergeants had

made a Junta, and your father was its secretary. They were going to lead the troops out into the streets at daybreak. And your father lay down to sleep in the sergeants' room and told the others to wake him. I don't know whether they forgot or he didn't hear them. But General Martinez Campos, who was then in power, had got wind of the story, and when they opened the gates of the barracks to march the men out into the street all the sergeants were taken prisoner and shot. And your father went on sleeping in his bed like a blessed baby. Nothing happened to him, because his comrades didn't give him away. But the General who was at the head of the rising was hanged . . . I think your father had too many illusions about it all, though, because if things had turned out well for them, the Republic would have been a Generals' Republic, and then they might as well have stuck to the King."

We were well off in those days. I was earning, and Rafael had also found a post as accountant with a Catalan contractor who had come to Madrid to get a share of the contracts for the projected public works. His chief had already obtained a few road-building orders, but he was after the fat contracts for building estates of cheap dwelling houses, planned in the suburbs of Madrid.

Then Rafael came home from work with the news that his chief had been given the contract for two of these building estates:

"If all the business deals of the Directorium are the same as this, it's going to be a nice kettle of fish. You know, my chief had friends in the Ministry who kept him informed of the other tenders. At the last moment they told him bluntly that he could have the contracts, but only if he was willing to pay a tip of a million pesetas, cash down. Of course he hasn't got a million at his disposal to pay out in banknotes; he's working on the credit he gets from the Urquijo Bank. So he went to his bankers, first of all to settle about the million in cash, and secondly to find out whether they were willing to give him a loan for the work until the State pays him. And everything's in order. Now he's got the two contracts and the bank has given him a loan for the total expenses, on the condition that the contracts will be taken over by the bank's nominee if he doesn't pay back the loan and the interest. Just a trifle—ten million pesetas."

"But after all it's a good thing that poor people should get homes of their own, even if it costs a lot of money," said my mother.

Rafael gave her a scornful glance: "But do you imagine, then, that those so-called cheap houses are built for poor people? They're going to build two housing estates of little houses, each with its garden and its fence, and they'll be let at 150 to 350 pesetas per month. The cheapest as much as my monthly salary."

"I'm sorry it's another swindle. Do you know that our old garret for

which we paid nine pesetas a month is let for twenty-five pesetas now?
I told you those Generals only make things worse."

She paused thoughtfully, and added:

"If at least that man would finish the war in Morocco—but how could
a General finish with wars?"

7. Villa Rosa

T H E year 1924 marks a deep incision in my life. If the later evolution
of my country had not had the effect of a catalysis on me, as on twenty
million other Spaniards, the course of my inward and outward existence
might have been fixed then.

I married and I changed my social status in that year.

My family, and above all my mother, cherished the conviction that I
could find a wife with every quality which goes into the making of a
so-called "good match." I had a girl friend, just as had every young man
of my age in Spain, because it would have been humiliating not to have
one. My family did not expect this girl to become my wife, and neither
did I; so far, I had not been thinking seriously of marriage. Other rela-
tionships satisfied my sexual needs, and "my girl" meant simply an exhibition of my manliness. I pushed the thought of matrimony away until
the time when my financial position would be better. Yet apparently other
people began to think that I had reached the marrying age.

Old Ungría called me to his room while his daughter, an attractive
girl of about twenty-three, was with him. He began to dictate a few
notes to me and she left us alone. When he had finished, he took off his
glasses and asked:

"What do you think of Conchita?"

"She's very nice—and she's very pretty." I said what I thought, and
he was shrewd enough to note it.

"She's the kind of girl that makes a good home and she ought to get
a good husband. But she hasn't found him yet."

"Isn't she engaged?"

"She has several admirers, yes—Señoritos. But I want a husband for her who knows the meaning of work, and if possible somebody who understands this business of ours. I'm getting old—don't grin, I've still got twenty years of life before me—or perhaps I haven't. Well, anyhow, the best thing for Concha would be a husband like you. Have you got a girl?"

"Yes."

"Tell me who she is. Is she of good family?"

"If you mean, is she of a well-to-do family, then she isn't, she's very poor. And if you call a 'good family' a family of distinction, hers isn't that either."

"But, my boy, then you're being very foolish. What you need is a marriage which definitely puts you on a decent level. You need a wife such as Conchita. After all, she has her dowry, and as her husband your future in our firm would be secure. You'll understand that there's nothing against taking one's son-in-law into partnership."

"Do you mean this as a suggestion, Don Agustín?"

"Take it as you like. We old people haven't much to consider, but you ought to think of what's best for you. Then you would no longer be a Sir Nobody."

"But supposing I don't please Conchita?"

"The girl does what I want her to. And anyhow, women don't know which man they like or not so long as they haven't been to bed with their first."

And there the conversation ended. I never could make out whether the initiative came from the father, the daughter, or the mother, who used to show a great liking for me.

But I had near me a living example of the consequences of Don Agustín's marrying zeal in the person of his son-in-law Domingo. He used to say that his father was an engine driver on express trains, but the statements which he let fall made it obvious that his father had been a stoker in the station yard at Albacete. They were a large family. Domingo, who had a good head for figures and beautiful handwriting, was sent by his father to Madrid to seek his living. The young man turned from one thing to another, always hungry and never finding his way to a career. When he was thirty, he came to work for Ungría, like so many others, accepting a miserable existence to escape starvation. Don Agustín's eldest daughter found the clerk attractive and greeted him warmly from her balcony which overlooked the office rooms. She was a plain woman of thirty-odd years, but he had gone hungry for a long time. They married. Don Agustín set up house for them, assigned him a salary of 250 pesetas, which was quite a lot at that time, and made him his proxy. The couple was prolific. Don Agustín gave Domingo a rise of twenty-five pesetas per child.

Sometimes he would call him to his room: "You're a silly brute. If you weren't my son, I would chuck you out this very instant. Be grateful to your wife, who's a saint, and to your children—my grandchildren—if I keep you at all. I'll put you on to copying accounts. You're supposed to be my proxy? You're a complete idiot."

The whole staff heard these rows. Don Agustín enjoyed making them in public, and Don Domingo's defense was to curse, also in public, the hour in which he had tried to escape from his misery by marriage.

Don Agustín's offer did not appeal to me. But I told my mother about it.

"And what did you answer him?"

"Nothing. The girl doesn't interest me, but that's something I couldn't very well tell her father. It would have been too rude."

"And what are you going to do?"

"Nothing. I told you that the whole affair doesn't interest me in the least. I've only got to look at Don Domingo to see the consequences of that kind of thing."

"But you're much more intelligent that Don Domingo."

"So what? Perhaps the old man wouldn't tell me that I'm a stupid brute, as he tells Don Domingo, but some day or other he would tell me that he lifted me out of poverty."

She thought for a while and then said:

"You know, you'll be very unhappy if you don't marry for love, and that's a very rare thing."

Though my mother did not follow up this discussion, she told some of her friends and relatives of it. As a result, I had to listen for days on end to well-intentioned advice that I should not spoil my chance. At the same time, the general opposition against the girl with whom I went about became very outspoken. It came also from her own family. Her parents and her sister considered that, as I would not decide either to marry or to leave her, she was wasting her time with me. I resented both attitudes. One day I announced that I was going to marry her. And we married.

Almost simultaneously one of the heads of the best-known patent agency in Spain died unexpectedly. I knew that it was difficult to find a replacement for him, because his work needed highly specialized qualifications, and went to see the Director of the firm. He knew me, as we all knew each other within the narrow circle of the profession, and we came to an agreement. I would be Technical Manager of the firm, with a salary of five hundred pesetas and a commission. My married life started under good financial auguries. Though I realized that there was little in common between my wife's mind and my own, I was confident that a few months of living together would convert her to my ideas about relations between man and wife.

Within a few months I had mastered my new task and had failed in my marriage.

Her father came to seek me out.

"I want to speak seriously with you," he said. "The girl has told me how things are. You've got a lot of modern ideas in your head and want to change the world, that's what it is. But now look here. A woman is either married, and in that case she's got to keep the house clean and feed the kids, or else she's a bitch and a street walker. So don't you set your mind on something different. The man must support his home and children, that's his business. And if you've got an itch to amuse yourself ... well, you go and find a woman somewhere, amuse yourself without a scandal, and that's all there is to it. Listen to what I'm telling you, I'm getting on for sixty and I know what I'm talking about. If you go on as you are, things will come to a bad end."

"All right. But I think that only a fool would marry just to have a woman in his bed. What I want is that my wife should be my best friend, besides being my bedfellow."

"Pooh, that's just romantic nonsense. Look here, a man marries to have a home of his own and a woman to nurse him when he's ill and to look after his children. And everything else is just modern claptrap."

I tried not to want more from my wife than she wanted to give. Our marriage was soon destroyed and consisted of nothing but the physical relationship. But if one's own wife differs from other women only by the color of her hair, the cut of her face and the shape of her body, she becomes one among the many women who are attractive to the man, with the disadvantage of being at hand day and night and having her attraction submitted to the relentless test of proximity without tenderness.

Señor Latre was a man of seventy years, so perfectly conserved that no one would have taken him for more than fifty. He spoke three languages fluently and knew the world outside Spain. As the owner of one of Madrid's few novelty shops, he had traveled widely and frequently, in addition to having studied at a German university. He had remained a bachelor and was now retired from his business. Groping in my isolation, I thought that I could not bear the reaction of most of my countrymen to my problems, which would only have been a repetition of my father-in-law's counsel on a different level. I spoke to Latre.

"I don't know what to do. I can't formulate any concrete complaint against my wife. Physically she pleases me and I think I please her. Anyhow, I'm sexually satisfied and I've no kind of jealousy. But apart from that we are as complete strangers to each other as if she were the woman on the nearest street corner and I a regular customer of hers. My life and my person do not interest her, and whenever I try to take an interest in her I come up against an insurmountable barrier. She usually says: 'Those are matters for women.' I can't call it incompatibility. We aren't incompatible and not even antagonistic, I should say. We simply live in different worlds and there is no communication between them."

"After that, what can I tell you? You're a patient who's given his own diagnosis. But there's no remedy I know of for the disease. The problem doesn't lie in you or in her—or rather, if anything, it does lie in you. But in any case, one can't do anything about it."

"I don't quite see what you're driving at."

"The problem is complicated in detail, but simple in its general outline. You see, in Spain boys and girls grow up in two separate, watertight compartments. The boy is told that he mustn't go near the girls or play with them, and if he does it all the same, he's called a sissy. The girls are taught that boys are brutal and beastly, and a girl who likes playing with them is not a 'little woman' but a tomboy, which is considered something very bad. Later, the school teachers get busy teaching the boys that Woman is a vessel of impurity and teaching the girls that Man is the incarnation of the Evil Spirit, created only for the perdition of women. So the boys form their masculine society and the girls form their feminine society, and when sex awakens, the young man goes to a brothel to learn about it and the young woman sits and waits until one of the men who come glutted from the brothels invites her to go to bed with him. Then some agree to do it through matrimony and others without it, and the first become so-called decent women, and the others whores. How do you expect real, complete marriages to grow from this soil?"

"I know all that, but I still don't understand why, after marriage, the two people can't adapt themselves to each other."

"Well, do you adapt yourself to your wife, or don't you rather think she ought to adapt herself to you? But apart from your case, they can't do it because the whole weight of the society of their own sex is against them. I'll describe to you what happens in daily life, and you will admit that you have seen it for yourself countless times.

"Two young people marry because they're more or less in love with each other. During the first two months they go everywhere together arm in arm, kiss each other in public, and people say: 'How charming, how much they're in love!' But after the honeymoon, the great offensive begins and it's very effective even while it is unconscious. One day when he's finished working, the young husband's friends will say to him:

'Come along with us to So-and-so's house and drink a bottle of wine.'
'No,' he'll say, 'I'm going home.' 'What, still in love? Your wife won't
run away from you. Partridge every day grows boring.' The man may
fence them off, but they will renew their attack, and it will be more
direct. 'Well, well, you seem to be pinned to your wife's petticoats. A man
mustn't be ruled by women.' If the husband doesn't give in, his male
friends will drop away, he'll be left alone and people will say of him that
in his house it's the woman who wears the trousers.

"And it's the same with the young wife. If she shows her fondness for
her husband too openly, her friends and even her mother will begin to
criticize her. They will say: 'What, your honeymoon isn't over yet?' And
in the end they'll say to her: 'My dear girl, you're behaving like a bitch,
always running after him.' So she won't dare to show that she's really fond
of him, because she's afraid of the strictures of the other women, and she
will become convinced that he's right if he keeps to his male society and
his amusements, and that he's not a real man if he doesn't. It will end as
most marriages in our country are doomed to end, with a great emptiness.
As things are, anything else would be a miracle."

There was no remedy. I tried to form part of male society. I did not
want to be shut up in loneliness. For a short time I frequented the little
tavern of the clerks in the Calle de Preciados. But quickly all the customers knew of my new job and I lost my old companions. A discussion would
start, but almost at once whoever was holding forth would interrupt himself:

"Of course, Don Arturo"—now I was 'Don' Arturo to them—"won't
be able to agree with me. I quite understand. He's in a different position
from us now. He's become a *bourgeois* and there are certain things he
can't see as we see them . . ."

On other occasions the talk would take a more aggressive turn:

"What we need is a revolution. We must make a clean sweep and
execute all the generals and all the priests. And we must burn down the
churches and . . ."

"In the end you'll be the only one left, isn't that so?"

"Of course, you're a *bourgeois*. They've bought you already. You've
sold yourself for a mess of pottage. My dear friend, you'll get fat and
you'll buy a diamond ring and you'll attend Mass with the Jesuits. I've
seen only too many like you."

One Sunday after a bullfight in which a famous and much disputed
torero had taken part, we were sitting in the tavern discussing his feats.
One of his enthusiastic supporters made a statement which I contradicted.

"Of course," he said, "you've seen him from nearby. As Don Arturo belongs to the upper class, he can afford to sit in the front row and see what we others can't see from far up under the roof."

In this manner our discussions sank to a ridiculous level. If somebody said that it was cold and I answered that I didn't think so, I was told that I didn't feel the cold because I could afford a good great-coat. Sometimes I reacted sharply, at other times I turned it into a joke. And in the end I went there no longer.

I took refuge in the tavern of The Portuguese, in the company of Luis Plá. He had known me as a boy and as a man, he would not misunderstand me. After a few months, Plá was the only one in the circle to defend me, and even his defense was sometimes fainthearted. My membership card of the U.G.T. had become a double-edged weapon. To those above me it seemed a disgrace that I, the manager of a big firm, should mix with the "mob" of the People's House. To the workers, including the white-collar workers, I seemed an intruder.

I buried myself in work, and it had much to attract me. I had not been able to become either a Mechanical Engineer or a mechanic, but I was now the adviser of inventors. Often I helped them in their research work, as an escape for myself. I wrote juridical and technical articles for two professional magazines, and my chief let me start a technical review as a propaganda organ for his firm. My work brought me into the realm of big industry and my journeys to the two industrial centers of Spain— Catalonia and the North country—became more frequent. And all the time I was more and more losing the habit of personal contact with people.

Yet I still liked being among people. I became a regular customer in two widely different places, in the Villa Rosa and in Serafin's bar.

The Villa Rosa was one of the best-known night establishments of Madrid, a *Colmado*—an Andalusian winehouse—with extensive basements in the Plaza de Santa Ana. I used to go there when I was eighteen, with money in my pockets and a predilection for Andalusian wine. Nothing was left of that period to link me with the Villa Rosa but my friendship with the old waiter Manolo. He had scolded me or even maneuvered me out of the place when I had more wine than was good for me, like an old retainer. He had given me advice about life with the picaresque humor of an old rake and with an honesty seldom found in Spain except among rogues and cynics with a code of conduct of their own. Now I met him in the street by chance and we dug out reminiscences. He looked half like the dignified steward of an aristocratic house and half like a buffoon grown aged and wise, with an infinitely sagacious face under his gray hair.

"I'm still at the Villa Rosa," he said. "Do come and visit us there."

"I'll be there tomorrow night, I promise you."

And I went. To those young and old men-about-town Manolo the waiter vouched for my quality as a gentleman.

About the same time I passed by the tavern of Señor Fernando in the Calle de la Huerta. In that tiny bar, frequented by workers from Avapiés, by the tarts of the Plaza de Antón Martín and by their pimps, I had drunk my first glass of wine in public. When Rafael and I were boys, we were sometimes sent there to fetch a bottle of wine. Then the owner, Señor Fernando, would give us a glass of lemonade or a few coppers for sweets, and we would play with his plump little son Serafin when he was not too busy rinsing glasses and bottles under the tap. Now, a strong, plump young man in a black-and-green striped apron was standing at the door when I went by and stared at me. He made a step forward.

"You're—I beg your pardon, are you Arturo?"

"And are you Serafin?"

He dragged me into the empty bar. The hacking dry cough of Señor Fernando sounded from the back room. I sat down with them and told them about my life. Their own had not changed; they had their business and their old customers, grown a little older, and a few new ones to replace those who had died. "Come and visit us," said old Fernando, "that's to say, if you're not too proud for us."

"I'm still the son of Señora Leonor, thank God. I'll come."

When I did not go to the Villa Rosa to exchange jokes with Manolo I went to Fernando's bar, or rather to Serafin's, for his father died soon after I had met them again. There they accepted me as a proletarian because Serafin had played with me, and because Señor Fernando had known my mother when she still took her bundle of washing down to the river.

Manolo came to my table, wiped it with his napkin and asked: "What's yours today? The usual? And a little glass for me, please, because I'm thirsty."

"Bring half a dozen."

"We've got a merry party in there today. I'll tell you about it later."

He brought me a tray with six small glasses filled with Manzanilla and raised one of them:

"Your good health!" He leaned over to me: "Do you know who's in the Patio?"

The Villa Rosa had a glass-covered courtyard imitating an Andalusian Patio, filled with flower pots, its arches and walls covered with arabesques in plaster of Paris.

"Well, who is it?"

"Don Miguelito."

"What Don Miguelito?"

"Good gracious, how stupid you are! Whom do you think I mean? The king of Spain! Primo de Rivera. And I bet he's out on a spree tonight. He's got *La Caoba* with him and some flamenco singers, and they want to paint the town red. After the rush hour, we're going to close to the general public."

"So that's why I've seen some funny figures outside."

"Of course, the detectives. He doesn't want police protection, but they follow him and stay outside."

Manolo went away to look after his own customers, but soon he came back and hovered around.

"What do you think of Don Miguel, Manolo?"

"Hm, what do you want me to say? I don't meddle in politics. He's a man with guts. That's why I like him. But you see, those Señoritos who are always with him, they're ne'er-do-wells and can't carry their wine. Between you and me, he'll come to a bad end. All that crowd are simply sponging on him and making up to him: 'Don Miguel, do drink a little glass . . .' and another, and another. In the end—I've seen it myself— they get him to give a road-making contract to a little friend of theirs, or a job in a Ministry, or a letter of recommendation. And when the cow won't give any more milk, they'll send it to the butcher's. Wait and see."

Manolo winked like a wise old gypsy soothsayer.

"I would like to see him from close to," I said.

"Haven't you ever met him, then?"

"I haven't even seen him, except in photos."

"Then wait a bit, I'll present you."

He disappeared for a while, only to come back and whisper into my ear: "Come along."

He stuck his head through the door of the Patio: "If Your Excellency will give me permission . . ."

"Come in, Manolo."

"Well, sir, I've got that young gentleman with me who's an old friend of mine and would like to pay his respects to you."

"Let him come in."

Somewhat excited and confused I entered the Patio, met by the stare of the whole party. General Primo de Rivera was lolling in a wicker arm-chair and a dark, gypsy-like woman was at his side. In the opposite corner was a group of gypsies with guitars and two girls with wide, swinging skirts. The small tables were pushed together to form a single big one, covered with glasses and bottles, and around it sat a crowd of men and women, the men of all ages, the women all young except for two who looked like procuresses.

"How do you do? Have something," said the General.

"Thank you very much, sir."

It was an embarrassing situation. What could I say to this man, and for that matter, what was he to say to me? I took a glass of wine. What the devil was I going to say? To toast the Dictatorship was something I could not do. To say "Your health," or something like it, seemed ridiculous to me. The General saved me from my difficulty.

"If you want a really first-class Manzanilla, gentlemen, go to Montillano's in Ceuta. That man knows what wine is."

"You're quite right, sir," I said boldly.

"Caramba, you know Montillano?"

"I've been a sergeant in Ceuta, sir, and General Serrano took me there a few times."

"Those were good times! When did you leave Morocco?"

"Almost a year ago, sir."

"Good, good. And what's your opinion about Morocco?"

"Well, sir, it's difficult to say. I was there as a soldier, but it wasn't too bad. Others have gone through worse, not to speak of those who died there."

"That's not what I'm asking you. I'm speaking of Morocco. Ought we to give it up or not?"

"These matters are too high for me, sir."

"All right, but I want to know what you think. You've been there—what would you do in my place? Be honest."

"Well then, frankly,"—fleetingly I wondered whether I was so courageous because of the wine—"I've served there in the ranks and I've seen much misery, and worse things than misery. I believe, sir, that the man who wants to rule Spain must give up Morocco, because it is nothing but a slaughterhouse."

In the background Manolo echoed me with a single gypsy exclamation: "Éle!"

"General Primo de Rivera believes the same, my boy. And if he can, he'll do it. And he can, the Devil take it!"

The General had half risen from his wicker chair to say that, but now he slumped back heavily against the curved back. His fatherly mien changed to sullenness. He said nothing more.

"My apologies for having disturbed you, gentlemen. Have you any orders, *mi general?*" Suddenly the automatic routine of the army came to my support. I felt sorry for the old man in his chair who had a beaten look at that moment.

"It's all right, my boy. Thank you."

Manolo accompanied me back to my table. "What do you think of the General?" he asked. "He's a good fellow, isn't he?"

"Manolo, do you realize that I could get a thousand pesetas for telling what the General said in there?" I visualized my impromptu interview on the front page of the papers. Manolo turned very grave:

"By your mother's life, Don Arturo, don't be silly and don't do things which would compromise us all and only land you in prison for so many years that you would get gray hair. Listen to an old man who has never yet deceived you. And I think you'd better go now."

Up to the time when I joined the circle in Serafin's bar, Señor Paco had lorded it there. Then I did. He might have resented my taking from him a right acquired in twenty years of political discussion round the marble table in the right-hand corner. But with all his revolutionary aplomb, Señor Paco was a simple man who felt stupefied by everything he did not know.

What he knew well were the four walls of his carpenter's shop, the thousand-and-one sorts of wood he used for his work, the information contained in the more vehement papers of the Left, particularly in the satirical reviews, the topography of the whole quarter of Avapiés, and the River Jarama where he liked to fish and in the summer to bathe.

"Nowadays trade has gone to the dogs. Give me a massive walnut table, and that poor stuff made of pine wood with mahogany strips on top as a veneer is simply nowhere. Or oak. Oak is the finest wood in the world. But you must know how to work it, or the tools slip off it as if it were a piece of iron. My master who taught me the trade, Señor Juan —God rest his soul—kept me sawing oak for a whole year. I was fed up and one day I threw the saw on the bench. He tweaked my neck— that's what an apprentice got in those days, and sometimes even a journey-man—and said: 'You believe you know all about it, don't you? All right, then, you'll work with the plane.' And he gave me a jack plane and an oak board, and I had to smooth it. I should like to see one of you do it. That damned tool gets stuck in the wood and doesn't cut, even if you sweat your guts out. It took me two years to learn how to plane oak and make my shavings as thin as paper. But now . . . you saw with a machine, you plane with a machine, and you burnish with a machine. At the most you cut pine and stick a few thin sheets of mahogany varnished with a pulverizer on top of it!"

"But, Señor Paco, machines mean progress. Now which is it to be? You're always talking big of Socialism and Progress and then you start cursing the machines!"

"Man alive, I'm not saying anything, but it's a fact that there are no real workmen nowadays. I can work wood but people now can't work as much as this," and he made the nail of his thumb crack. "Everything is mechanical nowadays. And what happens is that they manufacture things in big heaps, like buns, and then, of course, when the workers ask the master for a rise he tells them: 'Get out of here. I can get anybody to work the saw, even women.'"

"And what's wrong with a woman working a saw?"

"Women are here to wash dishes and suckle children."

"And you call yourself a Socialist?"

Señor Paco was helpless when, mockingly and cruelly enough, I exposed the contradictions in his emotional socialism.

There was a night when the papers contained the information that Abd-el-Krim had cut the communication lines between Tetuan and Xauen. They did not say it in so many words; they only spoke of a few engagements and the loss of certain positions whose names meant nothing to the common reader, although they spelled disaster to those who knew the battleground. Not only had the insurgents cut off Tetuan from Xauen, but they also threatened to cut it off from Ceuta. They had captured several points of the Gorgues massif, the mountain which dominates Tetuan, and from there they had the choice of attacking the city or overrunning the railway line and the road of Ceuta. The *kabila* of Anyera, whose ramifications cover the whole stretch of coast between Tangier and Ceuta, gave signs of insubordination. Apparently the tribesmen had been given arms as a political measure and were now inclined to use those same arms for an assault on Ceuta and Tetuan, in league with Abd-el-Krim.

I spread the newspaper out on the marble table in the right-hand corner at Serafin's. Señor Paco took it out of my hand and read the headlines.

"Just the same old story all over again! They'll never finish in Morocco. That henpecked old fellow, Primo de Rivera—always promising that Morocco will be finished with, and all the time tricking us just as we were tricked while I was there."

"It's serious this time, Paco. Abd-el-Krim has got under our skin."

"Rubbish! Just the old tricks of the Generals. I know them by heart. A pity they don't kick us out from there once and for all. Let it cost ten thousand men, but at least it will be over. It's a slow blood-letting process going on and on as it is now."

"I'll tell you something." I put my elbows on the table in an impressive pose. Serafin shut the glass door. "A few weeks ago I spoke to Primo."

"What the Hell!" cried Señor Paco.

"Well, believe it or not. But Primo wants to clear out of Morocco."

The circle of friends waited in suspense to see whether this would turn out to be one of my usual jokes. Señor Paco became grave.

"I'm not swallowing it this time, Don Arturo. You make a joke of a fellow because he's not an intellectual like you, but it isn't right to mock at us. For less than this I've given a man a lot bigger than you two slaps in the face. I'm too old to have my leg pulled."

"I was talking seriously, Paco."

"And I tell you that it's finished with our friendship."

I stood up: "All right. I'll keep the peace. Serafin, a round of wine for the party."

We drank in sulky silence. Señor Paco suddenly dumped his glass on the table.

"Primo de Rivera is a son of a bitch like all generals, past, present, and future, but . . . Well, you've been pulling our legs and I won't forgive you for it. But joke or no joke, if Old Whiskers really clears out of Morocco, Paco the cabinetmaker will stand up in the middle of the Plaza de Antón Martín and tell the world that he's the greatest fellow ever born in Spain. I've said it; and now, Serafin, another round. I don't want this to finish with a bump."

A few days later the operations for the liberation of besieged Xauen started. In a speech in Malaga, General Primo de Rivera announced that he intended to withdraw the army to the so-called "sovereign places," Ceuta, Melilla and Larache, which did not form part of the Moroccan Protectorate but were directly under Spanish sovereignty. At once the *kabila* of Anyera revolted and communications between Ceuta and Tangier as well as Tetuan were cut. Thousands of men were poured into Morocco. The press published nothing but war news.

Señor Paco devoured the papers and commented in his way:

"Now you can see how it's going to finish. Another disaster of Melilla and another fifty thousand dead. And in the end, Abd-el-Krim will make peace and get a nice post and a lot of money. Then things will go on until the next chieftain makes a rising."

"This time it's different, Paco."

"What's different? I wish it were. Everything's a racket. That's why they made the Dictatorship. First, so that it should not become known what the King has done—where have those papers of Picasso's gone to, eh? And secondly, so that they can make another dirty deal and get profits by the million. Cannon fodder is cheap. You go on having children so that they can be killed. God damn it all!"

Señor Paco wiped his brow; the summer of 1924 was very hot. He added:

"And don't tell me any more damned fool stories. Morocco hasn't been settled and it never will be. It's Spain's evil spirit, and all our misfortune will always come from there. You'll see in time, all of you."

Primo de Rivera went to Morocco to take over the Supreme Command. The withdrawal was carried through. It was a strategic victory and a catastrophe. All the Moorish *kabilas* in the zone of Ceuta had joined the insurrection. Primo de Rivera's tactical method was to extricate the garrisons of the isolated positions and blockhouses as best he could, some by battle, others by bribery with money or munitions. Many garrisons were rescued at the price of surrendering their armament to the Moors who, in addition, received as much armament again in bribes; that is to say, they gained two rifles per rescued man. The Spanish forces flocked into the Zoco del Arbaa, disarmed and demoralized. From there they still had to reach Ceuta, passing through hostile forces which closed in on them. Twenty thousand men and an incalculable amount of war material were lost.

I knew that terrain step by step, and thus I could follow the catastrophe step by step. I used to buy the evening papers and sit down in the Villa Rosa to read them. I felt unable to discuss matters with Señor Paco any more.

Towards the end of 1924 the greater part of the Spanish forces had been discharged. Strong garrisons were left in Ceuta, Melilla, and Larache. The insurrection had swept the whole Spanish Protectorate. Primo de Rivera decreed the blockade of the territory. Press and public opinion acclaimed him as the savior of Morocco.

8. The Endless Track

O N E night at the end of 1924, a sergeant of the Engineers came into the Villa Rosa. I was sitting at my little table in the corner and saw nothing but his back while he leaned over the bar. There was something familiar about him which made me go on watching. I wanted him to be somebody I knew. I was alone, and among people ignorant of that Morocco which still obsessed me.

The sergeant turned sideways and I saw his profile. It was Córcoles.
Friendship between people who have been in a war together is an odd
thing. The army forces strangers to share the same tent or to peel potatoes for the same bucket, and turns them into so-called comrades-in-arms.
War catches them together and imposes a solidarity which is not that of
men, but rather that of animals in a common danger; this solidarity becomes a friendship. The day the army service ends, each of the friends
goes home to his own place to be swallowed by the mass of the people.
Each of them, telling stories to his intimates, will occasionally recall the
other and turn him into a figure in a tale. And sometimes he will exclaim:
"That was the best friend I ever had!" Yet this friend has dissolved into
thin air, has ceased to exist: he counts for nothing in the new life. Then
one day the two meet face to face, and in a flash a piece of life is resusci-
tated which is unforgettable, however hard you may have tried to bury it.

The two slap one another's backs, babble, speak, talk, and then they
separate, perhaps forever. But every such encounter stirs the sediments
dormant in the mind of anyone who has been a soldier and tries to forget it.

Córcoles and I hugged each other so boisterously that we drowned the
noise of the crowded bar. We would have silenced the chatter in the most
crowded café in Europe. Córcoles had escaped from the slaughter, he had
gone through the retreat from Xauen, and now, when he was on leave
in Madrid, every nerve in his feline body was unleashed.

I had never realized that I was fond of the man. Now I felt like crying.
I shouted:

"Manzanilla—Manolo—Manzanilla—one bottle or two, as many as you
like! Come and drink with us, it's on us, it's on me. Wine, quick, we
must get drunk. Look at him, he's got out of it safe. You can't kill a
wildcat!"

When Córcoles was in the grip of emotion, he used to stutter' and his
vowels came out like a hen's cackle:

"Wi-i-ine, o-o-old man!"

"Who's an old man here, you shaver? I could still leave your mother
with a child!"

"Manolo, don't be a brute!"

"I'll split this fellow's lip, Don Arturo."

"You'll damned well show respect to this fellow, you braggart."

"All right, all right. Now, let's see. Are you a friend of Don Arturo's,
or what?"

"Manolo, don't be a damn fool. This is the best friend I had in Africa.
Can't you see his face?"

"Well then, what's all the shouting about? The bottle is on me and

you can both shut up. Wine, wine! You just come and tell Manolo: 'I'm
Don Arturo's friend,' and true as gold, Manolo will be here for you. But
no talk about gray hair, eh? The stoutest fellow here is me, and then
it's me again. And now let me ask you—didn't they bump you off in
Morocco?"

"What the devil d'you mean? Don't you see I'm here?"

"Oh no, you're just a ghost, with those bones of yours and those clothes.
I'll get you a snack, some nice little sausages, and you'll get fatter at
once."

"He's got me, that old fellow, he's got me."

Manolo and Córcoles took to each other with a sudden affection that
might have made me jealous. Manolo showed it by surrounding Córcoles
with enticing dishes, more than enough for a full meal, instead of the
little tit-bits usually served with the wine. He stood by and watched him
eating, with his white napkin over his shoulder:

"You eat and drink. You're thinner than a piece of mending cotton.
And don't look at that tart. What you need is food and drink; you
keep your oil in your oil-skin."

Indeed, if you had shorn off Córcoles's mop of unruly curls which
made his head twice its size and peeled off his uniform, he would have
been nothing but a frame of bones in a coffee-colored skin. His Adam's
apple protruded from his collar, his eyes were sunk in his skull, and his
hands were like five shaven dog's tails. But his wit was more biting and
more cynical than ever. He had the insolence of a man who has taken
the measure of Death.

"How are you here?"

"As you see me—all bones. When we arrived in Ceuta they had to send
me to hospital in bits and pieces because I'd fallen apart. And then the
doctor said to me: 'Two months' sick leave—where d'you want to go?'
I'm a Ceuta man, and you can imagine I didn't want a summer holiday
there. 'To Madrid,' I said. 'But haven't you got your family here?' 'Yes,
sir,' I said, 'but—do you want me to leave the hospital and go home so that
my mother and sisters can nurse me? They'd be saying all day long: "Be
quiet—Don't move—Go out in the sun—Here's a nice cup of something
that'll help you—Keep warm—and so on."' The doctor had to laugh and
he gave me a free voucher to go bathing in the Manzanares."

He turned round to stare after a girl.

"You've got some damn fine women! Manolo, get me more ham, I'll
raise your tip. I'm spending half the budget of the road from Tetuan to
Xauen here . . ."

Hardly any business is done in the week between Christmas and New
Year. I asked for a few days off and devoted my time to acting as Cicerone

for Córcoles who did not know Madrid. And bit by bit he told me about his experiences.

"You see, old man, it was fine in Xauen. You didn't know it as it was then. Even Luisa has set up a branch of her house there, and there is a tavern at every street corner. Well—there was. Because now there's nothing left there, not even the rats. It was the same old story as always. The Moors attacked one or the other convoy and killed a man or two, but in Xauen it was quieter than it is here with all these trams—I can't get used to their noise. And then one day we heard that they had attacked Uad Lau, and the next day had attacked Miscrela, and the third—well, it went on like that. But we didn't bother about it. Then suddenly they told us things had gone wrong. We couldn't go to Tetuan any more. And there we were, running round in circles, and the Moors pulling long faces, and nobody coming to market any more. We hadn't anything to eat then. They wouldn't sell us food, and so we took it. We cleared up every corner in Xauen, my lad. Well, in the meantime they were peppering us with bullets. We had plenty of ammunition, otherwise we wouldn't have got out of it alive. They started throwing stones at us. Then the *Tercio* came and they said at once: 'It's over, we're going.' Going where? 'Yes,' they said, 'we're all going back to Spain and the war is over.' The war may have been over all right, but not even the devil could have stayed on in Xauen. They were plastering us with bullets by day and by night. Well, the Legion stayed there; they got reinforcements and Franco had come along. Then the peninsular troops were evacuated and marched to the Zoco del Arbaa in the daytime. There was a bit of shooting on the way, but we were well covered and nothing much happened.

"You know the Zoco. I took you there first, remember? Well, it was bad when we got there. Thousands of men coming up from every side, all hungry, eaten by lice, dying of thirst, without arms, and half-naked. We all looked as if we were only fit to go begging for alms in the street. And all the brass-hats were there in the Zoco: Millán Astray, Serrano, Marzo, Castro Girona—well, all the first lot. Nobody knew what to do. The canteens had no water left. And two days after that, the Legion arrived at midnight. They had been stuffing uniforms with straw all day long and then they had got out of Xauen by night and joined us in the Zoco. They'd left the puppets leaning on the parapets, with sticks at their sides as if they were rifles. I suppose the Moors must have torn their hair next morning. But the Legionaries made us hurry: 'Get off before they find out.'"

Córcoles finished his glass of wine and drew lines on the table with his finger.

"You must remember the site of the Zoco. It's on the top of a hill, and if you go from there to Tetuan, at first there's a steep slope with a wood on the right. You remember a burned lorry lying there when you first came to join the Company? The Moors had ambushed a convoy just before. Well, about that slope. You go down and pass through a gully all overgrown with trees—that's where the wood begins—and then you climb up another slope. Afterwards the road goes straight to Ben-Karrick. Well, when we were going down the slope we ran into a hail of bullets. The Legion pushed on down the gully and the rest of us threw ourselves down in the ditches. The Moors got all those who didn't duck quickly enough. It took us four hours to get to the bottom of that ravine, and two hours to climb the other slope until we were in open country. It was the worst butchery I've ever seen, my lad. They killed nearly all the officers of the *Tercio*, they killed General Serrano, they wounded Millán Astray again. And you can imagine that the men were falling in hundreds if that's what happened to the big bugs. You couldn't see a thing in the bottom of the gully, what with the dust and the smoke, and the shrieks and the curses, and you kept treading on people who'd fallen. It was worse in Ben-Karrick. They were firing at us from the hills by day and night. Well, then we arrived in Tetuan, half of us, or a little less. And in Tetuan those dirty swine kept on firing from Mount Gorgues all day and all night long."

Córcoles drank another glass of wine.

"Yes. But now listen. I can't stomach those fellows in the *Tercio*. Every one of them has either killed his own father or something like it, or else he's fit for the madhouse. But the truth is that without them the rest of us would never have got out alive. That fellow Franco is madder than the rest. I saw him in that gully, as cool as cucumber, shouting his orders: 'You there, duck your head, you idiot! ... Two men to that stone on the right ...' A soldier would stand up and—boum—down he would go. An officer would come up to him to report—boum—down he would go. But Franco didn't get a scratch. He frightened me more than the bullets."

He finished another glass and changed the subject:

"D'you remember the camp where the tortoises invaded us during the night and you had two little green ones in your shirt when you woke up? And you remember the camp where we had to clear out because of the fleas?"

Then came a night when we touched upon the political problems which at that time centered round Morocco.

"I don't understand a word of all the muddle over here," said Córcoles, "but in Morocco things are boiling over."

We were in the Villa Rosa. Manolo brought a tray laden with little wine glasses and stayed leaning against the back of a chair. Córcoles shut up like an oyster.

"Go on," I said.

"All right, then, I'll go on. In Morocco people are saying that we're going to clear out from there for good."

"And we are clearing out," stated Manolo, "and you'll have to go on with your racket somewhere else."

Córcoles said: "I thought I should have shut up!"

"You go on," I said. "But you let other people speak too for once, Manolo."

"All right, I won't say anything. But I won't go away."

"You can stay, then," said Córcoles. "You didn't like what I said? Well, my dear friend, you'll hear a bit more. Morocco is a disgrace."

Some of the customers turned round. Córcoles, inspired by his public, raised his voice:

"Yes, sir, a disgrace. We Spaniards have no right to abandon Morocco. What they've done to us is a dirty trick. They let thousands of our men be killed, just because the politicians thought it would be nice to get rid of Morocco. But we in the Army have got our honor, and things can't go on as they are now. They won't go on, I tell you, even if Primo de Rivera himself wants them to."

A man came up to Córcoles:

"You keep quiet—General Primo de Rivera is the Head of the State."

Another man came after the first and pulled him by the sleeve:

"It's you who ought to keep quiet. The sergeant here's quite right. What's this—letting our men be killed and then giving up what they've paid for with blood? And using the Treaties as toilet paper, eh? You're a cad."

Manolo stiffened:

"You little playboy, you pansy, shut up. Go on, Sergeant."

A large crowd had gathered round our table. Most of the men vociferated that we ought to clear out of Morocco, but there was a minority which insisted on the opposite. Suddenly, the newspaper seller shouted:

"Hell—the gentlemen don't want to clear out? Long live the Republic!"

The shout was so absurdly unexpected that there was silence for a moment. Then glasses and bottle and stools were flying about. Manolo got hold of the two of us and pushed us into the corridor. He opened the private door into the Calle del Gato:

"Get out of here. You know nothing about what happened. I'm going back, I must see if I can't box the ears of one of those young fellows in there."

The street called the "Street of the Cat" is three yards wide and paved with large old flagstones. It is one of those odd little alleys you find in the heart of every big city: you enter there, and life is different. No vehicles pass, and hardly any people; the noise of cars and trams sounds very distant. The houses are tightly shut and shuttered. There is a tavern whose door is always closed; a shop for rubber goods; a café with waitresses and a few old hags, swollen with syphilis and gin, sitting in the entrance to wait for customers who never come. Cats walk serenely in the street, making love and snarling at the stray passers-by. Some of the street lamps on the house fronts are dark, but even those which are lighted give no light from their trembling flame, they only fill the darkness with shadows.

Córcoles and I pushed through the door of the tavern just in front of us and dived into the fumes of fried fish, spilled wine, and stale tobacco smoke. We sat down at a table and ordered fish and a couple of glasses.

"What a mess," said Córcoles. "I wouldn't have liked to sleep in a police station, especially while I'm in uniform."

"Well, that's that. Now tell me what you really think, but without patriotic attacks. I know you."

"The patriotism was for the gallery. But to tell you the truth, lad— where should we go to? If it's all over with Morocco, I can see myself stranded with 150 pesetas just now when I've got a girl I'd like to marry. And if I leave the army what can I do? It's the same for all of us. Take one of the Colonels with a pay of 999 pesetas 99 centimos, take him away from his pastures in Morocco, bring him here, with Mrs. Colonel accustomed to have a party every week-end, and what do you think will happen to him? Primo has got a swollen head from his almightiness. But I can tell you now, this Morocco business will have a sting in its tail. Our people out there are prepared to rebel for better or for worse if they get orders to embark for Spain.

"And there's another thing. It's easy to say that Spain will keep Ceuta and Melilla, but have you any idea of what's happening out there now? Nowadays you can't even go on the mole by night, because the Moors of Anyera cut your throat, empty your pockets and throw you into the sea. If things go on like this, on the day we expect it least they'll pour into Ceuta and chase us into the sea. It's as much as your life is worth to travel from Ceuta to Tangier, because we hold only the narrow lane of the road and the railway line, and on both sides the Moors fire at you as they please. Primo wants something which is simply impossible: to stay there and not to be there—to have the cake and eat it."

"Well," I said, "I don't know things as they are now over there, but I do know that everybody here is convinced we're going to leave Morocco.

Primo de Rivera has undertaken to do it, he's promised it publicly to the country."

"You can't make wheat grow by preaching. Neither the generals nor we—the sergeants—want to leave. If necessary, Sanjurjo will rise against Primo, and Franco with him, and the *Tercio,* and the *Regulares.* And then there's another factor."

Córcoles had his mouth full of fried fish and let me wait.

"What other factor? The King?"

"No, sir. Bigger than that. Now look here. In Africa people talk a lot and they tell a lot of stories. Half of them are just talk. But this seems to be serious. By our retreat we've left the French with their bottoms bare. Firstly, they've lost their business of selling rifles to the Moors, and secondly, they're having the hell of a lot of bother with Abd-el-Krim. But the worst thing for them is that if we clear out of Morocco, the Germans or the English or the Italians will get hold of it, and that's something the French won't stand for. To cut a long story short, they've told Primo in all friendliness that he's got to honor the Treaties and that if he doesn't he'll have to bear the consequences. And apparently they've negotiated with Sanjurjo. They've been well in with Franco ever since he was in Paris for his studies under old man Pétain, and it looks as if everything was settled. So that in a few months we'll begin the reconquest."

"The whole story sounds like a thriller. You must write me a letter when you get back and tell me the next instalments," I said.

We went out into the dark little street and back into the lights and the noises a hundred steps further away.

Various things happened between January and June 1925.

The troops of Abd-el-Krim and the Raisuni had joined forces to throw the Spanish garrison out of Xauen, but when it came to sharing the spoils they quarreled. Xauen belonged to the territory of the Jebala, the domain of the Raisuni, but the Riff warriors established themselves there as the lords and masters. The Raisuni, himself immobilized by dropsy in his mountain of Jebel Alam, sent out his supporters; the two chiefs waged war on each other. But the Raisuni was powerless against the machine guns and the artillery at the disposal of Abd-el-Krim. The war lasted not more than a few days. Then Abd-el-Krim captured the Lord of the Mountain in his castle at Tazarut, took his treasure, many millions' worth, and carried him as a prisoner to the Riff, where he died in April of the same year.

While the Chief won this victory, his brother Mohammed went to London, made a series of visits and published sensational statements in which he promised peace as soon as the European nations recognized the independence of the Riff. Simultaneously, the raids and thrusts into the French zone grew more frequent. In April, French troops sent to Morocco from the motherland launched an offensive. In May, Primo de Rivera took the most daring step of his career: he negotiated an armistice of three months with Abd-el-Krim.

The French forces suffered defeat after defeat at the hands of the Riff tribes; riotous clashes in the Chamber had their repercussions in the streets; Jacques Doriot, the Communist leader, issued a manifesto in which he branded the French Empire as the aggressor and demanded the recognition of the independence of the Riff as well as the withdrawal of France from the Moroccan Protectorate. The sending of expeditionary forces for a colonial war roused resentment and discontent in the French masses, still aching with the fresh memories of the Great War. By the end of May there were daily turbulent scenes in the Chamber and the French Government seemed powerless in its efforts to lessen the tension.

In that period I was trying to follow and to understand the development of the two great opposing ideas, Fascism and Socialism—or Communism—outside Spain. In my own country I found it difficult to fit the political movements into the orthodox pattern. The workers' movement, to which I felt I belonged, had small and articulate but uninfluential parties, and big, stirring, inarticulate masses driven by forces and feelings which defied organized expression. Primo de Rivera's dictatorship borrowed openly from the political system which Mussolini had erected; it established the "Single Party" and Corporations. And yet few of us called Primo de Rivera a Fascist. I myself hated and distrusted the rule of generals, and still I hoped that the old man, honestly blundering, would rid Spain of the Moroccan incubus and of the wave of frightening violence. Even then I was afraid of the other forces gathering strength behind the scene; I had seen them in the making over there in Morocco, but I hardly understood what I had sensed. This vague dread made me turn to the scanty information in the press, as though by realizing what was happening outside my own country I would discover the right angle, the right perspective to gage what was happening to us.

Doriot's action perturbed and puzzled me. It seemed to me obvious that a revolt of the French masses, led by the Communist Party under a flag borrowed from Abd-el-Krim, would inevitably provoke counter measures from all the Powers which had signed the Treaty of Algeciras. It would drive the French military caste to an immediate and effective activity. In fact, the immediate effect of Doriot's manifesto was that M. Malvy visited Primo de Rivera in Madrid and that, willy-nilly, the two Governments decided to crush Abd-el-Krim by joint action. At the time I thought that Doriot's tactics were so blatantly stupid as to equal those of an *agent provocateur*. His later career makes it possible to question whether he was not less of a clumsy demagogue than an efficient servant of his masters.

It was in the early summer of 1925 that I received a letter from Córcoles. He wrote:

"We can't know what will happen, but I think that Primo won't last long. You will have heard that Franco offered his resignation as Chief of the Legion. There is a story going round here which ought to amuse you. When Primo came to Melilla, Franco and the officers of the *Tercio* and the *Regulares* invited him to a big banquet in their mess and played a nice little joke on him. All courses were just egg dishes, fried, poached, boiled, omelettes and so on. He asked—so they say—why there was such a surfeit of eggs, and got the answer that those who wanted to get out of Morocco had no further need of their eggs—they were only needed by those who wanted to stay.[1] There was a terrible row and one of the officers is said to have drawn his revolver against Primo. Franco sent in his resignation and all officers here have declared their solidarity with him. The sergeants of the Engineers sent him a declaration of loyalty, too, and nearly all signed it. I have signed it myself."

The Kings of Spain built a great and famous road which leads from Madrid to the North. Philip II was the first, he built it when he erected the huge stone pile of El Escorial. Later kings constructed their places of refuge nearer to their Palace, at La Granja and El Pardo, but always on the road to the Guadarrama range. It became the road of King Alfonso XIII when he visited his castles or when he drove his fast car to the Cantabrian coast. And it is a road fit for kings. Thousand-year-old trees grow to its right and left, survivors from the primeval forests that once surrounded Madrid. For a stretch of the way the river Manzanares runs alongside, and there are sandy inlets, reeds and willows. A chain of hillocks covered with elms, poplars, pines and horse-chestnut trees lines up to the right until, near El Pardo, it is followed by a dense, wild, oak forest, once the property of the King.

On Sundays I used to take a book with me and walk along the North Road to the pines. Sometimes I did not plunge into the woods before I had entered the chapel of Saint Anthony, at the very beginning of the road, and looked at the ceiling painted by Goya.

In the early mornings only a few old women would be at prayer, lost in the shadow of the chapel, but the stout, hearty priest would sit in the doorway of his house or in the shade of the thick, spreading trees. He

---

[1] This joke turns on an untranslatable pun: "eggs" is one of the Spanish slang synonyms for testicles and thus for the "attributes of masculinity," of which Primo de Rivera himself had spoken in his manifesto.—Author's Note.

knew that I had not come to pray. He would fold up his newspaper, or shut his breviary, and greet me as an old friend. Then he would take me to the sanctuary and turn on the lighting of the dome so that I could see the frescoes, bright behind the film of a century of candle smoke. The old women would turn their heads, stare at us and then look upwards. The priest and I used to discuss details of the painting in a church whisper. He found pleasure in pointing out the figure which is called *La Maja de Goya* and is supposed to be the Duchess of Alba, a girl in a red dress by the side of the holy hermit.

"Friend," he would say, "those were different times. The Kings stopped here and the church was crowded. Now, the only people who come here are washerwomen who light a candle to the Saint because he's saved one of their children, or young girls who want a husband and pray on their knees to the Saint for this miracle."

One Sunday when we came out on to the sun-dappled terrace I saw a newspaper spread on the stone seat. It was *El Debate*. Big black headlines announced an attack on the Riff coastline, in the Bay of Alhucemas. The war in Morocco had broken out afresh. The landing had been made by Colonel Franco at the head of his Legionaries.

I went into the pine woods of the Moncloa and threw myself down on the carpet of slippery needles. While I watched the Sunday antics of the crowd at the foot of the slope, I thought of Morocco; and the road of the Kings running through the trees down there made me think of the road I had helped to build.

I saw the track of the road from Tetuan to Xauen, pushing onwards between the hills; I saw the men slowly digging the ground and crushing the stones.

There was something that had happened before the track had quite reached the fig tree, which was then still the crossroad between the mountain paths the Moors used on their way to the Zoco on Thursdays.

A blind Moor came slowly downhill, beating his stick against the rocks and testing them so as not to lose the thin trail on its meanderings through the thorn bushes. Suddenly the foot path came to an end and the blind man's stick tapped in the void. There was no firm ground in front of him. The Moors and the soldiers had stopped work and watched the blind man, jesting. I left my place under the fig tree and took the man by the arm to guide him down the cut in the ground. He grunted something in Arabic, which I did not understand.

"Are you going to the Zoco, old man?" I said. "If you are, come along here. We're building a road and there is no footpath any more."

At my words he lifted his seamy, sun-bitten face. He had a dirty white beard and red eye sockets, with rheumy lids folded back into the hollows.

"A road?"

"A road, yes, up to Xauen. It will be an even road, grandfather, where you can walk without stumbling."

The blind man broke out into sharp, convulsive laughter. He hit the heaped soil and the trunk of the fig tree with his stick. Then he extended his arms as though to outline the wide horizon, and shrieked:

"An even road? I'll always walk on the path, always, always! I don't want my sandals to slip in blood, and this road is full of blood, all of it. I see it. And it will fill with blood again and yet again and a hundred times again!"

The mad blind Moor climbed back on the trail which had brought him, and for a long time we could see his dark shape on the hills, fleeing from that luckless road which pushed forward to the city.

I had forgotten him. Now I remembered. Twice already that road had been soaked with Spanish blood.

Yet in those days many thousands of men were building the tracks of new roads through all Spain.

ARTURO BAREA

THE
CLASH

CONTENTS

PART I

PART II

... *honour eternal is due to the* BRAVE AND NOBLE PEOPLE OF SPAIN, *worthy of better rulers and a better fortune! And now that the jobs and intrigues of their juntas, the misconduct and incapacity of their generals, are sinking into the deserved obscurity of oblivion, the* national resistance *rises nobly out of the ridiculous details* ... *That resistance was indeed wild, disorganized, undisciplined and Algerine, but it held out to Europe an example which was not shown by the civilized Italian or intellectual German.*

RICHARD FORD, *Handbook for Travellers in Spain and Readers at Home.* London, 1845

Part I

1. The Lost Village

T H E August heat was melting the starch. The inside of my collar had become a damp, sticky rag, the outer tissue kept its stiffness, the edge chafed my sweaty skin. As I pushed my handkerchief between neck and collar to get relief, I suddenly saw before me my Uncle José, sliding a neatly folded silk kerchief between his strong throat and starched collar, while we waited for the coach to Brunete, thirty years ago.

I hated waiting in the heat.

Many people and many things die in thirty years. One feels hemmed in by ghosts, a ghost oneself. The little boy who waited on this spot thirty years ago was myself; but that boy no longer existed.

The old inn of San Andrés was the same: there was the shadowy gateway, the courtyard with the chickens pecking between the cobbles, the little taproom where they still sold wine from a goatskin. I checked the inventory of my memory, and the outlines were identical. But I myself was a little dazed and blunted—or maybe things looked flatter and bleaker in this harsh glare. I used to delight in the shops of this street. The street was unchanged, the same old taverns, the same old shops brimming over with farming tools, coarse cloth, sticky sweets and gaudy color prints for the customers from the villages of Castile and Toledo.

I knew that by the rules of geography Toledo belongs to Castile. Never mind: Toledo is different. It has always been an island in the old map of Spain. It bears the imprint of Roman legions, of the flower of Arab invaders, of knights-in-armor and of Cardinals, royal bastards, who left their Mass for the sword; of generation after generation of Moorish and Jewish craftsmen who hammered their steel, tempered it in the waters of the Tajo and inlaid it with wire of gold.

I had to go there, soon, if I could make myself free to go.

The bus was here at last. Not so very different from the old diligence.

The passengers were taking it by assault as they had done when I was that little boy. It was as easy as then to disentangle the two opposite worlds of the villages of Castile and Toledo. Here were the leàn, gaunt men from the meager wheat lands, from Brunete, and their thin, bony wives with bodies exhausted from childbirths and faces made taut by sun and frost. There were the people of the vale of Toledo, from the wine lands of Méntrida, the men a little pot-bellied and hearty, with fair skin under the tan, their women generously plump and noisily gay. I felt a pleasure, which I knew to be childish, in thinking that I was a crossbreed, my father Castilian, my mother Toledan. Nobody could label me, nobody was able to range me within one of these two groups. I looked different from both.

I was out of place. Just as my stiff collar and town suit were out of place among the country clothes of the others. My fleeting pleasure turned sour. The live people around me made me feel a stranger among my own kindred, and the dead who crowded my memory were ghosts.

I took my seat beside the driver. Antonio wore a laborer's jacket, and when the brakes screeched he cursed like a carter. He was out of place at the steering wheel. He should have been handling the long whip which reaches to the ears of the leading mule.

People sorted themselves out while we coasted downhill. They shouted across the bus—family news, shopping news—and the street outside was full of noises. But when the car changed gear to climb the long slope of El Campamento, the drone of the engine, the sun, the dust, and the acrid smell of petrol enforced silence. When we reached the dun-colored plain of Alcorcón, with its dry harvested fields and dried clay houses, the passengers were dozing or chewing the cud of their thoughts.

So we passed Navalcarnero and Valmojado, and followed the boundary between Toledo and Castile, until we left the main road at Santa Cruz de Retamar, turning east. Now we were on Toledan soil. It is an ancient highway. When Madrid was nothing but a famous castle, this was the great artery linking Toledo with Avila. Along this road people fought and traded. Moorish warriors descended from the Toledo mountains into the valley of the Alberche, to scale the Sierra and reach the Castilian uplands. And from the high tablelands of Avila and Burgos, knights streamed down to cross the river plains and to wrest Toledo, City of Stone, from the Moors.

I knew that I was showing color prints of history to myself. But why not? It was a diverting game.

Now the highway was asleep. Nobody used it but the people from the villages along it, with their carts and their donkeys, and sometimes a lorry with local produce. The road led nowhere in these days. It was merely a link between a few forgotten villages.

On this old warrior route, between Santa Cruz de Retamar and Torrijos, lay Novés. I was on my way to Novés now, and I wondered why. Of course I knew why. I had rented a house for my family in Novés, and this was the first week-end I was going to spend there, at my "country house." What had possessed me to take a house at the back of beyond? I had long wanted a house in the country near Madrid. Two years before, in 1933, we had spent almost a year in the foothills of the Sierra, in Villalba; but I had disliked the shoddy tourist atmosphere. I had wanted a real village for my week-ends. Novés was a real village.

But this was not the real reason why I chose it.

I had no wish to disentangle once more the complicated reasons which I had so often set out to myself. They were not pleasant, but inescapable. Some time ago I had resumed the joint household with my wife, after a separation of nearly a year. It was because of the children, and it did not work. A house in the country at some distance from Madrid meant regaining my liberty to some extent; it would avoid our having to live together. It was also a decent excuse—or what people call decent—in the eyes of others, while it circumvented a new separation which would have smacked of the ridiculous. And it would be good for the health of the children; and for Aurelia, who had been ailing ever since her last childbed. And the weekly rest and change would do me good. I could afford it after all.

Very good and correct reasons. But I would not deceive myself by repeating them over again, even though they were true as far as they went. The worst of introspection is that one cannot stop it at will.

The country outside was drab and monotonous and I was a stranger to the other passengers. There was no escape into contemplation or conversation.

I wondered whether Novés was not simply another defeat of mine, a flight from myself.

There was Maria. Our affair had lasted six years, which was not bad. But I had hoped to shape her to my measure, as I had hoped with Aurelia, a very long time ago. And Maria had developed in her own way. I had failed. Perhaps I was wrong. One cannot force companionship. It was certainly not her fault. But the worst of it was that she was very much in love with me and that she had become possessive. She wanted to absorb me. And that made it so clear that I was not in love with her. The house in Novés meant that I would be able to avoid the inevitable Saturday afternoons and Sundays with Maria.

It would give me a chance to escape from my wife during the week and from my mistress during the week-ends. A most satisfactory state of affairs!

But it was not the problem of the two women alone. Going to Novés meant that I could get away from my weekday isolation into another isolation. The change would be a relief; my isolation in normal life was making me restless. In theory I had resigned myself to a nice bourgeois existence, keeping up the appearances as far as my wife and my household was concerned, spending agreeable hours with Maria, and indulging in my private taste and whims. The truth was that I was tired of both women and had to force myself to play up to them. Money was not really important to me, it never had been. And my ambitions had long been buried—that to be an engineer as well as that to be a writer. When the Republic was young I had cherished political hopes and illusions while I worked hard to organize the Clerical Workers' Union. But I must have lacked the flexibility one needs to became part and parcel of a political organization and to make a political career. And it was sheer ingenuousness to believe that good will was sufficient to do good work.

Yet I could not seriously give up any of my ideals. I could not settle down to be a contented bourgeois.

I still believed that somewhere there existed a woman with whom I might have a contact beyond the physical, with whom I would have a complete life of mutual give and take. I was still unable to keep my fingers off any piece of mechanism in need of repair. I still plunged for months into difficult technical problems which arose in the course of my work, but in reality had nothing to do with it. I disliked the cheap writing which flooded the Spanish book market and continued to believe that I had more to say than many others. I was still a socialist.

But I had to carry on the life in which I was caught, or which I had made for myself.

I could feel that I was in an intellectual and even physical deadlock. I knew I broke out in spasmodic explosions, in violent disputes and bursts of rage against all around me. It was because I was impotent before the facts of my own life, and my country's.

Novés was a flight from all this. It was my total defeat, because it meant declaring myself an egoist in cold blood.

I did not like this label.

It meant declaring myself disillusioned, hopeless and in need of a refuge. That was it.

We were still in the plain, but the ribbon of the road before us lost itself in a horizon of hills.

Antonio nudged me:

"There's Novés—over there!"

I only saw the line of the road, topped by a gilded ball and cross.

"That's the church tower."

The bus dived into a gully and lurched through a village street until it came to a stop in the market square before an inn. The shadows were already lengthening, but the sun was still burning fiercely. Aurelia and my eldest daughter were waiting for me; the family had traveled to Novés with the lorry which moved our furniture.

"Well, how far have you got with the house?" I asked.

"Nowhere, we've been waiting for you. The children leave one no time for anything."

"Papa, our house is very big, you'll see."

"I've seen it, silly. Do you like it?"

"Yes, but it frightens me just a little. Because it's empty, you see, and ever so big."

The men had piled up our furniture along the walls by the entrance, a big heap of bedding, suitcases, trunks, and boxes in the middle. The three children were tumbling about, getting under everybody's feet.

"Children or no children, you'll have to lend me a hand."

"Well, there's a woman of the village who wants to come and be our maid-of-all-work. You must talk to her. I told her to come along as soon as she heard the bus hooting."

There she was, flanked by a girl of about sixteen, and a man in the forties. The three stood stock-still in the wide doorway looking at me. The man took off his cap and the woman spoke up for them:

"Good evening. My name's Dominga and this here's my girl and my husband. Now you just tell us what you want done, sir."

"Don't stand there in the doorway, come in. Now, what do you want?"

"Well, the lady will have explained. As she said to Don Ramón—that's the one that keeps the stores—you'll be wanting a daily woman so I've come, sir. So if it's all right with you, here we are."

"How much do you want, then?"

Peasant fashion, she avoided a direct answer:

"Well, the girl would come and help, and between the two of us, never you fear, we'll have the house shining like a new medal."

"But, frankly, I don't need two people here."

"No, sir, the girl would just come to help me, it wouldn't cost you a thing. Of course, if you wanted her to eat here she could, for as I always say, where three eat, four can eat as well. But for everything else there'd only be me. I was in service in Madrid before I married, and I know what the gentry like. And we're honest, you can ask anyone in the village. . . ."

"What wages do you want, then?"

"We can start at once, that's what Mariano's come along for, just to lend a hand, as he's out of work."

"Yes, but now do tell me what wages you're wanting."

"Well, if it suits you, twenty-five pesetas [1] a month and my meals. Don't worry about beds, we'll be sleeping at home, just round the corner, and if you ever want me to stay a night, you just say so, sir."

That seemed to be that. The taciturn husband, Mariano, helped me to put up beds and shove furniture about, while the women took care of the children, the supper, and the clothes. The house was a vast old single-storied farm building of no less than seventeen rooms, some of them enormous. In what was to be our dining room, the table seemed a little island in the middle and the sideboard a forlorn ornament against the wall, wherever we put it.

Night was falling. We lit three candles and stuck them in the necks of empty wine bottles. They made three pools of light on the table, while all around them was penumbra, alive with black shadows.

"The best thing would be to light a fire, even if it is August," said Dominga, and so we did. There was a huge open fireplace, bell-shaped, as large as one of the smaller rooms in our Madrid flat. Mariano heaped dry broom on the hearthstone, and the flames leaped up to man's height, drenching the room in dusky red and drowning the puny flicker of the candles.

Even when we had distributed all our furniture, the house was empty and our footsteps sounded hollow. Those rooms would have needed heavy old oaken chests, sideboards with three tiers, canopied beds with four heaped-up mattresses, such as our grandparents had. We soon went to bed, in weary silence, but my two Alsatians howled outside in the courtyard for many hours.

I got up early the next morning. Outside the door, I found Dominga, her daughter, and her husband, waiting. The women scurried off into the house, but the man kept standing there and twisting his cap round and round.

"I believe there's nothing more for you to do, Mariano," I said to him. I thought he was hoping for a tip such as he had been given the night before.

"Well, it's like this, sir. I haven't got a job, so I said to myself: 'Let's go there.' So now you just tell me what to do." He gave me a look and added quickly: "Of course, I don't ask for anything. But some day, if you feel like giving me anything, well, then you'll give what you like, and if

---

[1] In 1935, 25 pesetas were slightly more than 12 shillings, or about three dollars, at an exchange rate of roughly one dollar = 7 pesetas. This exchange rate applies to all sums in pesetas mentioned in this book, previous to the Civil War.

not, well, that's all right too. After all, I can always help the women sawing wood and fetching water."

There was a cobbled farmyard at the back of the house, with room for half a dozen carts and their mule teams. The mangers were ranged along the walls. I took Mariano there.

"Let's see if we can't do something here. Get rid of the cobbles and we'll try to make a garden with a few flowers."

So I had acquired a family of retainers. At midday I went to see my village.

Novés lies at the bottom of a ravine scooped out of the plain, and is built on the pattern of a fish's spine. There is a very wide main street, through the middle of which flows a stream blackened by the refuse of the whole village. On both sides, short alleys like ribs lead up the steep, rough slopes. When it rains, the bottom of the ravine becomes the bed of a torrent which sluices away the heaped-up muck. Then people are forced to use the bridges which span the whole width of the street at intervals. One of them is high, humpbacked, made of fitted stones; it is Roman. Another is of concrete and the road passes over it. Most of the houses are built of sun-baked clay with a thick coat of whitewash. They all look alike and they all implacably reflect the glare of the sun. There is a square with a few small trees, the church, the apothecary, the Casino, and the Town Hall. And that is all there is of Novés: some two hundred houses.

I followed the dirty brook downstream, because I had nothing else to do. After the last small houses, the ravine opened into a valley sheltered from the winds of the plain and gently green even in August. On both sides of the stream were market gardens with fruit trees, flowers, and vegetable plots. Each garden had its own well and chain pump. A slight murmur of water and clanking of iron was in the air all the time. A mile further on the valley folded up and the little river ran again through a barren ravine sunk into the arid, dusty plain. This was the whole wealth of Novés. Walking back, I noted that most of the chain pumps were silent, and remembered that it was Sunday. But then I began to see more. Many of the garden plots lay abandoned or badly neglected. There were a few small beds of melons which had been cared for, but the big market-gardens looked as though nobody had worked there for months. The earth was baked in hard lumps. I looked down a well-shaft by the wayside. The chain with the buckets was rusty, green weeds floated on the water. Nobody had used the pump for a very long time. Back at my house, I talked to Mariano about it. His answer was to the point.

"It's a sin against God, that's what it is. The men without work, and the land abandoned. You won't believe it, but something's going to happen here, something nasty. It's been like this for the last three years, almost as long as we've had the Republic."

"But how's that? I know the big landowners are refusing to employ labor nowadays, but here in the village, I didn't think there were any big landowners."

"We've only got four rich men in the village. Things wouldn't go so badly if it weren't for Heliodoro. The others aren't really bad. But Heliodoro has got them all where he wants them, and there's a war on all the time."

He was no longer taciturn, and his gray eyes came alive in his heavy face.

"I'll tell you something of what's going on here. Before the Republic came, some of our young people joined the Socialists and some joined the Anarchists, well, less than a dozen in all. I don't know how they had the guts to do it, because the Civil Guards were after them all the time and beat them up often enough. But of course, when the Republic came, the Corporal of the Civil Guard had to lie low at first, and a lot of us joined. Nearly the whole village is with the Socialists or Anarchists now. But Heliodoro has always been the boss here and managed the elections for the deputy of Torrijos. And so now he's doing what he's always done, because before the Republic he was sometimes a Liberal and sometimes a Conservative, but never on the wrong side. And when the Republic came, well, then he joined Lerroux's crowd and now, because the Right's been getting strong after what happened in Asturias, he's become one of Gil Robles' crowd. And when our lads asked for decent wages Heliodoro got the four rich men of the village together and said to them: 'Those rascals must be taught a lesson.' So then they started chucking people out and only giving work to the ones who swallowed the old conditions. Because there are some like that, too. And then, you know how things happen in a village, most of us have a bit of land and there's always something the matter with the wife, or the garden gets flooded by the rains, and so lots of people owe Heliodoro money. And because he's the man whose word goes in the village, he got hold of the Municipal Secretary and the Mayor and took out papers against everyone so that he could keep their land. And so things are getting ugly. They were ugly two years ago. People went and messed up the gardens. But now it's worse, because now it's the other side that has the power."

"And the young people, what about them?"

"What d'you suppose they could do? Keep their mouths shut and tighten their belts. When things happened in Asturias[1] two or three of

---

[1] The various references to events in Asturias in this and the following chapters allude to the events of October 1934, when the workers' associations called a general strike, which

them were taken away, and now nobody dares to say a word. But something will happen some fine day. Heliodoro won't die in his bed."
"Have you got Trade Unions here, then?"
"We've got nothing. The men meet at Eliseo's. He's got a tavern and he's turned it into a Workers' Casino, and there they talk. Eliseo went and joined the Anarchists out there in the Argentine."
"I suppose you've got a club secretary, or something of the kind?"
"We haven't got a thing. What the men do is to meet and talk. Because nobody wants trouble with the Corporal."
"I must go and have a look at your Casino."
"You can't go there, sir. It's only for the poor. You've got a Casino in the market square, that's for the gentry."
"I'll go there, too."
"Well, then, they'll chuck you out of one or the other, sir, to be sure."
"And what are you a member of, Mariano?"
"I hope you won't get annoyed, but it's like this: When the Republic came, the same thing happened to me as to the others, we were all for it, and I joined the Trade Union—the U.G.T. But there, you see, it hasn't helped us much, to tell you the truth."
"I'm a member of the U.G.T., too."
"The devil you are." Mariano stared at me with great seriousness. "What a mess! Well, you've got yourself into a tight spot here!"
"We shall see. I don't expect the Corporal will beat me up."
"You never know."
In the afternoon, Mariano and I went to the "Poor Men's Casino," as he called it. The place was a former stable, a huge room with crossbeams, a billiard table in the middle, a small bar at the back, and a score of scratched tables along the bare walls. An ancient radio set built on sham Gothic lines stood in a corner. The billiard table fascinated me; I could not imagine how it ever landed in Novés. It had eight elephantine legs, and eight men could have slept comfortably on its top. The cloth was riddled with tears drawn together with twine. Apparently the table was used for everything, even for an occasional game of billiards; a match was just going on, in which the twine and chance directed the balls. Mariano led me to the bar.

"Give us something to drink, Eliseo."

The man behind the bar filled two glasses with wine without saying a word. There were about forty people in the room. Suddenly I tumbled to the fact that they had all fallen silent and were watching us. Eliseo stared straight into my eyes. At the first glance, his face gave you a shock. An ulcer had gnawed away one of his nostrils, and a few hairs were sticking out between the livid, greenish seams of the wound. It looked like a biblical, a medieval sore. But the curious thing was that the man was so detached from his blemish that he provoked neither pity nor physical revulsion. Eliseo was in the middle forties, short and squat, dark, suntanned, with quick, shrewd eyes and a sensual mouth. The way in which he looked me up and down while he drank a sip of wine was a provocation. When I set down my empty glass, he said:

"And you, why have you come here? This is the Workers' Casino, and if you hadn't been with Mariano, I wouldn't have served you."

Mariano intervened:

"Don Arturo is one of us, he belongs to the U.G.T."

"Is that true?"

I handed Eliseo the membership card of my Trade Union. He scanned every page and then called out:

"Boys, Don Arturo is a comrade!" He turned to me: "When we heard you were coming here we all said: 'Another son of a bitch, as if we hadn't enough of them anyhow!' "

He left his corner behind the bar to join me, and in the center of the clustering men I had to report on events in Madrid: how the Right was organizing and how the Left was coming to life again after the "Black Year" of repression. The wine was cheap, the drinks were on me and they began to talk. There were great hopes and great plans. The Left would come back into the Government and things would be different this time. The rich would have to choose between paying decent wages and giving up their land so that the others could work it. Novés would have a big communal market garden with a lorry of its own, which would carry greens and fruit to Madrid every morning. And they would finish the school building.

"The scoundrels!" said Eliseo. "Have you seen our school? The Republic put up the money for it and they sent us a beautiful drawing from Madrid of a house with big windows and a garden. But Heliodoro and his gang convinced the Madrid gentlemen that the school should be built out in the plain, above the valley. And there they started building. Heliodoro got a lot of money for the site, which was his, of course, and up there in the dust you can see the four unfinished walls."

"Next time we'll build it ourselves, down in the orchards. They're so beautiful, it's a real blessing from God," said another.

"You can't imagine, Don Arturo," said Eliseo, "how glad I am that you're one of us. Now we'll show them that we aren't just a few poor yokels. But you'll have to look out. They'll try to get you."

That evening I went to the "Rich Men's Casino."

There was the obligatory big saloon with marble-topped tables and men drinking coffee or coffee-and-brandy, a billiard table, and a tobacco-laden atmosphere, and behind it a smaller room crowded with card players. A plump little man, womanish in voice, skin, and gestures, made a beeline for me:

"Good evening, Don Arturo, that's right, you've come to join us, haven't you? You already know our Heliodoro, don't you?" I knew the tight-lipped man to whose table I was gently propelled. He was my landlord. The plump little man babbled on: "Excuse me for a tiny little moment, I've got to get the coffee ready, you know, but I won't be long." Everything was arranged for me. Heliodoro introduced me to the two black-coated men at his table—"Our two doctors, Don Julián and Don Anselmo"—and asked me the obvious questions: had I settled down, had the move been difficult, and so forth. I have never been good at small talk, and this was as boring as any. The effeminate little man brought coffee and asked me the same questions all over again, until one of the doctors cut him short:

"José, enter Don Arturo in the list."

José produced a fat leather-bound notebook and thumbed it, giving me a glimpse of pages filled with columns of figures and headed by names.

"Now, let's see. How many are there in your family?"

"But surely I won't have to enter all my children as members of the Casino!"

"Oh, this hasn't anything to do with the Casino. This is our local Medical Aid Association. I put you on the list and it gives you a right to medical assistance whenever you need it."

"But I've got a doctor in Madrid."

Don Julián grunted:

"All right, if you don't want it, we won't put you down. But I warn you, if you've an urgent case in your family and you aren't a subscriber, my colleague here will send you a nice little bill. If you've a splinter in your thumb and he lances it, he'll put it down as 'for a surgical operation, two hundred pesetas.'"

"And if I call you in?"

"It's he who makes out the bills in any case. It would come to the same thing."

"All right, then, put me down. My wife, four children, and myself. Six in all."

"In what category, please, Don Julián?"

"Don't ask obvious questions, José. In our category, of course."

"Five pesetas per month, Don Arturo. And what about your servant?"

"Isn't she a member of your Association already?"

"Well, yes, she's on our list, but she doesn't pay. So she's been struck off. And if she has an accident at work, you'll have to pay."

Don Julián sniggered:

"Say she burns her hand on the frying-pan. For a surgical operation and treatment, two hundred pesetas."

"Put the servant down, then."

"Two pesetas. D'you want to pay now? I'm the cashier. It won't take me a second to make out the receipts."

José pocketed the seven pesetas and tripped away, to reappear with a pack of cards.

"One hundred pesetas in the bank, this deal."

He went straight into the back room and sat down on a high chair behind the biggest table.

"One hundred pesetas, boys, if nobody stakes more."

Baccarat. The customers flocked to his table, the most important looking monopolizing the chairs. José was still shuffling the cards when a haggard man in mourning called out: "Banco!" and put a hundred-peseta bill on the table. He seemed to be the local gambler, for people murmured behind his back and nodded sagely when José dealt and raked in the stakes. A large-boned old man muttered behind the loser: "A bad start, Valentín."

"Just the usual thing, Uncle Juán. Anything to avoid a change."

The old man said no more, and the man called Valentín went on staking against the bank and losing. The others rarely played more than two pesetas; they were following the duel between the bank and Valentín. "The same as every night," said someone near me. People began to play against Valentín, who after an hour announced that he had used up all his cash. José asked for a continuation. The gambler protested:

"That's not fair."

"But, my dear Valentín, it isn't my fault if you've run out of cash."

"Heliodoro, give me a hundred pesetas."

They went quickly.

"Heliodoro, I'll sell you my mule."

"I'll give you five hundred pesetas for her."

"Let's have them."

Heliodoro was pushing the five banknotes along the table, when the old man who had spoken to Valentín before interposed his hand:

"Don't sell your mule, Valentín."

"I've a right to do as I like."

"All right, then, I'll give you one thousand for her."

"When? Now, at once?"

"Tomorrow morning."

"I don't need them tomorrow." Valentín took the five bills and Heliodoro scribbled a few lines on a piece of paper.

"Here, sign the receipt, Valentín."

The luck changed. Valentín heaped up bills in front of him and José had to restock the bank with cash again and again. Suddenly somebody opened the door from the street and shouted:

"Good evening!"

José gathered in the cards and his money, the others grabbed theirs, and in an instant all were sitting at the marble-topped tables and chatting boisterously. Horses' hoofs sounded on the cobbles and stopped outside the Casino. A pair of Civil Guards entered, a corporal followed by a constable.

"Good evening, gentlemen!"

José contorted himself, bowing and scraping. The Civil Guards kindly accepted a coffee each. Drinking his cup, the Corporal suddenly lifted his head and stared at me:

"You're the stranger, eh? I know already that you went to Eliseo's this afternoon." He waxed avuncular: "I'll give you some good advice—no one here will interfere with you, you can do as you like. But no meetings, eh? I want no gentlemen Communists here."

Carefully he wiped his mustache with a handkerchief, rose and walked out, followed by his silent henchman. I was dumbfounded. José sidled up to me.

"Better be careful with the Corporal, Don Arturo, he's got a foul temper."

"As long as I committ no offense, I'm no business of his."

"It's not for me to say anything, but it isn't right for you to frequent Eliseo's. Nobody goes there except the rabble from the village, and that's God's own truth. But of course, you don't know the people yet."

Heliodoro said nothing; he listened.

The man Valentín joined us with a shining face and a fistful of bank notes.

"You've cleaned up today," said Heliodoro.

"Enough to make up for this evening, and for yesterday, and if the

Guards hadn't turned up, blast them, I'd have taken the shirt off little
José's back." He thumped José's plump shoulder.

"You wait till tomorrow," said José.

"Here are your six hundred pesetas, Heliodoro, and thanks."

"What's this?"

"Your six hundred pesetas."

"You don't owe me anything—well, yes, the hundred pesetas I gave
you a while ago. The five hundred were for the mule."

"But d'you think I'd give you my mule for five hundred? She's worth
two thousand at least!"

"You won't give her? You *have* given her. Have you sold me your
mule, or not? Yes or no? Here are witnesses, and I've got your receipt
in my pocket. So there's nothing more to discuss."

Valentín leaned forward:

"You son of a bitch——"

Heliodoro laid his hand on his hip pocket and smiled. He was a quiet,
inconspicuous man, with taut lips.

"Look here," he said, "let's keep things straight and quiet. If you don't
want to lose, don't gamble. Good night, gentlemen."

He walked off with dignity, without looking back, but a man I had
not noted before stepped up, watching Valentín's every movement. Old
Uncle Juán tried to steer the gambler away.

"Now, you keep quiet, and no foolishness! You've sold your mule and
you can't alter it. If only it would teach you a lesson."

"But that son of a bitch——" Valentín's eyes were watering with rage—
"here's his tame gunman to cover him, too——"

José went round with a tray full of glasses of brandy.

"Now then, now then, let's have peace. After all, I've lost more than
anyone."

But the game did not start again. Soon afterwards we all went out into
the moonlit night. Old Juán joined me.

"We're going the same way. What do you think of our village?"

"I don't know what to say. There's food enough for thought in one
day!"

"We've been discussing your visit to Eliseo's in the Casino. I think the
Corporal only came to have a look at you."

"But there is no Civil Guard post in this place, is there?"

"No, they've come over from Santa Cruz. But news spreads quickly.
I must say, I for one don't think it's wrong to have done what you did,
and so I told the others. But if you don't take a firm stand, you'll find
life difficult in our village."

"Now look here, I've no intention of getting mixed up with things in this place. After all, I'm only coming here on two days a week, and then I need a rest. But if I want to drink a glass of wine wherever I like, no one's going to prevent me."

I knew I was skirting problems, and I felt in my bones that I would not be able to skirt them for long, as I listened to the calm voice of the old man telling me a story I seemed to have heard hundreds of times, only to hate it more each time. Heliodoro was the lord and master of the township. His position as political boss was inherited from his father and grandfather who had been the usurers and *caciques*[1] of the place. Half the ground and the houses were his, and the few men who still worked their own land were dependent on him. At the coming of the Republic, people had hoped for a decent way of living. A few of the independent landowners had dared to pay higher wages. Heliodoro had proclaimed that people had to work for him at the old terms or not at all; his own living was not dependent on the land. Two years ago, the men had become desperate and destroyed trees and fields on Heliodoro's property. From that time on, he employed no labor at all, and since his latest political patrons had come to power, he gave no peace to the other proprietors.

"He fixed us with his lorries, mainly. He has got two, and so he used to carry our grain and fruit to Madrid. Most of us sold our produce direct to him. Then he refused to buy any more and our people tried to hire his lorries from him. He said no. They hired lorries in Torrijos, but because the Deputy comes from there and needs Heliodoro, the hire of the lorries was stopped. Then they hired lorries in Madrid, which was much more expensive. They had to pay double, but still, they sold their stuff in town. Then Heliodoro went to Madrid himself."

Old Juán explained how the fruit and vegetable market in Madrid was worked. A group of agents called *asentadores*, allocators, had a monopoly on the market sites. They received all produce, fixed the price according to quality and the daily market rates, and allotted the goods to the various stalls. They undertook to sell on behalf of the producer and to pay him the proceeds minus their commission.

"Well, and then, after Heliodoro's visit to Madrid, Paco, who's one of our biggest and wealthiest market gardeners, went with a lorry full of big red pimentos to market, and they were a sight for sore eyes too, and worth a lot of money. Pimentos were fetching two pesetas a dozen, and more, at that time. After three days, Paco came back from town in a fine stew and told us in the Casino what had happened to him. One after another of the allocators had told him that there was no stall available

[1] *Cacique* is the current term for the local political "boss" of the Spanish countryside, who often is the local moneylender as well.

for his pimentos, and that he would have to wait. The fruit had to stay in the lorry till the evening, and then Paco had to rent storing space. Next day, the allocators told him the same old story, and said that the market was flooded with pimentos, but they offered to take the lot off his hands at five hundred pesetas. He refused, naturally, and so another day passed. On the third day, the pimentos were squashed and dripping juice. Paco had to accept three hundred pesetas for the lot, and out of that to pay his storage, his stay at the inn, and the lorry. It was touch and go whether he would not have to pay more money out of his own pocket. When he'd finished telling the story—you can imagine in what a rage—Heliodoro laughed and said: 'You people don't understand business. No one in Novés can sell fruit in Madrid except me.' And so it was. Now, of course, people have to bring him their stuff, take what he decides to pay and dance to his tune if they want to sell anything at all. So that's why he lets his land lie fallow while the village is starving, and earns more money than he ever did from the few of us who still work. And that's why the man you saw in the Casino, and who was his father's electoral agent, has to trail round with him as his bodyguard. Because one thing is certain: Heliodoro will get it in the neck one day. Well, here you are —good night, and come and see me in my mill. It's still working."

I waited, hand on the doorknob, listening to Old Juán's footsteps dying away. They were the steps of a strong and healthy man, beautifully even. While I tried not to lose the sound, my ear was caught by the noises of the night. Frogs were croaking in the pools of the dirty stream, cicadas were shrilling tirelessly in the gully. There were little splashes and jumps, and the thin whirring sound of nocturnal insects, and the sudden creaking of old beams in some house or barn. A moon of white metal cut the street into two bands, one deep black—where I stood—and the other aggressively white, gleaming on the smooth chalk walls and glinting on the sharp flint stones. The sleeping village was beautiful in this light, but I thought I could hear the heart-beat behind the white walls, a hidden force.

My house was asleep, too. The flames in the fireplace threw huge, fugitive shadows on the walls and the two slumbering dogs were black heaps rimmed with red. I sat down between my dogs and let myself be hypnotized by the twisting flames.

The house felt empty, as I did.

2. Spiders' Webs

IN the north-west corner of the Puerta del Sol, Madrid's heart and center, begins the Calle de Alcalá, which is its most important street. The entrance is as narrow as an alley. In the peak hours, the two streams of passers-by are bottled up on strips of pavement hardly more than a yard wide. The middle of the street is a single compact mass of cars, broken up only when a tram cuts through; when two trams coming from opposite directions pass each other there, the whole street is blocked. You cannot escape and must let yourself drift with the slowly moving crowd. You are smothered in the smell of burning petrol from the cars, of hot metal from the trams, and of the human beings round you. You rub elbows with a porter and a demi-mondaine, and you have the smell of acrid sweat and cheap heliotrope in your nostrils.

Every time you pass the open door of one of the cafés, a thick gust of tobacco smoke and crowd hits you in the face, and further on you dive through the fumes of the frying-pan in which the tavern keeper of Number 5 fries his sardines under the doorway of his establishment. It is useless to cross over to the opposite pavement. There, too, are crowded cafés and another tavern with another frying-pan.

But the two frying-pans mark the end of your labors. Once you have come so far, the street and its pavements widen, you breathe more freely and can rest your ears. For while you are caught in the narrow thoroughfare you are deafened by tram bells and klaxons, by the cries of street hawkers, the whistles of traffic policemen, the high-pitched conversations, and by the patter of the crowds, the rattle of tram cars, the screech of brakes.

Then the street becomes aristocratic. On its gently sloping pavement twelve persons can walk abreast, the tram lines are lost somewhere in the middle, and on both sides cars can pass comfortably three at a time. The buildings are ample and solid, stone to the left in the palaces of the old Customs House and the Academy of San Fernando, steel and concrete to the right. This is a street of banks and big offices and fancy shops, sprinkled with smart clubs, bars, and cabarets, flashing with neon lights at night. At its bottom end the stone building of the Bank of Spain rises on one side, and the War Ministry, hidden in gardens, on the other. Between them is the wide expanse of a square, in its center a fountain where the goddess Cybele rides in a triumphal chariot drawn by lions and spouting jets of water: silver-gray pavement, white buildings, green trees, and a vast sky whose light drenches and obliterates the foolish architectural details. This length of street, no more than a quarter of an hour's walk from the Puerta del Sol, is the Calle de Alcalá.

You may cross the Plaza de la Cibeles and follow for a further hour a street which bears the name Calle de Alcalá, but to the people of Madrid it is no longer the same street. It is an artificial appendix whose construction we watched at the beginning of this century. We call it "the other side of the Calle de Alcalá," to make it clear that it is not our street.

In the winter, the winds of the Sierra de Guadarrama sweep down the street and people who have to pass through it walk rapidly. But in fine weather its pavements are turned into a promenade, and the owners of the cafés put their marble tables out in the open. At sunset an enormous, milling crowd moves slowly up and down between the Bank of Spain and the Calle de Sevilla on one side, and between the War Ministry and the Calle de Peligros on the other, without entering the bottleneck at the top. Gesticulating, noisy groups of well-known people sit at the café tables, and the strollers cluster round them to see the famous torero, or politician, or writer, and to listen to what they have to say. The newspaper boys cry out the evening papers until the street is full of their shouts, and people go on waiting for the later editions. Then they gradually disperse in search of their supper.

During the day everything is business; people hurry up and down the Calle de Alcalá and the revolving doors of the banks gyrate incessantly, their glass panes flashing. But by day and night the street has a population of its own, which seems to live on those pavements: toreros without engagement, musicians without orchestra, comedians without theater. They tell each other their difficulties and miseries and wait for a more fortunate colleague to arrive and solve the problem of a meal for them, for one more day. There are streetwalkers who come and go in the nearest bar, looking anxiously round to make sure that no policeman is near to stop them on their journey. There are flower sellers with their bunches of violets or tuberose buttonholes, assailing the customers of expensive bars and restaurants. There is the man without legs in his little wooden contraption which he propels with his hands; coins rain into his cap day after day, he has never missed a bullfight, good or bad, and Ministers and beggars greet him.

Much later, in the small hours of the night, something like a bundle of clothes lies in the porch of Calatrava Church. It is a woman with an infant in arms who sleep there, wrapped in the same huge shawl. You can see them in the same spot winter or summer. I have watched them during twenty-five years, and to me they were the greatest mystery of the

Calle de Alcalá. Were they a phantom, that never grew older? Or was the place a fief passed on from generation to generation in the beggars' guild?

It was in this bit of the Calle de Alcalá that I had my office. My room was on the top of a tower in one of the highest business buildings. It was a cage of glass and iron, with only two walls of masonry, one which separated it from the other rooms of the office, and another which joined it to the next house. The ceiling was of glass, big, transparent glass slabs in a framework of steel girders. The floor was of glass, smaller, dim glass tiles fitted into a net of steel bars. Two walls, one facing the street, the other facing a wide roof terrace, were plate-glass sheets in steel frames. In winter two enormous radiators fought against the icebox atmosphere. In summer, the cage was shaded with canvas covers, the huge windows and the door to the roof terrace were opened, and the drafts battled against the torrid heat of the sun on glass and steel. I could see the endless, luminous sky dwarfing the white city buildings, and the insect-like crowds in the street below.

My office was a cage suspended over the city, but I called it my confessional. Here the inventors shut themselves up together with me. We discussed their affairs, lying back in the deep leather armchairs or leaning over the draftsman's table, and it was often as though I were their confessor.

The humble, visionary inventor would arrive with his drawings in a leather briefcase bought especially for the purpose—he had never used a case of the kind himself and fumbled with the lock—and let himself drop into the armchair.

"Would you mind shutting the door?" he would ask.

I would turn round to Maria at her typewriter and say:

"All right, Señorita, please leave us alone for the moment. I'll call for you later."

She would shut the door carefully.

"Well now . . . I've come to see you because Don Julián—he's an old client of yours, of course—told me I could trust you and speak freely."

The man would entangle himself in his words, trying to evade the necessity of showing his drawings, for fear of being robbed of the millions surely awaiting him.

What a labor it was to convince people of the fact that their "invention" had been known to the world for years, or that their machine could not function because it was against the laws of mechanics. A few, a very few, saw it and left, bowed down under their knowledge, shattered. You had killed their spirit, and you felt compassion for them. But the great majority looked at you out of feverish eyes, pitying you greatly, and demanded that you should register a patent for them. You were unable to understand their genius. They had come to see you, not in order to convince you of their ideas, but simply to register their patent through you; then they would convince the whole world of their invention.

And since a Spanish patent is a document granted to whoever applies for it in the correct legal form and pays the fees to the State, you had to give in. The inventor was perfectly contented and invited you to lunch with him, and you had to listen to the story of how he had conceived the idea, of the calvary he had passed through, and of his extravagant hopes.

"Imagine," he would say, "that one out of every thousand inhabitants of Spain buys my apparatus. At five pesetas. That makes one hundred thousand pesetas. And then we take it to America, with a market of millions and millions of people—it'll be millions of dollars, you'll see."

Yet those were the innocents among the many who passed through my confessional. More frequently the deep leather chairs held great figures in industry and commerce who laid bare all their sense of power, all their cynicism: "Business is business, you know."

A professor of chemistry at Madrid University discovered a process by which hitherto insoluble alkaline earth salts became soluble. His discovery implied a revolution in various industries, and the inventor knew it. There was a side to it which immediately affected the general public. In the process of extracting sugar from beet or cane molasses, only fourteen to seventeen per cent of the sugar content of the solution was obtainable, because insoluble alkaline earth salts obstructed the separation of the remainder. By the professor's method, eighty-five to ninety-two per cent could be extracted. This meant that from the same quantity of raw material, five times as much sugar could be obtained as before, and that production costs would be reduced to a fifth.

While the patent was pending in several countries, the managing director of an alcohol distillery turned up in my confessional. His firm figured as Spanish, but German capital was behind it, and it possessed a virtual monopoly of industrial alcohol in Spain.

"Barea, I want to see a copy of that patent."

"It's still pending, and I can't let you have it without an authorization from the inventor."

He handed me a letter from the inventor, authorizing me to give him a copy of the patent and further detailed information. When he had read through the material, he asked:

"What's your opinion of the patent?"

"I think it's very interesting. England and Germany have granted it."

"But do you believe the process will work?"

"He's demonstrated it to me in his laboratory. I don't know about its commercial exploitation, but in the laboratory it's child's play."

"Hm. I want you to take action for an annulment of the patent."

This man's company was an old client of ours.

"I'm sorry, but we can't undertake it. We are the inventor's agents, after all."

"I know that. What I want is that you should take charge of the affair, that's to say, that you should handle it without figuring in public. The only one to figure will be the firm's lawyer. But he doesn't know the first thing about patent law, and so I want you to direct him."

"But do you realize that an action wouldn't have an earthly chance? The patent is solid, it's genuine, and it can't be declared null and void just like that."

"I know all that, but . . . well, I'll explain how things are. We buy all residues from molasses for our alcohol production from the Sugar Refinery. The inventor has signed a contract with the Sugar Refinery. That means that, in future, their molasses residues will contain about five per cent of sugar instead of eighty-five per cent. You will understand that we have a right to defend our business interests. As soon as we start proceedings against the patent, the Sugar Refinery must suspend the contract."

"But that won't give you the annulment of the patent."

"Of course not. But the inventor is a university professor. And we have a capital of several millions. The case will go through all the stages of appeal and it will last years and years. The firm's lawyer gets his fees from us anyhow, so that the only extra expenses will be your fees, and the cost of the action. We won't get the patent annulled, but we'll ruin the inventor."

We did not accept that deal, but we undertook the defense of our client, the inventor. His contract with the Sugar Refinery was cancelled. The lawsuits consumed his private means, a family fortune of some two hundred thousand pesetas. His patent remained valid. But big business had the last laugh. For five years I had to handle that man's affairs and follow his bitter experiences. A Dutch firm which produced sugar in the Dutch East Indies showed interest in the patent. When this firm had tested the process, it offered five thousand guilders for all patent rights. The inventor rejected the proposal with indignation. The answer was that they only wanted to acquire the patent in defense of their interests—for who would want to put it into practice, with a sugar surplus on the world market and the sugar business in a crisis owing to surplus production? A U.S. enterprise was even more brutally direct: "We don't know what to do with the Cuban sugar, and you want us to pay cash

for the right to produce five times more of a product we cannot sell?"
I felt no interest in the inventor as an individual. But I was fascinated
by the economic problem the patent case represented. In Spain, sugar was
one of the most expensive of all primary commodities. It was the un-
official monopoly of a trust which controlled the sugar-beet prices and
had its strong tendrils in politics, so as to maintain prohibitive customs
duties on imported sugar. The sugar-beet growers in Aragon were paid
starvation prices for the raw material; the consumer, who had no other
choice in buying, had to pay an exorbitant price for the finished product.
To the Spanish poor, sugar was a luxury article, and had been ever since
Spain lost Cuba. I remembered only too well the frugality with which my
mother had measured the small spoonful of sugar for her beloved coffee.

And this was not an isolated case by any means. Through my confessional of glass and steel passed dozens of the big sharks, each with
his own special, discreet recipe for multiplying his capital, whatever the
cost. To my confessional came men who crossed Europe by air and signed
fabulous contracts between the coming and going of a plane. Expensive
agents of their masters who kept somewhere in the dim background, they
arrived in impeccable clothes which did not always suit them, polished,
suave, bland, convincing in their deals, often incredibly brutal and primitive in their enjoyments after business. I had to see them dressed to kill,
and naked, in business and at play, for it was my job to be the agent of
those agents.

I have met many sane businessmen and industrialists, honest within
the limits of their human search for more money and greater scope, and
I never believed they were evil just because they were businessmen. But
there were those others, those who hadn't names like Brown or Mueller
or Durand or Pérez, but who were called the "British," the "Nederland,"
the "Deutsche," the "Ibérica," with the impunity of the anonymous; who
destroyed countries to increase that intangible, irresponsible power of
theirs. Their agents and managers, the people someone like myself would
meet, had only one standard: dividends. But to the trust or combine it
was important that they should appear legally honest. If it was necessary
to bribe a Minister, the firm gave the money, but its agent had to know
how to do it in such a form that no one would ever be able to prove
where the money had come from.

From my vantage point in the economic machinery I came to know
those concerns which could afford to give free shares to impoverished
or avaricious kings, and to make or unmake a Government, only to have
laws passed of which not only the country at large but often even Deputies of the Chamber were ignorant.

But they were too powerful for mere words to reach them.

I knew who had paid two hundred thousand pesetas for the vote of the highest law court in Spain, in order to procure a decision in his favor in a lawsuit which determined whether Spain should have an aircraft industry of her own or not. I knew that the Catalan cloth manufacturers depended on the mercy of the chemical concern, Industrias Químicas y Lluch, which was nominally Spanish but in fact belonged to none less than the I. G. Farbenindustrie. I knew who had given and who had taken thousands of pesetas to procure a verdict which meant that the Spanish public would not be able to buy cheap radio sets. I knew the intricate story of how, thanks to the stupid blindness of Spain's barrack-room dictator, an international firm assumed control of the whole Spanish milk industry, ruined thousands of small businessmen, ruined the dairy farmers of Asturias, and forced the public to pay dear for milk with reduced nutrition value.

But what could I do about it?

Those men and those things passed through my confessional. I was a very small cog in the machinery, but the driving power had to pass through me. And yet, I was given no right to think and see for myself; they considered me as complementary of them, as one man more who was starting on their career. And they confessed themselves to me.

At school I had found myself caught in the wheels of a hypocritical educational system which traded in the intelligence of its charity pupils, so as to attract as boarders the sons of wealthy mine-owners. In the army, I had found myself caught in the wheels of the war-makers, shackled by the Military Code and by a system which made it impossible to furnish proof of corruption, but easy to destroy a little sergeant, had he tried to rebel. Now I found myself caught in yet another system of cogwheels, seemingly less brutal, but infinitely more subtle and effective. I could rebel—but how?

You might go to a judge and tell him that the manager of a certain alcohol distillery was attempting to rob an inventor of the fruits of his work, and a nation of cheap sugar. But the judge did not exist for such matters; he existed so as to prosecute you if you committed the offense of violating professional secrets. Those other things were not an offense, they were legitimate business. The company had the legal right to combat a patent it thought invalid; the inventor had the legal right to defend himself. If he was unable to do so, lacking the millions he would need to fight an anonymous concern during five years of lawsuits, that was not the fault of the judge or the law, but the inventor's bad luck.

If I denounced the deal before a judge, he would laugh me out of his presence, and my boss would put me in the street. I would lose my name as a loyal intelligent worker and find all doors shut to me. I would starve,

haunted by my family's reproaches. They would call me an idiot. I might
have to go to prison for slander. For slandering those who took the cream
from the milk of Madrid's children, who stole sugar from them, for
slandering honorable and decent people who followed their legitimate
business.

I thought of all this while I listened to the lawyer of the German Embassy, young Rodríguez Rodríguez. He was explaining the action by
which we were to attack the patents for the manufacture of bearings for
railway coaches. What was at stake was an order of the Northern Railway
Company for several thousands of special bearings, an order which involved a million pesetas or so. The bearings the patents for which he
wanted to attack were the speciality of a French company, and the com-
petitor was the German Reichsbahngesellschaft.

Rodríguez Rodríguez was the prototype of a Madrid playboy. His
father had for years been the lawyer of the Germany Embassy—and of
many concerns of German heavy industry. He himself had succeeded his
father, although he had nothing but the title and degree of a lawyer. He
served the Germans in a double capacity. The lawsuits he undertook
did not gain public attention, as those of greater forensic lights would
have done; and he loaned himself to all kinds of machinations with an
easy unconcern. Immensely vain of his position, he had come back dazzled
from his last journey to Berlin. As soon as we had finished discussing the
patent action he proposed, he poured forth praise of German doctors and
hospitals as he had found them when he was treated for a broken arm.
And then they had made him a member, not just of the National Socialist Party, but of the S.S. He showed me a photograph of young men
in black shirts, he himself in the middle.

"Now, what do you think of that?"

"You look superb in uniform. . . . Now, tell me frankly, Rodríguez,
what the hell do you want out of this Nazi business? You're Spanish."

"Of course I am, and they wouldn't have taken me if I hadn't been
a member of Falange. It's an honor to become a member of the S.S., don't
you see? And besides, I'm convinced Hitler's ideas are right. They're what
we Falangists want for Spain. We need the sort of thing here that Hitler's
done in Germany. Remember what the mob did in Asturias. If they
hadn't been made to feel a firm hand, we would now have a Spanish
Lenin and be Russia's colony."

"I won't discuss your ideas about the workers and the Republic, they're
your affair. But don't you think you're going to make us into Hitler's
colony, which surely means going to the other extreme?"

"So what? I should be delighted. That's exactly what we need in Spain —a whiff of German civilization."

"Now look here, friend Rodríguez—we've worked together for quite a few years—you know what's happening in Germany better than I do. You know what we may expect from Junkers, and Schering-Kahlbaum, and the I.G. Farben. You can't deny to my face, after all we've seen, that they are the masters of Germany."

"My dear Barea, in this world there are only two possible attitudes: either you get eaten yourself, or you eat the others. Of course I have to look after my future. And after my country's too."

"That's why you put on a German uniform?"

"But I'm working for my country that way. It's not a disguise. It simply means that we are working to make Spain into a strong nation."

"Who's working?"

"Our friends, the Germans, and a handful of good Spaniards like myself, who will have to put things into practice. Believe me, I'm not the only National Socialist in Spain."

"No, I know there are quite a lot of them, unfortunately. I don't know whether they all have their Party uniform, but they're in it somehow."

"Of course they won't let just anyone put on their uniform, and they don't make them members like me. But after all, in my position, I'm almost a German subject."

"With the slight difference that you're a Spaniard. I know they send you to Germany with a diplomatic passport, and a lot of errands and messages. But all the same, I don't think it's good business that you've let yourself in for."

"Time will show. And you'll change your mind, Barea. You'll have to, you see."

He left. I had my lunch and took the bus to Novés.

A little bridge rising in a steep hunchback over a damp, green gully lined with aromatic herbs and populated by thousands of frogs. All around, the dun earth of Castile, cut into parallel lines by plowed furrows. In front of the bridge, the gate of the flour mill, overhung by the grape vine on the wall. The big house a single splash of whitewash, made to look harder and whiter by the sunlight and the background of gray soil, by the gay frame of the vine and the green band of the gully which carries live blood through the dry fields.

I entered the flour mill and found myself in a cool gateway. Light, white dust floated in the air. In the corner gyrated two cone-shaped stones which crushed grain for fodder. The grain steamed under the pressure and a fine vapor arose, greedily inhaled by two patient donkeys at the door.

To the left, behind a wooden partition with a window, was Old Juán's office. So he said with a flourish, but at the same time he laughed at the description, for he found it difficult to write with his knotty fingers. In his grandfather's time accounts were cut on wooden slats with a knife, a notch for each sack of milled grain.

He chuckled and showed me a bundle of tallies, polished by the hands which had handled them for many years.

"I still keep the accounts for many people of my own age this way. But I have to keep those damned books as well!"

He led me through a narrow door into the mill proper, and it was as though we had come out of the land of sun into the land of snow. The roof of the hall was some fifty feet above our heads and had big, plate-glass windows. From the roof down stretched a thicket of beams and tubes, wheels and belts. But none of it was of iron, all was wood. And in the course of the years, the fine dust of milled grain had settled in the minutest cracks and crannies, and had clothed each piece in white velvet. It was like a snow-bound forest. Spiders had scaled the heights and hung their webs from rafter to rafter, from corner to corner. The white dust had lined them, and they were like pine branches laden with snow. The panes of the high, tall windows, powdered with impalpable dust, let through a pale winter sun which laid gray shadows on the machinery. The monotonous noise of the rocking cradle which sifted flour from bran was almost like the sound of a lumberman's saw in the mountains.

"Here you see our whole wealth."

"This is an old place, Uncle Juán."

"My grandfather built the mill. He must have been a progressive man for his time, because he installed a steam engine. It's still there."

When I looked at the steam engine, I realized what people will think of our own notions of mechanics in a thousand years time. It was an ancient thing with a misshapen flywheel, half buried in the ground, red with the rust of half a century, fretted by wind, sand, and dripping water, chinky, cracked, crumpled. It stuck out of the ground like the skeleton of an antediluvian animal struggling to the surface, its rods the broken arms and its enormous piston the neck of a monster stricken and twisted by a cataclysm.

"I've had an electric engine for many years now."

"And do you make money?"

"I used to make it. They brought wheat from Torrijos and Santa Cruz to my mill. At times even from Navalcarnero and Valmojado. Then Torrijos built a mill for itself, and so did Navalcarnero. It was Navalcarnero that did me most harm, because it's on a railway line. But you know, what finished us off was politics. Since the time of the dictatorship, one's had to live on the village, and must be grateful to live as it is. Well, I can't complain. I'm nearing seventy-five, my sons have their living, and I'll die here in peace." He stopped and pondered. "If they let me. . . ."

"I don't think anyone will quarrel with you. And as you say, when one's seventy-five, one doesn't expect many more changes in one's life."

"I don't know—really, I don't know. We old people see many things, or we feel them. It may be just our inborn fear of dying. When in '33 the lads went out to the fields and cut down my trees and killed my few heads of cattle and burned the ricks and destroyed the vegetable garden—believe me, it didn't frighten me very much, because something like that had to come. But then things happened in Asturias and now it looks as if we were all going mad. Things will come to a bad end. To a very bad end. And very soon too, Don Arturo. The people are starving, and hunger is a bad counselor. . . .

"There's nothing but misery in the village. The half-dozen people who could give work to the others won't do it, some out of anger and some out of fear of Heliodoro. The land lies fallow and the people haven't got enough to eat. Don Ramón, God bless him——"

"Who's Don Ramón?"

"He's the village grocer. You must have seen his shop behind the Casino. He's a good, kind man, only he's crazy about the Church, and it's just as if they'd bewitched him. Don Ramón is one of the best—which doesn't mean that he wouldn't give you a few grammes under weight, though. Well, it used to be like this: every time anybody came to him and said: 'Don Ramón, do let me have some beans, or a bit of dried cod, and bread, and I'll pay you as soon as my husband starts working again,' he let the woman have something and put it down in his books. If they paid him, it was all right, but they often didn't or couldn't. When people had some misfortune, or when somebody in their family died, he took his pencil and ran it through the account: 'Don't worry, woman, that's settled. And may God forgive me, as He may forgive the one who's dead.' But then, between Heliodoro and Don Lucas——"

"Now, who's your Don Lucas?"

"Our priest, and he's one of the sharp kind. I was going to say, between the two of them, they've won him over, and now he doesn't give a bread-crumb to the poor any more. Because Don Lucas told him it was a mortal sin to help the godless, and Heliodoro said it was necessary to get a tight grip on those rascals, and if Don Ramón wanted to help them, he—Heliodoro—would get a tight grip on Don Ramón."

He made a long pause.

"The worst of it is that the people take it all in silence. In the morning they sit down in the plaza, on the stone wall along the road, and keep silent. In the evening they go to Eliseo's Casino and keep silent there. In '33 a few of them came near my mill, but they had some respect for me and knew they could always get a piece of bread in my house when they needed it, and so they went away again. But next time they come—and they will come—I don't know . . . For they'll come soon. You'll see."

Suddenly, Old Juán's pride as a host swept away his pessimism. He took an old earthenware Talavera jug, ingenuous blue flowers on a milky ground, and led me to a huge wine jar stowed away in a small room.

"Let's have a drink. You won't get another like it in Madrid."

Slowly we drank the cool, rough wine which frothed in purple bubbles against the glaze. We handed each other the jug and drank from the same side, as in an ancestral peace rite.

Aurelia was in a bad temper that day. After lunch we took the children for a walk in the orchards. She had prepared a snack which we went to eat by a stream at the bottom of the green gully. But her face did not change. In the end, she said:

"This village is so boring."

"What's the matter now?"

"Nothing. It's just as if we belonged to a different race."

"Well, what's happened now?"

"Nothing has happened, exactly. But you must see that those people are boycotting us. Because of course the better families in the village know by now that you're a Socialist and don't go to Mass and are seen in Eliseo's Casino. And naturally, all one gets in the street is a 'Good morning,' if that. And you must understand that I won't make friends with the country people."

"Why not? I should like you to."

"You would. But I think you ought to preserve your standing and——"

"And what? Go to the parties of the Reverend Father and invite Heliodoro's wife to our house? I'm sorry, but I won't. You can do as you like, but I haven't come here to go to parties."

"Of course, you go away early on Mondays, and I stay here the whole week long."

We grew sharp and bitter, both of us. The rest of Sunday passed in heavy boredom. When I left to catch my bus on Monday morning, the whole house was sleeping. I went away with a sense of liberation.

3. Unrest

I WAS about to finish signing my bunch of letters. It was the pleasantest hour in the confessional. The sun had sunk behind the tall buildings on the top of the Calle de Alcalá. A cool breeze blew into my room and made the canvas curtains belly and crackle. In the street down below, people began to cluster for their daily stroll. The noise of the beehive came up as a dull drone punctuated by the cries of the newspaper boys selling the early evening papers, the shrill tinkle of tramway bells and the bark of klaxons. It was a noise we no longer heard, but which was there, day after day.

When a sudden silence fell, it was so strong and unexpected that I stopped writing. Maria interrupted her typing and turned her head. The typewriters in the outer office stopped. It lasted only an instant. Then a shot sounded, and it was followed by a deafening roar from the multitude. Amidst the shouts I caught the sound of people running in all directions and of iron shutters being pulled down with a clatter. Then came a few more shots and the musical note of breaking glass. We ran out on to the roof terrace.

A wide space in the street below was deserted. At the fringe of this sudden void, crowds of people were running madly. Opposite us, at the corner of the Phoenix Building, some half-dozen people were leaning over a bundle on the ground. It looked ludicrous from our height. We could see the street in its full length. At our feet it widened into a sort of square, where the Gran Vía and the Calle de Caballero de Gracia joined it. Some cars were standing, probably abandoned by their occupants, and a tram had stopped and was quite empty. From our altitude the men in the little group were soundless and small, they were gesticulating like puppets in a show. Two of them lifted a still smaller figure, doubled up at the waist. A stain was left on the gray asphalt of the pavement. It looked black. A heap of newspapers beside it flapped in the wind.

Shock Police[1] arrived in an open lorry. The men clambered swiftly out, truncheon in hand, as though they intended to attack the lonely group.

[1] The *Guardia de Asalto,* here translated Shock Police, was set up by the Spanish Government in the early days of the Republic, as a corps loyal to the Republican authorities and qualified to replace the old Civil Guard, the rural constabulary which traditionally served the interests of the great landowners and their *caciques.*—Author's Note.

A taxi appeared in the still square. The wounded man and those who
supported him boarded it, and the taxi sped up the street. The Shock
Police hurried to the doors of the cafés. People again flooded into the
street and formed groups which the police dispersed.

I finished my mail and we all went downstairs. But police stopped us
on the first floor of the building. The Café La Granja had a door which
opened on to our staircase, and there the police had been posted. They
demanded identity papers and searched all of us. When we reached the
front door, we found the wife of the concierge sitting on a chair and
recovering from an attack of nerves under her husband's care, while a
police officer took notes. There was an intense smell of ether in the air.
The woman was saying:

"I was just standing in the doorway and looking at the people walking
past until the lads came who sell the *Mundo Obrero*. 'Now there'll be a
row as usual,' I said to myself. Because the young gentlemen of *FE* were
already standing in the door of the café with their papers and their sticks.
But nothing happened. The boys with the *Mundo Obrero* came running
and crying out their paper just as they do every day, and then the young
gentlemen started crying out their *FE,* but nobody paid much attention.
So it looked as if nothing was going to happen this time, until one of the
lads of the *Mundo Obrero* stopped here at the corner with two of his
friends. And then a group of four or five of the others came up at once
and pulled away his papers, and they came to blows. The people all
around ran away, and then one of the young gentlemen drew something
out of his pocket and shot the lad with the papers. Then everyone ran
away and the poor boy was left lying because he couldn't get up."

For weeks, it had been a daily occurrence that the Falangists waited
for the Communist paper to appear in the streets, and then began to cry
out their own review, *FE.* The people who sold those papers were not
professional newspaper vendors but volunteers from each party. After a
few moments the two groups would be involved in a row which ended
in faces being slapped, in an occasional broken head, and, inevitably, in
soiled and trodden newspapers scattered all over the pavement. Timorous
people would feel frightened and hurry off, but as a rule the passers-by
considered these scenes a stimulating spectacle in which they themselves
often felt moved to take a hand.

This time it was serious.

The next afternoon, signs of unrest became visible from half-past five
onwards. Workers who had finished in their shops at five seemed to have
agreed to meet in the Calle de Alcalá. You could see them arrive and
walk up and down in little groups with their meal packets under their
arm, exhibiting themselves provocatively between the tables on the ter-

race of the Aquarium, the smart café in which the bigwigs of Falange met. The number of police posts had been increased; people were made to pass on. You could see groups of Falangists passing groups of workers, exchanging looks and mumbling insults. The conflict was still to come. When the first shouts of *Mundo Obrero* came, they were answered by shouts of *FE*. For a few minutes, the cries filled the street with their challenge, and the supporters of each party flocked round their newspaper sellers to buy a copy. Suddenly one of the groups—from our altitude we could not see which—scattered; there was a scuffle, and at once the whole street became a battlefield. The Shock Police hit out with their truncheons at everyone within their reach.

Very soon the superior strength of the workers became clear, and a group of Falangists took refuge in the Aquarium. All the window panes in the door of the café were smashed. Glass showered on the pavement, and broken chairs and tables rolled on the ground. A carload of Shock Police fell upon the assailants. Once more the Calle de Alcalá was left deserted except for the Shock Police and a few passers-by who hurried through.

After supper I went to the People's House. In the half-empty café I found a group of men I knew, discussing the events of the evening and the day before. When each one had made an excited speech, an elderly man said:

"The worst of it is that all these violent happenings are only cooking the stew for the benefit of the Communists."

"So what—are you afraid of them?" said another mockingly.

"I'm not afraid, but what I see is that they're getting into our own ranks. To the Falangists everyone is a Communist, and of course we'll defend ourselves when they hit out at us. But at the same time we have to tell people to be patient, and so they go over to the Communists."

"Well, you're one of Besteiro's reformists, aren't you? You believe that things can be settled with velvet gloves. And that's a mistake. The Right is united—and we pull in all directions, each group on its own, and what's worse, each of us calls the others dirty dogs. The whole thing's mucked up."

The man who spoke banged a bundle of papers down on the table.

"Just read this, they're all our papers, Left papers. And what's in them? The Communists attacking the Anarchists, and the other way round. Largo Caballero together with Araquistain attacking Prieto, and the other way round. I'll leave out Besteiro, because nobody listens to him any more, and anyhow he never talks about revolution in the streets. But all those others talk about it, each about his own brand of revolution. If we don't get together quickly, the same thing will happen here as happened in Austria: Gil Robles and Calvo Sotelo dictators, and the Vatican dictating."

"That won't be so easy. The people will rise as they did in Asturias."

"And the same thing will happen as happened then, or worse, don't you see? Don't think I'm talking of what might happen in the moon. That old ditherer, Chapaprieta, won't be able to save his Government, and as soon as they've got him to resign—as they will—our dear Mr. President, old 'Boots,' will have to do one of two things, either make Gil Robles Premier, or dissolve the Cortes. And he won't dare to dissolve the Cortes, because it would cost him his job, whether the others win the elections or we do."

I did not take much part in the discussion, but I thought the pessimist was largely right. I was afraid he was right.

The then Premier, Chapaprieta, was clearly the head of a transition government, intended to mark time. He was a man without the backing of a political party, without a majority in the Cortes, in office only to steer the Budgets through. Gil Robles, the leader of the Right, would not fail to exploit the opportunity of bringing things to a head.

It was the most favorable situation for the parties of the Spanish Right. The parties of the Left were utterly disunited. It was not so much a disagreement between Republicans pure and simple and Socialists or Anarchists, but the deep split which followed from the fight for the masses in which each Left party had staked its bid. Azaña, the leader of the Left Republicans, commanded a large section of the middle class and could hope to win over a considerable part of the workers. The socialist trade unions of the U.G.T. controlled a million and a half workers, the anarchist unions of the C.N.T. the same number or more. The number of adherents was difficult to establish exactly, and the boundaries of influence were shifting. And both fought for the decisive influence among the workers. But there was also a struggle within each of the organizations. Officially, the U.G.T. acknowledged the principles of the Socialist Party, the C.N.T. those of the Anarchist. The opinions among their members were not always governed by the official line. The Socialist Party itself, and with it the trade unions under its influence, were divided into a left wing under Largo Caballero, a center under Indalecio Prieto, and a right wing under Besteiro. The C.N.T. was split, less clearly but no less deeply, into the supporters of "direct action" and the supporters of "syndical action," political anarchists and anarcho-syndicalists. In both great trade union centers there was a group which favored, and a group which opposed, the fusion of both into a single trade-union association. On the whole, it was the left wing of the Socialists and the U.G.T. which worked for such a rapprochement. But to complicate matters, it was in this left wing that the influence of the Communists began to make itself felt, and there existed an open and ingrained hostility between Communists and Anarchists.

It is very Spanish to "let oneself be blinded only to rob a neighbor of his eye," as the proverb says. So it could happen that Anarchists were pleased when Communists were attacked by Falange, and that Communists did their best to attack the Anarchists by means of official oppression, coming from a government equally hostile to the Communists themselves.

I think all of us who did not belong to a party bureaucracy counted those divisions and subdivisions of the Left over and over again in mental despair. And yet it seems to me now that, in stressing the splits of the Spanish Left, we were and are falling into a grave error.

For all those paralyzing splits and fights obsessed only the political leaders of each group and their collaborators, or immediate supporters—a minority. The average man who belonged to the Left felt differently. Out of instinct, out of emotion, if you prefer it, and without theoretically marshaled arguments, the vast majority of the Spanish working class Left wanted a union which would wipe out the resentments and differences that had scarcely ever been real to them. Yet the experience of the result of union was very real: the Republic had been born out of an agreement between the organized Left parties. In the Asturias rising, the miners had fought under the slogan of U.H.P., "Union of Brother Workers." And the longing for such a "union of brothers," mystical and strong, was alive among the masses in that second half of 1935, when it was clear that without it the Right would assume absolute power and send many thousands more into the prisons, to rot with the political prisoners who had been there since Asturias.

It took a long time before the confused urge of the members and supporters was converted into measures of common self-defense by the leaders of the Left.

The united front of the Right, however, embracing leaders, members and sympathizers, impressed itself on me—and others like me—in daily incidents.

I saw it most clearly on the minute battlefield of Novés.

I like walking in the lonely, vast lands of Castile. There are no trees and no flowers, the earth is dry, hard and gray, you seldom see the outline of a house, and when you meet a laborer on his way, the greeting you exchange is accompanied by a distrustful glance, and a savage growl from the wayfarer's dog who refrains from biting you only thanks to the harsh order of his master.

But under the sun of the dog days, this desolate landscape has majesty. There are only three things, the sun, the sky, and the earth, and each is pitiless. The sun is a live flame above your head, the sky is a luminous dome of reverberating blue glass, the earth is a cracked plain scorching your feet. There are no walls to give shade, no roofs to rest your eyes, no spring or brook to cool your throat. It is as though you were naked and inert in the hand of God. Either your brain grows drowsy and dulled, in passive resignation, or it gains its full creative power, for there is nothing to distract it and your self is an absolute self which appears to you clearer and more transparent than ever before.

A burning cigarette in the midst of the deserted plain assumes gigantic proportions, like a loud-spoken blasphemy in an empty church. The flame of the match disappears in this light and becomes less flame than ever. The blue smoke of the match mounts in slow spirals, gathers and thickens in the still air to a whitish little cloud and sinks down to your feet, grown cold and invisible. The earth swallows it. The air presses it down to the earth. The light dissolves its blue against the blue of the sky. When you throw away your cigarette stub, the white smoking patch seems more disgraceful than if you had thrown it on the richest carpet. There it stays to tell everyone that you have passed.

Sometimes I have felt so intensely like a criminal leaving a trail that I picked up the stub, crushed it out on the sole of my shoe and put it in my pocket. At other times, when I found a cigarette end lying in the field, I have picked it up out of sheer curiosity. If it was still damp, it meant that somebody was near. A cigarette rolled with coarse paper would indicate a farm worker, a machine-made cigarette a man from the town. Brittle edges and yellowing paper meant that the man had passed days or even months ago. When I saw those signs I would breathe more freely, for in the lonely plains of Castile, an instinctive fear is reborn in you and you love solitude as a defense.

That morning I had gone for a solitary walk in the fields round Novés and come back with an active mind, my brain washed clean, but my body tired and parched. I sat down at one of the tables José had put before the entrance of the Rich Men's Casino.

"Something very cool, José!"

He produced a bottle of beer covered with dew. He leaned over my tables and asked, as they all asked:

"How do you like our place?"

"Well, I like it. I prefer villages which are not townified. Perhaps it's because I'm fed up with the town."

"If you had lived here all your life like me you would want to get away."

"Of course. . . ."

Opposite the Casino the road dipped down and a low stone wall bordered it on the side of the gully. A dozen men were lined up along it. They were watching us in silence.

"What are they doing there, José?"

"They're waiting for something to happen. For a windfall. But if the moon doesn't fall. . . . You see, Don Arturo, it's customary for the men who are out of work to come here in the mornings and wait until somebody hires them for some small job or other."

"But it's almost noon, and Sunday into the bargain. Who the devil would hire them today?"

"Oh, they just come because they're used to it. And then, on Sundays the gentry come here for their glass of vermouth, and sometimes one of them has an errand to be run, and that means a few coppers. And sometimes one of the men dares to beg a little money. The poor devils must do something after all. They deserve what they've got, though."

"Do you mean they deserve to starve to death?"

"Goodness me, I don't mean starve to death, as you put it, because one isn't quite hard-hearted, after all. But it's a good thing for them to learn their lesson. That'll teach them not to get mixed up with Republics and things, and to go wanting to put the world in order. Because you've no idea, sir, what this place was like when the Republic came. They even let off rockets. And then they started at once demanding things, for instance, a school. There it is, up there, half finished. If they don't put the money up themselves, their Republic won't."

On the road there emerged a horseman on a black horse covered with scars and sores. A gaunt figure encased in tight black trousers which molded his calves like the fashionable trousers of the nineteenth century, a black riding coat with rounded tails and a bowler which must have been black in its time, but now was the color of a fly's wings. A Quixote in his late seventies, with few teeth left, but bushy brows over lively black eyes, a goatee and a few snow white tufts of hair sticking out from under his hat. He dismounted, threw the reins over the horse's neck and beckoned one of the men sitting on the stone walll.

"Here, take him to my house."

The man caught the reins and dragged the horse past the Casino into a doorway beside the pharmacy, some ten yards from where I sat. The rider came towards me, beating a tattoo on his shin with his riding whip.

"How d'you do, I've been waiting to meet the Madrileño. Do you mind if I sit down here?" He did not wait for my assent but simply sat down.

"What's yours? Beer? José, two beers." He paused and looked at me. "Possibly you don't know who I am. Well now, I'm their accomplice"—he nodded towards the two village doctors who had just arrived and sat down at another table, hunting in pairs as usual—"that's to say, I'm the apothecary, Alberto de Fonseca y Ontivares, Licentiate in Pharmaceutics, Bachelor of Science—Chemistry—landowner and starveling to boot. These people here never fall ill, and when they do fall ill, they haven't any money, and farms produce nothing but lawsuits. Now tell me about yourself."

He was amusing, and I gave him a brief sketch of myself and my work. When I explained my profession, he clutched my arm.

"My dear fellow, we must have a talk. Do you know anything about aluminum?"

"Yes, of course. But I don't know exactly what interests you about aluminum and whether my kind of knowledge is likely to be any good to you."

"Never mind, never mind, we must have a talk. I've made a most interesting discovery, and we must have a talk. You'll have to give me advice."

I was by no means pleased at the prospect of having one of those cranky inventors next door to me in the village, but it was impossible not to respond.

The man who had led away the horse came back, took off his cap and stood there, waiting, a couple of yards from us. Don Alberto gave him a stare.

"What are you waiting for? A tip, eh? All right, this is a red letter day—here you are—but don't think it will happen every time. And what's that you've got there in the pocket of your blouse?"

The man reddened and mumbled:

"Doña Emilia gave me a piece of bread for the kids."

"All right, all right, may you enjoy it."

I stood up. Don Alberto wanted to discuss his discovery, but I had not had my meal and I did not like looking at the silent men lined up along the wall.

We had our discussion later in the day, in the back room of the pharmacy. Doña Emilia listened, her knitting needles clicking. Her chubby hands moved swiftly. Otherwise, she consisted of tight rolls of fat in calm repose. Sometimes she looked at her husband over her spectacles. A sleepy cat in an old rep armchair opened its eyes, two green eyes with a vertical black slit, whenever its master raised his voice. The room was dark, not because of lack of light, for light entered freely through a wide window opening into the sunlit street, but because everything inside the room was dark: dark purple, almost black curtains and carpets, the four arm-chairs raisin-colored, darkened by age, the wall paper a blackish blue with tarnished gilt scrolls.

Don Alberto explained:

"As I told you this morning, I'm a landowner. May God give us good earth! I've got a big field rather like a graveyard, all studded with stone slabs, and four miserable cottages in the town. The tenants don't pay rent, and the ground lies waste. But I have to pay the taxes every year, like clockwork. Thank goodness, we've got a bit of our own and this pharmacy to live on. As you saw, every day, no matter what weather God sends us, I saddle my horse and we go off for a ride in the fields. You can't imagine how often I've taken a ride across my fields. Then, one day, I saw a fellow squatting on the ground there and digging little holes. I wondered what he was up to, so I accosted him and asked: 'What are you doing, my good man?' and he answered in poor Castilian: 'Nothing, just pottering. Do you know who owns this land?' 'I do,' said I. 'It's quite good soil, yes, isn't it?' he answered. 'Not bad if you want to sow paving stones.' He stared at me and changed the subject and started telling me that he was a German and liked Spain very much, and so on. He told me he thought of building a little house in the country. He found the landscape round here very pleasant, he said. Now, you see, you've got to have a very thick skin to say that without blushing. Because that landscape is as bare as my palm. I said yes to everything and thought: 'Now what has this rogue got up his sleeve?' When he was out of sight, I went back to my piece of land, collected a few lumps of the soil and shut myself up here in the back room. My dear friend"—Don Alberto said this very solemnly—"my soil is bauxite. Pure bauxite."

He gave me no time to show my amazement, but changed from enthusiasm to rage with lightning speed.

"And that German is a scoundrel. That's why I called you in."

Doña Emilia dropped her knitting in her lap, raised her head, wagged it and said: "What's your reason, Albertito?"

"Be quiet, woman, let us talk."

The knitting needles resumed their monotonous seesaw, and the cat again shut its green eyes. Don Alberto went on:

"A few weeks ago he turned up here. He had decided to build himself a house in this marvelous spot, he said. He had liked my land so much. And as it wasn't arable land, he assumed that I would be willing to sell it cheaply, because he wasn't exactly rich. I couldn't refrain from saying: 'So it's a little house in the country you're wanting to build—a little house with big chimneys, eh?' He showed himself most astonished. 'Yes, yes, don't play the innocent now. You think I don't know what you're after.

Luckily, I haven't quite forgotten my chemistry.' My good German chuckled broadly and said: 'Good, now we will understand one another better, yes? You must realize that I have to look after my business and if you hadn't got wise to what's in your soil it would have been more economical from my point of view. But never mind. How much do you want for your land?' I said: 'Fifty thousand duros—two hundred and fifty thousand pesetas.' My German laughed loudly and said: 'Now, don't let us waste our time. The site has been registered in accordance with the Law of Mining Sites. So we have the right to expropriate your ground and the adjacent land. I offer you five thousand pesetas in cash and twenty thousand in free shares of the company we will set up. Think it over and you'll see that it's best for you.' I told him to go to the devil. But now he's sent me a summons to appear before the judge to settle the question of the expropriation of my land in amity. What would you advise me to do? Those scoundrels think they'll get my land for a chunk of bread."

What advice could I give to this village apothecary? If Germans were mixed up in the affair, the prospectors were doubtless financed by some important firm in Germany; and no one knew the power and the means at the disposal of those people better than I. Don Alberto had the choice between getting a handful of pesetas and entering on a law suit, with the result that the pesetas he might be paid in the end would not cover the costs of the brief. Obviously, they had him in a trap and there was no escape for him.

I explained the legal situation and advised him to try to hold out for the biggest possible sum, but not to involve himself in litigation.

He waxed indignant.

"So those rogues come from abroad and rob us of the fruits of our labor? That's the whole history of Spain. Those people come here where no one wants them and take the best for themselves. There you have Rio Tinto and the Canadiense and the Telephones and the Petrol Monopoly and I don't know what more. And in the meantime, we can starve! What we need is a strong Government. What we need is that the Chief should take the whole thing into his own hands."

"The Chief? What Chief?"

I knew very well whom he meant. Gil Robles was being built up as the great Leader, the *Jefe,* and his name coupled with the title "Chief" was being dinned into our ears. But I did not feel like accepting this chieftainship unchallenged.

Don Alberto said: "There's only one Chief. The man who'll save Spain: José Maria Gil Robles. The man whom the whole nation backs."

It had always been one of my incurable weaknesses, one which had earned me much enmity, that I tended to revert in the middle of a serious, polite conversation to the mode of expression of a Madrid street urchin and of a soldier in the African Army—to blurt out what I thought with the greatest directness and in the worst language.

I answered Don Alberto with a grin:

"Well, I don't think that our country will be put in order by that church rat."

Don Alberto turned a flaming red, more intensely red because of the white frame of his hair; he rose and flashed a wrathful glance at me. The knitting needles stopped short and the cat got to its feet, arched its back and clawed the rustling chair cover. Solemnly and melodramatically, Don Alberto pronounced judgment:

"You will realize, Don Arturo, that you and I cannot continue to exchange words."

I had to leave, somewhat ashamed and annoyed with myself for having lost my sense of fitness, and yet rather amused by the attitude the good man had struck. But there came a sequel to that conversation, one week later.

I was standing before the church tower, figuring out its structure. Its foundations were Roman, and the brick walls built on the square hewn stones very many years later were doubtless Moorish work. It would have been pleasing to know the hardships the ancient tower had gone through at the time it was a fortress, or a watchtower, or whatever it might have been.

A fat voice spoke to me from under the porch:

"Sightseeing, eh? Haven't you the courage to come into the church? We don't devour anybody here."

Don Lucas, the priest, was standing in the porch of the church and watching me with a slightly mocking glance.

"I was looking at the architectural muddle of this tower. But I would indeed like to have a look at the church, if its Cerberus has nothing against it."

"Cerberus has nothing against it. This is God's House, open to everyone. Of course, if it's antiquities you're after, there'll be little for you to see. This is just a big barn of a building."

The church deserved the term. Smooth walls, whitewash on mortar and stone, with half a dozen altars ranged along them, each with its saint in life size, made of papier-mâché and painted in gaudy colors. A wealth of embroidered altar cloths, stiff with starch, bronze candelabra and paper flowers smothered in dust. A confessional on each side of the High Altar. Behind the entrance a Christ on the Cross, the Holy Water stoup on one side and the font on the other. Two rows of benches down the middle,

and a score of chairs with straw seats scattered here and there. The only
pleasant thing was the coolness of the nave.

"It's true that there isn't much to see."

"I'll show you our treasure."

He took me to the sacristy: two huge commodes with plated locks,
presumably the most valuable stuff in the whole church, a vaulted niche
with an old wooden carving of the Child Jesus, a pulpit, a bench along the
wall, a monkish armchair, some church utensils laid out on the commodes.
On the front wall the oil painting of a Saint Sebastian with a somewhat
feminine body, a painting of the chromolithographic school of the late
nineteenth century.

The priest—well filled and fleshy, rather like a pig with his very small
eyes and thick, bristling hair and stubble on his chin, bristles on the
broad, heavy hands, thick, red lips, altogether a peasant polished by the
Seminary—sat down in the armchair and invited me to take a seat on
the bench beside the pulpit. He took out a leather cigarette case and we
both rolled ourselves a cigarette. He puffed some smoke and then looked
straight at me.

"I've noticed, of course, that you don't go to church on Sundays. I know
you're one of those Socialists and have dealings with the low people of
our village. I must tell you, when you set up house here and I saw your
wife and children, I thought: 'They seem the right kind of people. Pray
God it be so.' But—it seems I was mistaken."

He did not say this in an insulting manner. When he made his little
pause after the "but," he did it with a mild, almost evangelical smile, as
though he apologized for his daring. Then he stopped, looking at me, his
two heavy hands on the table.

"Well now. It's quite true that I have socialist ideas, and that I don't
go to Mass on Sundays, nor my people either. And it's also true that, if
all that means being the wrong kind of people, well, then we are the
wrong kind of people."

"Don't get bitter, Don Arturo. I didn't want to molest you. But you
see, I can understand it in a way if one of those yokels doesn't believe in
God and the Devil. But to find someone who appears to be an intelligent
man thinking as they do . . ."

"The fact that I don't go to Church doesn't necessarily mean that I
don't believe in God."

"Now don't tell me that you're one of those Protestant heretics—it
would pain me greatly—but in that case I would not be able to tolerate
your presence in this Sacred House for a single moment."

"In this Sacred House which is the House of God and therefore open
to everyone, isn't it? Don't be afraid. I'm no heretic. It didn't occur to

me to change the label. The trouble with me, I think, is that I've suffered from too much so-called religion all my life. You can rest assured, I've been brought up in the lap of Holy Mother Church."

"But why don't you go to church, then?"

"If I tell you the truth, we shall probably quarrel."

"Just speak out. I prefer to be plain and to know where I am."

"Well then, I don't go to church because you clergy are in the Church, and we don't get on together. I was taught a faith which by its doctrine was all love, forgiveness, and charity. Frankly, with very few exceptions, the ministers of the faith I have met possess all sorts of human qualities, but just not those three divine qualities."

Don Lucas did not enter this field. He chose a tangent:

"What should we do then, in your opinion? For instance, what should I do? Or, to put it clearly, what would you do if you were in my place?"

"You're pushing me into the personal sphere. It is possible that you yourself are one of those exceptional priests I've mentioned, and some of whom I have known and still know. But if you want to hear what I would do in your place if I were a priest, it's quite simple; I would drop the post of Chairman of Catholic Action—that's what you are, I think—so as to obey your Master's Law 'Render unto Caesar that which is Caesar's,' and that other Word which says that His reign is not of this world. And then I would use the pulpit for teaching the Word of Christ, not for political propaganda, and I would try to convince all people to live together in peace, so that the poor need no longer perish, lined up along the stone wall of the road waiting for a piece of bread as for a miracle, while the rich let the soil lie waste and each night gamble away enough money to wipe out all the hunger in Novés."

It was now that the priest took offense. His lips went grayish white and quivered.

"I don't think you can claim the right to teach me my duties. In this place there are a good many of the rabble who need one thing, and one only: the stick. I know you think our Chief is a 'church rat.' But whether or not it pleases your friends, the revolutionaries, who want to push Spain into the greatest misery—he is the man who will create a great Spain. I'm sorry to say that you and I can't be friends. You've come to disturb the tranquillity of this place. We'll each fight for his own side and God will help those who deserve it."

I left the church in a pensive mood. This was a declaration of war in due form from the masters of the village, although I had not yet interfered in the village life.

It also gave me a practical demonstration of the unity within the Right Wing. Don Alberto was an old Monarchist. Don Lucas was a politicizing priest. Heliodoro was nothing but a ruthless usurer, exploiting the political game. The two doctors had not the slightest interest in the Church or in politics, so long as they had their racket. Valentín gambled his farm away. Others believed they had the bounden duty to stand against the workers, simply because they themselves belonged to the landed class. None of them had strong political or religious ideals, and yet they sallied forth as one man to defend a policy and an ideal. Was it precisely their lack of convictions which permitted them to unite? Was it the existence of ideals which made it difficult for us of the Left to be united?

The logical inference was that those men united to defend their property and their position. But why could not the leaders of the Left unite to defend what position and chance of position they had? Why was it that the men in the street, the common people, the workers, the farm laborers, and the miners, were always ready to get together—and not their leaders?

It was not I who asked this. In those days of the Indian summer of 1935 all Spain asked this question, even our enemies.

4. Ballot

UNREST and uncertainty made me seek for something unchanged and secure in human relationship. But my mother was dead.

My mother had died in harness, seventy-two years old, tirelessly working, however tired she may have felt, helping my sister Concha through her many pregnancies, taking over the care of the children and the housework, helping her by taking a post as concierge in a tenement house so that Concha and Agustín, her husband, should have free lodging, helping them with her own scanty earnings through the long periods when Agustín, a skilled cabinet maker, was out of work during the series of strikes in his trade.

There had been a hard time, before I myself had won through to comparative prosperity, when my mother and Concha had to accept the assistance of charitable institutions. There existed a Home for Washerwomen, founded by Queen Maria Christina; my mother applied, not for herself, but for children's clothes on Concha's behalf, and received help from the nuns who ran the Home. There also existed a State institution called "Drop of Milk," *Gota de Leche,* where mothers of small children could obtain free milk. Concha applied, and was granted a daily milk ration for which she waited in a queue, while our mother looked after the children. But they had to pay for this charity by figuring in the lists of those who regularly attended Mass, and by presenting the parish priest's certificate to show that they had partaken of Holy Communion. This did not make it easier to accept charity.

My mother never grew bitter. She was proud of her usefulness and bore with the "things of life," as she would say, with a cheerful resignation and skeptical hopefulness. But it made me bitter, and at times, when I felt least able to help, unjust towards my sister.

It was natural that my mother should go to help her daughter. But it hurt and irked me that my mother was so little part of my own home because she was unable to get on with Aurelia. Clearly as I realized the defeat and emptiness of my marriage, I could not bear strictures from others, not even from my mother, still less from my brother, my sister, my brother's wife, and my sister's husband, who all agreed in disliking the woman who was, after all, my wife.

My mother died in 1931. I had little inner contact with the rest of the family. But now, when the open failure of my marriage was an accepted fact and I felt the chill of a great change in my bones, I resumed a closer friendship with my brother and with my brother-in-law. We three had been much together when we were young boys. We knew a lot about each other, without having to explain anything. The women, my wife, my sister, and my sister-in-law, hated one another and met as little as possible. Agustín, short, square, slow to speak and slow but capable in his movements, with a hidden vein of shrewd satire and plenty of horse sense, placid and reliable, gave me a feeling of rest and safety, and when he spoke he was as infallible as Sancho Panza at his best. But it was difficult for him to go out and leave Concha with the nine children, harassed and overworked as she was.

Thus Rafael, my brother, thin, colorless, and acid, more restless and more skeptical than I, became more than ever my silent companion.

When I dissolved my home in Madrid and set up my family in Novés, he let me have a bedroom in his flat. Escaping from the stale, sour atmosphere and the shallow gossip of his wife, we would go out after supper to walk through the streets, to stay for a while in cafés or bars where we had friends, and then to walk on in heated and pointless discussion

or in the familiar morose silence. And on some of the evenings I would
go out with Maria.

But my relationship with Maria was also in a stage of restlessness.

When I first came to the office, Maria was the least attractive of the
four typists. She was seventeen then, with black eyes and hair, angular
and bony. Her olive skin looked dirty, her neck was long and thin, her
chest flat. And she was highly strung and active, rapid of comprehension.
She was not particularly well educated, but quick on the uptake and a
good typist. I took her on as my secretary and we worked well togther.

Maria's face was pitted with pockmarks. This made her very unhappy
and she was continually conscious of it. It gave her comfort when I began
to tell her about the difficulties of my married life and my hopes of finding The Woman, because I tried to explain that I did not think so much
of physical beauty as of mutual understanding, of harmony, of fusion. I
was unaware at the time that I was seducing the young girl. Maria's plain
face denied her that homage which is freely given to attractive women in
the Spanish streets. She had no other contact with men than myself. And
I imagine that I had the kind of fascination for her which mature, experienced men so often have for very young women. In slow stages our intimacy grew. During those years the scrawny girl became a ripe woman
with a harmonious body. We slid into a love affair, inevitably, since I
wanted to find someone to whom I could give affection and who would
understand my language. The community at work and her ardent will
to please me were a substitute for love.

We were discreet in our relationship, but did not try to hide it. It was
an open secret. In the true tradition of a Spanish marriage, in which the
wife does not overmuch mind an affair of her husband's, as long as it
does not absorb him forever and as long as there are no illegitimate children, I had no great trouble with Aurelia. She did not feel her funda-
mental position threatened by Maria, and we had a few acrimonious
discussions, but no more. There was no difficulty on the side of Maria's
family either. She lived with her mother, a brother, and a younger sister.
The mother knew of our relationship, but ignored it in silence, I think
because she regarded Maria as a girl who would never marry and therefore had the right to enjoy her life as best she could.

We had agreed that we would both remain completely free, but six
years had created a very close intimacy between us. Even though I had
never been in love with her, I had been content in those six years.

Now I was no longer content. Nor was she.

One Saturday morning Maria tackled me:

"Are you going to Novés this afternoon?"

"Yes, of course."

"I'm fed up with this arrangement. Every Sunday I'm left alone, and I'm getting bored. My sister goes out with her girl friends and I can't go with her."

"I don't see why not."

"Most Sundays they go to a dance. If I go I must dance too, because they all know I love dancing, and I can't pretend I don't."

"Well, what more do you want, then? If you feel like it, go to a dance and dance yourself, of course. You know I'm not jealous. But I can't stay here on Sundays. We're together all the week. Anyhow, we thrashed all this out in advance, and you agreed with me about it."

But Maria insisted that I should stay in Madrid. She did not want me to stay every Sunday, only from time to time, and particularly this time. I sensed she had something definite in her mind and let them know in Novés that I would not come for the week-end.

On Saturday night we went to the theater together. Maria showed more interest in the details of life in Novés and in discussing my wife's behavior than in the plan. On Sunday we made a day of it and went to El Escorial. When we were lying in the grass, before us the overpowering range of mountains which encircles the monastery, Maria suddenly said:

"Now, what do you intend to do?"

"What about?" The question had caught me by surprise and produced no mental association in me, although we had discussed my matrimonial affairs off and on during the day.

"About Aurelia."

"You mean, what can I do? I can only get a divorce, and I can't see why I should. It would be bad for the children, they would be much worse off without me, and it wouldn't do me any good either. I'd have to stay alone and live in a boarding house, or stay for good in my brother's flat. I'd live less comfortably and spend much more money. It would have been worth while if I'd found my woman."

I did not mean to be cruel. I had been talking spontaneously, just as I had talked for years, about my own problems. Maria watched me, and her eyes were full of tears.

"I don't mean anything to you, then . . ."

"But—child—our case is something quite different."

"Of course it's different. For you a pastime and for me a closed door." She began to weep bitterly.

"But listen, what is it you want me to do? To get a divorce and live with you? Or to marry you?"

She wiped away her tears and smiled.

"Of course, you silly."

"But don't you see that it wouldn't do? Now, everybody is tolerant about us and shuts both eyes. The moment we do what you want, they would all be against us, and particularly against you. Can't you see? In the office they wouldn't keep you on, probably neither of us, but certainly not you. . . ."

"Once we lived together it wouldn't matter. I would stay at home."

"All right, granted. But you don't see things as they are. If we lived together, they would treat you as an ordinary tart. If we married, they would treat you as the woman who has seduced a married man and destroyed a home. Even your family wouldn't like it, I presume."

"Never mind about all those things. I'm of age and can do as I like. If it's only that—it doesn't matter to me what people call me."

"But it matters to me."

"Look how little you love me!"

The conversation rang hollow and false, but we went on and on. From that excursion we came back in an antagonistic mood. I understood Maria's attitude and hopes, but I had no intention of realizing them. A divorce followed by a joint household or marriage would have meant no more than an exchange of one woman for another, with the prospect of more children and the boredom of married life without love. Maria was in her own right while she worked with me as my secretary and listened to my personal worries and problems; she was in her own right as my comforter. She would lose all this in a marriage. I would lose the secretary and the comforting listener.

My attitude and line of action were coldly and pointedly selfish. I knew that. It gave me a chill feeling in the pit of my stomach. I did not like myself, and I did not like her. She had broken our pact. I knew she was right in her way, and I thought I was right in mine. It was not as though she just wanted to get her man; she was convinced that her affection for me would make me happy, that even if I was not in love, I was very fond of her, and that I had no hope of ever meeting the woman of whom I used to talk and think. After all, she knew very well that I was thirty-eight years old, an age at which a man begins to be a fatalist in matters of love, or a skeptic.

But I was not altogether a skeptic. And it was not that I wanted to get rid of her or to exploit her coldly. We had had our good times. But I knew that the imposition of a life together would destroy the friendship and fondness born out of loneliness and grown in loneliness.

Our discussion was closed, but it left a tension in the air. Maria did not repeat her demand, but she intensified her attentions to me, down to the smallest matters. She wanted to show me that she was a perfect woman not only as a lover but also as a housewife. Her tactics were wrong. I was not interested in living with a good housewife. She only made me feel irritated and bored. It amused but also annoyed me to see how Maria tended to behave as though we were a good bourgeois couple. We often went to a night club to dance, but now Maria began to tell me that we ought to behave more discreetly.

"If anyone saw us like this, he would think there was something behind it."

"My dear girl, he would only think what's true."

"But I don't want people to think I'm one of those women. I love you just as if you were my married husband."

By the end of 1935, I was in a state of acute irritability and desperation. I avoided contact with both women, and I could not escape either.

At that time began the campaign for the impending elections. For several weeks the mass excitement and the knowledge of what was at stake swept all private problems from my mind.

When Premier Chapaprieta submitted the Budgets to the Cortes, the Right began a systematic obstruction. Chapaprieta had to resign. President Alcalá Zamora—"Boots"—was an old fox in politics, a *cacique* from Andalusia who during the Monarchy had kept himself in power by managing elections in his district, and who in the last stage of the Monarchy had turned himself into a Republican. Chapaprieta's resignation involved the position of the President. Gil Robles held the majority in the Cortes, and the President would have to call upon him to form a Cabinet. Alcalá Zamora was not opposed to a Right Wing and Catholic Government; he was a militant Catholic. But he preferred to become the Dollfuss of Spain himself, rather than to leave this role to Gil Robles. And Gil Robles had attempted to put pressure upon Alcalá Zamora, a fact which the old boss could not easily forget.

The President entrusted Portela Valladares, an independent Republican, with the formation of the Government. The idea was that he would use all the resources of governmental power to prepare elections in favor of the moderate Center, the group which Alcalá Zamora wanted to represent and which would then sway the votes of the Cortes in one or the other direction.

But the game was obsolete. It had been played with success in support of the Monarchy ever since 1860. But now the country was no longer politically indifferent; it was full of effervescence, deeply divided into two opposite camps. Alcalá Zamora's game had no chance of success; it was never even properly started. As soon as Portela Valladares announced his Cabinet, it was attacked by both Right and Left. He resigned. In December 1935, Alcalá Zamora dissolved the Cortes and announced the 16th of February 1936 as the date for the new elections.

The constitutional rights of citizens were restored. The propaganda battle began. The Right hoisted the anti-Communist flag and frightened prospective voters with accounts of the great damage which a Left victory at the elections would do to the country. They predicted chaos, and gave color to their prediction by multiplying provocative street incidents. The parties of the Left formed an electoral bloc. Their list of candidates comprised all shades from Republicans to Anarchists; they focused their propaganda on the atrocities which had been committed against the political prisoners after the Asturias rising and on the demand for a general amnesty. Yet at the same time the dissension between the parties of the Left grew. The Left press devoted at least as much space to mutual attacks as to attacks against the Right. Everyone feared a Fascist *coup d'état* and voiced this fear, and proclaimed his particular brand of Revolution as the only way out. Largo Cabellero accepted the title of Spain's Lenin and the support of the Communists. His group told the masses that a victory at the elections would not be the victory of a democratic bourgeois· State but of a revolutionary State. The Anarchists also announced the coming victory of a revolutionary State, not after the pattern of Soviet Russia, but based on "libertarian" ideals. After the "Two Black Years" of oppression, it was like an intoxication. The lid was off. Every single individual was discussing the political situation and taking active part in the propaganda for his ideas.

I entered the fray in Novés.

Eliseo received me with a shout of welcome when I entered the Poor Men's Casino:

"We've been waiting for you. We've decided to prepare for the elections here, and we want to set up an Electoral Committee."

"A very good idea."

"But we want you to organize the whole thing. We don't know anything about anything here, and we do want to do things well. Heliodoro and his gang have got it all organized on their side. They're promising the people everything under the sun, and at the same time they threaten them if they don't behave. And hunger is a bad counsellor. Now, you've got friends in Madrid, so if you help us we'll get meetings and make propaganda. Anyhow, you know what I mean."

I had my roots in Madrid and not in Novés, but I could not refuse to take an active part in what I believed to be a decisive moment for Spain and for our socialist hopes. These people needed someone who could not be intimidated by the Corporal of the Civil Guard or trapped by dubious maneuvers, someone who could save them from committing foolish or illegal acts and thus giving the other side a handle. It crossed my mind that it would give me satisfaction and diversion to plunge myself into the elections and that it would keep me aloof from the two women as well.

I saw instantly that a victory of the Right, and even perhaps a victory of the Left, would mean that I would have to leave the village at once. But Novés was drawing to an end for me anyhow.

I accepted the task.

The first thing I did was to seek contact with Carlos and Antonio.

Carlos Rubiera was an old member of the Socialist Youth Organization, whom the Party put forward as a candidate at the elections. We had worked closely together in 1931 to found the Clerical Workers' Union in Madrid; our trade union had flourished and gained victories, Carlos was well away on his political career. He had often invited me to join the Socialist Party as a member or to become an official of the trade union; I had refused, because I felt unfit for a political career, but we had remained good friends. He was a very gifted orator and organizer.

Antonio was a Communist, and an old friend of mine. I knew exactly how honest, how poor, and how narrow-minded he was. He had been a little clerk who earned a pittance and had no prospects in life other than to go on earning a pittance and keep himself and his mother just above starvation level. In 1925, while Antonio was in a sanatorium with tuberculosis, his mother died in misery. When he reappeared in Madrid, cured, he earned just enough to live. It would not have been enough for any vice, but smoking and drinking had been cut out by his tuberculosis, and Antonio had become afraid of women since his illness. He became a Communist, one of the earliest Communists in Spain, and he followed his faith with the zeal of a fanatic. In 1936 he was a minor party official.

Rubiera and Antonio let me have propaganda material for Novés, gave me hints on organizing an electoral committee, and promised to send Left speakers to the village.

The next Saturday afternoon we set up the Electoral Center of the Popular Front in Novés.

That evening José called me aside and led me to his house, at the back of the Rich Men's Casino. While his wife served coffee to the customers, José hauled out a bottle of cognac.

"You'll excuse my inviting you here, but we must have a talk. I've got to give you some advice."

"Oh, well, thanks. But I don't remember having asked you."

"Don't get annoyed, Don Arturo. It's a friend's advice, because friends must show themselves when they're most needed. I've a great respect for you and your family, and I can't keep my mouth shut any longer. It's not as if I had a personal interest in the question. I'm concerned with my business, and that's all. But I know our village, and you're a stranger here. You won't change it."

"And what exactly is your advice?"

"That you shouldn't get mixed up in these elections. Let the people settle their own affairs, and don't play Don Quixote. Of course—if you've got it into your head to go on working with Eliseo's gang, you'll have to get into the bus as soon as the elections are over, and never come back. If they let you go, that is . . ."

"You mean to say, if the Right wins the elections."

"Or the Left. You believe things will change here if the Left wins, but that's your mistake. Things will go on here as always. They won't let their land go, one way or the other. And where there's money there's a way. You never know what's going to happen. After all, we're all mortal."

"Good. That's the message Heliodoro gave you for me?"

"If you want to take it that way. . . . It's true he told me that you ought really to be warned and that he couldn't very well do it himself. But this is my own idea, because of my esteem for you."

"Many thanks, José. But I don't think I'll change my mind. It may well be that you're right and that I'll have to pay for this by getting out of the village. But I have to stick to my people."

"Well, think it over. And just in case—but this is really my own idea —don't walk about too much at night when you're alone. Our people here are very rough, and there's been trouble at every election."

When I reported this conversation in Eliseo's Casino, it caused a great stir; whenever I went out at night afterwards, two hefty young men with cudgels accompanied me everywhere.

I went to Santa Cruz de Retamar to see the Corporal of the Civil Guard about the legal formalities. He received me with a surly face.

"And who ordered you to get mixed up in all this?"

"I've a right to do so, haven't I? I'm a householder in Novés and have the right to take part in the village life.' '

"All right. Here are your papers. I should stay quietly in my house, if I were you, because if I'm not very much mistaken, there'll be trouble at the elections. For me the situation is quite simple. It's my duty to maintain order, whomever it may affect. So you have been warned. Look out."

Carlos Rubiera and Antonio kept their promise. Four speakers of the Popular Front were coming to Novés on Sunday: one of the Republican Left, one Socialist, one Communist, and one Anarchist. With the exception of the Republican, who was a middle-aged man, they were all young lads, completely unknown in politics. The news produced an upheaval at Eliseo's.

"We need the ballroom!"

The ballroom belonged to the inn where the bus stopped and where the post office was installed. I went to see the owner.

"We should like to rent your ballroom for a meeting next Sunday."

"You'll have to ask Heliodoro, he's booked it for the whole time until Election Day for meetings of the Right. I can do nothing for you." ·

Heliodoro received me in his office with the pomp of a great man of affairs, entrenched behind a huge walnut table and surrounded by piles of paper. He answered with a frosty little smile:

"I'm extremely sorry, but I can't help you. I need the room."

Discouraged, I went back to Eliseo's. We could not arrange an open-air meeting in the middle of January. But Eliseo hit upon the solution.

"They're dirty rogues, those people. Heliodoro can't rent the ballroom, because, you see, it is rented by the municipality. The Municipal Council pays Rufino"—the inn-keeper and postmaster—"so-and-so much per year, and the only right he's got is to set up a buffet when there's a dance. He just can't sublet it."

I returned to Heliodoro. He bridled.

"I've rented the ballroom, and I've got the receipt here. If you want to enter a legal action against Rufino and the Municipal Council, you're welcome, but please leave me out of it. . . ."

I went to the Corporal and explained the case. He shrugged his shoulders. There wasn't anything he could do. I lost patience.

"Now listen. The other day you told me you were here to maintain order, whomever it might affect. The ballroom is here for the free use of the whole population. I won't cancel the meeting, and the meeting will be held in the ballroom. You can settle it however you like, that's to say, if you don't want the thing to go beyond mere words. And I can tell you something: this won't be a matter of a few village lads. Tomorrow I shall inform the parties which organize the meeting, and report the things that are going on here, and the responsibility will fall on you, because it's your obligation to solve such questions without further trouble."

The Corporal of the Civil Guard beat a retreat. There was unrest in the villages and towns of the province, which had suffered particularly severely from the vindictiveness of the landowners during the Two Black Years. The Corporal foresaw that it would come to an open conflict for which he would be made responsible in the end. That same night he spoke to Heliodoro. And Heliodoro conceded me the ballroom.

"This is a personal favor out of consideration for you and the Corporal. I don't want trouble which would lead to a serious incident, any more than you. What we want is public order."

During those weeks, I spent almost every evening in Novés and went back to Madrid early each morning. On one of those evenings, Aurelia handed me a letter:

"Here, José brought it for you. And he's been telling me plenty of things. I can't think why you've got to go and interfere in those elections."

The letter was a communication from the Novés Farmers' Circle—the official name of the Rich Men's Casino—informing me that the General Assembly had decided unanimously to cancel my membership. We celebrated it at Eliseo's that night. The Novés Workers' Circle made me its honorary member. After that, we went out to stick the posters of the meeting on walls and hoardings.

It turned out a radiantly sunny day. The plain in which Novés is ensconced is one of the coldest spots of Spain in winter. The winds from the Sierra de Guadarrama which sweep it freeze the soil deep down. But the village in its gully is sheltered from the winds, and on sunny days people prefer to stay out in the open, so as to get away from their dismal houses. The place comes alive. The women sit on low stools outside their house doors and chat, and their children run round playing; the men stand in groups in the market square and the young people go for walks in the orchards, holding hands.

That Sunday the village looked alien. From the early morning onwards, people from the near-by villages arrived for the meeting of "those Madrid people." The main street was filled with peasants and land workers accompanied by their wives and children, all shouting greetings at each other, all noisy and excited. The ballroom was hung with Popular-Front posters and its door stood wide open. People went in and out in a continuous stream to show each other the new sight. At midday a number of women turned up with chairs which they planted along the walls, determined not to lose the spectacle or their seats, even if it meant waiting for hours.

The ballroom was an old stable converted into a place for entertainment by the simple expedient of putting up a wooden platform and framing it with draperies of red calico. A little side door led to this dais from the inn stableyard. A sheet hung between the two red draperies served as a screen for films or as a curtain for theatrical performances. When there was a dance, the band occupied the dais. At the other end of the room a sort of balcony had been fixed to the wall; it would be reached by a ladder with a cord for a railing, and was reserved for distinguished guests at theatrical functions, and for the film projector at other times. The floor was beaten earth, and some tiles were missing in the roof so that the sunbeams came through, or the rain, or the snow.

On the dais we had set up the table for the chairman, with a dozen chairs in a semicircle behind it, and a smaller table for the speakers, both covered with the tricolor of the Spanish Republic in calico. The meeting was to start at three in the afternoon and we had arranged that the speakers should first have a meal at my house. Some of the village lads went to the edge of the gully and lined up at the side of the road to warn us of the coming of the car. At noon the pair of Civil Guards arrived and took up their posts outside the ballroom door. They loaded their carbines with ostentatious care.

"Are you going to kill us, then?" an elderly woman asked with a smile.

The Corporal gave no answer, but looked at the woman out of lackluster eyes. A few of the men went at once to Eliseo's and told me of the incident.

"You can't imagine what his eyes were like when he looked at the poor woman. Do you think there will be trouble?"

Eliseo brought a pistol out of his house and stuck it under his belt, in the pouch of his blouse.

The car arrived at half-past twelve and was received by the cheers of hundreds of people. Heliodoro must have hated it. I had to shut the doors of my house to prevent an invasion.

The only one of the speakers who knew the village was the Socialist, a member of the Land Workers' Union of Toledo. The three others were from Madrid. The Republican was a short little man who looked like a natty clerk. He spoke slowly and with great emphasis, and was unable to say a single sentence without mentioning Azaña. The Anarchist was a young waiter, bright and agile, who seemed to be rehearsing for the meeting by indulging in a stream of words whenever he said anything. He found his match in the Communist, a young metal worker who let loose a torrent of phrases sprinkled with quotations from Marx and Lenin. The four of them were a little nervous.

"Now tell me what the people in this place are like," said the Communist.

"Just as in all the other villages. They're above all interested in the land and the school."

"That's one of the things the Party will do first—we're going to organize the Komsomols—I mean, the Kolkhoses—in Spain as they've done in Russia, with model farms and cattle and splendid dairies. In the Ukraine——"

I cut him short: "Listen, it seems to me that you won't establish any dairies here, not even with goats. There are no more than two cows in the whole village, and I don't think they've ever seen a pasture in their lives!"

"Well, what have they got here?"

"Excellent orchards, corn land, and a *cacique* who owns half the village."

"All right, we'll liquidate him." He said it as simply as if he had destined a chicken for the oven.

"Democracy's what we need, democracy and tolerance—a lot of tolerance," said the Republican. "Don Manuel"—Azaña—"is right. Don Manuel said to me one day: 'Those Spanish villages, those rotten boroughs, need schools, friend Martínez, schools and bread, and the elimination of their parasites.' "

"Don't kid yourselves, we Spaniards are all Anarchists at heart. We can't make do here with Socialism or Communism, and you"—the Anarchist addressed the Republican—"have nothing to lose here. What we need is a new society with the cornerstones——"

"Hear, hear! But first, I don't want to have to listen to your speeches twice over, secondly, let's leave our dirty linen at home, and thirdly, we're going to eat now," I said. I was not happy about the meeting, particularly when the conversation at table followed the same channels.

When we entered the platform from the side door, we saw before us a moving carpet of heads and a splash of motley gay color in the background. They had put the women in the "boxes" as a precaution, and their garish kerchiefs and blouses shone out. The men were standing; outside the entrance there were over two hundred people who had not found room in the ballroom. The doors stood wide open so that they should hear the speeches, and the men jostled each other and stretched their necks to see.

Teodomiro, the Mayor, a creature of Heliodoro's, was sitting on one of the chairs behind the presidential table.

"Well, well, what are you doing here?" I asked him.

"I represent the authorities."

There was nothing to be said against this. I opened the meeting. The Communist, as the youngest of the four speakers, took the first turn. He started by explaining the assets of a Popular Front. He spoke rather well, with a certain nervousness and big gestures, but with fluency and conviction. The public, well disposed in advance, lapped up his words and interrupted him from time to time with applause. Then he touched on the subject of the Asturian rising.

". . . one of the great aims of this alliance of the Left is to free our prisoners. We all have a prisoner to set free, a murder to avenge. In the name of those who were assassinated at Oviedo . . ."

Applause interrupted him. The Mayor rose, waving his hands, then banged his fist on the table.

"Silence, silence!" A surprised silence fell. What was that fellow going to say? Teodomiro turned to the Communist: "If you mention Asturias once more, I'll suspend the meeting. I represent the authorities here."

I told the speaker in a whisper to limit himself to propaganda for the elections and to leave out Asturias, since this was better than to lose the meeting. But Teodomiro clearly had his instructions; he interrupted the speaker at every sentence after that. In the end the young man was thrown out of his stride. The Republican leaned over to me.

"Let me deal with this. I'm an old fox."

I told the boy to come to an end in the best possible manner, and then Azaña's little man faced the public.

"I wanted to speak to you and explain my personal opinions, which in very many points coincide with those of my friend, the previous speaker. But we must respect the authorities as represented by our friend the Mayor, and as I don't wish him to interpret my words in an adverse way, I will speak to you in the words of Don Manuel Azaña, words which he pronounced at the public meeting of Comillas and to repeat which I do not believe his Worship the Mayor will refuse me the right."

"Quite so, quite so," said Teodomiro.

"Well then, at Comillas Don Manuel said . . ." and the little man, who must have had a fabulous memory, recited entire passages of the famous speech which had moved the whole of Spain, passages which denounced the policy of the Church, the oppression of Asturias, the tortures inflicted on political prisoners, the scandals of racketeering and corruption, the deeds of violence committed by Falange. The public roared applause and hardly let him finish. Teodomiro was purple in the face and took council with the Corporal. The Corporal shook his head. There was nothing to be done.

The Socialist followed, and he had learned his lesson. Slyly he asked Teodomiro:

"I suppose you've nothing against my quoting words of Largo Caballero?"

The struggle was won. The Socialist and the Anarchist spoke, and the public was delirious, just as much because "their" speakers had scored a victory over the local powers and had carried through the meeting, as because of what they said. Everyone felt that this was less a defeat of the Mayor's little game than of his boss, Heliodoro, and the Corporal of the Civil Guard.

When at the end of the meeting, some people started singing the Internationale, I rose.

"I'll only say a few words to conclude this meeting. You saw what happened, and I suppose you also saw what might have happened. If you want all this to finish well, go out slowly, don't sing, don't shout in the street, don't stand about in groups—go home, or wherever you want to go, but don't give any occasion for trouble."

"Do you mean to insinuate that I've come here to put my foot in it and provoke something?" grunted Teodomiro.

"Oh, no, you've come here to represent the authorities and to avoid disturbances. There haven't been any disturbances during the meeting, thanks to you, and now I don't want any to arise in the street. Let him who hath ears . . ."

The meeting of Novés became famous in the region, and meetings were held in all the little villages around. The Popular Front found ample ground between Santa Cruz de Retamar and Torrijos.

But what happened in Novés on a small scale, happened throughout Spain, not always with the same turn of events. During the period known as the Two Black Years, the parties of the Right had entrenched themselves in the countryside and now they spared neither coercion nor promises nor gifts. Their efforts were particularly hectic in the cities. A giant poster showing Gil Robles addressing the multitude covered the whole front of a big house in the Puerta del Sol. So as to sow confusion among the members of the Anarchist trade unions, they published posters against the Communists, signed with the initials C.N.D.T., very similar to the Anarchist "C.N.T." Cardinal Gomá, Primate of Spain, issued a declaration in which he claimed that the Pope himself had asked him to appeal to the Spanish Catholics so that they should give their votes to the parties defending the Faith. Inmates of charitable institutions, cloistered nuns and the servants of big houses were taken to the ballot box in groups. In the working-class districts the offers of payment for each vote in favor of the Right rose to fifty pesetas.

The elections of February the 16th were a victory of the Popular Front. The Chamber met with 265 Deputies of the Left, 64 of the Center, and 144 of the Right.

The highest number of votes had fallen to Julián Besteiro, who was not a professional politician and whose theories were not shared by a great many workers, but who seemed to embody the longing of the Spanish people for culture, decency, and progressive social development.

When the high tide of enthusiasm had passed, the mass of voters went home. The politicians resumed their fight for power. The Popular Front began to disintegrate after the first session of the Cortes. It appeared as though the voice of the people had not been heard.

Novés underwent a change. The public offices were given to the people who had the best contact with the Popular Front Deputy for Torrijos. But the men who met at Eliseo's had played out their role as soon as they had voted, and Heliodoro brought the full weight of his economic power to bear upon the new administrators. There was no more work than before for the men who waited sitting on the stone wall along the road. "It will come very soon now, you'll see," said Old Juán. "You won't change things without trouble." A fortnight after the elections I moved my family back to Madrid.

5. Lining Up

I HAD found a large and inexpensive flat in the Calle del Ave María, a street hardly more than three hundred yards from the Puerta del Sol, yet belonging to the oldest working-class quarter of the city. I liked it because it was near the center and my place of work. But it had another attraction for me. It was one of the streets which led to El Avapiés, the quarter which had dominated my boyhood. My mother had lived three streets further down. My old school, the Escuela Pía, was so near that I could hear its clock striking the hours at night. Each street and each corner held a memory for me, and there were still old friends of mine living in the shabby tenement houses.

Aurelia, my wife, went there reluctantly. She admitted that the flat had the advantage of size, important enough for the four children, but all the other tenants were merely workers, and she considered ourselves as belonging to a higher social category, too good for such surroundings.

I suppose what I wanted was to get back to my own roots.

It was on the very morning when the lorry with our furniture arrived that Angel and I met.

The men who had come with the lorry began to unload and carry things upstairs. One of them was different from the four others who were big, heavy, sluggish porters. He was in the middle forties, short and very wide across the shoulders, his round face mobile like a monkey's. He worked harder that anyone else, smiling all the time and showing two rows of tobacco-blackened teeth. He drove the others on, pushed each piece of furniture into its exact place, made faces at the children or told a funny story to enliven his work, and bounded indefatigably to and fro.

When everything had been moved in I gave a twenty-five-peseta note to the driver, to be distributed among the five. When the little man bounced up to him, and asked for his duro, the driver stared.

"Why the devil should I give you a duro?"

"What d'you think? I've worked for it like the others."

"And who asked you to work? If the gentleman called you in he'll pay you himself."

"I thought he was one of your men," I said.

"Oh no, sir, we thought he belonged to you."

"Now look—I'll explain. But can I have a fag?" I gave him a cigarette. He lighted it, very much at his ease, and said: "I'm Angel, you see. They call me Angelito hereabouts. I've got nothing to smoke and I'm out of work—and it's not because I don't want to work but because there just isn't any. I saw the car with the furniture and said to myself: 'Let's lend a hand. We'll get something out of it, even if it's no more than a glass of wine.' Now, if you people don't want to shell out a bean, that's just bad luck for me. I won't ask anything of the gentleman, because it's you whom I've saved a lot of work, and so it's you who ought to pay me. But if you won't, never mind. *Salud!*"

He spat on the pavement and stalked away composedly.

I called him back.

"Don't go off like that. It's true that you might have asked before-hand. But we'll find something for you."

The lorry drove off and I felt like a drink, so I invited Angel to the bar in the ground floor of the house. In the doorway he asked me:

"Do you like wine?"

"Indeed I do."

"Then let's go to the tavern at Number Eleven, they've got a white wine that's good. I mean, if it's all the same to you. Because in this bar they ask forty centimos for a glass of beer, and for the same money I can drink four glasses of wine, the same size, over there. And I'll tell you something, I've been hungry for a glass of wine for months!"

We went to the tavern, I gave Angel his duro, and he told me his story.

He lived in the next street, the Calle de Jesús y María, as a concierge in a poor tenement house; he was married, but luckily he had no children; he had started as an errand boy in a chemist's shop, become a helper in the laboratory, and ended as an employee in one of the big pharmaceutical stores.

"And then, two years ago, I had words with one of the bosses, because I told him I had no intention of going to Mass. So they chucked me out. And I've been out of work ever since."

"Because you didn't go to Mass?"

"That's what I'm telling you. After Asturias they went and set up the Sacred Heart, with its little altar and all, in the middle of our store. And they told us we had to be there with a burning candle at the Feast of Consecration. They turned eight of us out into the street. Then, when I was applying for another job, those dirty swine wrote a letter saying quite simply that they had had to dismiss me because of Asturias. What had happened was that at the time when the fight was on in Asturias, our Trade Union told us not to go to work, and so I stayed at home two days. I'm only sorry because of my wife, she's had a thin time of it. Now I want to send her to her own people, they're quite well off and have got a farm in the province of Burgos. And I'll take the firm's Asturian certificate, and they'll have to take me on again and pay my arrears."

It was one of the Popular Front projects to enforce the re-engagement of staff dismissed during the reprisals for October 1934.

On the following day Angel turned up at my new flat. "I've come because, what with the moving-in, you'll be needing a lot of things here in your flat. I can install the light for you, paint the rooms, go shopping, or take the children for a walk. I've taken a fancy to your family."

For a few weeks Angel spent his time tearing layers of old paper from the walls, filling holes with plaster and painting the rooms. He continued to come when everything was in order; he helped in the house, and took the children for walks in the Retiro in the evenings. I liked him and he gave me the affection of a privileged family valet. He was the classical Madrileño, bred in the streets, cocky, carefree, and alert as a bird, always merry and very shrewd. In a few weeks' time he belonged to the circle that met every night in Emiliano's bar downstairs.

And so did I. For I could not take friends into the chilly emptiness of my so-called home life, and I did not want to stay there in irritation and isolation, or in empty disputes. Nor did I want to go out with Maria every night. But I needed to be with people who would make no demands on me, when I had finished with the complicated, often repellent and often disturbing operations of my day's work.

Every night after supper Rafael came to fetch me and we went down to Emiliano's bar to drink our coffee. There we met Fuñi-Fuñi. He had been at school with Rafael, and I had known him since I was a boy. He had been given his nickname at school because he first sniffed—"fnn-fnn" —and then sneezed every time he lifted his head and sniffed after every second word he talked. His nose was a tiny, soft blob with two holes stuck on to his round face, and he could not breathe through it properly. He was very shortsighted and wore big round glasses; his optician had to figure out a new kind of bridge for them, because otherwise they would never have stayed on. The mustache above his broad lips rose in rough bristles like a porcupine's quills, and the whole looked rather like the moon-shaped face, fringed with spikes, of some grotesque fish.

Fuñi-Fuñi lived close by and used to come to the bar to have a political discussion with Manolo, our concierge's young son. Fuñi was an Anarchist intellectual, imbued with political theory and abstract philosophy; Manolo was a skilled mechanic with communist sympathies, who swallowed every book on Marxism that fell into his hands. Rafael and I used to sit down with them, and Angel would join us.

For several nights Angel sat listening to the conversation with strained attention, losing the thread between names and quotations which meant nothing to him. From time to time he interrupted Fuñi.

"Who's the bird you're talking about now?"

Fuñi-Fuñi would explain about Kant, or Engels, or Marx, or Bakunin, and Angel would make odd faces while he listened. Then one night he hit the table with his flat hand and said:

"Now it's my turn. All those things you've been talking about day after day, and all those things you've just told us are just stories. I'm a socialist. All right. And I've never read that Marx or that Bakunin, and they don't interest me a bit. I'm a socialist for the same reason that you're an anarchist and Manolo a communist. Because we're fed up with things. There you go and get born into this world, and when you're beginning to understand what's what, you find that Father's out of work, Mother with child, and the cooking pot empty. Then they send you to school so that the Friars should give you food by way of charity, and as soon as you can, even before you've learned to read, off with you to work like a man. You get four coppers from the master and nothing from your mates, but all the time it's: 'Boy, bring me a glass of water.' 'Boy, take out those pails.' 'You'll get a kick in the pants.' And you get it too. Until you're a grown man, and then you earn a duro. A measly five pesetas. So what happens? You get infatuated, you marry, you have children, and next thing, you're out of work. Then your wife goes a-charing, the kids go to the Friars' school to get free soup, and you can run round in circles in the streets and curse. Well, and that's why I'm a socialist, because of all the ugly things yours obediently, Angel García, has had to swallow in the forty-odd years of his life. And now I tell you—shut up about Bakunin and Marx. U.H.P.! Do you know what that stands for? Union of Brother Workers. Just like the people of Fuenteovejuna, all as one. That's what counts. Because we don't get anywhere with all that balderdash from one side and the other, we just kick each other instead of getting together. And that's why the others will thrash us!"

Angel's rhetorical fire and gesticulations had attracted the other customers and they pressed round our table. When he ended they cheered him, and from that evening on he was the most popular speaker in all the taverns of the quarter. There he would stand and hold forth: "What about the priests? Well, the priests can go and say their Mass and let anyone who wants it have his confession or extreme unction. I won't say anything against that, because everyone is free to believe what he believes. But they shouldn't get a centimo from the State, and they should have to pay taxes on their business. So-and-so many Masses per year, so-and-so much income tax . . .

"And the rich? I wouldn't do away with the rich. If someone makes a lot of money because he's smart, well let him do what he damn well likes with it. But when he dies, then his money and his property go to the State. None of your inheritances, and none of your wealthy young gentlemen doing nothing. And there'll be limits to being rich. Beyond that limit not a centimo. Because in this business of the rich, it's the money we've got to settle, not the men. If someone has got money let him spend it, or put it in a drawer, but there won't be any more people living on dividends and interests. The State will have to look after their business and there'll be an end to all that coupon cutting. You understand me, something like what they've got in Russia. Over there, they give one of the Stakhanovites a hundred thousand roubles as a bonus, but he's got to go on stakhanovizing, because they've no Treasury bonds or shares which bear interest there. Here, if they give someone a hundred thousand duros, he puts them in the bank, and starts on the high life, and chucks his hammer on the scrap heap. And that's all wrong."

Angel treated me as though he were my henchman and wet-nurse at the same time. But he never knew how much moral support he gave me. The foolish and funny things he said when he was trying to brush away intellectual and political complications outside his ken were exhilarating, because behind them stood his sturdy loyalty and common sense, his belief that sooner or later all the working people would get together and settle their world sensibly and firmly. And he seemed irrepressible and indestructible.

Most days, before I went home for supper, and coffee and discussion downstairs in the bar, I left my office together with Navarro, our draftsman, and had a glass of wine with him at the tavern of the "Portuguese." There I looked at the melancholic, drowsy drunkard in the corner who was my old friend Plá, an aging and hopeless bank clerk, and listened to Navarro's problems, thinking of my own.

Navarro had dreamed of becoming an artist when he was young, and had become a draftsman in the Topographical Institute. His civil serv-

ant's pay was pitiful, and in the afternoons he made commercial publicity drawings, or mechanical sketches to accompany our patents. He
knew nothing about topography, publicity, or mechanics, but he had
learned how to make impeccably correct drawings, just as a shoemaker's
apprentice learns how to put nails into shoe soles. His drawings were
perfect in line, but they had to be checked very carefully because it meant
nothing to him to have left out a wheel or a screw.

He was married and had two sons, sixteen and twenty years old. His
work permitted him to keep his household on a comfortable level and to
let his sons study for a professional career. But he himself had become
a money-making automaton. His wife ruled the house, and she was entirely under the influence of her Father Confessor, a Jesuit, on the one
side, and of her brother, a Captain in the Civil Guard, on the other. Between them, the three of them managed the house and the sons who had
realized as young boys that their father was a nobody, while The Family,
their family, was the mother's, with an illustrious surname and a Captain
Uncle who had fierce mustaches and a post in the Ministry of the Interior. Both went to the Jesuit College in the Paseo de Areneros, and they
represented Navarro's gravest problem.

"I can't think what to do with the boys, Barea. Their uncle has put
them into that Falange thing, and now they go round with life pre-
servers in their pockets, and provoke rows with students at the university.
They egg them on at their school and send them to the university to
make trouble. What should I do?"

I could speak frankly and even brutally to Navarro:

"To tell you the truth, Juanito, you're simply not capable of doing the
only thing which would solve the problem. And the worst of it is that
it's you who will pay the piper."

"But what can I do, in God's name? Tell me what I can do."

"Buy a strong stick, get hold of the Captain, the Father Confessor—
and your wife—and tickle their ribs a bit. And then take the boys and
deal with them."

"You're a barbarian, and you wouldn't dream of doing it yourself."

"All right, I'm a barbarian, and that's exactly why I would not have
got myself into that particular mess of yours. But you're good, meek, and
helpless."

"But I don't want my boys to get mixed up in politics! Ever since
their uncle came back from Villa Cisneros where they sent him for taking
part in the August Revolt, he's been filling their whole mind with stories
about heroism and heroics. And they'll be badly caught one day. But
what can I do, Arturo, what can I do?"

His only consolation was to drink a glass of wine at the Portuguese's and to see all the Walt Disney films shown in Madrid. As one of his few intimate friends, I saw him quite often in his home and came to know the atmosphere of absolute, freezing intolerance in which this modest and tolerant man had to live. His wife eternally quoted her brother or her Father Confessor: "Pepe told me . . . Father Luis said we ought . . ." Navarro was haunted by a hopeless longing for a home where he could sit in his armchair in the midst of his family, with gaiety and warmth around him.

He arrived at the office one morning with a deeply worried face and wanted to speak to me.

A few days before, a tumultuous row had broken out between Right- and Left-wing students at the Central University. It had started with cuffs and blows as usual and had ended in shots: there had been one dead. Somebody had fired a pistol and a Republican student had been killed. During one of the following nights, Navarro had been working very late at home and had found himself without matches; he had looked for a box in the pockets of his elder son's jacket and found a short club made of a lump of lead tied with cord to a stick. The lead was stained with dried blood. In the morning, just after the son had left home, saying he was going to the University, the police had come to fetch him. He was hiding in his uncle's house.

Navarro was desperate: "Of course, the police will find him sooner or later. Or, what's worse, the others will have singled him out and they'll get him as soon as they can. Because each group keeps a list of the ones who stand out on the other side."

"It's just a youthful affair," I said unconvincingly.

"Youthful—stuff and nonsense. That's the work of grown-up men. People like his uncle and the black frocks get the boys involved and use them as cannon fodder so that they kill each other. I wonder if they won't employ my Luis, though. If the Right wins, it's on the cards that they will call in my Luis, and give him a living. And they'll promote the Captain to Major and Father Luis to Canon. It's I who have all the worries. His mother is in high spirits because of the boy's feat, his uncle calls him a hero, and his little brother has brought me a letter from the Reverend Fathers saying that they lament what happened—I don't yet know what has happened—but that we must all be patient because it's in the service of God and Spain. And here am I, his father, made a complete fool of!"

I was thinking that Navarro was unable to influence the course of his own life because he was shackled by his own character and his circumstances, and was just feeling an almost supercilious pity, when I caught myself up: was I not in a very similar state? Was anything achieved if one decided to submit to things as they were? Was it not better—perhaps —to rebel once and for all, and to know that it was one's own fault if everything crashed?

All the signs indicated that everything was going to crumble and crash. The country was drifting towards a catastrophe. Though the Right had lost seats in the Parliament, it had gained in the sense that all its supporters were now prepared to wage war on the Republic in every possible field. And they were in good positions to do so. The Right could count upon a great part of the Army officers, the clergy, home-grown and foreign capital, and the barefaced support of Germany.

The Republican parties, in the meantime, were subject to the pressure of the country which demanded that the reforms promised during the election should be put into force without further delay, and each of the parties exploited this demand to attack the others. Alcalá Zamora had been deposed as President of the Republic, and Azaña had been appointed in his place; this robbed the Republic of one of its ablest constructive brains. The Basque Countries and Catalonia increased the difficulties by their particular claims. The workers distrusted a Government in which there were no socialists of any shade whatsoever and which kept on temporizing. The debates in the Cortes were nothing but a mêlée in which the Right made the best use of the situation. Gil Robles, doubly defeated because his claims to Chieftain had been so flamboyant and his electoral strategy so unsuccessful, disappeared as the leader of the Right, and Calvo Sotelo replaced him.

As soon as the Government began negotiations about the Statute of the Basque Countries, then Galicia, Valencia, Old Castle, and Léon in their turn presented a claim to autonomy. When it came to the point of reinstating the workers and employees who had been dismissed from their posts after the October Rising in Asturias, some of the firms affected closed down, and others refused to take the men back. Angel had applied for his re-engagement; he was still out of work. Strikes broke out all over Spain and fantastic rumors were rampant. Everybody expected an insurrection of the Right. The workers were ready for a violent counter-move.

In the higher civil service and in the judiciary, the obstruction was barely disguised. The young man who had shot at the Socialist Jiménez de Asua was acquitted, although he had killed the detective who was guarding the Deputy; the acquittal was granted on the ground that he was mentally deficient and infantile—just a boy to whom his father, a high Army officer, used to give pistol ammunition "to melt down and make lead soldiers, because it kept the boy amused."

Day after day I stumbled on object lessons in my contacts with the Ministry of Labor and with our clients.

When I was a child, the Puerta de Atocha was the easterly boundary of Madrid. Beyond it was only the terminus of the Saragossa and Alicante railway lines, and a few houses scattered in the hills. Sometimes, when my mother wanted to escape from the unbearable summer heat in our attic, she prepared a cold supper and we went down the Atocha valley, to lie in the grass and eat our supper in the open. It was a poor people's outing. Dozens of workers' families camped near us in the yellow grass.

At that time, the Basilica of Atocha, never to be finished, and the Ministry of Public Works were under construction. The Madrid milkmen sent their goats to browse on the hillocks between the heaps of building material. My childish imagination was deeply impressed by the immense excavations, by the cemented foundations and the stone blocks straggling in the field, which were to become the new Ministry. Sculptures by Querol, destined for the frontispiece, were lying about half unwrapped: gigantic horses' legs, naked female bodies, all sawed into bits as though by a monstrous crime.

The edifice cannot claim great artistic merit. It was planned around 1900, and is a huge bulk of mixed Doric, Roman, and Egyptian elements, striving to be monumental and succeeding merely in being disproportionate. But to my child's eyes it was a cyclopic work which was to outlast centuries.

In the ground floor of this building I passed a long stretch of my life. And I was to see the giant pillars of the entrance, which had loomed in my infancy, crash down in splinters, hit by a bomb.

When the big building became the Ministry of Labor, the Patent Office was housed on its ground floor. For fifteen years I went nearly every day into those vast stone halls and glass-roofed office rooms.

The fields in which I had eaten my supper and played thirty years before had been converted into pretentious modern streets. But farther on, white stone blocks still littered the waste ground at the foot of the unfinished basilica's ugly white-and-red tower, and women, tired from work as my mother had been, sat in the evenings on the benches of the dusty gardens.

The chief of the Patent Office, with the title of Director-General, owed his post to a political appointment and changed with every Government. I had to deal with the three permanent officials, and to crowd all my business into the brief hours when they were available.

Don Alejandro, Departmental Chief, was tall, scrawny, with glittering blue eyes, thin lips and nose. His impeccable dignity hid a clever trickery, ever ready to pull a fast one if it involved no risk.

Don Fernando, Head of the Patents Department, was a merry, fat man with a pendulous belly, always harassed, always in a hurry, and always too late; he had a moon face and a savage appetite embittered by flatulence and hyper-acidity which he tried to drown in bicarbonate. His favor was not for sale, but a case of champagne bottles softened him, a letter from a Deputy calling him "My dear friend" melted him He had been young in a period when politicians appointed and dismissed the civil servants, when each change of Government meant a hundred posts suddenly vacant and quickly refilled. He had been bred in awe of politicians, and still felt it.

Don Pedro, Head of the Trade Marks Department, was a tiny, fragile man, with a little shaven head crowned by a toupee, rather like the cowlick of a naughty boy, and a gentle, womanish voice. He came of a wealthy family and was deeply religious, without vices great or small, methodical, meticulous, fastidious, the only man who came to the office in time and who never left before the end of office hours. He was incorruptible, and impervious to political pressure. Only a priest could ever make him change his mind, for a priest was infallible to him.

I had to steer the interests of about a thousand clients past these three men. I had to remember that Don Alejandro admired the Germans and sent his sons to the German College, that Don Fernando kowtowed to Deputies, and Don Pedro obeyed the Church. I could obtain astounding results by fencing cleverly with a few bank notes, an amiable letter from a German personage, an amiable letter from a politician, or an amiable letter from a prominent Father.

And I knew from direct experience that the Patents Office was only a small sample of Spanish Administration.

There had been the case of the representative of a foreign firm who had come specially to Madrid by air, to settle the account for aircraft engines supplied to the Spanish Army. The account amounted to a hundred thousand pesetas and had been endorsed by the Finance Ministry. Our client thought he would only have to call and receive the money. I had to explain about the forms he would have to fill in so that the date for payment would be fixed—and that some of the money owed by the State to veterans of the Cuban War had not been paid because the date of payment had never been settled. I had then to indicate to whom a commission might be acceptable; the client left by the next passenger aircraft, carrying with him the money of his firm minus twenty thousand pesetas—five per cent commission.

I worked out the reasons for, and the inferences from, this state of affairs in the long hours while I waited in the cool stone halls of the Ministry. A great many of the civil servants came from the middle class and remained in the middle class, trying to live up to an ideal of independence and ease which was not within the reach of their meager salaries. They had felt the power of connections. They had found it easier to cede to pressure than to resist, easier to accept a tip than to wax indignant, because indignation meant the risk of transfer and banishment to an obscure provincial post. Or if they were independent, like Don Pedro, they were still bound to their education and class, doubly submissive to the moral rule of their spiritual advisers in this general hopeless corruption.

How could these administrators have been other than opposed to the Republic which threatened their benefactors and advisors, and their own precarious position in the machinery of the State?

And on the other side there were the clients.

There was Federico Martínez Arias. He was the manager of a rubber manufacturing company in Bilbao. He was an old client and on friendly terms with me. Of humble origin, he had worked himself up to a safe position in the society of Bilbao; he was the Consul of two Latin-American Republics. In Spain he had become wealthy, in America he would have reached the millionaire class. He used to have endless discussions with me on social and economic problems. He was greatly influenced by Taylor and Henry Ford, and mixed their ideas with a dose of Spanish feudalism.

"I belong to the school of thought which says that a worker must be well paid. In our factory we pay the best wages in the whole of Bilbao."

Beyond the pay, he wanted to organize and supervise the workers, giving them decent houses, decent cities, comfort, schools, culture, leisure, but all under the rule and control of the factory.

"The workers have not the right qualities to do it for themselves. They are like children, you've got to lead them by the hand so that they don't stumble. . . . The worker does not need more than a good house, good food, a bit of diversion, and the certainty that his living is safe."

"But in your opinion he must accept it and not start thinking and discussing."

"He doesn't want to. Just look what Ford has done with his thousands and thousands of workers. What Trade Union has ever given them as much as Ford? Labor must be organized by the State. The worker is part of the State mechanism."

"Goodness me, have you turned Nazi, Don Federico?"

"No, but I do admire the Germans. It's a marvel what that man Hitler has achieved. We want a man of his kind here in Spain."

But he was not a political fanatic, nor a religious one. He believed. He believed in the divine mission of the Leader as the head of the national family, a very Catholic and Spanish concept; he also believed in the submission of the serfs. "Even if the Leader is wrong—what would become of an army if the soldiers were to start discussion?"

"If the soldiers could speak out, we might not get wars, Don Federico."

"Certainly. And what would it lead to? Life is a struggle, even the grass blades bore through a stone so that they can grow. Read Nietzsche, Barea."

"But you call yourself a Christian, Don Federico."

"I know, I know—pacifist blah. 'Peace on earth'—yes, but remember what follows: 'to men of good will.' You aren't going to tell me, I hope, that those Socialists and Communists preaching red revolution are men of good will?"

Don Federico called on me at the office, and after talking over his outstanding affairs, he said suddenly:

"I've come to take you with me to Bilbao."

"What for?" I was not astonished, for our business often made it necessary to go to the other end of the country at a moment's notice.

"What for? To work for me. Get out of this hole. You'll never get anywhere here. I offer you the post of attorney to the firm, at one thousand pesetas per month and a commission."

The offer was tempting. The salary was high as salaries go in Spain, the chances it opened were better. It would have meant surmounting the last barrier between me and an upper-class existence. Attorney to the Ibérica in Bilbao would have meant being accepted into the society of Bilbao, one of the most powerful groups in Spain. It would have meant a prosperous future. It would have meant renouncing once and for all everything—everything, that is, of which I still had Utopian dreams!—and hadn't I told myself I had to be a good bourgeois?

I did not know then as I know now that this incident was a critical juncture in my whole life. It was nothing but the voice of my instinct which prevented me from accepting.

"Don Federico, I'm afraid you can't very well take me on. Do you know that I'm almost a Communist?"

He gaped.

"Of all the absurd things I've heard in my life, this beats the lot. You a kind of Communist! Don't talk nonsense. Pack your suitcase and come to Bilbao. I know you can't do it tomorrow. Tell your chief he's got to find someone in your place, I'll leave you three months for it. And I'll pay you your salary as from today so that you can arrange for the move comfortably. Don't say anything now. I will write you an official letter as soon as I am in Bilbao, and you can answer then."

The letter came, a very formal business letter, and I answered it in the best business style. I did not accept.

A few days later Don Federico's great friend, Don Rafael Soroza, owner of an important dolomite deposit, came to the office. He patted me on the shoulder.

"So you're coming to join us in Bilbao, eh?"

"No, sir, I'm staying here."

"But, my dear fellow, you're an idiot—forgive my frankness. Just in these days . . ."

"What about these days?"

"In these days we need men like you."

He launched forth into politics and economics. While I listened, I remembered Don Alberto de Fonseca y Ontivares, the apothecary of Novés. The man before me represented a parallel case, with a different final twist. Soroza was in the late fifties, sturdy, expansive, and cheerful; but the later half of his life had been disturbed by business. He came of a patriarchal family from the Asturian mountains. Though his father had made him study law and follow the career of a lawyer, he had lived quietly in his little village after his father's death, farming his land. Then German prospectors arrived.

Few people know with what meticulous thoroughness German agents investigated the soil and subsoil of Spain for some twenty years. And few know that there exist dozens of companies, apparently of genuine Spanish complexion, which serve as cover for the most powerful German concerns, often not so much to do business themselves as to prevent others from doing it.

The Germans found dolomite in one of Don Rafael's Soroza's properties, and tried the same game with him which they had played so successfully with the apothecary of Novés. But by pure accident the piece of land was already registered as a mining site, because it included an abandoned coal mine, and the rights were the property of Don Rafael's family. The Germans set up a limited company, installed Don Rafael as its manager, and so Don Rafael began to earn money without knowing how he did. Germany took shiploads of dolomite.

"You just imagine the amount of magnesia consumed all over the world because of people's digestion. The Germans buy all the magnesia I am able to extract from the dolomite, and now they're asking for greater quantities. It's an excellent insulator, and they're going to use it for refrigerators and for covering all the pipes in the ice factories. It's better than asbestos. We must take out a patent."

Don Rafael registered innocuous patents which protected the rights to use magnesia as a non-conductor of heat. The Rheinische Stahlwerke, the I. G. Farbenindustrie, and Schering-Kahlbaum sent us patents protecting the extraction of magnesium from dolomite and its exploitation for mechanical purposes. German firms were busy investigating the use of magnesium and its alloys in internal combustion engines. The raw material was to come from Spain, and a ring of patents impeded its industrial exploitation.

When Don Rafael had ended his discourse, I told him:

"In short, you've turned Falangist."

"No, Barea, no. It's something much bigger. I'm a member of the National Socialist Party. You know that my partners are Germans, and they've let me join, although I'm a foreigner. Now what do you say, Barea?"

"That you've got yourself into a mess, Don Rafael."

"Nonsense, man. The Cause is making progress with giant strides. In one or two years' time we'll have Fascism here, and then we'll be a nation such as we ought to be. It won't last more than a year as it is. Mark my words. . . . And now, tell me, when are you going to join Don Federico? He belongs to us too."

"As a matter of fact, I'm staying in Madrid. The climate of Bilbao is bad for me, and I'm in a sound position here."

"I'm sorry to hear it. Well, you know your own business best."

I did not dare to tell him that I was a Socialist as I had told Don Federico. He would have fainted. But what the devil had he to do with the Nazi Party? I could figure it out in the case of Rodríguez Rodríguez, who had spent his life in the German Embassy. But this Asturian gentleman-farmer?

He supplied me with the answer himself when he called me to his Madrid office to decide on a few pending matters.

"I'm leaving tomorrow, and wanted to settle these points with you before I go." With childlike gaiety he added: "I've got guests at home, you know."

"Are you going on a bear hunt?"

Bears are still to be found in the mountains where Don Rafael had his manor house.

"Nothing of the kind. They've sent a few German lads to me. They're on a research tour—geology, mines, topography—and some engineers are coming as well, I believe, to look round for a good airport site. It's a pity we have the Republic, for, believe me, with the help of the Germans and with what we have ourselves, this could be a great country."

"You have not done so badly, personally."

"No. But that is how things are in the whole of Spain: we're treading wealth under our feet and don't know it. Spain is the richest country in the world."

"Yes. And look how our people live!"

"But why is it so, tell me, why? It's the fault of that handful of demagogues who have become the masters of this country. Remember what they did to Primo de Rivera and how they would not let him run things as he wanted to. But all this won't last much longer. We're going to make an end of all those Freemasons, Communists and Jews, at a single stroke, Don Arturo—at a single stroke."

"But there aren't enough Jews in Spain for your stroke, Don Rafael, unless someone invents them."

"We shall find them, Barea."

6. The Spark

DON MANUEL AYALA had wired us to meet him on the airfield at Barajas. We were waiting for him, my chief and I.

A Douglas used on the lines to Barcelona and to Paris stood out glaringly new between the old Fokkers. I went up to it and studied the fuselage. Something at the back of my mind made me uncomfortable and marred my pleasure. I did not know what, and it bothered me, because I had always been in love with aviation. I had to grope for it.

Whatever I knew of the theory of aerodynamics I owed to the Junkers *v.* Ford case, in which I had been acting for our client. It was some time now since the last Junkers and Heinkel patents had passed through my hands. I wondered what they were up to just now.

When Captain Barberan in Morocco had taken me up into the air in his crate and when he spoke of his dream of a Transatlantic flight, it had been beautiful.

I remembered the first flights I had ever seen, and my delight as a small boy. There was that long, exciting walk in the flat grounds of Getafe while I waited for the arrival of Vedrines, the first man to fly from Paris to Madrid. There were the three afternoons when I tramped through the fields to the Velodrome at Ciudad Lineal until the weather was fine enough and Domenjoz could show us what looping-the-loop was.

I would have liked to fly in that Douglas to Barcelona high above the wild coast of Catalonia and the translucent water, and see the shimmering, shifting light of sun and clouds on range beyond range of distant mountains.

I stopped and focused my troubled memory.

It had happened in the 'twenties, when Junkers had built a four-engined aircraft to tour the world and bring home contracts for the big airlines planned just then by various countries. Junkers was our client. The Germans tried to obtain a commercial air base in Seville, where the tower for the anchorage of the Zeppelin had been constructed. Spain could be a key position in the network of communications with America. There had been many and complicated moves in the game, and one of them was the law suit between Junkers and Ford about the patent for aircraft with wings placed below the fuselage.

My old chief and I had had to go to the airport of Getafe when the four-engined Junkers was due to arrive in Madrid on its propaganda tour. A solemn reception was planned and the King of Spain was to be there. When the monster arrived, a little after the scheduled time, the King and his aides-de-camp inspected it thoroughly; the King insisted on being taken up for a trial flight, and diplomatic engine trouble had to be evolved. But while the official formalities were still going on, a German scientist explained the features of the machine to several Spanish officers who had come with the possibility of an army contract with Junkers in mind, and my chief and I went with them.

The man had the title of doctor, but I never caught his name. He was small and thin and sandy-haired, with thick glasses riding on the bridge of a pendulous nose. His hands were enormous. I remembered having thought that they looked like the skinned hands of a big ape. When he moved his bony fingers, the articulations seemed to jump out of their sockets and to assume strange shapes.

First he folded those hands on his back, behind the heavy tails of his coat, and led us through the cabin where the luxurious armchairs for the passengers were lined up. Then he took us through tunnel-like passages which ended in the engine rooms, and finally we came to the pilots' compartment, separated from the passengers' cabin by a sliding door.

The pilots' compartment was shaped like an elongated hemisphere, corresponding to the curved part of the aircraft's nose. Its outer wall consisted of a duraluminum frame and glass panels. The seats of the two pilots were raised in the center of the half globe, as though suspended in mid-air, and commanded a free field of vision in almost all directions.

Here the little doctor freed his hands and began to explain in Spanish: "Now that you have seen the machine"—he stopped all praise by weaving those bony fingers in the air—"I will show you something more interesting."

With surprising agility he bounded along the curved glass floor and began to unscrew some of the cylindrical rivets placed where the duraluminum bars crossed. Hollowed sockets with a screw thread appeared underneath.

"As you see, it suffices to unscrew the rivets to uncover the threaded socket into which you can screw the legs of a machine gun in a few moments—these—and these—are for the machine gunner's seat. You take away this glass panel here, and the barrel of the machine gun is adjusted so that it protrudes. Here on both sides—here—and here—there is room for two more machine guns, so that the airplane is protected and equipped to attack another airplane. And now come with me, gentlemen."

He ran in front of us with small, bouncing steps to the passengers' cabin. There he showed us how the legs of the armchairs were screwed to the floor.

"They can be taken off in two minutes, and this room is empty. Into these sockets you screw equipment for airborne troops and if necessary for bomb storage and releasing gear. Here are the trapdoors. . . . Now I will show you where the bombs are to be installed."

Underneath the huge wings he unscrewed other mock rivets and demonstrated the sockets which were to receive the bomb racks. He bounded on his toes and his bony fingers danced while he gloatingly repeated the procedure:

"Here—you see—and here! Now what do you think of it? In a single hour we can transform the planes of a commercial airport somewhere in Germany, say in Berlin, and come to bomb Madrid. Ten hours after the declaration of war we can bomb the enemy's capital. And if it is we who declare war, five minutes after the declaration. Ja, ja, this is Versailles!"

The old and famous balloon pilot who was with us and whom I knew well turned to me and muttered:

"That fellow is as loathsome as a spider. One feels like squashing him underfoot."

I had been very glad at the time that the Spanish Army contracts for bomber aircraft did not go to Junkers, in spite of the enticing demonstration the cadaverous doctor had given the staff officers.

I had managed not to think of the incident too often since then. But it had changed my views on the future of aviation. It had poisoned my pleasure in flying. It was bothering me just now. There had been Abyssinia. There was Hitler. It was so easy to drop bombs on defenseless towns: you took the rivets off the sockets and fixed the machine guns and bombing gear.

I was getting morbid, I told myself. This Douglas with its sober English comfort was nothing but a luxury vehicle to make flying a pleasure.

The plane from Seville circled and made its landing. We went to meet our client. He was not alone, and I did not recognize his companion. A funny pair they made, plodding across the field.

Don Manuel Ayala was short and squat, in the middle seventies, desiccated and burned by the sun, a sharply pointed nose in the wrinkled, furrowed face, bright mouse eyes behind old-fashioned gold-rimmed glasses fastened to his lapel with a black silk cord, a white, tobacco stained mustache drooping over his small and very thin mouth. The man with him was old, heavy, and uncouth. I thought he was big until I realized that only his extremities were big: hands and feet so huge as to be shapeless, and a large head lolling on disproportionately wide shoulders. He had a coarse peasant face, clean shaven, but blue black from the roots of the hair. What made him look comic was his suit. It was as though a giant had been ill in hospital, lost half his weight, and now came out into the street for the first time in his old clothes. They hung loosely on him, as on coat hangers. But he walked with sure, firm steps.

Then I recognized him. I had never seen him out of his clerical garb before. He was our client's brother, the Jesuit—Father Ayala.

Whenever Don Manuel Ayala had come to Madrid, he had asked me to accompany him. He had lived seventy years of his life cloistered in a small village in the province of Huelva and never gone further than on a sporadic visit to Seville. He administered the landed property he had inherited from his father and sold its produce, but otherwise he led the life of a recluse. He grew exquisite wines which were treated with care, and in his old age he suddenly decided to launch them on the market. Somebody gave him an introduction to our firm, and we provided a set of trade marks, labels, and model bottles for his wines and cognacs. He was merry and loquacious, easygoing and a little cynical about himself. He considered his wish to become a famous winegrower as the sudden whim of old age, but was resolved to indulge it, just as he suddenly took to air travel when he came to Madrid.

"At my age one is no longer afraid of anything. Why shouldn't I give myself the pleasure? I'm only sorry to be so old just when all these new things are turning up."

He felt awe and pride for his brother, the Jesuit, who was so holy and so important that nothing might be said about him. In 1930, the year before the coming of the Republic, he had taken me along for the first time when he went to see his brother at the Jesuit Residence in the Calle de Cedaceros. I had found Father Ayala repulsive. He was dirty and greasy, his habit slovenly, his huge, stiff-soled boots never cleaned, the nails of his splay fingers edged with black. I had no glimpse of his mind, but I knew the strength of the man. At that time, the threads he held in his fingers led to the Royal Palace, to the Cortes, to aristocratic salons, and to officers' rooms in important garrisons. But he never appeared in public. I knew he now lived in civilian clothes in a Seville tenement house together with two other Jesuits. Why did he suddenly accompany his brother on this trip to Madrid, by air, unexpectedly? What new spider's web was he weaving?

Father Ayala left us when we reached our office and Don Manuel apologized for him: "The poor man is very worried about what is going to happen."

He went on explaining while the lift took us upstairs.

"You know, when the Republic dissolved the Order, my brother went to Seville and took a tiny little flat with two others. They're still living there, a communal life. There are hundreds like them in Spain. Of course, quite a lot left the country, but gradually they've been coming back. Now things are going to change, and their place is here, don't you see?"

When we had finished our business talk, Don Manuel invited me to have lunch with him, "because my brother has abandoned me and you know the best corners."

The old man was deeply religious; he lived a bachelor's life and had hardly had any contact with women. But he had a weakness for good food and good wine. When we were installed in one of those "corners" he liked, Don Manuel asked me:

"Now tell me how things are going in Madrid, politically."

"As far as I am concerned, I'm very pessimistic. The Left groups are quarreling with each other, and the Right is out to ruin the Republic. And now some idiot has had the idea of making Azaña President and so immobilizing a man—perhaps the only man—who might have been able to govern the country in its present state."

"Yes, yes, and that's a great advantage for us. Believe me, Largo Caballero and Prieto ànd all those people aren't important. The only dangerous man is Azaña. Azaña hates the Church and he's the man who's done us most harm. Now his teeth are drawn. Otherwise it would have been necessary to eliminate him before doing anything."

"*Caramba*, Don Manuel, that's a side to you I'd never suspected—that you should think of killing anyone!"

"Not I, no, I can't kill a fly myself. But I must admit that certain things may be necessary. That man is the ruin of Spain."

"The ruin of your Spain, you mean."

"Man alive, of yours as well. Because you're not going to tell me you're on the side of that Communist rabble!"

"Perhaps not. But certainly not on the side of the Falangists. Now look, Don Manuel, I don't believe in the Monarchy. I'm for the Republic with my whole heart."

"Psh, I don't care about Monarchies or Republics. There you have Portugal with an ideal Republic. An intelligent man at the top, the Church respected and in the place that's due to Her—that's what I like."

"You talk as if you were your brother."

"If you only could hear my brother! And I agree with him. Communism! Do you know that the Society of Jesus solved the social question centuries ago? Read history, my dear fellow, just read it. Then you'll see what the missions in America did, particularly the one in Paraguay. The Society administered the country and no one went hungry. No one, get that straight. The Indians have never been so happy as they were then. When one of them needed a blanket, he got it, as a gift, not for sale. The Fathers even found them wives, if necessary. They needed no money. It was a paradise, and a model administration."

"And a mine of wealth for the Holy Fathers, I presume."

"Now don't be a demagogue. You know that the Soceity is strictly poor."

"You won't deny that it had influence, and still has it."

"I won't deny anything. But neither can you deny that the Society had many enemies and that the poor fellows must have means of defense." He stopped and thought. "If only they had done as my brother told them in time . . . but they wouldn't listen. When Don Alfonso said he would go, and make way for the Republic, my brother advised against it. With a few regiments everything could have been settled in a couple of days. Well, you saw what happened."

"I know your brother has excellent contacts."

"Oh no, no, the poor man never left the Residence except for a little walk. But the Holy Fathers consulted him, because—although it's not for me as his brother to say so—he's a great person. But always his simple self. You have met him after all. Don't you agree?"

It was true. Father Ayala had never changed. There were others of his Order to be men of the world. He had shown his uncouth contempt and guarded his power. I told Don Manuel that I agreed. Mellowed by the meal, he expanded.

"Good times are just round the corner, Barea. Nearer than you think. Now we have the means, and we have the leader. This Calvo Sotelo is a great man. He's the man of the Spain of the future—of the very near future."

"You don't think we shall get another military rising as in 1932? Or do you?"

"And why not? It's a patriotic duty. Rather than get Communism we have to man the barricades. But it won't be necessary. The whole nation is with us, and all the muck will be swept away at a single stroke. Maybe not even that will be necessary. Calvo Sotelo will become the Salazar of Spain."

"Yes, most people seem convinced that it will come to an explosion overnight. But if the Right take to the street, I think there'll be few of them left to tell the tale. The country is not with them, Don Manuel."

"If you call that mob 'the country,' no. But we have the Army and the middle class, the two live forces of the country. And Azaña will not get rid of that with a laugh, as he did in August 1932."

"Then, according to you, Don Manuel, we shall have a paternal Government, Paraguayan or Portuguese style, in August 1936?"

"If God grants it, Barea. And He will."

We finished the lunch pleasantly joking, for neither of us wanted to go further in showing his thoughts to the other. I never saw either of the two brothers again.

On Monday I sent my eldest daughter on a holiday to the mountains with Lucila, Angel's wife, who was going to stay on her family's farm near Burgos, while her husband was still out of work.

It was the 13th of July 1936. When I had seen them off, I went directly to the Ministry with my brief case.

The rooms of the Patent Office stood empty. A crowd of people clustered round the door to Don Pedro's office. I saw Don Pedro himself gesticulating and vociferating behind his desk, his eyes filled with tears. I asked one of the employees:

"What the devil is going on here?"

"Good Lord, don't you know? They've killed Calvo Sotelo!"

Many of the staff belonged to the Right, particularly four or five typists, daughters of "good families," and a far larger group of sons of similarly good families, some of whom were members of Falange. Now they were standing round Don Pedro's desk, making a sort of chorus to his outcries at the assassination of the political leader.

"It's a crime against God! Such a man, so clever, so good, such a Christian, such a gentleman, killed like a mad dog——" he moaned.

"We'll settle the account. They'll have little time to rejoice. Now the only thing we can do is to go out into the street." Thus the response of the chorus.

"No, no, for God's sake, no more bloodshed—it is not Christian. But God will punish the evildoers."

"God will do it? Well then, we'll lend God a helping hand," replied a very young man.

I went away. There was no work to be done in the Patent Register that day.

The news had caught me by surprise, as it had caught the whole town. Yet it was obvious that the killing of Calvo Sotelo was the answer to the killing of Lieutenant Castillo of the Republican Shock Police. The only question was whether it would prove to be the fuse which would light the powder keg. And my daughter in the train to Burgos! If I had known in time, I would have stopped the journey. Though she might be better off in a small hill village than in Madrid once things started to happen. But—small village? I had seen what could happen in Novés. And the only thing I knew about Lucila's family was that they were well off and considered important people in their village, which was not exactly a guarantee of safety if the countryside was in an uproar. I walked on to the Glorieta de Atocha, not knowing what to do.

The wide expanse of the square was like an ant heap, not because of the assassination of Calvo Sotelo, but because of the preparations for Saint John's Fair, the *Verbena de San Juán.* The foundations for the hundred and one amusements of the Fair were set up on the paving stones. There were the simple wooden frames for the canvas walls of the junk stalls, there was the circle of steel rails for the merry-go-round. A row of men clinging to a cable slowly raised a tall pole from which flapped a circular canvas. Two mechanics streaked with grease adjusted and hammered the pieces of an old steam engine. The men were in vests, with bare arms, and sweated profusely in the July sun. Peeling and flaking pieces of bedaubed wooden horses were piled up in a heap. Smoke rose from the minute chimneys of the caravans of the fair people. And the female tightrope walker was walking around with drooping breasts, her armpits sweaty, looking after the food and helping out the artists who had turned themselves into carpenters. Wagons and lorries unloaded packing cases and indefinable, bulky objects. The children and the onlookers contemplated the assembling of the stalls with ecstatic attention.

Madrid was preparing for its amusement. Who thought of Calvo Sotelo?

I was wrong. Nobody failed to realize the significance of his death. The people of Madrid felt the fear of soldiers about to depart for the front. Nobody knew when and where the attack was to begin, but everybody knew that the hour had come. While the fair people were setting up the merry-go-rounds, the Government had proclaimed a "state of alert."

The Building Trade Union of the C.N.T. declared itself on strike, and some of the U.G.T. members, who wanted to go on working, were assaulted. The Government shut down all centers of the Right-wing groups, without distinction, and arrested hundreds of their people. It also closed the *Ateneos Libertarios,* the local centers of the Anarchists, and arrested hundreds of their members. It was clear that they intended to avert the conflagration.

In the Calle de Atocha, I met my Communist friend, Antonio, with four others.

"Where are you going?"

"We're on sentry duty."

"Don't be stupid. They'll only arrest you. Anybody can see a mile off that you're out on business. Your friend there couldn't show more clearly that he's carrying a pistol if he tried."

"But we've got to be in the streets to see what's going on. We must protect our branch!" The local branch of the Communist Party, of which Antonio was secretary, had its office near by. "And we don't even know whether the police aren't going to close it down. Of course we've cleared all our people out of the office."

"What you should do is set up a stall at the Fair."

Antonio gasped: "This isn't a joke, you know."

"No, it certainly isn't a joke. I mean it. It's quite simple. Go and buy a few toys in a store, at once, now, get hold of a few boards for a trestle table, and a blanket, and set up a stall in the Fair. I know a tradesman quite near, in the Paseo del Prado, who's a friend of mine and will let you use his telephone even during the night, because he doesn't close his bar during the *Verbena.* So you can stay there and keep informed without making yourselves conspicuous."

They did it, and I helped them. That very afternoon Antonio set up a stall with cheap toys at the side of the Botanical Gardens. The members of his local branch who manned the pickets came and went, stopped to finger the toys and pass on their news. The first sensational piece of news came in the middle of the afternoon: the Socialist Party, all the trade unions belonging to the U.G.T., and the Communist Party had concluded a mutual assistance pact and pledged their support to the Republican Government. Antonio was full of enthusiasm and impatience behind his toys.

"Why don't you join the Party?"

"Because I'm no good for your discipline, as you know."

"But we need people now."

"I'll think it over. First let's see what happens."

None of us doubted that the Right would carry out its rising. My

brother Rafael and I went to the *Verbena* that night, fetched Antonio
away from his post and sat down in the open outside my friend's bar.
The Fair was not yet in full swing and there were few people merry-
making, although there was no lack of groups of police, Shock Police,
and workers. The public at large, usually so ready to enjoy summer
nights in the open, was afraid of gatherings.

"The greatest problem," said Antonio, "is the Anarchists in the C.N.T.
They're capable of making common cause with the Right."

"Don't be an idiot."

"I'm not an idiot. Now look here, who can understand their going on
strike just now and starting to shoot up the U.G.T. people? We've already had to give protection to some of our comrades on their way home
this evening. It's worst in the University City. Particularly since the Government has been stupid enough to shut the *Ateneos*. Not that I like the
Anarchists—I'd like to get rid of all of them—I'd like to get rid of all of
them—but all the same we can't afford to let them go over to the Fascists!"

"No fear. Did they go over in Asturias? When the hour comes to
fight—if it does come—they'll be with us."

"You're an optimist. And I'm afraid you've got a soft spot for the
Anarchists."

I was stubborn in my hope.

That week was one of incredible tension. Calvo Sotelo's funeral was
turned into a demonstration by the Right and ended in shooting between
them and the Shock Police. In the Cortes, Gil Robles made a speech in
Calvo Sotelo's memory, which was officially described as a declaration of
war. Prieto asked Casares Quiroga to arm the workers, and the Minister
refused. Detentions and assaults were on the increase in all districts of
Madrid. Building trade workers of the U.G.T. went to work in the University City under police escort, for the C.N.T. continued to attack them.
Expensive cars, with their luggage carefully covered so as to escape attention, left the town in considerable numbers on the roads to the north.
People began to flee from Madrid and from Spain.

On Thursday rumors ran riot. Fantastic stories circulated, and the
evening papers loaned color to them. Officially, nothing had happened.
The Army had not revolted in Morocco, nor had a military rising taken
place in southern Spain. The phrase used to calm the public was as
equivocal as the rumors: "The Government has the situation well in
hand." To stress this fact, broadcasts were started on the same subject.
They had the opposite effect. If nothing was happening, why all this
nervousness?

Outwardly, Madrid looked as though it were celebrating its fiesta. In
that broiling heat, the people lived more in the streets at night than in

their asphyxiating houses. The café terraces, the doorways of bars and taverns, the gateways of tenement houses were choked with groups of people who talked, disputed, and passed on news or rumors. But in spite of all the tension, an undercurrent of vague optimism survived.

On Friday night—July the 17th—our circle in the bar of my house was very large. At eleven o'clock, the Calle del Ave María seemed to overflow. The balconies of the houses stood wide open and the voices of the radio sets poured through them. Every bar had its loudspeaker on. The people sitting on the terraces carried on their discussions in shouts and screams. Gossiping women were sitting in the doorways and flocks of children played and made a noise in the middle of the street. Taxis carrying members of the Workers' Militia on their round drove up and down the slope. Their brakes screeched when they stopped outside one of the bars.

The loudspeakers bawled out news, and the street submerged in silence to listen and to hear.

"The Government has the situation well in hand."

It was strange to hear the phrase proclaimed in a badly synchronized chorus along the street, from different altitudes. No two voices were the same: they reached one's ear clashing and repeating each other. A loudspeaker in a fourth floor room somewhere down the street was left behind and shouted into the silence the word "hand."

"They should leave it in our hands," said Fuñi-Fuñi.

"Yes, so that you can shoot us," cried young Manolo.

"We Anarchists are as good anti-fascists as you are. Or better. We have been fighting for the revolution in Spain for nearly a century, and you only started yesterday. And now, as things are—you're sending your masons to work like a lot of sheep, and the Government refuses you arms. What do you expect? Do you think the Fascists are going to give you higher wages in the University City because you're good little boys? You're a nice lot. The builders going to work——"

"We're disciplined. Do you want to give the others a handle so that they can say we have gone into the streets? Let the Fascists do it, and then you'll see."

"Yes, yes, leave them to it, and you'll see what happens once they're in your house, while you're on your way driving lorries with cement for their public works!"

"And if only you go on shooting at our own people, the Fascists won't get into our houses, I suppose? What logic!"

"The logical thing about it is that you have not yet found out that the hour has come to make the revolution."

"Of course I haven't found it out. What has come is the hour to defend ourselves when they attack us. After we've crushed them, thanks to the action they've taken, we can make the revolution."

"I don't agree."

"All right. Go on killing builders."

On the following day, Saturday, July the 18th, the Government openly announced that there had been insurrections in many of the provinces, although it continued "to have the situation well in hand." Rumors and news, inextricably mixed, chased each other: Morocco was in the hands of Franco; the Moors and the Foreign Legion were disembarking in Seville; in Barcelona the battle was raging; in the provinces a general strike had been declared; the Fleet was in the hands of the rebels—no, it was in the hands of the sailors who had thrown their officers overboard. In Ciudad Lineal a few Falangists had attempted to seize the transmitter of the Navy Ministry, or, according to other reports, they had seized the buildings of film studios in Ciudad Lineal and had installed their headquarters there.

Under the avalanche of contradictory reports, the people reacted in their own way.

"They say that . . . but I don't believe it. What can four generals do? As soon as they start leading the troops out into the street, the soldiers themselves will finish them off."

"Well, I've been told that . . . but it's just the same with me as with you, I can't believe it. It's all an old wives' tale. Maybe some drunken playboy has marched into the street to proclaim a rising—in Villa Cisneros."

Villa Cisneros was the place in Northwest Africa where the Republican Government had deported Right-wing promoters of the Anti-Republican military rising in August 1932.

As the afternoon neared it end, it was no longer rumor, it was an admitted fact that a military rising had taken place in several of the provincial garrisons and that there was street fighting in Barcelona. But "the Government had the situation well in hand."

My brother and I went down into Emiliano's bar to have a quick coffee. Our friends had gathered.

"Sit down here," cried Manolo.

"No, we're going to the People's House to see what they're saying there."

We were just about to leave when the radio interrupted its music and the voice we had begun to know so well said brusquely:

"An urgent order has been issued to the members of the following trade unions and political organizations to report immediately to the center of their respective groups." The speaker went on to enumerate all the trade unions and groups concerned; he enumerated all the groups of the Left. The bar was in a tumult. A few of the men drew pistols.

"Now it's the real thing. And they won't catch me unprepared!"

Within two minutes the bar had emptied. Rafael and I hurried back to our flats to tell our families that we might not come home during the night, and then we met again. Together we hastened to the secretariat of the Clerical Workers' Union. There they were doing nothing but drawing up a list of the members who reported, and telling us to wait. We decided to go to the People's House after entering our names.

I had a funny feeling in my throat when I saw the streets of Madrid.

Many thousands of workers were on their way to report to their trade union, and many of their organizations had their seat in the People's House. From the outlying districts to the center of the city the houses were pouring forth men all going in the same direction. On the roof of the People's House burned a red lamp which was visible from all the attics of Madrid.

But the People's House lay in a narrow, short street lost in a maze of equally narrow and short old streets. And so it happened that the House seemed more and more unapproachable the more the multitude thickened. At the beginning, sentries of the Socialist Youth Organization checked the membership cards in the doorway. Then they had to demand the cards at the two corners of the street. By ten o'clock sentries were guarding the entrances to all the streets in a two hundred yards' radius of the House, and within this circle thronged thousands of persons. All the balconies of all the houses stood open and countless loudspeakers were shouting the news:

The Right had taken to open insurrection.

The Government was tottering.

Rafael and I dived into the living mass of the crowds. We wanted to get through to the tiny room where the Executive Committee of the Socialist Party had its office. The stairways and the narrow corridors of the People's House were blocked. It seemed impossible to advance or recede a single step. But those workers in their boilersuits asked us:

"Where do you want to go, compañero?"

"To the Executive."

They flattened themselves against the wall and we were pushing through, when we were deafened by a surging shout, by the roar:

"Arms! Arms!"

The cry was taken up and re-echoed. At times you heard the whole syllable and at times a cacophony of "a-a-a." Suddenly the multitude was welded into a single rhythm and repeated:

"Arms, Arms! Arms!"

After the third cry there was a pause, and they started afresh. The clipped rhythm leaped along the corridors and down the stairs, and won through to the streets. A fine dust silted down from the vibrating ceiling. Through the open windows, with a bodily impact, came the shout of a hundred thousand people:

"Arms!"

7. The Clash

I FELT sluggish after the meal and tired from my night without sleep. It was good to rest my drowsy head on Maria's thigh and relax like a contented animal. I stared upwards into the tops of the pine trees and the bits of blue, luminous sky between their branches. Maria began to play with my hair and to stroke my neck. A quick wave of desire lapped over my weariness and repose. The scent of resin was clinging to the skin.

Then we lay side by side in the pile of dry pine needles.

"Let me sleep a bit, will you?" I said.

"No, I won't. Tell me what happened last night."

"Nothing at all happened. Let me sleep now. I'll tell you later."

"But I don't want to let you sleep. Tell me what happened. What should I do with myself while you're asleep? Get bored?"

"Sleep a bit, too."

"I won't let you sleep. Look, if you like, we can walk down to the village early this evening and stay at the inn overnight. But I won't let you sleep now."

We were enmeshed in a senseless, unfriendly discussion. My nerves were raw and taut from last night's excitement, from the weary listlessness which always invaded me after sexual contact, from the blurred, distorted, nagging vision of the happenings of the last twenty-four hours, from sheer hunger for sleep. In the end we shouted at each other. I rose.

"Now we'll go to the station at once. I'm going back to Madrid. If you like come with me, and if not, do as you please."

We walked down through the pine wood, silent and sullen. To slide on the pine needles which polish one's shoe soles until they shine had always been exhilarating; that afternoon we only cursed when we skidded on the slope. We found it irritatingly ludicrous to slip and to land on our backsides. And we had to walk down a long slope for more than an hour until we reached the little village in the hills.

"No train until five. Let's drink a glass of beer."

There were few people in the inn: four or five couples of holidaymakers and four Civil Guards playing cards, their belts unstrapped, their coats unbuttoned. Two of them sat there in their shirtsleeves. They gave us a glance and went on with their game. After a few moments one of them turned round and said paternally:

"A little quarrel, eh?"

A young man in the corner stood up and came towards us. I had not seen him; his table was in the gloom and I was still blinded by the sun outside.

"What are you doing here, Barea?"

"Spending Sunday in the country. And you?"

"I'm staying here for a month or so, to have a good rest. I feel almost like going back to Madrid, what with the things that are happening, but my wife says I'd be silly to do it, and I suppose she's right. A few shouts for Calvo Sotelo, and then—a pricked balloon! Last night when I heard the radio I thought it was going to be serious, but this morning people came out here with their snacks and their bottles of wine to spend the day here, just like other Sundays. Just like you yourself. There have been fewer of them, though, to tell the truth."

"I don't really know what to say to you. Last night I too thought it was serious. Today I can't make up my mind what to think. I was almost inclined to stay here for the night, but I've had a row with the girl and I'm going back at five."

"Stay here."

"What for? I would if it were only to stay with you for a while and have a talk. But I prefer going back to staying a night with a bad-tempered face beside me. And anyway, I'm done up, my nerves are all on edge."

"You can come home with me if you like."

"No thanks. I'll take the train back."

One of the Civil Guards was watching us all the time. It did not surprise me, for Hernández was known as a Socialist and in the small mountain village everyone was aware of it. He went there every summer to strengthen his weak lungs; his work—he was a printer—was bad for his health, and he used to rent a woodcutter's shack among the pines for himself, his wife, and his children.

When Maria and I rose at half-past four, the Civil Guard Corporal who had watched Hernández and myself put on his uniform coat. While he was buttoning it up, I went to Hernández' table to say good-by.

"So you're really going?"

"Yes. Come to Madrid with me."

"I'd like to. But I'll only go when they send for me. They know where I am. As long as they don't call me back, things can't be very serious."

The Corporal went out of the door in front of me and turned round in the road.

"Your papers."

He looked twice at my *cedula personal,* the identity paper which also registers the category of the owner's income. I saw that he was impressed and astonished. He stared at me doubtfully.

"How is it you know Hernández?"

"I've known him since we were boys," I lied.

"Do you carry arms?"

"No."

"By your leave." He passed his hands over my body. "All right. You can go."

Twenty-four hours later the Civil Guard had taken over the little village in the Sierra. Early in the morning, they shot Hernández by the roadside. But I learned this, and knew that I had escaped the same fate by a narrow margin, only many days later. At the time, Maria and I climbed the torturous road which led up to the tiny station building, in morose silence.

The railway track runs on a ledge of the Sierra between two tunnels, the village lies embedded in a circle of serried, pine-grown hills. Only at the bottom of the valley is there a meadow where cows graze. It was very peaceful to look down from the bench on the station. The cows were gently browsing, the air was drenched with the scent of pines, the blue sun-filled sky was calm, without a breath of wind. When one of the cows raised its head, the air carried up the clear, mellow sound of its bell.

The station canteen-keeper said:

"It's early for you to be going back."

"Yes, but it will be very crowded later on."

"And how are things in Madrid?" As though Madrid were thousands of miles away. The canteen-keeper's small children clung to his trousers and watched us with wide-open eyes. Smiling, I answered his question:

"It's a little confused at the moment."

The train, a short train which came from Segovia, carried few passengers. The people who had gone to the Sierra from Madrid had not yet abandoned the pleasure of the pine needle carpet. An elderly couple in our compartment, well-to-do provincials, looked at us questioningly. After a while, the man offered me a cigarette.

"Did you come from Madrid this morning?"

"Yes, we did."

"Are things very unruly there?"

"Oh well, much ado about very little. As you see, people went to the Sierra as usual for their Sunday."

He turned to his wife.

"Now you see I was right. These women are always afraid of something. A new Government, that's all."

"You're probably right. But I shall have no peace until we're with Pepe. Don't you agree?" She turned to Maria for support, and told her about their son who was at the University in Madrid and—"God guard us!"—had gone in for Left politics. He belonged to the Students' Association. And she could not stay quiet.

The women went on talking, and I withdrew into my corner and reviewed in my mind the happenings of the past night.

Rafael and I had succeeded in pushing our way through to the cubicle at the end of a long passage where the Socialist Party Secretariat was housed. Carlos Rubiera was there, Margarita Nelken, Puente, a couple more whom I knew by sight, tackling a torrent of people, telephone calls, shouts and written notes which were passed to them from hand to hand along the corridor.

Carlos Rubiera saw me.

"Hullo, what brings you here?"

"I've come to see if I can be of any use."

"You're just in time. Go and help Valencia." He showed me an officer in the Engineers' uniform who was sitting at a small table. "Hey, Valencia, here's someone you may be able to use."

We shook hands and Valencia asked:

"You've been in the Army?"

"Four years in Morocco—Sergeant in the Engineers. We belong to the same Arm."

"Good. At present I'm in command of the guard here. We've got Puente and his boys, and an inexhaustible number of volunteers. The bad thing is that we have no arms and no ammunition, and that most of the lads have never handled a rifle in their whole life. They're all in the big room on the terrace. We'll see what Puente says." Puente was the commander of the Socialist Militia.

It amused me to note the contrast between the two. Valencia was very much the officer, slim, erect, his uniform fitting like a glove. A long, oval

face, gray eyes, a fine, straight nose and full mouth. In his early forties.
The gray mass of his hair, black and white threads mixed and swept back
in faint ripples, gave a sternness to his head which the gay eyes and the
mouth belied. It was impossible not to sense his firm energy.

Puente, a baker by profession, must have been about ten years younger,
although his round, fresh face made it difficult to assess his age. But the
lines of his face were blunted and harsh. He had a town suit which did
not fit his solid, strong body. He looked as though it would have suited
him better to stand there in a sleeveless vest and exhibit his naked muscles
and hairy chest.

It was Puente who steered Rafael and myself through the clogged passages and stairways to the saloon. There one could breathe. It was a
large assembly room which opened on to a roof terrace. No one who did
not belong to the Militia had been allowed through; there were no more
than fifty persons, standing about in groups. In every group one man
was holding a rifle and the others were mobbing him, because each one.
wanted to hold the rifle for an instant, handle the trigger and take aim,
before passing it on to the next. Puente clapped his hands, waiting for
the men to line up before the dais.

"All those who don't know how to handle a rifle—to the left!"

"Shall we get rifles?" shouted a few voices.

"Later, later. Now listen. Our friend Barea here has been a sergeant in
Morocco. He'll explain to you all about how a rifle works. And you"—he
turned to those who had gone to the right and therefore claimed to be
familiar with rifles—"come along with me. We'll relieve our comrades
who are posted in the streets."

He marched off with his men, and there we were left standing on the
platform, Rafael and I, in front of thirty-odd curious faces. I wondered
whether I had forgotten the mechanism of a rifle in twelve years, selected
a Mauser and began to take it to pieces, without saying a word. It was an
old Mauser of 1886. My fingers found their way back instinctively to their
old practice. The red cover of the table before me was soon plastered with
oily parts.

"If there's any mechanic among you, step forward." Five men pushed
themselves to the front. "I'll explain to you how the pieces fit together.
You will find it easier to understand than the others, and later you can
explain it to them in groups of two or three. In the meantime my brother
here will explain the theory of firing to the rest."

Rafael took another rifle and marched his men out on to the terrace. After half an hour each of the mechanics was ready to take
on a small group. Rafael was left with two difficult cases, men who
seemed incapable of holding a rifle straight. "You've got the oaf

platoon," I said into his ear. I went and looked down from the terrace. The house on the other side of the street, some six yards away, had all of its balconies open and all its lights lighted for me to see. There were dining rooms with a lamp in the middle illuminating the table. In one, a woman was collecting what was left over from supper. In another, the empty table was covered with a dark-green cloth with embroidered flowers along its edge. The owner of the flat was leaning in shirtsleeves over his balcony railing. In the flat below the family was having supper. Then there were bedrooms and sitting rooms, all different, each with its own personality, and all alike. From every flat came the voice of a radio set, all the same, each with its own pitch, pouring music over the heads of the mass packed in the street, a dense, black mass of moving heads. A wave of heat rose from below; it smelled of sweat. Sometimes a soft breeze swept this billow of human warmth from the terrace, and then it smelled for a few seconds of trees and flowers. The noise was so intense that the building throbbed with it, as though it were trembling. When the music stopped and the hundred loudspeakers cried: "Attention! Attention!" you heard the multitude fall silent with a dull rolling sound which died away in the distance in the streets of the quarter. Then only coughs and grunts came, until someone commented on a piece of news with a joke or a blasphemy. A firm voice shouted "Silence!" and a hundred mouths repeated the command, drowning everything else for seconds. As soon as the announcement was over, the rumbling noise grew worse than ever.

By midnight the Government had resigned. A new Government was being formed. Over my head a voice said: "Dirty dogs."

I looked upwards. On the top of the roof swayed a red flag, almost invisible in the darkness of the night; above it, the red lamp. From time to time, when a shiver of the flag dipped a fold into the red glare, it flashed in a sudden blaze. In a corner of the wall, a winding iron staircase led to the roof. Somewhere on the top I saw the faint glow of a burning cigarette. I climbed up. At the highest point, on an open platform above all the roofs, I found a militia lad.

"What are you doing here?"

"I'm on watch."

"Because they might come over the roofs?"

"Yes, because they might."

"Whom do you mean?"

"The Fascists, of course."

"But you can't see anything from here."

"I know. But we've got to watch out. Imagine what would happen if they caught us by surprise."

The iron platform rose into the dark. Below was the bulk of the building, crudely lighted. The sky was clear and powdered with flickering stars, but there was no moon. Round us shimmered the glow from the lights of the streets of Madrid and dwindled away into darkness. The street lamps of the suburbs cut through the fields in parallel threads of beads, white flames which seemed to flicker like the stars. The noise of the street came to us muffled through the huge bulk of the house. Twenty steps, and it seemed a different world. I leaned my elbows on the railing and stayed for a long while, quiet.

Then they called us to a belated supper. From somewhere they had produced roast lamb and some bottles of wine for the guard. We ate and talked. The people were still calling for arms. Puente said to me: "We've got twenty rifles and six cartridges per rifle in the building."

"Then we're in the soup."

"Well, it will all be settled now. I suppose they'll give the Government to our Party, to the Socialists. Anyhow, it will have to be settled soon. The Fascists are in Valladolid, and marching for Madrid. But don't tell any of the lads here."

I went back to the terrace, while Puente had to inspect his men. The long waiting began to wear down the crowd. Some people nodded, sitting on the stairs and in the passages, others leaned against the wall and dozed. I climbed up to the little platform and saw the dawn begin as a faint white sheen in the east.

The loudspeakers started again: "Attention! Attention! . . . The new Government has been formed!"

The speaker made a pause and then read the list of names. People fished hastily in their pockets for a piece of paper and a pencil. All the sleepers had awakened and were asking: "What did he say? What did he say?"

The speaker went on with his litany of names. It was a national Government, he had said. Then the name of a Minister without Portfolio rebounded over the heads: Sánchez Román. It was impossible to hear more. The multitude burst into a roar: "Traitors—treason!" And above the medley of curses and insults surged the cry: "Arms! Arms!" The roar grew and swelled. In the stairways and corridors the crowds wanted to move, to go up, to go down. The building quivered as though it were worn out and ready to crumble in a cloud of dust.

A new shout rose: "To the Puerta del Sol!" The short word "Sol" whipped through the air. The dense mass in the street swayed and moved. The People's House poured forth an unending stream from its doors.

"Sol! Sol!" The cry was still cracking through the air, but from farther away. The crowd below thinned out. Daylight slowly filled the street with a pale, almost blue haze. The People's House was empty. The first rays of the sun caught us with Puente and his Milicianos, left alone on the terrace. Up on the roof, from his iron balcony, the sentry cast a long, misshapen shadow over the tiles.

"What are we going to do?" I asked Puente.

"Wait for orders."

Down in the street a few groups of people were standing in heated discussion. Isolated words drifted up to us.

"Don't you think we ought to go to the Puerta del Sol?" I asked.

"No. Our orders are to wait. We must keep discipline."

"But not under this Government."

The Milicianos echoed my words. One of them began to cry openly. I said to Puente:

"I'm very sorry, but I can't help it. I came here last night of my own will to help in any way I could. I was willing to go everywhere with you, and to be posted anywhere. But I'm not willing to serve under a Sánchez Román. You know as well as I do what his being a Minister means. It means that this Government will try to make a deal with the generals. I'm sorry."

I shook hands with him. It was not easy. The militiamen turned round, and some of them leaned their rifles against the parapet of the terrace: "We're going too."

Puente swore at them, and they took up their rifles again, except two who marched out behind Rafael and myself. We walked through the emptied house. A few people moved on the stairways like ghosts. We gulped down a scalding cup of coffee in the bar and went out into the deserted street.

A street cleaner was spraying the pavement with the jet from his hose and the smell of a moist dawn hung in the air.

But from the center of Madrid, from the Puerta del Sol, sounded a tremendous clamor, a muffled bellow which made the air throb and which grew louder as we came nearer. At a street corner a tavern stood open, with a table in the doorway. On the table, a coffee urn on a charcoal heater, a basin with water, cups and saucers, a row of liquor bottles. We stopped to take another cup of coffee and a glass of cognac. The tavern's radio interrupted its crooning: "Attention! Attention!" The tavern keeper increased the volume: "A new Government has been formed. The new Government has accepted Fascism's declaration of war on the Spanish people!"

One of the two Milicianos who had come with us from the People's House said: "Then it's all right. Salud." He walked off and then turned

back. "But one never knows with those Republicans in the Government."
When we reached the Puerta del Sol, the crowd had dispersed and
the shutters of the bars were clanking open. The people who carried on
their discussions in groups and clusters along the pavement went in to
have their breakfast. A radiant sun rose over the houses. The day was
going to be hot. Taxis passed by, cluttered with militiamen; many of
them carried flags with the inscription "U.H.P." The Sunday buses lined
up to carry the people into the open country. Beside us a conductor
shouted: "Puerta de Hierro! Puerta de Hierro!" Groups of boys and girls
and whole families came in driblets to climb into the buses with ruck-
sacks on their backs.

"What a night!" exclaimed a man as he sat down.

I remembered that I had arranged to meet Maria in the Puerta del Sol
at seven in the morning on Sunday and to go to the Sierra with her for
the day. This was Sunday. It was half-past six. I did not want to go home
—there was nothing I could do—and it was a splendid morning.

"Listen," I said to Rafael, "tell Aurelia that I won't be home till late
tonight. Give her some explanation, say I had work to do at the Union.
Or anything. I'll wait for Maria here and go with her to the Sierra. I've
had enough."

That was what had happened on the night of the 18th. Last night—
though it seemed far away. The conversation of the others droned on
and on. I was tired, annoyed with the whole day, annoyed with Maria,
annoyed with myself, unwilling to go home and be shut in with my wife
on top of it all.

Then we were in Madrid. People stormed the tram. We preferred to
walk. The first buses crowded with holiday-makers came back from the
banks of the Manzanares. Outside the station was a traffic block. A policeman with a white helmet was trying to unravel it with great shouts
and gesticulations. There were lorries full of people singing at the top
of their lungs. A luxury car with suitcases heaped on the luggage rack
coasted by.

"They're running away, they're running away!" yelled the men in the
lorries. The big car swept past them in silence; the road which led away
from Madrid was free. Yet the shout had not been threatening; it had
been excited, but merry: the crowd made fun of people who fled from
Madrid out of fear.

The gaiety died out in the streets as soon as we had passed the hill
of San Vicente. Pickets of Milicianos asked for our papers at the street
corners. Police had drawn a cordon at the entrance of every street leading to the National Palace. Few people were about, and they all hurried.

More cars with Party emblems painted on their doors and the inscription "U.H.P." passed us at great speed. People greeted them with the raised fist. A dense smoke column rose at the bottom of the Calle de Bailén. A loudspeaker told us through an open window that General Franco had demanded unconditional surrender from President Azaña. The Republican Government had answered by a formal declaration of war.

A few churches were burning.

I took Maria to her house and hastened home. The streets round the Plaza de Antón Martín were choked with people. They were filled with an acrid, dense smoke. They smelled of burned timber. The Church of San Nicolás was on fire. The dome had a helmet of flames. I saw the glass panes of its lantern shatter and incandescent streams of molten lead run down. Then the dome was a gigantic, fiery ball with a life of its own, creaking and twisting under the impact of the flames. For an instant the fire seemed to pause, and the enormous cupola cracked open.

The people scattered, shouting:

"It's coming down!"

The dome came down with a crack and a dull thud and was swallowed by the stone walls of the church. A hissing mass of dust, ashes, and smoke rose. Broken glass tinkled shrilly. Suddenly made visible by the fall of the cupola, a fireman's ladder was swaying in the air. A fireman at the top was pouring his jet on to the market stalls in the Calle de Santa Isabel and on the walls of the cinema beside the church. It was as though a harlequin had suddenly been left alone, ridiculous and naked, in the middle of the stage. The people cheered, and I did not know whether they meant the fireman or the collapse of the dome. The fire roared on, muffled, behind the stone walls.

I walked into Serafín's tavern. His whole family was in the back room, the mother and one of his sisters in hysterics, and the bar was full of people. Serafín was running from the customers to his mother and sister and back, trying to do everything, his round face streaked with sweat, half-crazed and stumbling at every step.

"Arturo, Arturo, this is terrible, what's going to happen here? They've burned down San Nicolás and all the other churches in Madrid, San Cayetano, San Lorenzo, San Andrés, the Escuela Pía——"

"Don't worry," a customer who sported a pistol and a red-and-black scarf challenged him. "There are too many of those black beetles anyhow."

The name Escuela Pía had shaken me: my old school was burning. I hastened down the Calle del Ave María and found Aurelia and the children outside the house among the neighbors. They greeted me with cries:

"Where have you been?"

"Working all day long. What's going on here?"

Twenty neighbors started giving me information: Fascists had fired at the people from the churches, and so the people had stormed the churches. Everything was burning . . .

The quarter smelled of fire, a light rain of ashes filtered down. I wanted to see for myself.

San Cayetano church was a mass of flames. Hundreds of people living in the tenement houses alongside had dragged out their furniture and stood there, dumbly staring at the fire which threatened their own homes. One of the twin towers began to sway. The crowd screamed: if it fell on their houses, it would be the end. The tower crashed on the pavement.

In front of San Lorenzo a frenzied multitude danced and howled almost within reach of the flames.

The Escuela Pía was burning from inside. It looked as though shattered by an earthquake. The long wall of the school in the Calle del Sombrerete, with its hundred windows of cells and classrooms, was licked by tongues of fire which stabbed through the window grilles. The front was demolished, one of the towers crumbled, the porch of the church in ruins. Through the side door—the entrance for the poor pupils—firemen and Milicianos came and went in ceaseless action. The glow of the central fire in the gigantic building shone through the opening.

A group of Milicianos and a Shock Police officer came out of the door. They carried an improvised stretcher—boards across a ladder—and on it, wrapped in blankets, a small figure of which nothing was visible but the waxen face under a thatch of white hair. A pitiful old man, quavering, his eyes filled with fright: my old teacher, Padre Fulgencio. The multitude opened a path in silence, and then men put him into an ambulance. He must have been more than eighty years old. A stout woman beside me said:

"I'm sorry for poor old Father Fulgencio. I've known him ever since I was a tiny little girl. And to think of him going through all this now! It would have been better for him if he had died. The poor man has been stricken with paralysis for many years, you know. Sometimes they carried him up to the choir in a chair so that he could play the organ, because his hands are all right, but from the waist down he's like dead. He wouldn't feel it if you were to stick pins into his legs. And you know, all this has happened because the Jesuits got hold of the school! Because before that—and believe me, we can't stand the black frocks—but all of us here liked the old Fathers."

"Padre Fulgencio was my chemistry teacher," I said.

"Then you know what I mean. Because that must have been quite a long time ago. Well, I mean to say, you aren't old. But it must have been a good twenty years ago."

"Twenty-six."

"There, you see. I wasn't far out. Well, as I was telling you, some years ago, I don't remember if it was before the Republic or just after, the school changed so that you wouldn't have recognized it."

The fire was crepitating inside the church. The building was a shattered shell. The woman went on, hearty and verbose:

"The Escolapians—you know, they were nice and, mind you, I don't like the black frocks generally—went and joined one of those Catholic School Associations, or whatever they were called, but it was all managed by the Jesuits. You remember how it was when the Father Prefect used to go to the Plaza del Avapiés and give us coppers, and my own mother went and kissed his hand. But you see, all that was over and done with when the Jesuits came. They started that what-d'you-call-it, the Nocturnal Adoration, and then the fine young gentlemen came and prayed. Nice prayers, I can tell you! Didn't we see them drilling in the schoolyard and getting in arms? And then, would you believe it, this very morning they started firing at us with a machine gun from the windows up there and people could hear it in the whole quarter!"

"And were there any casualties?" I asked.

"They caught four or five over there in the Mesón de Paredes Street and Embajadores Street. One was killed on the pavement there, the others have been taken away, no one knows where."

I went home in profound distress. I felt a weight in the pit of my stomach as if I wanted to cry, and could not. I saw flashes of my boyhood, I had the sensation of the feel and smell of things I had loved and things I had hated. I sat on the balcony of my flat without seeing the people who walked through the street and stood there in groups, talking loudly, trying to sift the conflict within me. It was impossible to applaud the violence. I was convinced that the Church of Spain was an evil which had to be eradicated. But I revolted against this stupid destruction. What had happened to the great library of the College, with its ancient illuminated books, its unique manuscripts? What had happened to the splendid collections of Physics and Natural Science? All that wealth of educational material! Had those priests and those Falangist boys really been so incredibly stupid as to expect the College to serve as a fortress against an enraged people?

I had seen too much of their preparations not to believe in their use of churches and monasteries for their stores of arms. But I still hated the destruction, as much as I hated those who drove the people to it. For a moment I wondered where Padre Ayala was, and whether he liked the outcome of his silent work.

What would have happened if our old Father Prefect had thrown open the gates of the Church and the College and stood there himself under the lintel, in the face of the crowd, upright, his gray hair stirred by the wind? They would not have attacked him, I was sure of it.

Later I was to learn that my dream had not been vain: the parish priest of the Church of Santa Paloma had put the keys into the hands of the militia and his church with its art treasures was saved, although the papier-mâché saints were smashed and the metal ornaments used for the war. And similarly San Sebastián, San Ginés, and dozens of other churches had been preserved, some of them for the bombs to come.

But that evening I felt leaden. The fight was on, it was my own fight, and I was repelled and chilled to the core.

Rafael took me to Antonio's stall at the Fair. There were still people about and the customary amusements functioned. But Antonio was wildly excited and about to leave. The garrison of the big barracks, the Cuartel de la Montaña, had fired from a machine gun at a lorry carrying members of the Socialist Youth returning from the Puerta de Hierro. The police had drawn a cordon round the barracks. It was the headquarters of the insurrection in Madrid, it seemed.

"We must go there," Antonio said. I refused. There was nothing I could do. I had seen enough, I was dead tired. Rafael went off with Antonio and I returned home. I slept four hours and woke just after four in the morning. It was bright daylight. In the street below people were talking and disputing. I dressed and went down. A taxi with Milicianos stood in the Plaza de Antón Martín. The men were drinking milk at the dairy which belonged to Serafín's brother-in-law. I joined them and drank two glasses of cold milk out of the icebox.

"Where are you going?"

"To the Cuartel de la Montaña. It's getting serious there."

"I'm coming with you."

Shock Police stopped our car in the Plaza de España. I walked on to the Calle de Ferraz.

The barracks, in reality three different barracks joined together, is a huge building on the crest of a hill. In front of it lies a wide glacis on which a whole regiment has room for its drill. This terrace slopes down to the Calle de Ferraz on one side and is cut short above the Northern Railway Station on the other. A thick stone parapet runs along its whole length, with a sheer drop of twenty feet to a lower glacis which separates the barracks from the public gardens of the Calle de Ferraz. At the back, the building looms high over the wide avenue of the Paseo de Rosales and the open country to the west and northwest. The Cuartel de la Montaña is a fortress.

Rifle shots were cracking from the direction of the barracks. At the corner of the Plaza de España and the Calle de Ferraz a group of Shock Police were loading their rifles in the shelter of a wall. A multitude of people were crouching and lying between the trees and benches of the gardens. A wave of furious shots and cries was surging from them, and from others I could not see, nearer to the barracks. There must have been many thousands ringing the edifice on its hill. The pavement on the other side was deserted.

A plane came flying towards the barracks at great altitude. People yelled: "It's one of ours!"

The day before, Sunday—that Sunday on which we had gone to the Sierra in the morning, hoping that the storm had blown over—groups of officers on the two airfields of Madrid had attempted an insurrection, but had been overpowered by the loyal forces.

The machine flew in a wide curve and banked down. I could not see it any longer. A few moments later the ground and the air shook. After dropping its bombs, the plane made off. The crowd went mad with joy, some of the people in the gardens stood up, waving and throwing their caps into the air. A man was making a pirouette when he fell, shot. The barracks was firing. The rattle of machine guns rose above all the other noises.

Shouting and screaming, a tight cluster of people appeared on the other side of the Plaza de España. When the mass arrived at the street corner, I saw that it had in its midst a lorry with a 7.5 centimeter gun. An officer of the Shock Police was trying to give orders on how to unload the cannon. The crowd never listened. Hundreds of people fell upon the lorry as though they wanted to devour it, and it disappeared beneath the human mass like a piece of rotting meat under a cluster of black flies. And then the gun was on the ground, lifted down on arms and shoulders. The officer shook himself, and shouted for silence.

"Now as soon as I've fired it off you're to carry it over there as quickly as you can, do you understand me?" He pointed to the other end of the gardens. "But don't kill yourselves. . . . We've got to make them believe that we've got plenty of guns. And off with all of you who aren't helping."

He fired off the field-gun and even before the barrel had come to rest the dense mass of men closed in and carried it one hundred, two hundred yards further on. Again the gun roared, and again it started on its crazy run over the paving stones. It left in its wake people hopping on one foot and screaming with pain: the wheels had rolled over men's feet.

Machine-gun bullets were spraying the street very close to us. I took cover in the gardens and threw myself down behind a stout tree trunk, just behind two workers lying on the lawn.

Why the devil was I here—and without any kind of weapon in my pockets? I knew perfectly well that it was sheer useless folly. But how could I be anywhere else?

One of the two men in front of me raised himself on his elbows. He gripped a revolver with both hands and rested it against the tree trunk. It was an enormous, ancient revolver with a nickel-plated barrel and a sight that stuck out like a wart. The cartridge drum was a shapeless bulk above the two hands clutching the butt. The man pressed his face perilously close to the weapon and pulled the trigger, laboriously. A terrific bang shook him and a pall of stinging smoke made a halo round his head.

I almost leaped to my feet. We were at a distance of at least four hundred and fifty yards from the barracks, and the front of the building was completely screened by the trees of the gardens. What did that damned fellow think he was firing at?

His companion took him by the shoulder. "Now let me have a shot." ,

"No, I won't. It's my revolver."

The other swore. "Let me have a shot, by your mother!"

"No, I won't, I've told you so. If they bump me off the revolver is yours; if not, you can just lump it."

The other turned round. He had a clasp-knife in his hand, almost as big as a cleaver, and he brought it down on his friend's behind. "Give me the revolver, or I'll prick you!" He stabbed at his buttocks with the point of the knife.

The man with the revolver jumped and bellowed. "It's gone in!"

"Now you see—you let me have a shot or I'll puncture you."

"Here you are, but hold tight, it kicks."

"D'you think I'm an idiot?"

As though following a fixed ritual, the other raised himself on his elbows and clutched the butt with both hands, so deliberately and ceremoniously that it looked almost like a supplication. The nickel-plated barrel lifted slowly.

"Go on, get it over!" shouted the owner of the revolver.

The other turned his head.

"Now it's you who's got to wait. It's my turn. Now I'll show those bastards!"

Again we were shaken by the crash, again the acrid smoke clung to the ground around us.

The bangs of mortars and the rattle of machine guns went on at the barracks. From time to time the gun roared at our back, a shell made the air throb, and the explosion resounded somewhere in the distance. I looked at my watch: ten o'clock. Ten! It was impossible.

Just then a silence fell, followed by a pandemonium of cries and shouts. Through the confused noise rose the words: "Surrender! White flag!" People burgeoned from the ground. For the first time I saw that there were women as well. And all of them started running towards the barracks. They swept me along. I ran with them.

I could see the stone stairways in the center of the parapet which led from the lower to the upper glacis; they were black with tightly packed people. On the terrace above a dense mass of bodies blocked the exit.

A furious burst from the machine guns cut through the air. With an inhuman shriek, the crowds tried to scatter. The barracks spouted metal from its windows. Mortars sounded again, nearer now, with a dry crack. It lasted some minutes, while the wave of cries was more frightful than ever.

Who gave the order to attack?

A huge, solid mass of bodies moved forwards like a ram against the barracks, against the slope leading upwards from the Calle de Ferraz, against the stone stairs in the wall, against the wall itself. An immense cry rose from the multitude. The machine guns rattled, ceaselessly.

And then we knew in an instant, though no one told us, that the barracks was stormed. The figures in the windows disappeared in a flash, other figures whipped past the windows after them. The tide of screams and the firing now sounded inside the building. A Miliciano emerged in a window, raising a rifle high into the air and throwing it down outside. The multitude answered with a roar. I found myself part of a mass which pushed on towards the barracks. The glacis was strewn with bodies, many of them twitching and slithering in their own blood. And then I was in the barracks yard.

The three tiers of galleries enclosing the square yard were filled with running, yelling, gesticulating people who waved rifles and called senselessly to their friends down below. One group was chasing a soldier who forged ahead, crazed, but swerving aside whenever anyone crossed his path. They had run almost the whole round of the gallery when somebody tripped the soldier up. He fell. The group of people closed round him. When they separated, there was nothing to be seen from the yard where I was.

A giant of a man appeared in the highest gallery, bearing on his huge hands a soldier who threshed the air with his legs. The big man shouted: "Here he comes!"

And he threw the soldier down into the yard. He fell, revolving through the air like a rag doll, and crashed on the stones with a dull thud. The giant lifted his arms.

"And now the next!"

A crowd had gathered in the corner of the arms depot. The rifles were there. One militiaman after the other came out, brandishing his new rifle, almost dancing with enthusiasm. Then there was a new rush at the door.

"Pistols—Pistols!"

The depot began to pour forth black boxes, passed from hand to hand over the heads. Each box contained a regulation pistol—a long-barreled Astra caliber 9—a spare cartridge frame, a ramrod, and a screwdriver. In a few minutes the stones of the yard were spattered with black and white patches—for the inside of the black boxes was white—and with grease-stained paper. The depot door was still spitting forth pistols.

It has been said that there were five thousand Astra pistols in the Cuartel de la Montaña. I do not know. But that day, empty black-and-white cases dotted the streets of Madrid. What was not found, however, was ammunition. It had been seized at once by the Shock Police.

I walked out of the barracks.

When I served my first few months in the Army, a conscript soldier destined for Morocco, it had been in these barracks; that was sixteen years ago.

I had a glimpse of the officers' mess in passing. Dead officers were lying there in wild disorder, some with their arms flung across the table, some on the ground, some over the window sills. And a few of them were young boys.

Outside on the glacis, under the glare of the sun, lay corpses in hundreds. It was quiet in the gardens.

8. The Street

O N Tuesday morning, the day after the storming of the barracks, I went to the office and had a conference with my chief on what course to follow in the circumstances. We decided that our office would continue to function and the staff come to work in the mornings as usual. We even attempted to co-ordinate our work for the day, but gave it up as soon as we realized that postal communications had been uncertain. I took a brief case full of papers which had to be registered and submitted in the Patent Office and left for the Ministry.

Two floors below us was the head office of Petróleos Porto-Pí S.A., a company set up by Juán March after the organization of the Oil Monopoly, with scarcely any other purpose than that of claiming fantastically high compensation for alleged oil-bearing properties from the Spanish State. The door stood open and I saw two Milicianos with rifles slung over their shoulders and pistols in their belts rummaging through the drawers. One of them turned round and saw me standing at the door.

"Come in!"

I entered. The Miliciano went past me to the door and shut it. Then he addressed me:

"Now, my fine bird, what brings you here?" He had grasped his pistol and held it with the muzzle pointing to the floor. "Just you drop your nice little case there and put your hands up!"

He did not search me for arms but simply emptied all my pockets on to the desk. My notecase attracted his attention. He drew out the wad of papers and began to scan them. In the meantime the other Miliciano rifled the briefcase.

"I think you're barking up the wrong tree," I said.

"You shut up and speak when you're spoken to."

"All right. I suppose one is allowed to smoke. Tell me when you're through."

I had not yet lighted my cigarette when the man shoved the U.G.T. membership card under my nose.

"Whose is this?"

"Mine, I should say."

"Do you mean to tell us that you're one of us?"

"I do. But it's a different question whether you're going to believe me or not."

"I'm not swallowing fairly tales. Whose is this *cedula personal?*"

"Mine too, I imagine."

He turned to his companion. "I told you this was a good rat trap! We've caught a bird already. A *cedula* of the hundred-pesetas class, just like the bigwigs, and a U.G.T. card! What do you have to say to that?"

"It's possible, but it's a bit unlikely, it seems to me. Leave him for a moment and look at what I've got here."

When they had finished thumbing official and legal documents and trying to decipher the complicated designs for a liquid-air installation, they resumed their cross-examination.

"Explain who you are and what all those scrawls mean."

I gave them circumstantial explanations. They took me down to the concierge, who was pale with fear but confirmed what I had said.

"It seems we've got to take a look at that office."

We went up to our office in the lift and I led them into the confessional.

"Now, what is it you want to know?"

"Well, we want to know what kind of office this is and what people you've got here."

"I'll show them to you, that will be the best way." I said to Maria: "Tell everybody to come here——"

"Don't you move," one of them said to her and pushed the button on the desk. Carlitos, our office boy came in.

"Hullo, kid, you're buttons here, aren't you? Now listen, get every one of the staff in here, just as if this gentleman here had sent for them. You know who he is?"

"Hell, of course I know. You're on the wrong track, pal."

But he brought in our employees one by one. They stood in a silent semicircle and waited.

"Now you can introduce them," the leader of the pair said.

"The best thing will be for you all to show your Union cards. The only person here who hasn't got one is our chief—here he is—and he's one of the partners of the firm."

The two Milicianos accepted the facts, although they clearly showed their desire to search the office. Before they left, they fired off their parting shot:

"All right—but we'll come back. This outfit will have to be taken over. It's good-by to employers now, and you"—this was directed to our chief— "can look round elsewhere for your meal-ticket."

It was getting late for the Ministry; the Patent Departments would close within an hour, and there would be no taxis to be had. I walked down the stairs with the two Milicianos. Now they turned friendly.

"You know, my lad, what with you looking like a bourgeois louse and with the figure on your *cedula,* we thought you must be one of those Falangists. Because they carry our Union cards in their pockets, you know. And then you turned up in the door of that robbers' den!"

"I looked in precisely because I was astonished to find anyone in that place just now—and so you've made me late for the Ministry with these papers of mine!"

"We'll take you there in a jiffy, don't you worry."

Outside was a car and two militiamen with pistols from the Cuartel de la Montaña in their belts. When they saw us coming, they laughed broadly.

"Have you bagged him?"

"No, he's one of ours, we're going to take him to his Ministry."

That was my first experience in a requisitioned car with a self-appointed driver. We started with a violent jerk and shot down the Calle de Alcalá in defiance of all traffic regulations. Passers-by raised their clenched fists, and we all, including the driver, returned the salute. The car responded with a swerve and the driver tore at the wheel so that we tumbled over one another. There was nothing to be done except to wait for the moment when the madly careering car would crash into another mad car or lorry passing us, brimful with Milicianos who would raise their clenched fists, or when it would dash on to the pavement, crush a couple of pedestrians and end up against a lamp post. But nothing happened. We crossed the Paseo del Prado through a maze of boards and girders, the dismantled skeletons of fair-stalls and merry-go-rounds.

When we came to the Ministry, my companions decided that they wanted to have a look at it; they had never been in a Ministry.

Shock-Police posts at the entrance would not let anyone through who did not possess a pass; when the militiamen walked up the broad stairs, trying to follow me, a corporal barked at them:

"Where are you going?"

"We're going in there with him."

"Are they coming with you, sir?"

"Yes."

"Have they got passes?"

"No."

"Then you have to ask for forms over there and wait for your passes."

"Well, if you come in, you know where to find me," I said with a childish feeling of triumph.

In the Register everything was topsy-turvy. A dozen employees of patent agencies were waiting in the hall, but the places behind the windows of the counters were deserted. A few of the employees of the Ministry were standing in the middle of the hall and discussing the latest events with the others. One of the Register people saw me and said:

"If you've got anything for us, Señor Barea, let me have it, I'll register it for you. It's not exactly my job, but no one else has turned up. Well, one has—Don Pedro himself."

"I should have thought he would prefer not to leave his house today."

"You don't know him then. Go in and see him."

Don Pedro was buried in mountains of papers and working feverishly.

"How are you, Arturo, do you want anything?"

"Nothing, sir. They told me you were here, and I came in to say good morning. I tell you frankly that I didn't expect to see you today."

"What should I do in your opinion? Go into hiding? I've never done harm to anyone and I haven't ever meddled in politics. Of course—I have my opinions which you know, Barea." He changed to the more distant form of address.

"I know them; they seem to me a little dangerous just now."

"Of course they are. But if one has a clear conscience, one isn't afraid. What I am, though, is shocked and horrified. Those people respect nothing. One of the priests of San Ginés came to my house. He is still there, shivering and trembling, and making my sisters almost die of fright. And those burning churches . . . I can't believe that you approve of all this, although you do belong to the Left."

"I don't approve of it, but then I don't approve of rifles stored in churches either, nor of conspiratorial meetings held by Christian Knights at two in the morning."

"They were forced to defend themselves."

"So have we been, Don Pedro."

There we were off again, careful not to hurt each other's feelings too much, neither of us hoping to come to any agreement with the other, yet both trying to behave as though discussions were still of value. I was not very attentive. I knew his arguments as much by heart as I did my own. I thought about the man himself.

His religious faith was so strong, his integrity so complete, that he was unable to admit even the possibility that anyone professing the same faith might have a lower moral standard than he himself. He was a simple, childlike man who after the death of his parents had taken refuge in an almost monkish life together with his sisters; he had a private chapel in his house and thus was aloof from the political life of the sacristies; he neither smoked nor drank, and I imagined that he had never known a woman.

There was something else I knew about him. In 1930, a clerk in a patent agent's firm had developed tuberculosis. He was earning 200 pesetas per month, was married, and had two children. His illness had presented him with an insoluble problem. To give up work or to apply for admission to one of the State Sanatoria would have meant starvation for his family. The illness made rapid progress, and the moment came when he was unfit to go to work. His firm paid him three months' salary and dismissed him. The employees of the private patent firms and of the patent departments in the Ministry collected money for him, and I asked the three chiefs of the Patent office for their contribution. A few days later Don Pedro called me to his room and shut the door. He inquired about the result of the collection, and when I told him that it had netted four hundred pesetas, he exclaimed: that was bread for one day, and hunger for the future. I explained that we were not able to do what would be necessary to provide a place in a sanatorium for the man and financial support for his family in the meantime. Don Pedro said that everything was settled, including the recommendation to the sanatorium which would cut short all the red tape; he was going to pay for the cure; I was to tell the consumptive man's wife that his friends had collected enough money to pay her 200 pesetas per month for the duration of her husband's illness. "Nobody will know, because we can manage all this between you and me."

It had been arranged as Don Pedro suggested. The clerk was cured, he lived with his family in the north of Spain. Neither he nor his wife ever learned what had happened. When the young man was dismissed from the sanatorium, Don Pedro had wept with joy.

How could I have quarreled with this man, whom I respected, much as I disagreed with all his beliefs and political ideas? The discussion dragged on painfully. In the end Don Pedro rose and held out his hand. "I don't know what is going to happen here, Barea, but if anything does happen . . ."

"If anything happens to you, let me know."

I went out into the streets.

The workers' militias had occupied all the barracks of Madrid: the conscript soldiers had been discharged. The police had arrested hundreds of persons. News from the provinces was still contradictory. After a fierce battle, Barcelona was finally in the hands of the Republicans. So was Valencia. But the list of provinces which the insurgents had caught by surprise was long.

Crossing the Plaza de Atocha, I wondered what course the War Ministry would follow. A general mobilization? General Castello had the name of being a loyal Republican. But would he dare to arm the people? Would President Azaña bring himself to sign the decree?

Milicianos had drawn a cordon across the Calle de Atocha.

"You can't get through, man, they're firing from the roof up here. Get yourself under cover round the corner." I heard the crack of a rifle shot. Two Milicianos on the other side of the street fired back, one with a rifle, the other with a pistol. In the doorway of the house where I stood there was a cluster of people and two more militiamen.

"I think I can get through as long as I stick to the front of the houses."

"All right, if you like. Have you got papers?"

I showed him the U.G.T. card and he let me through. Shots crackled from the roof. I kept very close to the wall of the house and stopped when I had passed it. A group of men came out of the entrance. Two of

them were carrying the limp body of a boy of sixteen. His head was oozing blood, but he was alive. He moaned: "Mother—Mother——"

The whole quarter of Avapiés seemed in an uproar round the Plaza
de Antón Martín. Shots sounded from many roofs. Milicianos were chasing snipers over the roofs and through the skylights. Somebody said that
two or three Fascists had been killed in the Calle de la Magdalena. But
the people showed little alarm. Men, women, and children from the
tenements were in the streets, all looking up at the upper stories of the
houses, all shouting and shrieking.

A strong voice shouted the order which I then heard for the first time:
"Shut the balconies!"

The street resounded with the clatter of the wooden laths of window
and balcony blinds. Some windows stayed open, and people pointed at
them with their fingers.

"Señora Maña!" someone kept on shrieking. After a while a fat woman
came out on an open balcony. "Shut your balcony, quick!" And the fat
woman rolled down the blinds without a word.

Then it grew quieter. The houses showed blinded fronts. A little boy
squeaked: "That window's open, over there!"

On a third floor a window stood wide open and its curtain flapped,
leisurely. A Miliciano growled: "Some son of a bitch could fire at us from
behind that curtain." People round him began to scream: "Shut that
window!" The curtain went on flapping, like a challenge. A militiaman
took up his stance on the opposite pavement and loaded his rifle. He
took aim. The mothers clutched their children and edged away from the
man, who stood in the middle of the deserted space and fired. Broken
glass clinked. One of the men entered the house and came out with a
little woman, shrivelled and humped by old age, who cupped her hand
to her ear. The others shouted in chorus:

"Who's the tenant of the flat up there, Señora Encarna?"

When at last the old woman understood, she answered with perfect
gravity:

"And that's what you've called me for, children? That's the staircase
window. The Fascists live on the first floor. They're bigoted devils, they
are."

Within a few seconds the balconies of the first floor were thrown open.
A Miliciano leaned out from the last window in the row: "There's nobody
here—they've flown!"

Furniture and crockery rained down on the paving stones.

The loudspeakers interrupted their music, and the crowd clamored for
silence. The shower of furniture ceased. The Government was speaking:

"The Government, on the point of finishing with the criminal sedition fostered by military who have betrayed their country, requests that the order now about to be re-established should remain entirely in the hands of the public forces of law and order, and of those elements of the workers' associations which, subjected to the discipline of the Popular Front, have shown such abundant and heroic proof of lofty patriotism.

"The Government is well aware that Fascist elements, in despair at their defeat, are trying to sham solidarity and join with other turbid elements in an effort to discredit and dishonor the forces loyal to Government and People by displaying an alleged revolutionary fervor which expresses itself in incendiarism, looting, and robbery. The Government commands all its forces, whether military or civilian, to quell any such disturbances wherever they may encounter them, and to be prepared to apply the utmost severity of the law to those who commit such offenses. . . ."

The pieces of furniture stayed there, strewn over the pavement. Milicianos stood guard beside the spoils.

The people clustering in ardent discussions were cheerful; now the insurrection was beaten, the Right would soon realize what Socialist rule would be like. The blindfolded, somber street became illuminated and almost festive.

At the entrance of the Calle de la Magdalena appeared three lorries packed with standing Milicianos who shouted rhythmically: "U.H.P.—U.H.P.—U.H.P."

The street took up the cry, with raised fists. When one of the lorries stopped and the militiamen came tumbling out, the crowd clotted around them. Many of the men had rifles and army leather straps; there were some women in men's clothes, in blue boiler suits.

"Where have you come from?"

"We've had a good day—we've given the Fascists a beating they won't forget so quickly—we've come from the Sierra—the Fascists are in Villalba, but they won't have much guts left to come to Madrid. We met a lot of soldiers going in the other direction when we were coming back."

"But how is it that they let you come back?" a stout woman asked a man who seemed to be her husband, a mason by the traces on his overall, in the middle forties, somewhat the worse for drink.

"Now listen to her! Who would have the right to stop us? When we saw it would soon be getting dark, we all said it's time to go home to bed, so that the ladies shouldn't get frightened without us. Some of the lads stayed behind, but they had taken their wives along."

After supper a boisterous crowd thronged the streets, fleeing from the suffocating heat of their houses and still optimistically discussing the Government declaration and the impending end of the insurrection.

Rafael and I set out to make a round of the most popular meeting places of the quarter. I wanted to see the people.

First we went to the Café de la Magdalena. It is a very old café and music hall, where, in the last century, generations of gypsy dancers and flamenco singers had paraded, to be followed by "national and foreign dancers" who came nearer and nearer to strip-tease acts as the era of the cakewalk, machicha and rumba passed. There was always a core of simple-minded customers, workers, and strangers who came to have a drink and stare at crude variety numbers, and round them a fringe of prostitutes with their pimps lying in ambush and the police never far away.

That night some two hundred people blocked the entrance, all trying to get in. Two Milicianos with rifles over their shoulders guarded the door. Rafael and I were determined to get through, and we made it. The rowdy who was porter and ticket collector at the same time never asked for our tickets, but greeted us so unctuously with a "Salud, comrades" that Rafael muttered: "He thinks we're plain-clothes cops."

The huge saloon was crammed with couples of sweating men and women, who swayed and pushed in a futile attempt to follow the strident tune of the dance band, all braying brass and bleating saxophones. Above their heads hung a streaky pall of bluish smoke turned gray by the dust. They smelled like a truckload of sheep doused with cheap eau-de-Cologne. The men and women were clad in workmen's overalls as though in a uniform, and a pistol was stuck in almost every belt. The big Astra pistols from the Cuartel de la Montaña glinted blue, and their burnished mouths glittered in the garish light.

When the band stopped, the mass howled: "More—more!" They struck up the *Himno de Riego,* the Republican anthem. The multitude sang the chorus to the words of the popular parody:

> *Simeon had three old cats*
> *And gave them food on a plate . . .*

When it was over, they howled louder than before. The small jazz band intoned a crazy Internationale, with drums, cymbals, and jingling jazz bells. All the people stopped, raised their clenched fists, and sang religiously:

> *Arise, ye starvelings from your slumbers,*
> *Arise, ye criminals of want . . .*

A swarthy, bulky man with frizzed black hair falling over his ears and neck, a black-and-red scarf wound round his throat, towered above the others and roared: "Long live the F.A.I.!"

At the Anarchists' war cry, it seemed for an instant as though it would come to a brawl. The air was thick with insults. Black-and-red scarves gathered at the back of the saloon. Nervous fingers fumbled at belts and hips. Women squealed like cornered rats and clutched at their men. The Internationale broke off as though choked by a huge fist.

A little man in the ludicrous coat of a waiter had jumped on to the dais and was screaming something, while the big white drum behind him made a frame for his contortions and punctuated them with its thuds. The crowd fell silent, and the little man shrieked with a grating voice: "Comrades"—he must have thought that he had better not use the Communist style of address alone, and corrected himself "—or fellow workers! We've come here to have a bit of fun—don't forget we are all brothers in the struggle against Fascism, all brother workers—U.H.P.!" The saloon shook when the crowd repeated the three magic letters in a staccato rhythm. Then the band struck up a galloping fox trot, the couples started to dance in a furious whirl. They had more room to dance now; many had left.

Rafael and I were edging out, when a mass of flesh bulging out of a tight boiler suit hooked itself on to my arm, with opulent breasts almost at the height of my shoulders and a wave of cheap, cloying scent: "Come on, sweetie, buy me a drink. I'm dying of thirst."

I had seen her many a night walking on her beat at the corner of the Plaza de Antón Martin. I freed my arm.

"I'm so sorry, but we've got to go. We've been looking for a friend, but he isn't here."

"I'll come along with you."

I did not dare to give the woman an aggressive refusal; a mischievous phrase could easily provoke an attack from those temperamental so-called Milicianos, particularly as Rafael and I were too well dressed for the place. The woman clung to us until we came to the Plaza de Antón Martín. There we took her into the Bar Zaragoza, bought her a beer, and disappeared. She was swallowed by a delirious mass of half-drunken men and women, of pistols and black-and-red handkerchiefs, menacing splotches of color in a swaying sea of heads.

We crossed the street and went into Serafín's tavern. The small bar was cluttered, but we walked through to the back room. There were familiar faces. Old Señor Paco was there, the politicizing carpenter, with a new, shiny leather belt and the straps of a soldier, a rifle between his knees, holding forth to an enthralled audience:

"As I say, we had a fine day in the open, there in the Sierra. Just as if we'd gone shooting rabbits. Near Villalba a post of Shock Police stopped us in the middle of the road, and sent us up to a hill top between rocks and scrubs with a corporal and two constables. The wife had cooked a tortilla to take along, and Serafín had filled my leather bottle with wine in the morning, so everything was fine. The worst of it was that we all got scorched among the stones there, because the sun shone straight down on us. But we didn't see the tip of a Fascist's nose, and we've had a very nice day. There were some shots from the direction of the road, and for a time we heard machine guns, but very far away. The corporal said he had posted us there so that the others shouldn't sneak through the hills, and he also said things were very serious over near Buitrago. Well, so that was that. We've eaten splendidly, my nose is peeling from the sun, and we've had a first-class day. Most of us came back in the evening. The Lieutenant of the Shock Police wanted us to stay, but what the hell, we aren't soldiers, I said. Let them stay there, that's what they're paid for."

"Are you going back tomorrow, Paco?"

"At six in the morning, if God will it. Well, of course, that's just a manner of speaking, because we've done with that sort of thing now."

There was a man in the circle whom I had never seen before. He smelled of gasoline and had cold gray eyes and thin lips. He said:

"We've had an even better day. We've made a clean up."

"Have you been chasing Fascists across the roofs?"

"That's for kids. We've been selling tickets for the Other World in the Casa de Campo. We led them out like sheep. A shot in the neck, and that was that. We haven't got much ammunition to spare." While he was speaking, his hand made a gruesome shadow play in the air. Cold shivers ran up and down my spine.

"But that's all the Government's affair now, isn't it?"

He stared at me with his frosted eyes.

"Pal—the Government, that's us."

We talked of him while we walked home, Rafael and I. If that kind of person got power there would be a frightful slaughter. But it was to be hoped that the Government would step in. We looked at each other and shut up.

When we came to the street corner, where two Milicianos stopped us and asked for our papers, we heard from the far end of the Calle del Ave María the noise of shouts, running feet, a shot and a cry. Then the running feet sounded again, further away, and the street lay silent. The pair of Milicianos did not know what to do. One of them turned to us: "Shall we go?"

The street was deserted, but I sensed the people whispering behind the closed doors of the houses. One of the Milicianos loaded his rifle, the other followed suit. The bolts clanked loudly. Down the street someone cried: "Halt!"

The militiamen answered the shout. Two shadows moved towards us, keeping close to the walls. Before our groups met, we saw the dead man. He was lying across the gutter, a tiny black hole in his forehead. He had a cushion of blood under his head. The fingers of his outflung hands were contracting. The body jerked and then lay still. We bent over him, and one of the Milicianos lighted a match close to his mouth. The little flame burned unwaveringly and lighted up the gaping face and glazed eyes. The big black-and-red scarf looked like a wound in the throat. It was the man who had shouted "Long live the F.A.I.!" in the Café de la Magdalena.

One of the Milicianos said philosophically: "One less." Another went to telephone. Three mounted guard over the corpse. The house doors opened and curious faces drew near, gray disks in the darkness.

I could not sleep. The heat choked me, and through the open balcony entered the noise of the street and the music from the loudspeakers. I got up and sat on the balcony in my pajamas.

I could not continue to drift.

When I had gone to the People's House on Saturday, I had done so because I wanted to serve in the ranks of the anti-Fascist formations in the capacity in which I would be most useful. I knew that what we lacked and needed above all were officers, closely knit groups of trained men who could lead and organize bodies of militia. I was ready then to do such work and to exploit my hated experiences in the Moroccan War. But Azaña had nominated the Government of Martínez Barrio with Sánchez Román as a discreet negotiator, a Government clearly created so as to make a deal with the rebels, and when the Commander of the Socialist Militia had told his men to accept it with discipline, even while the masses were roaring with fury and forcing the President to rectify his step within an hour, I had walked out. I was unable to submit to this sort of blind political discipline.

I had rubbed elbows with the mass of Milicianos, of people calling themselves Milicianos and accepted as such, for three days and nights. This was a pseudo-military machinery of which I did not want to become a part.

But I could not continue on the fringe of events. I felt the duty and I had the need for action. The Government stated that the rising had finished, but it was evident that the contrary was true. The rising had not yet begun in full earnest. This was war, civil war and a revolution. It could not finish until the country had been transformed either into a Fascist or into a Socialist state. I did not have to choose between the two. The choice had been taken for me by my whole life. Either a Socialist revolution would win or I would be among the vanquished.

It was obvious that the vanquished, whoever they would be, would be shot or locked up in a prison cell. That bourgeois life to which I had tried to resign myself and against which I had been struggling had ended on the 18th of July 1936. Whether I would be among the victors or the vanquished, a new life had begun.

I agreed with Prieto's statement in *Informaciones:* This was war, and a long war at that.

A new life meant hope. The revolution which was the hope of Spain was also my own hope for a fuller, cleaner, more lucid life.

I would get away from the two women. Somewhere I would be needed. I would shut myself up in work as though behind the walls of a fortress. For the Government simply had to take things in hand.

And supposing it was unable to do so? If revolution meant the right to kill with impunity—where would we end? We would kill each other for a word, for a shout. The revolution, Spain's hope, would turn into the bloody orgy of a brutal minority. If the Government was too weak, it was up to the political groups to take the lead and to organize the fight.

But I was still under the impression of what I had seen that very night in the quarter of El Avapiés. I had seen the mass of prostitutes, thieves, pimps and gunmen in a bestial frenzy. This was not the mass which had stormed the Cuartel de la Montaña, mere human bodies against machine guns. This was the scum of the city. They would not fight. They would not carry through a revolution. But they would rob, destroy, and kill for pleasure. That carrion had to be swept away before it infected everything.

I had to find my own people. We needed an army. Tomorrow, today, I would go and see Rubiera. We would work together again, as we had done years before, and we would achieve something useful.

For a short time I dozed on the balcony. One of the children in the room behind me began to cry. I wondered what would happen to my children. The office was going to stop work. On what were the people out of work going to live? I had the means to hold out for months; but what would happen to those who lived on their weekly wages and had received their last pay envelope on Saturday the 18th?

A motor horn was barking impatiently down in the street. It was daybreak. My boy in there was crying more loudly. The door of our house clanked open and Manolo, the concierge's son, came out, leather straps, rifle and all. I called down: "Where are you going?"

"To the Sierra, with the boys here. There will be a bit of shooting. Do you want to come along?"

The lorry was full of militiamen in the blue boiler suits which by now seemed to have become a uniform. Most of them wore the five-pointed star of the Communists. There were three girls among them.

The lorry lumbered up the street, its occupants singing at the top of their voices. Downstairs a door was thrown open; the smell of freshly made coffee was wafted up to my balcony. I dressed and went down to Emiliano's bar. The manager, Emiliano's brother, had red-rimmed eyes, puffed with sleeplessness.

"It's a dog's life. Emiliano will have to come here and do his own work. Tomorrow I'm going to the front."

The first customers drifted in, the night watchman, the Milicianos who had been on guard in the street, the baker's men, a driver.

"Salud!"

"Salud!"

A band of sparrows was pecking among the paving stones and hopping on the balcony rails. From a window high up came the call of a caged quail: "Pal-pa-la—pal-pa-la!"

The street was deserted and flooded with peace.

9. Man Hunt

T H E work at our office was practically at a standstill. The firm was faced with the problem of whether to carry on in a void or to shut down altogether and risk being taken over by a workers' committee. For at that time, such committees had begun to take control of private firms, factories, and tenements in each case in which the owners were known to sympathize with the Right or had deserted their offices and buildings, either because they were guilty of conspiracy with the rebels or because they were afraid of staying on. In this emergency, the workers and employees set up committees which carried on the work; other committees were formed by trade unions, and imposed their control on firms the owners of which were suspect.

This movement was an act of self-defense against economic collapse. It developed without order or concerted action, and there were many cases of bad faith or crude theft. Yet with all its blemishes and errors, it prevented Madrid from being starved within one week, and it prevented the black market from flourishing.

Our chief decided that to maintain his unproductive business would be a lesser evil. It looked as though the situation would soon be settled by events outside his control. Already on July the 18th, one of our staff had disappeared and not even his family knew his whereabouts. Two of our men who had been officers reported to the War Ministry and were posted away from Madrid. Our two German employees had vanished. There were three men and four typists left, apart from myself and Carlitos, the office boy. We agreed to keep the office open from ten to twelve. There were no further difficulties, since the patent business had nothing to do with the war, involved nothing but papers, and did not arouse the interest of any of the workers' groups which assumed control of undertakings whose products had more immediate value.

My brother Rafael was the accountant of a perfumery wholesaler's. His chief was an intelligent autocrat hated by the whole staff; within twenty hours of the murder of Calvo Sotelo he had crossed the frontier together with his family. His staff took over the store, with the backing of the Communist Party to which the most active of the employees belonged, and tried to carry on the business on which their living depended. As I had time hanging on my hands, I often went there and observed how it worked; but the same thing happened in some hundreds of warehouses and stores all over Madrid. Simultaneously, each trade union and each party group began to organize its own militia. That was the time of the militia battalions with high-flown names apparently taken from penny dreadfuls, such as the "Red Lions" or the "Black Eagles."

It was also the time of the vouchers.

One morning, two militiamen with rifles over their shoulders and the black-and-red scarf of the Anarchists wound round their throats turned up at my brother's store and presented to him, as the man in charge, the following voucher:

Valid for
        5,000 safety razors
        5,000 sticks of shaving soap
    100,000 razor blades
        5,000 bottles of branded eau-de-Cologne
            10 50-liter flagons of barber's eau-de-Cologne
        1,000 kilos of toilet soap

My brother refused to accept the voucher: "I'm sorry, but I can't give you what you ask for. And by the way, whom do you want all this for?"

"Look at the stamp: the Anarchist Militia in the Círculo de Bellas Artes. . . . What do you mean, you can't let us have it? That's a joke." "No joke at all, pals. I wouldn't accept that kind of voucher unless it was endorsed by the War Ministry." "All right, then we'll take you with us."

To be taken to the Círculo de Bellas Artes meant the risk of being found at dawn in the Casa de Campo, with one's neck shattered by a bullet. The two Milicianos were alone, while there were plenty of men with pistols in their pocket about in the store. My brother told the two to wait and rang up the command of the Anarchist Militias in the Círculo. They had not heard of the voucher and asked my brother to bring the two Milicianos and the voucher to them. There it turned out that the men had attempted a bold theft; the Anarchists shot them that night.

Yet vouchers which had to be accepted piled up on my brother's desk, papers which no one would ever redeem. The only money which reached the cashier came in payment for the scanty orders from tradesmen carrying on their business, but as no credit was granted any more, they bought nothing but goods whose sale was absolutely certain. Food began to be frighteningly scarce.

The trade unions which enforced the acceptance of their vouchers could not refuse to issue meal vouchers to their members. They had taken over many cafés and restaurants in the city; when a trade-union member wanted a meal, he was given a stamped voucher from his organization and went to one of its restaurants. Meal vouchers became valid tender when wages began to peter out. At first, people squeezed in at small café tables as best they could. Then the tables were pushed together in the middle of the room and converted into long mess tables. People sat down next to each other as they arrived, though they tried to snatch a seat near the kitchen door. Meals were distributed at one o'clock sharp. There was no bread; many people brought a roll or a chunk of bread along in their pockets. A stream of women and children passed through, all coming to carry their food home in a pot tied into a napkin or large handkerchief. The menu was based on rice and potatoes boiled with meat, the ration was practically unlimited. Albacete was in the hands of the Government, so that communications with Valencia were safe, and Valencia poured the rice and potatoes into Madrid, where all supplies were taken over by the trade unions. Each organization seized as much as possible and shared the food out among the communal restaurants under its control. Empty churches served as storehouses. The smell of a badly kept grocer's shop streamed out into the streets from wide open church doors.

In my brother's office the staff distributed the money among themselves at the end of the month, and the meal vouchers every day. But their stock of perfumery goods was rapidly dwindling. They were beginning to feel desperate.

The Government was powerless in the face of the chaos. There was no group which would accept orders from it.

The political parties were subdivided into their local branches, the trade unions into trade groups as well as local branches. Each of the groups and branches set up its own communal feeding center, its own supply service and storehouse, its own militia battalion, its own police, its own prison, its own executioners, and a special place for its executions. They all made propaganda to attract new members, except for the U.G.T. The walls of Madrid were covered with appeals: "Join the C.N.T." "Join the Communist Party!" "Join the P.O.U.M." The Republicans pure and simple did not count. People flocked to the centers of the organizations, let themselves be introduced by one or two old members, and obtained a. membership card.

Fascists found this a useful subterfuge. They selected the groups which were least strict in their requirements and joined in large numbers. Some people paid heavily for a membership card antedated by two or three years. With this backing, Fascists would commandeer their own cars and use them to save their friends and to kill off their enemies. Criminals found cover by the same method. They, too, would form their own police and proceed to rob and kill with impunity. No one was safe. Consulates and embassies opened their gates to refugees; some of them set up refuges on a grand scale, ran them as luxury hotels and bought whole houses for the purpose.

Side by side with all that chaos, misery, and cowardice, the other thing which was alive behind the bombastic names of Red Lions and Black Eagles began to assume shape. The excursions to the Sierra were stopped. Positions were established in the hills. Loyal officers set out to mold that embryo of an army. Every group could create a militia battalion, but now the arms, the few arms available, were in the hands of the War Ministry; they were distributed to the volunteer militias, but they in turn had to accept the Ministry's rule in order to exist. At the same time, parties and trade unions competed in showing each other a model of discipline and bravery.

The Rebel Army under General Mola was thrown back behind Villalba; Toledo was retaken; Saragossa was attacked through the province of Huesca; a force was landed in the Balearics; Ceuta was raided.

But there was still no cohesion, although there was plenty of enthusiasm. Party pride seemed stronger than the feeling of common defense. A victory of an Anarchist battalion was paraded in the face of the Communists; a victory of a Communist unit was secretly lamented by the others.

The defeat of a battalion was turned into ridicule for the political group to which it belonged. This strengthened the fighting spirit of the individual units, but also created a hotbed of mutual resentment damaging the military operations as a whole and circumventing a unified command.

I had gone to see Antonio, the Communist, and Carlos Rubiera, the Socialist. I told Antonio that I wanted to work, but refused to join a party militia; the leaders of the Clerical Workers' Union, which I had helped to found together with Rubiera five years earlier, told me that I might be useful in helping to organize the Clerical Workers' Battalion. I tackled the task with something like despair. I doubted the response of the white-collar workers.

They allotted us a commandeered house with a tennis court in the aristocratic Barrio de Salamanca. Fifty volunteers started their military training on that court. We had our theoretical instruction in the enormous marble hall with its pretentious Doric columns; there we ranged benches taken from a near-by school, installed a dais, a huge blackboard and a map of Spain. The War Ministry let us have two dozen rifles and one spare cartridge case per rifle.

I made them form platoons on the tennis court and began to lecture them on the handling of a rifle. Before me I had a double file of anemic faces perched on starched collars, with a sprinkling of coarser heads topping blouses or braided, tight-fitting livery coats; most of my volunteers were clerks, but a few were office boys and messengers. Some were very young and some old. Many had spectacles which made their eyes glitter and their faces look nervous.

After the first two minutes of my instruction one of the recruits stepped out of the file.

"Now look here, all that's stuff and nonsense. The only thing we need to know is how to shoot. Then give us a rifle and we'll march to wherever we have to. I haven't come here to play at soldiers."

I ordered them to fall out, took them to the hall and stepped on to the platform.

"Now, you all want a rifle and you all want to go to the front to fire off your rifle and to kill Fascists. But none of you wants to go through the military instruction. Now, suppose I give a rifle to every one of you this moment, pack you into a couple of lorries and place you on the crest of Sierra—in face of Mola's army, with its officers and sergeants who are used to giving commands, and its soldiers who are used to obeying orders and who know what each order means. What would you do? Each of you would run about by himself and fire off bullets, I suppose. Do you think the men you would have to face are just rabbits? And even if you went shooting rabbits in a party of ten or twelve, you'd have to know how to do it if you didn't want to shoot each other."

We went back to the tennis court and continued the instruction. Many times I was interrupted when someone exclaimed: "We're wasting our time—anybody knows how to throw himself down when he's got to!" It was the same with each new batch of volunteers. But slowly a unit began to emerge, although it still had nothing but two dozen rifles passed from platoon to platoon. It was the beginning of the Battalion *La Pluma*, The Pen.

In those days, Angel practically lived in my flat. Since his wife had gone away, he helped Aurelia with the house, the children, and the shopping, as he had done in the first weeks of our acquaintanceship. He knew so many people in the quarter in which he had been born and bred that he always found something for our meals. One day he turned up pushing a wheelbarrow with two sacks of potatoes, and followed by a train of women. He stopped before the door of our house and cried:

"Make a queue, please."

The women obediently stepped into line, and Angel produced a scale and weights out of thin air, by a conjurer's trick.

"Two pounds each, my girls, and mind no one comes twice!"

When the potatoes in the first sack had disappeared, Angel opened the second sack and swept the queue with a glance.

"Friends, I need potatoes myself. These here are for me." He weighed out twenty pounds and put them in the first sack. "And now let's get rid of what's left."

Angel went for potatoes to the market of Mataderos where the goods trains were unloaded. His quick tongue always secured him the friendship of the man in charge of the distribution to the tradesmen. He was a street vendor himself, he would say; that was what he did for his living, and the poor people of El Avapiés got something to eat as well. "Now look, pal. Here you are giving the potatoes to a shopkeeper of the Barrio de Salamanca, so that he can feed the rich and the Fascists. Won't you let me have two sacks?" Then he would invite the man to a cup of coffee and cognac early in the morning and get his two sacks. Once the Anarchists from a branch in the neighboring street wanted to expropriate the two sacks of potatoes, but the women almost rioted against them, and Angel obtained the protection of the Anarchists' leaders.

Then came days when even Angel found no potatoes, because no potatoes reached Madrid. Aurelia took the children to her parents. I was about to leave the flat, when Angel said: "If you'll come to my room with me, I'll go along with you. I've nothing to do today."

I accompanied him to the Calle de Jesús y María. The street begins in the Plaza de Progreso, among the houses of the well-to-do people, and for a stretch of fifty yards the inhabitants of its old houses are small tradesmen and skilled workers. So far the street is paved with big square porphyry blocks. Then it narrows down and changes its face. The paving is made of sharp edged pebbles, the houses are low, squalid, and rickety, the people who live in them are very poor workers and prostitutes. The tarts lounge in the open doors and fill the street with their quarrels.

Angel lived on the ground floor of a small tenement house stuck between two brothels. His flat was a single big room divided into a bedroom, dining room, and kitchen by thin partition walls. There was nothing in the bedroom but a double bed and a night table. The kitchen was half the size of the bedroom. Light and air entered through the door and through a barred window which opened on to a courtyard three yards square, containing the lavatory for all the tenants of the ground floor and the water tap for the whole house. The room, now deserted, smelled of mildew and urine. I waited for Angel while he changed in the bedroom.

Suddenly, an explosion shook the house. Angel came out, still struggling into his coat. Piercing cries and the patter of feet sounded outside. Angel and I went out into the street. People were running wildly. A few yards away, several women were lying on the ground and shrieking. One of them was dragging herself along on a belly torn to bleeding tatters. The walls of the houses and the paving stones were spattered with blood. Then we were all running towards the injured.

In the last house of the wide stretch of the street was a clinic for nursing mothers. At that hour there had been a queue of women, most of them carrying a child, waiting for the distribution of milk. A few yards further down, prostitutes had been following their trade. A bomb had fallen in the middle of the street and sprayed the mothers and the street walkers. A woman propped up on her bleeding arm stump gave a scream and let herself drop heavily. Near me was a bundle of petticoats with a leg sticking out, bent at an impossible angle over a swollen belly. My head was swimming, I vomited into the gutter. A militiaman beside me cursed and was sick. Then he began to tremble and broke out into spasmodic laughter. Someone gave me a glass of neat brandy and I poured it down my throat. Angel had disappeared. Some men were busy picking up the wounded and the dead and carrying them into the clinic. A man stuck his head out of the gate, white hair and spectacles over a blood-stained surgeon's overall, stamped his foot, and yelled: "No more room! Take them to Encomienda!"

Shrieks sounded from the Plaza del Progreso. Angel was beside me, his coat and hands splashed with blood.

"Another bomb in the Plaza del Progreso!"

Groups of people came running down the street in frenzied fear, pairs of men carrying someone between them, women with children in their arms, all screaming and shrieking. I saw nothing but arms and legs and bloodstains in motion, and the street rocked before my eyes.

"Go to Encomienda! There's been one here too."

The whirling mass of arms and legs disappeared through the Calle de Esgrima.

We went back to Angel's flat and washed. Angel changed again. When we came out of the house, the neighbors told us that a plane had flown low over Madrid from north to south, dropping bombs all along its course. It had left a trail of blood from the Puerta de Toledo to Cuatro Caminos. By accident or because the pilot guided himself by the open spaces, most of the bombs had fallen in public squares and many children had been hit.

That was on the 7th of August 1936. That evening and that night, Fascists were firing from windows and from skylights. Many hundreds were arrested. There were mass executions of suspects during the night.

Antonio sent for me while I was at home in the evening. The local branch of the Communist Party was organizing pickets to paint the street lamps blue and to see to the blackout. Rafael, Angel, and I went. We worked in small groups, each protected by two armed Milicianos; but it was an almost hopeless task to improvise a blackout in August, in Madrid. Shuttered houses were stifling. It was impossible to stay in any public place with the shutters closed. We had to compromise. People were to avoid the rooms facing on to the street and stay in the inner rooms, using only candles. It was easy to paint the street lamps blue, with a mixture of water, aniline dye, and plaster; only a few tenuous, white rays filtered through. We turned off every other lamp.

The streets looked ghostly in our wake, night black, with white dots on the pavements and blue, sickly blobs of light a little higher up in the dark. Sometimes the front of a house was lighted by the fugitive glow of a candle carried through a room in the house opposite, which turned a balcony into a yellow square of light, streaked by the black lines of the railing, and leaped distorted along the walls. The people thronged the streets as they did every night, but they were only half visible in the penumbra, shapeless black bulks from which voices came and, at intervals, the dazzling spark of a lighter or the little red glow from a cigarette outlining a few heads.

Some lorries arrived carrying Milicianos returning from the Sierra and from Toledo. Their headlights were switched on; the crowds caught in their beams looked livid and naked. The cry went up: "The lights—turn out the lights!"

Brakes screeched, and the lorries rolled slowly on amid the sound of breaking chairs and pitchers. The red light of the rear lamps glowed like a bloodshot eye. In the darkness it was as though nightmare monsters were panting there, about to spring.

By midnight the whole quarter lay in deep shadow. In the Calle de la Primavera we stopped under a street lamp which had been forgotten. One of us climbed up, while another reached him the brush soaked in blue dye. A shot cracked, a bullet ricocheted on the wall above the lamp. Somebody had shot at us from one of the houses opposite. The people lounging in the street took refuge in doorways. We marched out the tenants of the four houses from which the shot might have come. The concierge and neighbors identified them one by one. Then we weeded out those who had been in the street from the others, and started to search each flat in turn. All the tenants surged after us and asked us to go into their flats with them; they wanted to clear themselves, and at the same time they were afraid that a stranger might have hidden in their rooms. We searched through attics and lofts full of cobwebs and old rags, we climbed up and down stairs, we caught dust and dirt on our clothes and banged against rafters and invisible nails. At four in the morning we had finished; we were filthy and sleepy, it was broad daylight, but we had not found the sniper. Somebody had brought a huge pitcher filled with steaming coffee and a bottle of brandy. We drank greedily.

One of the men said: "That bird's saved his skin." As though in answer, Angel exclaimed: "Let's go to Mataderos and see the ones who were polished off this time."

At first I refused to go, and then I suddenly gave in. It was easier. I dug my fist into Angel's ribs and said to him: "You're a brute—after what we saw yesterday afternoon, too!"

"God save us—come along, then you'll get rid of the bitter taste of seeing those mangled kids yesterday. Do you remember the woman with child, who had her leg doubled up on her navel? Well, she was still alive and she gave birth in the clinic. Then she died. A boy, it was. Nobody in the whole quarter knows her."

The executions had attracted far more people than I would have thought possible. Families with their children, excited and still drowsy with sleep, and militiamen with their girls were walking along the Paseo de las Delicias, all in the same direction. Requisitioned cars and lorries were passing by. Crowds and cars had collected at the entrance to the vegetable market and the slaughterhouses at the Glorieta. While carts and trucks with green vegetables came and went, militia pickets on duty meandered round and asked anyone who caught their fancy for his papers.

Behind the slaughterhouses a long brick wall and an avenue with stunted little trees, not yet rooted in the sandy soil under that ruthless sun, run along the river. The landscape is arid and cold with the chill of the cemented canal, of sand, and of dry, yellow tufts of grass.

The corpses lay between the little trees. The sightseers ambled from one to the other and made humorous remarks; a pitying comment might have provoked suspicion.

I had expected the bodies. Their sight did not shake me. There were about twenty of them. They were not mangled. I had seen far worse in Morocco and on the day before. But I was shaken by the collective brutality and cowardice of the spectators.

Vans which belonged to the City of Madrid arrived to collect the corpses. One of the drivers said: "Now they're going to water the place and make it nice and spruce for tonight." He chuckled. It rang like fear.

Somebody gave us a lift back to the Plaza de Antón Martín. We entered Emiliano's bar to have our breakfast. Sebastian, the concierge at Number Seven, was there with a rifle leaning behind him. He left his coffee when he saw us and started to explain with extravagant gestures: "What a night—I'm dead beat! I've accounted for eleven."

Angel asked: "What is it you've done? Where have you been?"

"In the Pradera de San Isidro. I went with lads of my union and we took some Fascists with us. Then friends from other groups turned up and we had to lend them a hand. I believe we've got rid of more than a hundred this time."

I felt hollow in the pit of my stomach. Here was somebody whom I had known almost since I was a child. I knew him as a cheerful, industrious man who was fond of his children and of other people's children; doubtless rather crude, with little brains, but all the same honest and forthright. Here he was turned into an assassin.

"But, Sebastian—who dragged you"—I used the formal pronoun *usted* instead of the customary, familiar *tú*—"who in the world has dragged you into such things?"

He looked at me out of shame-filled eyes.

"Oh well, Don Arturo"—he did not dare to speak to me in the way he had spoken for over twenty years—"you're not going to start with sentimentalities, I hope. We must make an end of all those Fascist swine."

"That's not what I was asking you. I want to know who dragged you into these doings."

"Nobody."

"Then why are you doing it?"

"Well, someone has to."

I said nothing and he began to stammer.

"The truth is . . . the truth is, to tell you the truth in confidence . . . it's like this. You know I found work a year or so ago with a recommendation from the C.E.D.A., which my landlord got for me. And after the February elections I didn't need their scrap of paper any more and went back to my own Union, of course. The boys all pulled my leg because I had belonged to the C.E.D.A., and because they said I had turned a reactionary, and so on. Naturally I told them I was as good a revolutionary as they. Then one day they took some Fascists for a ride and one of our boys said to me: 'Now then, up with you, come on, as you're always talking of killing Fascists.' And you can imagine the rest. I was between the devil and the deep sea, because it was either the one or the other, either I had to finish off one of those poor devils, or the lads would have bumped me off. Well, since then I've simply been going there, and they tell me when there's something doing."

He stopped and pondered, and then shook his head slowly.

"The worst of it is, you know, that I'm beginning to like it."

He stood there with a drooping head. It was repulsive and pitiful. Emiliano's brother gulped down a glass of brandy and swore. I swore too. Then I said:

"Sebastian, I've known you all my life, and I used to respect you. But now, I tell you—and you can denounce me on the spot—that I won't ever speak to you again."

Sebastian lifted the eyes of a whipped dog, full of water. Emiliano's brother blasphemed and smashed his empty glass on the marble slab: "Get out!"

The man walked out meekly, with bowed shoulders. None of us saw him again, and days later we heard that he had gone to the front. He was killed by a bullet, in an attic in front of the Alcazar of Toledo.

At eleven o'clock that morning, a middle-aged woman in black came to see me in the office. She was tearful and agitated: "I'm Don Pedro's sister. They arrested him this morning. I've come to you because he told me to get in touch with you if anything happened. . . . I don't know where they've taken him, I only know that the men who came for him were Communists and took him away in a car."

I went to Antonio and explained the case. "If I were you, I wouldn't interfere in this mess," he said. "From what you tell me he's a Rightist and known as such. So no one can help him."

"All right, maybe we can't save him, but we must try, and you've got to help me try."

"I'll help you to find him if it's true that our people have arrested him, but I won't interfere in any other way. I've got enough unpleasantness with these matters as it is."

We found out to which tribunal Don Pedro had been taken, and went there together. The men in charge let us see the denunciation. Whoever had written it knew the Ministry inside out; it described in great detail how Don Pedro had behaved on the day of Calvo Sotelo's assassination, explained his religious creed and stated that he had a private chapel in his house and kept a priest in hiding there. The denunciation ended with the statement that he was a rich man and possessed a numismatic collection of considerable value.

"You see, there's nothing to be done," said the man who showed us the papers. "Tomorrow we're going to take him for a ride."

I took a deep breath and said: "You accuse him of belonging to the Right. He does. It is also true that he is a practising Catholic and a rich man, if that's an offense, and that he has a collection of antique gold coins. But I don't think that's a crime."

"It isn't. We know that the fellow who denounced him is a son of a bitch who only put in that bit about the collection so as to make us go for the old man. Don't you worry. We may take him for a ride, but we aren't thieves."

"I know, or I wouldn't be working with the Party. But as you see, the only concrete thing against him is the story about the priest he's hiding. It doesn't surprise me of the man. I believe he would be capable of hiding me too if the Fascists were after me. But tell me, has the priest taken active part in the rising?"

"I don't think so. He's just a priest of San Ginés who's got the jitters and gone into a burrow like a rabbit, but I don't believe he's any good for a man's job any more, he's over seventy."

"Then you must admit that it wasn't a crime to hide him. And now I'm going to tell you another thing the man you've arrested has done." I told them the story of Don Pedro and the consumptive clerk. "It would be a crime to execute a man who had acted like that," I ended.

"I can't do anything about it, my lad. What you can do, if you like, is to stand surety for his good faith yourself. The other members of our tribunal will see whether they find it a strong enough guarantee. But I would advise you not to do it, because we might just as easily have to lock you up yourself."

Don Pedro was set free that afternoon. I went again to see Antonio and reported the fact to him.

"I knew it. They asked me plenty of questions about you. And apparently they couldn't find anything concrete against the old man. It's a pity that we can't investigate every single case in the same way, but it's quite impossible, I assure you."

He stopped and went on after a long pause: "You know I'm counsel for the defense on one of the tribunals? Come with me this afternoon, you can stay as a witness. We must finish half a dozen cases tonight. I personally believe that the Government ought to take the whole thing into its own hands. On the day of the bombing, the tribunals didn't even sit and pass sentence, everyone who was brought in was shot, and that was that. The people wouldn't listen to reason. The same thing happened when Badajoz was taken by the Fascists and our people were slaughtered in the bull-ring there. Before that you could straighten out some of the cases, but now it's getting more and more difficult every day. The worst thing about this job I've taken on is that, in the long run, one is drawing suspicion on oneself by defending others and trying to see that things are done decently. I think I'll chuck it up and let them do their dirty work alone."

He took me to one of the most popular churches in Madrid, which had been turned into a prison and a tribunal. The offices had been installed in the priest's house, the prison in the crypt. The church stood in a small, dingy street, but the priest's old, two-story house was imbedded in high, modern buildings in one of the big streets of the town. We entered a narrow doorway and walked through a long corridor with stone walls and stone floor, dark, dank, and oppressive. Then the corridor turned at a right angle, and we stood in the entrance to a wide, flagged courtyard with two carpets of well-tended lawn in the middle and potted flowers along the walls. Before us was the huge colored glass window in the back wall of the church. The sun shone on the bits of glass in their leaden frames and made them glint. Sparks of blue, red, green, and purple fell on flagstones, grass and walls, and the flagstones were mottled with green and the lawn with deep purple. While we walked past, each piece of glass in turn sent out a flash of its own pure color. There was an age-old grapevine covering the south wall with its green leaves and golden-green grapes, and a flock of sparrows which did not scatter at our steps.

The militiamen on sentry duty sat on canvas chairs in the shade, smoking and contemplating the birds.

Antonio and I climbed a narrow stairway and found ourselves in a room, which must have been the parish priest's. A missal lay open on a lectern near the balcony. Half of its left page was covered by a huge gilt Q fringed with red arabesques. The book was printed in a clear, old letterpress and the first letter of each chapter and each verse was painted by hand. The initials of the chapters were gilded, the initials of the verses were smaller and painted only in red. A voice at my back said: "It is prohibited to take away the prayer book." A Miliciano was sitting in the upholstered leather armchair behind an old, massive desk covered with green cloth. He was a boy of twenty-three or so, strong, with broad shoulders, a broad grin and broad, milk-white teeth.

"You wouldn't believe how many people are after that book. But it looks pretty here, don't you think? One of our comrades can sing Mass and sometimes he does it for us."

While we were chatting, another man entered, in the forties, with a fierce mustache, black and crooked teeth and lively gray eyes. His *Salud* sounded more like the growl of a dog than like a salute, and he started at once to swear, displaying an inexhaustible vocabulary of blasphemies. When he had vented his bad temper he dropped heavily into a chair and stared at us.

"Well," he said after a while, "today we'll liquidate all the Fascists we've got here. A pity it's only half a dozen, I'd prefer six dozen."

"What's bitten you today, Little Paws?" asked the young Miliciano.

I looked at the older man's hands. They were huge, with knotted fingers, and broad, chipped nails like spades, rimmed with black.

"You can call me Little Paws as much as you like, but if I get hold of one of those dirty dogs today and smack his face, his head will fly off its socket. Do you know whom we found this morning in the meadow when we counted up? Lucio, the milkman, as cold as my grandfather in his grave. They shot him in the neck and the bullet came out through his Adam's apple. You can imagine the row. One of our oldest Party comrades, turned to cold meat under our very noses! They stuck one of those little rubber balls for kids into his mouth so that he shouldn't crack a joke. And for all I know, we rubbed him out ourselves, because we helped out some other comrades when they came with their lot, and we didn't know them. Somebody's playing tricks on us. We went to see Lucio's mother and she told us that last evening three comrades had come to fetch him in a Party car. She must have seen something in our faces, because she insisted we should tell her what had happened. And so we told her, and I won't say any more about it. Now we've got to warn all our comrades to be on their guard and not fall into a trap, and we must try and catch out the others. What have you got there?"

"Three new-comers."

"That's not much. All right, let's settle yesterday's lot."

The young Miliciano, Little Paws and a third taciturn man constituted themselves a People's Tribunal, with Antonio as counsel for the defense. Two Milicianos brought in the first prisoner, a twenty-year-old boy, his elegant suit dirty with dust and cobwebs and his eyelids reddened.

"Come nearer, my fine bird, we won't eat you," Little Paws jeered at him.

The militiaman in the armchair took a list from the desk and read out the name and the details. The accused belonged to Falange; several comrades had seen him selling Fascist newspapers, and on two occasions he had taken part in street fights. When he was arrested, a lead bludgeon, a pistol, and a Falange membership card were found on him.

"What have you got to say for yourself?" the judge in the chair asked.

"Nothing. I've had bad luck." The prisoner fell back into a defiant silence, his head bent, his hands rubbing against each other. Little Paws leaned forward from his chair:

"All right. Take him away and bring the next one."

When we were alone, the judge asked: "Are we all agreed?"

The three of them and Antonio all answered in the affirmative; the Fascist would be taken out and shot that night.

The next to be brought in was a gray-haired man near the fifties, his face distorted by fear. Before the judge began to speak, he said:

"You're going to kill me, but I'm an honest man. I've worked all my life and I've earned everything I possess by my own labor. I've never mixed in politics."

Little Paws rose with a threatening movement, and for an instant I thought he was going to hit the man. "You shut up, you mangy cur!"

The judge searched among the papers. There was a wallet among them, which Antonio grasped and searched. The judge said:

"Be quiet, Little Paws. . . . We don't kill anyone here if it isn't necessary. But you've got to explain a few things. We have a concrete denunciation; it states that you're a bigoted clerical."

"I'm a Catholic, but that's no crime. There are priests who are Republicans."

"That's true, there are some—though I wouldn't trust them an inch. But the denunciation says that you've given money to the C.E.D.A."

"That's a lie."

"Thirdly, one of your nephews who often comes to stay in your house is a Falangist, and one of the worst at that."

"I won't deny it. But what have I got to do with it? Haven't any of you a relative who belongs to the Right?"

Antonio had been checking and comparing papers. Now he called me to him while the accused man went on explaining that he had a shop in the Calle de la Concepción Gerónima, that he never left his shop, that he never mixed in politics. . . .

Antonio silently handed me two papers, one the denunciation, the other an I.O.U. for ten thousand pesetas, lapsed months before. "The same handwriting," I whispered. Antonio nodded. "That's why I wanted you to look at them!" He turned round and interrupted the prisoner in his stream of words:

"Explain this." He held out the I.O.U.

"But there's nothing to explain about it, it hasn't anything to do with politics. I loaned the money to an old friend of mine who was in difficulties. I hoped it would help him to get out of them, but it didn't work. He's a rolling stone, and he just spent it. I forgot about the I.O.U., I simply happened to have it in my pocketbook with the other papers."

"We must check up on it. What's your friend's address?"

When he had given it, Antonio told the two Milicianos to take the prisoner out of the room. Then he put the two papers on the desk side by side.

"We must clear up this story. We must get that other fellow here at once. You know I'm dead against those anonymous denunciations. If someone has something to denounce, let him come and do it face to face. As it is, we're liquidating people who haven't done anything, or who are just bigoted, and some who are just fools."

The young judge nodded, Little Paws muttered something. While they waited for the denouncer to arrive, they proceeded with the other prisoners. Three were sentenced to death in the half-hour's interval. Then two militiamen brought in the man whose address the prisoner had given. He was still young, thin, with a tired face, his hands and legs trembling. Antonio showed him the anonymous letter at once.

"You wrote this, didn't you?"

The man stuttered: "Yes . . . yes . . . I'm a good Republican, I'm one of your people . . ." Then his voice gained a little firmness: "That man is a dangerous Fascist, brothers."

"Now, then, we're not your brothers or anything of the sort. They didn't feed me out of the same trough as you," growled Little Paws.

Antonio spread out the I.O.U. and asked:

"And this paper here—brother—won't you tell us what it means?"

The man could not speak. He trembled and shook. Antonio sent the guard for the prisoner and waited until the two stood facing each other. Then he said: "Well—here you have the man who denounced you."

"You, Juán—why? What have you got against me? You aren't political either. And I have been like a father to you. There must be a mistake somewhere, gentlemen. But, let me see—this is your writing——" He suddenly screamed, shaking the other by the arm: "Answer me!"

The denouncer lifted a pallid face with bluish lips which quivered helplessly. The other let go his arm and stared at us. Nobody spoke. Then Little Paws rose and let his hand fall on the shoulder of the denouncer, who jumped, and said: "That settles you, friend."

"What are you going to do to him?" asked the older prisoner.

"Nothing. A bullet through his head, that's all," said Little Paws. "This swine's blood must be blacker that the priest's frock." He jerked his thumb towards the silken cassock hanging behind the door.

The judge got up. "Well now, this affair is cleared up, you are free. And this other man stays here."

"But you can't kill him for this. After all, it's me he has denounced, and I forgive him as I hope God will forgive me."

"That's our affair, don't worry."

"But no, no, it's my affair. I can't go away from here before you give me your word that nothing is going to happen to him."

"Now look here, don't be a damn' fool, and get out of here," said Little Paws. "You caught us in a soft hour, now don't try to make us turn back, because then we might take you both for a ride. Hey, you there, take that man away and lock him up."

The two Milicianos led the denouncer away, but the man he had denounced refused to go. He implored and begged the tribunal and in the end knelt down.

"I beg you, gentlemen—for the sake of your own mothers—of your children—of whatever you love in the world! I would never be free from remorse all my life. . . ."

"This fellow must have been to the theater more often than was good for him," shouted Little Paws. He took him by the elbow and lifted him from his knees without visible effort. "Now be off with you, go home and say a paternoster if you like, and leave us alone."

I stood on the balcony and saw the man stumbling down the street. A cluster of people from the next house stared at him, then stared at the rectory door, and whispered among themselves. An elderly woman cried after him: "Got out by the skin of your teeth, eh?"

The man glared at her as though he were drunk.

The sixth prisoner was a coal merchant from the same street, a primitive man of tremendous physical strength, with a brutal, bloated face. The judge snapped at him: "So you've been paying money to Gil Robles—to the C.E.D.A.—have you?"

"Me?" The coalman opened his bleary eyes. "And you've dragged me here to tell me that? I've got nothing to do with that cur. I'm here because somebody's out for my blood. But I've got nothing to do with that lousy fellow. I'm an old Republican. By this cross!" He blew a loud kiss on his crossed thumbs, black as cinder. The judge laid a receipt on the desk. "Then what's this?"

The coalman took it between his huge fingers and began to spell out: "Confederación Española de Derechas Autónomas—C.E.D.A.?—what the hell—ten pesetas." He gaped at us. "I don't know what to say. I did pay them. But to tell you the truth, you see, a poor fellow like me isn't much good at books and so on, and so when I saw all those stamps and that bit about Confederation, I thought 'It's the insurance.' And now it looks as if those dirty swine had stolen two duros out of my pocket and got me into the soup as well."

"Do you realize that we can shoot you for paying money to the C.E.D.A.?"

"Me? Damnation! After they've stolen my money, too? You're crazy, the lot of you."

Little Paws hit him in the ribs so that he swiveled round and faced him. "You there—look me in the eyes and answer: Did you or did you not know that the money was for the C.E.D.A.?"

"Hell, how often have I got to tell you the same thing over again? If I say so, then it is so, gospel truth. They've diddled me out of those two duros, as sure as my name's Pedro. May God grant that they have to spend it on the doctor's bill!"

"You speak of God quite a lot," grumbled Little Paws.

"As it comes, lad. It's useful to have Him at hand so that you can swear at Him sometimes, and then He sometimes helps you out."

When the coalman was told that he was free, he said: "I knew it anyhow. The wife started weeping like a waterfall when your boys came to fetch me, but I told her you wouldn't take me for a ride. Not me. The whole quarter's known me for the last twenty years, and they can tell you whether anybody's ever seen me mixed up with the priests. I was the first to vote for the Republic. Never mind, boys, anybody can put his foot in it from time to time. Come along and have a drink on me now!"

We heard him lumbering down the creaking stairs.

"That's all for today," said the judge.

"You've put a fast one over on me—two out of six have got away. But at least we've got that stool pigeon left. I'll settle accounts with him tonight," said Little Paws.

We walked through the big, cool, stone nave of the church, through pools of deep shadow and swathes of colored light. Someone was singing a flamenco song high up in the dusk; metal tinkled. A Miliciano perched on the top of the High Altar was wrenching off brass candelabra and throwing them down into the hands of another who stood at the altar's foot and dropped each piece on a mountain of metal scraps. "That's all for cartridge shells," said Antonio.

The wood of the altars was bare and ugly. The crippled images lying on the ground had lost their respectability. Old, worm-eaten wooden statues leered with noseless faces. Plaster-covered stuffing stuck out from many-colored robes. From the gilt screen in front of the High Altar hung a collection box, its lid secured with a big lock and smashed by a hammer blow. The Child Jesus lay on one of the altar steps, a sky-blue ball spangled with silver stars, dangling a pair of minute feet and topped by a two-pronged stick. One of the prongs ended in the papier-mâché head of a fair-haired child with blue eyes, the other in a chubby, pink hand, its thumb doubled on the palm, the four other fingers sticking out rigidly. The tunic was missing, but a shabby coat was wrapped round the stick and turned it into a scarecrow, with the blond head hanging sideways and smiling archly.

"Put a cigarette in his mouth, then he'll look like a good proletarian," the Miliciano shouted from the height of the altar. "Imagine all the money they got out of the silly, bigoted old women with the help of the little angel! But if one of them had lifted the petticoats and seen that broom-stick underneath, she would have fainted, don't you think?"

I thought of the stage-setting in the Church of San Martín as I used to see it when I was a boy: the image taken out of its niche on the eve of the Saint's Day; the rural landscape rigged up with lamps hidden behind boards and empty sardine boxes loaned by the fishmonger of the Calle de la Luna; the priest cursing the smell, while the pious women of the parish covered up those boxes with rugs and sheets in the sacristy; scarlet, gold-studded cloth hoisted on to the High Altar, the holes gnawed by mice in the course of the years disappearing in its rich folds; the trappings taken down at the end of the Novena, in a shower of dust and cobwebs, while the Saint's image lolled on the floor like the wax doll in an empty shop window.

Bit by bit, I recognized the pieces of scenery in the despoiled church before me. Here were the ladders of worm-eaten pinewood, which had been blazing with votive candles. Here was the shrine, open and void. It smelled of rancid wax and crumbling wood. The empty space in the golden arch where the Child Jesus had been was festooned with spiders' webs.

Yet above the broken trumpery rose the inaccessible stone pillars and cross-vaults, dark with age and smoke. The organ towered across the nave and aisles. Late sunlight filtered through the windows in the slender lantern of the dome.

10. Menace

T H E Battalion *La Pluma,* the battalion of the penpushers, was organized; it had its officers and formations which took over the new recruits; it had still no arms and no equipment. Gregorio, one of my office colleagues, was made its captain, mainly because his experience in dealing with Ministry officials seemed to make him particularly fit for negotiations with the War Ministry. He went there day after day, came back with empty hands and exclaimed that only the Anarchists were able to squeeze arms out of the Ministry's depots, because they called the officers Fascists and traitors and threatened them with being taken for a ride if they did not give them arms.

My own work as organizer and instructor was over. I had nothing to do. The couple of hours at the office were nothing. I hated having to go round Madrid as did so many thousand others, raising a clenched fist when a car filled with Milicianos passed, shouting "Long live" or "Down with" together with the crowd, saluting the body of fallen militiamen carried past under a red shroud, and being afraid of an error, a denunciation, a sniper's bullet.

In Serafín's tavern we were talking of a man who had fallen in Toledo. Serafín asked me whether I had known him. "Since he was so high," I said and raised my flat hand to indicate the height of a young boy. Two minutes later a couple of armed militiamen entered, with a little man at their heels, who pointed me out to them. The Milicianos took me by one arm each and said: "Come along." It was lucky that I was surrounded by people who had known me all my life. In the course of the explanations it emerged that the little man had denounced me as having given the Fascist salute.

One morning, Navarro, our draftsman, came to me with a crazed face. His two sons had been arrested and taken to the Circulo de Bellas Artes; the younger one had come back at midnight, set free because he was not yet sixteen. He knew nothing about his brother's fate. Could I do anything? I went to Fuñi-Fuñi and discussed the case with him, but not hiding my opinion that it was hopeless, because the boy had been mixed in university brawls and in all probability wounded one of his adversaries. But we could at least attempt to find out his fate for certain.

Fuñi-Fuñi found it out. The student had been shot in the Casa de Campo during the previous night; the family could try to find and take away his body, but it might already be buried in a cemetery. I told the father. After this I did not see him for many days. Then I happened to go into the Tavern of the Portuguese, and there I found Navarro, drunk. He called me to his table and I sat down. We said nothing for a long while. Then he looked at me and said:

"What can I do, Barea? I don't belong to the Right, as you know. I belong to you. But your people have killed my son. What can I do?" He flung his face down on his crossed arms and sobbed. His shoulders heaved in jerks, as though someone were hitting him on the chin at regular intervals from under the marble table. I got up softly and left him.

Angel established himself as my bodyguard. "You're much too trustful, and say just what comes into your mind to anybody," he declared. "Think of your row with Sebastian. If he takes it into his head to denounce you to his gang they'll bump you off." He went with me to the office in the mornings and waited patiently in the doorway until I came out. When I was talking to somebody he kept out of sight, but not out of reach of my voice. Whenever I tried to put him off, he would say: "I won't go. You look too much like a Señorito, someone will have a go at you some day. But not while Angelito is with you."

In desperation I took Angel along when I visited Antonio another time to see whether he could not give me something useful to do. In one of the rooms of the Party Secretariat I saw thousands of books dumped on the floor. "The boys in the Sierra have asked for books, and so we've cleared out the libraries of some of the Fascists," said Antonio. "Let me handle this for you," I begged him. "I don't think all these books are good reading for the Milicianos out there." Nobody else seemed to bother, so I dived into the surf of books, together with Angel. There were some rare old editions which I salvaged, and text-books which were put aside and turned out to be very useful at a later stage. But after a week, when the books were classified, I was again left without anything to do.

Then I remembered the patent of a very simple hand grenade which had gone through my hands. Its inventor, Fausto, was an old mechanic whom I had come to know well. The ordnance factory at Toledo had just taken up its production when the insurrection broke out. This was the kind of weapon which was needed now. I saw Fausto and asked what had been done about his invention.

"I really don't know. The officers of the factory have all disappeared, and now they've got a workers' committee, and nobody knows anything about anything. I've been there."

"Would you like to get things going?"

He was delighted, but skeptical. I spoke of the matter to Antonio, who had proved most accessible to me, and he in his turn sent me to see the Comandante Carlos of the 5th Regiment.

The Communist Party had taken the first big step towards the formation of an army by organizing the 5th Regiment, not as a loose militia, but as a closely knit and disciplined body. Volunteers flocked to it. The idea caught on among the masses outside the political groups, because it seemed something beyond party ambition and propaganda. In those late August days the 5th Regiment was already a myth, as well as a very concrete fact.

Its commander, Carlos, came from somewhere in Central Europe, I imagined, but he had lived in America for years and spoke excellent Spanish. I showed him the model of the grenade, explained its possibilities, and when I left he gave me an authorization to collect the several hundreds of grenades in stock in Toledo and to investigate the chances of resuming their production. He accompanied me through the vast building. I saw recruits drilling, who moved and acted like trained soldiers, and I said so, profoundly impressed, but Comandante Carlos shook his head discontentedly. He wanted to show me a workshop for hand grenades set up by Asturian miners; it did not belong to the 5th Regiment, but supplied all the fronts.

In the workshop, men and women were filling pieces of iron tubing with dynamite and fixing short fuses. We stumbled over dynamite cartridges, filled bombs and cigarette stubs in a hellish medley. I felt most uncomfortable.

"But, Carlos, this place is going to blow up any minute."

"I can't do anything about it. They are free to do as they like. They're under no kind of discipline, and nobody will ever persuade them that they are crazy, because they have been handling dynamite all their lives and think they know everything there is to know about it."

At eleven in the morning we left the workship. At half-past eleven an enormous explosion shook the district of Salamanca, and the hand-grenade workshop was wiped out.

A few days later, Fausto and I went to the ordnance factory in Toledo in a little car which the Communist Party had put at our disposal.

The city of Toledo was in Government hands, but the Alcazar was held by a strong force of cadets, Falangists, and Civil Guards with their families, under the command of General Moscardó. They had ample ammunition and food stocks, and the old fortress, with casemates scooped out of the living rock, defied the armament of the militia. The struggle had gone on since the beginning of the rebellion. The militia had occupied all the buildings which dominated the Alcazar and set up a battery outside the town on the other bank of the river Tajo. Several assaults had failed. At the time we went there, the Government had offered to pardon the rebels if they surrendered, and they had rejected the offer. There was talk of a new and final assault. There was also talk of the advance of an enemy column towards Toledo and Madrid. Oropesa had been taken by them.

When we arrived at the ordnance factory down in the valley, we knew only that a workers' committee had taken the plant under its control; but it became clear at once that there reigned an atmosphere of mutual distrust. Nobody knew anything, nobody was ready to make a decision. Fausto remembered in what part of the building the grenades were stored. We found them, but the man in charge said:

"You can't take them away without an order from the War Ministry, approved by the Workers' Committee."

"Never mind, we'll settle that," Fausto answered. "But the main thing is that you should go on producing them."

"Well, you see . . . it's like this: we do produce something."

They were producing "something" indeed, something which consumed material and justified the payment of wages. They had been producing thousands of screws needed for the grenade, and two workers at automatic lathes were continuing to produce them. Miles of steel wire had been turned into springs, and percussion pins were still being produced on a large scale, but none of the other parts of the grenade, not even the explosive charge.

"We had to shoot the explosives expert," said the *Responsable*. "For sabotage. He absolutely refused to give us explosives for rifle cartridges, so we confiscated his whole stock. But then the cartridges exploded. So we had to shoot him."

"Of course, if you put mitramite, which is what was in stock here, into a rifle cartridge, it blows up the whole rifle," said Fausto.

The man shrugged. "I tell you, the cartridges exploded in the rifle, and that's sabotage."

Before we went away, depressed and helpless, the man took us with a mysterious mien into a corner and showed us a switchboard. "What do you think of that? If the Fascists come here we've prepared them a nice surprise. If you pushed down this lever now, not one of the workshops would be left. They're all mined, with a dynamite charge underneath. But that's a secret."

In the car Fausto said: "I don't know whether to laugh or cry. We shall have to produce the thing in Madrid. Carlos might help. Let's have a look at Toledo."

We were at the bottom of the sun-drenched valley. The Tajo purred where it flowed into the reservoir of the power plant. Poplars hemmed the path with their green and their shade, people were picnicking, drinking, and laughing in the river meadow. The towering rock of the town showed its tawny flanks flecked with tufted grass and cistus, and its crown of city walls. Far away on the other side of the river a cluster of men dispersed and revealed the outline of a toy cannon, at its muzzle a wad of cotton-wool smoke. Something went screeching through the air. Then came a dull thud followed by a second thud from behind the city walls on the crest of the hill. The echo of the two shots rumbled between the sheer rock walls of the gorge at Alcántara Bridge.

Now we could hear the crackle of rifle shots up in the town, but they sounded like squibs let loose on a fairground.

We went as far as the corner of the Zocodover, the market square of Toledo. Broken chairs, trees with their branches lopped off, twisted iron bars, the bandstand smashed, clothes and old papers scattered here and there, the fronts of the houses scarred, jagged glass splinters fringing the window frames, the balcony of a hotel swinging loose in the air. In the middle of the square was nobody, there seemed to be nothing but a silent void. Taking cover from the fire of the Alcazar in doorways and behind jutting corners, Milicianos and Shock Police in dark blue uniforms crouched in ridiculous positions, vociferating and gesticulating, letting off shots, shouting orders, blowing shrill whistles. Sometimes a puff of smoke, as though from a smoker sitting behind a window, was wafted out of the rosy, enigmatic façade of the Alcazar, but it was impossible to hear the sound of the shot among the hundreds of shots from the crowd at the foot of the fortress. It was like a sound film when the synchronization of sound and picture goes wrong: the actor opens his mouth to speak, but you hear the voice of the woman who listens to him with closed lips.

"Let's get out of it," Fausto growled. Later on he said: "We're going to lose the war if this is a symbol."

We passed commandeered cars and lorries. Militiamen and militia girls were making merry; they were laughing and singing, the men drank from leather bottles and their girls tickled them in the armpits so that the wine spattered. Once more the shots sounded like fairground squibs, and the cannon on the other side of the river decorated its muzzle with a fluff of cotton wool. In tomorrow's papers we would see the photograph of a pretty girl letting off a gun.

Near Getafe a small plane was doing stunts in the air, a sun-gilded fly showing off its glinting back and belly. People stared at it and blocked the pavement; a convoy of militia cars blocked the road. Fausto sounded the motor horn.

"Go to hell," shouted one of the Milicianos and stayed there in the middle of the road, staring into the air.

When we came to Toledo Bridge we had to give the right of way to a municipal van coming from the Pradera de San Isidro. Fausto glanced at me: "Do you think it's carrying something? It's a bit late for that."

The garbage vans collected the bodies of those who had been executed and took them to the cemetery.

Fausto drove faster, and we overtook the van. Its iron doors were shut. Then it bumped over a hole in the road, and loose iron bars clanked in its hollow bowels. It was empty. I wiped some drops of sweat from my forehead.

Antonio had left a message at home; he wanted to see me as soon as possible. I found him in the Party Secretariat, very busy and surrounded by Milicianos who had come from the Sierra. He asked me curtly: "Do you know English?"

The militiamen turned round and watched me with curiosity.

"Well, I don't speak English, but I read it and I translate from it quite fluently. If that's any good to you."

"Go into the next room and speak to Nicasio."

"Antonio told me you want some work to do," the other secretary said. "The Foreign Ministry needs people who understand English. So if you like——" He scribbled out a note and rang up somebody.

"Go there and ask for Velilla, he's a party comrade and will tell you all you want to know."

Shock Police guarded the Foreign Ministry. I had to wait in the enormous entrance where the sergeant on duty had a desk. All except one of the iron doors were shut. It looked like the reception desk of a prison. Then a young man, masked by big, horn-rimmed glasses and a mop of unruly hair, came straight towards me. "You're Barea, of course." He took the note out of my fingers and tore it up without having read it. "They need people who know languages in the Press Department."

"I know French well, but I don't speak a word of English. I can translate from it, though."

"You won't need more. Let's see the Head of the Department."

A single desk lamp threw a circle of light on heaped-up papers and a pair of white, cushioned hands. Two palely glinting disks stuck on to an egg-shaped blob moved in the dusk beyond the region of the beam from the lamp. Then I took in the head, a pallid, hairless dome, and smoked glasses in tortoiseshell rims. The two soft hands rubbed one against the other. Then a three-cornered tongue pushed out between the lips and curved up towards the nostrils; it looked almost black in that light.

Velilla introduced me to Doń Luis Rubio Hidalgo, who invited me to take a seat, tipped up the conical light shade so that the room, he himself, and his heavily lidded eyes without lashes became visible, and began to explain.

He was the Chief of the Press and Propaganda Department at the Foreign Ministry. His office included the censorship of foreign press reports; he would like me to join them as a censor for press telegrams and telephonic press dispatches. The work was done in the Ministry during the day and in the Telefónica during the night, from midnight to eight in the morning. It was for this night work that he needed me. I could start the following evening. The salary was four hundred pesetas per month. I would be taken to work by one of the Ministry's cars. It was sufficient for him that I could translate from English.

I accepted the job. It sounded interesting. But I disliked my new chief, and said so to Velilla. "Nobody likes him," he answered, "but he is in the confidence of the Minister. We distrust him. There are two boys in his department who are comrades, but we must see that we get the whole thing into our hands. Come and see me as often as you can. You will have to join our cell, there are eleven of us." He ran on, with an engaging mixture of simple faith and involved argument. He believed that the war would be over in a few weeks and Spain become a Soviet Republic. I disagreed, but found him likable; I felt ready to work with him.

When I told the whole story to Angel, who had waited for me outside the Ministry, he grumbled because it would mean being out at night when, as he said, the Milicianos shot off their rifles at anything that moved because they were afraid, and when the phantom cars of Falange went about their murderous business. But he would look after me. When I told him I would be fetched by car and he would have to stay at my flat so that my wife and children should not be left alone, he grumbled again and was proud. All my friends in Emiliano's bar were pleased and intrigued by my new job. It dominated the conversation, until all its aspects had been thrashed out. Then everyone began to discuss politics. A few days before, Largo Caballero had taken over the Government, Manolo summed up the general opinion by saying: "Now something will get done. This is a war government, and now the rifles will go to the front. No more parading up and down the streets—Prieto will show those people something!" Prieto had been made Minister of War.

"Yes, you watch out," said Fuñi-Fuñi. "No more trips to Toledo for you!"

"But I'm already a member of a battalion, only it hasn't got any arms yet. As soon as they give us arms, I'll be the first to go."

"All right, so it's no more Toledo, is it?" the other insisted, and the customary quibble began. It was cut short by a distant noise which came nearer: motorcycles, motor horns, sirens. We all rose. A dispatch rider came racing down the street, the exhaust of his motorcycle open, his siren sounding ceaselessly. In those days, when Madrid had no air raid warning system, the alarm was given by the motorcyclists of the Town Council who had sirens mounted on their vehicles.

The women and children of the house came down to take shelter in Emiliano's cellar. The men crowded into the bar. The iron shutters clanked down, and a few women screamed at the noise. Then the people grew quieter and spoke softly, for they all listened. The drone of planes came close and went away, came back, and seemed to hover overhead. Downstairs in the cellar a child began to cry, other children followed suit, some of the mothers shrieked in hysterical rage. Up in the bar the men stared at each other.

Then the hum of the engines no longer sounded in our ears. Somebody rolled up the shutters. We flocked out into the street. It was very still, the night was dark and decked with stars. People went to their flats to see with their own eyes that nothing had happened, but the men soon came down again. Nobody seemed able to sleep. The women came after the men: the children were afraid that the planes might come back. At dawn the street was crowded. Newcomers brought news from other quarters of the town: bombs had fallen in the district of Cuatro Caminos, and there had been many casualties. We had not heard the bombs. After sunrise, Manolo's militia friends arrived in their car. They were going to Toledo. He had not slept? Nor had they. "Come along, we'll have our siesta out there."

They rolled down the street, singing the Internationale. In the evening they brought Manolo back, dead. While they were taking their siesta in the fields, a plane had dropped a bomb close to the car. Manolo had a tiny orifice in his forehead. He had not wakened. He still slept placidly, pale from the sleepless night.

The Fascists had entered Talavera de la Reina.

At six that evening I went to the Foreign Ministry and Don Luis introduced me to my future colleagues and the work. I read through the journalists' output from the day before and he explained the principles of his censorship. I was given an official pass which authorized me to go anywhere in Madrid at night, and an identity card. At a quarter to midnight a car came to fetch me from my house. All the neighbors saw me off.

I felt elated and light-headed. During the day I had been sorting out the new situation with Aurelia and with Maria. I had explained to myself and to the two women, one after the other, that I would have to work during the night and to sleep during the day. I would no longer be able to meet Maria in the afternoons, as she had demanded. I would no longer have to struggle with the other's clinging and cloying nearness at home, where I had stayed more since the air raids had begun. At daybreak I had discussed my future work with Aurelia; she had been quick to see the disadvantage which it implied for her, and she had opposed my "getting mixed up in those things." In the afternoon I went to see Maria; she had resented my absence from the office in the morning and had her doubts about the new arrangement, but accepted it with good grace. It separated me more clearly from my home; it coincided with her belief that a victory of the Government and the social revolution in its wake would bring about my final separation from Aurelia and my agreement to a life together with her. She found it natural that I wanted to take an active part in the war. Her own young brother had just joined a volunteer battalion. Thus my new work held out new hope to her. I saw it, but made no comment. I would be inside the fortress of my work.

The car carried me through deserted streets, their darkness streaked with the feeble rays of light filtering through blinds and tavern doors. It was a new, chilling Madrid. Five times in the course of our short route a pair of Milicianos gave us the "Halt!," dazzled us with their pocket lamps and scrutinized our papers. The official Ministry Pass did not impress them; when at last I held out my U.G.T. card, one of the sentries said: "Why didn't you show that one first, comrade?"

The last control was at the door of the Telefónica. It was too dark to see anything but smooth concrete walls towering over the narrow Calle de Valverde. A Shock Police sentry in the door took me to the guard room, where a lieutenant examined the Ministry papers and then passed me on to the Workers' Control.

The control desk was a sort of counter at one side of the big entrance hall, manned by a dark-skinned, unshaven, burly man who had tied a huge black-and-red scarf round his throat in a slovenly knot.

"What d'you want, brother?"

He pushed aside the official papers. "O.K.—but what is it you want here?"

"As you see, I'm going to censor the reports of the foreign journalists."

"What's your organization?"

"The U.G.T."

"All right, you'll find one of your people up there. He's daft. But we'll have to settle that business with the foreigners. They're Fascists, all of them. The first one who does anything wrong—you just bring him to me. Or simply ring me up. And keep your eyes skinned when they talk their lingo. I can't think why they're permitted to talk their own language. Hell, if they want to make reports, let them do it in Spanish and pay for a translator. Then they come down the stairs with a lot of noise, talking their English, and nobody knows when they're calling one the son of a bitch. Well, your office is on the fifth floor, and these two will go with you."

A pretty, flirtatious girl took me and the two Milicianos up in a lift; then we walked through long, dim, twisting passages with many doors and entered the last door of all. The narrow room smelled like a church and the darkness which filled it was suffused with a violet glow. A small circle of light was sharply outlined on the desk. The glow and the smell of wax came from the violet carbon paper wrapped round the bulb in place of a blackout shade. The censor on duty, a tall, bony man, rose and welcomed me. Two shadowy bulks at the other end of the room moved: the orderly and the dispatch rider, the smooth moon face of an elderly valet and the meager, dusky face with lively eyes of a bootblack.

Then I plunged into the work and did not emerge for many nights. The organization was simple. The journalists had their own room on the fourth floor; there they wrote their reports in duplicate and submitted them to the censor. One copy was returned to the correspondent, stamped, and initialed, the other sent to the telephone room by orderly. When the connection with Paris or London was established, the correspondent read out his dispatch, while a switch censor sitting by his side checked the text and through his earphones controlled the service conversation as well. If the journalist wanted to transmit his report by telegram or radio, the censored copy was sent by dispatch rider to Transradio.

The big American agencies and Havas had teams of reporters who worked in shifts and produced a stream of what they called snaps; the more important British and American newspapers had their special correspondents. The majority spoke English, but there were a number of Frenchmen and a sprinkling of Latin-Americans.

My colleague and I were supposed to deal with all of them. He knew colloquial English, I could read the English of technical reviews and of books. His French was very thin, mine was not bad. But none of us had ever worked with the Press. Our orders were strict and over-simple: we had to cut out everything that did not indicate a victory of the Republican Government. The correspondents battled against this rule with all their wit and technique. Perea and I pooled our knowledge and often called in one of the switch censors; we searched the dictionaries for double meanings and cut out a phrase when it remained obscure to us. At the beginning I thought that I would soon have a clearer view of the work and be able to turn it into something positive. But the opposite happened. As the autumn went on, the Republican forces suffered one defeat after another, and the journalists did their level best to get their reports of the facts through; the Frenchmen used *argot*, the Englishmen and Americans their respective slang, and they all tried to catch the switch censor napping by putting some insinuating words into their conversations with their editors, or by inserting into their dispatches little phrases not contained in the original text.

The most important battle in September was that for the Alcazar of Toledo. Colonel Yagüe's column was marching up the Tajo valley and drawing near to Toledo. The Government forces tried to take the fortress before the relief column arrived. Part of the Alcazar was blown up; but the defenders held out in the rock casemates and in the ruins. On September the 20th—I remember the date because it is my birthday—big tank cars were driven to Toledo and the Alcazar's cellars were flooded with petrol and set on fire. The attempt failed. On the same day a well equipped column of volunteers coming from Barcelona paraded through the streets of Madrid and was cheered by the crowds: the men had come to fight Yagüe's army.

At that time the Government tried to suppress the wild tribunals by creating a new, legalized form of Popular Tribunal in which a member of the judiciary acted as the judge, and militia delegates as his assessors; it authorized militia squads to track down and arrest Fascists, so as to eliminate the terror of the man hunt. But the tide of fear and hatred was still rising, and the remedy was hardly better than the disease.

It was the official policy to pass only reports according to which the Alcazar was about to fall, Yagüe's column halted, and the Popular Tribunals a pattern of justice. I felt convinced that our news and censorship policy was clumsy and futile. But when I dealt with the journalists I disliked the glib assurance with which they took our defeat for granted and tried to squeeze out sensations, and then I carried through the official orders with a savage fury, as though by cutting out a phrase I were cutting out a hated and dreaded fact.

When I went to the Foreign Ministry in the evening to receive my instructions for the night, I usually had a talk with Don Luis, who seemed to single me out. He would tell me stories of how extremists had threatened him because he had let through an unfavorable piece of news, or of how he had been taken to task because some correspondent or other had sent out reports in the diplomatic bag of his embassy; of how he had fallen under suspicion and was afraid of being taken for a ride one fine day. He was on good terms with the Communists—after all, I was there

because they had recommended me!—and Don Julio, the Minister, who
backed him, was very much favored by them. But the Anarchists . . .
He would end each of his perorations by opening the drawer of his
desk and showing me a pistol. "Before they get me, I'll get one of them!
Well, anyhow, take great care and don't let anything pass, and above
all, watch over your colleague who is weak, very weak!"

In the last week of September, Fausto, the inventor of the hand grenade, came and fetched me away from my day sleep. He had a written
order of the War Ministry to collect the grenades stored in the ordnance
factory, but he had no means of transporting them. The hundreds of
cars and vans which were driven aimlessly round Madrid were in the
hands of Milicianos, the Ministry had no control over them. Each militia
group would willingly fetch the grenades for its own unit, but not for
the Army Depot.

"If Prieto hears about it, the bombs will be fetched," I said.

"Yes—but will Prieto know about it before the Fascists enter Toledo?
I'm going there myself and I want you to come along."

I went with him. The Toledo road was choked with Milicianos and
cars, coming and going. Some shouted that the Alcazar had fallen, and
some that its fall was a question of hours. Near Toledo the crowds thickened. The rock was wreathed with the bursts of explosions. Ambulances
drove slowly over Alcántara Bridge, and the people greeted them, raising
their clenched fists. We drove on to the ordnance factory, but gave up
all hope as soon as we heard that the factory lorries stood ready to transfer to Madrid the whole stock of brass tubing and the machinery for
cartridge production. Fausto was in despair. Neither of us was in a mood
to drive up to Toledo. I suggested going back to Madrid via Torrijos so
that I could stop at Novés.

In Torrijos the streets were blocked by carts. People were loading them
with clothes, mattresses, and furniture, jostling each other and shouting.
"The Fascists are coming," said an old man in answer to my question.
"The Fascists will get us. Yesterday they dropped bombs from their
planes, and killed a lot of people, and this morning we could hear their
guns. And the people who've passed through here! They've come from all
the villages, even from Escalonilla, which is only half an hour from here."

Novés was almost deserted. A few women hurried through the street.
Both casinos had their doors shut. I asked Fausto to drive on to Old
Juán's mill. There I found the old man tying up bundles with his two
mill hands. He was amazed at seeing me. "You'll have to hurry, the
Fascists are coming. We're moving to Madrid tonight."

"They won't be here as quickly as all that," I said.

"Listen, Don Arturo, those fellows are already on the road. They dropped bombs here two days ago. They killed two cows of the village, and Demetria and her child and husband. People saw pickets of Moors on the Extremadura Road early this morning. I tell you, if you don't hurry, you won't get away. We'll meet in Madrid, Don Arturo, and then I'll tell you what happened here. It was horrible."

We left Novés in the direction of Puebla de Montalbán so as to reach the Extremadura Road. When we got there Fausto glanced round and stopped the car. "So that's that. What shall we do? Go back via Toledo?"

"The road to Madrid is still free, I believe. Let's take it—but step on it."

The road was deserted. It was strewn with heaps of clothing and armament, caps, coats, straps, blankets, rifles, tin plates, and mugs; the ditches were littered with them. Rifle and machine-gun shots sounded in the distance, from the direction of Toledo we heard the dull explosions of five bombs. Fausto drove on at top speed. We began to pass Milicianos sitting by the road, barefooted, their boots or sandals lying beside them. There were more and more of them; then we overtook others who were marching on laboriously, most of them without their rifles, in shirtsleeves or open vests, their faces and bare chests burned red. They shouted at us to give them a lift, and screamed insults when our little car drove past them. We expected a shot in the back. Then the road became crowded. Trudging Milicianos mingled with peasants walking at the head of a mule or donkey which carried their wife and children, or driving a cartload with bundles and crockery, their family perched on top of the bedclothes. So we reached Navalcarnero.

An officer and a few men of the Shock Police had drawn a cordon across the road. They stopped militiamen in their flight, made them deliver their arms and ordered them to line up in the plaza. The little garrison had a solitary machine gun set up in the square: it stemmed the threatening panic. The people of Navalcarnero were packing and shutting up their houses.

They stopped our car, too. Fausto and I scrambled out and explained the aim of our journey to the officer, whose face was a mask of sweat-streaked dust. We simply had to get through to Madrid and report to the War Ministry, Fausto concluded, so that army lorries could be sent out to collect the ordnance material before the Fascists arrived and got it.

At that instant a group of Milicianos with rifles pushed through the crowd and seemed about to break through the cordon by force. The officer left us standing and climbed on to the roof of our car. "Halt—go back, or we fire! Now, listen . . ."

"Shut up with your lousy commands. Let us through, or we'll get through by our guts," shouted one of the Milicianos.

The officer shouted back: "All right, you may pass through, but listen to me first!" The disarmed Milicianos surged round the car. Fausto muttered: "If we get out of this, today's our real birthday!"

But the officer spoke well. He called the militiamen cowards to their faces, he made them see how shameful it would be to go back to Madrid in their state, he told them that they had been dirty curs to throw their rifles into the ditch. Then he explained that they could reorganize in Navalcarnero and stay there until the forces arrived which were under way from Madrid. In the end he shouted: "That's all—those of you who've got guts will stay, the others can go on. But they must at least leave us their rifles so that we can fight!" A deafening clamor drowned his last words. He had won.

The officer jumped to the ground and at once sent armed pickets back along the road to collect as many rifles as possible. Then he turned to us, wiping his brow: "Now you can go on, comrades."

It was almost dark when we reached Madrid. We had left the vanguard of the refugee carts in Alcorcón. I went straight to the Foreign Ministry and spoke to Rubio Hidalgo. "Don't worry," he said. "The Fascists have already been halted, and the Alcazar won't last out this night. A few Milicianos have stampeded, that's all. The most important thing is that you shouldn't let through any news of this kind. Tomorrow morning there will be good news, you'll see."

That night I had to battle against the journalists. One of them, a young, supercilious Frenchman who worked for the *Petit Parisien,* tried so many tricks and blustered so much that I threatened him with arrest. I don't remember more than that I shouted myself and gripped my pistol. In the morning it was no longer possible to conceal the fact that the rebels had advanced as far as Maqueda on the Extremadura Road, a village nearer to Madrid than Puebla de Montalbán where we had passed a few hours earlier, and as far as Torrijos on the Toledo Road. Their column on the Extremadura Road threatened Madrid, the other threatened Toledo. The Government capped this piece of news with the announcement that the Alcazar had fallen; this had to be officially denied later on. Some days afterwards, on September the 27th, the rebels entered Toledo. The ordnance factory was not blown up and they occupied it intact.

The censorship work was turned into an unending nightmare. My colleague on the night shift was so panic-stricken that he had to go; I worked alone from nine in the evening to nine in the morning, hardly knowing what I did. The nearer Franco's forces drew to the capital, the more cryptic became the dispatches of the journalists, the more pressing their manner. With the mounting menace and fear, a new wave of killings swept the city. The food situation grew more and more difficult, only the communal restaurants were able to provide meals. There was a strict curfew starting at eleven o'clock; it was dangerous to be out in the streets. On September the 30th the Government decreed the incorporation of all militias into the regular army, which did not exist yet. I ate in the canteen of the Telefónica or in a near-by café and Angel took food home to my family. Snipers' shots cracked through the dark under my windows. I lived on black coffee and brandy during those nights.

When I crossed the street in the early morning to have breakfast I saw the thin stream of refugees from the villages, with their donkeys and carts and gaunt, yellow dogs. They traveled by night for fear of being bombed in daylight. The first batches were billeted in big, requisitioned houses, those who came later had to camp in the avenues of the city. Mattresses were heaped up under the trees in the Castellana and Recoletos, and the women did their cooking at open fires on the pavement. Then the weather changed and torrential rains chased the refugees into the overcrowded houses.

Old Juán of Novés came to see me one morning. I took him to my café and he began to tell me his story, in his slow, equitable manner.

"I was right, Don Arturo. Old people are not often fooled. The things that have happened! When the rebellion broke out, our people went mad. They arrested all the rich men of the village and all those who worked with them—me too. But they let me out after two hours. The lads knew that I never mixed in politics and that there was always a piece of bread in my house for everyone who needed it. And then, you see, my boy is in the Shock Police, and so I became a Republican through him. Well, they set up a tribunal in the Town Hall and shot all of them, including the priest. Heliodoro was shot first. But they buried them all in hallowed ground. The only one who escaped was José, the one from the Casino, because he often gave a peseta or so to the poor people when they hadn't anything to eat. It's always useful to light a candle to the devil! Well, so the families of the men who were shot went away, and our people at first wanted to share out their land, and then they wanted to till it communally. But they couldn't agree and there was no money. They requisitioned my mill, but of course they hadn't any grain to mill, and it was much the same thing in all the other villages. A few joined the militia in Madrid, but most of us stayed on and lived on our garden produce and on what had been stored in the rich men's houses. Then the rebels came nearer, and the people who'd been most active, like Elisro, got away. But we others thought we had nothing to fear and stayed on. A few left when the first bombs fell, but you know how attached one is to one's own home and land, and so most of us stayed. Until the people from other villages passed through on their flight and told us that, when they enter

a village, the Fascists shoot all the men and shave the women's hair
off. . . .

"So, what with one thing and another, we all decided to get away. But
it was at the very last minute, the day you passed through. The others
were already in Torrijos and Maqueda, and their two groups joined and
cut us off from Madrid on the roads. So we had to walk across the fields.
They were chasing us. When they caught a man he got a bullet through
his head. They drove the women back to the village with their rifle butts.
The Moors gleaned the fields afterwards, and when they got hold of a
young woman they tumbled her on the ground. You can imagine the
rest. They did it to a girl who was a servant at Don Ramón's. They threw
her down in a plowed field and called their comrades, because the girl's
very pretty. Eleven of them, Don Arturo. Marcial, one of my mill hands,
and I were hidden in a thicket and saw it happening. Marcial was so
scared that it upset his innards and he dirtied himself. But afterwards he
dared to come with me and we picked her up. She's here in the General
Hospital, but they don't know yet whether she will be all right or not.
Because, you see, we couldn't manage to carry her on our backs, and so
she had to walk along with us across the fields for two days, until we got
to Illescas, and from there they took her to Madrid in a cart. . . . I'm
all right here, I'm with relatives, and so are some of the others. But
there's something I want you to see, Don Arturo, because it's so frightful.
It's the place where they've put the poorest of our people, those who
haven't got anybody here in the town."

After a meal in the canteen, Old Juán made me go with him, although
I was stupid with tiredness. He took me through a marble portal with
wide marble stairs and Doric columns, into a big hall. When he opened
the entrance door, the stench of excrement and urine hit me in the face.
"But what is this, Uncle Juán?"

"Don't ask me. It's sheer misery. All the lavatories are broken and
blocked. The people were bewildered by this place, you see, and didn't
know what to do with it, so they smashed it all up. . . . I told you it
was frightful."

In one of the reception rooms of the palace, a horde of women, children,
and old people, filthy, unkempt, evil-smelling, lived in a litter of truckle
beds, crockery and pieces of furniture. A woman was washing napkins
in a washbowl; the dirty water slopped over and trickled under one of
the camp beds, in which an old man was lying in his drawers, smoking.
Three women were quarreling round a table. The blue-green tapestry
hung from the walls in shreds, the marble mantelpiece was chipped, the
fireplace choked with refuse and muck. Two small children were squall-

ing; and a third sat in a corner, clutching at a dirty little mongrel which barked ceaselessly and shrilly. In another corner stood an iron bedstead, with a goat tied to one of its legs.

While I stared, Old Juán said: "Here are the people of Novés—you don't recognize them? Well, I told you they were the poorest of all, and I don't suppose you ever saw them. They were too poor to talk to you. In the other rooms are people from three or four other villages. They all hate each other, and they're always fighting because one's got a better place than the other, and some have a washbasin and some not, and so on. In the end they destroy everything so that the others shouldn't get it, the mirrors, and the lavatory bowls, and the pipes. There's no water left except in the garden pond."

"But can't someone put it in order? Somebody must have brought them here, after all."

"Nobody. When they arrived with their donkeys and carts, some militiamen got hold of them in the middle of the street and put them in here. They do send them meal vouchers, but nobody cares about them apart from that."

It was on that day that Franco proclaimed himself the Caudillo—the Dictator—of Spain, I remember.

During the days that followed, the caravans of donkeys and carts with tired men, women, and children squatting on their bundles, never ceased. Battalions of Milicianos were hastily organized and sent out. Every day news came which showed how the armies of the rebels were fanning out like locust swarms, advancing on Madrid from all sides, from the Sierra de Gredos and the Alberche valley, passing by Aranjuez, through Sigüenza, in the Sierra de Guadarrama. Many people thought the war would end quickly; if the rebel armies closed the ring, if they cut communications with Albacete, Valencia, and Barcelona, Madrid would be lost.

On October the 13th, Madrid heard enemy gunfire for the first time.

I had lost my hopes and plans of arriving at a better understanding of the foreign journalists' way of working, and of thus gaining some influence on their attitude. The journalists, their reports, my life in the Telefónica by night, the life of Madrid by day, were converted into a rapidly moving strip of pictures, some clear, some blurred, but all so fleeting that it was impossible to focus attention on any one of them. I could no longer decipher the hand-written sheets some of the correspondents submitted to the censorship; it looked as though they were made intentionally illegible. In the end I made a ruling that every dispatch had to be typed. It helped a little. One of the Frenchmen made it his excuse for leaving, but when he protested against my "high-handed measure" I saw that he was afraid. He was an exception. While I slashed their reports according to orders, I admired the personal courage of the correspondents, although I resented their detachment. They went out, risking the bullet of a foreigner-hating Miliciano, or the capture by Moors in the fluctuating fighting, so as to produce a few meager lines of a military report, while we could not pass the sensational articles they would have liked to write —or did write and pass on in some unimpeachable diplomatic bag.

So I saw myself sitting there in the darkness, behind the livid light-cone, working in the dark, when everybody thought I knew what was happening. I knew nothing except that the ring round Madrid was drawing closer, and that we were not equipped to meet the menace. It was difficult to sit still. Sometimes, when I walked past a group of slightly tipsy pressmen who had tried to get the better of me the whole night long, and had perhaps got it, I longed to have a row with them. What to us was life and death, meant nothing but a story to them. Sometimes, when the Anarchist of the Workers' Control in the hall downstairs told me again that all those foreign journalists were Fascists and traitors, I felt a twinge of sympathy. When I saw a certain one of them sprawling on the bed in the telephone room, snoring while he waited for his call to come through, I remembered how he had baited us in the certainty of Franco's prompt entry into the town, and I hated the brute.

I found it impossible to be friendly with Maria when she rang me up and demanded that we should meet. All our lives had come to a dead end.

The air raids became an almost daily occurrence. On October the 30th a single aircraft killed fifty little children in Getafe. The Building Trades Unions sent out men to dig trenches round Madrid and to construct pill-boxes and concrete barricades in the streets. The streets filled with refugees no longer from outlying villages, but from the suburbs of Madrid, and the nights were punctuated with distant gunfire. Elite units went out to man trenches not very many miles away; militiamen came, fleeing from the contact with tanks. La Pasionaria met them on the outskirts of the town and mustered her best strength to put new heart into them. The C.N.T.—the Anarchist Trade Union Center—sent two Ministers into the War Government. The journalists were writing reports which tried to say that we were lost, and we tried not to let them say it.

In the evening of November the 6th, when I went to the Foreign Ministry to receive my orders for the night, Rubio Hidalgo said:

"Shut the door, Barea, and sit down. You know, the whole thing is lost."

I was so inured to his dramatic statements, that I was not impressed and only said: "Really? What's the matter?" Then I saw papers burning

in the fireplace and others stacked and packeted on the desk, and asked:
"Are we going to move?"

He wiped his gleaming pate with a silk handkerchief, passed his dark,
pointed tongue over his lips, and said slowly:

"Tonight, the Government is transferring to Valencia. Tomorrow,
Franco will enter Madrid."

He made a pause.

"I'm sorry, my friend. There's nothing we can do. Madrid will fall
tomorrow."

But Madrid did not fall on the 7th of November 1936.

Part II

. . . When the senses
Are shaken, and the soul is driven to madness,
Who can stand? When the souls of the oppressed
Fight in the troubled air that rages, who can stand?

WILLIAM BLAKE

1. Madrid

T H E siege of Madrid began in the night of the 7th of November 1936, and ended two years, four months, and three weeks later with the Spanish war itself.

When Luis Rubio Hidalgo told me that the Government was leaving and that Madrid would fall the next day, I found nothing to say. What could I have said? I knew as well as anybody that the Fascists were standing in the suburbs. The streets were thronged with people who, in sheer desperation, went out to meet the enemy at the outskirts of their town. Fighting was going on in the Usera district and on the banks of the Manzanares. Our ears were forever catching the sound of bombs and mortar explosions, and sometimes we heard the cracking of rifle shots and the rattle of machine guns. But now the so-called War Government was about to leave, and the Head of its Foreign Press Department expected Franco's troops to enter. . . . I was stunned, while he spoke on urbanely. The drawer in which he kept his melodramatic pistol was half open.

"We're going tomorrow, too," he was saying. "Of course, I'm referring to the permanent staff only. I should very much like to take you with me to Valencia, but you'll understand that I'm unable to do so. I hope—the Government hopes, I should say—that you will remain at your post up to the last moment."

He paused, and moved his smooth face sideways, and his smoked glasses glinted. I had to say something, for he made a pause. "Of course," I said.

"That's good. Now I'm going to explain the situation to you. As I mentioned already, the Government will move to Valencia tonight, but no one knows it yet. Written instructions will be left with General Miaja, so that he can negotiate the surrender with the least possible loss of blood. But he doesn't yet know it himself, and he won't know until after the Government has gone. Now you will realize the task that falls upon you. It is absolutely necessary to keep the Government's move a secret, otherwise a frightful panic would break out. So what you have to do is to go to the Telefónica, take over the service as usual—and not let a single reference through. I'm going to leave early in the morning with my staff and with all the foreign journalists who can't risk being found here when Franco enters. I'll spend the night at the Gran Via Hotel, and if necessary you can report to me there."

"But if you take the journalists away, they must know what is going to happen."

"Not that the Government's moving. They may guess something, and of course, we've told them that the situation is extremely grave, so grave that the Government must ask them to leave, and is putting cars at their disposal. Some will stay, but that doesn't matter. I told them that they won't have our censorship facilities any more, because the military are taking over, and that there won't be any service in the Telefónica. So those who are staying behind are the correspondents who are safe in their embassies, risk nothing, and will be glad to be on the spot when the troops enter."

"Then you feel sure that they will enter?"

"My dear fellow, what do you think half a dozen Milicianos can do? Tell me: what could they do against the Foreign Legion, the Moors, the artillery, the tanks, the aviation, the German experts—what could anyone do? I grant you that they may not enter Madrid tomorrow on the dot, but that would not make any difference, except that there would be more victims—they would enter the day after tomorrow, that's all. Well, I meant to tell you: you can pass the report that as a precautionary measure the Government has organized the evacuation of the press services. Everybody knows that by now. Tomorrow there'll be a proclamation that the Government has decided to move to Valencia, to conduct the war from a focal point, free from the impediments which must hamper any war administration in a front-line town."

"What shall I do tomorrow, then?"

"As there will be nothing you can do, you will close the censorship when your shift is over, go home, and take care of your own skin, because nobody can tell what may happen. I'll let you have the wages for our commissionaire who acts as your orderly and for the dispatch riders; you can pay them tomorrow, and they can go home, or do whatever they feel like. I'm going to leave you some money for yourself, so that you have something on which to fall back if things go badly for you."

He gave me two months' salary, eight hundred pesetas, then he rose and took my hand, shaking it solemnly as though at a funeral. I could not tell him anything of what I felt, so I looked down. From his desk, big glistening photographs showing rows of dead children stared at me, and I stared back.

Dully I asked: "What are you going to do with these photographs?"

"Burn them, and the negatives as well. We wanted to use them for propaganda, but as things are now, anybody on whom they were found would be shot on the spot."

"So you won't take them with you?"

"I'm cluttered up with papers anyhow," and he went on explaining something, but I did not listen. I knew the pictures. They had been taken in the mortuary in which the school children of Getafe, killed by bombs from a low-flying Junkers a week before, had been lined up, each with a serial number on its chest. There was a small boy with his mouth wide open. I felt as though Rubio in his fear were sacrificing those dead children over again. "Let me take them," I said. He shrugged his shoulders and handed me the photographs and a box with negatives. "If you care to take the risk. . . ."

On my way home I concentrated on the problem of how to save the photographs from destruction. There would be a fight. I knew, without giving it much thought, that our people would try to get at the men behind the steel curtain, with their bare knives if necessary. The others would not come in as easily and smoothly as that smooth, frightened man had said. But they might come in, they probably would come in, and then the denunciations, arrests, searches, and executions would start at once. It would be a death warrant to have those photographic documents in one's house. But I could not let them go. The faces of those murdered children had to reach the eyes of the world.

At home I found my sister Concha, her husband, and her seven children waiting for me. Agustin, unperturbed and slow as always, told their story. That morning, their district—the outlying workers' district on the other side of Segovia Bridge—had been attacked by the Fascists. They had fled together with all the neighbors, crossing the bridge under shellfire. Now the Fascist troops were entrenched on the other bank of the river and advancing into the Casa de Campo. Their house was a heap of rubble. They had saved some bundles of clothes and my sister's sewing machine. For the moment they were staying in Rafael's small flat, because Concha preferred not to live together with Aurelia, my wife.

It seemed absurd to make any permanent arrangements. Within twenty-four hours we might all be in the same situation. I suggested that everyone should get a few things ready for a sudden, last-minute flight. Then I left for the Telefónica.

I found the correspondents in the wildest excitement, waiting for their calls, passing on the latest news from the suburban front, and deputizing for one another if a call came through in the absence of the man who had booked it. The tables in the journalists' room were littered with coffee and spirits, all the telephones seemed to ring at once, all the typewriters were clacking. Nobody referred to the Government's move in my hearing.

From the window in the censorship I heard people marching out towards the enemy, shouting and singing, cars racing past with screeching motor horns, and behind the life of the street I could hear the noise of the attack, rifles, machine guns, mortars, guns, and bombs. Then I sat down to censor the dispatches.

Towards two in the morning somebody brought the news that the Fascists had crossed three of the bridges over the Manzanares, the Segovia, Toledo, and King's Bridges, and that there was hand-to-hand fighting in the courtyards of the Model Jail. This meant that they were within the town. I refused to pass the news so long as I had no official confirmation, and went to the telephone room to see that the embargo was kept. The big American, over six feet, two hundred and twenty pounds or so, who had drunk steadily throughout the evening, turned aggressive; Franco had entered Madrid and he was going to let his paper know about it, in one way or other. The Republican Censor hadn't any say any more. He took me by the coat lapels and shook me. I drew my pistol and put him under the guard of two Milicianos. He dropped heavily on to one of the emergency beds and started snoring wheezily. When the last correspondents had sent off their dispatches, the switch censors and I were left alone with the snoring bulk on the camp bed.

Our nerves were centered in our ears. We listened to the mounting noise of the battle. The American was sleeping off his whisky very noisily. Somebody had thrown a gray blanket over him, and his two enormous feet in black, thick-soled shoes stuck out, laid together as neatly as the feet of a corpse.

There was no need to talk, we were all of the same mind and knew it. The Gran Vía, the wide street in which the Telefónica lies, led to the front in a straight line. The front came nearer. We heard it. We expected from one moment to the next to hear under our window shots, machine-gun bursts, hand grenades, and caterpillar chains of tanks clanking and screeching on paving stones. They would storm the Telefónica. There was no escape for us. It was a huge trap, and they would chase us like trapped rats. But we had pistols and a few rounds of cartridges each. We would shoot it out through corridors and stairways, to the end. If we lost, it would be our bad luck. We would not wait for them to kill us. We would fight as best we could.

A puny young man, the Madrid reporter of the Barcelona agency *Fabra*, came into the room with a blanched, twitching face, drew me into a corner and whispered: "Barea—the Government has fled to Valencia!" "I know. Don't get scared, shut up. I've known it since six o'clock. We can't do more than we are doing."

He trembled and was on the point of bursting into tears. I filled him up with brandy like an empty bottle, while he lamented the fate of his children. Then he was sick and fell asleep.

The battle noise had abated. We opened the windows to the Gran Vía. It was a gray dawn. While the cold morning mist drifted in, a dense bluish cloud of tobacco smoke and human warmth streamed slowly out through the upper part of the windows. I made the round of the offices. Most of the correspondents had gone, a few slept on camp beds. Their room was fuggy with cold smoke and alcohol fumes, and I opened a window. The four men of the switch control were sleepily waiting for their relief. The girls sitting at the switchboards belonged to the morning shift, their lips were freshly painted and their hair slicked. The orderlies brought thick, black coffee from the canteen, and we poured a small glass of brandy into each cup.

One of the switch censors, a quiet, gray-haired man, untwisted a little roll of paper and brought out two lumps of sugar. "The last," he said.

Across the street a convoy of cars was lined up before the Gran Vía Hotel. I went down to take leave of Rubio Hidalgo. The newspaper vendors were selling their morning papers. It was no longer a secret that the Government had gone to Valencia. Madrid came under military law and would be governed by a defense council, the *Junta de Defensa.*

"And now what, Don Luis?" I asked. "Madrid has not fallen yet." "Never mind, stick to what I told you yesterday. Your work is done, now look after yourself. Let the *Junta de Defensa* take over the censorship with a couple of officers, while it lasts. Madrid will fall today or tomorrow—I hope they haven't cut the road to Valencia yet, but I'm not so sure we'll get through. The whole thing is finished." He was very pale in the sunlight and the nerves under his thick white skin quivered.

I went back to the Telefónica, gave Luis, the orderly, and Pablo, the dispatch rider, their wages, and said what Rubio Hidalgo had told me to say. Luis, an elderly commissionaire of the Ministry, ceremonious and a

little unctuous in his manner, a resigned, simple, and shrewd man underneath, turned ashen. "But they can't chuck me out, I belong to the Ministry staff, I'm a permanent employee of the State and have my rights!"

"Well, you could go to the Ministry and see if you can get anywhere
with your claim. I doubt it. They're clearing out, my poor Luis." I felt
savage. "I'm going home myself, our work here is over."

While I lingered on, a switch censor came to tell me that Monsieur
Delume wanted to book his early morning call to Paris and insisted on
transmitting his report. "We haven't received any orders to stop press
calls," the man said, "but how can I let the journalists speak with their
people abroad before their dispatches are censored? And now you say
you have shut down for good! Do you think we should cut their calls
off?"

I tried to state Rubio Hidalgo's case, but even while I was speaking I
made up my mind. I had entered the censorship not as a paid civil servant
but as a volunteer in the war against the Fascists. The foreign press, our
link with the outer world, could not remain without a censoring control,
but it could not be silenced either; nor was it right to leave everything to
the military censors of whom Don Luis had vaguely spoken. There existed no such thing, the military had other tasks and worries. At the best,
army censors would force the foreign correspondents, particularly those
eagerly waiting for Franco's entry, to use other channels of communication. Whatever Rubio or his kind might decree, only those who were
defending Madrid—whoever they were—had the right to order me to
abandon my post.

I interrupted myself in the middle of a sentence and told the man:
"I'll come along with you and talk to the others. We can't let things
go on like this."

I held council with the four switch control censors, who were employees
of the American Telephone Company, but had been commandeered to
help out the official censorship. We decided that I should go to the Ministry, and if necessary to the new defense authorities, and obtain a ruling.
In the meantime, they would censor the journalists' reports to the best
of their knowledge. I collected the Press Department stamps and went
to the Plaza de Santa Cruz.

The glass-roofed courts of the Foreign Ministry were filled with disputing and gesticulating groups. In the middle of the biggest group Faustino, the majestic Chief Doorkeeper, was holding forth, while the sergeant
of the Shock Police detailed to guard the building stood by.

"Those are the orders I've received from the Under-Secretary," Faustino
was declaring, "and you will leave the building this very moment, gentle-

men." He rattled a big bunch of keys like a sacristan about to lock up his church.

"What's going on here?" I asked.

The torrent of explanations was so unintelligible that I turned to Faustino for an answer. He hesitated. It was plain what was going on in his mind. I was a mere nobody, with no place in the official hierarchy, while he was the Chief Doorkeeper of Spain's chief Ministry, the power behind the throne of each Minister, more lasting than they, and the dictator in the basement of the old palace. But since his whole world had been turned upside down, he decided to answer me.

"Well, you see, sir, this morning the Under-Secretary rang me up and told me the Government had gone to Valencia, he was leaving that very moment, and I was to shut up the Ministry. He said the staff would have to go home as soon as they arrived."

"Has he sent you a written order to shut up the building?" I asked.

This had not occurred to him. "No, sir. It was the Under-Secretary's personal instruction."

"I beg your pardon. You said just now that it was a telephonic instruction."

"You won't tell me that I can't recognize his voice!"

"You won't tell me that voices can't be imitated." I addressed the sergeant in a tone of command: "On my responsibility, you will see to it that this Ministry is not closed unless by written order from a competent higher authority."

He stood to attention. "I wouldn't have gone anyhow, even if the building had been shut up, because I haven't received orders. But what you say seems O.K. to me. Don't worry, this place won't be shut up by anybody while I'm here."

I turned round to see what the others said.

There were some twenty of us standing in the middle of the frosty, flagged court: ten employees in stiff white collars, incongruous in that Madrid of the Militias, five or six commissionaires in blue braided uniforms, and half a dozen workers of the Ministry printing office. I saw an incredulous hope mixed with fear in all but five faces, and found it not difficult to understand. The Ministry, the part of the State machinery in which some of them had spent their whole life, had vanished overnight. They might have believed in the reality of the war, the revolution, the danger in which Madrid stood, the threatening entry of Franco and his troops, but they were incapable of believing that the edifice of the State could suddenly crumble, and in its fall bury the salaries, the social position, the basis of the existence of its employees. Those modest middle-class people with the luster of civil servants, most of them without any political conviction, saw the ground drop away from under their feet. They were helpless and homeless now that the Ministry was about to shut down. They did not belong to a trade union. Where could they go, what could they do? They would find themselves out in the street unsupported by a political group or union, unable to apply for protection from the immediate danger of being shot. On the other hand, the rebel army might enter the city that very day, and they would have been employees of the Republican Government almost up to the last hour. It was too late to join either of the camps. My intervention gave them new hope and spared them any responsibility for action. If Franco were to take Madrid, it would have been I, the revolutionary, who had seized the Ministry by brute force and compelled them to go on working. If Madrid were to hold out, they would be among the brave men who stayed on, sticking it out, and nobody would be able to deny them their rights as servants of the Republic.

They all shouted approval. They were backing me, and Faustino withdrew slowly from the scene, muttering and shaking his bundle of keys.

Torres, a young printer, offered to go with me to the *Junta de Defensa,* but neither he nor I knew where to find it. In the end we decided to appeal to Wenceslao Carrillo, an old labor leader whom we both knew and who was an Under-Secretary in the Ministry of the Interior. As we expected, he was still in Madrid and at his office, a cold, dank stone box, smelling of worm-eaten paper and cellar dampness. About two dozen people were crowded into the ridiculously small cubicle and the air was foul with smoke. Carrillo stalked up and down in the middle of the cluster of employees and Shock Police officers. The old socialist used to exude a robust, sanguine optimism, but that morning he was in a bad temper, his eyes suffused with red from a sleepless night, and his face congested. He spoke brusquely as always, but without his sly twinkle.

"Well—and you, what d'you want?"

I explained the situation at the Foreign Ministry: it was not right to shut the Ministry and its censorship while there were embassies and foreign journalists in Madrid. For the moment I had prevented it from being shut, but I needed an official order, something to regularize the position.

"And what do you want me to do? I'm in the same boat. They've gone and here's Wenceslao to face the music. The devil take them. Of course they didn't tell me they were going, because if they had told me. . . . Look here, settle it somehow among yourselves. Go to the *Junta de Defensa."*

"But where is the *Junta de Defensa?"*

"How the hell should I know, my boy? Miaja's the master, and Miaja's running round the town and letting off shots. Well, the best thing you can do is to go to the Party and get instructions there."

We did not go to the Socialist Party, which was what Wenceslao Carrillo meant. I had lost all confidence in its power of assuming responsibility and authority in a difficult situation, and my companion Torres, an old member of the Socialist Youth Organization, had recently joined the Communists. We went to the Provincial Committee of the Communist Party. There they told us that the *Junta de Defensa* had not yet constituted itself; but Frades, one of their leading men, would be the secretary to the Junta's Executive Committee. Frades explained that our case could not be settled until the Junta existed in due form; we should come to see him the following day, and in the meantime I had better not leave the Ministry. He did not question my intervention at the Ministry, nor did I ask his opinion; we never discussed this point, because it seemed obvious that no post of any importance in Madrid should remain abandoned.

Torres and I walked back, so immersed in our immediate problem and the danger from pro-Fascist elements within the bureaucracy which we both suspected that we did not think much of the battle going on two miles away. Luis, my orderly from the Telefónica, made an emergency bed for me in the press room at the Ministry on one of the huge, soft, mulberry-colored sofas. He was in his commissionaire's uniform, coming and going with the perfect tact of a trained flunkey, and wildly excited under the bland surface: Don Luis had wanted to throw him out into the street like a useless old rag, and I had saved his existence, he said. He was convinced that I would obtain official sanction for my act, and that I would stay at the head of the censorship. I thought it possible that I would be shot, but I was too exhausted to care. I telephoned to the switch control in the Telefónica and asked them to censor the dispatches during the night. Then I slept like a log.

The following day Torres and I went to the palace of the banker Juán March where the *Junta de Defensa* had installed some of its offices. Frades handed me a paper with the printed letterhead *Junta de Defensa de Madrid, Ministerio de la Guerra*—Defense Council of Madrid, War Ministry. It said: "This Defense Council of Madrid decrees that pending a new order from this same Defense Council the whole personnel of the Ministry of Foreign Affairs shall continue at its posts. The Secretariat. Signed: Frades Orondo. Dated: Madrid, 8th November 1936. Stamped with the stamp of the Junta's Executive Committee." I still have the paper.

When we arrived back at the Ministry, the portly Faustino came up to me and said in a hushed voice:

"The Under-Secretary is in his room."

"All right, leave him there. Hasn't he gone to Valencia, then?"

"Oh yes, but his car broke down."

"I'll see him later. Now be so kind as to call the whole staff to the press room."

I showed the order of the *Junta de Defensa* to the gathered employees and said: "I think what ought to be done now is to form a Popular Front Committee which will be responsible for the conduct of affairs. Apart from that, you will all have to stay at your posts until there are detailed orders from Valencia."

Torres, who was young and ingenuous, wanted to do things in the grand style. He asked Faustino to unlock the Ambassadors' room, and added: "As a lot of you don't belong to any political organization, all of us who do will meet in the Ambassadors' room."

There were nine of us, the six printers, two office employees, and myself. Torres took the chair. He was small and thin, and his insignificant body sank far too deep into the upholstery of the Minister's chair.

The Ambassadors' room was a long hall almost filled by an enormous central table. The walls were hung with red-and-gold brocade, the chairs had curved gilt backs, and red velvet seats, the claws of their legs bit deep into the flower bunches of the carpet. A leather folder with the coat-of-arms embossed in gold lay on the table in front of each seat. Torres in shirtsleeves addressed the six printers in their blue blouses and us three disheveled clerks with a solemn: "Comrades!"

The big room dwarfed and smothered us. We shouted loudly in our discussion. When we left, the carpet was smeared with cigarette ash and the brocade impregnated with smoke. While we filed out, Faustino came in and threw all the windows wide open to cleanse his sanctuary; but we were well content. We had formed a Popular Front Committee, of which Torres was chairman and I secretary. We had also founded the Foreign Ministry Employees' Union. An hour later all the personnel had joined.

The sergeant of the Shock Police called me into his room and shut the door with ostentatious care. "Now, what are you going to do with that fellow?"

"Which fellow?"

"That Under-Secretary. He ought to be wiped out."

"Don't be a damned brute."

"I may be a brute, but that fellow is a Fascist. Do you know what happened to him? He was afraid to go through Tarancón, because of the Anarchists, and so he's come back. Didn't you know the story? All Madrid knows it. The Anarchists of Tarancón were waiting for the Government and the bigwigs when they ran away last night, and wanted to shoot all of them. The only one who had guts enough to deal with them was our own Minister, Don Julio, but there were some who ran away in their pajamas and dirtied them too, I bet."

I went to see the Under-Secretary. Señor Ureña's eyes were dilated behind his spectacles, his face faintly green like a church candle. He offered me a seat.

"No, thank you."

"At your pleasure."

"I only wanted to tell you that I hold this order of the *Junta de Defensa* according to which the Ministry is not to close down."

"Well—it's for you to say——" There was no mistaking that the man was racked by fear and his mind haunted by visions of firing squads.

"That's all I wanted to say."

"But I must leave for Valencia this afternoon."

"There's nothing on my side to prevent you. You are the .Under-Secretary of Foreign Affairs, I'm just a wartime employee of the censorship. You, I suppose, have your instructions direct from the Government. The only thing I had to tell you was that this Ministry of Foreign Affairs would not close down. Nothing else concerns me."

"Oh, all right then, all right, very many thanks."

Señor Ureña left that afternoon, and Madrid saw him no more. Torres gave me an order signed by the Popular Front Committee to the effect that I was to take charge of the Press Department. In the day censorship room sat an elderly man with a white thatch of hair, the journalist Llizo, mild-mannered and of a shining honesty, who received me with a cry of relief.

"Thank goodness this is being settled. Do you know that the journalists put through their reports without any censorship yesterday?"

"What the devil—the switch censors were going to look after that!"

"Yes, that may be, and they certainly seem to have done so during the night. But you know, quite a lot of the journalists used to book their calls from here and telephone their dispatches through from the Ministry press room, because it was more comfortable, and we used to do the switch censoring here. The Telefónica people must have put through the calls because they believed the reports were censored and checked here as usual. Or perhaps it was just a muddle. Anyhow, here you can see what was sent out to the world yesterday."

I looked through the sheaf of papers and my stomach turned over. The suppressed feelings of some of the correspondents had flared up; there were reports breathing a malicious glee at the idea that Franco was, as they put it, inside the town. People abroad who read it must have thought that the rebels had conquered Madrid and that the last, weak, disjointed resistance would soon come to an end. There were just and sober reports as well; but the general picture that arose was one of a hideous muddle—which certainly existed—without the blaze of determination and fight which also existed and which was, in the slang of the journalists, the "real story." I had never been as completely convinced of the need for a war censorship as when I read those petty and deeply untrue reports and realized that the damage abroad had been done. It was a defeat inflicted by the man who had deserted.

On the same day, a haggard, shy man in mourning, who looked as though he suffered from stomach trouble, came to see me. "I'm the State Controller of the Transradio Company. I heard that you got things going here, and so I thought I would consult you. You see, I have to censor all the radio telegrams, and most of them are from foreign embassies. You belong to the Foreign Ministry, so you might be able to help me, since everybody else has gone away. Frankly, I don't know what to do. You see, I'm not a man of action." He straightened his tie and handed me a packet of telegrams. I explained that I had no authority to intervene in his affairs and tried to send him to the *Junta de Defensa*.

"I've been there. They told me to go on censoring as usual, that's all—but now look, what shall I do with this?" He picked out a telegram directed to "His Excellency Generalissimo Francisco Franco, War Ministry, Madrid." It was a flowery message of congratulation to the conqueror of Madrid, signed by the President of one of the smaller Spanish-American Republics.

"That's easy," I said. "Send it back with the service note: 'Unknown at the above address.'" But if this telegram was not particularly important from a censorship point of view, there were others in code from embassies and legations whose support of Franco was unequivocal. There were radio messages from Spaniards with a foreign embassy address—anti-Republican refugees—to "relatives" abroad, which showed the time-honored pattern of simple code messages. The most prolific telegram sender was Felix Schleyer, the German businessman whom I knew to be one of the most active Nazi agents, but who was protected by a spurious extra-territoriality as the Administrator of the Norwegian Legation in the absence of its Minister, then residing in St. Jean de Luz.

To help the controller of the radio company, I took it upon myself to decide which telegrams to hold back and which to send. But I was under no illusion. We were fumbling, we were not equipped to deal with the matters abandoned by those in charge. Yet we could not abandon them too. I was hot with resentment and contempt for the bureaucrats who had scrambled to safety, too sure of the fall of Madrid to make any provision for the continuation of the work. The case of the radio telegrams, which did not immediately concern me, brought it home to me that the breakdown had occurred in all the administrative offices of the State, and that those who had stayed on in Madrid had to set up emergency services following the rules of a revolutionary defense, not the rules of precedence.

I reorganized the foreign press censorship with the five members of the staff left behind by Rubio Hidalgo. Some of the journalists showed us a sullen resentment; they chafed under the re-established control. "Now they'll be sending out their poisonous stuff through their diplomatic bags," said one of the censors.

What we had set up was a very flimsy structure. We were cut off, without instruction and information, without any superior authority short of the *Junta de Defensa,* and the Junta had other worries than to look after the foreign press censorship. Nobody there was certain to which department we belonged. I could not get through to Valencia by telephone. Yet I felt pride in carrying on.

Around us, Madrid was swept by a fierce exultation: the rebels had not got through. Milicianos cheered each other and themselves in the bars, drunk with tiredness and wine, letting loose their pent-up fear and excitement in their drinking bouts before going back to their street corner and their improvised barricades. On that Sunday, the endless November the 8th, a formation of foreigners in uniform, equipped with modern arms, paraded through the center of the town: the legendary International Column which had been training in Albacete had come to the help of Madrid. After the nights of the 6th and 7th, when Madrid had been utterly alone in its resistance, the arrival of those anti-Fascists from abroad was an incredible relief. Before the Sunday was over, stories went round of the bravery of the International battalions in the Casa de Campo, of how "our" Germans had stood up to the iron and steel of the machines of the "other" Germans at the spearhead of Franco's troops, of how our German comrades had let themselves be crushed by those tanks rather than retreat. Russian tanks, A.A. guns, planes, and munition trucks were arriving. There was a rumor that the United States would sell arms to the Spanish Republic. We wanted to believe it. We all hoped that now, through the defense of Madrid, the world would awaken to the meaning of our fight. Therefore the foreign-press censorship of Madrid was part of its defense, or so I thought.

On one of those mornings, the new siege guns brought up by the rebels began their dawn bombardment. I was sleeping in an armchair at the Ministry, when I was awakened by a series of explosions in the neighborhood. The shells were falling in the Puerta de Sol, in the Calle Mayor, in the Plaza Mayor—three and two hundred yards from the building. Suddenly the stout walls trembled, but the explosion and destruction for which my nerves were waiting, did not follow. Somewhere in the upper stories there was shouting and running, half-clad people came pattering down the stairs, Faustino in a dressing-gown, his wife in a petticoat and bed-jacket, her spongy breasts flapping, a group of Shock Police in shirt-sleeves. In the west court, a cloud of dust silted down from the ceiling. A shell had hit the building, but not exploded. It had gone through the thick old walls and come to rest in the door to the dormitory of the Shock Police guard. There it was, monstrously big, lying across the threshold. The wood of the inlaid floor was smoldering, and on the wall opposite was a jagged hole. A row of volumes of the Espasa-Calpe Dictionary had been shattered. It was a twenty-four centimeter shell, as big as a child. After endless telephoning hither and thither, a man from the Artillery Depot arrived to dismantle the fuse; the shell would be fetched away later on. The Shock Police cleared the western half of the building, and we waited in the other court. After a short while, the ar-tillerist emerged triumphantly, in one hand the brass fuse cap, in the other a strip of paper. The guards carried the huge, harmless shell into the court and set it up. Somebody translated the words on the paper that had been hidden in the hollow of the shell. It said in German: "Comrades, don't be afraid, the shells I charge do not explode.—A German worker." The big wrought-iron gates were thrown open and the shell exhibited under the portal. Thousands of people came to stare at the shell and the strip of paper. Now the workers in Germany were helping us—we were going to win the war! *No pasarán, no pasarán*—They will not pass! A plane, glittering like a silver bird in the sunlight, was flying high over-head. People pointed to it: One of ours—the Russians—Long live Russia! The plane made a loop, banked and dropped a stick of bombs over the center of the town. The crowd scattered for an instant and then drifted back to restore its faith by looking at the dud shell on its table, flanked by Shock Police sentries.

I went home, fetched the photographs of the murdered children of Getafe, and took them to the Communist Party office, to be used for propaganda posters.

In the morning of November the 11th, Luis came to tell me that two foreigners were waiting for me in Rubio's office.

When I entered the dark, musty room which still carried the traces of sudden flight, I saw a youngish man with strong, high-colored mobile features, horn-rimmed glasses and a mop of crinkled brown hair, walking up and down, and a pale, slight woman with prim lips and a bun of mousy hair leaning against the desk. I had not the faintest idea who they were. The man slapped a bundle of papers on the desk, and said in bad Spanish, with a guttural accent:

"Who's the man in charge here? You, I suppose?" He put his question in an aggressive tone which I resented. I answered curtly: "And who are you?"

"Look, comrade, this is Comrade Kolzoff of *Pravda* and *Izvestia*. We come from the War Commissariat—and we want to know a few things from you." She spoke with a French accent. I looked at the bundle of papers. They were the press dispatches sent out without the censorship stamp on November the 7th.

The Russian snapped at me: "This is a scandal. Whoever is responsible for this kind of sabotage deserves to be shot. We saw them in the War Commissariat when somebody from the Ministry brought them in an envelope to be sent to Valencia. Was it you who let the journalists get away with it? Do you know what you have done?"

"I know that I have prevented this kind of thing from going on," I retorted. "Nobody else has bothered about it, and you too have come somewhat late in the day." But then I began to explain the whole story, less annoyed by Kolzoff's imperious manner than pleased because at long last someone cared about our work. I ended by telling them that so far I was in charge of the censorship by nobody's authority except my own and that of the improvised Popular Front Committee, consisting of nine men.

"Your authority is the War Commissariat. Come along with us. Suzana will provide you with an order of the Secretariat."

They took me in their car to the War Ministry where I found out that the woman called Suzana was acting as responsible secretary to the Madrid War Commissariat, apparently because she had stayed on and kept her head. She had been a typist. Groups of militia officers came and went, people burst in to shout that their consignment of arms had not arrived, and the man Kolzoff intervened in most of the discussions on the authority of his vitality and arrogant will. I was glad to come under the War Commissariat. Alvarez del Vayo, who was already my supreme chief in his capacity as Foreign Minister, had been appointed Commissar General. I did not yet know him personally, but I was swayed by the popular feeling for him: he was the first of the Ministers who had come back to Madrid and made contact with the front line of the besieged city. It was common talk that he alone had stood up to the Anarchist group at Tarancón like a man; people remembered that it was he who had told the truth about our war to the diplomats assembled at Geneva. I hoped that under the conditions of a state of siege, the foreign press censorship would remain divorced from the Foreign Ministry's bureaucracy in the Valencia rearguard.

The written order I received from the War Commissariat on November the 12th said:

"Having regard to the transfer to Valencia of the Ministry of Foreign Affairs and to the indispensable need for the Press Department of the aforesaid Ministry to continue functioning in Madrid, the General War Commissariat has decided that the aforementioned office of the Press Department shall henceforward be dependent on the General War Commissariat, and furthermore that Arturo Barea Ogazón shall be in charge of the same, with the obligation to render a daily report of its activities to the General War Commissariat."

On the evening of that day, Rubio Hidalgo rang up from Valencia; he was coming to Madrid to settle things. I informed the War Commissariat. They told me not to let him touch any papers, but to bring him to the War Ministry; they would speak to him.

"And supposing he doesn't want to come?"

"Then bring him here between two men from the Shock Police."

I had been avoiding Rubio's room. It belonged to an official head of the department who might sit there in state, undisturbed by the work of others. Moreover, I disliked the very smell of that room. But when Rubio Hidalgo arrived from Valencia, I received him in his own office, behind his desk, and at once passed on the order from the War Commissariat. He grew even more pallid and blinked his hooded eyes, but he said: "Let us go then."

At the Commissariat he kept still under the crude, outspoken reprimands, then played his cards. He was the Press Chief of the Foreign Ministry: the War Commissariat must be opposed to any wild and disorganized action, since it recognized the authority of the Government in which the Chief of the War Commissariat was a Minister. Rubio's legal position was unassailable. It was agreed that the Foreign Press and Censorship Office at Madrid would continue to depend on him in his capacity as Press Chief. It would be under the Madrid War Commissariat for current instructions, and through the Commissariat under the *Junta de Defensa.* The Foreign Ministry's Press Department would continue to cover the expenses of the Madrid office, the censored dispatches would continue to be sent to Rubio. He was suave and conciliatory. Back at the Foreign Ministry, he discussed the details of the service with me; the general rules for the censorship continued to be the same, while military security instructions would reach me from the Madrid authorities. We agreed that the censorship offices would have to be moved to the Telefónica altogether. The journalists were clamoring for the transfer; most of them lived in hotels near the Telefónica, and they found the repeated journey to and from the Ministry, through shell-spattered streets, most inconvenient. We also had an interest in relieving the Telefónica employees from their emergency censoring and in covering all the shifts with our own scanty staff. Rubio promised to send another censor from Valencia. He departed with expressions of friendship and appreciation for our arduous work. I knew that he hated me far more deeply than I hated him.

When we had settled down in the Telefónica, I went out for a few hours' walk. It was my first free spell since November the 7th. My brain was drugged, I wanted to have some air. It was unthinkable to go home. I walked towards the district of Argüelles, the residential quarter overhanging the Manzanares valley, which had been shattered by concentrated bombing in the first days of the siege, when the rebel tanks had stood ready to climb up the slope to the Plaza de España. They had begun climbing up the slope, but they had been thrown back, almost in sight of the bronze statue of Don Quixote. But the part of Argüelles around the Paseo de Rosales and the Calle de Ferraz, which was to have been the breach in the defense ring, had since been evacuated and declared part of the front-line zone.

The night fogs had gone and the sky was mercilessly brilliant. I saw every rent and hole in the Cuartel de la Montaña. The gardens at its feet were rank and dirty. Some of the holes framed the sunlit walls of an inner court. The building was a big, hollow shell which caught the sounds from the front and gave them back, amplified. The rattle of a machine gun down by the river echoed in the galleries of the barracks.

So far there were signs of human life, the noises of people in some part of the abandoned barracks, Miliciano units marching through the avenues in the direction of the front, sentries standing in doorways. I wanted to turn into the Paseo de Rosales, but a soldier sent me back: "You can't go there, brother, it's swept by the machine guns." So I went down the parallel street, the Calle de Ferraz. It was deserted. As I walked on, the dead street took hold of me. There were absurdly intact houses side by side with heaps of rubble. There were houses cleft through cleanly, which showed their entrails like a doll's house. In the few days that had passed, the fogs had peeled the paper from the walls, and long pale strips fluttered in the brisk wind. A tilted piano showed its black and white teeth. Lamps were swinging from the rafters of vanished ceilings. Behind the glass knife fringe of a window frame a shamelessly smooth mirror reflected a rumpled divan.

I passed bars and taverns, one whose floor had been swallowed by the black gulf of its cellar, another with the walls standing undisturbed, but the zinc bar corrugated, the clock on the wall a twisted mass of wheels and springs, and a little red curtain flapping in front of nothing. I went into a tavern which was not damaged, but only deserted. Stools and chairs were standing round red-painted tables, glasses and bottles were standing as the customers had left them. There was thick, slimy water in the rinsing basin of the bar. Out of the neck of a big square flagon, blackish with the dried dregs of wine, a spider crept slowly, stood straddled over the rim on its hairy legs and stared at me.

I walked away quickly, almost running, pursued by the stare and the cry of the dead things. The tram rails, torn from the paving stones and twisted into convulsive loops, blocked the path like angry snakes.

The street had no end.

2. In the Telefónica

WHEN you are in danger of death you feel fear, beforehand, or while it lasts, or afterwards. But in the moment of danger itself you attain something I might call power of sight: the percipience of your senses and instincts becomes so sharpened and clarified that they see into the depth of your life. If the danger of death persists over a long, unbroken period, not as a personal, isolated sensation, but as a collective and shared experience, you either lose your power of imagination to the point of insentient bravery or numb passivity, or else that power of sight grows more sensitive in you until it is as though it had burst the boundaries of life and death.

In those days of November 1936, the people of Madrid, all of them together, and every single individual by himself, lived in constant danger of death.

The enemy stood at the gates of the city and could break in at any moment. Shells fell in the streets. Bombers flew over the roofs and dropped their deadly loads, unpunished. We were in a war and in a besieged town; but the war was a civil war and the besieged town held enemies in its midst. No one knew for certain who was a loyal friend and who a dangerous hidden enemy. No one was safe from denunciation and error, from the shot of an overexcited Miliciano or of a masked assassin dashing past in a car and spraying the pavement with machine-gun bullets.

What food there was might disappear overnight. The air of the town was laden with tension, unrest, distrust, physical fear, and challenge, as it was laden with the unreasoning, embittered will to fight on. We walked side by side, arm in arm, with Death.

November was cold, damp, and hung with fogs. Death was filthy. The shell which killed the old street seller at the corner of the Telefónica flung one of her legs far away from the body into the middle of the street. November caught it, smeared its slime and mud on what had been a woman's leg, and turned it into the dirty tatters of a beggar.

The fires dripped soot. It dissolved in the dampness and became a black, viscous liquid that stuck to one's soles, clung to one's hands, hair, face, and shirt collar, and stayed there.

Buildings slit open by bombs exhibited shattered, fog-soaked rooms with swelling, shapeless furniture and fabrics, their dyes oozing out in turgid dribbles, as though the catastrophe had happened years before and the ruins stayed abandoned ever since. In the houses of the living, the fog billowed through the broken window panes in chill wads.

Have you ever leaned by night over the curbstone of an old well where the waters sleep far down? Everything is black and silent and you cannot see the bottom. The silence is dense, it rises from the bowels of the earth and smells of mold. When you speak a word, a hoarse echo answers from the deep. If you go on watching and listening, you will hear the velvet padding of slimy beasts on the walls of the shaft. Suddenly one of the beasts drops into the water. The water catches a spark of light from somewhere and dazzles you with a fugitive, livid, steely flash, as though of a naked knife blade. You turn away from the well with a cold shudder.

That is how it felt to look down into the street from one of the windows high up in the Telefónica.

At times the silence filled with dreaded sounds, that silence of a dead town, was ripped, and the shaft of the well came alive with piercing screams. Bundles of light swept through the street alongside the screeching sirens mounted on motorcycles, and the drone of bombers invaded the sky. The nightly slaughter began. The building quivered in its roots, the windows rattled, the electric lights waxed and waned. And then everything was choked and drowned in a pandemonium of hisses and explosions, of red, green, and blue glares, of twisting, gigantic shadows cast by crashing walls and disemboweled houses, of madly tolling fire bells, of whistles, of shouts, of cries. The broken glass showering down on the pavement tinkled musically, almost merrily.

I was exhausted beyond measure. I had a camp bed in the censorship room at the Telefónica, and slept in snatches by day or night, constantly wakened by inquiries or by air raids. I kept myself going by drinking strong black coffee and brandy. I was drunk with tiredness, coffee, brandy, and worry. The responsibility for censoring the international press had fallen on my shoulders, together with the care of the war correspondents in Madrid. I found myself in perpetual conflict between the contradictory orders from the Ministry in Valencia on the one side, and from the *Junta de Defensa* or the War Commissariat of Madrid on the other, short of staff, incapable of speaking a word of English and forced to face a horde of journalists nervously excited by their own work at a battle front barely a mile away. And we had to work in a building which was the landmark for all the guns shelling Madrid and all the bombers flying over the city, and which every one of us knew to be a mantrap.

I stared at the journalists' reports, trying to make out what they wanted to convey, hunting through pedantic dictionaries to find the meaning of their double-edged words, sensing and resenting their impatience or hostility. I never saw them as human beings, but merely as grimacing puppets, pale blobs in the dusk, popping up, vociferating, and disappearing.

Towards midnight an alert was sounded and we went into the narrow corridor which offered shelter from flying glass in the little lobby behind the door. There we continued to censor reports by the beams of our electric torches.

A group of people was groping through the passage. "Can't those journalists keep quiet while the raid's on?" one of us grunted.

They were correspondents who had just come from Valencia. A couple of them had been in Madrid before and gone away on November the 7th or so. We exchanged greetings in the semi-darkness. There was a woman among them.

I took them back to the office when the brief alert was over. I could not make out the faces of the newcomers in the dim light of the lamp wrapped in its purple carbon paper. Other journalists arrived with urgent messages about the raid, which I had to dispatch at once. The woman sat down at the desk: a round face with big eyes, blunt nose, wide forehead, a mass of dark hair that looked almost black, too-broad shoulders encased in a green or gray coat, or it may have been some other color which the purple light made indefinite and ugly. She was over thirty and no beauty. Why in hell had those people in Valencia sent me a woman, when I had my hands full with the men anyhow? My feelings towards her were strictly unfriendly.

It was irritating having to look up the many new words war and its weapons threw up every day; it made me very slow at my work. The woman was watching me with curious eyes. Suddenly she said in French: "Can I help you with anything, *camarade?*"

Silently, I handed her a page with a number of baffling idioms. I was displeased and slightly suspicious when I saw how quickly and easily she ran her eyes along the lines, but I consulted her about a few terms, to get rid of the heap of papers. When we were alone I asked her: "Why did you call me 'comrade'?"

She looked up with an expression of great astonishment. "Because we are all comrades here."

"I don't think many of the journalists are. Some of them are Fascists."

"I have come here as a Socialist and not as a newspaper correspondent."

"All right, then," I said, "let it pass at comrades." I said it harshly and against my inclination. That woman was going to create complications.

I checked and endorsed her papers, billeted her in the Hotel Gran Vía, just opposite the Telefónica, and asked Luis, the orderly, to pilot her through the dark street. She walked down the passage, straight and terribly serious in her severe coat. But she knew how to walk. A voice behind me said: "She's a member of the Shock Police!"

When Luis came back he exclaimed: "Now there's a woman for you!"

"What, do you find her attractive?" I asked him, astonished.

"She's a fine woman, Don Arturo. But perhaps too much of a good thing for a man. And what an idea to come to Madrid just now! She doesn't even know five words of Spanish. But I think she'll be all right if she's got to be out in the streets all by herself. She's got plenty of guts, that woman."

The following day she came to the censorship for her safe-conduct and we had a long talk in conventional French. She spoke frankly about herself, ignoring, or not even noticing, my resentment. She was an Austrian Socialist with eighteen years of political work behind her; she had had her share in the February Rising of the Viennese workers in 1934, and in the underground resistance movement following it; then she had escaped to Czechoslovakia and had lived there with her husband, as a political writer. She had decided to go to Spain as soon as the war broke out. Why? Well, she thought it was the most important thing in the whole world for Socialists, and she wanted to do something for it. She had been following events in our country through the Spanish Socialist papers which she deciphered with the help of her French, Latin, and Italian. By University training she was an economist and sociologist, but for many years she had invested her time in propagandist and educational work within the labor movement.

I groaned internally: so a highbrow woman intellectual had fallen to my lot!

Well, since she was determined to get to Spain, she had got there, goodness knows how, with borrowed money, on the strength of the promise
of some Left papers in Czechoslovakia and Norway to take her articles,
but without a salary or budget for telephone reports or cables, with nothing but a few powerful letters of introduction. The Spanish Embassy in
Paris had sent her on to the Press Department, which had decided to
pay for her food. Rubio Hidalgo had taken her back to Valencia in
his convoy, but she thought that at least one labor journalist ought to report directly from Madrid, and so she had come back. She would write
her own stuff and serve as a kind of secretary to a French and an English
journalist, who were willing to pay her quite a lot; so she would be all
right. Not that this was very important. She had put herself at the disposal of our propaganda department and considered herself under our
discipline.

A neat little speech. I did not know what to do with her; she seemed
to know too much and too little. Also, I thought her story a bit fantastic,
in spite of the letters she had shown me.

A plump and jovial Danish journalist came into the room, one of the
men who had arrived together with the woman. He wanted me to pass
a long article for *Politiken*. I was very sorry: I could not censor anything
in Danish, he would have to submit it to us in French. He spoke to the
woman, she glanced through the handwritten pages and turned to me.

"It is an article on the bombing of Madrid. Let me read it for you. I
have censored other Danish articles for the Valencia censorship. It would
make it difficult for his paper if he had to re-write and send it in French."

"I cannot pass reports in a language I don't understand."

"Ring up Valencia, ask Rubio Hidalgo, and you'll see that he will let
me do it. It's in your own interest, after all. I'll come back later to hear
what he says."

I did not much like her insistence, but I reported the case to Rubio
when I had my midday telephone conference with him. I found that I
could not pronounce the woman's name, but there was no other foreign
woman journalist in the town. To my surprise, Rubio agreed at once
and asked: "But what else is Ilsa doing?"

"I don't really know. She'll write a few articles, I suppose, and type for
Delmer and Delaprée for a living."

"Ask her to join the censorship. The usual pay, three hundred pesetas
a month, plus her expenses in the hotel. She might be very useful, she
knows a lot of languages, and is very intelligent. But she's a bit impulsive
and naïve. Ask her today."

When I invited her to become a censor, she hesitated for a brief moment and then said: "Yes. It isn't good for your propaganda that none of

you can speak with the journalists in their professional language. I'll do it."

She started that very night. We worked together, one on each side of the wide desk. The shadow from the lampshade fell on our faces, and only when we were leaning over the papers did we see the other's nose and chin in the light cone, foreshortened and flattened by the glare. She was very quick. I could see that the journalists were pleased and talked to her in rapid English, as though to one of themselves. It worried me. Once she put the pencil down and I watched her, while she was absorbed in her report. It must have been amusing, because her mouth curved in a faint half-smile.

"But—this woman has a delightful mouth," I said to myself. And I suddenly felt curiosity and wanted to see her more closely.

That night we talked for a long time on the propaganda methods of the Spanish Republican Government, such as we saw them mirrored in the censorship rules I explained to her, and such as she had seen them in the results abroad. The terrible difficulties under which we labored, their causes and effects, had to be suppressed in press reports. Her point of view was that this was catastrophically wrong because it made our defeats and social diseases inexplicable, our successes unimportant, our communiqués ludicrous, and because it gave foreign Fascist propaganda an easy victory. I was fascinated by the subject. From my own experience in written propaganda, although I had worked from a commercial angle, I believed our methods to be ineffective. We tried to preserve a prestige we did not possess, and lost the opportunity for positive propaganda. She and I saw with astonishment that we wanted the same, although in different formulas and coming from widely different starting points. We agreed that we would try to make our superiors change their tactics, and that we were in a key position to do so in the Foreign Press Censorship of besieged Madrid.

Ilsa did not go back to her hotel room. She admitted that the night before, when Junkers and Capronis had showered down incendiary bombs, she had not liked being there, cut off and useless. I offered her the third camp bed in the office and was pleased when she agreed. So she slept in snatches and censored in snatches through the night, as I did while Luis gently snored in his corner.

We worked round the clock during the following day, and we talked at every free moment. Rafael asked me how I could find so much to talk about with her; Manolo told her that her conversation must be singularly fascinating; Luis nodded his head sagely. When she went out to type her own articles and stayed away with some of the English-speaking journal-

ists, I was impatient and restless. News from the front was bad. The noise
from the trenches knocked at our windowpanes the whole day long.

After midnight I threw myself on my camp bed under the window,
while Ilsa took over the censorship of the night dispatches.

I could not sleep. It was not only that people kept coming and going.
I was in that stage of nervous exhaustion which makes one go on and on
in a weary circle, in mental and physical bondage. During the past nights,
I had not slept because of the raids, and I had had my brief share of fire-
fighting when incendiary bombs fell in one of the courtyards of the Telefónica. Now I was drugged with black coffee and brandy. A dull irritation was mounting in me.

Then Ilsa, too, lay down on the bed along the opposite wall and soon
fell asleep. It was the quietest time, between three and five. At five one
of the agency men would come with his endless early morning chronicle.
I dozed in a sullen, semi-lucid stupor.

Through my dreams I began to hear a tenuous purr very far away,
which quickly came nearer. So I would not sleep this night either, because the bombers were coming! I saw through the purple-gray darkness
that Ilsa opened her eyes. We both propped our head on one of our hands,
half sitting, half lying, face to face.

"I thought at first it was the lifts," she said. The big lifts had been
humming all the time in their shafts behind the wall.

The airplanes were circling directly overhead and the sound drew
nearer. They were coming down, slowly and deliberately, tracing a spiral
round the skyscraper. I listened stupidly to the double-toned whirr of
their propellers, a low note and a high note: "To sleep—to sleep—to
sleep."

Ilsa asked: "What are we going to do?"

What are we going to do? Like that. In a cool, detached voice. Who
was this woman that she thought it was a joke? My head kept on hammering the stupid words in time with the engines: "To sleep—to sleep—to
sleep." And now that idiotic question of hers: What are we going to do?

And was she going to make up her face now? She had opened her
handbag, taken out a powder puff and passed it over her nose.

I answered her question brusquely: "Nothing!"

We stayed on, listening to the drone of the engines circling inexorably
overhead. Otherwise there was a deep silence. The orderlies must have
gone down to the shelters. Everyone must have gone down to the shelters.
What were we doing here, listening and waiting?

The explosion lifted me from the mattress by at least an inch. For an
infinitesimal moment I felt suspended in the air. The black curtains billowed into the room and poured a cascade of broken glass from their

folds on to my blanket. The building, whose vibration I had not been feeling, now seemed to swing back into place in a slow movement. From the streets rose a medley of cries. Glass was crashing on stone. A wall crumbled softly. I guessed the muffled thud of the wave of dust and rubble pouring into the street.

Ilsa rose and sat down at the foot of my bed, in front of the flapping curtains. We began to talk, I do not remember of what. We needed to talk and to have the feeling of a refuge, like scared animals. The damp fog, carrying a smell of plaster, came in gusts through the windows. I felt a furious desire to possess that woman then and there. We huddled in our coats. Overhead the drone of aircraft had ceased. There were a few explosions very far away. Luis poked his frightened face through the door.

"But did you stay up here, you and the lady? What lunacy, Don Arturo! I went down to the basement and they sent me out with a rescue party while the bombs were still falling, and I had to carry a few who were just a nasty mess. So perhaps it would have been better to stay up here. But I didn't think I was leaving you alone, I thought you would come down too, of course——"

He ran on with his nervous, jerky chatter. One of the agency correspondents came with the first "snap" on the big raid. He reported that a house in the Calle de Hortaleza, twenty yards from the Telefónica, had been totally destroyed. Ilsa went to the desk to censor his dispatch in haste, and the faint gleam that came through the purple-gray carbon paper round the bulb illuminated her face. The paper was being slowly scorched and smelled of wax, the odor of a church in which the big candles of the Main Altar have just been put out. I went with the journalists up to the twelfth floor, to see the green fires which ringed the Telefónica.

The morning came with a watery sun, and we leaned out of the window. The Calle de Hortaleza was partly closed to traffic by a cordon of Milicianos. The firemen were helping to clear away debris. People were rolling up their blinds and drawing back their curtains. All the window-sills and balconies were littered with glass. Someone started sweeping the glittering heap down into the street. It tinkled on the pavement. Suddenly the figure of a drowsy woman or man wielding a broom appeared in every balcony door and window. The broken glass rained down on both sides of the street. The spectacle was absurdly funny and hilarious. It reminded me of the famous scene in *Sous les Toits de Paris*, when a human figure appears in every lighted window and joins the chorus of the song. The glass clattered gaily on the stones, and the people who were sweeping it down exchanged jokes with the Milicianos in the street who had to take cover from the downpour.

I saw it as something apart from myself. My own anger was still mounting. Now I would have to find another room for our office, because one could not even dream of new windowpanes.

At ten o'clock Aurelia arrived, determined to persuade me that I should come home for a short while; I had not been there for at least a week. She would arrange it so that the children would stay with her parents, and we would be alone in the flat. For two months or more we had not been alone. I was repelled by the proposal, and our exchange of words became acrid. She jerked her head towards Ilsa and said: "Of course, since you are in good company . . . !" I told her that she would have to take the children away from Madrid. She said that I only wanted to get rid of her; and, seriously as I felt about the removal of the children from the multiple dangers of the town, I knew that she was not quite wrong. I tried to promise her that I would come to see her the following day.

At midday we were installed on the fourth floor in an enormous conference room. It had a huge table in the middle and four desks lined up under the four windows. We ranged our three camp beds along the opposite wall, a fourth one in the far corner. The windows opened to the Calle de Valverde, facing the battle-front of the Manzanares valley. The big conference table had a shrapnel scar; the house in front of us was slashed by a shell; the roof of another behind it was gnawed away by fire: we were in the wing of the Telefónica most exposed to artillery fire from the blue hills beyond the maze of low roofs. We replaced the missing panes with cardboard and hung mattresses over the windows behind the desks which we selected for censoring. The mattresses would keep out shrapnel, and nothing would keep out a shell anyhow.

We were gay while we made our preparations. The big room was bright and friendly compared with the one we had abandoned. We decided that it should be our permanent office. Ilsa and I went to lunch in one of the restaurants still functioning in the Carrera de San Jeronimo; I was tired of the canteen food, and did not feel like sitting with the journalists in the Hotel Gran Vía, only to listen to a conversation in English I could not understand. While we passed the deep crater of the bomb which had smashed through the gas main and the vaulting of the Underground, Ilsa took my arm. We were crossing the expanse of the Puerta del Sol, when someone plucked at my sleeve.

"Can you spare me a moment?"

Maria was standing behind me with a hag-ridden face. I asked Ilsa to wait for me, and went a few steps with Maria who burst out at once:

"Who's this woman?"

"A foreigner who's working with me in the censorship."

"Don't tell me stories. She's your lover. If she isn't, why should she be glued to your arm? And in the meantime, you leave me alone, like an old rag one throws away!"

While I tried to tell her that it didn't mean anything to a foreigner to take a man's arm, she poured forth a torrent of insults and then started to weep. Openly crying, she walked away, down the Calle de Carretas. When I joined Ilsa, I had to explain the situation; I told her briefly of the failure of my matrimony, of my state of mind between the two women, and of my flight from them. She made no comment, but I saw the same faint astonishment and disgust in her eyes which I had caught in the morning when I had been quarreling with my wife. During lunch I felt driven to annoy and provoke her; I wanted to break through her calmness; afterwards I had to make sure that I had not destroyed the frankness of speech between us, and talked, mainly of the torture of being a Spaniard who could not do anything to help his people.

By midnight, after a day when we had had to carry the main load of the censorship, with little help from other staff, our fatigue became overpowering. I decided to close down the office between one o'clock and eight in the morning, except for very urgent and unforeseen cases. It was a liberation to think that I would not have to read through long, futile military surveys at five in the morning. It was impossible to go on working eighteen hours a day.

While one of the other censors dozed at the desk, Ilsa and I tried to sleep on our hard camp beds. The cracks of rifle shots and the occasional rattle of machine guns were sweeping in waves through the windows. It was very cold and damp, and it was difficult to shut out the thought that we were in the direct firing line of the guns. We went on talking as though we were holding fast to each other. Then I slept like the dead for a few hours.

I do not remember much of the following day. I was doped by sleeplessness, black coffee, brandy, and despair; I moved in a semi-lucidity of senses and brain. There was no raid, news from the front was bad, Ilsa and I worked together, talked together, and were silent together. That is all I know.

At midnight, Luis made the three beds and pottered round the room. He chose the bed in the far corner for himself; there he hung his braided coat over a chair, took off his boots and wrapped himself in the blankets. Ilsa and I lay down on our camp beds, at a foot's distance from each other, and talked softly. From time to time I stared at the profile of the censor on duty, pallid in the shaft of light. We talked of what we had lived through in our minds, she in the long years of revolutionary fight and defeat, I in the short, endless months of our war.

When the censor packed up at one o'clock, I bolted the door behind him and turned off all the lights except the desk lamp in its carbon-paper shade. Luis was snoring peacefully. I went back to bed. The room was in darkness outside the purple-gray pool on the desk and the small, ruddy island round the single electric stove. Fog filtered through the windows together with the sounds of the front, and made a mauve halo round the lamp. I got up and pushed my bed close to hers. It was the most natural thing in the world to join our hands and close the circuit.

I woke at dawn. The front was silent and the room quiet. Fog had thickened in it, and the halo of the desk lamp had grown to a globe of purple-gray, translucent and glowing. I could see the outlines of the furniture. Cautiously I withdrew my arm and wrapped Ilsa in her blankets. Then I pushed my bed back into its old place. One of the iron legs screeched on the waxed floor boards, and I stopped in suspense. Luis continued his rhythmical breathing, scarcely a snore any more. Recovering from my fright, I drew my blankets tighter and went to sleep again.

In the morning, the most extraordinary part of my experience was its naturalness. I had not the feeling of having known a woman for the first time, but of having known her always; "always," not in the course of my life, but in the absolute sense, before and outside this life of mine. It was the same sensation we sometimes feel when we walk through the streets of an old town: we come upon a silent little square, and we know it; we know that we lived there, that we have known it always, that it has only come back into our real life, that we are familiar with those moss-grown stones, and they with us. I had not even the masculine curiosity that watches out in the morning for what the woman with whom we have slept will say and do. I knew what she was going to do and what her face would look like, as we know something which is part of our own life and which we see without watching.

She came down from the washroom of the telephone girls with a fresh face, powder specks still adhering to the damp skin, and when Luis went out to fetch our breakfast we kissed gaily, like a happy married couple.

I had an immense feeling of liberation, and seemed to see people and things with different eyes, in a different light, illuminated from within. My weariness and annoyance had gone. I had an airy sensation, as though I were drinking champagne and laughing, with a mouth full of bubbles which burst and tickled and escaped merrily through my lips.

I saw that she had lost her defensive seriousness and severity. Her gray-green eyes had a gay light in their depths. When Luis spread out the breakfast on one of the tables, he stopped and glanced at her. In the security of knowing that she did not understand Spanish, he said to me:

"She's good to look at today."

She realized that he was talking of her. "What is it Luis said about me?"

"That you are better looking this morning." She blushed and laughed. Luis looked from one to the other. When he and I were alone, he came up to me and said: "My congratulations, Don Arturo."

He said it without irony and quite without roguery. In his straight-forward mind, Luis had seen clearly what I did not yet know with my brain: that she and I belonged together. With all his profound devotion to me, whom he considered to have saved his existence, he decided simply and clearly to be the guardian angel of our love. But he did not say any further word of comment.

For it was so that at that time I did not know what he knew. While all my instincts had felt and seen that this was "my woman," all my reason battled against it. As the day went on, I found myself caught in those carefully formulated mental dialogues which arise from a reasoned struggle against one's instincts: 'Now you're in it . . . now you're tied up with yet another woman . . . you've run away from your own wife and you're running away from your mistress of many years' standing, and now you fall for the first woman who comes along, after knowing her five days. She does not even speak your language. Now you are going to be together with her all day long, without any possible escape. What are you doing? What are you going to do? Of course, you do not love her. It's just an odd attraction. It's impossible that you should be in love with her. You have never been in love yet."

I put myself in front of Ilsa, looked into her face and said with the wondering voice of one who states a problem he cannot solve:

"*Mais—je ne t'aime pas!*"

She smiled and said in a soothing voice: "No, my dear."

I was angry.

In those days, members of the International Column, who had known Ilsa, or known about her, from her life outside Spain, began to visit the Censorship and to have long conferences with her. One day Gustav Regler came, a German with a pasty, furrowed face, in big boots, a heavy jacket with sheepskin collar, his whole body twitching with nerves. Ilsa had just thrown herself on her camp bed to take half an hour's rest, and I was censoring at the desk. The German sat down on the foot of her bed and talked to her. I watched them. Her face was animated and friendly. While she spoke, he laid one of his hands on her shoulder, and then he laid it on her knee. I felt an overpowering desire to kick him out.

When he had gone, with a casual nod for me, I went over to her and said: "He wanted to make love to you."

"Not really. The International Column is in the thick of it, and he's no soldier. He tries to escape from his nerves by pretending that he needs a woman—and I happen to be here."

"Do as you want," I said roughly, and sat down on the edge of the bed. For a moment I leaned my forehead on her shoulder, then I straightened up and said furiously: "But I'm not in love with you."

"No," she said serenely. "Let me get up. I'll take over the shift, I'm quite rested. Now you have a sleep."

She went to the desk and began to read, while I looked at her from my camp bed and kept on thinking that the wall behind her faced the front. Isolated shrapnel shells burst over the roofs. I was happy.

During the night we listened to the ring of mortar explosions. In the gray, wet dawn we went to the window and heard the horizon of noise quieten down. One of the men from the Workers' Control came and showed me a Mexican rifle: Mexico had sent arms. The fighters circling overhead were ours; they were sent by Soviet Russia. In the Casa de Campo, German and French comrades were fighting and dying for us, and in the Parque de Oeste the Basque unit was digging in. It was very cold, and our windowpanes were starred with small holes. The foreign journalists reported small, infinitely costly, local advances of the Madrid forces, and small, dearly bought, threatening advances of the ring of encirclement. But there was a joyful hope in us, underneath and above the fear, menace, muddle, and petty cowardice which went on, inevitably. We were together in the fear, the menace, and the fight; people were simpler and friendlier to each other for a time. It did not seem worth while to pretend; there were so few things that mattered. Those nights of fire and fighting, those days of stubborn, grinding work were teaching us—for a short time—to walk gaily in step with Death and to believe that we would win through to a new life.

The siege and defense of Madrid had lasted twenty days.

3. The Siege

T H E assault was over and the siege was set.

A small stair leads from the last story of the Telefónica up to its square tower. There the city noise recedes, the air grows more transparent, the sounds more clear. A soft breeze blows on days of calm, and on windy days you seem to stand on the gale-swept bridge of a ship. The tower has a gallery facing with its four sides to the four points of the compass and you can look out over a concrete balustrade.

To the north are the pointed crests of the Guadarrama, a barrier changing color with the course of the sun. From deep blue it turns into opaque black; when its rock reflects the rays of the sun it grows luminous, at sunset it glows in copper tints; and when the darkened city puts on its electric lights, the highest peaks are still incandescent.

Over there the front began, invisibly curving round distant crags and gullies. Then it turned west, following the valleys, and bending towards the city. You saw it first from the angle of the gallery between its north and west sides, a few smoke plumes and shell bursts like puffs from a cigarette. Then the front came closer, along the shining arc of the river Manzanares which took it south and through the city itself. From the height of the tower, the river appeared solid and motionless, while the land round it was shaken by convulsions. You saw and heard it move; that part of the front sent out vibrations. The ground carried them to the skyscraper, and there they mounted its steel girders until they were amplified under your feet to a tremor as of distant railway trains. The sounds reached you through the air, unbroken and undisguised, thuds and explosions, the clatter of machine guns, the dry crack of rifle shots. You saw the flashes from the gun muzzles and you saw the trees in the Casa de Campo swaying as though monsters were scraping against their top branches. You saw ant-like figures dotting the sandy banks of the river. Then there came bursts of silence when you stared at the landscape, trying to guess at the secret of the sudden stillness, until ground and air trembled in spasms and the shining smoothness of the river broke up in quivering ripples.

Up on the tower, the front seemed nearer than the street at the foot of the building. When you leaned over to look down into the Gran Vía, the street was a dim, deep canyon, and from its distant bottom vertigo dragged at you. But when you looked straight in front, there was the landscape and the war within it spread on a table before you, as though you could reach out and touch it. It was bewildering to see the front so close, within the city, while the city itself remained intangible and aloof under its shield of roofs and towers, below the red, gray, and white divided by a labyrinth of cracks which were its streets. Yet then the hills across the river spat out white points, and the mosaic of roofs opened up in sprays of smoke, dust, and tiles, while you still heard the ululating shells pass by. They all seemed to pass by the tower of the Telefónica. Thus the landscape with its dark woods, tawny fields, and glittering river sand was fused with the red tiles, the gray towers, and the street down below, and you were plunged in the heart of the battle.

The stories above the eighth floor of the building were abandoned. The lift usually arrived empty at the thirteenth floor, where a few artillerymen manned an observation post. The men's boots thumped on the parquet of the wide rooms and made them ring hollow. A shell had crashed through two floors, and the snapped rods, the bent steel girders of the frame were hanging like tatters into the jagged hole.

The girl who took up the lift, perched on her stool like a bird, was pretty and merry. "I don't like coming up here," she would say. "It's so lonely now, I always think the lift is going to shoot out of the tower into thin air."

Then you dropped down into Madrid like a stone, while the walls of the shaft closed up above you, the metal doors clanked and a smell of grease, hot iron, and sprayed varnish enveloped you.

The town was alive and tense, palpitating as a deep knife wound in which the blood wells up in gusts and the muscles twitch with pain and vigorous life.

They were shelling the center of Madrid, and this center overflowed with people who talked, shouted, pushed, and showed each other that they were alive. Platoons of Milicianos—soldiers, we were beginning to call them—were coming from the front and marching to the front, cheered and cheering. Sometimes people broke into song with raucous gusto. Sometimes steel grated and clanked on stone when a tank passed, its turret open and a small figure peeping out with its hand upon the lid, like a jack-in-the-box escaping from a giant pot. Sometimes a big gun passed and stopped at the street corner so that people could finger its gray-green paint as if they were afraid of its being unreal. Sometimes a huge ambulance, red crosses on milk-white ground, passed and left silence in its wake, and the silence was torn by a stuttering motorcycle weaving its way round people and cars. Then somebody would shout: "You'll be late!" and the din of the crowd would burst out afresh.

Everything was as fleeting as pictures on a screen, fleeting and spasmodic. People talked in shouts and laughed in shrill outbursts. They drank noisily with a great clatter of glasses. The footsteps in the streets sounded loud, firm, and quick. In daylight everyone was a friend, by night everyone might be an enemy. The friendliness was shot with a feeling of drunkenness. The city had attempted the impossible, it had emerged triumphant and in a trance.

Oh yes, the enemy was there at the gates, twelve hundred yards from this corner of the Gran Vía. Sometimes a stray rifle bullet made a starred hole in a windowpane. So what? They had not entered that night of November the 7th, how could they enter now? When shells dropped on the Gran Vía and the Calle de Alcalá, starting at the higher end near the front and tracing "Shell Alley" down to the statue of the goddess Cybele, people clustered under the doors on the side of the street which was considered safer and watched the explosions at thirty yards' distance. Some came from the outlying districts to see what a bombardment was like, and went away contented with shell splinters, still faintly warm, for a keepsake.

The misery of it all was not on exhibition. It was hidden away in cellars and basements, in the improvised shelters of the Underground and in the hospitals where they had neither instruments nor medicaments to deal with the never ending stream of wounded people. The flimsy houses in the working class districts collapsed from blast, but their inhabitants were swallowed by other flimsy, overcrowded houses. Thousands of refugees from the villages and suburbs were stowed away in deserted buildings, thousands of women and children were taken away by evacuation convoys to the east coast. The clutch of the siege was still tightening and more units of the International Column, grown to two brigades, were poured into the gaps of the defense. Yet the elation which carried us beyond our fears and doubts never petered out. We were Madrid.

Life was slowly going back to settled conditions in our new censorship room. We looked round and found each other hollow-eyed, drawn, begrimed, but solid and human. Newcomers among the journalists were inclined to treat those who had settled in as veterans, and Ilsa, the only woman, as a heroine. The guards in the Telefónica changed their tone; some of the foreigners had overnight become comrades. Others were just beyond the pale, such as the big American, who faded out of the picture and was replaced by a man of a very different caliber, commanding trust.

Ilsa was silently given the right of citizenship in the Telefónica by most of our men and followed by the whispering hostility of most of the women. I left it to her to deal with the English-speaking journalists, not only because her energies were fresh and I overwrought and exhausted, but also because I had to admit that she was doing what we had never been able to do: by handling the censorship with greater imagination and leniency, she improved relations with the foreign correspondents and influenced their way of reporting. Some of the censorship employees resented it and I had to back her with my authority, but through Suzana of the War Commissariat came qualified approval from the General Staff, where the censored dispatches were read before going to Valencia. Soon Ilsa's method was put to a hard test.

National Socialist Germany had officially recognized Franco and sent General von Faupel as a special envoy to Burgos. Most of the German citizens had been evacuated by their Embassy, and the Embassy itself had closed down. But there was no declaration of war, only German nonintervention, in the guise of technical and strategical support for the rebels. On a gray November day, our police raided the German Embassy in Madrid and confiscated papers and arms left there. It was technically a breach of extra-territoriality, but the foreign correspondents who had witnessed the raid submitted reports speaking with unexpected accuracy of the links between the Embassy and the headquarters of the Fifth Column. Only—according to our strict official rules—we had to stop their reports: we had to suppress any reference to police measures unless they were released in a communiqué from Valencia. The correspondents were furious and bombarded us with demands and requests. It grew late, and they were afraid of missing the deadline. I rang up the War Commissariat, but only Michael Kolzoff was there to give instructions and he told me to wait for an official statement.

Ilsa was less furious and more worried than the journalists. When an hour of waiting had gone, she took me aside and asked me to let her pass the reports in the order in which they had been handed in. She would sign the dispatches with her initials, so that the responsibility would rest on her, and she was prepared to face the very grave situation which would arise from her breaking a clear order. But she was not prepared to turn the good will of the correspondents into bad will against her better knowledge and to let the German version monopolize the morning press of the world. Somewhat melodramatically, she said: "I'm responsible not to your Valencia bureaucracy but to the labor movement, and I won't allow this to be messed up if I can help it." I refused to let her shoulder the responsibility alone. We released the reports about the raid on the Embassy.

Late at night I was rung up by Kolzoff and threatened with courtmartial for myself and Ilsa. On the following morning he rang up again and took everything back: his own superiors, whoever they were, had been delighted with the results of our act of insubordination. Rubio, speaking from Valencia, followed the same line, although he stressed the serious character of the step Ilsa had taken in "her impulsive manner," as he called it. But for the time being she had carried the day and, aware of her advantage, attempted to follow it up.

After the first week when the bombing and shelling of Madrid was news, the correspondents began to chafe under the restrictions imposed on their reports from the front. Ilsa argued that we should give them access to new material, on the principle that "you must feed the animals at the zoo." There was nobody except our own office to deal with them. The military could not be expected to release more than they did. The journalists, on the other hand, were little interested in the social aspects of our fight; or if they were interested, they either turned them into black-and-white left-wing propaganda for readers already convinced, or into bogies to scare comfortable people abroad. We could not suggest subjects for them, but we ought to enable them to write something of the story of Madrid. It was our opportunity, since we were at the switchboards.

One day when Gustav Regler came from the front, heavy-footed in his new dignity as political commissar with the XIIth Brigade—the first of the International Brigades—he launched forth in an impassioned speech in German. Ilsa listened attentively, and then turned to me: "He's right. The International Brigades are the greatest thing that has happened in the movement for years, and it would be a tremendous inspiration to the workers everywhere, if only they knew enough about it. Think of it, while their governments are organizing Non-Intervention . . . Gustav is willing to take journalists to his headquarters and General Kleber would see them. But there's no point in it if we don't pass their stories, on principle. I'm going to do it."

Again it was an audacious step and an immediate success. The correspondents, headed by Delmer of the *Daily Express,* and Louis Delaprée of *Paris-Soir,* came back with glimpses of the best there was in the International Brigades, genuinely impressed and with a news story bound to make headlines. The ball was set rolling. Yet after a week or so it appeared that only the International Brigades figured in the press dispatches, as though they were the sole saviors of Madrid. Ilsa was beginning to feel qualms; she had got more than she had bargained for. I was angry, because I found it unjust that the people of Madrid, the improvised soldiers in Carabanchel and the Parque de Oeste and the Guadarrama, were forgotten because there was no propaganda machine to publicize them. Even before instructions came from the General Staff in Madrid and the Press Department in Valencia, we restricted the space for reports on the International Brigades. It left me with a bitter feeling of cleavage between us, the Spaniards, and the world.

In those days Regler asked me, as the only Spaniard with whom he had
any contact, to write something for a front-line paper of his Edgar André
Battalion. I wrote a jumble of conventional praise and personal impressions; I voiced my early instinctive fear that the international units would
be like the Spanish Foreign Legion I had known in its selfish courage,
brutality, and recklessness, and my relief at realizing that there existed in
them men driven by a clean political faith and by love for a world without slaughter.

Ilsa worked her way through the article because she was to translate
it; she was beginning to read Spanish fairly fluently, though we still had
to converse in French. Then she said unexpectedly: "Do you know that
you can write? That is, if you cut out all the pompous ornaments which
remind me of the Jesuit Baroque churches and write only your own
style. This thing is partly awful and partly very good." I said: "But I've
always wanted to be a writer," stuttering like a schoolboy, hot with pleasure at her and her judgment. My article was never used, it was not what
the Political Commissar had wanted, but the incident was doubly important for me. She had disinterred my old ambition, and I had admitted my
suppressed resentment against the foreigners in so many words, talking
myself free of it.

It was thrown back at me in a caricature, on the same day, I think. The
Austrian labor leader, Julius Deutsch, made General of the Spanish Republican Army in honor of the Workers' Militia which he had helped to
organize and which had fought the first battle against Fascism in Europe,
came to visit Ilsa. He was touring our zone together with his interpreter
Rolf, and he had been given not only a car but a militia captain as a political commissar and guide. While the two were speaking with Ilsa,
trying, as I saw clearly and with annoyance, to persuade her to leave the
dangers of Madrid, their Spanish guide told me that they were spies
"because they were always speaking that lingo instead of speaking like
Christians." The man was really upset and excited: "Now tell me, *Compañero,* what do they seek in Spain? It can't be anything decent. I tell
you they are spies. And the woman there must be one too." It made me
laugh and gave me a shock even while I was talking sense to him: I was
one of those Spaniards, too.

Angel was standing before me in the motley uniform of a Miliciano,
blue boiler suit over several layers of torn pullovers, a greasy peaked cap
with a five-pointed star, a rifle in his hand and a huge sheathed knife in
his belt, everything caked with mud and his grimy face split by an enormous grin.

"Christ alive, I thought I'd never find you in this labyrinth. Well, so here I am. I didn't die, oh no, sir, and they didn't kill me, either. I'm going strong, I am."

"Angel, where have you sprung from?"

"From somewhere over there." He pointed with his thumb over his shoulder. "I was getting bored in my dispensary and things were getting hot somewhere else, so I went there. So now I'm a Miliciano, and a real one, I can tell you."

In the middle of October, Angel had been taken on as dispensary assistant in one of the first emergency hospitals. He had vanished on the evening of November the 6th and I had not heard of him since.

"Yes, on the evening of the 6th I went down to Segovia Bridge. Well, what should I tell you? You know they gave us a thrashing—the Moors, the Legionaries, and the tanks. As though the world had come to an end. They killed nearly all of us."

"But you were left."

"Yes. But . . . well, I don't know about that, because you see, I don't really know if I am left. I'm only beginning to realize it now. Somebody came up to me yesterday and said: 'Angelillo, you're going to be a corporal.' So I said: 'Hell, why?' And the other bird said: 'Because you've been made one.' I was thinking he'd made a mistake, because as far as I knew, we weren't exactly in barracks, but in a hole in the earth digging hard to make a trench. So then I began to get onto things. The *Tercio* and the Civil Guard were peppering away at us from a couple of houses. And there it was. They hadn't killed me. So I asked a fellow by the name of Juanillo, a neighbor in our street: 'Juanillo, lad,' I said, 'what day is it?' He started counting on his fingers, scratched his head and said to me: 'Well—I don't rightly know.'"

"Angelillo, I believe you're a bit drunk."

"Don't you believe it. It's just that I'm afraid. I only took three or four glasses in company with my friends, and then I said to myself, I'll go and see Don Arturo—if they haven't killed him yet, that is. Your missus told me you don't ever get out of this place, so I came here. But I won't say I wouldn't like to take a glass with you, if you've no objection. . . . All right, then, later. And I've nothing to tell you, as I said before. Nothing. It's just been a lot of bangs all the time since the 6th until today, because we've finished our trench now. Of course, they're still shooting, but it's different. Before, they were peppering us in the middle of the street, and round the corners, and even inside the houses. But now we've set up a real hotel, I can tell you."

"But where are you now?"

"The other side of Segovia Bridge, and we'll be in Navalcarnero in a couple of days, you'll see. And what's been happening to you?"

It was as difficult for me as it was for him to give an account of things. Time had lost its meaning. November the 7th seemed to me a date in the remote past and, at the same time, yesterday. I remembered flashes of things seen and done, but they bore no relation to the chronological order of events. We could not narrate what we had lived through, Angel and I, we could only seize upon incidents. Angel had spent those days killing, drowned in a world of explosions and blasphemies, of men killed and left behind, of crumbling houses. He remembered nothing but a blur, and a few lucid moments in which something had printed itself on his memory.

"War's a crazy thing, you don't know what's happening," he said. "Well, of course, you do know a few things. For instance, one morning a Civil Guard stuck his head out from behind a wall and I tried to take aim at him. He wasn't looking at me, but somewhere over to my right. He knelt down outside the cover of the wall and drew up his rifle. I fired, and he fell like a sack, with his arms spread out. I said: 'So there, you swine.' At that moment, somebody beside me said: 'I've got a sharp eye, haven't I? I laid him out.' So I said: 'It seems to me you've got a bit mixed up.' So then we ended by punching each other there on the spot, about whether it was him or me that had killed the man. We're always together now, and when we sight a Fascist, we take it in turns to fire first, once him and then me. I've scored three by now. But to talk of something else—Doña Aurelia's told me all sorts of things, that she can't go on like this, and that you've got mixed up with a foreign woman here in the Telefónica, and that she'll have to do something desperate one day. Hell, you know what women are!"

I introduced Angel to Ilsa. He took to her at once, winked at me twice and began to tell her endless stories in his rapid Madrileño slang. She did not understand more than a few stray words, but listened with the right expression of interest until I took him away to the bar of the Gran Vía Hotel across the street. We were drinking their golden Amontillado when shells began to fall outside.

"Does it often get like this, then?" Angel asked.

"Well, only every day and at any time."

"I'm going back to my trench. We're more polite there. It doesn't suit me at all to be on leave here and get smashed up. . . . What do we think of the war out there? Well, it'll end very soon. With Russia helping us, it'll all be over in a couple of months. They've been doing us fine. Have you seen our fighter planes? As soon as we've got a few more of them, it will be good-by to Franco's German friends. That's one of the things I just can't understand. Why did those Germans and Italians have to go and get mixed up in our row, when we've done nothing to them?"

"I think they're defending their own side. Haven't you noticed that this is a war against Fascism?"

"Now listen—haven't I noticed? If I started to forget it, they'd remind me every hour with their mortars. Don't think I'm as dumb as all that. Of course, I damn' well know that those generals on the other side are hand in glove with the generals down there in Italy and Germany, because they're all pups from the same litter. But still, I don't understand why the other countries are just keeping quiet and looking on. At least, yes, I can understand it about the people at the top, because they're the same everywhere, German and Italian and French and English. But there are millions of workers in the world, and in France they've got a Popular Front Government. And what are they doing?"

"I don't understand it either, Angel."

He paid no attention to me and went on: "I won't say they ought to send us an army of Frenchmen, because we're good enough ourselves to cut those sons of bitches to pieces. But at least they ought to let us buy arms. That's something you don't know about, because you're in the town here, but out there we're fighting with our bare fists, and that's God's own truth. At first we hadn't any rifles to speak of, and we had to agree that whoever was nearest the enemy should have a shot at firing. Then the Mexicans sent us a few thousand rifles, blessed be their mothers. But it turned out that our own cartridges were a bit too big for their barrels and stuck. So then they gave us hand grenades, at least, that's what they called them. They're tin cans like water coolers and they're called Lafitte bombs, and you've got to give a tug at a kind of fork and throw them very quickly and then run away, because otherwise they explode in your hand. And then they gave us some pieces of iron tubing filled with dynamite, which you've got to light with your burning cigarette. And the other side are hotting up things for us with their mortars, and the mortar bombs drop on your head without your noticing them. Have you seen one of their mortars? It's like a chimney pipe with a spike at the bottom. They set up the pipe at an angle and drop a bomb the size of an orange in its muzzle, with little wings and all, to make it fly well. When the bomb hits the spike at the bottom of the pipe, the powder in its bottom takes fire, and it shoots sky-high and falls down right on our heads. And there's nothing you can do about it unless you want to spend the whole day gaping at the sky, because it doesn't make any noise. The only thing we can do is to build our trench in angles and stay in the corners. They may kill one of us, but not a whole row as they did to begin with."

"Stop a bit and have a rest. You're running on like a clock-work toy."

"It's because your blood boils when you start talking about all those things. I'm not saying the French haven't done anything at all, because they did let us have some machine guns, and people say a few old planes too, but the point is that they don't do things openly as God wants them to. If Hitler sends planes to Franco, why can't the French let us have planes, and with a better right too? After all, we're defending them as well as ourselves."

I felt too much as he did to say anything, except to remind him that there was Soviet Russia and the International Brigade.

"I'm not forgetting them, but they don't count. Soviet Russia's under an obligation to help us anyway, more than anyone else. A nice thing it would be if Russia shrugged her shoulders and said things just can't be helped!"

"The Russians could have said it. After all, they're a long way away, and there was no need for them to risk war with Germany."

"You say things you don't really believe, Don Arturo. Russia's a socialist country and has got to come and help us, that's what they've got Socialists—well, Communists—over there for. And as to Germany declaring war: Hitler's just one of those big dogs that bark a lot, but if you hit them with a stone they run away with their tails between their legs. . . . And now I must go back to my own place. I'm getting used to mortar shells out there, but I don't like the noise of your shells here. It doesn't sound right in town. *Salud.*"

A convoy of Foreign Ministry cars was leaving Madrid to take stray members of the staff and their families to Valencia. Aurelia and the three children were going with them, and I was seeing them off.

It was good so. The children would be safe. Aurelia had wanted me to come with them and the last days had been burdened with disputes and bickerings that seemed more futile than ever. She had been convinced from her first glance that the "woman with the green eyes," as she called Ilsa, was the current cause of my attitude; but she was less afraid of the foreigner, who in her view was only having a brief adventure with me, than of Maria, who might establish herself more firmly if I stayed alone in Madrid. She had suggested that I should install her and the children in the basement of the Telefónica, which had been thrown open to nearly a thousand homeless refugees. I had taken her through that pit of misery, noisy and evil-smelling, and explained why it would be wrong to put the children there; but though she had given up her idea, she had insisted that I should go away as the rest of the Ministry had done. In her eyes I only wanted to stay on in Madrid to have more license to roam. She repeated it even while I was saying good-by to the children.

I went back to the Telefónica. In the narrow Calle de Valverde there was an endless queue of women and children, drenched by the frosty morning drizzle, stamping their feet, clutching shapeless bundles. Four evacuation lorries, with crude boards for benches, waited a bit further on. Just as I came to the side door of the building, a group of evacuees filed out, women, children, old people, greenish faces, crumpled clothes which carried the stench of the overcrowded shelter in their creases, the same shapeless bundles which the people in the waiting queue carried, the same bewildered, noisy children, shouts, cries, blasphemies, and jokes. They clambered on to the lorries and settled down somehow, a single mass of bodies, while the drivers started their cold, coughing engines.

Now the women in the queue surged past the sentries into the narrow door. The stream caught me and carried me past the Workers' Control Post, down the basement stairs, through the maze of passages. Before and behind me mothers pushed on to seize a free place. Shrill voices were crying: "Here, Mother, I'm here!" Bundles opened and poured filthy bedclothes into a miraculously free corner, while the occupants of the pallets right and left cursed the newcomers. At once the damp clothes began to steam and the thick, sour air became more dense and muggy. "When are we going to eat, Mother?" cried a dozen children around me. The refugees were starved.

I fought my way upstairs and back to the big, cold, gray room where Ilsa was sitting on her camp bed, listening to the complaints of three people at once, arguing and answering with a patience which seemed wrong to me. I turned to our orderlies: they were cursing as I did.

Rubio rang up from Valencia and told me that I should transfer there. I said I could not go, I was under orders from the Madrid Junta. He gave me instructions about the office. Half an hour later Kolzoff gave me another set of instructions. I shouted through the telephone, in despair; I had to know whose orders I was supposed to follow. There was no decision to be had from either quarter.

I took Delmer, who alone of the English correspondents emerged from the fog of my indifference, to see the clowns Pompoff and Teddy; he made an article out of them. I spoke for hours with Delaprée on French literature and on the utter hatefulness of violence. It did not help much. It irritated me when I saw Ilsa advising and helping some newcomer or other after fifteen hours of work, pumping the last ounce of her energy into an unimportant conversation, only to turn to me with a drawn face and fall silent.

At four in the morning I went down into the second basement which was asleep under the glare of electric bulbs. The silence was full of snores, groans, coughs, and mumbled words. The men of the Shock Police post were playing cards. They gave me a glass of brandy; it was tepid and smelled of sleep. The rooms had the warmth of flesh slowly stewing in its own exudation, of a broody hen, and the brandy had the same warmth and the same smell.

I leaned out of the window for a long while afterwards to rinse my lungs and throat. I could not sleep. I was under a spell. I wanted to take the generals who called themselves saviors of their country, and the diplomats who called themselves saviors of the world to the shelters in the basement of the Telefónica. To put them there on the pallets of esparto grass, damp from November fog, to wrap them in army blankets and make them live and sleep in a space of two square yards, on a cellar floor, between crazed hungry women who had lost their homes, while shells were falling on the roofs outside. To leave them there one day, two days, more days, to drench them in misery, to impregnate them with the sweat and the lice of the multitude and to teach them living history—the history of this miserable, loathsome war, the war of cowardice in top-hats gleaming under the chandeliers of Geneva and of traitor generals coldly murdering their people. To tear them away from their military bands and tail-coats and top-hats and helmets and swords and gold-knobbed canes, to dress them in fustian or blue twill or white twill like the farmhands, the metal-workers, the masons, and then to throw them out into the streets of the world with a three days' stubble and fug-reddened eyes.

I could not think of killing or destroying them. It was monstrous and stupid to kill. It was sickening to see an insect crushed under one's foot. It was marvelous to watch the movements of an insect for hours.

Everything round me was destruction, loathsome as the crushing of a spider underfoot; and it was the barbaric destruction of people herded together and lashed by hunger, ignorance, and the fear of being finally, totally, crushed.

I was choked by the feeling of personal impotence in face of the tragedy. It was bitter to think that I loved peace, and bitter to think of the word pacifism. I had to be a belligerent. I could not shut my eyes and cross my arms while my country was being wantonly assassinated so that a few could seize power and enslave the survivors. I knew that there existed Fascists who had good faith, admirers of the "better" past, or dreamers of bygone empires and conquerors, who saw themselves as crusaders; but they were the cannon fodder of Fascism. There were the others, the heirs of the corrupt ruling caste of Spain, the same people who had maneuvered the Moroccan war with its stupendous corruption and humiliating retreats to their own greater glory. We had to fight them. It was not a question of politicial theories. It was life against death. We had to fight against the death-bringers, the Francos, the Sanjurjos, the Molas, the Millán

Astrays, who crowned their blood-drenched record, selling their country so as to be the masters of slaves and in their turn the slaves of other masters.

We had to fight them. This meant we would have to shell or bomb Burgos and its towers. Cordova and its flowered courtyards, Seville and its gardens. We would have to kill so as to purchase the right to live. I wanted to scream.

A shell had killed the street vendor outside the Telefónica. There was her little daughter, a small, brown, little girl who had been hopping round between the tables in the Miami Bar and the Gran Vía café like a sparrow, selling matchboxes and cigarettes. Now she turned up in the bar in a shiny, bright black cotton dress.

"What are you doing?"

"Nothing. I come here since they killed my mother. . . . I'm used to it, I've been doing it since I was so small."

"Are you alone?"

"No, I'm with Grandmother. They're giving us meals at the Committee, and now they're going to take us to Valencia." She hopped up to a big, beefy soldier of the International Brigades: "Long live Russia!" Her voice was high and clear.

No, I could not think in political terms, in terms of party or revolution. I had to think of the crime it was to send shells against human flesh and of the need for me, the pacifist, the lover of Saint Francis, to help in the task of finishing with that breed of Cain. To fight so as to sow, so as to create a Spain in which the command of the Republican Constitution: "Spain shall renounce war" would be truth and reality. The other thing —to forgive—was Christ's alone. Saint Peter took to the sword.

Over there, the front was alive and sent the echo of its explosions to our windows. Over there were thousands of men who thought vaguely like me and fought, hoping for victory in good faith, ingenuous, barbarous, scratching their lice in the trenches, killing and dying and dreaming of a future without hunger, with schools and cleanliness, without overlords or usurers, in sunshine. I was with them. But it was difficult to sleep.

When all those visions and emotions, thoughts and counter-thoughts crowd into one's brain, when day and night shells and bombs shake the walls and the front line draws nearer, and when sleep is sparse and work long, difficult and full of contradictions, one's mind takes shelter behind the tiredness of the body. I did not work well. Everything was clear and safe while I was together with Ilsa, but as soon as she worked and I looked on, I was uncertain even of her. She did not suffer the civil war in her own flesh as I did; she belonged to the others who went the easy

way of political work. In the evenings, when I had drunk wine and
brandy to get over my tiredness, I told stories until I found a reason to
shout with excitement, or had sudden rows with any journalist who
seemed to treat Spaniards more like natives than the others. Every second
day I demanded clear and unified instructions for our work from Valencia and from the War Commissariat, and every time I was told by
Rubio that I was actually in Madrid against his orders, and by Kolzoff
or his friends that everything was in order. When Maria rang up, I was
first rude to her and then took her out for a drink because there was so
much pain everywhere and I did not want to cause more.

Ilsa looked at me out of quiet eyes which seemed full of reproach, but
she did not ask me about anything which had to do with my private life.
I wanted her to ask, I would have had an outburst if she had done so.
She held the work of the office in firm hands while I tortured myself with
doubts. Then came the day when Rubio told me over the telephone that
I ought to realize that I was under the authority of the Ministry, not
under that of the *Junta de Defensa,* and when the people in the War
Commissariat told me the exact opposite, I rang up Rubio again. He
gave me strict orders to report to him in Valencia. I knew that he hated
me and was waiting for an opportunity to take me away from the work
I had usurped, but I was tired of shilly-shallying. I would go to Valencia
and have it out, face to face. At the back of my mind was the urge to
escape from an ambiguous situation.

The Junta refused to give me a safe-conduct to Valencia, because my
job was in Madrid and no orders from Valencia could relieve me from
it; Rubio Hidalgo had not the power to give me a safe-conduct. It was
an impasse.

Then I met my old friend Fuñi-Fuñi, the Anarchist, now one of the
leaders of the Transport Workers' Union. He offered me a safe-conduct
and a place in a car to Valencia for the following day. I accepted. Ilsa
said very little. She had once more refused Rubio's invitation to go to
Valencia.

On December the 6th I left Madrid, feeling like a deserter who is going
into a grim battle.

4. The Rearguard

T H E car that took me to Valencia belonged to the F.A.I. and carried three leaders of the Anarchist militia. One of them, García, was their commander at the Andalusian front. Although they knew that I was not an Anarchist and although I told them that I had collaborated with the Communists, they accepted me as a friend, since their Madrid head-quarters had given me the freedom of their car. And I accepted them because their harsh comments on the men who had abandoned Madrid to its fate fitted my mood. I was convinced that the officials who had gone to Valencia on November the 7th were now working hard to regain control of the capital without having to go back there themselves. I was one of the chief witnesses of cowardice and lack of responsibility, and so they would obviously try to get rid of me in an unimpeachable manner. That was why I had been called to Valencia and that was why I obeyed the order.

I began to speak of the problems which choked me. García listened carefully, and his shrewd questions helped me to go on speaking. It was a relief. I described the story as I saw it, the censorship before the night of November the 7th, the functioning of the office in the Telefónica, the role of the Defense Junta, the orders from Valencia, the muddle, the strain, the neglect. The road to Valencia is long, and I talked on to clarify my own mind, while García continued to listen and to put terse questions. When we arrived in the city, we went into a bar to have a drink together before going our separate ways. Only then did García say:

"Well, *compañero,* now give me that fellow's address. We'll pay your boss a visit tonight."

I was startled: "What for?"

"Never mind, people sometimes disappear overnight here in Valencia. They're taken to Malvarrosa, or to Grao, or to the Albufera, get a bullet in the neck, and then the sea carries them away. Sometimes they're washed ashore, though."

His face was as gravely thoughtful as ever. I tried a different line of approach.

"I don't think he deserves all that. Firstly, I don't believe that Rubio's a traitor to the Republic. He worked with Alvarez del Vayo for a long time, you see. And secondly he's one of the few people we have who

knows something about the foreign press. And then, after all, my affair
is my own personal affair."

García shrugged his shoulders: "All right, if you say so. You'll have to
lie on the bed you've made for yourself. But I tell you, one day you'll be
sorry for it. I know that type. We're going to lose the war because of
them. Or do you believe we don't know about the many things the censors let through? That man is a Fascist, and we've been realizing it for
quite a long time. We've warned him too, more than once. You can say
what you like, he'll be taken for a ride sooner or later."

It shook me out of my smoldering resentment against the Ministry.
I knew only too well that the foreign censorship committed far more
blunders by banning than by passing news or comment; I saw how distant from those Anarchists I was in my judgment, how distant in my
feelings, despite the anger and indignation which linked us together.

I went alone to the Press Office.

It was early in the morning. The sun shone from a cloudless sky. After
the December fogs and gales of Madrid, the air of Valencia was heady
wine. I walked slowly through an outlandish world where the war existed
only in the huge anti-Fascist posters and in the uniforms of lounging
militiamen. The streets were blocked by cars and thronged with boisterous, well-dressed people who had time and leisure. The café terraces were
crowded. A band was playing march music in the middle of the big
market square. Flower-sellers carried sheaves of white, red, and rose-pink
carnations. The market stalls were heaped with food, with turkeys, and
chickens, with big blocks of almond paste, with grapes, oranges, pome-
granates, dates, pineapples. A shoe-cleaner assaulted me, and I let him
polish my dusty shoes. There was no whistle of shells in the air. When
I passed a lorry with evacuated children from Madrid I wanted to speak
to them, because I was as bewildered as they were.

The Press Office had been installed in an old palace. I climbed a shabby,
sumptuous staircase and found myself in a reception room with faded
red brocade on the walls; from there a casual orderly sent me on through
a chain of small rooms overflowing with typewriters, roneos, rubber
stamps, and packets of paper. People I did not recognize came and went.
I stood there like a yokel, until the commissionaire Peñalver discovered
and welcomed me as though I had returned from the realm of death.
"You simply must stay with us while you're in Valencia," he said. "There
is no room anywhere, and your brother's already sleeping with us. I'll
tell Don Luis at once that you're here."

He received me in state, very much the head of the department despite
the squalid pomp and disorder of his surroundings, affable, urbane, non-
committal, his saurian eyes half hidden by the smoked glasses and the

dark arrowhead of his tongue flickering across his lips. I said nothing of what I had meant to say when I left the Telefónica. In Madrid I had cut easily through his bland phrases; but here in Valencia he was in his own fief, and I but a quixotic fool, unable either to submit and conform or to take the way of savage decision which García, the Anarchist, had offered.

Rubio Hidalgo told me he was sorry, but he had not the time to discuss outstanding matters with me that day; I might come back the next morning. I went away. From a street hoarding the blank eyes of the children killed in Getafe, the children of the salvaged photographs, stared at me. A propaganda poster. A very effective appeal. It crossed my mind that I had imagined it differently, and yet I had passed on the negatives of those photos for that very purpose.

I did not know what to do with myself.

In the afternoon I went to see my children and Aurelia in the small village where they had been given a billet. The narrow-gage railway that took me there was as slow as a mule-drawn cart. The village was under the administration of an Anarchist workers' committee which had commandeered a few big houses for the Madrid evacuees. I found Aurelia in a huge farm building with mighty rafters and decaying mortar-and-stone walls, large reception rooms, a bewildering number of stairs, a damp, somber garden and an orchard with a few orange trees. It sheltered only mothers with their children, twenty-two families, about a hundred persons in all. The committee had requisitioned beds and bedding and set up dormitories in the biggest rooms. It looked like a hospital or one of the old wayside inns with communal bedrooms.

In Aurelia's room ten beds were ranged in two rows along the main walls. She and the three children shared two beds close to the balcony which let in a blinding flood of sunlight. The place was clean and whitewashed, the four mothers seemed to get on well together. Within the first quarter of an hour of my stay I found that there existed a violent group antagonism between the various dormitories. The women were well cared for and had little to do beyond looking after their broods and being interested in each other. The committee provided milk for the children and issued vouchers for food rations. One of the women in Aurelia's dormitory, whose husband had been killed in the first days of the rising, was being entirely supported by the committee and received a daily shower of small gifts from the village people, clothing for the children, sweets, and flowers.

The children had settled down happily in the strange surroundings and were playing in the orchards. Aurelia paraded the husband who was "something in the Foreign Ministry" before all the inmates of the big

house, including the hostile clans of the other rooms. Towards the evening she asked me:

"What are your plans for tonight?"

"I'm taking the last train back to Valencia. Peñalver's let me have a
bed in his house. I'll come and see you again as soon as possible."

"No. Tonight you are going to stay here. I've arranged the whole
thing."

"But there's no room for me here."

"Oh yes, there is, I told you I'd arranged everything. The women are
going to sleep in other rooms tonight, as soon as the kids are asleep, and
so we'll be alone."

"Do stay, Papa . . ."

I felt an infinite repugnance and at the same time a wave of affection
and pity. We had lost our home in Madrid and everything that makes
life pleasant; the children hemmed me in and did not let me move;
Aurelia's eyes implored. I stayed.

That night I did not sleep at all. It is so difficult to lie.

The room was lighted by two little oil lamps whose sickly glow filled
it with shadows. Within reach of my arm, the children slept placidly in
the other bed. Aurelia slept beside me. And I was lying by being there.
I lied to the children by pretending a harmony with their mother which
did not exist. I lied to their mother by feigning a tenderness which was
dead and had turned into physical revulsion. I lied to Ilsa there in Madrid. I lied to myself by finding false justification for my presence in a
bed in which I did not want to be, should not have been, could never be
any more.

In the morning I took the first train to Valencia and slept in the close
carriage until fellow-travelers woke me. I went to Peñalver's house and
slept on there until midday. In the afternoon Rubio told me that he had
no time for our talk and was forced to postpone it. The following day
he had gone to Madrid. When he came back I heard from others that
he had installed Ilsa formally as head of the Madrid office. He told me
nothing, except that he would settle my case as soon as he had time. I
waited, and did not force the issue. I waited from one day to the other.
Once Rubio went to Madrid on a hurried journey; when he came back
he put me off more openly, with a more insolent tone in his voice. I had
a violent altercation with him, but I stayed and waited. My fight, so clear-
cut in Madrid, appeared hopeless and meaningless in Valencia, where I
was alone and helplessly floundering.

A week passed, nerve-racking and slow. The sky was uniformly clear,
the nights uniformly peaceful, the life of the city unbearably gaudy. Every
night my hatchet-faced landlord, Peñalver, produced a packet of cards

and a bottle of gin. My brother Rafael, who had gone to Valencia after the evacuation of his family, sat around, silent and morose. At midnight Peñalver would go to bed, befuddled. I could not sleep.

I was collecting stories. With the pressure of Madrid on my mind, I tried to understand the process of the organization of the war. But as I was waiting, idle and supernumerary, I never met any of the people who must have been working feverishly at the time. I only saw the hangers-on, the small fry of the bureaucracy settling down in safety to justify their existence. The minor employees of the Foreign Ministry, who had left Madrid because they had been ordered to do so or because they had been afraid, told malicious tales, and often the point of their malice was turned against the fools who had stayed in Madrid and muddled things up. They all thought that I had come to Valencia to stay, because it was the sensible thing to do. According to their version, the high State functionaries were greatly annoyed because those who organized the defense of Madrid behaved as though they had been heroes and the official evacuees to Valencia cowards. "You must admit that you people arrogated powers," someone said to me. "Yes, because you had written off Madrid," I retorted. But it was patent that anything I could say would fall into a void, would sound empty and declamatory. I remembered the Anarchist García with an uneasy feeling of comradeship, mixed with loathing; so I fell silent, listening, and watched.

They told me that Rubio Hidalgo had said he would put me into the Postal Censorship at Valencia "to rot there," and that I would not be allowed to go back to Madrid. They told me that he had spoken with great indignation of the day when I had been quick to usurp his chair and desk in the Ministry. They hinted that Ilsa was to be left in the Madrid office until things were settled—unless she committed a blunder at an earlier stage; Rubio would manage her easily, it was felt, because she was a foreigner without backing and without any knowledge of Spanish to speak of. Others told me that she was politically inconvenient and would shortly be expelled from Spain, especially if she continued to be so friendly with foreign journalists as to make herself suspect. With all that, she had become a legend.

I visited my children regularly, but I did not spend another night in the village. After a bitter quarrel I spoke no more to Aurelia and she knew that I would never come back.

I sat with my brother in cafés and bars, dazed by the noise, and went out to the beach to watch the people swirling round the fashionable beach restaurants or to stare at the frying-pans in the open kitchen of *La Marcelina,* where rice simmered under wreaths of chrome-red crawfish and chunks of golden-skinned fried chicken. The rice in the Gran Vía

Hotel of Madrid, which we had been eating day after day, was a sickly pink paste. On the wooden platforms overlooking the sands and the sea, where tables had to be booked in advance, the women of the town evacuated from Madrid were fighting a grim battle of competition with their colleagues of Valencia. A wealth of loose cash was spent in hectic gaiety. Legions of people had turned rich overnight, against the background of the giant posters which were calling for sacrifices in the name of Madrid. A new brand of organizers was invading the offices.

My landlord, Peñalver, commissionaire in the Foreign Ministry, awoke one morning with the inspiring idea of setting up a Cyclists' Battalion recruited from the ranks of Ministry orderlies. He had a bicycle and was able to ride it, so were his two sons, both dispatch riders at the Ministry. He started canvassing his idea in the various other departments and after a few days appeared in a brand new captain's uniform, with an order authorizing him to organize a battalion and a voucher for expenses in his pocket. After this, he began to consider leaving the Ministry for good as soon as he had assembled his unit. But in the meantime he had his innings.

I heard that Louis Delaprée had died. During the last days of my work in Madrid he had had a row with his paper, the *Paris-Soir,* because his impassioned reports of the killing of women and children by indiscriminate bombing had not been published, not being topical any more. That was in the days when Mrs. Simpson monopolized the front pages. When I had said good-by to him he had been sitting on my camp bed, his face more pallid than ever, a brick-red scarf round his throat, and had told me that he would have a very serious word with friends in the Quai d'Orsay about the French consulate's brazenly pro-Fascist conduct. "I hate politics, as you know, but I'm a liberal and a humanist," he had said.

He had left in a French aircraft; it also carried a Havas correspondent and a delegate of the International Red Cross who had investigated the killing of political prisoners from the Model Jail at the beginning of the assault on Madrid. Not far from the city the French plane was attacked, machine-gunned, and forced down by an unidentified aircraft. The Havas man lost his leg, the Red Cross delegate was unharmed, the pilot bruised, and Delaprée died a painful, lingering death in a Madrid hospital. Rumors claimed that the attacking aircraft had been Republican, but Delaprée denied it in the endless lucid hours of his agony. I could not believe it.

It was to attend the funeral service that Rubio Hidalgo had hurried to Madrid with a sheaf of glowing flowers in his car, and it was after his return that I had heard the spate of stories about Ilsa's strong but precarious position and my own impending exile in the postal censorship.

Journalists came to Valencia from a spell in Madrid, and their effusive praise of Ilsa's régime worried me more than the vague rumors. I saw her exposing herself to envy, entangling herself in a net of bureaucratic rules which she ignored or did not know, and I saw her going away from me, on her own road.

I began to write a diary-like letter to her, in French. It was stiff, uneasy, and self-conscious, and I knew it. As I had entered the Madrid censorship on the recommendation of the Communist Party and grasped the reins after November the 7th with their consent, I went to see one of the party secretaries. He had told me that the censorship muddle would have to be cleared up by the Government, that we all had to support the reorganization of the State machinery in every way, that I was in the right but would have to wait for an official decision. I waited. It was all very reasonable and it drove home to me that I did not belong.

There came a letter from Ilsa in answer to a note in which I had urged her to join me in Valencia. She would come for a few days' leave, after Christmas, and she hoped that I would return with her to Madrid. Luis, our orderly, would give me more details, she was about to send him off to Valencia for a brief holiday and he ought to arrive shortly after her letter. I went to the Ministry; no car had come from Madrid. When I returned a few hours later, somebody mentioned vaguely that he had heard of a car accident in which two journalists and an orderly had been wounded. No, they did not know exactly who they were.

The hospital of Valencia was an enormous building looking like a convent, with vaulted rooms, cold stone walls, dark corners, where the dying were hidden away, and a slab with the name of a saint on the door of each room. The stone flags and huge tiles of the floor rang with footsteps, glasses and crockery clicked, the air was dense with the odor of carbolic. The old order was broken up by the war. A crowd of visitors had installed themselves on chairs and bedsteads, closing in on the sick and wounded. The vaults hummed like a giant beehive.

Nurses and medical orderlies had become gruff and exasperated. They pushed their way through the clustering people without answering questions. I tracked down the English journalist; he had nothing but scratches, he would sleep in the hotel that night. But he passed me on to Suzana of the War Commissariat who had taken him along in her car: she had a deep gash on her forehead which had to be stitched up, and she knew that Luis was gravely injured. I could not find him. Nobody knew where he was. A bed to which I was directed stood empty. He might have died, or it might all have been a mistake. I walked through a maze of cold corridors and found him, in the end, on a stretcher outside the door of the X-ray department.

The tenderness on his face when he saw me was so intense that it hit me like a blow. I knew he was doomed. A thin thread of saliva mixed with blood ran out of the corner of his mouth, his gums were greenish and had receded from his teeth, his skin had turned ashen and his limbs were totally paralyzed. Only his eyes, lips, and fingers were alive. The doctor let me accompany him and showed me, in silence, the shadow picture on the other side of the fluorescent screen: the spinal column broken in the middle of the back, two of the vertebrae an inch apart.

Afterwards I sat down by the side of his bed. Luis labored to speak, and said:

"The letter, in my jacket." I found a fat envelope in the coat hanging at the foot of the bed. "Now it's all right. You know I'm going to die?" He smiled, and it was a grimace. "It's funny, I was so afraid of the bombs. Do you remember that night in the Telefónica? If you want to run away from Death you run straight into Her arms. Life's like that. I'm sorry because of my daughter. Not because of my wife." He put a bitter stress on his "not." "She'll be glad, and I too. Give me a cigarette."

I lighted the cigarette for him and pushed it between his lips. From time to time his fingers closed round the stub and lifted it away, and he spoke.

"Don Arturo, don't let that woman get lost. I was right. She's a great woman. Do you remember that night she came to Madrid? And she loves you. We've talked a lot. Do you know that she speaks Spanish already? At least, we understood each other, and we spoke a lot about you. She's in love with you and you're in love with her. There are many things I see clearly now. You know, it's always said that one doesn't see things clearly until one's about to die. Don't let her go, it would be a crime, for you and for her. She's coming here on the 26th. You'll be happy, both of you, and you'll remember poor Luis. You've got her letter safe, have you? I was worrying about it all the time."

The agony of peritonitis is shattering. The belly lifts the sheets, steadily, inexorably swelling. The bowels are crushed by the tremendous pressure and in the end pushed out of the mouth in a loathsome paste of mixed excrement, blood, and bubbles of gaseous stench. Luis' wife could not stand it and deserted her place at the head of his bed, and I stayed on alone for long hours, ceaselessly wiping his mouth. His eyes were to the last moment alive, resigned and affectionate, and he said good-by to me very softly, choked by froth.

Ilsa came to Valencia on December the 26th. They put flowers into her hotel room on behalf of the department because she was a "heroine." She was tired and her round face looked haggard, but she was strong and buoyant. When I met her, everything in the world fell into place again. The following midday, her friend Rolf came to look for me in the smoking room of the hotel: an agent of the Political Police had waited for her at the reception desk and taken her away. She had met Rolf on the stairs and told him to notify me and Rubio Hidalgo.

I saw the avenue near the abattoir of Madrid, its rickety, dusty little trees, tumbled bodies in the gray light of dawn, the nervous titter of passers-by, the ugly blasphemies of evil people, I remembered the old woman I had seen dragging a small boy by the hand and pushing a piece of pastry into the half-open mouth of a dead man. I saw the tribunal where Little Paws had asked for more people to be taken for a ride. I saw Ilsa before a tribunal of men who believed anything of a foreigner, and I saw her stretched out on the sand of the beach, the water lapping at her feet. The clock in the room ticked slowly. I had a pistol. We all had pistols.

I rang through to the Press Department and asked for Rubio Hidalgo. He cut me short. He had heard, he would do everything in his power and would soon find out what had happened. Yes, I said, he would have to find out soon. He told me that he would come to the hotel at once. There were other strangers around me; Rolf had brought Julius Deutsch, the Austrian, who knew her well. I think he rang up Largo Caballero's secretary. Rubio came and monopolized the telephone. I had laid my pistol on the table before me. They all looked askance at me as though I were a madman, and told me to be calm.

I said it did not matter whether she appeared that night or not, other people would die in Valencia, that was all. I put two filled cartridge frames on the table. Rubio rang up the Foreign Minister.

Then they told me that the whole thing was cleared up; it had been a stupid denunciation, nothing more; she would be back soon. I did not altogether believe them. The clock went very slowly. She came back two hours later, smiling and self-possessed. I could not speak to her. The other people crowded round and she told them her story with a wicked relish. The agent who had detained her had asked her questions on the way to the police, which indicated that she had been denounced as a "Trotskyist spy." There had been no concrete accusation, but her friendship with the Austrian Socialist leader Otto Bauer had loomed large. While two people cross-examined her—in a very clumsy and uncertain way, she said, which gave her the feeling of being mistress of a ludicrous rather than a dangerous situation—the telephone had started ringing. After the first call they had asked her whether she was hungry; after the third or fourth they had brought her a sumptuous lunch; after the sixth or seventh they had asked her opinion about the man Leipen who had apparently denounced her, a little Central-European journalist who for a time had worked in the Press Department and whom I did not even know. She had told them that she thought him a twister, but nothing worse, and left it at that. In the end they had treated her with the greatest affection, as a friend of the family. It did not matter that she had never realized the whole extent of her danger. She was back again, alive. I stayed with her.

That night the moon of Valencia shone like molten silver. Valencia has gardens and fountains, it has a wide promenade flanked by palm trees, it has old palaces and churches. Everything was dark, from fear of enemy aircraft, and that polished moon lorded it over the city. The small, bright disk rode on a blue-black sky studded with tiny, white, flickering flames, and the earth was a field of black and silver.

After supper we went out and walked through the light and darkness. There was a scent of cool, moist soil, of thirsty roots drinking the sap of the ground, of breathing trees, of flowers opening to the moon and the shadows. We walked along the pillars of palm trees whose broad fans rustled like parchment, and the sand crunching under our feet caught sparks from the moon as though the world were of crystal. We spoke softly, so that the moon should not shut her eyes and leave the world blinded.

I do not know what we said. It ran deep as talk runs in a nuptial night. I do not know how long it lasted. Time had no measure and stood still to watch us walking beyond its orbit. I do not know where we went. There was garden and moon, sand, and leaping fountains, rustle of dry leaves in pools of shadow, and we went on, hand in hand, disembodied, following the murmur of the cradle-song.

In the morning we went to the sea, speaking soberly of the struggle in front of us, until we would go back to our posts in Madrid and work together. We walked past the village of El Cabanel, white, frail-looking huts of fishermen and workers. Where the beach curved away from people and houses, we sat down in the sand. It was yellow, fine, and warm like human skin. Sea and sky were two shades of the same soft blue, fusing without a borderline in the dim haze. Shallow waves ran up the beach and their glassy crests carried flicks of sand. The sand grains rode on gaily like mischievous gnomes until the wave toppled over with a gentle splash and left them ranged in long motionless ripples, the trace of the sea's lips.

My neck was lying on her bare arm, skin on skin, and I felt the currents running below our skins, as strong and imperious as the forces beneath the blue surface of the sea.

"I don't know any more where I end and where you begin. There is no borderline."

It was peaceful. We had no need to talk much about ourselves. We had each said a few sentences: she would have to write to her husband and tell him that their marriage had come to an end. I would try to straighten out my own private mess with the least possible hurt to those whom I had involved.

"You know that it will be a lot of pain for the others, and pain for ourselves as well as happiness. One's got to pay, always."

"I know."

But everything seemed apart from our life together, the only life we could feel. The muddled, complicated, entangled matters of which I knew in my brain referred to somebody else. I told her of my boyhood, of my delight when I could bury my head in my mother's lap and feel her light fingers in my hair. That was my self still. It belonged together with Ilsa's slow smile and the small shells she dug out of the sand, shells white as milk, golden as bread from a peasant's oven, deep rose as a woman's nipples, smooth and polished as a shield, curled and grooved as a perfect fan.

Then we were hungry and plodded through the yellow sand to a small beach tavern. There we sat on the wooden platform, looking at the sea and talking of Madrid. The waiter brought an earthenware pan with the saffron-yellow Valencian rice and pointed to two slender red crawfish on its top: "From the comrades over there." A fisherman at the corner table rose, bowed, and said: "We thought that the foreign comrade ought to have a chance of eating the real thing. We've only just caught those *langostinos*, they're quite fresh."

The rice smelled tangy and we drank tart red wine with it.

"Hasn't the new year begun today?"

"Still three days to go."

"You know, it's odd, but it's only today that I found out that we can share a life in daylight and gaiety, a normal life."

"Will you always tell me things I've been thinking of?"

It was beautiful to be childish. I felt as strong as never before. We walked out on the beach, lay in the sand, and collected more of the golden and pink shells. When we went home in the crowded, clattering tram, the shells in Ilsa's pocket clicked like castanets.

5. Front Line

"THE story has moved from Madrid to Valencia because of the non-intervention racket," I heard a foreign correspondent say. "Of course, everything still depends on whether Madrid holds out or not—I've heard that the Nationalists are going to resume their offensive against the Great North Road—but we've got to stay in contact with the Valencia Government."

It was true. Madrid was in the war, but Valencia was in the world. The laborious work of administrative organization and diplomatic traffic had come into its own; it was necessary although it bred a parasitic life. Yet I knew that I could not become part of it without losing my last shred of faith. I had to go back to Madrid. I wanted to have a share in the handling of foreign propaganda from there. This meant that I would have to learn how to exert an indirect influence on the outside world, converting that which to us was naked life and death into raw material for the Press. It also meant that I would have to return to Madrid, not in opposition to the "proper channels" of the Press Department, but in agreement with them.

This was difficult to work out within myself. I revolted against it even while I believed in Ilsa's diagnosis. She was profoundly uneasy at the thought of once again having to face the Spanish authorities by herself, at the head of a key office, yet without the slightest knowledge of official rules and regulations. She wanted me there to help her in collecting the factual material which she would hand out to journalists in search of copy. It now seemed worth while to me. I read foreign papers in Valencia and forced myself to observe their methods of reporting. Ilsa hoped that Julio Alvarez del Vayo, with his journalistic experience, would see her point, but she was very doubtful whether the Minister's friendliness towards her would outweigh his Press chief's venomous dislike of me. I was skeptical, yet willing to let her try her best.

Suddenly all obstacles dissolved into thin air. I was waiting in an anteroom of the Ministry when Ilsa came out from an interview with Don Julio with a blank expression that sat oddly upon her, and told me that Rubio Hidalgo was waiting to see us both. He received us with great warmth and informed me that he was sending me back to Madrid as Head of the Foreign Press Censorship with Ilsa as my deputy. Ignoring my bewilderment, he went on smoothly: his secretary would settle the administrative details; our salaries would be slightly raised; the Ministry would foot our living expenses; otherwise, there was not much he could tell me; I knew the ropes, none better; and Ilsa seemed to have bewitched the foreign journalists into a constructive attitude—although I would have to guard her from an excess of kindness and indulgence, to which she was inclined.

It was just as well that I had donned my official face; I was at a complete loss. Ilsa seemed to know something about the background of the sudden change, for she chatted with a studied impulsiveness, mentioned by the way that she was glad Rubio had realized the impracticability of his plan to send his Valencia censors to Madrid in turn, and expressed her concern at the appointment of Major Hartung. Was he to be our chief, or just liaison officer with the General Staff?

Who the hell was Major Hartung?

"That man has nothing whatsoever to do with you," said Rubio. "You, Barea, are responsible for the department in Madrid together with Ilsa, and you both work directly under me. I am sure you will do it better than ever before. We'll send you food parcels and whatever you need. Take care of yourselves. I'm sorry, but you will have to leave for Madrid tomorrow."

Everything was arranged, the car, the petrol quota, the safe-conducts, the Ministry papers, even rooms in the Gran Vía Hotel, since it would be too strenuous to go on sleeping on camp beds in the office. This time our work would run in regular grooves. I gave the answers that seemed expected of me. Rubio Hidalgo slapped me on the shoulder and wished us good luck.

Not even Ilsa knew exactly what had happened, but at least she had grasped one thread of the tangle. An Austrian, calling himself Major Hartung, had turned up in the Telefónica on Christmas Eve, sent to Madrid by official car on some undefined mission. He had talked a lot about the need for a military Press Office, casting himself for the role of Chief Publicity Officer with the General Staff in Madrid, stressed his allegedly enormous journalistic experience, and boasted of his acquaintance with the Minister. Ilsa had regarded him as a jovial braggart and failed to take him seriously. He was now in Valencia, apparently about to go back to Madrid with some kind of Press appointment in his pocket. Rubio Hidalgo saw in him a menace to his own office, and turned to us in his quandary. So, through no merit or act of our own, the road back to our joint work was cleared.

The road from Valencia to Madrid had changed in the bare four weeks since I had traveled in the opposite direction. There were fewer control posts at the roadside, many of the pickets and barricades in the villages had disappeared, the remaining sentries had a businesslike air and scanned our papers carefully. The most important crossroads were in the hands of the Shock Police. We overtook military vehicles and a chain of light tanks moving towards Madrid. The air of the hills was crisp and exhilarating, but at dusk, when we climbed the uplands, the wind bit into our skin. From the height of Vallecas, the white skyscrapers of the city rose out of a pool of dark mist and the front rumbled in the near distance. Our car plunged down the slope, past the concrete pillars of street barricades, and then we were suddenly back at home; in the Telefónica.

Two days later, the Rebels launched two attacks, one at Las Rozas against the North Road, the Corunna Road, which was the link with El Escorial, and the other in the Vallecas sector, against the road to Valencia. They captured Las Rozas and penetrated deeper into the north-western fringe of the city. A new stream of peopde in flight swept through the streets and choked the tunnels of the underground stations. The International Brigades stopped the gap at Las Rozas. The Government attempted to organize a large-scale evacuation of noncombatants to the Mediterranean coast. We heard the swelling roar of the battle through the windows of the Telefónica during our working hours and through the windows of our hotel room during the few hours of sleep. Those were days of hunger and cold. The lorries which entered the city carried war material, not food. There was hardly any coal left, and the cardboard in place of the broken windowpanes did not keep out the bitter frosts. Then a thick blanket of chilly fog spread over the town and smothered the noise. The shelling stopped. The offensive was broken off. Only then did I look round and take stock.

While I had been away, the foreign journalists had come to take it for granted that the Censorship Office should help them personally, as well as censor their dispatches. Men of the International Brigades came and went, bringing us their letters and snatching a few words with people who spoke their language. Correspondents who had no assistant to pick up material for them came and exchanged impressions and information with us. Our office provided newcomers with hotel rooms, and helped them to get petrol vouchers. Ilsa had established official relations with *Servicios Especiales,* a branch of the Military Security Police, which at our request granted safe-conducts for certain sectors of the front to foreign journalists. The Political Commissars of the International Brigades visited us as a matter of course and gave us information which we could pass on to the journalists.

The Russian General Goliev, or Goriev, who was attached to Miaja's staff as an adviser and at the same time as chief of the detachments of Russian technicians and tank-men detailed to the Madrid front, sent regularly for Ilsa in the small hours of the morning and discussed current Press problems with her. So far as I could make out, his appreciation of her work had gone far to strengthen her difficult position and to neutralize the enmity of those foreign Communists who considered her undesirable because she was critical and independent of them. Sometimes, when Goliev's Spanish Adjutant, childishly proud of his post, came to fetch Ilsa at three in the morning, I went with her.

The Russian general perturbed and impressed me. He was fair, tall, and strong, with high cheek-bones, frigid blue eyes, a surface of calm and constant high tension underneath. He was not interested in people unless they forced him to consider them as individuals; and then he was curt. His Spanish was good, his English excellent; his capacity for work was apparently unlimited. He was watchful and correct in his treatment of Spanish officers, but ruthlessly detached and cold in his discussion of Spanish problems, in so far as he touched upon them at all, that is to say, whenever they impinged on his military considerations. He lived, ate, and slept in a gloomy, dank cellar room. There he saw the bald, bullet-headed Mongolian commander of the tankists, a man with a cellophane-covered map forever under his arm, or the employees of the Soviet Embassy, and dealt with them rapidly and, to judge by the sound, brusquely. Then he would turn to us, giving his concentrated attention to the problems of Press and propaganda. He never attempted to give us orders, but clearly expected us to follow his advice; at the same time, he accepted a surprising amount of argument and contradiction from Ilsa, because— as he said—she knew her job but was no Party member.

Every morning he scrutinized the censored press dispatches of the previous day, before they were sent on to the Ministry in Valencia by a War Commissariat courier. Sometimes he disagreed with our censoring, and said so, sometimes he explained points of military intelligence value of which we ought to be aware, but as a rule he focused his attention on the trends of foreign opinion revealed by the correspondents, and more particularly by reports to conservative and moderate newspapers. The noticeable change in their tone, from open animosity against Republican Spain to straight reporting, had impressed him. He had conceived a predilection for the sober articles of the *New York Times* correspondent, Herbert Matthews, and for the *Daily Express* reports of Sefton Delmer's, whose carefully dosed shrewdness disguised by a whimsical style amused him as much as his erratic typing; but he showed a cavalier disregard for the reports of Communist newspapermen.

From time to time, Goliev probed into Ilsa's political ideas which he found inexplicably near to and far from his own, so that he would stare at her in puzzled interest. Once he ended by saying to her: "I cannot

understand you. I could not live without my Party Membership card."
He tended to leave me alone because he had classified me as an emotional,
romantic revolutionary, useful enough in a way, but unreasonable and
intractable. No doubt he was right from his point of view. He was so
honest and blatant about it, that I accepted his manner and repaid it in
kind, by my silent scrutiny of this new breed, the Red Army officer,
single-minded, strong, ruthless, and beyond my touch. He seemed a man
from Mars. But he was more or less of my own age, and I could not help
imagining what his experiences had been in 1917.

A few doors further on in the cellar passage, and in a different world
altogether, was General Miaja. Operations were directed by the General
Staff, and he, the nominal C.-in-C., had little say in them. And yet he
was more than a figurehead. In that period, when the role of the Defense
Junta had shrunk and the new administration did not yet function, he
acted as Governor of Madrid and held a considerable part of the administrative power in his hands, without making much use of it. He had the
sly shrewdness of a peasant who does not want to be entangled in things
beyond his understanding, and he knew to a nicety his own value as a
symbol of Madrid's resistance. He knew that he was at his best whenever
he could sum up the feelings of the men in the trenches and the streets
in rude, blunt words, such as he liked and shared with them, and that
he was at his worst when it came to the game of politics or the science
of strategy.

Miaja was short, paunchy, red in the face, with a long thick nose and
incongruous spectacles which made his eyes frog-like. He liked drinking
beer even more than he liked drinking wine. When the Foreign Press
Censorship, which he neither understood nor cared about, came under
his authority by the rules of martial law and the state of siege, he found
it mainly awkward. With Ilsa, who was saved from his dislike of intellectuals only by her plumpness and her fine eyes, he never quite knew
how to deal, but he thought me a good fellow: I enjoyed drinking with
him, cursing highbrows and politicians together with him, and matching
the barrack-room language in which he found relief from his official dignity. As long as I did not embroil him with "those fellows in Valencia"
he was willing to back me within his own kingdom of Madrid.

The courtyard of the Ministry of Finance, into which you emerged
from the underground headquarters, had been cleared of the litter of sod-
den papers that filled it in the days of November. Then you had trodden
on reports on economic planning and taxation reform of the eighteenth
century, on bleached State Loan certificates and sheaves of agrarian statis-
tics, all thrown out from the vast archive vaults when they were being
converted into bomb-proof offices. Now, the courtyard was packed with

lorries, cars, motorcycles, and occasionally a bevy of light Russian tanks just arrived from a Mediterranean port. The smell of damp mold and of rats' nests still stuck to the stone slabs which the sun never touched, but it was mixed with the stench of petrol and hot metal.

On the first floor of the drab building were the offices of the Military Government of Madrid, the Army Judiciary, and of *Servicios Especiales*. This Intelligence Department was headed by a group of Anarchists who had taken over the abandoned office when the Government machine had been rushed to Valencia in the early days of November. I have never dealt with any police authority which tried to be so meticulously just, so sparing in the use of its power; and yet some of the agents attached to the department were shady and obnoxious, very much the *agent provocateur* type, mixing old spy methods with a new, truculent brutality which was alien to the ideas of their temporary chiefs.

The man who dealt with matters connected with foreigners was Pedro Orobón, whose brother had been famous among the collaborators of the great Anarchist Durruti. Pedro was small, dark, thin, with shrewd, sad, kind eyes in an ugly monkey face, a childlike smile and nervous hands. He was utterly unselfish, an ascetic believer with a burning, incorruptible sense of justice, of the breed which gave Spain a Cardinal Cisneros and an Ignatius Loyola. Frank, helpful and ready to be your friend as soon as he trusted you, he would have shot his best friend had he found him guilty, and you knew this about him all the time. But you also knew that he would have fought with all the strength of his being against any punishment he believed unjust, that he would never have accused anyone without being convinced of his guilt, and before having exhausted every means of clearing or justifying him. To him, an aristocrat had the moral right to be a Fascist, because his environment had molded him in a certain way; Pedro would have liked to give him pick and shovel and make him earn his bread with his hands—and he would have thought it possible that this way of living might open the aristocrat's mind to the ideals of Anarchism. But a worker gone Fascist or a traitor pretending to be a revolutionary were to him past redemption; they had sentenced themselves. He had respect for other people's convictions and was willing to work with all militant anti-Fascists; he and Ilsa trusted each other, and he treated me as a friend. Yet even while he himself worked as part of the war machine without dimming his ideas, he was worried about the Anarchist Ministers' participation in the Government, because he feared the trappings of power and the dilution of ideals for them.

I had soon every reason to be grateful for Orobón's scrupulous fairness.

Hartung, the Austrian whose vague promotion had made Rubio Hidalgo send me to Madrid, had turned up armed with papers which made him Chief Press Officer with the Army at the Central Front. He was extremely loquacious, expounded his plans—he would of course manage everything with the General Staff, provide our office with a fleet of cars and whatever else its importance warranted, and so forth—and went off. Soon we heard that he had presented himself everywhere in his brandnew uniform of a Spanish Artillery major, thrown out grandiloquent and nebulous hints, and left distrust behind him wherever he had entered. When I broached the matter in one of my telephone conversations with the head office in Valencia, Rubio Hidalgo told me to disregard that madman and swindler as well as his papers which seemed to make him my superior. The journalists began asking embarrassing questions about the new man.

Some days later, two agents of the Military Police came and asked Ilsa whether she had had anything to do with a countryman of hers, a so-called Major Hartung; when I intervened and explained the connection, they told us both to come with them. In *Servicios Especiales* we found our Anarchist friends puzzled, somewhat worried, yet ridiculing any idea that we had been arrested. Nevertheless we were not allowed to leave the building and spent hours in the dingy ante-room, together with a motley collection of people who had been seen speaking or having a drink with Hartung: there was an attaché of the Soviet Embassy, the correspondent of a Swiss newspaper, a Norwegian woman journalist, and Professor J. B. S. Haldane. The Russian walked silently up and down, the Norwegian was frightened, Professor Haldane sat down at a deal table and filled in a number of old blanks bearing the signature of His Gracious Majesty King Alfonso XIII, giving himself beautiful titles and interesting things to do. Ilsa spoke to the German girl Hilda who worked with the Anarchists in *Servicios Especiales,* and explained that the huge man in the leather jerkin which rode up his belly was a famous scientist, Nobel Prize winner and a great friend of the Republic's, upon which Hilda shyly invited him into their room. Haldane came out soon, rather disgruntled, and all I could understand of his English harangue was that he was disappointed because they had not threatened to shoot him at dawn, but had offered him, of all things, a cup of tea!

From the guarded remarks of our friends, I realized that Orobón and his colleagues were resisting pressure from the Special Military Judge in charge of the Hartung affair to put us all into jail on suspicion of conspiracy with a foreign spy. The Judge, an army officer and a Freemason with a strong bias against Socialists and foreigners, found it most suggestive that all the people rounded up by the agents as having had contact with Hartung were foreigners, with the exception of myself. The chiefs of *Servicios Especiales* objected to the summary injustice against people who, in their opinion, had proved their loyalty more clearly than the Judge himself, and against journalists who had happened to stray into Hartung's hotel. In the end, Orobón rang up General Goliev and let Ilsa speak to him; then I spoke briefly with General Miaja, who said that the Judge was his friend and that he could not interfere with the judiciary, but anyhow, he would speed up matters and see to it that we should not be kept away any longer from our work.

Once again I felt caught in a trap, when I entered the faded reception room where a natty Colonel sat enthroned behind a paper-laden desk, a perfectly groomed young girl in riding breeches beside him as his secretary. In clipped tones the Colonel asked me a number of questions, of which the young girl took notes, with an occasional giggle. The brocade chairs gave out a stale odor of dust and damp.

What were my relations with Hartung? I answered that I had seen him only once, in my official capacity. The Colonel had an outburst of barrack-yard rage: "None of your tales! You're in with a pack of foreign Fascists, and I know how to deal with the likes of you . . . !" I was just calling him a sabotaging Fascist, when the 'phone rang and I heard the Colonel say, "Yes, *mi general* . . . of course, *mi general* . . . at your orders, *mi general.*" He was scared, of the telephone and of me. After putting down the receiver, he started tendering me carefully worded apologies: maybe the whole thing was a mistake; Hartung might well be nothing but a dangerous kind of lunatic, the man had not slept during the night and devoured any food he got hold of. "Even that sort of rice the Milicianos eat," said the Colonel with contemptuous disgust.

Ilsa's interrogation lasted a few minutes, during which the Colonel tried to make her say that the shady man Hartung had been promoted to a position of power by Alvarez del Vayo and Rubio Hidalgo because they had dark reasons of their own; but she had found it easy to parry his clumsy insinuations. Haldane ambled off with a chuckle, tugging at his leather jerkin. I believe he put on the fantastic tin hat from the last war which he sported in Madrid, as though it were Mambrino's helmet. The Norwegian was almost in tears, the Russian disappeared quietly. We went back to the Telefónica. Hartung was kept imprisoned and it was never cleared up whether he was more than an adventurer with a touch of megalomania. The incident was closed. Rubio Hidalgo was affectionate during our telephone conversations the following days: there had been no scandal and everything was nicely settled. Yet I knew well that, but for the refusal of *Servicos Especiales* to send us all to prison without further ado, and but for the intervention from higher quarters, we might have been caught in a purposeless, dangerous tangle, caught in the cogwheels of machinery hostile to everything we stood for.

They rang me up from the Military Emergency Hospital in the Palace Hotel. A wounded Miliciano wanted them to get in touch with me. His name was Angel García.

I felt convinced that Angel was in grave danger. In my confused mind I saw him doomed, as all the simple men of good faith seemed doomed in the unequal struggle. The day was foggy and dirty. The battle noise to the south of the city was carried through the streets by gusts of wind. I took Ilsa with me, afraid of being alone with a dying Angel.

We found him stretched out on his belly, splashed with mud, streaks of drying blood on his torn, dirty shirt. There it is, I thought. He turned his face and grinned. His eyes crinkled in impish merriment. A huge, grimy bandage covered him from the waist downwards and another spanned his shoulder blades.

"Now, that's nice! Well, here I am: I've been born again! Those Moors, the dirty bastards, have been trying to violate me."

I had seen cases of that sort in Morocco, and felt sickened. But Angel burst into a guffaw. His teeth, which ought to have glistened white in his berry-red face, were stained a dark brown by tobacco juice.

"Now you're on the wrong track, Don Arturo. What d'you think of your Angelillo? Oh no, it's not that. It's only that those gentlemen have shot me through the ass, I beg your pardon, ma'am. And a nice shot it was, too. You see, we made a night attack on a machine-gun nest that annoyed us, and they sprayed us with bullets, so the only thing we could do was to stick to the ground like limpets and bury our heads in the mud. I've still got some on my face—see? Well then, a bullet struck me in the shoulder, grazed my spine and went right through one of my buttocks, and all the way along it touched nothing but flesh. No bones broken. If I hadn't stuck so flat to the ground it would have made a tunnel through me from my shoulder blade to my footsole. But they don't get me, no, sir."

I was gulping down hysterical laughter. Of course, what other wound would have been right for Angel? It was just like him. Wasn't he indestructible? Doomed—nonsense, he was more alive than I was. He stank of mud, sweat, blood, and carbolic acid, but he winked at me and wriggled on his belly, babbling on about the nice shelter he had rigged up for himself at the front in Carabanchel and how we would get drunk together the first day he was out of bed, because you didn't need your buttocks for drinking, did you? Nor for other things.

A young boy lying in the bed opposite was getting irritated by Angel's flow of jokes. He launched forth in a bitter tirade. He had been wounded near the Jarama, and his wound was no joke. His unit, the 70th Brigade, had been sent into action without sufficient armor and automatic weapons, just because they were Anarchists of the F.A.I. and the C.N.T., and the neighboring brigade, which was Communist, was excellently equipped but kept in the rear.

"We made three attacks, *compañero,* and the Fascists gave us hell. The third time we got the position we wanted, and we mightn't have stuck it if we hadn't wanted to show those other rogues who we were. But it was a lousy trick of theirs. We'll have to shoot it out with the Communists sooner or later."

Angel grew angry and screwed round his neck to glare at the young boy. "Listen, you fool, I'm a Communist myself and I won't let you insult my people. We can shoot too, if that's your game."

"I didn't mean you. I meant your bosses. It's always, the poor devils who pay, people like you and me and the many others who don't live to tell the tale."

"What bosses?" said Angel. "No boss puts a fast one over on me. There's our Captain, he's been my neighbor for ten years and he's younger than me, and now he starts talking of Party discipline and Army discipline and what not, because you see, it's true, we're an Army now and he's right, only I don't tell him so. They've started peppering us with mortars and we got orders to clear out of the huts we were using as shelters and get down into proper dugouts. But you won't catch me sleeping in a dugout, I don't want to be buried alive and it's too damp for my rheumatics. So when the Captain told me to get myself a dugout, I said to him, you can't tell me anything, I was a Socialist and a Communist and what you will when you were still afraid of your Father Confessor, and I won't be ordered about. So he called me Corporal García and ordered me to get myself a mortar-proof shelter, and he didn't mind if I got it in hell. So I did. I got a lot of doors from ruined houses, and a lot of spring mattresses, and I propped up the doors inside my hut, plenty of them, until it looked like a builder's store, and then I tore off the roof of my hut and put another lot of doors across. The upright doors were like beams, see? Then I shoveled earth on the top of my hut, two feet of it, and then I planted a heap of spring mattresses on top of the earth, and that was my roof. I fixed the springs with wire so they couldn't slip, and the Captain said I'd gone mad."

"And hadn't you, Angelito?"

"Don't you see? It's all a question of ballistics. Now, when a mortar bomb hits my roof while I'm asleep, it falls on something springy and bounces off. Then one of two things happens: either the bomb explodes in its bounce in midair, and that's O.K. by me, or it goes on bouncing up and down on my mattresses like a rubber ball until it comes to rest on the bed, and then all I've got to do is to collect the mortar bomb next morning and send it back to the other side. So I've obeyed my Captain's orders, you see, discipline and all, and I shan't get buried in a filthy damp dugout either. The others've started collecting spring mattresses too. What price your bosses, you young idiot? We're a revolutionary army, we are." And he wriggled on his paunch and grinned at the Anarchist who growled: "You make jokes about your being cannon fodder."

We were hilarious, Ilsa and I, when we walked back to our office. "You could turn Angel into a symbol like the Good Soldier Schwejk," she said, and told me about the book of the Czech rebel. Yet then we had to go on censoring bleak reports of skirmishes and shellings written by people who did not know Angel and his kind.

An extremely competent English journalist who had recently arrived to write human interest stories for the London branch of the Republican Agence Espagne had written up the pluck of Gloria, one of our lift operators, in taking her cage down from the top floor to the basement while shell splinters were clattering on its roof. It was one of the classic tales of the Telefónica, but he had to describe her as a dark Spanish beauty, with a red rose behind her ear, because "readers in London want their spot of local color and wouldn't like to miss the Carmen touch." He was shivering in his greatcoat. Herbert Matthews handed me an account he wanted to send on to his editor, including various items for the treatment of chilblains; to demonstrate that it was no secret code, he pointed a long, sausage red finger, swollen and split open, at a purple chilblain on the tip of his melancholy nose.

Doctor Norman Bethune, the dictatorial chief of the Canadian Blood Transfusion Unit, came stalking into the room with his escort of lumbering, embarrassed young helpers. Ilsa must come with them at once, they had found hidden papers in the flat where they were billeted. And as some were in German, Ilsa would have to translate them. She went and returned hours later with a bundle of letters and filing cards. The card index was that of the members of the German Labor Front in Madrid: employees of Siemens-Halske, Siemens-Schuckert, the A.E.G., and other big German firms. The letters were the correspondence between my old acquaintance, the lawyer Rodríguez Rodríguez, and his friends in Germany; among them was the photograph he had showed me, centuries ago, to boast his place of honor among the Nazis. Ilsa translated the letter of a high Nazi official, which defended Rodríguez Rodríguez against criticism by saying that his membership in the Catholic Falange was only natural, as Falange corresponded to the National-Socialist Movement under Spanish conditions. A number of small incidents which belonged to my former office life fell into place: here was part of the material about the Nazi network in Madrid. But Bethune claimed the letter. In immaculate battledress, his frizzy gray hair slicked back on his long, narrow head; he stood there swaying slightly on his feet and proclaiming that he would take these important papers—his own treasure trove—to Alvarez del Vayo, in the Blood Transfusion van. He knew nothing about the former owner of the flat where his unit was installed. It had been empty.

I came back to the office harassed by an hour's talk with Maria, who had asked me with a dreadful tenderness to give her at least those moments of contact every day, since she was threatened by the loss of the only worthwhile thing in her life. She refused to accept my union with Ilsa; she would get me back; I would see who was stronger in the end; it could not be true that I loved that foreigner. I knew that she was desperately alone; she was a stranger for whom I was sorry. How to end it?

In the Telefónica I found Ilsa tense and excited. Her husband had rung up from Paris. Through an unfortunate coincidence he had never received her letter from Valencia in which she explained to him that she had broken away from their marriage. Over the crackling wire and in precise French, Ilsa had told him what had happened to her, because she did not want to speak to him for a moment under false pretenses, but the cruelty of the thing she had done to him left her shaken. She hardly spoke to me. The young censor on duty kept staring at her through his glasses and wagging his horselike head. "I couldn't help listening," he said. "The way she did it—it was one of those things one reads about in novels—I never thought it could happen in real life—it must be a great experience, but I couldn't do it."

That night she telephoned to Paris again and arranged to go there by air from Alicante; the Spanish Embassy booked a seat for her: she was going to discuss propaganda matters in Paris and to meet her husband so as to define the situation once and for all.

I was in a panic, but I had not the right to ask anything of her. It appeared to me that outside Spain she would be caught by her other life. Her many friends and her political work would drag her back. She had still a profound affection for Kulcsar, who was working at the time as adviser to the Spanish Legation in Prague. Suddenly I could not imagine in my Spanish brain that a woman was capable of going to meet her husband, only to tell him to his face that she had left him for good and meant to link herself to another. Was it that my own muddled life, my dark temper, had exhausted her? Was it that the experience of love had been mine only? It was so difficult to love, even while it was so easy. It seemed to have no place in life as we knew it. Was she leaving me? I had no right to ask anything from her.

She left the next day, alone in a small car. I was afraid for her and afraid of Paris. The Telefónica was an empty shell and the work sense-less. I did not sleep unless I drugged myself with brandy. My brain was revolving round the hundred and one chances that she would never come back, against the one chance that she would. The enemy thrusts south-east of Madrid foreshadowed a new drive to cut off the roads. She might come back and her driver, not knowing the new front lines, might blunder on the side roads near the Jarama and land her in a Fascist po-sition. She might come back and be hit by one of the shells which raked the town. Or she might decide to stay abroad and leave me alone.

She came back after six endless days. I was so weak with relief that I gave her a meager welcome. Her driver told a long tale of how she had bullied the Military Governor of Alicante into giving her one of the of-ficial cars, and of how he had obtained petrol by telling the guards at the filling stations that she was the daughter of the Soviet Ambassador—wasn't it crazy anyhow that she had made him drive by night through the snowdrifts of the Mancha? They had got the last petrol at Toboso.

Ilsa had obtained a promise from her husband that he would agree to a divorce as soon as she gave the word after the end of the Spanish War. He had seen that she was utterly certain of herself, but he still hoped that she would snap out of her infatuation with me. The reactions of the outer world to Madrid had depressed her deeply: too many people had wanted to know whether it was true that the Communists held all the safe posts, instead of trying to understand that spirit of Madrid out of which the Left press was making stirring headlines. Still, an increasing number of foreign writers and publicists were coming to Madrid and we would have to look after them; I myself would have to do some journalistic work for the Agence Espagne until the arrival of another correspondent.

I had not much time to spend on arranging my private affairs then, because the wave of work and danger was mounting once more. But I decided to get my divorce from Aurelia and to make the position clear beyond any misconception to Maria; the torture and relief of Ilsa's jour-ney had made it impossible for me to go on in a mesh of relations which had become untrue and wrong. It was not enough that Aurelia was my wife in nothing but in name, and that my contact with Maria was re-duced to an hour in a café or a walk in the streets. For the time being, people accepted and respected my life with Ilsa, because we raised it be-yond the level of an affair by complete frankness and naturalness; but I knew that this somewhat romantic indulgence would not last and that we could not carry it off indefinitely without giving and taking offense. I did not talk this over with Ilsa; it was my own difficulty, while it was unreal to her, and she only felt that she hated the tangle. But just when I tried to summon my courage for an unequivocal break, Maria told me of the death of her younger brother at the front, and I did not dare to wound her even more. I had to go on meeting her every second day for a drink and a brief walk, feeling nauseated with myself and resentful of her, yet trying to be as gentle as possible within the cruelty of it all.

In desperation I took Maria with me while I traced the damage done by a single three-engined Junkers which had circled low and slowly over the jerry-built cottages of Vallecas, on the evening of January the 20th, and dropped a stick of bombs on the little square where women were sewing and children playing. I had met the father of three of the murdered children, and I thought that I would do what the professional journalists did not do because minor raids were no longer a story for them. The little house of the man, who was a fish-hawker, had been smashed by seven light bombs. His wife had been killed on the doorstep, with a baby in her arms. The two older girls had been killed. A six-year-old boy had lost one of his legs. The smallest girl, aged four, had over a hundred scratches and wounds from shrapnel dust in her little body. The eldest boy, bleeding from his torn eardrums, had carried her to the First Aid Post in his arms. I visited the one-legged boy in the Provincial Hospital and heard the father, Raimundo Malanda Ruiz, tell the story, while the boy looked at me out of staring, opaque eyes.

I imagined that this was a good case history to illustrate nonintervention, but presumably I did not understand the market of foreign public opinion well enough.

Maria did not see what I saw, because she was only interested in keeping something of me; and this indifference made me give up the attempt to find a basis of friendship with her in the common experience of us all. I persuaded her to take up work outside Madrid, aware that I was only putting off the final injury to her.

February was a dark and bitter month. While the battle on the Jarama, the battle for the southeastern approaches to Madrid, was being fought and while skeptical journalists discussed the possibilities of the fall of Madrid after the cutting of its lifeline, the Rebels and their Italian auxiliaries took Malaga. Madrid was being starved of food and wine and the tunnels of the Underground, like the basements of the Telefónica, were still clogged by thousands of refugees. And we knew that on the road from Malaga to the east a stream of refugees were trudging on or hiding in the ditches from the machine guns of low-flying German and Italian planes. There were no large-scale air raids on Madrid, only a few bombs were scattered on its outskirts from time to time as an evil reminder. The shelling went on and on. Most of us scurried across the Gran Vía when we went to the hotel for lunch, and I never lost my resentment at Ilsa's slow pace while I was waiting for her in the doorway of the bar, counting the seconds before the next, close-by shell burst.

The horizon of Madrid was suffused with flashes and flares to the south, east, and west. In the southeastern sector, the International Brigades had halted the enemy advance on the Jarama at a terrible price. One of the Englishmen, a longshoreman with simian arms and a low brow, came to see Ilsa and tell her of the death of his friends who used to take him to the Telefónica, of the Cambridge archeologist, and of the young writer, and gave her a pitifully funny photograph of himself in an impressive pose, hand on a plush chair.

But then the first smell of spring was in the air, with a dry, scented wind and fast white clouds sailing the bright sky.

The battle noise coming from the west, heavy mortar thuds and sharp rattle of machine guns, was grateful to our ears. We knew that there, on the slope below the Model Jail where four months earlier Miaja had rallied a handful of crazed volunteers against the invading Moors, Antonio Ortega's Basque regiment had reconquered the Parque de Oeste, inch by inch, and was pressing back the enemy.

Ortega, a bony man with a face carved in wood yet mobile as rubber, had organized his sector so well and was so proud of it that we liked to send him journalists and foreign visitors in search of a whiff of the front. But we ourselves had to know what we wanted others to see. After an interminable, sumptuous, and very gay meal in Ortega's headquarters, and after half an hour of singing songs with his young officers, among them a young painter and an international footballer, he took us through a narrow tunnel. We emerged in the park, in the intricate network of well kept trenches which crossed the unkempt sand paths. The trees were slashed and torn, but the young leaves were just bursting out of their buds. In the zigzagging trenches the soldiers were peacefully occupied oiling and burnishing metal parts. A few were sitting in dugouts and dozing or reading. From time to time there was a swishing sound and a soft plop, and another star-shaped flower with white splinter petals blossomed on one of the tree trunks.

And then we were in the first line. The trench was surprisingly dry and clean, as Ortega pointed out with professional pride. In the places where a trickle of water came down the hillside, the ground was covered with doors taken from the bombed houses of the Paseo de Rosales. Through slits in the parapet I snatched a glimpse of an earthen ridge where little dust clouds spurted from time to time.

There was the enemy, a hundred-odd yards from us: Moors—Falangists —Legionaries—Italians—a sprinkling of Germans—conscript soldiers from Old Castile. The vast buildings of the University City loomed heavy and shell-pitted in the background. A doll-like figure passed behind a window hole and high up, under the roof of the brick building of the Faculty of Medicine, a machine gun cackled, but I could not think where the bullets went. The sun glittered on a loop of the river.

With the city at our back and the big Basques and Asturians cracking their jokes around us, the enemy was nothing. You had to laugh. We were safe here, the city was safe, victory was safe.

Then Ortega showed off a primitive mortar; the bomb was released by a big spring, as from a catapult. The Basque in charge of the mortar made ready to fire: "As you're here, comrades, you must see the fireworks. Let's tickle them a bit."

At the second attempt, the missile went off without a sound, and a second later a sharp explosion shook us. Then the front broke loose. The cracks of rifle shots ran along the parapets and a machine gun to our right began to rattle. The buildings of the University City joined in. A thin "eeee" sounded in my skull. The hidden power of the explosives was unleashed. We were no longer playing at safety.

Ten days later, armored Italian divisions launched a big offensive in the stony plain of Alcarria, to the northeast of Madrid. Their tanks overran our forces; they took Brihuega and Trihueque, they were before Torrija and nearing Guadalajara. It was a bid to cut off our northern salient and to seal the road through Alcalá de Henares, which had become essential to Madrid since the Valencia road had to be reached by side roads.

General Goliev took the retreat coolly; he spoke as though we had got the wide spaces of Russia in which to maneuver. I do not think that many people in Madrid realized the gravity of the situation. The foreign journalists knew that this was the first open action of the Italian Army in Spain. Here was a great story. But when they reported that Italian armor and Italian infantry formed the spearhead of the advancing Rebel forces, they came up against the censorship of their own editors. The fiction of nonintervention had to be conserved. Suddenly, our censorship and the foreign correspondents were thrown together in the wish to get the news of what was happening across to the people and the papers in England, France, and the United States.

Herbert Matthews had a service conversation after reading out one of his telephone reports, in which the man at the other end of the wire, somebody at a desk in Paris, told him: "Don't always speak of Italians, you and the Bolshevik papers are the only ones who use that propaganda tag." Matthews, tied down by our censorship rules, came to my desk with tight lips and submitted a service cable he wanted to send: If they had no confidence in his objective reporting, he was going to resign. The answer from the *New York Times* office said nobody thought he wanted to make propaganda, only that he might have fallen for the official handout of the Republicans.

Herbert Matthews won this fight. Yet when I read, months later, in what form various British, American, and French newspapers had published the reports we had passed in Madrid, I found that most of them had changed the terms "Italian tanks," "Italian infantry," etc., to "Nationalist" forces, tanks, infantry, or whatever fitted, so as to eliminate the awkward evidence of an international war.

Then the tide turned. The Republican fighter planes, provided by Soviet Russia, those "Ratas" and "Moscas" which seemed so marvelous to us, battered the advance forces. An Anarchist unit led a big Italian formation into a trap. The International Brigades moved up. The loudspeakers of the Garibaldi Battalion called to the Italians on the other side. Then they advanced, anti-Fascist Italians and Germans together with Spanish units. They took back Trihueque and Brihuega, they took more than a thousand prisoners—all Italians—and they captured the mail bag and documents of a Brigade staff.

Gallo, the Communist Commissar of the International Brigades, and Pietro Nenni, the Italian Socialist leader who was everywhere with his unobtrusive friendliness, brought us postal orders sent home to their families by Italian soldiers in Spain, blood-stained diaries, still uncensored field-post letters, which we gave to correspondents who wanted irrefutable proof of their correctness in reporting on nonintervention. War Commissariat cars took journalists out to recaptured towns. I think that their reports after the victory of Guadalajara made good reading, so that they could no longer be bowdlerized; they turned it into a propaganda victory of ours.

The front line was stabilized much farther to the northeast than it had been before the Italian rout, although hopes of a decisive advance towards Aragon petered out. Yet after Guadalajara, Madrid was no longer isolated; the semicircle of the siege was no longer threatening to become a ring. There was a steady trickle of visitors. No one spoke of the fall of Madrid any more. The reorganization of the civil authorities was speeded up. Rubio was more curt on the telephone. Foreign delegations arrived, were led through Argüelles and Cuatro Caminos, through the Duke of Alba's Palace and, if they felt like it, through Ortega's trenches; they paid their respects to Miaja, looked at one or the other model factory under the workers' control, and at one or the other school for adults and home for orphaned children, and left.

One of the delegations we had to show round was headed by the Austrian Social-Democrat Friedrich Adler, then Secretary of the Labor Socialist International. He hated the existence of a Popular Front and the collaboration with the Communists so much that he never asked any of us a question; he disapproved of Madrid in offensive silence, and the young Right-Wing Socialists who had been tactfully detailed by the Junta to accompany him asked me who the unfriendly old man was and why he was so much like a walking corpse. He left a feeling of hostility behind, which was the only result of his visit.

Then more journalists and writers came. Ernest Hemingway arrived, was taken over the battleground of Guadalajara by Hans Kahle of the International Brigades, and worked with Joris Ivens at the film "Spanish Earth," while his bullfighter-secretary, Sidney Franklin, went round the offices to get petrol, permits, and gossip. Martha Gellhorn arrived and was brought to the Telefónica by Hemingway, who said: "That's Marty —be nice to her—she writes for *Collier's*—you know, a million circulation." Or was it half a million—or two million? I did not catch it and did not care, but we all stared at the sleek woman with the halo of fair hair, who walked through the dark, fusty office with a swaying movement we knew from the films.

Drinks at the Gran Vía bar and drinks at the Miami bar. Apart from some hard-working "veterans" of Madrid, such as George Seldes and Josephine Herbst, the foreign writers and journalists revolved in a circle of their own and an atmosphere of their own, with a fringe of men from the International Brigades, Spaniards who touted for news, and tarts. March had turned into April. It was hot in the streets but for the hours when the sharp wind blew from the Sierra. In the evenings, the streets were thronged and the cafés full, people were singing and laughing, while far away machine guns burst out in short spasms as though the front were spluttering with rage. There was no menace in the air for the time being.

I started my divorce proceedings after obtaining Aurelia's unwilling consent. I was restless. The work had no longer much hold over me. We had had our share in the fight, but now everything seemed flat. Propaganda had seized upon the cliché of Heroic Madrid and had become easy and shallow, as if our war were not growing in scope and evil ramification.

Whenever Angel came on an evening's leave and, half tipsy, told me of a new trick they had invented in the trenches, of his abortive adventures with women, and his hopeless longing for his wife, he helped me. Agustín, my brother-in-law, helped me when he explained how life among his neighbors and in the workshops went on. I took Ilsa to Serafín's tavern, where I had been at home as a young man, and was glad when she liked the baker and the butcher and the pawnbroker who were my friends, or when an unknown worker sitting on the bench of the back room gave her a few edible acorns out of his pockets, just because he liked her face. All this was real. Other things were wrong. But my own life cleared.

On an April afternoon, when Ilsa for the first time wore her new gray coat and skirt instead of her soldier-like jacket, I walked with her through the oldest, narrowest and most crooked lanes of Madrid and showed her the *Cava Baja* where I had waited for the diligence to Brunete as a boy and for the bus to Novés as a man. I showed her corners and fountains in deserted, ancient streets, where I knew every stone. While we walked across the sun-filled squares and through shadowy alleys, women in the house doors looked after us and gossiped. I knew exactly the words in which they were discussing us.

From the escarpment of Las Vistillas, near a gun emplacement, I looked down at the Viaduct across the Calle de Segovia and beyond the river to the Casa de Campo, where the enemy was, and saw myself trotting up the slope with my mother, tired from her washing by the river. I told her tales of my childhood.

6. The Shock

THEY had sent us a delegation of British women politicians from Valencia; our office was to look after them during their brief stay in Madrid. They had a guide of their own, the putty-faced Simon of Agence Espagne, and the Valencia departments were very much concerned about them. There were three M.P.s, the Duchess of Atholl, Eleanor Rathbone, and Ellen Wilkinson, and a society welfare worker, Dame Rachel Crowdy. It took Ilsa some time to din their names, political attributes, and range of interests into my head; I was not feeling too kindly towards the stream of well-meaning but usually self-centered visitors who had been touring Madrid ever since the victory of Guadalajara had eased the grip of the siege. In exchange, the grip of bureaucracy was tightening;

I was acutely aware of a change in the air, and the fashion of sightseeing seemed to me part and parcel of it.

I left the personal contacts with the party to Ilsa and arranged a tour of Madrid on the obvious lines: introduction to Miaja in his musty cellar vault; visits to the flattened-out workers' houses in Cuatro Caminos and to the empty ruins of Argüelles; Sunday morning in the Protestant Church of Calatrava, with its ingenuous, honest parson and a few earnest young men in uniform singing hymns; a glimpse of the front from some comparatively safe place; a reception by Miaja in due form; a visit by the Duchess of Atholl—without any of us to guide her—to the gutted palace of the Duke of Alba, where she would be able to check and disprove on the spot the Grandee's hostile statements to the Press. The shelling, which had become singularly intense during the last few days, would provide the background noise.

First came the introductory visit to Miaja. The four women waited in the ante-room, looking excited, while we cajoled Miaja into seeing them. He liked having an opportunity to grumble at the demands of the many people who came to pay him their respects. Twice he asked Ilsa who the hell those women were, and twice he asked me why the hell I did not produce young and pretty women, or at least sensible people who supplied arms for our troops. "If they're making me into a vaudeville turn they ought at least to give me presents, a machine gun or a plane, and then I'll sign a photograph for them if they like." But he came out meekly enough and listened to their little speeches "to the Defender of Madrid," looking down his long nose and answering with a few gruff words. Ilsa did her translating with a hidden flourish which made me suspect that she had edited what both sides had said. Miaja grunted: "Tell them to come to a tea party tomorrow afternoon, since you think they're so important. As they're English we must give them tea. The devil take it. They shouldn't expect too much of us, tell them, because there's a war on here. *Salud.*"

I felt almost as surly as he did. I was unable to take part in the English conversation, but I wanted very much to ask them rudely whether they couldn't do anything about nonintervention without a sight-seeing trip. Moreover, I resented Simon's slick showmanship. When we walked through a side street in Cuatro Caminos where the only thing left of a row of houses were the outlines of their flimsy foundations, an old woman came up to show us, with a dramatic instinct and sparse words, the place where her hearth had been. Simon looked as pleased as though he had stage-managed the encounter, or so I thought. I was in no mood to be just; it was a good thing that I had to do nothing but to provide the silent Spanish background.

The shelling was still growing in intensity, and it was spraying the center of the town along "Shell Alley." When we drove back from the suburbs, wisps of gray smoke floated in the air the whole length of the Calle de Alcalá, and people walked very near to the house doors on the so-called safe side of the street. We hustled our guests into the Gran Vía Hotel.

I wanted the women to have lunch with us upstairs in our room, partly because I did not want them to get their image of Madrid from the tawdry cosmopolitan atmosphere of the public dining room. But they preferred to see life in the basement, and so I arranged for lunch there. The foreign correspondents rose from the long table, where they were sitting with their friends from the International Brigades, and chose their victims among the visitors, while a crowd of soldiers, tarts, and anxious mothers taking shelter with their children were milling about, shouting, eating, drinking, and waiting for a lull in the bombardment. Through the skylights came the sound of shell bursts and the wafts of acrid fumes, but the noise and the smell inside drowned them. It was a successful lunch.

After the black coffee I took the party up to the entrance hall; we were scheduled to visit Ortega's artillery observation post and our two cars were waiting outside.

In the hall there was a thin haze of smoke and an unusually dense crowd. The manager made a beeline for me:

"Don Arturo, would you please come along at once? There's been a fire in your room upstairs and the firemen are just dealing with it. It must have been a shell." .

I had heard the firebell tinkling while we were finishing our meal.

We pushed our way through the curious people blocking the stairs and the corridor. Our room was gray and smudged with smoke. There were burns on one wall and on the wardrobe, the chairs were tumbled on the ground, two firemen were just withdrawing a hose and another was tearing a smoldering curtain from its rod.

No shell had hit the room, so much was clear at a glance. But a big, triangular piece of a shell was lying on the table. It was still warm. Before it dropped, its force spent, it must have been hot enough to set the curtain on fire. That was all. Two eggs in a bowl on the side table were intact. My cigarettes had disappeared. The tablecloth was torn, a few plates were smashed; the table had been set for Ilsa and me as it was every day. Her shoes which had been lined up on a rack under the window, covered by the long curtain, were a pitiful heap of scorched, twisted, tortured-looking leather. There were stains of soot and water on pillows, and clothes. It had been nothing.

Ilsa stared ruefully at the small leather corpses of her shoes and complained that a new blue pair, much beloved by her, was shriveled and shapeless. The Englishwomen kissed her, because they had saved her life through their presence. Hadn't she said that except for them she and I would have been lunching at that table even while the shell fragment struck it?

I heard Ilsa saying that it didn't look as if it would have been as serious as all that, even if we had been in the room; the women were making much of her, while I said nothing. Nothing had happened. I took them down to the entrance once more. Our drivers were waiting, and it was not right to let them stay much longer in the Gran Vía during the afternoon shelling.

The street was filled with glaring sunlight and curls of slowly thinning smoke. Dull thuds sounded from further up Shell Alley. The porter informed me that our drivers were waiting round the corner in the Calle de la Montera, which was safer. I walked ahead of the women to find the cars. At the corner itself a gust of the familiar acrid smell hit me. Out of the corner of my eye I saw something odd and filmy sticking to the huge show window of the Gramophone Company. I went close to see what it was. It was moving.

A lump of gray mass, the size of a child's fist, was flattened out against the glass pane and kept on twitching. Small, quivering drops of gray matter were spattered round it. A fine thread of watery blood was trickling down the pane, away from the gray-white lump with the tiny red veins, in which the torn nerves were still lashing out.

I felt nothing but stupor. I looked at the scrap of man stuck on to the shop window and watched it moving like an automaton. Still alive. A scrap of human brain.

Like an automaton, too, I took the elbow of the elderly woman beside me, whose honest red face was paling, and made a few steps forward to help her on. There was a fresh gray-white scar in the paving stones at the corner. The post of the old newspaper woman. I stopped. What was it I meant to do? I was hollow inside, emptied and without feelings. There seemed no street noise in the void around me.

I strained myself to hear. Somebody was calling me.

Ilsa was clutching at my arm and saying in a rough, urgent voice: "Arturo, come away from here—Arturo!"

There were those foreign women. We had to take them somewhere. Ilsa was supporting the heavy, gray-haired one. The car was just in front of me. But my feet were sticking to the ground and when I tried to lift them I slithered. I looked down at those feet of mine. They were standing in a small sticky puddle of coagulating blood.

I let Ilsa push me into the car, but I never knew who else was inside. I believe that I rubbed my shoes on the car mat once, and I know I said nothing. My brain was blocked. Stupidly, I looked through the window and saw buildings and people move past. Then we were outside the tall house in which Ortega had set up his observation post with the telemeter of which he was so proud. He was there himself to do the honors. His young officers were ragging me because I had turned myself into the guide of a duchess. Everything was normal and it was easy to answer their jokes.

They took us up to the top floor. The wide windows overlooked a large sector of the front and of the city. One after the other our guests looked through the telemeter and let Ortega show them enemy gun emplacements, camouflaged trenches, the white and red buildings of the University City, the flash and smoke of a firing battery and the place where its shells hit their target. While he led them out on to the balcony to explain the lines of the front, I looked through the telemeter myself.

It was focused on a low building wreathed in white smoke-puffs. They were shelling it, and I wondered what their target was. I adjusted the telemeter. What I recognized in the field of vision was the chapel of the Cemetery of San Martín. The place where I had played on countless days of my boyhood while my Uncle José was there on his official visits. I made out the old brick building, the courtyards, the gallery with its white niches. One of the smoke wads dissolved and I saw the hole the shell had torn into the thick wall.

As though I had been looking into a magic crystal globe, I saw the images of my childhood in the frame of the telemeter lens.

The old cemetery with its sunlit courtyards. The row of rose-trees laden with flowers. The old chaplain, and the cemetery keeper with his flock of boys more or less my own age. The transfer of long-buried people when the cemetery was closed down. My Uncle José inspecting the decorations in the chapel before the funeral ceremonies. Bones of an ashy gray color spread out tenderly on a sheet so white that it looked bluish. Hollow bones thrown into the bonfire of the keepers, together with the moldy planks from burst coffins. Myself chasing butterflies and tiny lizards between the trellises and cypresses.

"We must go," Ilsa murmured into my ear.

Through the balcony I saw streets filled with sun and people, and in the open grounds of Amaniel, green with spring grass, a dark patch, spires of cypresses wreathed in another white cloud, very far away and daintily small.

We had to go to Miaja's tea party for the British ladies.

The General had invited a few people from the Propaganda Ministry to help him with the foreigners. They had prepared a sumptuous spread in one of the big rooms of the underground department. The walls were stained and flaking, but orderlies brought bunches of flowers and served the unfamiliar tea with a smirk on their faces. While I kept up a running banter with the staff officers, Ilsa acted as interpreter in the conversation between the General and the Duchess, toning down questions and answers.

"Why the devil is she asking about Russian instructors to our air force? Tell her that we've got splendid lads of our own—why the hell isn't she interested in them?"

"Oh, I know the way generals talk from my own husband," the Duchess said briskly.

When the drinks came, Miaja lifted his glass and said in his best French: "To peace!"

The Duchess gave back: "And to liberty, for peace can be bought at too dear a price."

"*Salud!*" Ellen Wilkinson cried from the other end of the table.

When our guests had gone back to the Hotel Florida, we worked for a few hours in the Telefónica and then walked across the street to the Gran Vía Hotel. They had given us a couple of airy new rooms, on the same side of the house as the one that had been hit. We were very tired, but while Ilsa shrank away from more noise, I had to be among people. Simon was giving a party to a few Americans and some Germans from the International Brigades on another floor of the Gran Vía, and I went with him. There was nobody I liked. Major Hans was everything I imagined a raw-boned Prussian officer to be; Simon petted a white-blonde girl with a baby-skin and a hard mouth; they were all drinking and showing off their toughness, and none of them thought of the war as our war, as Spain's torture and pain. I drank with them and burst out into a tirade to which only one person, an American film critic whose name I never knew, listened with sympathy. I shouted at them that they had come to Spain to seek their own ends, not out of a simple faith, and that they were not helping us; that they were smug and glib and we barbarians, but that at least we felt and knew what we were doing. Then my excited mood died down. I was a complete stranger among people who had every right to dislike me as I disliked them. I went down and found stillness with her.

When I woke up at eight in the morning, I did not want to wake Ilsa. The blackout curtains were split by a thin, bright gap. I wanted to take a bath, but found that we had forgotten to move soap, shaving tackle, and toothbrushes over from our old bathroom. I went out to fetch them.

Our old room was flooded with sun. It still smelled of smoke and scorched leather, and there were half-dried pools of water on the floor. It was a radiant morning. The smooth front of the Telefónica across the street was dazzlingly white. I stood by the window and looked down into the street to see whether they were not just sprinkling the pavement and producing the scent of moist earth I loved. An explosion sounded from the upper end of the street. The morning shelling had begun, punctual like the milkman. There were few people about in Shell Alley. Idly I watched a woman crossing the street a little higher up, and suddenly I wondered: wasn't that Ilsa? She was sleeping in the near-by room, I knew it, but this woman was so like her, the same size, the same body, seen from the back, the same dark-green costume. I was staring at the woman's back when the high whistle of a shell tore through the air. It hit the Fontalba Theater just above the booking office. The woman swayed and fell, and a dark stain began to spread. One of the Shock Police sentries ran up to her, two men sprinted across the street beneath my window, and the three picked up the body. It sagged and slipped through their hands. Her limbs hung as though all her joints had been smashed by hammer blows.

I went back to our room and found Ilsa standing by the window in her dressing-gown. I looked at her and my face must have been odd, because she came over to me and said: "What's the matter with you?"

"Nothing."

There was another whistle, and my eyes instinctively followed the direction of the sound. A window opposite us in the fifth floor of the Telefónica was boarded up. The boards buckled in and spat splinters into the air, a dark phantom shape entered the hole and then the torn boards bulged outwards again. I ducked and dragged Ilsa down to the floor with me; we were in the line of flying shrapnel and masonry.

Squatting on the floor I had an attack of nausea, a sudden violent contraction of the stomach as when I had vomited in the shambles of the Moroccan War fifteen years earlier. But at the time I did not remember that. I cowered in a corner, trembling, unable to control my muscles which had acquired a life of their own. Ilsa led me down to the vestibule of the hotel, into a dark corner behind the telephone boxes. I drank a couple of brandies and my trembling ceased. The dark corner where I was sitting faced across the shadowy hall to the entrance. The sun was glittering and licking through the revolving doors. It was like being in a cave opening out into the fields, like awakening from a vivid dream within strangely distorted bedroom walls. At that moment my whole life suffered a distortion.

The others did not notice it. Even Ilsa only thought I was feeling a transitory after-effect of yesterday's shock. The British party had gone, and we resumed the strenuous daily routine. Yet I refused to lunch upstairs, as Ilsa wanted, and insisted on our taking our meals in the basement at the noisy table of the journalists, where I never spoke much and people were used to my morose face.

When we went up to our room before going on duty again, I saw a tiny orifice in the cardboard which replaced one of the window panes, and found a steel splinter embedded in the opposite wall.

We were arranging our books on a shelf beside the window. It was quiet, people were strolling and chatting in the street, everything had the light, color, and smell of spring. The sky was clear blue and the stones of the houses looked warm with sun. A Shock Police sentry at the corner of the Telefónica paid compliments to every girl that passed him, and from my window it was easy to see that some of the girls crossed the street only to stroll past him and hear what the handsome lad had to tell them. The revolving door of the Telefónica behind him kept turning, and the glitter of its panes threw bundles of light across the shadow at the foot of the building.

Three people were crossing the Grand Vía, a soldier and two girls. One of the girls wore a black dress and carried a parcel wrapped in pink paper, bright and gay against the black. Ilsa remarked that the girl walked like a young animal, and I told her:

"If a woman walks like that we say she is *una buena jaca,* a fine filly, because she moves with the grace of a young and skittish horse."

Then the shell whistled, and it felt as if it had passed a few yards from our faces. The soldier threw himself flat on the ground, his arms flung over his head. The shell burst in front of him with a flash and a cloud of thick black smoke. The Shock Police sentry disappeared as though swallowed by the wall of the building. The two young girls dropped like two empty sacks.

I was clinging to the window-sill, my mouth filled with vomit, and saw through a haze how people hurried away with the two bodies. Then the street was deserted and the pink parcel lay there in the middle of dark stains. Nobody collected it. The deserted street was gay and spring-like, with an inhuman indifference.

It was the hour when our afternoon shift began. We crossed the street to the other corner of the Telefónica.

I sat at my desk and stared at the meager dispatches of journalists who had nothing to report except that the shelling of Madrid continued with unabated and monotonous intensity. Ilsa was pacing up and down, her poise shattered. Suddenly she sat down at a typewriter and wrote something at great speed. When she had finished she rang up Ilsa Wolff, the German journalist who ran the U.G.T. Radio which broadcast to foreign workers in various languages, and in distinction to whom our Ilsa used at that time to be called *Ilsa de la Telefónica*.

They spoke in German and I was not interested. But then Ilsa rose, took her coat and said to me: "I must do something, otherwise I can't forget that pink parcel. I must speak to my own workers at home—they'll still know my voice in some places—and I've told Ilsa Wolff that I simply must broadcast today instead of her."

I knew at once what she meant. There had been many duds among the shells, and we were all firmly convinced that there was some sabotage in the German factories which supplied Franco with armaments. Ilsa was going to cry out to her Austrian workers. But few of them would hear her. When she went out into the street I sat there listening for the sound of bursting shells.

There was too little work to do. I was obsessed with tracing the course the shells might have taken. The piece of metal which had set the curtain of our window on fire had followed a curve which meant that it would have hit her head, if we had lunched in our room as usual. The minute steel splinter which a few hours ago had pierced the cardboard in the window-frame of our new room had bored deep into the opposite wall. Had we eaten there as Ilsa had wanted, her head would have been midway between the hole in the pane and the hole in the wall. I was haunted by images of her, in the shape of the woman whom I had seen hit in the street that morning, or sitting at our table with a hole in her head.

Journalists came and went, and I spoke as much or as little to them as usual; in the end I handed over the censoring to old Llizo and started to write.

I do not remember that story well; it would be of interest to a psychiatrist. Like a dream it mixed sights and visions: the shop window of the Gramophone Company, a display of black disks showing the white, cock-eared dog on their gaudy labels; the smooth pane reflecting the passing multitude, a phantom multitude of living beings without life; the black records enclosing in their furrows a multitude of ghost voices; everything unreal, and the only real thing above them—on the surface of that solid glass pane—a scrap of palpitating brain, still living, the antennae of its severed nerves lashing out in a desperate voiceless cry to a deaf multitude. And then I put the woman behind the glass panel, lying still, a hole in her head, the corners of her lips like a question mark in a faint smile, very serene. It was no story.

When Ilsa came back, quietened and tired, I was still sitting at the typewriter. I handed her the pages I had written. When she came to the description of the woman, she gave me a scared glance and said without thinking:

"But it's me you've killed here."

I took the pages from her and tore them up.

The routine work went on, but we had a guest whom I liked and respected, John Dos Passos, who spoke about our land workers and peasants with a gentle understanding, looking from one to the other out of wondering brown eyes. He helped us that evening; I saw that Ilsa's eyes were following my gestures with a suppressed anxiety and that she kept the conversation going so as to lead me back into normal contacts.

I find that John Dos Passos mentions this encounter in one of his sketches in *Journeys between Wars*. This is what he says:

"In the big quiet office you find the press censors, a cadaverous Spaniard and a plump little pleasant-voiced Austrian woman. . . . Only yesterday the Austrian woman came back to find that a shell-fragment had set her room on fire and burned up all her shoes, and the censor had seen a woman made mincemeat of beside him. . . . It's not surprising that the censor is a nervous man; he looks underslept and underfed. He talks as if he understood, without taking too much personal pleasure in it, the importance of his position as guardian of those telephones that are the link with countries technically at peace, where the war is still carried on with gold credits on bank ledgers and munitions contracts and conversations on red plush sofas in diplomatic ante-rooms instead of with six-inch shells and firing squads. He doesn't give the impression of being complacent about it. But it's hard for one who is more or less of a free agent from a country at peace to talk about many things with men who are chained to the galley benches of war.

"It's a relief to get away from the switchboards of power and walk out into the sunny streets again."

But I was chained to myself and split in myself.

When I was seven I went to school one morning and saw a man running round a street corner towards me. Behind him sounded shouts and the patter of an invisible crowd. The stretch of street where we were was empty except for the man and me. He stopped close to me and pushed something into his mouth. There was a bang, I saw the man's cap hurled into the air, and black scraps flying, there was a flash, and then I found myself at a first-aid post, where people were pouring water with a penetrating odor down my throat.

When I was nine years old, I was sitting on the balcony of my uncle's flat one morning reading a book. Suddenly I heard a dull thud in the street down below. On the opposite pavement lay the body of a woman, smashed on the stones. She had her eyes tied with a white handkerchief which was turning first red and then almost black. Her skirts were gathered above her ankles with a green curtain cord. One of the tassels of the cord dangled over the curbstone. The balcony began to sway and the street to reel before my eyes.

When I was twenty-four years old, and I saw the room in the barracks of the Civil Guard at Melilla, which looked as though the dead men leaning over the window-sills and in the corners had splashed each other with their blood as during a battle in a swimming pool in the summer, I had vomited. With the stench of slashed bodies eternally in my nostrils, I had been unable to stand even the sight of raw meat for over three years. It all came back.

I was listening with my whole body for the whistle of a shell or the drone of an aircraft among the thousand noises of the street; my brain was trying feverishly to eliminate all the noises which were not hostile and to analyze those which held a threat. I had to fight ceaselessly against this obsession, because it threatened to tear the weave of whatever I was doing, hearing, or saying. People and things near me grew blurred and twisted into phantom shapes as soon as they were out of direct contact with me. I was afraid of being shut up and alone, and afraid of being in the open among people. When I was alone I felt like an abandoned child. I was incapable of going alone to my hotel room, because it meant crossing the Gran Vía, and I was incapable of staying alone in my room. When I was there, I stared at the white front of the Telefónica, with its bricked-up window-holes and black window-holes and the pock-marks of dozens of shells. I hated it and I stared at it. But I could no longer bear to look down into the street.

That night I ran a high temperature and although I had not eaten, I vomited bitter stomach juice in spasmodic convulsions. The following day my mouth filled with the sour liquid at the sound of a motorcycle, a tram, the screech of a brake, at the sound of air-raid sirens, the drone of planes, and the thud of shells. The city was full of those sounds.

I knew what was happening to me and fought against it: I had to work and I had no right to show nervousness or fear. There were the others before whom I had to be calm if I wanted them to be calm. I clung to the thought that I had the obligation not to show fear, and so I became obsessed with a second kind of fear: the fear of being afraid.

The people, apart from Ilsa and my brother-in-law, Agustín, who had become senior orderly at our office, only knew that I was not feeling well and seemed in a particularly black mood. The journalists themselves were urging a transfer of the censorship office to safer quarters; at their request, the telephonic room was installed downstairs in the basement of the Telefónica, yet even so they had to cross Shell Alley too often. It had become an unreasonable risk. Ilsa had been almost the only person to defend our continued stay in the Telefónica; she had an affection for the very walls of the building and felt part of it. But by then the situation had become untenable even for her.

We changed our rooms in the hotel to the back where our windows opened into a chimney-like yard that caught and held every sound. I was shaken by bouts of fever and bouts of sickness. I neither slept nor ate. For a day, I stayed in the dark corner of the hotel hall, doing office work other than actual censoring, while Ilsa carried on in the Telefónica. It was she who obtained Rubio Hidalgo's consent to move our office to the Foreign Ministry. Some of the journalists urged the transfer to one of the quiet and almost shell-proof suburbs, but it would have taken a long time and a lot of wiring; in the Ministry the press-room and censorship were still wired and had thick stone walls, even though the building was within the habitual range of the siege guns.

The Telefónica had been hit by over one hundred and twenty shells, and although not a single life had been lost within its walls during that time, the journalists and censors alike had a feeling of impending disaster.

On May the 1st the Foreign Press and Censorship Department of Madrid moved back to the Foreign Ministry in the Plaza de Santa Cruz. I waited for the move in my corner at the back of the hotel vestibule, fighting myself and lost within myself. I did not know at that time that Ilsa was crossing the shelled street and working on the fourth floor of the Telefónica for eight days with the absolute conviction that she was doomed to be killed. I even left it to her to collect all papers and bring them to the Ministry with the help of Agustín.

The day after they left the Telefónica, a shell entered through one of the windows of our deserted office and exploded by the main desk a few minutes after five. At five sharp every afternoon Ilsa had taken over and sat down at that very desk.

The Foreign Ministry is built round two big, flagged, glass-covered inner courts and divided by a monumental staircase which leads up from the triple entrance. Arched galleries circle the two courts in two tiers; the upper gallery has a parqueted floor and gilt railing, the gallery on the ground floor has large flagstones and it echoes under the heavy vaulting. The office rooms open on to the galleries. The building is of stone

and brick, with enormously stout walls. Two towers with pointed slate
roofs flank it. It is an island amid silent old streets, near the old Plaza
Mayor of the Auto-da-fés and bullfights, and near the noisy Puerta del
Sol. Below the building are vaulted cellars and mighty passages dating
from an older age.

The Ministry is dignified, chilly, and unfriendly, with its stones, which
seem to sweat dampness on rainy days, and the heavy iron bars before its
windows. The cellar vaults once belonged to the jail of the Royal Court.
Second-rate sculptures made by artists whom the Spanish State subsidized
stand stupidly and incongruously around the courts.

Ilsa and I installed ourselves in one of the small rooms. The censorship
moved back to its old quarters, and Rubio Hidalgo's office was opened
for formal occasions, but hardly ever used. It smelled stale. To save the
journalists unnecessary trips through the spatter of shells, a kind of canteen was set up; orderlies brought food—poor food—from the Gran Vía
Hotel in a service car. Whenever the shelling moved near and thuds came
from the Pláza Mayor there was the vault of the cellar staircase with
fifteen feet of stone and mortar thickness above it, a perfect shelter.

The noise and bustle of the transfer had torn me out of my daze. Away
from the glaring façade of the Telefónica I lost one of the elements of
my obsession, but the others did not disappear with the move as I had
secretly hoped. I went down to the Ministry library in the basement
vaults and listened from there for the sound of Ilsa's heels on the flags
of the court. I forced her to stay within the building, but I could not force
her to stay in my sight, because she had to do two men's work to cover
up the fact that I was not working. She was amused with the Ministry,
content because the journalists seemed to like it, and busy making our
small room livable; she, and Agustín's steady, good-humored common
sense kept me from lapsing into a broody melancholy dangerously near
to something worse.

After a few days, when I saw I was not sleeping in the new place either,
I asked the Ministry's physician to examine me and give me some drug.
He gave me a medicine based on morphine. Ilsa thought I should rather
fight it out mentally, but she did not understand: I simply could not sleep.
That night I went to bed early, reeling with exhaustion and sleeplessness,
and took the prescribed dose.

I sank down into a gulf. The outlines of the room dissolved. Agustín
was nothing but a shadow moving against endless yellow walls which
lost themselves in dark depths. The light was a faint glow which grew
steadily more faint. My body lost the feeling of weight and I was floating.
I slumbered.

An infinite terror invaded me. Now, at that very moment, the shelling was going to start afresh. I would be tied to my bed, unable to move or to protect myself. The others would go down to the basement and leave me alone. I battled desperately. The drug had worked upon the motorial nerve center and I could not move. My will did not want to submit, it did not want to sleep or to let me go to sleep. Sleep meant the danger of death. My brain sent out urgent orders: move—jump out of bed—speak —scream! The drug held its own. I was shaken by waves of deep-seated nausea, as if my entrails had torn loose from me and were moving furiously, with hands, claws and teeth of their own.

Someone was speaking close above my head, trying to tell me something, but it was too far away, although I saw the shadows of enormous heads looming. I was being hurled into bottomless pits, falling into voids, with a horrible pressure in my stomach, and at the same time trying to push upwards and to resist the fall and the crash at the invisible bottom of the abyss. I was being dismembered; my limbs were converted into a shapeless, woolly mass and then became invisible, although they were still there, and I was trying to recapture those arms and legs, those lungs and bowels of mine which were dissolving into nothingness. Phantasmagoric faces and monster hands and floating shapes caught me, lifted me, dropped me, carried me hither and thither. And I knew that at that very moment the explosions would start again. I felt myself dying of disintegration of the body, with only an incommensurable brain left to pit all its energies against death, against the dissolution of the body to which it was attached.

I have never been certain whether it was the threshold of death or madness at which I stood that night. Nor did Ilsa ever know whether she saw me drifting towards death or madness.

Slowly my will was stronger than the drug. At dawn I was awake, covered with cold sweat, mortally exhausted, but able to think and move. There came a second wave of frenzy in the afternoon, when I rolled on my bed and fought to retain my senses while Ilsa, who dared not leave me alone, had to answer the questions of unfriendly Polish visitors—Alter and Ehrlich—by the table in our room. I saw their faces in distorted, leering shapes and tried not to cry out. It seems that I did moan, however.

The worst part of my experience, and of all the stages of experience through which the war shock took me, was that I was the whole time aware of the process and its mechanism. I knew that I was ill and what I had to call abnormal; my self was fighting against my second self, refusing to submit to it, yet doubting whether I had the strength to win my fight—and thus prolonging the struggle. I doubted whether that other self which produced the abject fear of destruction was not really right, and I had to suppress those doubts so as to live on among the others.

When I got up and returned to work, I felt set apart from the others, who themselves appeared abnormal to me because they did not share my own anguish. I could not emerge from introspection, because I was forced to keep a conscious check on myself, and this constant self-observation made me observe the others in a new way.

I lost my interest in the office work which the others carried on in set tracks and against a growing passive resistance from the head office in Valencia. What occupied me was how to understand the springs that moved other people in our war, and to understand the course of the war itself.

It seemed to me that small, unreasoned and unreasonable things were driving each individual to fight, things which stood for shapeless and deep emotions. A particle of palpitating gray matter had set off a hidden train of thoughts and emotions in me. What was it that set off others? Not what they said in well-ordered words.

A few days after I had recovered from my nightmare ride, I wrote my first short story, about a Miliciano in a trench who stayed there because the Fascists had destroyed his wife's sewing-machine, because he had to be there, and finally because a blindly hitting bullet had crushed a fly 'which he loved to observe on a sunlit spot of the parapet. I brought it to Ilsa, and I saw that it struck her. If she had said that it was no good, I think I would never have tried to write again, because it would have meant that I was unable to touch hidden springs.

But this was only a slight relief. I could not get away from the vision of the war with which I had risen from my stupor. Our war had been provoked by a group of generals who were in their turn maneuvered by the sectors of the Spanish Right most grimly determined to fight any development within the country which might threaten the privileges of their caste. But the rebels had committed the mistake of resorting to outside help and of converting the civil war into an international skirmish. Spain, her people, and her Government no longer existed in a definite form; they were the objects of an experiment in which the States standing for international Fascism and the State standing for Communism or Socialism took part, while the other countries looked on as vitally interested spectators. What was happening to us was a signpost for the future road of Europe and possibly the world.

The spectator countries favored one or the other of our two fronts; their ruling classes leaned towards the camp of international Fascism, a part of their working people and intellectuals leaned more or less clearly towards international Socialism. An ideological guerrilla warfare was going on in Europe and America. Recruits for the International Brigades came from all countries, and all countries refused to supply the Spanish

Republic with the arms it needed. The avowed reason was to avoid an international war; yet some groups may have hoped that Spain would provoke war between Soviet Russia and Germany and many were curious to see the strength of the two opposing political ideologies tested, not in the field of theory but of arms.

It seemed to me beyond doubt that the ruling groups of Europe expected to retain mastery of the situation after a defeat of Communism and a weakening of militant Fascism, which could then be usefully exploited and handled by them. Thus it was part of their game to protect Fascism from the danger of finally losing its war in Spain, for Fascism was the lesser evil, or rather a potential boon. This meant nonintervention, and the surrender of the Republican Government into the hands of Soviet Russia, of the rebels into the hands of Germany and Italy.

We could not win the war.

The statesmen of Soviet Russia would not be so foolish as to carry their intervention to a point when it would mean war with Germany, in a situation in which Russia would be left alone and Germany enjoy the support of the ruling classes and of the heavy industries of all the other countries. Soon the Russians would have to tell us: "We can't do more for you, carry on as well as you can."

We were condemned in advance. And yet we were carrying on a ferocious fight. Why?

We had no other choice. Spain had only two roads before her: the terrible hope, worse than despair, that a European War would break out and force some of the other countries to intervene against Hitler's Germany, and the desperate resolution to sacrifice ourselves so that others should gain time for their preparations and so that one day, after the end of Fascism, we would have the right to demand our compensation. In any case we would have to pay in blood, in the currency of a savage destruction of our own soil. It was for this that the many thousands who faced death at the front were fighting with a Credo and a political conviction, with faith, and with the hope of victory.

When I had reached this conclusion, it was sheer intellectual torture. I had nothing with which to soften it. I saw in mind the corpses piling up, the destruction spreading without cease, and I had to accept it as necessary, as inevitable, as something in which I had to take part, although I lacked the consolation of a blind faith or hope. At that stage, it became more intolerable than ever to see that there was so little unity on our side. Among the leaders of the struggle, the ideal to save the Republic as the basis for democratic growth had evaporated; each group had turned monopolist and intolerant. For a short time I had forgotten the atmosphere there was away from the front of Madrid. Now came the news of street fighting among anti-Fascists in Barcelona. The civil servants sent back to Madrid from Valencia were very meticulous about their political label. We who had tried to carry on in the days of the November crisis were out of place, and it had become dangerous for us to vent our feelings.

But there were still many men like Angel and the shy, gawky Milicianos he brought to the Ministry to see Ilsa and me, boys who clutched a pitiful bunch of rosebuds in their fingers, who had come from olive fields and brick kilns to fight for the Republic and wanted to hear me read Federico García Lorca to them. There were the men I met when I took Ilsa to Serafín's tavern on quiet evenings, tired workers, fatalistic, grumpy, and unshaken. There was the girl who ushered people into her porter's lodge during shellings because her grandfather had done so until shrapnel had killed him.

I wanted to cry out to them and to the world. If I was to stay on fighting against my nerves and my mind, relentlessly aware of myself and the others, I had to do something more in this war than merely supervise the censorship of increasingly indifferent newspaper dispatches.

So I continued to write, and I began to speak on the radio.

7. Crying Out

AT the outbreak of the Civil War, Spanish radio stations, the semi-official ones as well as the numerous amateur transmitters, had been commandeered by political groups and used for their propaganda, not so much of a general as of a partisan and sectional character. The outcome was confusion and muddle, less noted since few of the stations were at all audible abroad, and none in all parts of Spain. When the Government regained its hold on public life, it began by accepting this state of affairs as a lesser evil, but then, step by step, imposed its authority and ended by decreeing the cessation of all party stations and the functioning only of transmissions under official control.

One morning, the State Controller of Transradio, the same shy, haggard civil servant who had made me shoulder his worries about radio-telegrams in the first days of the siege, turned up at the Ministry to confront me with a new puzzle.

The Spanish State had a contractual right to use the short-wave station EAQ, the transmitter of the Transradio Company, during certain hours every day. This service came under the authority of a Government Delegate, but the Controller did not know which was the competent Ministry. A small team of speakers had been broadcasting official communiqués in Spanish, French, Portuguese, English, and German, and culled items from the Spanish press to compose their news bulletins. Since the beginning of the reorganization of broadcasting matters, however, the Government Delegate had failed to pay the speakers' salaries, and by now only the Spanish and the Portuguese broadcaster were left to carry on.

The Controller had officially nothing to do with the broadcasting side; but he was worried at this neglect of one of the best weapons at the disposal of the Republic, and he had discussed matters with the Workers' Committee whose members felt as he did. Something had to be done, otherwise the only short-wave station of Madrid would close down so far as propaganda was concerned. The speakers could not weather it out any longer. The Portuguese was half starved anyhow, and went about in shoes without proper soles. He, the Controller, had attempted to argue the case with one of the Junta's secretaries in the Ministry of the Interior and with his own superiors, the postal authorities, but when they found that the EAQ broadcasts were destined for foreign consumption they had lost all interest. At bottom, they thought foreign propaganda a useless luxury; they knew nothing about it; and anyhow, the only official body concerned with foreign matters was the Foreign Ministry. The Foreign Ministry was in Valencia, and I knew, said the Controller, how impossible it was to get Valencia to do anything for and in Madrid. But now I was back in the Foreign Ministry. Would I do something?

I was no less ignorant of the whole affair than the Controller. Miaja, as the Governor-General of Madrid, could have intervened, but I felt that it was futile to approach the General with this intricate problem. Yet I shared the Controller's conviction that we had to act. The only thing which occurred to me on the spur of the moment was that the Portuguese speaker might eat in our canteen and, if he had nowhere to go, sleep on a divan in one of the Ministry's empty, dust-sheeted rooms. I asked the Controller to send me the Portuguese and promised to think over the entire problem.

I was glad to be given something concrete with which to grapple. The censorship was running in settled grooves. Ilsa had the help of a new censor, the white-blonde Canadian girl Pat whom I distrusted. The head office in Valencia, where Rubio had left the reins in the hand of his new assistant, Constancia de la Mora, was balking our requests on behalf of the journalists with tiresome consistency. There were more visitors and more special correspondents on lightning trips to the Madrid front; General Goliev had been transferred to the Basque front. The shelling went on and on; and my nightmares lasted.

The Portuguese Armando came to see me, slovenly, unshaven, a skeleton frame covered with twitching nerves, his clothes miserably frayed. His bony, hooked nose and the gapped teeth in his wide mouth did not matter; his eyes were alive and intelligent under a domed forehead and his hands long and slim, with terse, neat gestures. He spoke without pause of the political crimes being committed out of indifference and corruption of the mind, and he caught my imagination with his picture of what could be done if the radio station were used for intensive propaganda directed to the Americas. When I broached his own situation, he countered all proposals with a savage pride: he wanted no alms, the salary for over three months' work was due to him, and he had no cause to accept charity from anyone. If he starved to death, it would be a good, clear case of official sabotage. In the end Ilsa talked him round, and he joined me at the long table of our improvised canteen, where journalists and passing visitors ate together with the censors, dispatch-riders, and orderlies.

It may have been because his burning, relentless, high-pitched indignation at things as they were coincided with my own frame of mind: we became friends.

I learned from Armando not only about the unexploited possibilities of the EAQ station, but also about the need for a directing control and censorship of the broadcasts. It had happened before—and now I realized how—that journalists, whom we stopped sending off a piece of news because it was banned by Military Intelligence, protested sharply and proved that the same report had gone out on the air for all the world to hear.

Among the regular visitors to my office was a man I will call Ramón, a Spanish journalist attached to Miaja's headquarters and used by the General as a private secretary and publicity agent. I spoke to Ramón of the radio muddle, and he quickly understood that I thought Miaja ought to intervene, but did not know how to make him. Two days later Miaja sent for me.

"Now what's this damned story about the radio? You boys are always trying to drag me into one of your messes. One day I'll chuck the whole damned bunch of you out."

Ramón gave me an accomplice's grin. After my simple explanation, the General wiped his eyeglasses and called his secretary.

"Make out a paper thinggammyjig for Barea. He's in charge of the radio censorship now. And you know, my boy—you're a sucker!"

I started to tell him about foreign propaganda, the EAQ station and its potential importance, but Miaja cut me short and Ramón produced a few bottles of beer out of the bedroom. A few days later, however, I was summoned again: the General gave me a "paper" with his signature, which made me his Commissioner at the EAQ station, with full powers.

My most urgent task was to find out which official department had to pay the speakers. I called in the Government Delegate—whom I had superseded—and asked him to render an account of his administration on the following day; he never turned up. The Workers' Committee brought me a bundle of letters from sympathizers overseas who had sent small donations of which there was no trace. This made it a matter for the police, and I handed it on; not however to my friends the Anarchists, for Pedro Orobón had been killed by a shrapnel splinter and the tolerant, human, selfless leadership of his friend Manuel replaced by a new system, more impersonal and more political, under a young Communist.

I still did not know which Ministry would pay the speakers and put up the money for the special valves bitterly needed by the station. Rubio Hidalgo, when I raised the point in one of our sporadic telephone conversations, made it perfectly clear that he was annoyed at my having meddled with something outside my office. Broadcasting was a matter for the Propaganda Ministry which had a Delegate in Madrid, Don José Carreño España. I sent a memorandum to Don José and received no answer.

At this, I called a council of war consisting of the Controller, the Workers' Committee, and the two speakers. I told them that I had not yet solved the financial question. I believed in the importance of their work. If they wanted to cease broadcasting in view of the difficulties and the official neglect, I could do nothing. If they were willing to go on until I found a way out—which I thought I could find—I would do my best. The speakers could eat in our canteen, since the food problem would otherwise be insoluble for them, and I would help with the programs. Ilsa would find friends in the International Brigades to broadcast in foreign languages.

They agreed to carry on, skeptically, yet too much in love with their station to let it close down.

I solved the matter of the speakers' pay by sheer chance. Carreño España and I met in Miaja's room, and the General presented us to each other. I said: "I'm glad to know you exist after all." "How's that?" Miaja grunted, and Don José asked the same in more elaborate words. "Because memos addressed to you seem to get nowhere." Then, of course, the whole story came out; we all agreed that it had been an office blunder; the Madrid Delegate of the Propaganda Ministry declared that the commitment would be honored, and I had made yet another friend in official circles. . . .

In those weeks, the Madrid front held little military interest. Hemingway had to find material for his articles by investigating the reactions of his friends in the bull-fighting world and by keeping in contact with the Russian colony in the Hotel Gaylord; when we stood in the ring of inane, marble statues in the Ministry court, his jokes told me how near he was to understanding Castilian double meanings—and how far, in spite of his obvious wish to speak to us man to man. Delmer (who was deeply annoyed because we failed to procure from either Valencia or from Carreño España a permit to use his big camera) and Herbert Matthews visited the Aragon front and came back disgusted with the sector held by P.O.U.M. units. Most of the correspondents only stayed on in Madrid because something was bound to break, in their opinion. But what came was the collapse of the northern front.

We were self-centered in Madrid; we thought that the rearguard—the "rotten rearguard"—of Valencia and Barcelona belonged to another world which we did not even try to understand. But Bilbao was fighting, Asturias was fighting, and they seemed to belong to us. And Bilbao fell.

I heard it first from foreign correspondents whose editors in London and Paris wanted them to report on Madrid's reaction to the news which had been broadcast from the other side. We knew nothing, officially. Rumors had been going round, but there were strict orders to press and radio not to publish anything except official communiqués; so far no communiqué had told the story of the fall of Bilbao, but many had spoken of its victorious defense. This news policy was humiliating in its stupidity. I went to Miaja and stated my conviction that this night's broadcast to America would have to deal with the fact of Bilbao's fall; if we were going to be silent about it, it would hurt our moral standing more than the fall itself. Miaja refused to make a decision: any order had to come from Valencia, he could not assume the responsibility and he did not know how to give the news. I suggested that I would write a talk on the subject and show it him before broadcasting.

"I can't imagine how the devil you can put it so that it doesn't hurt us," Miaja said. "But you can write it by all means; there's still time for me to tear it up and leave the Valencia people to cope."

I wrote a talk. As a device, it was directed to the blockade-running ship's captain nicknamed Potato Jones, and it was merely a profession of faith. It said that Bilbao had fallen, it explained what it had meant to our Spain and what it would come to mean again; that we were fighting on and that there was no time to weep for Bilbao. Miaja read it, thumped on his desk, and ordered me to broadcast the talk. He also rang up the only newspaper which was scheduled to appear the following day and told the editor to print my piece. In this form, Madrid read about Bilbao. That was the first time I spoke into a microphone. The engineers and guards of the building thronged the narrow room and I saw that I moved them. I had a lump in my throat and the feeling that here was a force entrusted to me. So I told the Workers' Committee that I would broadcast a talk every day after the news bulletins for Latin America, at a quarter past two in the morning. The speaker had announced me as "An Unknown Voice from Madrid," and I wanted this to remain my radio name. This was what I wanted to be.

The day was burdened with double office work since I had to censor all talks broadcast from Madrid. I went through it mechanically, forever listening to the thuds of shells. When the shelling came too near, I went down to the vaults of the library and wrote there. The new foreign journalists who came and went hardly ever became real persons to me. I remember the young Dane Vinding. He arrived with great plans, amusedly recalling that his father had fled from Madrid during the November raids, and then came to ask me for shelter, a trembling wreck, after seeing a little boy torn by a shell in the Gran Vía. I spoke to him about myself, so as to give him a fellow feeling; but at his first sally into the streets he was caught in a shooting brawl in one of the cafés and, escaping, faced a phantom car of the Fifth Column, swishing past with a rattle of tommy-guns: I had to send him back to Valencia. I also remember the German Communist George Gordon, crippled and twisted by the Nazis in body and mind. He worked for *Agence Espagne* and quickly began to agitate for people of a sterner political discipline to be put in mine and Ilsa's places, when he found that we did not let him monopolize all scoops and influence our treatment of the journalists. I found him slimy, with a crooked mouth, a sliding glance, sidling movements, and no spontaneous warmth or interest; I underrated him. From him and the circle of young foreign party workers he collected I turned more than ever to people I knew to be genuine.

· Torres, the printing worker who had founded the Popular Front Committee of the Ministry together with me, came to us with his difficulties. He had become secretary of the Communist cell, but he knew that he was ignorant and helpless and therefore submitted his political worries to Ilsa who, after conscientiously reminding him that she did not belong to the Party and was indeed disapproved of by it, would explain to him what, in her opinion, he ought to do, and what the Party line would be. He never found it odd that he let himself be guided by her, as long as it helped his work; he never admitted that he was acting against the discipline of his Party. But to me he came with other problems. He was married; he had not the courage to break away from it altogether as I had done, although he was unhappy and in love with another woman; he envied me; he wanted to speak of the relationship between men and women. Then again he told me of the Fifth Columnists he feared were among the bureaucrats of the Ministry. I contradicted him. There was nothing left in the building which could have been of interest to the enemy, and the people he suspected were scared elderly employees, faithful servants of the old ruling caste, such as the doorkeeper Faustino who greeted me with an obsequious bow and a bilious glance, but by no means dangerous. Then one day Torres arrived in great excitement and burst out:

"Now there you are, you and your talk of harmless scared old men. . . . In San Francisco el Grande, the Shock Police have caught one of them sending heliograph messages to the rebels in the Casa de Campo by tugging at the cord of a blind, and there was a pocket mirror tied to one of the slats, and that's how he signaled news of troop movements on our side. If you'd seen the man! He was just like a wrinkled old bat. And you see, the worst of it is, the art treasure left in San Francisco el Grande is our responsibility—I'm one of the Controlling Committee—and we thought we could trust some of those bigoted old fools because they've looked after it so long. But you can't trust anybody except our own people."

He pestered me to go with him and see the works of art still left in the old monastery which for half a century had been one of the National Monuments. It was his responsibility before the people and weighed upon him; but he wondered what I would think of it: was it really great art?

I began to go out again and to teach myself to behave as everybody else did. In the night I would speak to the outer world as the voice of Madrid, so I had to be one of the people of Madrid. With Ilsa, I spent quiet hours in the back room of Serafín's tavern while he told me stories of his street. He took me down into the pawnbroker's cellar where he and his friends slept on empty wooden shelves, the shelves where pawned mattresses used to be piled, so as to be safe from shells. The women slept in the neighboring cellar on camp beds. But Serafín had a purple bruise on his forehead which never waned and was the butt of countless jokes: every time he jumped because of an explosion, he bumped his head against the upper shelf and every time he wanted to get out of his bunk to help clear up the mess left by a shell in the street, he bumped it too. His fear and his courage both gave him bruises.

I told this story over the wireless, as I told the stories of street-cleaners watering Shell Alley and washing off dark trickles of blood, of tramway bells tinkling and giving me courage during raids, of a telephone girl crying until her eyes and nose were swollen, but sticking to her post while the windowpanes were shattered by blast, of old women sitting and knitting under the porches of a front-line village where Pietro Nenni took me in his car, of children picking up shell-fuses, still warm, in the street behind the Ministry and making a game of it. I believe that all the stories I wrote and broadcast at the end of a day in the bleak, echoing Ministry, were stories of ordinary people living in that mixture of fear and courage which filled the streets of Madrid, and its trenches. All their fears were mine, and their courage warmed me. I had to pass it on.

Miaja had put a driver and a small car, one of the Italian Balillas captured after Guadalajara, at mine and Ilsa's disposal for our broadcasting. After one o'clock, when the Press Censorship was closed, it took us through empty streets where sentries stopped us and asked for sign and counter-sign. The station was in the Calle de Alcalá, in a tall building whose top floor had housed big, well-equipped studios. The shelling had made the upper floors uninhabitable, and an emergency studio and office had been installed in the basement. You walked down a small concrete staircase and found yourself in a dirty, narrow passage, dank and pervaded by the smell of the doorless lavatory which opened into it, exhibiting white tiles and dripping water pipes. The small cubicles ranged along the corridor had originally served to store coal; each had a grating set high in the wall and opening out into the street just above pavement level. One of those coal cellars had been cleared out and converted into a studio by the simple means of army blankets strung up on the walls for sound-proofing. It held a gramophone turntable, a small switchboard and a suspended microphone.

The coal cellar next door had been turned into the office. It had half a dozen chairs and two huge, old, ink-stained desks. A big iron stove in the middle was kept burning even on the hottest summer nights, because the cellars sweated dampness. Thus the room was filled with steam, thickened and colored by tobacco smoke. The passage and the empty cubicles were littered with pallets stuffed with esparto grass. There slept the family of the concierge, the engineers, a few employees of the company, the messenger boys, the militiamen posted there, two Assault Guards, and an assortment of children who had nowhere else to go. Everybody talked and shouted, the children squeaked, and the concrete walls resounded. Sometimes it was necessary to cut the transmission for a moment and to shout for silence, with a couple of curses to lend force to the command.

At the far end of the passage a round hole opened, like a well shaft;

a winding iron stair led into a cellar hole, ten feet square and of solid concrete, where my friend the Controller had his office. Under the green glow of the lampshade he looked like a ghost, with his thin frame and loose clothes, and the sudden silence behind the thick walls made you feel as though you had descended into a tomb. There we would sit with the Secretary of the Workers' Committee, a spare man from the Mancha with jutting cheekbones and small, glinting eyes, and plan our programs. There we would read the first letters addressed to the "Voice of Madrid." One was from an old Spanish miner in the United States. He said—and I think I remember the exact words of his utterly simple letter: "When I was thirteen I went underground to dig coal in Peñarroya. Now I am sixty-three, and I am still digging coal in Pennsylvania. I am sorry I cannot write better, but the Marquess and the priest of our village did not grant us any schooling. I bless you who are fighting for a better life, and I curse those who do not want our people to rise."

While I read my nightly talk, the entire population of the basement used to assemble in the blanketed studio. The men seemed to feel that they had a share in my broadcasts, because I spoke their language, and they were possessively critical of them. The control-room engineer in Vallecas made a point of ringing me up and telling me whether I had once again been too soft for his taste or not. The simplest among the men had a predilection for biblical denunciations of the powers of evil on the other side; some of the workers were shocked and fascinated by the harshest pieces of realism I wrote; the employees found my style too uncouth and devoid of rotund, polished passages, not literary enough; most of them were astonished that they could follow every sentence easily, without intellectual stumbling. I had no theory; I was fumbling to express what they dimly felt, in the clearest possible language, and to make people overseas see below the surface of our struggle.

The man whose reactions were most illuminating to me was the sergeant in command of the Shock Police post at the Ministry. He held himself at my disposal with the unquestioning loyalty of a henchman, following the orders of his predecessor who had stood by me on November the 7th. Convinced that I was a worthwhile target for the Fifth Column, he refused to let me out of his sight after dark and accompanied me to the radio station with a silent, childlike pride. There he would stand in a corner, towering above the others, and blink when he was touched. His face was flat and rugged, as though carved out of a weather-beaten stone slab, and his eyes were pale. After a few weeks of listening to my broadcasts he entered my room, gulped, blinked, and handed me a few sheets; he had written down the bad things he had done and seen being done in his years of service in the Army and the Civil Guard. Now he wanted me to turn his story into a broadcast, as an atonement to the people. His handwriting was much like the old miner's who had written from Pennsylvania.

The new Republican Government under Dr. Negrin had been in office for some time. Negrin himself had made his first, grimly sober broadcasts; Indalecio Prieto was rumored to have cleaned up the General Staff; Army discipline was being tightened up, the Party character of the units reduced, the role of the Political Commissars restricted. There were troop movements on the sectors west of Madrid, the roads from the coast saw a constant flow of war material, many more new fighter planes were flying overhead, war correspondents arrived from Valencia. I was given a series of stringent orders by H.Q.: Prieto was in the town, but his stay was to be kept secret; as soon as the operation started, no reports other than the war communiqués were to be passed by the censorship; private as well as diplomatic telegrams and radio messages were to be held up for several days; correspondents were not allowed to go to the front.

Offensive operations began in a broiling July heat. The Lister, Campesino, and International Brigades were in action. The battle for Brunete was joined. The Republican thrust, supported—for the first time—by successful air operations, gained ground due west of Madrid in a bid to cut the enemy's lines, turn his flank and force an evacuation of his positions in the University City. But then the offensive was halted; in spite of their remarkable technical improvement, our forces were too weak to increase their pressure before the enemy had time to bring up reinforcements. After the advance came a reverse; Brunete and Quijorna, taken at great cost, were lost again and wiped out in the process.

Torres and I climbed the crooked, cobwebbed stair to the western turret of the Ministry. Through the skylight we looked down on the chessboard of slated roofs and on the vast battlefield. Far away in the plain, too far for our eyes to make out any detail, was a mass of smoke and dust, split by flashes, and from its dark base an immense smoke column rose into the bright sky. The war cloud heaved and quivered, and my lungs trembled with the vibration of sky and earth. Fine dust floated from the old beams of the turret, clearly visible against the light that came through the panes. Down on the Plaza de Santa Cruz people were going about their affairs, and on the roof opposite a black-and-white cat sat down by a chimney, stared at us, and began to slick its ears.

The dreaded nausea crept from my stomach into my mouth. There, below the apocalyptic cloud, was Brunete. In my mind, I saw the dun-colored village, its mud walls whitened with chalk, its miry pond, the desolate fields with their dry, bleached, stone-hard clods, the merciless sun of the threshing floors, the powdered wheat chaff stinging one's throat. I saw myself as a boy walking down the village street, the Madrid Road, between my Uncle José and his brothers, he in his town suit and they in their cor'uroys, but all of them carrying their smell of dry earth and sweat dried by sun and dust; for even after many years in town, my Uncle José still had the skin and smell of a peasant from Dry Castile.

There, behind that dark, flashing cloud, Brunete was being killed by clanking tanks and screaming bombs: its mud houses crumbled in dust, the mire of its pond spattered, its dry earth plowed up by shells and sown with blood. It seemed to me a symbol of our war: the forlorn village making history by being destroyed in a clash between those who kept all the Brunetes of my country arid, dry, dusty, and poor as they were, and the others who dreamed of transforming the dust-gray villages of Castile, of all Spain, into homesteads of free, clean, gay men. It was also a personal thing to me. The soil of Brunete held some of the roots of my blood and of my rebellion. Its harsh, dry heritage had always battled within me against the joyful warmth I had received, as a legacy, in the other stream of blood from that other village of my youth: Méntrida with its wine lands, its green meadows, its slow running river between reeds—Méntrida, a speck out there in the plain, far from the sinister cloud, yet in the bondage of the men who were turning the fields of Spain into barren waste.

In the night after that day, I cried into the microphone what I had felt in the tower facing the front.

The journalists, so close to the focus of the war and yet unable to report on it, were persistent and angry. They all sent out air force and army communiqués, but they quarreled with me, and I quarreled with them, because I stuck to orders and did not let them say more. At the start of the offensive, the precautions were clearly necessary. The radio-telegrams which the Controller put on my desk, and which we delayed four days, included a good many messages that sounded highly suspicious; the German agent Felix Schleyer, still administrator of the Norwegian Legation, produced an outburst of private telegrams; an astonishing number of people with an impeccable diplomatic address had developed family trouble. Yet once operations were in full swing, I thought it in our own interest to let the journalists send out reports of their own. I went to Prieto in the General Staff, and after a heated discussion obtained a relaxation of the rules.

Yet my relations with the journalists had suffered under our mutual irritation; they noted that requests for permits, which had been so quickly dispatched before, were being delayed, and had little idea of the struggle between our office and the reborn bureaucracy which lay behind it. To them I was the source of the trouble, and I did not even try to undeceive them or to soothe them down, although I knew that they raised complaints with Prieto and the Valencia office, and that the Valencia staff, at least, was not displeased with this fact. George Gordon came back from a trip to Valencia, shrouded in political importance, and I went out ·of my way to be more than usually rude to him. Rubio Hidalgo appeared for half a day, insisted that the temporary contract with the girl Pat should not be prolonged because she had passed a dispatch calling Prieto the "roly-poly" Minister (which in his opinion was against the national dignity), expounded a plan to install a Spanish journalist, mainly known for his feud with the *Times* correspondent, as Madrid propaganda director for both press and radio, found me more refractory than ever, and worse than that when he hinted at the bad impression caused by my divorce and my relationship with Ilsa.

It was evident that more than one campaign of a personal and half-political kind was under way. I was too exhausted to care, or it may have been that I secretly welcomed them.

When the offensive was over; my divorce in its final stage; the International Anti-Fascist Writers' Congress, with its exhibition of intellectuals posturing on the background of fighting Madrid and discussing the political behavior of André Gide, over and done with, I fell into a stupor.

Maria came once a week to threaten and implore me; I worked myself up into a state of rage, disgust, and dislike until I was able to be brutally frank to her. She never came again, but wrote anonymous letters. Aurelia's mother, who recognized her daughter's share of responsibility in the wreck of our marriage, formed the habit of visiting Ilsa and me regularly; when she first came, the employees of the Ministry watched through half-open doors so as not to miss a thrilling row, and when they found that the old lady was on affectionate terms with her ex-son-in-law's future wife, it gave them an even more sensational, because more revolutionary spectacle. "It's still like in a foreign novel," said the horse-faced censor to me. "I wouldn't have thought that Spanish people could behave like this." I listened to everything and did little except write my broadcasts.

At that time people who were no more than casual acquaintances began to speak to me about my mistake in wanting to marry the foreigner instead of merely carrying on with her; so long as they believed that a Spaniard had "conquered" a foreign woman, their male fellow-feelings had been tickled, but now they saw me breaking their whole code of behavior and thought it morally wrong. It chimed in with Rubio's hints and filled me with a weary loathing, an additional excuse to despise the whispers I caught about my growing slackness, my outbursts of anger, my insecure health. Those whispers almost pleased me and I courted them.

Only when I saw how Ilsa was worried and harassed, and when Torres, or my old sergeant, or Agustín, or Angel, or the old friends in Serafín's tavern showed their belief in me, did I shake myself into spasmodic action.

While I was in the throes of this crisis, Constancia de la Mora came on her first visit to Madrid. I knew that she had virtually assumed the control of the Censorship Department in Valencia and that she did not like Rubio; that she was an efficient organizer, very much a woman of the world who had joined the Left of her free choice, and that she had greatly improved the relationship between the Valencia office and the press; I was also aware that she must have found it irksome that we in Madrid invariably acted as if we were independent of their—of her—authority. Tall, buxom, with full, dark eyes, the imperious bearing of a matriarch, a schoolgirl's simplicity of thought, and the self-confidence of a granddaughter of Antonio Maura, she grated on me, as I must have grated on her. Yet when she advised Ilsa and me to take our long overdue and obviously much-needed holiday, I was prepared to trust her intention. I had to relax and sleep; and I wanted to find out what the Valencia people meant to do with us.

Ilsa was pessimistic. She had evolved a theory that we had become mere survivors of the revolutionary pioneer days, since we had failed to adapt ourselves to the changes in the administrative system. She was no more prepared than I to surrender her independence of judgment and her unbureaucratic ways, but she had begun to think that there was no room for them any more, and that I had outgrown my position—she knew that I had deliberately brought my insubordination, impatience and anger to the notice of the powers that be—as she had outstayed her welcome and usefulness as a foreigner without party backing. I brushed her apprehensions aside, not because I thought them wrong, but because I did not care if they were right.

General Miaja asked me to arrange for an acting radio censor, gave permission to use the driver and car during our holiday as "the only pay you'll ever get for courting trouble," and supplied us with safe-conducts from and to Madrid.

The road to Valencia was not the straight road across the Arganda bridge which we had traveled in January. We had to go a round about route through Alcalá de Henares, scaling bare red hills and returning to the hot, white road after weary hours. I slept most of the time on Ilsa's shoulder. Once our car stopped to give room to a long file of miserable, mangy, spavined mules, donkeys, and horses. Dust and flies were clogging the sores of the exhausted beasts which seemed to carry all the ills and evils of the world on their sagging backs. I asked the gypsy who

squeezed past our mudguard: "Where are you taking this collection?"
"Meat for Madrid. Give us a fag, comrade."
On the hills lavender was in bloom, a blue haze, and when we came
down into the valley, the stream was edged with clumps of rose-red
oleander. Then the hollow of Valencia wrapped us in moist and sticky
heat, in noise and the smell of crowds.
We reported to Rubio's office. He was devastatingly polite: "If you had
let us know you were arriving this evening, we should have received you
with flowers, Ilsa. . . . No, we won't discuss shop any more. You go
and have your rest—what's your address? Altea? Very nice indeed—and
don't you worry about the Madrid office. We'll see to everything, you've
done your bit."
After a fitful sleep in the steaming, mosquito-infested hotel room we
escaped into the bright, hot morning. The town was gaudy and crowded.
I left Ilsa to herself while I went to visit my children and speed up the
final divorce formalities with the local magistrate. It meant some greasing
of palms; and it meant that I had to harden myself against the sense of
the injustice I was inflicting on the children. I was astonished at being
so callous. Aurelia was at the hairdresser's, and I had long hours alone
with them. It would have pleased me to take my younger daughter with
me, but I knew that no compromise was possible.
On my return to town I found Ilsa at our meeting place in the café,
talking gravely to the same police agent who had arrested her in January.
He was a hulking man with a deeply furrowed, humorous face, who addressed me before I could say anything: "I'm sorry you were first with
Ilsa, I'd have liked to try out my chances with her. Never mind, it's because of her that I'm about to tell you something as a friend."
What he told us with a wealth of detail was that, according to his au-
thoritative information, Rubio and Constancia had no intention of letting
us go back to our posts in Madrid. Constancia had fixed my successor, a
secretary to the League of Anti-Fascist Intellectuals recommended by
Maria Teresa León. "You see, those Spanish women don't like a foreign
woman having so much influence. And then, they're all new and eager
party members." There had been more than one complaint against us.
Ilsa, for instance, had passed an article for the Stockholm Labor paper,
which criticized the elimination of the Socialist and Anarchist Trade
Unions from the Government, and this was taken to be a pointer to her
own political sympathies. Some of the German Communists working in
Madrid (I at once thought of George Gordon) maintained that she was a
Trotskyite, but so far their campaign had been discredited by the Russians. Ilsa's old enemy Leipen was bombarding the authorities with denunciations of her, in which he advised against letting her leave Spain,

because she knew too many people in the international labor movement. Aurelia was filling the Ministry with abuse of Ilsa and myself whenever she came to fetch my salary, which I had transferred to her and the children. We would do better, in sum, to set our own friends in motion and to cut our stay in Valencia short—it was not healthy for us.

There was very little we could do on the strength of his confidential information. It all fitted, but how could we prove anything? How could we fight this combination of personal dislikes, political intrigues and the ineluctable laws of a state machine during a civil war? Del Vayo was no longer Foreign Minister; his successor, a politician of the *Izquierda Republicana,* would not have known about us; it would have been childish to demand an explanation from Rubio Hidalgo, and I could not have trusted my self-control. We spoke to a few people who were in a position to act, should we disappear without any trace. Our only way was to go back to our place in Madrid as soon as we had recovered some strength for the coming test.

We went to Altea.

The road along the rocky coast of Levante, the *Costa Brava,* took us across terraced hills at the foot of the blue, barren mountains, through crumbling towns with resounding names—Gandía and Oliva and Denia and Calpe—through stony, herb-grown gorges and past whitewashed farms with an arched portico and curled tiles on their roofs. At the first vineyard I stopped the car. The old field guard came, looked at the number plate, grumbled: "From Madrid, eh? How are things there?" and gave Ilsa a heap of golden-green grapes, a few tomatoes, and a cucumber. We passed through villages, bumping on the cobbles, and saw old women in black sitting on low stools outside the swinging bead curtains of their house door, by their side a box heaped with long bars of the greenish soap which country people of the region made of the residues of their oil-press and caustic soda. In Madrid there was no soap.

By dusk we reached the little roadside inn at Altea, a whitewashed, clean-smelling hall, dark polished dressers, rush-plaited chairs and a breeze from the sea. Our tiny bedroom was filled with the smell of the sea mixed with a scent of garden and freshly watered earth, but outside our window was nothing but a dark haze, water and air fused, a star-powdered blue-black sky above it, and a chain of gently swaying specks of light drawing away into the blue darkness. The men of Altea were out fishing. That night I slept.

Altea is almost as old as its hill; it has been Phoenician, Greek, Roman, Arabic, and Spanish. Its flat-roofed white houses, plain walls pierced by window-holes, climb the hill in a spiral which follows the mule-track with its age-polished, worn stone steps. The church has a slender tower, the minaret of a mosque, and a blue-tiled dome. The women walking from their silent, dark houses down to the shore where the men are mending their fishing nets carry on their heads water pitchers of a light yellow clay, with a swelling curve, a narrow base, a graceful neck, an amphora-shape of their own which the local pottery reproduces only for Altea after the ageless pattern. The ancient port is deserted, but the lateen sails of the Altea fishermen still reach the African coast on fishing and contraband trips. Around the hill are olive and pomegranate groves, and terraces of cultivated land scooped out from the rock. The coastal road is new, and round it a new village has sprung up, wealthier and less soil-bound than the town on the hill, with a police station, a few taverns and inns, and the villas of rich people from the outside world. It has left the hill-town more secluded in itself than ever. After all the changes it absorbed it has become immutable.

I felt the shock of this peace and immutability in my marrow. It made me sleep in the nights and think during the days. This place ignored the war. The war only served to increase the market value of its fishing hauls. Politics? Only a few young men with a bee in their bonnet had volunteered for the fight, and if age classes were being called up now, it was a cruel injustice. Politics and wars were always the same, a matter for a few politicians and a few generals quarreling for power, each out for himself. There had been supporters of the Left and Right in Altea, there had been a few rows, but now everything was at peace. If the others, the Fascists, came, the people of Altea would go on just as they were now. Sometimes the sound of naval guns or of bombs was carried to the village by the wind. Then it was better not to leave the waters of the port, to leave fishing for another night. Prices were rising.

A few miles from Altea the war was knocking at the coast. On the Rock of Ifach, "Little Gibraltar," as it was called, there was a naval observation post in the ruins of the ancient watchtower. Men of the International Brigades, sent to the hospital of Benisa to recover from wounds and exhaustion, came every day in lorries to bathe in one of the three shallow, scalloped little bays at the foot of the rock. When we did not go to the African beach of Benidorm, with blue mountains and palm trees and dung-beetles making their tracks in the hot sand, we went to the Rock of Ifach and stayed with Miguel, the tavern keeper whom I called the Pirate, because he looked like the free, bold pirate of the tales.

He sold wine in an open, reed-covered shack with long benches and plain trestle tables, protected from the glaring sun by plaited rush curtains. He had seen shacks like that in Cuba, he said. His eyes were gray-blue and distant, and his skin golden. He was no longer very young, but he was strong and moved noiselessly like a cat. When we first came into the cool shade he looked us up and down. Then, as though conferring a favor, he brought us wine in a glazed jar and drank with us. He looked at Ilsa and suddenly offered her a packet of Norwegian cigarettes. Cigarettes were very scarce then. "You're a foreigner. Good.. You're with us." He stated it simply. Then he took us into the smoky kitchen to meet his young, dark-eyed wife and his little son in the cot. A sturdy five-year-old girl silently followed each of his steps. His wife stood by the hooded fireplace and said nothing, while he explained:

"Look, this comrade here has come from far away to fight with us. She knows a lot of things. More than I. I told you that women can know about things too, and that we need some of them."

But she did not like it, she looked at Ilsa with quiet hostility mixed with awe, as though she were a strange monster.

He left the kitchen with us, brought another jar of wine and sat down. "Look," he said to Ilsa. "I know why you've come here. I can't explain. Perhaps you can. But there are many like us in the world. We understand each other when we meet for the first time. Comrades or brothers. We believe in the same things. I would know what you believed even if you didn't speak a word of Spanish."

He drank his wine ceremoniously. "*Salud!*"

"Miguel, what are you?"

"A Socialist. Does it matter?"

"Do you believe we shall win the war?"

"Yes. Not now, perhaps. What's this war? There'll be others, and in the end we shall win. There will be a time when all people are Socialists, but many will have to die before then."

I went to see him whenever I was cloyed with the drowsy peace of Altea. He never told me much about himself. He had gone night fishing along these coasts with his father, in a boat with a lantern in the stern. Then he had gone to New York. He had been twenty years at sea. Now he had married because a man must sink his roots into the soil at some stage. He had what he wanted, and he knew what was wrong with the world. I was too tense, I ought to sit in the sun, fishing. He loaned me a rod. That day—I caught a single blue-scaled fish—he himself cooked us a meal: a bucket of fish, fresh from the sea, glinting in the colors of the rainbow, were cooked until the water had sucked out their goodness; then he boiled plain rice in this juice of the sea. That was all. We ate it with gaiety and drank rough red wine.

"You learned it when you were a pirate, Miguel."

"There aren't any pirates."

The lorry load of men from the International Brigades arrived. Some had their arms and legs in plaster, some had half-healed scars which they exposed to the wind and sun, lying in the wet sand by the pale, over-scented sand-lilies. At noon, when the sky shimmered with heat, they stormed the shack and shouted for drinks and food. Miguel served them silently. If he had to keep them in order, he always had a strong curse in the right language ready. Later in the afternoon, the men were half drunk and started rows. A Frenchman was the noisiest. Miguel ordered him and his cronies out of the shack. The others left submissively, but the Frenchman came back and reached for his hip pocket. Miguel lunged, caught him and threw him through an opening in the rush curtain as though he were a doll. An hour later he slouched in again. Miguel looked straight through him and said in a very low voice: "Get out."

The man never came back. But a few tourists sitting at a small table had witnessed the scene. One of them, a woman with the face of a par-rot, said as soon as the lorry had left: "Now tell me, why are those for-eigners here? They ought to have stayed at home. They're having a racket at our expense."

Another woman who was sitting with her said: "But they helped us to save Madrid. I know it, I was there at the time."

"So what?" said the unfriendly woman.

Miguel turned round: "Those men have fought. They're with us. You're not."

The husband of the parrot-woman asked hastily: "What do we owe you?"

"Nothing."

"But we've had——"

"Nothing."

They went away, cowed. A few old men from the small white houses by the beach had climbed up the road, as they did every evening. They sat down on low stools outside the rush curtain. Their glowing cigarette ends drew cabalistic signs in the dusk. "That war—they'll come here too," one of them mumbled.

Miguel, his face lit by the flare of his match and turned to stern bronze, asked: "What would you do then?"

"What can an old man do? Nothing. I'd make myself so small they wouldn't notice me."

"You can do nothing, if they really come," said another. "They come and go, but we've got to stick it out here. . . . You know, Miguel, there are some people in Calpe who are waiting for the Fascists to come, and you're on their black list."

"I know."

"What would you do, Miguel?" I asked.

He took me with him to a shed behind the shack. There were two big drums of petrol. "When they come here," Miguel said, "nothing will be free. I'll put my wife and the children in my boat and burn all this. And I shall light a fire on the rock where they used to have a beacon in old times, to tell the people along the coast to flee. But I shall come back one day."

In front of the dark, rustling curtain, the burning cigarette ends of the old men were a chain of red points. Far out to sea, the lanterns of the fishing boats were a swaying chain of sparks. It was very still and down by the beach a fish jumped.

The next time I was about to visit Miguel, I received a registered letter; Rubio Hidalgo informed me that his department was granting Ilsa and me indefinite leave "for the benefit of our physical and moral recovery," after which we would be used for work in Valencia. I had, however, taken away an official car of the department without a permit, which I ought to send to Valencia at once. I answered by sending in Ilsa's and my own resignation from any war work in the Foreign Ministry; we were going back to the posts in Madrid from which General Miaja had given us sick leave; the car had been put at our disposal by the General and had nothing to do with the Press Department; we would not accept indefinite leave, because we did not intend to draw pay for work not rendered.

I felt a bitter pain in the pit of my stomach.

8. In the Pit

BACK to Madrid. The dull ache which possessed me never lifted.

As though to mock the war and those who were fighting it, the whole breadth of the Spanish landscape unfolded: salt plains by the shimmering Mediterranean; the palm forest of Elche in the noon haze; eyeless, blindingly white Moorish houses on the slope of bare yellow dunes, petrified in the shape of waves; gnarled oak and pine on rocky ridges, unbearably lonely under the infinite dome of the sky; a neat carpet of well-watered, green fields and garden plots spread out before the tall, squalid old houses and many squat church towers of Orihuela; a slow river, women beating linen on flat stones by the water; more desolate bleached hills with blue shadows in their sharp folds; the fiery depth of the sky turning into a soft blue glow; the emerald-green garden of the Murcian plain, with the basalt rock of Monteagudo soaring, fantastically, into an amber evening sky and holding up a many-towered, battlemented fairy-tale castle; then the city of Murcia itself, dingy baroque palaces and bazaar life wrapped in the warm, intimate dusk.

The only beds we could obtain in the overcrowded hotel were camp beds rigged up in an airless lobby. The three open galleries running round the huge stair-well were filled with the strident voices of women and drunken men. The restaurant was overflowing with soldiers, rich farmers, and food-racketeers; food and wine were excellent and preposterously expensive. It was easy to place the Murcians who looked askance at the birds of passage: there were small groups of the old rural owner caste, uneasy, sullen, and silent; there was a self-confident majority of the tenants of old, men who had been cruelly exploited, but had themselves been wont cruelly to exploit their primitive farm laborers, and who now earned undreamed of riches from the food ramp; and there were the workers, clumsy, noisy, boisterously showing off the freedom they had won and sporting the black-and-red scarves of the Anarchists so as to scare their hated former masters. There was an atmosphere of forced good cheer and underlying distrust, of electric tension and desperate enjoyment in the place. But the war was there only in the uniforms, and the revolution was there only in the deliberate exhibition of newly acquired affluence and power by those who had been the proletariat of wealthy Murcia.

I hated the place; I think Ilsa was scared by it. We stayed no more than a couple of hours in the stench of our improvised bedroom, and left in the early morning. Hilario, our young driver, shook his head. "This is a worse rearguard than Valencia. And the food they waste! But what can you expect of those treacherous Murcians anyway?" For in the rest of Spain the people of Murcia have the reputation of being crafty and treacherous.

And on through the hills, long slopes covered with withered grass where sheep were cropping, on to the uplands of Castile.

Great billowing clouds, sailing slowly to the east, laid splashes of shadow on the bleak conical hills which rose out of the plain. There were no trees, few birds—black-and-white magpies and lonely cruising hawks —and no human beings. The plain was tinted yellow, dun, tawny, russet, umber, and elephant-gray, but rarely green. In that great field of loneliness I no longer wanted to shout or scream: we were too little.

Past the ugly garrison town of Albacete, center of war supplies and the International Brigades; barracks, stucco houses, dusty stunted avenue trees, military traffic, repair shops, refuse heaps. And then we were in Don Quixote's Mancha. The white road fringed by telegraph poles cut an almost straight line through endless, undulating vineyards; their black grapes were covered with thick white dust. A lime pit showed the shallow top layer of fertile, ashy-brown earth, no more than a foot deep, and the lifeless white chalk underneath. The sun burned fiercely and my mouth was filled as though with dust and ashes. But there was no village and no wayside tavern for long hot hours. Then we reached La Ronda. It was market day. Straight-backed women in dusty, black cloth dresses were sitting, motionless, behind boxes of cheap thread and buttons, or behind baskets of grapes. They all looked old before their time, yet ageless, burned into likeness by the same pitiless sun, frost, and winds, made haggard and fierce by the same hopeless fight with the dry soil. On the background of their discolored mud-brick houses they were a frieze in black, brown, and parchment-yellow. None of them seemed eager to sell. They did not deign to speak. Their dark, shuttered eyes followed Ilsa with a bitter interest. When we acquired a pound of the purple-black grapes from one of them, it seemed a victory over their hostile silence.

I decided to take a secondary road from La Ronda to the Valencia trunk road where we would find a place to give us lunch. The Mancha was inhospitable. But after a mile our car floundered in deep, powdery white dust where the wheels did not grip; we had to slow down to five miles an hour. Now there was something simple and straightforward which could be blamed for our misfortune: my stubbornness in insisting on the side road against the advice of the driver. The three of us broke out into childish jokes which showed how strong our feeling of depression had been. It seemed very funny to be slower than a cyclist wobbling in the deep dust. And then there were trees, pine copses which hid a field airdrome with "Moscas," the small, fly-like fighter planes supplied by the Russians; and there was a little river, and a mill, and fields. There was life. It did not matter that Hilario had to repair one of the springs in the village forge, after we had limped into Motilla del Palancar. I took Ilsa to the threshing floor where we saw the chaff eddying in the wind, and I took her to an old inn where they gave us eggs and bacon in a cool, flagged room with a hooded fireplace. The light fell through the inverted funnel of the chimney on to the clean brick hearth, and there were old red clay pitchers and jars on the wide mantelpiece. In the wagon yard chickens were pecking grains. We stared at them: starved Madrid was so very near.

A chain of tanks caught us and carried us on towards the city front.

The Valencia road was blocked by two streams of military traffic, one coming and one going. It slowed us up. We spent a night in Saelices where we slept on feather mounds in high, old-fashioned beds whose linen had not been changed for months. The mutton stew they gave us was rank with grease. To make up for it, the innkeeper presented Ilsa with an enormous tomato weighing well over two pounds, the pride of his heart and, so he maintained, with a flavor better than cooked ham. Carrying the red, glistening ball, we entered the Ministry on the following morning.

The pale, inhibited girl Rosario who had been appointed chief of the Foreign Press and Censorship Department in my place was plainly embarrassed to see us, but she was courteous and tried to be helpful. Once again, people stared at us from behind half-open office doors. Old Llizo came bravely to tell me how sorry he was that our common work, begun on that unforgettable November the 7th, had ended; he would never change towards me or Ilsa "who had made the censorship an office of diplomatic importance." My old sergeant wrung my hand and muttered something about what he would like to do to those bastards, and so forth; he remained at my orders. Yet I could not delude myself into underrating our quandary. Agustín turned the key in the lock of our room. "I've had to keep it locked the last few days—Rubio wanted to throw out your things just like that. There was a story they gave out that the police had arrested you because you had absconded with the car. None of them thought you would come back to Madrid. Now the girl's ringing up Valencia to tell them you're back, and you'll see: they won't let the journalists speak to you, much less to Ilsa."

I reported to General Miaja: we would resume our job with the radio, but we were no longer employees of the Foreign Ministry. I told him the story of the car which had been meant as a trap for me. Miaja grunted. He disliked the whole muddle. I had better take care of what those fellows in Valencia would do next: "We in Madrid are only muck to them, my boy." It was all right about the car, we would have to go on using it as long as we did night work at the radio. And there wouldn't be any trouble about the radio—yet. He would tell Carreño España. But it might be wise if I got the new Civil Governor of Madrid—"Yes, my boy, I'm no longer Governor General, and glad I am to get rid of all that trouble"—to endorse me as chief radio censor. People were getting damned formal these days; that girl Rosario—not much to look at, is she?—had been accredited to him and the Civil Governor and Carreño España, and the devil knew whom with all sorts of pomp and circumstance, and she would have every facility for which I had shouted in vain, just because her official papers were beautifully in order. Journalists would find that she could get things done for them. I should have a look at things and get wise—if I could ever get wise. But I wouldn't.

I had a drink with Miaja after his sermon and left him with that cold, nauseating lump in the pit of my stomach. Yes, our position was extremely precarious. I was still Radio Censor of Madrid and Commissioner of the EAQ station by Miaja's order, but obviously Miaja himself did not think that his orders would stand very much longer. The fact that I received neither salary nor fee would probably give me some more time in which to go on working. But nobody would back me. Ilsa was nothing but my voluntary helper in languages I did not understand, with Miaja's knowledge, but without any appointment. She, too, would be left to carry on the work she had begun, the organization of foreign language broadcasts to the Americas, until the moment when one of the Ministries decided to turn it into a paid job. I might go to the new Civil Governor of Madrid. But I had no stomach to beg for a favor where I had created something in which I believed and which was already bearing fruit. Hundreds of letters from overseas were waiting for the "Unknown Voice of Madrid," some of them abusive, many naïve, and many touching; all of them showed that those people were listening avidly to something personal and human, off the beaten track. I was convinced that I had chosen the right way of speaking to them. But I was determined not to move a finger for myself. If "they"—all those people who were going in for a new formal bureaucracy—had so little interest in the essence of the work, they would do better to push me away, as they had pushed away Ilsa and me from the censorship.

I did not speak to anybody more than I could help, and I did not make it easy for anybody to help me. On the day after our arrival, we moved into the Hotel Victoria on the Plaza de Santa Ana, where the Propaganda Ministry had reserved a number of rooms; while we did a full time job for them (and immediately after our return the work piled up for both of us) they would have to pay our expenses in place of any other compensation. As there was no radio censorship office, I stayed in a small unused room of the Foreign Ministry, waiting for an official instruction to clear out, which was never given; very unwillingly, Rosario told me that Ilsa and I would have to continue the radio censoring there for the time being. She did it reluctantly, because our mere presence in the building created a difficulty for her. The veteran correspondents, most of whom had been absent at the time of our leave and dismissal, were too experienced in their trade not to keep on the best terms with the new authorities, but they still sought out Ilsa, as a colleague, to discuss news with her; the censors still asked our advice when nobody observed them; we still took over foreign guests from Rosario, whenever a short-wave broadcast had to be arranged. It was a division between official and intellectual authority which was hard to bear for both sides.

Rosario did her best to fit me into a secure place; she took me to a banquet given by the Civil Governor, expecting me to settle the matter of the radio censorship with him so that he should find a proper office for me, away from the foreign press. I had been to the front of Carabanchel the day before, I believe, and I had been fighting the old sick feeling that rose in me every time the explosion of a shell had shaken the Ministry; my brain was on fire and I bitterly hated the well-behaved crowd moving decorously from the bar to the side tables. They were all so anxious to shed the last odor of the rude, lousy, desperate rabble which had committed so many atrocities and, incidentally, had defended Madrid when the others left it. The Civil Governor was a well-meaning, well-fed Socialist, evidently prepared to meet me half way when Rosario introduced me. But I did not want to be met half way. I gulped down a few glasses of wine, but they neither warmed nor cooled my overheated mind. Instead of explaining about the radio censorship, I burst into a loud, incoherent, desperate harangue, in which I mixed the rats I had seen in a trench of Carabanchel, and the stupid, simple people who believed that the war was fought for their future peace and happiness, with accusations against sated, reactionary bureaucrats. I wanted to be "impossible." I was impossible. I belonged to the impossible, intractable people, and I did not belong to the hedged-in administrators. Whenever I met Ilsa's anguished eyes I shouted more loudly. I felt that I might cry like a hurt child if I stopped shouting. It was soothing to know that I had broken my own neck, and not left it to others.

Then, at a quarter-past two in the morning, I went to the microphone in the blanketed cellar room and described the trench in Carabanchel which our men had wrested from the Civil Guards, the stinking shelters through which Angel had guided me, the rotting carcass of the donkey wedged in between burst sandbags, the rats and lice and the people who fought on down there. The secretary of the Workers' Committee, that acidulous man from the Mancha (I thought of the gaunt, black-dressed women in the market square of La Ronda), smiled thinly and said: "Today you've almost made new literature." My old sergeant blinked and snuffled, and the engineer of the Vallecas control room rang to say that for once I had spoken as if I had guts.

I felt hilarious and triumphant. When we emerged into the starlighted night, its stillness punctuated by shell thuds, our car would not start; and the four of us, the sergeant, Hilario, Ilsa, and I, pushed it down the deserted slope of the Calle de Alcalá, singing the refrain of *La Cucaracha:*

La cucaracha, la cucaracha
Ya no puedo caminar,
Porque la faltan, porque la faltan
Las dos patas de atrás . . .

The poor old cockroach, the poor old cockroach
Can no longer walk or run,
For her two hindlegs, for her two hindlegs
Are forever lost and gone!

There were nights when the success of an ambitious feature broadcast or of a new series of talks in English or Italian made me believe for a short while that we would be allowed to carry on with work which was so clearly useful. Carreño España agreed to cover our basic living expenses and to let the Portuguese Armando eat in the Hotel Victoria as well, since he had no home and found it impossible to cater for himself. Bread was very scarce in Madrid at that time. Thin slices of bully-beef were the best fare the hotel could provide; on the rare occasions there was meat it made me think of the diseased mules and donkeys on the Valencia road: "Meat for Madrid."

But in the Ministry, during the brief hours when we worked there to censor radio talks, the air was laden with tension.

Torres, faithful and worried, reproached us with having missed the right moment to convert ourselves into regular civil servants and employees of the Ministry, with full trade union rights; he began to throw out dark hints of threatening dangers. The sergeant, like a big, clumsy dog, did not know how to express his allegiance; one day, he arrived with a solemn invitation from the Shock Police barracks, took us religiously through every room and workshop there and filled Ilsa's arm with a sheaf of tall snapdragons, yellow, salmon, and scarlet. He, too, warned us of vague and sinister plots. Llizo, the white-haired censor, tried to teach Ilsa the Andalusian way of playing the guitar and apologized for not being able to be with us more often, as this displeased his chief.

George Gordon came, swaggering, and told me—his Spanish was very good—that I might be permitted to keep the radio if I approached the Party in the right way, but he rather thought it was too late; we had played a lone hand too long and this was a thing liable to be misconstrued—or perhaps to be correctly interpreted. Young Pat, the Canadian for whom Ilsa had fought tooth and nail, much against my feeling and advice, at a time when the girl had been jobless and in difficult straits, maneuvered not to see us when we passed her. The Australian wife of our English radio announcer, a young Communist whom Constancia had sent from Valencia at our request, was at least honest; she made it clear that, to her, we were dangerous heretics or lepers. The more experienced among the correspondents were perturbed but not particularly surprised at seeing us in disgrace; things of the sort were happening all the time. Some of them asked Ilsa to do journalistic work for them, which helped us financially, and most of them were more personally friendly than they had ever been. Ernest Hemingway, back in Madrid, said with a worried frown: "I don't understand the whole thing, but I'm very sorry. It seems a lousy mess." He never changed his behavior towards us, which was more than could be said of many lesser people, Spaniards and non-Spaniards. A tight net was closing in on us; we knew it, and had to keep still.

In the end, after weeks of a muffled, intangible warfare, an English correspondent who felt under an obligation to Ilsa—for in the early days she had risked her position to defend him against political accusations which might have had serious consequences for him—told her in so many words what was going on: George Gordon was asking the other journalists not to have any dealings with us because we were suspect and under police supervision. The story he had told uninformed foreign visitors so as to keep them effectively apart from us (it was my impression that Tom Driberg had been one of those warned off) had lurid features: according to it, Ilsa was either a Trotskyist and therefore a spy, or had committed imprudent acts, but anyhow she would shortly be arrested and at the very least expelled from Spain, while I was so deeply entangled with her that during my broadcasts the transmission was cut and I was speaking into a disconnected microphone without knowing it.

Not even the ludicrous character of those details could diminish the reality of our danger. I knew only too well that, if some people belonging to foreign Communist groups wanted to get rid of Ilsa for personal or political reasons, they would join forces with those Spaniards who rightly or wrongly hated me, and through them would find means to make use of the Political Police.

In those days, the shelling of Madrid grew in intensity after a slack period. There was a night when eight hundred shells were reported by the Fire and Rescue Services to have fallen in ten minutes. The bitter juice of nausea never left my mouth; but I did not know whether it was produced by the recurrent nervous shock which I had only partly under control, or by my despairing, helpless anger at the thing that was happening to us. Again I felt ill, afraid of being alone and afraid of being in a crowd, forcing Ilsa to go down to the shelter and hating the shelter because down there you could not hear the sound of explosions, only feel their tremor.

And I did not know how to protect her. She was very quiet, with a fine-drawn face and big, calm eyes which wounded me. Matter-of-fact and in possession of all her cool power of analysis as she was, I saw her stretched on the rack. But she did not say so. That was the worst.

All her friends tried to show her that she was not alone. Torres brought a young couple to keep her company in the evenings, a captain in a Madrid regiment and Luisa, his wife, organizer of the district branch of the Anti-Fascist Women's League. The girl, lively and eager to learn, was happy to speak to another woman without the undercurrent of envy and jealousy which poisoned her friendship with Spanish girls of her age, and Ilsa was glad to help her by answering and listening. Luisa had organized a sewing and mending workshop at the regimental headquarters and suffered tortures when she saw her husband flirting with a pretty girl there. She was caught between the new rules of conduct and the old, half thinking that, as a male, her man had to play the game with other females and half hoping that he and she might be complete friends and lovers. The old women of her tenement house told her that her husband did not love her, since she was allowed to go out alone to her meetings in the evenings; and Luisa never knew whether they were not somehow right. "But I can tell you—a Spanish woman would try to take him from me—I'm sure he loves me. And he wants me to work with him. It does happen. Arturo loves you, doesn't he?" And she looked hopefully at Ilsa.

In the empty afternoons, Ilsa played songs for the hotel waiters and for me. She had an untrained, husky voice, deep and soft when she did not strain it, and I liked her singing Schubert. But the Anarchists among the waiters were happy when she played their fighting song, after the Republican anthem and the Internationale. When we sat in the dining room, the waiters brought us their stories about the newcomers. I remember an American delegation which caused a stir because one of the women —the humorist Dorothy Parker—sat at table in a cyclamen-colored hat shaped like a sugar loaf, surely the only hat worn in Madrid that day. The waiter came and whispered: "What d'you think's the matter with her so that she can't take the thing off? Perhaps her head is shaped like a cucumber. . . ."

But the days were long. The radio work Ilsa still had to do could not fill them, nor did it exhaust her energy. She began to translate some of the talks I had written; she collected propaganda material; she still furnished the many journalists who came to see her with sidelights on events or with a vision of political developments. It seemed impossible for her not to exert this intellectual influence in some form or other, but it recoiled on her. Cut off from the censorship, shunned by those who were afraid of catching the infectious disease of disfavor, she still had a hold on foreign propaganda from Madrid which remained no secret.

Torres brought me a message from a friend who was a Shock Police captain in the political branch of the police: he offered me a bodyguard, one of his own young men, to watch over Ilsa because otherwise she might be arrested on some pretext and taken for a ride. The captain, whom I then met for the first time, was a Communist; the young policeman, who from that day accompanied Ilsa when she went out alone, and stood on guard outside the hotel when she was indoors, had also joined the Communist Party. Both appeared deeply incensed at the thought that by means of complicated intrigues, "a few Foreigners and a few fascist-minded bureaucrats," as they put it, were trying to harm somebody who had passed the great test of November 1936 in Madrid, whether as a member of the Party or not. It was curious to see how the growing dislike those men felt for "interfering foreigners" melted away in her case, because they were bound to her by the overpowering common experience of the early defense of Madrid.

It was so bitter having to accept the bodyguard that it did not bear discussion. It was worse to think of the possibility which we were trying to forestall. I fought not to think of it; I could not longer talk openly to Ilsa, because I could not let her see my whole fear. And she kept quiet, quieter even than before. Anger and hot despair choked me. When she walked off with young Pablo, the guard, talking about John Strachey's book on Fascism which she had loaned him in the new Spanish translation, I felt easy in some part of my mind. He was willing to fight for her. But then it all came back, the whole cruel senselessness of it.

What could I do? I tried to do something. I went to Miaja; but he only explained that nobody had anything against me personally, while there were people who had their knife into Ilsa, and I would doubtless be promoted and protected if I were no longer mixed up with her. Further he did not dare to go openly. I went to see Antonio, my old friend, who was by then a great man in the Provincial Secretariat of the Communist Party. He was profoundly embarrassed and muttered something about the time I had kept him hidden in my flat to save him from prosecution. He was still my friend, so—frankly, why had I obtained a divorce? Was it necessary? I had always arranged my private life before. It wasn't a good thing for somebody recommended by the Party for an important post such as the censorship. And as to that foreign woman—he didn't know anything officially, but he had heard that some of the German comrades, or Austrian—anyhow, people who ought to know—considered her a kind of a Trotskyist, although it could not be proved because she had been too clever to commit any false move inside Spain. That was it, she was too clever for safety. I had been taken in by her. I ought to leave her; after all, she was only my mistress.

I asked him whether this was the official opinion of the Communist Party; he denied it anxiously, it was only his friendly advice to me. I sent him to hell, and was glad that I was able not to hit him. Later I realized that he had been bewildered, unhappy, and trying to be helpful in his stupid way, but at the time I did not think so.

Up till then I had still found my refuge in the talks I broadcast night after night. In them I forgot the personal side of the matters which burned in my brain, and spoke for the people I met at Serafín's, in the streets, in the shops, in the little park of the Plaza de Santa Ana where not even the shells drove away the lovers, the old women, and the sparrows. But when the nights turned cool, on one of the first days of October, a man with a written instruction from the Valencia Propaganda Ministry was waiting for me in the office: he was the new radio commissioner and censor. And he was a German called Albin, very Prussian to my eyes, something like a Puritan inquisitor to judge by the expression of his bony face. To Ilsa he was barely civil; he just listened to her report on the foreign broadcasts which were scheduled, and turned away. His Spanish was halting and bare, but correct. Would I submit my next talk to him, please? I did, and he passed it. I broadcast two more before I asked him whether he expected me to go on. If he had said yes, I might have done it because my heart was in the work. But he told me coldly that it had been agreed to drop the talks by the "Unknown Voice of Madrid."

Some days later, two police agents came to search our room while Ilsa was still in bed. Pablo, her guard, came up at once and smartly told them that his department would see to it that we received fair treatment; they were guaranteeing us. The agents had brought along a sallow, gangling German boy who had to translate every scrap of paper written in French or German; while he was doing so he cast agonized looks at us, twisting his thin arms and legs in pitiful embarrassment. The documents which illustrated mine and Ilsa's range of work during the first year of the siege seemed to impress and disconcert the agents. They took some of my manuscripts, most of our letters, all photographs, and my copy of a Mexican fable—*Rin-Rin-Renacuajo,* the young tadpole, a poem which had pleased me when I heard it during the visit of a delegation of Mexican intellectuals—because President Azaña had mentioned "toads croaking in their pond" in a recent speech and the fable might contain a hidden political meaning. They also took a copy of Dos Passos's *Forty-Second Parallel,* signed for us by the author, because he had declared himself in favor of the Catalan P.O.U.M. and Anarchists, and this was a suspect possession. They confiscated my pistol and small arms permit. But then they were at a loss what to do next. The denunciation they were following up had hinted at dark conspiracies plotted by Ilsa, but they had found her record impeccable, our papers all to her credit, and me an almost exemplary Republican. Above all, they did not want trouble with another police group. They looked at Pablo, looked at us, and said they would have lunch with us downstairs. Then they shook hands and left. The deadly cloud had lifted. The anti-climax made us laugh. It was no longer likely that the police would be used to get rid of Ilsa. I had lodged a sharp complaint against the denouncers, not sparing the man whom I suspected behind the move. At lunch, while we were sitting in amity with the police agents, I had seen George Gordon's face flushed and twitching. A couple of days later he made a movement as though to greet us, but we overlooked it.

I wanted to be merry. I took Ilsa round the corner to the Andalusian bar, Villa Rosa, where the old waiter Manolo greeted me as a lost son, examined her thoughtfully, and then told her that I was a rake, but not a genuine rake, and that she was the right woman to cope with me; he drank a little glass of Manzanilla with us, tremulously, because the war had made him very old. He did not get enough food. When I let him have some tins given us by a friend in the International Brigades, he was so humbly grateful that I could have cried. In the evening we went to Serafín's and plunged into the warm welcome of the cronies. Torres, Luisa, and her husband came with us, gabbling with pleasure. They thought that now our troubles were over and that soon we would do work in Madrid again.

But Agustín, who had staunchly visited us every day, though it could do him no good with his boss Rosario, told me bluntly that we ought to leave Madrid. As long as we stayed on, certain people would resent our very existence. Intrigues might not always go through official channels, and we could not walk about for good with a bodyguard. Moreover, I was going crazy, in his opinion.

I felt in my bones that he was right. But I was not yet ready to leave Madrid. I was tied to it with hurting, quivering nerve-strings. I was writing a story about Angel. If they did not let me broadcast any more, I had to talk through print. I believed I could do it. My very first story (the story of the militiaman who made a fly his pet) had been printed, incongruously enough, in the *Daily Express,* and the fee had overwhelmed me, accustomed as I was to the rates of pay of Spanish journalism. I realized that the story had been published mainly because Delmer had liked it and provided a witty headline and caption, such as: "This story was written under shellfire by the Madrid Censor—who lost his inhibitions about writing by censoring our dispatches." All the same, my first piece of simple story-telling had gone out to people who, perhaps, would through it get a glimpse of the mind of that poor brute, the Miliciano. I wanted to go on; but what I had to say had its roots in Madrid. I would not let them drive me away, and I could not go before I had cleared the red fog of anger out of my brain. It swept me, together with the relief that she was alive and with me, every time I watched Ilsa. All my submerged violence rose when I saw her still bound to her rack, still lashed by the ugliness of the thing which people of her own creed were inflicting on her, and still quiet.

The man who helped me then, as he had helped me through the evil weeks that went before, was a Catholic priest, and of all those I met in our war he commands my deepest respect and love: Don Leocadio Lobo.

I do not remember how we first came to talk to each other. Father Lobo, too, lived in the Hotel Victoria, and soon after we had moved in he became a regular guest at our table, together with Armando. The mutual confidence between him and Ilsa was instantaneous and strong; I felt at once the great attraction of a man who had suffered and still believed in human beings with a great and simple faith. He knew, because I said so, that I did not consider myself a Catholic any more, and he knew that I was divorced, living in what his Church called "sin" with Ilsa and intending to marry her as soon as she had her divorce. I did not spare him violent outbursts against the political clergy in league with the "powers of darkness," and against the stultifying orthodoxy I had come to hate in my schooldays. Nothing of all this seemed to impress him or to affect his attitude to us, which was that of a candid, detached friend.

He wore no cassock, but a somewhat shiny dark suit. His strong, regular features would have made him an attractive man, had they not been deeply furrowed by his thought and struggle; his face had a stamp of inwardness which set him apart even in his frequent moments of expansion. He was one of those people who make you feel that they only say what is their own truth and do not make themselves accomplices of what they believe to be a lie. He seemed to me a reincarnation of Father Joaquín, the Basque priest who had been the best friend of my boyhood. Curiously enough the origins of both were alike. Father Lobo, like Father Joaquín, was the son of simple country folk, of a mother who had borne many children and worked tirelessly all her life. He, too, had been sent to the seminary with the help of the local gentry because he had been a bright boy at school, and because his parents were glad to see him escape from grinding poverty. He, too, had left the seminary not with the ambition of becoming a prelate, but with that of being a Christian priest at the side of those who were hungry and thirsty for bread and justice.

His history was well known in Madrid. Instead of staying in a smart, influential parish, he chose a parish of poor workers, rich in blasphemies and rebellion. They did not blaspheme less for his sake, but they loved him because he belonged to the people. At the outbreak of the rebellion he had taken the side of the people, the side of the Republican Government, and he had continued in his ministry. During the wildest days of August and September he went out at night to hear the Confession of whoever demanded it, and to give Communion. The only concession he made to circumstances was that he doffed his cassock so as not to provoke rows. There was a famous story that one night two Anarchist Milicianos called at the house where he was staying, with their rifles cocked and a car waiting at the door. They asked for the priest who was living there. His hosts denied that there was one. They insisted, and Father Lobo came out of his room. "Yes, there is a priest, and it's me. What's up?"

"All right, come along with us, but put one of those Hosts of yours in your pocket."

His friends implored him not to go; they told the Anarchists that Lobo's loyalty was vouched for by the Republican Government, that they simply would not allow him to leave, that they would rather call in the police. In the end, one of the Anarchists stamped on the floor and shouted:

"Oh hell, nothing will happen to him! If you must know, the old woman, my mother, is dying and doesn't want to go to the other world without confessing to one of these buzzards. It's a disgrace for me, but what else could I do but fetch him?"

And Father Lobo went out in the Anarchists' car, into one of those gray dawns when people were being shot against the wall.

Later on he went for a month to live with the militiamen in the front line. He came back exhausted and deeply shaken. In my hearing he rarely spoke of his experiences in the trenches. But one night he exclaimed: "What brutes—God help us—what brutes, but what men!"

He had to fight his own bitter mental struggle. The deepest hurt to him was not the fury vented against churches and priests by maddened, hate-filled, brutalized people, but his knowledge of the guilt of his own caste, the clergy, in the existence of that brutality, and in the abject ignorance and misery at the root of it. It must have been infinitely hard for him to know that princes of his Church were doing their level best to keep his people subjected, that they were blessing the arms of the generals and overlords, and the guns that shelled Madrid.

The Government had given him a task in the Ministry of Justice which was anything but simple: he had come to Madrid to investigate cases of hardship among the clergy, and he had to face the fact that some of the priests whose killing by the "Reds" had been heralded and duly exploited came out of their hiding, safe and sound, and demanded help.

I needed a man to whom I could speak out of the depth of my mind.

Don Leocadio was most human and understanding. I knew that he would not answer my outcry with admonitions or canting consolation. So I poured out all the turgid thoughts which clogged my brain. I spoke to him of the terrible law which made us hurt others without wanting to hurt them. There was my marriage and its end; I had hurt the woman with whom I did not share my real life and I had hurt our children because I hated living together with their mother. I inflicted the final pain when I had found my wife, Ilsa. I told him that Ilsa and I belonged together, complementing each other, without superiority of one over the other, without knowing why, without wanting to know, because it was the simple truth of our lives. But this new life which we could neither reject nor escape meant pain, because we could not be happy together without causing pain to others.

I spoke to him of the war, loathsome because it set men of the same people against each other, a war of two Cains. A war in which priests had been shot on the outskirts of Madrid and other priests were setting the seal of their blessing on the shooting of poor laborers, brothers of Don Leocadio's own father. Millions like myself who loved their people and its earth were destroying, or helping to destroy, that earth and their own people. And yet, none of us had the right to remain indifferent or neutral.

I had believed, I still believed, in a new free Spain of free people. I had wanted it to come without bloodshed, by work and good will. What could we do if this hope, this future was being destroyed? We had to fight for it. Had we to kill others? I knew that the majority of those who were fighting with arms in hand, killing or dying, did not think about it, but were driven by the forces unleashed or by their blind faith. But I was forced to think, for me this killing was a sharp and bitter pain which I could not forget. When I heard the battle noise I saw only dead Spaniards on both sides. Whom should I hate? Oh yes, Franco and Juán March and their generals and puppets and wirepullers, the privileged people over there. But then I would rather hate that God who gave them the callousness which made them kill, and who punished me with the torture of hating any killing and who let women and children first suffer from rickets and starvation wages, and then from bombs and shells. We were caught in a monstrous mechanism, crushed under the wheels. And if we rebelled, all the violence and all the ugliness was turned against us, driving us to violence.

It sounded in my ears as though I had thought and said the same things as a boy. I excited myself to a fever, talking on and on in rage, protest, and pain. Father Lobo listened patiently, only saying sometimes: "Now slowly, wait." Then he talked to me for days. It may be that the answers I gave myself in the quiet hours on the balcony, while I stared at the

Church of San Sebastian cut in two by a bomb, were fused in my memory with the words Father Lobo said to me. It may be that insensibly I made him into the other "I" of that endless inner dialogue. But this is how I remember what he said:

"Who are you? What gives you the right to set yourself up as a universal judge? You only want to justify your own fear and cowardice. You are good, but you want everybody else to be good too, so that being good doesn't cost you any trouble and is a pleasure. You haven't the courage to preach what you believe in the middle of the street, because then you would be shot. And as a justification for your fear you put all the fault on to the others. You think you're decent and clean-minded, and you try to tell me and yourself that you are, and that whatever happens to the others is their fault, and whatever pain happens to you as well. That's a lie. It is your fault.

"You've united yourself with this woman, with Ilsa, against everything and everybody. You go with her through the streets and call her your wife. And everybody can see that it's true, that you are in love with each other and that together you are complete. None of us would dare to call Ilsa your mistress because we all see that she is your wife. It is true that you and she have done harm to others, to the people who belong to you, and it is right that you should feel pain for it. But do you realize that you have scattered a good seed as well? Do you realize that hundreds of people who had despaired of finding what is called Love now look at you and learn to believe that it exists and is true, and that they may hope?

"And this war, you say it's loathsome and useless. I don't. It is a terrible, barbarous war with countless innocent victims. But you haven't lived in the trenches like me. This war is a lesson. It has torn Spain out of her paralysis, it has torn the people out of their houses where they were being turned into mummies. In our trenches illiterates are learning to read and even to speak, and they learn what brotherhood among men means. They see that there exists a better world and life, which they must conquer, and they learn too, that they must conquer it not with the rifle but with their will. They kill Fascists, but they learn the lesson that you win wars not by killing, but by convincing people. We may lose this war— but we shall have won it. They, too, will learn that they may rule us, but not convince us. Even if we are defeated, we will be stronger at the end of this than ever we were because the will has come alive.

"We all have our work to do, so do yours instead of talking about the world which doesn't follow you. Suffer pain and sorrow and stick it out, but don't shut yourself up and run round in circles within yourself. Talk and write down what you think you know, what you have seen and thought, tell it honestly and speak the truth. Don't produce programs which you don't believe in, and don't lie. Say what you have thought and seen, and let the others hear and read you, so that they are driven to tell their truth, too. And then you'll lose that pain of yours."

In the clear, chill nights of October it seemed to me sometimes as though I were conquering my fear and cowardice, but I found it very hard to write down what I thought. It is still difficult. I found out, however, that I could write honestly and with truth of what I had seen, and that I had seen much. Father Lobo exclaimed when he saw one of my stories: "What a barbarian you are! But go on, it's good for you and us."

One evening he knocked at our door and invited us to go with him to see a surprise. In his small room was one of his brothers, a quiet workman, and a farm laborer from his village. I knew that his people brought him wine for Mass and wine for his table whenever they could, and I thought he wanted to invite us to a glass of red wine. But he took me into his bathroom. An enormous turkey was standing awkwardly on the tiles, hypnotized by the electric light. When the countryman had gone, we spoke of those simple people who brought him the best thing they had, not caring whether it was absurd or not to dump a live turkey in the bathroom of a city hotel.

"It isn't easy for us to understand them," Father Lobo said. "If you do, it's a basis for art like Breughel's or like Lorca's. Yes, Lorca's. Listen." He took the slim war edition of the *Romancero Gitano* and started reading:

> *And I took her down to the river,*
> *Thinking she was a maiden,*
> *But she had a husband. . . .*

He read on with his strong, manly voice, not slurring over the words of naked physical love, only saying: "This is barbarian, but it's tremendous." And he seemed to me more of a man, and more of a priest of men and God, than ever.

In the worst weeks, when it took some courage to be seen with us, he spent long hours at our table, aware that he gave us moral support. He knew more about the background of our tangled story than we ourselves, but he never gave away what he had heard from others. Yet I did not dream of doubting his word when, after the campaign had passed its peak, he suddenly said: "Now listen to the truth, Ilsa. They don't want you here. You know too many people and you put others in the shade. You know too much and you are too intelligent. We aren't used to intelligent women yet. You can't help being what you are, so you must go; and you must go away with Arturo because he needs you and you belong together. In Madrid you cannot do any good any more, except by keeping quiet as you do. But that won't be enough for you, you will want to work. So go away."

"Yes, I know," she said. "The only thing I can do for Spain now is not to let people outside turn my case into a weapon against the Communists—not because I love the Communist Party, for I don't, even when I work with Communists, but because it would at the same time be a weapon against our Spain and against Madrid. That's why I can't move a finger for myself, and even have to ask my friends not to make a fuss. It's funny. The only thing I can do is to do nothing."

She said it very dryly. Father Lobo looked at her and answered: "You must forgive us. We are in your debt."

Thus Father Lobo convinced us that we had to leave Madrid. When I accepted it, I wanted it to be done quickly so as not to feel it too much. It was again a gray, foggy November day. Agustín and Torres saw us off. The Shock Police lorry, with hard loose boards for benches, rattled through the suburbs. There were few shells that morning.

Father Lobo had sent us to his mother in a village near Alicante. In his letter he had asked her to help me, his friend, and my wife Ilsa; he did not want to bewilder his mother, he said, and he had put down the essential truth. When I stood before the stout old woman with gray hair who could not read—her husband deciphered her son's letter for her—and looked into her plain, lined face, I realized gratefully Don Leocadio's faith in us. His mother was a very good woman.

9. Face to Face

THERE was no war, nothing but blue hills, the moon-sickle of a wide, shallow beach, and blue water. The cart track alongside the coast was carpeted with deep, loose sand. Where the ground became firm and the sea shells rare, small wooden shacks, half boarding houses and half taverns, had sprung up; for in peace time San Juán de la Playa had been a holiday resort. A mile further on was the village where Father Lobo's parents and his ailing sister lived a quiet life which drew its warmth from the sons and brothers somewhere at work in the war. For the mother, all life centered in her son the priest.

They had sent us to their friend Juán, the owner of one of the shacks and the most famous cook of rice dishes between Alicante and Valencia. He let me have a small room open to the sea wind and gave me the run of his house and kitchen. I learned how to make *paella* from him. Ilsa arranged with Juán to give lessons to his two girls, which permitted us to live very cheaply. We had little money left. Secretly I always suspected Juán of hoping that I was a hunted aristocrat in disguise, for despite his lukewarm Republicanism he hankered after the splendor of "quality" to grace his table and give his masterly *paellas* their due.

The November days were hot, still, and sunny on the coast of Alicante. In the afternoons, when the water began to chill, we let ourselves dry in the warm sand and watched the tide recede in gentle ripples. Sometimes I laid lines, but I never caught any fish. When the slow dusk crept up from the sea, we—and the village children—walked along the line of froth left by the lapping water, to hunt the minute crabs which betray their presence only by the tiniest of eddies in the wet, sleeked sand.

I began to sleep at night. By day, Juán let me work in his dining room or in his vine bower facing the sea. Few people came past, and the only other boarder was out, working in an aircraft factory in Alicante. I began to think out a book I wanted to write, my first book, primitive stories of primitive people at war, such as I had woven into my radio talks. But first I had to repair the small, battered little typewriter which Sefton Delmer had thrown away as scrap metal after he had learned how to type on it. I had asked him whether he could let me have it, and he had roared with laughter at the idea that it could still be used. Now it was our only wealth, but it did not yet work. I hated having to write by hand; it was too slow to catch up with my thoughts.

On the scrubbed deal table, I dismantled the typewriter, spread out its thousand-and-one pieces, cleaned them one by one, and put them together without hurry. It was good work. I seemed to hear my Uncle José saying:

"When I was twenty I started writing. At that time only rich people had the steel nibs you use. The rest of us had quills, and before learning how to write I had to learn how to cut and trim quills with a penknife. But they were too fine for my fingers, so I made myself a thick pen out of a cane."

I, too, had to make myself a pen before writing my first book, and though mine was a far more complicated pen than Uncle José's, I, too, was only about to learn how to write.

In those first days I was happy sitting in the sun, wrapped in the light, scent, and sound of the sea, reconstructing and healing a complicated mechanism (how I love machinery!), my brain confined within the maze of fragile bolts and screws, and the vision of a book, my first book, gaining shape at the back of my mind.

In a silvery night filled with the song of crickets and frogs I heard the heavy drone of planes coming near and waning, and coming near again. There were no more than three dull thuds, the last of which shook our flimsy house. The next day we heard that one of the bombs dropped by the Capronis—I had seen one of them glinting in the light of the moon like a silver moth—had fallen in Alicante, in the middle of a cross-road, laying flat half a dozen mud-built houses and killing a dozen poor workers who lived there. The second bomb had fallen in a barren field. The third had fallen in the garden of an old man. It had destroyed his tomato crop and killed nothing but a frog. It made me angry to hear the hefty aircraft mechanic laugh at the idea of the dead frog. The wounded garden caught hold of me. I could not conceive that a wound to any living thing was a matter of indifference. The whole war was there in the trees and plants torn by a bomb, in the frog killed by blast. This was the first story I wrote on the cured typewriter.

In the fourth week of our stay in San Juán de la Playa, I was awakened by a loud knock at our door; I opened, had a glimpse of Juán's scared face, and then two men brushed past him and filled the door frame: "Police. Here are our papers. Is this lady an Austrian called Ilsa Kulcsar? Yes? Will you please dress and come outside." It was before sunrise and the sea was leaden. We looked at each other, said nothing, and dressed in haste. Outside, the two police agents asked Ilsa: "Have you a husband in Barcelona?"

"No," she said, astonished.

"No? Here we have an order to take you to Barcelona to your husband Leopold Kulcsar."

"If the name is Leopold Kulcsar, then he is indeed my legal husband from whom I have separated. You have no right to force me to go to him —if he really is in Barcelona!"

"Well, we know nothing except that we have the order to take you with us, and if you don't want to go we have no other choice but to declare you arrested. Will you come with us voluntarily?"

Before Ilsa had time to answer, I said: "If you take her with you, you will have to take me as well."

"And who are you?"

I explained and showed them my papers. They went away to discuss the new problem. When they came back into the room, one of them started: "We have no order . . ."

Ilsa interrupted: "I will come with you, but only if he accompanies me."

The second agent grunted: "Let's take him, too; maybe we ought to arrest him in any case."

They gave us just enough time to settle our account with Juán, to ask him to take care of the things we left behind, and to pack a small suit-case. Then they hustled us into the car which was waiting outside.

"Don't worry so much," said Ilsa. "As it's Poldi who's started the hue and cry after me, it must be some kind of stupid misunderstanding."

But it was she who did not understand. I had read the stamp on the agents' papers: S.I.M.—*Servicio de Inteligencia Militar,* Military Intelligence Service. That story about Ilsa's husband was a blind; the trick which had miscarried in Madrid was being tried through another, more powerful agency, in a place where we had no outside help whatsoever. The only thing which astonished me was that they had not searched us. In my pocket I still carried the small pistol Agustín had given me on our departure from Madrid.

They took us along the coastal road to Valencia. After the first half-hour, the two agents began to ask questions, probing into our affairs with a certain guarded sympathy. One of them said he was a Socialist. We discussed the war. They asked me where we might get a decent lunch and I suggested Miguel's place by the Rock of Ifach. To my astonishment, they took us there. Miguel gave them a sour look, watched Ilsa's face and saw it serene, frowned, and asked me what he could cook for us. Then he prepared fried chicken and rice, and sat down with us. It was an unbelievably normal meal. As we slowly drank the last glass of wine, one of the agents said: "Don't you ever listen to the radio? For days there's been a message for this foreign comrade to get in touch with her husband in Barcelona." I wondered what we should have done, had we heard it. But whoever listens to police messages at the end of news bulletins?

Mellowed by the sun and the meal, they took us to the car again. Miguel shook hands with us and said: *"Salud y suerte!"* Good luck!

I dozed, exhausted by my own thoughts and by the impossibility of talking with Ilsa. She enjoyed the journey, and when we came to an orange grove she made the agents stop the car so that she could pluck a branch with fruits graded green, yellow, and golden. She took it with her to Barcelona. I could not understand her gaiety. Did she really fail to see her danger? Or, if that legal husband of hers was behind the whole thing, did she fail to see that he might want to take her away from Spain by force and—perhaps—get rid of me for good?

Suddenly, when it was near sunset, the more burly of the agents said: "If we come to Valencia before dark they'll saddle us with some other assignment. Let's go round the longer way by the Albufera, the foreign comrade will like it, too."

I sat stiffly and said nothing. The Albufera is the lagoon in which the corpses of killed people had been dumped in the chaotic and violent days of 1936. Its name made me shiver. Recklessly, I put my hand in my pocket and cocked my pistol. The moment they ordered us out of the car I would fire through my coat, and we would not be the only ones to die. I watched the tiniest movement of our guardians. But one of them half dozed and the other chatted with Ilsa, pointing out water-fowl, rice fields, fishermen's nets, explaining about the small villages and the size of the wide, shallow, reed-grown lake. And the car went on at an even pace. We had already passed several spots which would have been excellently suitable for a swift execution without witness. If they wanted to get it done, they would have to hurry up. This was the far end of the Albufera.

I set the safety-catch and let the pistol drop to the bottom of my pocket. When I pulled out my hand, it was cramped and I trembled. "Are you tired?" asked Ilsa.

It was dark when we arrived in Valencia and were taken up to the S.I.M. office. We were left waiting in a fusty ante-room, with people whispering behind our backs. Officers telephoned to Barcelona, where their head office had recently moved together with the Government; then they came to fire abrupt questions at us, and disappeared again. In the end one of them said, wonderingly: "They say you're to go to Barcelona with her. But I can't understand what the whole thing's about. Now, you explain to me." I tried to do so, briefly and noncommittally. They stared at me in distrust. I sensed that they would have liked to keep us in Valencia for investigation; but when I asked whether we were detained or free, I received the answer: "Free—only we've to keep you under observation since they want you so urgently."

In the small hours of the morning we left Valencia in another car. The agent who had taken us past the Albufera said good-by and regretted that he was not sent on with us: he had considered it almost a holiday. But when I was seated, I noticed that our small attaché case was nowhere to be seen, although I had asked for it and been told that it was waiting for us in the car. I went back to the office, I asked the drivers, but everybody disclaimed any knowledge. The case contained my manuscripts and most of the papers which documented our work in Madrid, as far as they were left to us. This meant that we had lost our most important weapon, which we might need bitterly in Barcelona, now the seat of the Government offices, of new bureaucrats who knew nothing of us, and of our old adversaries.

When the car stopped at the Barcelona headquarters of the S.I.M., it was so early that the chiefs had not yet arrived. Nobody knew what to do with us. For safety's sake, we were taken to still another ante-room with an apathetic guard at the door. Ilsa was certain that things would clear up quickly. I did not know what to think. Were we, or were we not arrested? We spent our time discussing the building, too small to be a palace, too big to be the house of a wealthy bourgeois, with showy tiles in the courtyard and deep-piled carpets in the corridors, old braziers and modern colored-glass windows showing a coat-of-arms.

A man entered brusquely. Ilsa rose and cried: "Poldi!" He whipped off his hat, threw me a somber glance and kissed Ilsa's hand in an exaggeratedly ceremonious and courtly gesture. She said a few sharp words in German and he drew back, almost reeling in astonishment. Later she told me that she had asked him: "Why did you have me arrested?" and that this accusation had stunned him.

Only then did she introduce us to each other, in French, saying no more than the names. I nodded. He bowed from the hips, a theatrical bow. We did not shake hands or speak.

Her legal husband: deep-set, brown-ringed eyes stared at me, feverish and intense. He had a wide, broad, powerfully domed forehead, made still higher by his incipient baldness; his head sat well on strong shoulders, he was slim, slightly younger and slightly shorter than I. Good-looking in his way. His jaws rigidly clamped on an embittered mouth whose upper lip had a smeared outline. His thinning hair looked dead. He took stock of me as I took stock of him.

Then he turned to her and sat down by her side on the velvet-covered bench. The guard had saluted him and disappeared. The three of us were alone. While the other two started to talk in German, I went to the window and looked down into the courtyard, first through a yellow, then through a blue, and finally through a red pane. The sunlit walls and the shadows under the arches assumed with each color new, unexpected depths and perspectives. For a few minutes I thought of nothing at all.

It was difficult for my Spanish mind to assimilate and to gauge the situation. This man had never been real to me before. Ilsa was my wife. But now he, her legal husband, was in the room, talking to her, and I had to keep my nerves quiet. How was he going to act, why had he come to Spain, why had he tracked us down through the S.I.M., why did the guard salute him so respectfully?

Both were talking in anger, though their voices were still low. Sharp question, sharp answer: they were disagreeing.

The wall opposite threw the warmth of the sun back into my face. The chill which had weighed me down melted away and left nothing behind but a great weariness, the fatigue of a sleepless night and of a twenty-four-hours' journey—God, what a journey! The room was heavy and drowsy with curtains, rugs, and tapestries. I had no share in their unintelligible talk. What I needed was coffee, brandy, and a bed.

Had that man come to claim his wife and take her away? I had the stubble of two days on my chin and felt my skin sticking to my bones in tiredness and tautness. I must have had a villainous face.

What will you do if he tries to take her away?—The question is whether she wants to go, and she doesn't.—Yes, but he is her legal husband, he is a foreigner who can claim the help of the Spanish authorities in taking his wife away; they might refuse her a further stay in Spain— and what then?—We would protest.—To whom, and on what legal grounds? I had not been able to protect her from persecution even in Madrid.

I tried to argue it out in an articulate dialogue with myself. But then their voices were no longer sharp. She was dominating him, convincing him with that warm voice which was so soothing after the icy edge it had before. At this hour the sun would already have warmed the sea on the beach of San Juán. To dip into the shallow water and then sleep in the sand!

Ilsa rose and came towards me: "We'll go now."

"Where?"

"To Poldi's hotel. I'll explain later."

The guards saluted when we left the building. Ilsa walked between him and me. Again, he started to speak in German, but she cut him short: "We'll speak French now, won't we?" We made the rest of the way in silence. The hotel hall was full of chattering people, among them half a dozen journalists we knew. I was very conscious of my state of squalor. Poldi took us up to his room and told Ilsa where to find his washing and shaving things; he did not speak directly to me. A huge blue trunk stood in the middle of the room, and he showed it off to Ilsa, opening drawers and compartments and pulling out the rod with the clothes hangers. It was all very complicated and did not work well. When he left us alone, Ilsa said in a motherly tone, which angered me:

"The poor boy, it's always the same with him. Any silly new luxury gadget makes him as happy as a child with a new toy."

I told her gruffly that I was not interested in imitation trunks, and showered questions on her. While we were washing and brushing, she explained. He was in Barcelona on some official mission or other, not yet understood by her; but he had also come to take her away from Spain, forcibly, if she was not willing to go. The reason was that he had heard not only rumors of the political campaign against her, but also stories about me which made him anxious for her fate: that I was a confirmed drunkard, with a litter of illegitimate children, and that I was dragging her down into the gutter with me. He had indeed intended to use his legal standing as her husband to take her away against her will—just as I had imagined—not under the illusion that she would resume her married life with him, but so as to save her and give her the chance of recuperating in sane, peaceful surroundings. The mode of our detention in San Juán de la Playa was due to the fact that he had been unable to get our address in Madrid (an odd thing, as several people had it, both officially and privately) and thus been driven to enlist the help of radio and police; and the S.I.M. policemen seemed only to have acted according to their lights. Apparently he had dropped his original plans after seeing her calm, self-possessed, clear-eyed, and happier than he had ever known her, in spite of the obvious difficulties. Now he wanted to discuss things with me and to help us. She ended triumphantly: "Here you are, with all your nightmares! I told you he would never play me a dirty trick."

I was not yet convinced; I knew the force of possessive instincts too well. But when the three of us sat together at lunch and I saw more of the man, I began to change my mind. Ilsa was so perfectly natural in her behavior to him, so friendly and unselfconscious, that he lost the demonstrative arrogance toward me, against which I would have had no defense since he had every right to protect his own pride as best he could. I saw him twisted and straightforward at the same time. A small incident broke the ice between us. We had no cigarettes and tobacco was almost unobtainable in Barcelona. Poldi demanded a packet of cigarettes from the waiter, in an imperious tone which drew nothing but a smile and shrug from the man. It was the overbearing accent of a young boy who does not know how to give orders and tips, and is afraid that the waiter might see through his varnish of worldliness. I intervened, chatted with the man, and in the end we had cigarettes, good food, and good wine. This impressed Poldi beyond measure, so much that I could guess at his adolescent dreams and his difficult youth; he said wistfully: "You seem to have a knack which I never possessed." I realized how much his lordly manner was a flimsy armor to cover an inner insecurity and lack of poise.

Yet now that he had accepted me as a man, he was simple and dignified in talking to me about Ilsa. She was the most important human being in the world to him, but he knew, finally, that he had lost her, at least for this period of his life. He did not want to lose her altogether. She would have her cake and eat it, he said: she would have her life with me, as I seemed to be able to make her happy, and she would keep his devotion and friendship. And if I were to hurt her, I would still have to reckon with him.

Poldi said he would try to arrange a divorce, but it would be extremely difficult for the time being. They were married according to Austrian law, and both fugitives from Fascist Austria. In the meantime, he understood that neither of us was doing any practical work in the war, mainly because we had mismanaged all our official relations. We had been crazy to have done important propaganda work in Madrid, without making sure of the appropriate trappings and emoluments. He had known Ilsa to be a romantic, but he was sorry to find me, too, a romantic. She would have to leave Spain until the campaign against her had died down; though only a few persons were behind it, our bureaucratic quarrels had isolated us and brought us into bad odor. He would help us to get all the necessary papers, both of us, since she would not leave me, and we would find useful work to do outside Spain. In fact, Ilsa was much needed there and he was willing to accept her valuation of me. He realized that he had done us harm by unwittingly entangling us with the S.I.M. which considered everything grist that came to its mill; but he would remove any trace of ambiguity in our situation and recover the papers taken from us.

He tried to do all this the same afternoon. Back at the S.I.M. headquarters Poldi again donned the ostentatious behavior which I had noted and disliked. He was nervous and excited, as though he would soon slide into the depths of depression. He asked one of the S.I.M. chiefs to give us papers to show that the department had nothing against us, even though it had brought us forcibly to Barcelona; but the pallid young man gave him no more than a promise. However, he telephoned an urgent order to Valencia to send on our suitcase with its contents intact, without attempting to gloss over the fact that it had been silently confiscated. Without a paper to show why we were in Barcelona, we would have found no billet; therefore the S.I.M. man said he would send an agent along with us to the Ritz and we would be given a room. He would prefer us to stay there so they would know where to find us. The offer was an order; it demonstrated that, despite Poldi's explanations, the man intended his department to have a thorough look at us, since we had accidentally been brought to their notice. So we went to the Ritz, only recently thrown open to the public, with the red, thick carpets and me-

ticulous ceremony of peacetime but scant food and scanty lighting, and
were given a room opening out into the garden. We had not even toothbrushes with us.

The rest of my day was a jumble of conversations and silences, of waiting and walking alongside the others like a puppet on a string. When
we closed the door of our room behind us that night, we were too exhausted to talk or think, although we knew that we had been pushed onto the threshold of a new stage in our life. This man had said that I was
to leave Spain, to desert from our war, so as to be able to work again. It
sounded crazy and wrong. But I would have to think it out, later, when
things would have resumed their firm shape.

I was too tired to sleep. The balcony door was wide open and a pale
bluish light filled the alien room. My ears labored to identify a faint,
distant purr, and decided that it was the sea. A cock crowed somewhere
in the night and was answered by others, near and strident, distant and
ghostly. Their chain of challenge and counterchallenge seemed unending.

There followed ten unreal days while Poldi was in Barcelona and his
presence dominated our timetable. He spoke to me, he took Ilsa for
walks while I wondered at my absence of any conventional resentment
or jealousy, he arranged meetings with this or that official, diplomat, or
politician, he dragged us along to the S.I.M. headquarters to demand our
safe-conducts. The suitcase had arrived, but we were still without a
paper justifying our arrival in Barcelona. I tried to find my way through
his mind, and my own; I tried to find firm ground under my feet so that
I would be able to stay on and work with my own people; and I had
again to fight my body and nerves whenever the sirens went or a motorcycle engine spluttered in the street.

While Poldi discussed international affairs he fascinated me by his
knowledge and vision. He was convinced that closely knit, revolutionary,
Socialist organizations were the only forces able to fight international
Fascism wherever they met it, and that the most important battlefield
of that war was still the German working class, even while the most important battle was being fought on the Spanish front. He was throwing
all his energies into his work as secretary to Jiménez de Asúa, the Spanish
Minister in Prague, and his friends risked their lives crossing the frontier
to give warning of new bombs and shells being produced in German
factories for intervention in Spain. Yet serving the Spanish Republic was
only part of the greater war and preparation for the bigger battle to come,
the battle in which England and France would be ranged by the side of
Soviet Russia, in spite of their murderous and suicidal game of nonintervention. He told Ilsa bluntly that in his opinion she had deserted from

the main fighting line by submerging herself altogether in the Spanish war and dropping all her work for Austrian and German Socialism. He agreed that she was right in making no effort to mobilize one of her Socialist friends, such as Julius Deutsch or Pietro Nenni, when the political campaign against her became dangerous, because the shabby intrigue might have been magnified into an issue between Socialists and Communists by people inveterately opposed to the collaboration between the two groups, in the necessity of which both Ilsa and he believed.

I listened and marveled; I remembered that he had shown me the revolver he had been prepared to use against me, had he found it necessary to save Ilsa in this way. And then he agreed that she should throw away her life rather than do an imagined harm to a political principle? The two talked so easily, they used the same language, the same abbreviations of thought, the same associations and quotations; I saw them attuned in everything which touched their social and political ideas, while I was left outside, almost hostile to their analytical logic.

Yet there was an evening when Ilsa and Poldi argued on the aim of their Socialism. When she professed her belief in the human individual as the final value, he exclaimed: "I've always felt that our philosophy clashes—you know, this means that we are spiritually divorced." It sounded so high-falutin' to me that I made a silly joke; but then I saw that it had hit him very deeply, and I felt it within myself. In spite of our different logic and language of the mind, I met her where a gulf was between her and Poldi. It was the same as when he said to me: "She is difficult to understand, isn't she?" and I denied it, astonished. It had hit him and made him jealous as no physical fact could have made him jealous. For he had wanted to dominate and possess her, and his hunger for power and possession had destroyed their marriage.

I thought about myself and I found that my life had made me hate power and possession too much to want anything but freedom and spontaneous union. It was here that we clashed, he and she, he and I. He had had much the same proletarian childhood as I, he had hated the world as it was and become a rebel as I. But his hatred of power and possession made him obsessed with it; he had never outgrown the hurts to his self-confidence.

I saw it with pity and aversion on the day when we finally received our safe-conducts from the S.I.M. I had passed an ugly hour. Ordoñez, the young Socialist intellectual who had become chief of the department, had played at interrogation, with an equivocal smile and the cruelty of a weakling; but in the end he had ordered his secretary to prepare the papers at once, and we had them in our hands, eager to go. Poldi was scanning a heap of paper connected with his official mission, material on the foreign leaders of the Catalan P.O.U.M. who had been arrested under the suspicion of an international conspiracy. He spoke to Ordóñez, magniloquently as he was wont to speak within that building, gave an order to one of the agents who stood around, and buried himself in the papers again. The agent brought in a big, lumbering woman, and Poldi interrogated her in a tone which made Ilsa move restlessly in her chair. I too recognized the tone: he heard himself speaking as the great, cold judge— a dangerous ambition. I was pleased that I could answer in the negative when Poldi asked me whether I had ever seen the woman in Madrid.

Then the electric light was cut off. Somebody lighted a candle which threw yellow patches and immense shadows on the walls. The house quivered in its roots; a stick of bombs had fallen. I felt my fingers tremble and fought back the vomit which filled my mouth. Another agent brought in another female prisoner, a small woman with taut, bitter features and the wide, dark eyes of a hunted animal. She went up to Ilsa: "You're Ilse— don't you remember me—twelve years ago in Vienna?" They shook hands, and I felt Ilsa go rigid in her chair; but Poldi began to interrogate, the perfect prosecutor in a revolutionary tribunal, and it seemed shameless for us to stay on. I thought I heard how he made his voice ring in his own ears. He must have dreamed that scene; perhaps he had imagined it when he was imprisoned for his share in the great Austrian strike against the last war, an imaginative, uncertain, and ambitious boy. Now he did what he conceived to be his duty, and the terrible thing was that the power over others gave him pleasure. In the yellow light his eyes were hollow like a skull's.

After we had left the building (and I thought that I never wanted to see it again) he spent a long time explaining to Ilsa why he could no longer consider that woman a Socialist. The details escaped me; I had sympathy neither for the P.O.U.M. nor for their persecution. Poldi might have been right. But however careful and convincing his argument, there was a streak of madness in him. There was in me. But mine was born from the fear and hatred of violence, while his seemed to push him towards a fantastic dream of power. This impression grew in me so much that I did not pay great attention to his plans for Ilsa's and my work abroad. He had no sympathy with my manner of looking at the problems of our war; it seemed only sentimental to him. If he wanted to find work for me, it was as much because it gave him pleasure to have the power of helping me as because he imagined me to be a good propagandist. But I had to find my own way.

Whenever Poldi took us along to his many conversations with young officials of the various Ministries, I tried to assess them. It struck me that most of them were ambitious young men of the upper middle classes who now declared themselves Communists, not, as we had done in Madrid, because to us it meant the party of revolutionary workers, but because it meant joining the strongest group and having a share in its disciplined power. They had leaped over the step of humanist socialism; they were efficient and ruthless. They admired Soviet Russia for its power, not for its promise of a new society, and they chilled me to the bone. I tried to see where I might fit in, because it was torturing to know that nothing of what I had to give was exploited in the war. But the only thing I found to do for myself was to write the book of Madrid which I had planned. I was a has-been.

It was bitterly cold when Poldi left. He looked very ill and was suffering pain; he confessed to a serious stomach complaint rendered worse by his way of living, the late nights, the irregular food, the black coffee and the cognac which he used in the way I knew so well, to whip up his energies. Before going, he spoke again of Ilsa to me: she now looked as she had looked before he had twisted her gaiety and simplicity, and he was glad of it. We would be together often, the three of us, for "if it were not for Ilsa, blast her, you and I would have been friends." I did not believe it, but it was good that he felt so. There was no poisoning bitterness between us.

I was left face to face with myself.

In those dark December days, the air raids on Barcelona multiplied, and in January 1938 they grew worse. The Government troops were attacking on the Aragon Front, and Barcelona was the great supply center. Italian planes had a short way to go from the Balearic Islands. They stopped their engines far out over the sea and glided down over the city, released their bombs, and fled. The first warning was the tremor of a distant bomb, then the electricity was cut off, and much later the sirens sounded. I was back in the clutches of my obsession. I could not stand the bedroom once I woke up. In the street, every confused noise shook me and brought the humiliations of the vomit on me. First I stayed in the hotel hall, listening to the street, looking at the people. Then I discovered the bar in the basement, where I could chat with the waiters and sit under thick walls, and finally I found a small room which was wedged in behind the bar. It was in disuse, and the manager agreed to let me use it for working. There I put my typewriter, and there I worked days and nights, in a feverish excitement bordering on hysteria. When an air raid came I was down in the shelter anyhow and could hide from people; a small grating opening just above the pavement let me listen to the noises outside. I would have liked to sleep down there. I slept in snatches on the plush divan, twisting in nightmares from which I only recovered after drinking a glass of wine. I drank much and smoked much. I was afraid of going mad.

When I could work no longer because the words became blurred, I went out of my cubicle into the bar. There was a motley collection of Spanish officers and officials, of journalists, foreign and Spanish, of the Government's foreign guests and of international racketeers, with a sprinkling of wives and elegant tarts. The noise, the drinks, the discussions and the sight of people saved me from the deadly lethargy which fell on me as soon as I stopped working.

Sometimes, but rarely, I made myself go out and speak to people I knew in some department of the war machine. I still hoped that I might be useful and cure myself within Spain. Yet men such as Frades who had worked with me in the November days of Madrid—how far away they were in this town of business and bureaucracy, where the heart of the fight had grown cold!—told me that it was all very sad, but the best thing for me was to publish a book and then see what happened. Rubio Hidalgo had gone to Paris as head of Agence Espagne, but it was Constancia de la Mora who had succeeded him in Barcelona, and I did not dream of speaking to her of my affairs. The great man in the Foreign Ministry was Señor Ureña, who had certainly not forgotten my share on November the 7th; Alvarez del Vayo—whose wife showed great kindness to Ilsa—was not yet back at the Foreign Ministry, and anyhow he was bound to support others rather than me. I found no one to whom I could speak honestly, as I did to Father Lobo.

The Government and the war machine were working as they had never worked before. There existed an Army now, and an efficient Administration: you need both to fight even a small-scale modern war. I believed the reorganization to have been necessary; and yet it had ruined the urge for freedom, the blundering efforts to build social life anew. My brain assented, and all my instincts rose against it.

I went into the shop to buy a beret. The owner told me, smiling, that his business was improving; the wives of government officials were again being encouraged to wear hats as a sign that the turbulent, proletarian times were over.

It was all true. Perhaps the men who did not want to give me work in their teams were right. The only hope for Spain, the new Spain, was to hold out until the non-Fascist powers were driven to sell us arms because we were their vanguard—or until they were themselves forced to fight the looming greater war. In all that there was no room for dreams. There was no time or place for the premature fraternity of Madrid. Here, in the Barcelona of 1938, I could not talk to any man in the street as to a friend and brother. They organized a Madrid exhibition with huge empty bomb cases, with splinters and fuses of shells, with photographs of ruins, children's homes, and trenches. The faces of the murdered children of Getafe again looked down at me.

But Madrid was far away.

Teruel had been stormed by our troops. Correspondents came back with stories of death in fire and ice. Our Norwegian friend, Nini Haslund, organizer of international relief work, told of small girls cowering in a shelled convent and of old women weeping when they were given bread.

A feeling of inferiority was weighing me down. Our soldiers were dying in the snows of Teruel. We were destroying our own cities and men, because there was no other defense against the horror of life in Fascist bondage. And I ought to be there at the front—when I was not even capable of working in Barcelona where the bombs fell. I was a physical and mental casualty, crouching in a cellar room instead of helping the children or the men.

I knew that I could not alter my physical defects, neither my game finger nor my heart trouble nor the scar in my lung tissue. I knew that I was not willing to kill. But I was an organizer and a propagandist, and I did no work as either. I might have been less self-righteous, more elastic in my dealings with the bureaucracy; after all, I had worked with it successfully in the service of patents whose benefits went to the heavy industry I hated. Now, in the great clash, I had put my qualms and aversions above the work. I had driven myself out of my chosen post in the war, out of Madrid. But for my intransigeance and cherished individualism, Ilsa and I might still be doing work which, to the best of my belief, we did better and more unselfishly than most of the others. Or would my shattered nerves have betrayed me in any case? Would the sour, bitter juice of my body—the cud of my warring thoughts—have filled my mouth so that I could not have spoken any longer as the voice of Madrid? Did I escape into an illness of the mind because I could not bear to be face to face with the things my eyes saw, and the others seemed able to overlook?

Slowly, in fits, I was finishing the book which included something of the Madrid I had seen. In the nights I listened to the cocks challenging each other from the roof tops. While Ilsa left me alone in our bedroom I felt exposed to all terrors, an outcast, and when she came I took shelter in her warmth. But I slept little. My brain made its weary round, a blind mule chained to the wheel of a well.

After a period of grappling with the war and coming war, my thoughts always went back to myself. They no longer controlled the emotions which drove me; their net had become threadbare. I was afraid of the torture which precedes death, of pain, mutilation, living putrefaction and of the terror they would strike into my heart. I was afraid of the destruction and mutilation of others because it was a prolongation of my own terror and pain. An air raid would be all this, magnified by the crumbling walls, the rush of the blast, the image of one's own limbs being torn from one's living body. I cursed my faithful, graphic memory and my technically trained imagination, which showed me explosives, masonry, and human bodies in action and reaction, as in a slow-motion picture. To succumb to this terror of the mind would be stark madness. I was terrified of going mad.

It was a profound relief when the sirens went and the danger became real. I would make Ilsa get up and come with me to the basement. There we would sit with all the other guests in dressing gowns and pajamas, while anti-aircraft guns barked and the explosions rocked the house. A few times my mouth filled with vomit, but even so it was a relief, because all this was real. After a bombing I always fell asleep.

Then, in the morning, I would go down to the stale-smelling cubicle behind the bar and sit before my typewriter. For a short time, my brain would clear and I would think. Was it true that I had to leave Spain so as not to go mad, so as to be able to work again? I did not believe in Poldi's plans and negotiations. Things would develop by themselves. As each concrete situation faced us we would have to come to a decision. In the meantime the foundations of the future edifice were here, firm and real and indestructible: my union with Ilsa. Poldi had seen it as Maria and Aurelia had seen it, as Father Lobo had accepted it. There at least was no problem. I held on to this one plain thing.

On the evening of January the 29th—a Saturday—the manager came down to the bar to find Ilsa: somebody wanted to speak to her in the hall. When she did not come back for a while, the waiter said: "The Police, I think," and I went after her. She was sitting with one of the S.I.M. agents, her face was gray, and she held out a telegram: "Poldi died suddenly Friday. Letter follows." Somebody's signature. The agent had come to make sure that it was no code. She explained the situation carefully to the man and answered his chatty remarks on the hotel and its international racketeers with grave friendliness. Then, holding herself very straight, she walked down the stair to the bar in front of me. Father Lobo was with us then; he had met Poldi, declared him a great and fundamentally good man, and yet seen why Ilsa did not belong to him. Now he was gentle with her.

For a whole night she sat in her bed and fought it out with herself. There was little I could do but stay with her. She held herself responsible for his death, because she thought that his way of living since she left him had destroyed his health. She thought that he had not taken care of himself just because she had left him, and because he had to strengthen his hold on life in some other way than through his feeling for her. So much she told me, but she did not speak much. It did not make it easier for her that she felt no remorse, only sorrow at having hurt him mortally and at the loss of a deep, lasting friendship. They had been married fourteen years and there had been many good things in their life together. But she knew that she had failed him because she had not loved him, and it anguished her. She paid her price.

At three o'clock in the morning there was a raid. The bombs fell very near. A few hours later she dropped off into an uneasy slumber; I dressed and went down into the basement. There the charwomen were still at their work, and I had to wait in the hall. A young Englishman—the Second Officer of an English vessel which had been sunk by Italian bombs, as the manager told me—was wandering up and down, up and down like an animal in a cage. He had the eyes of a scared animal, too, and his jaw hung loosely. He paced the hall in the opposite direction to mine and we stared at each other when our tracks crossed.

That Sunday morning was brilliantly blue. Ilsa had promised to act as interpreter for one of her English friends, Henry Brinton, during an interview with President Aguirre of the Basques. Now she came down, still very rigid and pale, drank the morning beverage—lime-blossom tea with no bread, for the food situation of Barcelona was growing worse from one day to the other—and left me alone. I had enough of staring at the nervous young Englishman and went down to my refuge. My collection of tales was finished, but I wanted to read it through and make corrections. I was going to call the book *Valor y Miedo*, Courage and Fear.

Half an hour later the sirens sounded, together with the first explosions. I went quickly to the bar table; my stomach was rising, and the waiter gave me a glass of brandy. The young Englishman came down the stairs with trembling legs; at the last triangular landing he stopped and leaned against the wall. I went to him. His teeth were chattering. I helped him to sit down on a step and brought him some brandy. Then he began to explain in a laborious mixture of French and English: bombs had fallen on the deck of his ship and he had seen his mates torn to shreds, a couple of days before. It had given him a shock—and he hiccoughed convulsively.

A tremendous crash and roar shook the building, followed by the rumble of masonry knocking against the wall. Shrill screams from the kitchen. A second crash, rocking us and the house. The English officer and I drank the rest of the brandy. I saw my own hand tremble and his shake. The waiter who had run upstairs came back and said: "The house next door and the one behind us have been smashed. We'll make a hole through our kitchen wall, because there are people calling on the other side."

And Ilsa was out in the streets.

A herd of cooks in white overalls appeared in the corridor. The white was stained with the red of brick dust. The tall white cap of the *chef de cuisine* was dented. He guided a few women and children in torn, tattered clothes covered with dust. They were weeping and shrieking: they had just been rescued through a hole in the basement wall. Their house had fallen down on them. Two others were still stuck in the rubble. A fat, elderly woman held her belly with her two hands, gave a scream and began to laugh in great guffaws. The officer of the English ship stared at her out of wide-open blue eyes. I felt that my control, too, was slipping, pushed the officer aside with my elbow and slapped the woman in the face. Her laughter stopped and she glared at me.

Slowly the rescued women and children disappeared into the passages. The Englishman had drunk a bottle of wine and was lying across a table, snoring with a painfully contracted face. The waiter asked me: "And where is your wife?"

I did not know. My ears were full of explosions. Out there, in the street, or dead. I was in a stupor. Through the small windows in the ceiling came the sound of firebells and a fine rain of plaster. It smelled of an old house being torn down.

Where is she? The question hammered on my brain, but I did not try to answer it. It was a murmur like the beating of the blood in my temples. Where is she?

She came down the stairs together with Brinton, and she looked years older than the day before. Upstairs in our room we found only one of our panes cracked, but the house on the far side of the hotel garden had disappeared. The garden was invaded by Venetian blinds twisting like snakes, by broken furniture and strips of wallpaper, and by a big tongue of spilt rubble. Ilsa stared at it and then she broke down. She had been in the street during the bombing and it had not scared her; she had piloted Brinton through the interview with Aguirre, and there had been a flowering mimosa in the President's garden, and an anti-aircraft shell stuck in the pavement of the street. But then the chauffeur had told her that the Ritz was hit or almost hit and in coming back she had been steeling herself against the thing that waited for her. She had helped to kill Poldi. Now she thought that she had left me alone to be killed or to go mad. And I realized that I had thought her dead because of Poldi's death, without admitting it to myself.

That night the sound of pick and shovel, the shouts of rescue workers came into our room together with the crow of the cocks. I remember that

an English delegation—John Strachey and Lord Listowel among them—
arrived that evening and was taken to the heap of debris beside the hotel,
where men still worked by the flare of hurricane lamps to rescue the
buried. I seem to remember that the journalists spoke much about a public Mass Father Lobo had said that Sunday morning, and that Nordahl
Grieg—the Norwegian writer who was shot down in a British aircraft
during a raid on Germany six years later—told me how rescue squads
had hauled able-bodied revellers out of a night club where he had been
drinking. But I do not remember anything about myself. The following
days passed as in a fog. My book was finished. Ilsa was alive. I was
alive. It was clear that I had to leave my country if I was not to go mad
altogether. Perhaps I was already mad; I wondered about it with a feeling
of indifference.

Whatever was done in those weeks of February was done by Ilsa and
her friends. She finished the German translations of my stories and sold
them to a Dutch tobacco racketeer and general agent, so as to pay our
hotel bill. The Spanish manuscript of *Valor y Miedo* was, to my astonishment, accepted by. *Publicaciones Antifascistas de Cataluña*. A German
refugee—a girl who had been secretary to left-wing writers, had fled from
the Nazi régime, starved in Spain, and was suffering from a nervous
shock which made her a public menace in shelters—had obtained a visa
to England only because Ilsa had persuaded Henry Brinton to help her,
and the British Envoy in Barcelona to see the matter through; in her
gratitude, the girl took my manuscript to publishers she knew, and I had
to do nothing but sign a contract. It was good to know that something
of me would survive.

As I was not fit for active service, I was granted a permit to leave the
country; but it had to pass through complicated official channels. Julius
Deutsch helped, Del Vayo helped, I do not know how many others
helped to settle the countless formalities which had to be gone through
before we obtained our passports and the exit visa. On the few occasions
when I myself had no choice but to go out into the street, I thought of
little except how not to vomit. When I came back to the hotel I went off
into a doze or ennmeshed myself in an endless, pointless discussion with
somebody down in the bar. But I do not think people in general noticed
that I was fighting mental destruction. Dozens of time I told Ilsa that it
was hopeless to pit ourselves against the blind force of circumstance, and
every time she told me that if only we wanted to we would survive, because we had many things to do. When I felt beaten and went into a
doze, she was desperately furious with me, and made the impossible possible. My weakness forced her out of her own private hell; it gave her so
much to do that she almost forgot her fears for me. For she, too, was

afraid that I was going mad, and she was not able to hide this fear from my sharpened eyes.

She had learned by letters that Poldi had died from an incurable kidney disease which had already affected his brain and would have destroyed it, dreadfully, if he had lived on instead of dying quickly and mercifully; she had learned from her mother that he had come back from Barcelona quietened, almost happy, proud of her and friendly towards me, determined to rebuild his own life. This released her from her sense of responsibility for his death and left her with the abiding knowledge of the wound she had dealt him. She said that his death had ended her last lap of youth, because it had taught her that she was not stronger than everything else, as she had secretly believed. But now my illness drove her to tap her deepest reserves of strength. As she put it, she was working the miracle of Baron Münchhausen: pulling oneself out of the mire by one's own pigtail. But I saw most of it only through a haze of apathy.

There was one thing, however, a single thing, which I did alone. I procured the papers and took the steps necessary for our marriage. A week before we left Barcelona and Spain, we were married in due form by a caustic Catalan Judge who, instead of a sermon, said: "One of you is a widow, the other divorced. What could I say to you that you don't know? You are aware of what you are doing. Good luck."

When we went down the rickety stairs, I wondered that a mere formality could make my heart feel relieved, for nothing was altered. But it was right that we had no longer to fight for an acknowledgment of our life together. Out in the bright, empty street, the wind of early spring whipped my face.

10. No Truce

T H E clock of the Spanish church tower struck twelve—midnight—just as the customs official lifted his rubber stamp off its sticky inkpad. He pressed it on the open page of my passport, and the clock of the French church on the other side of the frontier tolled in answer. If we had reached La Junquera five minutes later, they might have turned us

back, for my permit to leave Spain expired with February the 22nd. I
I would have had to return to Barcelona and apply for a prolongation of
the permit. But I would not have had the strength to do it. Rather go to
hell and perdition in Barcelona. Our soldiers had lost Teruel again, they
were being driven back through the icy fields. Why should I flee from an
imagined madness?

Now the man was stamping Ilsa's passport.

It was she who had found the car to take us out of the town: one of
the cars of the British Embassy. No other vehicle had been available for
days ahead. The last week had been racked by air raids and hunger.
There was no bread in Barcelona, and no tobacco to assuage that nagging
suction in one's stomach. The morning before we left we had passed the
fish stalls of the Rambla de las Flores in our desperate search for cigarettes for me; there had been a single heap of little quayside fish spread
out on one of the boards, with a slip of paper stuck on a wire saying:
"Half-pound—30 pesetas." The monthly pay of a Miliciano had been 300
pesetas. While I watched the British pennant fluttering on the bonnet of
the big car, I had thought of that pitiful white paper flag.

The customs official was buckling up the straps of our three suitcases.

He had handled my manuscripts with care and respect; evidently he
believed that I was going to France on some mysterious mission, since we
had arrived at the customs house in a police car. For the beautiful British
car had broken down thirty miles from the frontier and the men in the
roadside garage had been unable to repair it. Again I had felt defeated by
fate, again I had seen myself as one of the soldiers reeling back from
Teruel, doomed by fire and snow; but the garage owner had rung up
the local police, and their rickety car had taken us to our destination. It
must have been the magic of the British flag and Ilsa's foreign accent.
Blind chance had rescued us from blind chance.

And so we had made La Junquera five minutes before twelve, after
driving through serried ranks of trees which sprang out of the darkness
into the light cone of the car lamps, and through sleeping villages where
the rubble of bombed houses littered the road. So it was true that I was
leaving my country.

Then we were standing on the road, in front of the barrier. A Spanish
carabinero on one side, a French gendarme on the other. The French
road was blocked by heavy lorries, with their rear bumpers turned our
way: no arms for Spain, I thought. We crossed the barrier, the frontier.
The gendarme looked at our passports, casually. I would have to lug our
suitcases up the slope to the French customs house, for Ilsa could not
carry them; I told her to wait for me by the third suitcase and the type-

writer. From one of the lorries a score of oranges came trickling down on to the frozen road, and two of them rolled past me, back to Spain.

When I came into the bare, narrow office, I was engulfed by the fumes of tobacco and a red-hot iron stove. Two men were dozing behind the counter, wrapped in capes. One of them stirred, stretched, yawned, suddenly gave me a sharp look. "You've just come out of Spain, eh?" and held out his cigarette case. I smoked one with greed before plunging back into the icy clarity of the night. There were no street lamps burning, no more than in Spain; La Junquera had been bombed a couple of nights before, and Le Perthus was next door to it, near enough for a share of bombs.

Ilsa was talking to the Spanish sentry, but I did not feel like it. I grasped the heavy suitcase, she took the typewriter, and we turned our backs on Spain. *"Salud,"* the sentry called out.

"Salud."

We climbed the long, bleak slope without a word.

There was no bed to be had in Le Perthus that night, because the drivers of the lorries which carried oranges from Spain to France had occupied the last free corner. I wished I had picked up one of those oranges. We were hungry and thirsty. The customs official, an elderly Frenchman with long, flowing, black-and-white and tobacco-yellow mustaches, suggested that his neighbor might be willing to take us to Perpignan in his car. He would like to let us stay overnight in the warm customs office, but they had to lock it up at one o'clock. I thought of our scanty money and of the ice-cold night, and decided to interview the man's neighbor. After long minutes of knocking and waiting on the doorstep, a sleepy fat man in a sleeveless vest and half-buttoned trousers opened. Yes, he would take us to Perpignan, but first we would have a drink. He put a bottle of wine and three glasses on the table: "To the Spanish Republic!"

Even while he was dressing, he and the other man plied me with questions about our war. Then the customs official said:

"I've been in the other war—muck and misery and lice! And now they're pushing us into still another. My boy's just the right age." From a paunchy, greasy wallet, he took the photograph of a hefty lad ensconced in an ill-fitting uniform. "That's him. That man Hitler's going to muck things up for us, and the second war will be worse than the first. I'm sorry for you people over there. We don't want wars, what we want is to live in peace, all of us, even if it's not much of a life. But those politicians —to hell with all politicians! And you, what are you?"

"A Socialist."

"Well, so am I, of course, if you know what I mean. But politics in general are muck. If they kill my boy . . . We didn't fight to have another war on our hands, but if they ask for it they'll get it in the neck again. Only, what I say is, why can't people live in peace?"

It was getting on for three when we reached Perpignan. The streets were deserted, but they were lighted. We gaped at the street lamps which exhibited their light so shamelessly. One of the light cones fell into our hotel room. I made a movement as if to draw the curtains and leave the light outside in the cold of the night.

Ilsa slept the sleep of exhaustion; she had warned me that once in France, she would let herself drop. But I listened to the street noises through the thin crust of my slumber. At seven I was wide awake and could no longer bear being shut up in the room. The walls were closing in on me. I dressed noiselessly and went out into a street full of bustling people and pale, frosty sunshine. A young girl in a white apron, a short black skirt and silk stockings, pretty as a servant girl in a comedy, was arranging the shelves in a baker's shop window. Rolls, buns, *croissants,* pastry, long staves of white bread, on trays whose golden-brown wood looked as though it had been toasted in the oven. The cold air carried a whiff of fresh bread to me; it smelled of sun-drenched women. The sight and smell of the bread made me voraciously hungry, voluptuously hungry.

"Can you give me some *croissants?*" I asked the girl.

"How many, monsieur?"

"As many as you like, half a dozen . . ."

She looked at me out of clear, friendly, compassionate eyes and said: "You've come from Spain? I'll give you a dozen, you'll eat all of them."

I ate some in the street and took the rest up to our room. Ilsa was still fast asleep. I put one of the *croissants* on the pillow close to her face, and its smell woke her.

We were walking lazily through the streets, because it was pleasant to stroll and to look at people and shops, although our errand was rather urgent. We had to go to the bank where Poldi had deposited money in Ilsa's name, in exchange for some of our own money which he had needed on his departure from Barcelona. The sum would be just enough to get us to Paris and to allow us two—perhaps three—weeks of rest without immediate financial worries. The future seemed simple and clear. I would soon get well, away from the air raids. In the meantime we would work for our people in Paris. So many articles waiting to be written by her, so many human stories waiting to be written by me. Then we would return to Spain, to Madrid. Everything would come right. We had to be in Madrid in the hour of victory, and we would. The only thing which still had power to hurt Ilsa was the fact that we had not stayed on in Madrid, as was our right and our duty.

But then there was no deposit in Ilsa's name at any of the banks in Perpignan. He must have forgotten about it; his brain had had blackouts.

We counted and recounted our money. At the official rate of exchange, we had brought four hundred francs out of Spain. Not enough for two third-class tickets to Paris or for a week's board at the hotel in Perpignan. We felt stunned. What was there we could sell? We had nothing but shabby clothes, papers, and an old Paisley shawl. Pawn the typewriter? But that would rob us of our tool.

I left Ilsa resting on the bed, escaping into sleep, and went down for a drink in the hotel courtyard. When I saw Sefton Delmer sitting there in the center of a boisterous group it bothered me. I did not want him to know about our quandary. But he took our presence in Perpignan for granted and spoke only of the new car he had come to fetch, in place of the old, war-worn Ford two-seater which he had taken across the frontier for the last time and would pension off now. I looked at the new car and listened to reminiscences about the exploits of the old little car, and wondered whether the Ford would be chucked on the scrap-heap just like the typewriter which I had mended. I felt a secret bitterness and envy, and asked Delmer what was going to happen to the Ford. Oh, his colleague Chadwick who had brought the new car from Paris would take it over— the fellow there with the sloping forehead. He was going to drive it back to Paris in a couple of hours.

Quaking with excitement, I asked as casually as I could whether Mr. Chadwick by any chance had room to take us along in the car. We had little luggage and wanted to go to Paris ourselves. Well—there might just be room if we didn't mind being uncomfortable. I said we did not mind, and went to' wake Ilsa, proud as though I had handled Fate well. At five in the afternoon we were on our way to Paris where our driver-host had to be by noon the next day.

The journey was our salvation and my nightmare. In the fading light, every twist of the road on the flats threatened destruction. I was sickeningly afraid of a malicious, senseless accident, of a sudden twist of the cogwheels to remind us that there was no escape from the crushing mechanism of life. When we began to climb the Central Plateau (on the map this looked like the shortest route to Paris) the roads were frosted and the car slithered on the hairpin bends. Chadwick was a bold and good driver, and I had enough road discipline not to say anything to him, but I had to press myself into Ilsa to still my trembling. With the same blueprint clarity with which I imagined the course and effect of a bomb, I now imagined the skid, the clash, and the cruel mutilation. Once we went into a lonely tavern to warm ourselves and have a quick supper. We lost our road, and found it again. The sleet turned into prickling snow. We went on and on, while I was digging my fingers into Ilsa's arm.

Then, shortly before dawn, when we were planing down somewhere near Clermont-Ferrand, Chadwick stopped the car. He was at the end of his resistance, he had to sleep for an hour or so. Ilsa stowed herself away in the hollow space between the toolbox at the back of the seat, and the low roof. Chadwick fell asleep over the steering wheel. I tried to do the same in my corner, now that I had slightly more room. The cold numbed me and I had to move, as I could not sleep. Cautiously I opened the door, and walked up and down the stretch of road. It was a gray misty dawn, chill and moist. The soil was frozen hard. A few trees along the road were gaunt skeletons. On the top of a near-by hill, a tall chimney overtowering the blurred, dark bulk of a factory was belching forth dark smoke. Workers were passing me on their bicycles, first single, then in droves; their red rear lamps dotted a side-path leading to the factory. Suddenly the screech of a siren split the air; dense white steam spurted from the side of the tall chimney-stack and curled away in the thinning gray mist.

Nausea gripped me when I was not prepared for it. I vomited in the middle of the road, and then I stood there, frozen, trembling, clammy with sweat, my teeth chattering.

Was there no cure for me? Here I had been watching the chimney and the very steam which produced the shrill whistle; I might have known that it was coming; I knew that it meant the beginning of a morning shift of work, and not an air raid. I knew that I was in France, in peace. And yet I was the puppet of my body and nerves. Not until nearly half an hour passed did I wake the others. Chadwick grumbled because I had let him oversleep past six o'clock; I said that I would have hated to wake him, exhausted as he was. I could not have told him that it would have shamed me too much, had he seen me pallid and trembling.

It was cold and sunny when we entered Paris. Chadwick, in a hurry, gave us the address of a cheap hotel in Montparnasse, and we went there in a taxi. The noise of the city bewildered me. Thinly joking, I said to Ilsa:

"Hôtel Delambre, Rue Delambre—if you pronounce it the Spanish way it become Hôtel del Hambre and Rue del Hambre."

Hunger Hotel and Hunger Street.

The small bedroom on the third floor smelled of cooking and a dirty street. It had wallpaper with pink and mauve roses like cabbages on a gray-blue ground, a big shameless bed which filled half the space, a yellow wardrobe which creaked but did not quite shut, a deal table, and a white enamel basin with nickeled taps and no hot water. Madame, the wife of the hotelkeeper, had been handsome and was by now formidable, with jet-black eyes and a thin-lipped mouth. Her husband had a big flabby walrus mustache, and a big flabby body; whenever he could, he slipped out of the parlor into the street and left his wife to keep guard behind the glass door. It was cheaper to rent the room for a month, but when we had paid for it in advance we had just enough money left to eat our fill during three days. The small restaurants of the quarter offered set meals at seven francs, with bread *à discrétion* included in the menu; coming out of Spain, one full meal a day seemed enough to us, once our first hunger was stilled. We imagined that we would manage to live on twenty francs a day. To tide us over, there were a few things—our watches, my fountain pen, the Paisley shawl—which we could pawn at the *Mont-de-Piété*, for sums small enough to make us certain of being able to redeem them. And I would begin to earn money without delay.

I went to the Spanish Embassy. The Counsellor, Jaime Carner, received me with sympathy and skepticism, gave me introductions to a couple of Left papers, but warned me that I would find it extremely difficult to break into the charmed circle of French literary sets without strong backing either by a party or else by one of the acknowledged writers. I knew that I would have neither.

Vincens, at the beginning Press Attaché, later head of the Spanish *Bureau de Tourisme*—one of the main propaganda agencies—invited us to lunch, which was very welcome, and gave me another introduction to yet another Left periodical.

Professor Dominois, who had been Poldi's friend, a French Socialist, staunch supporter of Republican Spain and expert on Central European politics, summoned us to the Café de Flore, tumbled out of a taxi, his bulging, stained waistcoat half unbuttoned, his gold pince-nez dancing on a black cord, and his briefcase spilling papers, and with immense goodwill expounded large-scale plans for our future propaganda work—for the Spanish Embassy.

With a bundle of amateurish translations of my Madrid stories I made the round of the editors. Some of the sketches were accepted and set up in print, only to perish "on the marble," on the slab which was the graveyard of unimportant contributions; some were published; and two were even paid. The proofs of a short sketch which the *Nouvelle Revue Française* took, but never actually published, helped us to impress Madame and the hotelkeeper for a whole fortnight. Ilsa was luckier; she placed articles of hers and a few translations of my tales in Swiss Socialist papers which paid punctually although meagerly. Later on we met a Swedish girl who out of enthusiasm (because she recognized Ilsa as the heroine of a broadcast by a Swedish journalist back from Madrid) translated two stories from *Valor y Miedo;* the stories were published and paid, miraculously. Collected in a folder, the sum total of our free-lance efforts during the first few months looked encouraging. We told ourselves and one another that, single-handed, we had made people abroad read about the Spanish war just when they were getting tired of it and when the Press treated it as stale news. But though it had taken all our combined energy to achieve even so much, it was shockingly little compared with the task, and it did not satisfy our need for work. Also, it brought us no more than a sporadic trickle of cash. Soon we were in arrears with the rent, chained by this debt to a hotel which we had learned to hate for its very air and for the tiny, greedy ants nesting in its walls; and we often went hungry.

Ilsa was no more fit for systematic work than I was. In the evenings she was feverish and almost immobilized by rheumatic pains; half an hour's walk would exhaust her to the verge of tears. When we had come to France, she had begged me to give her time to recover her strength. Now, it made me furiously angry and depressed when she had to go out in search of work or of a friend from whom to borrow a small sum to keep us going. She found a few lessons, but none of her pupils could afford to pay more than a pittance, and one of them was just able to pay her a white coffee and roll in the café where they met. I found an agency for commercial translations which paid at the rate of one franc per hundred words, with a guaranteed minimum of three francs. They had hundreds of people on their waiting lists, mainly for translations from and into German, but occasionally they sent Ilsa a few lines to translate into French from one of the Scandinavian languages, and they gave me Spanish work to do. Mostly it was a question of short advertisements netting five francs apiece, enough for bread and cheese. But once they sent me a patent to translate into Spanish. When I started to type, one of the letter-levers broke. It was nothing short of disaster, for the patent was long enough to promise warm meals for at least five days. I sat and thought for a long time, while Ilsa was trying to sleep. It was exhilarating and exciting to grapple with a purely mechanical adversity. When I hit upon my great invention and repaired the lever with piano wire, it made me happy for days. I am still proud of it, and the lever is still working.

Yet there were far too many days in endless weeks when we lived on bread and black coffee. This was before we were able to buy a little spirit-lamp, a stewing pot and a frying-pan; we had not even yet asked Madame's permission to cook in our room. The sluttish chambermaid had told us that Madame did not like dishwashing in the basin, and we were too conscious of our standing debt to ask for favors. But even a few consecutive days of bread and coffee at the counter—where the coffee is cheaper and thinner than in the café proper—made us very weak. Neither of us had quite got over the effects of the lean times in Spain. When I was empty of food, my brain grew feverish and sluggish at the same time. Often it seemed more reasonable to stay in bed and doze than to go out and pawn my watch once again, or to borrow five francs from people who had little more than ourselves—for it was still preferable to ask them rather than people who lived a normal, comfortable life. It had been very much easier to go hungry in Spain, together with everybody else and for a reason which made it worthwhile, than to go hungry in Paris because we found no work and had no money, while the shops were brimming over with food.

Sometimes Ilsa had a spurt of desperate courage and forced herself to ask help from one of her well-to-do friends, afraid that he might resent it as sponging. But she was so scared of meeting Madame's hostile eyes and of being asked when we would pay the rent, that it was usually I who sneaked past the glass door and went out in quest of money for bread and cigarettes. If I waited long enough at the corner of our street, outside the Café de Dôme, I would see somebody whom I knew from Spain, or one of Ilsa's refugee friends, people who would give away whatever they could spare, as easily and naturally as the waiters and I had pooled our cigarettes in Madrid, in the days of scarcity, aware that the other's turn to give or take would come any time.

If the only person I met had just enough money to pay me a coffee in the newly opened, glistening bar of the Dôme, I would gratefully stay there, accept a cigarette from the waiter, and listen to his stories, bandy jokes with the pretty German girl who claimed to be the only painter's model with a Renoir behind, stare back at English and American tourists who had come to get a glimpse of bohemian life, and then return to the hotel, defeated, only to make the journey a second time late at night. When I was lucky, I fetched Ilsa down, walking between her 'and the glass door in the hotel lobby; then we would eat sausages at the bar, in an elated and mischievous mood because Madame had not accosted us and because we were alive, no longer buried in our stale-smelling room.

Ilsa did not like to stay in the bar. The noise made her restless. She would have a chat with the flower-seller outside, a stout, florid, imperious woman who used to discuss her flowers and the articles in the *Humanité* with Ilsa. Or she would walk round the other corner to the secondhand bookshop behind a narrow blue-painted door, where the wife of the languid, handsome owner—a small, cuddly provocative girl with rolling black eyes and dyed yellow hair—let her browse among the books, bor-

row a battered volume for a franc, and, in days of affluence, buy a book
with the certainty that the shop would take it back at half the price. The
bookshop flaunted surrealism, in the primitive guise of absurd, incongruously matched toys hung up in a bird cage or dangling from the wall in
front of family portraits of the plush era. But they had very good books.
There were two cats, a beautiful dwarf Siamese she-cat and a huge black
Persian who was castrated and sat motionless while the Siamese, in heat,
dragged herself in frenzy along the floor in front of him.

I felt smothered in the backroom of the bookshop, and it did not give
me any pleasure to read pages out of books by André Gide, which seemed
beautifully, austerely unreal, remote and chill. I preferred to move among
the people in the street and the bar.

Every day, just after dark, a little man arrived at the bar of the Café
de Dôme and took up his post at one end of the horseshoe table. He
always wore the same shiny dark suit on his round little body and the
same rusty bowler hat on his round little head, topping a featureless,
round face with a very French mustache. He looked like any old clerk
of any old-fashioned notary, one of those notaries who live in ancient,
leaning houses and have a gloomy office, where stacks of dossiers tied
with red tape pile up in every corner, and an indigenous population of
rats grow fat and respectable on a diet of yellowed paper and crumbs of
bread and cheese scattered among the files.

The little man would lift his forefinger, slowly and deliberately, crook
it, and wave it at the waiter inside the horseshoe of the bar. The waiter
would put a glass of colorless liquid in front of the little man, pour into
it a few drops from a bottle, and a poisonous yellow-green cloud would
mount in the transparent fluid until the whole glass was aglow with it;
it was *Pernod*. The little man would plant his elbow on the bar table,
bend his hand outward at a right angle, rest his chin on his hand, and
stare at the greenish drink. Suddenly he would shake off his meditation;
his head would jerk free, his arm extend stiffly from the elbow, his forefinger point accusingly into the void, his eyes pop and swivel in their
sockets, in a swift survey of the circle of customers leaning at the bar.
Then his finger and eyes would stop, and aim straight at someone's face.
The victim would grin and wriggle. The stabbing forefinger would trace
signs, affirmative and negative, questioning and persuasive, while the
empty features of the little man would contract in a series of rapid gestures, illustrating the rhetoric of the finger. But his body would remain
motionless and the words and chuckles which his lips formed never became sound. The grimacing head looked like one of those toy heads of
painted rubber which move and gesticulate as you squeeze and release
their necks in your hand. Then the play would suddenly stop, the little

man would drink a sip of his Pernod and fall back into meditation for a few minutes, only to resume his mute soliloquy in an altered key, with the same mute vigor.

He would go on like this for hours, never moving from his place, from time to time crooking his finger to order another Pernod. People tried to make him speak, but I never heard a word come from his lips. When his eyes looked straight into yours you knew that they never saw you. They were the windows of an empty house; there was nobody left inside the skin of the body. The man had gone quietly mad.

But I was no longer afraid of going mad. My illness had been fear of destruction and fear of the rift within myself; it was an illness which equally threatened all the others, unless they were emptied of thought and will, gesticulating puppets like the little man at the bar. True, the others had built up more defenses, or possessed greater powers of resistance, or had fought their way to a greater spiritual clarity than I. But I might fight my own way to clarity, and I might be able to help others in the end, if I traced my mental disease—this disease which was not only mine—back to its roots.

In those noisy summer evenings when I was alone among strangers, I realized that I did not want to write articles and propaganda stories, but to shape and express my vision of the life of my own people, and that, in order to clarify this vision, I had first to understand my own life and mind.

There was no discharge, no release, no truce in the war I carried in myself. So much I knew. How could there have been, when the war riding its course in my country was being dwarfed by the forces lining up for the other war and by the deadly menace to all freedom of spirit?

The drone of passenger planes always carried a threat; it reminded me of the giant Junkers whose cushioned seats could so easily be replaced by bombing gear. I was waiting for German bombs to fall on Paris.

Every Thursday, the air-raid sirens of Paris blew their whistles for a quarter of an hour, beginning at noon; long before the test alert started, I was preparing myself for its impact, without ever preventing the bitter juice of nausea from filling my mouth.

Once I was waiting on a Métro platform and quietly talking to Ilsa, when I vomited; and only in the grip of the convulsion did I become consciously aware of the train rumbling overhead.

In the white-tiled, glistening underground passage of the Châtelet station I was obsessed with the vision of crowds trapped during an air raid combined with a gas attack. I looked at big buildings to assess their potential resistance to bombs.

I was sentenced to a perpetual awareness of the oncoming clash in its physical form, as I was sentenced to feel the helplessness and muddled violence of its victims and fighters in my own mind. But I could not speak to others than Ilsa about it.

The Frenchmen I knew were scarcely hiding their frightened impatience with the Spanish fight; they resented the writing on the wall, because they still clutched at their hope of peace for themselves. The political refugees from Austria whom I met through Ilsa were harassed by their knowledge of developments in their country, recently occupied by Hitler, and by the doom hanging over Czechoslovakia; yet even so they found cover behind their group doctrines, ambitions, and feuds. A single one of them, young Karl Czernetz, realized that international Socialism had lessons to learn from the case history offered by Spain's bleeding body and overwhelmed us with questions about the mass movements, political parties, social and psychological factors in the Spanish war; the others seemed to have their explanations pat. As to Spaniards, those whom I met in official and semi-official departments may have been seared by our war as I was, but they were profoundly afraid of anything outside the sheltering official or party line. I was as much a stranger to them as to the others, although I was far from glorying in an isolation which reduced my radius of action. The alternative, however, was worse, because it would have meant bartering away my independence of thought and expression in exchange for conditional support and help, and for a party label which would have been a lie.

Even in my own ears my purpose sounded crazily audacious: to make people abroad see and understand enough of the human and social substance of our war to realize how it linked up with their own latent, but relentlessly approaching fight. Yet as I strove to control and define my mental reactions, the conviction grew in me that the inner conflicts behind those reactions tortured not only me, the individual, but the minds of countless other Spaniards as well; that indeed they would rend the minds of countless men throughout the world once the great clash engulfed them.

If others, then, felt no urge to search for the causes and the chain of causes, I felt it. If they were content to speak of the guilt of Fascism and Capital and the final victory of the people, I was not. It was not enough; we were all bound up in the chain and had to fight ourselves free from it. It seemed to me that I might better understand what was happening to my people and to our world, if I uncovered the forces which made me, the single man, feel, act, blunder, and fight as I did.

I began to write a book about the world of my childhood and youth. At first I wanted to call it *The Roots,* and describe in it the social conditions among the Castilian workers at the beginning of the century, in the villages and slums I had known. But I caught myself putting down too many general statements and reflections which I believed but could not check, because they did not grow out of my own experience and mind.

I tried to wipe the slate of my mind clean of all reasoning and to go back to my beginnings, to things which I had smelled, seen, touched, and felt and which had hammered me into shape by their impact.

At the beginning of my conscious life I found my mother. Her work-worn hands dipping into the icy water of the river. Her soft fingers stroking my tousled hair. The black-coated earthenware pot in which she brewed her coffee out of a week's dregs. At the bottom of my memory I found the picture of the tall arch of the King's Bridge with the Royal coach guarded by red-and-white horsemen rolling past, high above our heads, washerwomen beating linen down by the river bank, boys fishing rubber balls out of the big black sewer canal, and an Asturian woman singing:

> *Por debajo del puente*
> *no pasa nadie,*
> *tan solo el polvo*
> *que lleva el aire . . .*
>
> Under the bridge
> nobody goes,
> only the dust
> that the wind blows.

There I started. I called the book *La Forja,* The Forge, and wrote it in the language, words, and images of my boyhood. But it took long to write, because I had to dig deep into myself.

About that time we had a windfall; Ilsa earned an English pound, worth 180 francs at the exchange rate of the week. We bought the spirit-lamp and the frying-pan of which we had spoken so much, and two plates, two forks, two spoons, and a knife. I remembered the smell and splutter of the frying-pan in my mother's old attic, and cooked Spanish dishes for us. They were poor people's dishes, but to me they tasted of my country: fresh sardines, potatoes, meat-balls, fried in sizzling oil, even if it was not olive oil. I had never cooked before, but I recalled the movements of my mother's hands: "Now what was it she did then . . ."

It was something of alchemy and white magic. While I was frying fat sardines in front of the black, useless fireplace, I told Ilsa about the attic, the passage, the staircase, the street, the sounds and the smells of El Avapiés. They overlaid the noises and vapors of the Rue Delambre. Then, before going back to the typewriter, I would stretch out on the floor, my head on Ilsa's lap and her fingers in my hair, and listen to her warm voice.

At the upper end of our short street was the market of the quarter. We went out together to select vegetables for a salad and to find the cheapest fish on the slab. Many times we were saved from another hungry day by cuttlefish, which few people bought and the fishmonger was glad to give away for a mere nothing. They looked ugly, slimy, and unclean. But I stripped off their many layers of transparent skin, until the only thing left was the firm flesh with its mother-of-pearl glints; I prepared a glorious sauce out of their own inky fluid, oil, bay leaves, fried garlic, and a drop of vinegar, in which I simmered the white strips of flesh. And then the whole room smelled like Miguel's kitchen at the foot of the Rock of Ifach. On other days, Ilsa would have an attack of nostalgic cooking and insist on preparing a Viennese dish for once, under my critical eyes. Late in the evening, when I no longer dared to go on typing, afraid of provoking a complaint by other lodgers, we would stroll down to St. Germain des Prés, watch the blue glow of the sky, and guard the frail bubble of our gaiety.

When we had a small sum of money beyond the needs of a single day, we were not reasonable. Instead of doling it out carefully, we would celebrate each small victory in a skirmish with existence by eating a full meal in a real restaurant, with the bottle of cheap red wine that went with it. Usually we sat under the striped awning of the Restaurant Boudet in the Boulevard Raspail, because I liked its blend of noisy American students, desiccated Parisian clerks, and stodgy provincial families on an outing, and because I liked gazing at the spacious boulevard with its air of shabby gentility and the fringe of paintings—sunsets, lilac in a blue vase, coy, pink-hued maidens—which was spread out along the curb on the other side. Also, Boudet's gave a good meal for eight francs or substantial dishes à la carte; and they were generous with their white bread, which circulated freely in big baskets filled and refilled by the waitresses.

On hot evenings, when I was smothered by the walls of our close room and wanted to see people and lights, to hear anonymous voices, and feel the slight breeze after dusk, we went to Boudet's even if we had no more than five francs between us. Then we ordered a single dish, sadly refused the wine which the waitress would automatically put on the table, and secure one of the baskets with much bread in it. But it happened early in the summer, when we ordered a dish of macaroni and a second plate, that the elderly, broad-faced waitress leaned over our table and said: "You must eat more, this isn't good for you." Ilsa looked up into the friendly face and said lightly: "It doesn't matter, we can't afford more today. Next time, perhaps."

Next time we asked for a single dish again, the waitress stood there, solid and firm, and said: "I'm going to bring you the set meal, it's very nice today. Madame says you've got credit with us and can order what you like."

I went to see Madame, like a stammering schoolboy. She was sitting behind her cash register, in a black dress, a black-and-white cat by her side, but unlike most of the proprietresses of French restaurants entrenched behind their cash-box, she was not florid and high-bosomed, nor did she wear her black satin like impenetrable armor. She was small, thin, and lively, short in her speech like a mother of many children. Oh yes, it was all right. I did not know when we would get money to pay accounts? That did not matter. We would pay in the end. She cut short my halting explanations of our financial situation: we would order what we needed, on account, and pay when we had the money. It was her risk.

We rationed our visits to Boudet's; but even so we went there often enough when we had no cash for food to cook in our room or when we wanted to breathe freely. By the end of September, we had accumulated a debt of almost six hundred francs. The kindly warmth of the two women never changed; they never assumed a proprietary air. Sometimes I went to eat there merely to bask in their human welcome. How much it helped us to overcome our physical depression, how much it helped me to work without the dread of the next hour when I would have to sneak out and hunt for a few pieces of silver, I cannot tell. But it was certainly my secret ambition then to pay my moral debt—I paid the cash debt, ludicrously, out of two thousand francs I gained on a single lottery ticket bought in·cynical despair, with my last ten francs, on a gray rainy day— and to pay it in the face of the world, in print, as I am now doing.

That blue-and-golden September was the September of Munich.

For weeks the Frenchmen round us had been discussing the chances of a peace at any price paid by others than themselves. They began to look askance at foreigners who embodied an uncomfortable warning and the threat of political complications. The ugly word *sale metèque* was spreading. Whatever its origin, its meaning was clear enough: it hit aliens other than Englishmen and Americans in the back. I heard a drunkard spit "Dirty nigger!" into the yellow-gray face of a half-caste who wore two rows of ribbons from the last war on his lapel. The workers to whose conversations I listened in the *bistro* were confused and uncertain; why should they fight for a bureaucracy going Fascist, for a Government of Big Business? Look at Spain. It showed what happened to the people who risked their lives to defend freedom—isn't it so, Spaniard? It was hard for me to answer them; they did not hate war more than I did; I distrusted their Government as much as they did. Whatever I said about the need to fight for one's chance of a better social order rang hollow, because it had been said so often; the word liberty sounded ironical.

An increasing number of refugees applying at the Préfecture for the monthly or bi-monthly prolongation of their Aliens' Registration Card (the *Récépisse*) were told that they would have to leave the country within eight days. At the corner of the Café de Dôme I heard about many who had left Paris to tramp the roads to the south rather than be arrested and taken across the Belgian frontier—or dumped on the German frontier and left to their fate.

Republican Spaniards, too, met with increasing official disapproval. Franco's armies had cut Loyal Spain into two shrinking areas and were threatening Catalonia. When, in our turn, we went to the Préfecture (on foot, because we had just the amount to pay the fee for the prolongation of our *Récépisse*), we discussed soberly what we would do if they refused us the permit to stay in the country any longer. Go back to Spain—my book half written—my sanity half restored—in the certainty that we would not be given work to do? We had a standing invitation to England, and Ilsa talked of going there almost as if it were her home; but how could we muster the money for the fare within eight days? It was a blind alley. Then, when the morose official prolonged our permits without the slightest hitch, we walked down the stairs hand in hand, like children coming out of school; but my legs felt hollow.

In the evenings people stood about on the boulevards in tight clusters, reading and commenting on the multiple late editions of *Paris-Soir*. Hitler spoke. Chamberlain spoke. What about Czechoslovakia? It was war or no war. In our streets, one of the grocery shops was shut: the owner had gone home to his family in the country. On the following day two more of the shops in the Rue Delambre were shut because their owners had taken their families to the country. It was a nightmare to think what would happen in this Paris if the war were to break out; the very first thing would be chaos in the food supply because those people had no thought but to escape from the bombs. It was bitter and strengthening to think of our people in Madrid who were still carrying on, with the second year of the siege approaching its end.

On July the 14th, when the dull detonations of holiday fireworks had shaken the town and colored flashes ringed the horizon, I had gone underground, into the shelter of the nearest Métro station, because I could not bear the sounds and the tremor of the earth; in the streets, people had been singing and dancing in a strained, hectic effort to recapture the joyous relief of a half-forgotten victory of freedom. Now, when I knew the threat to be real and not a figment of my brain, I could stand it, for war was inevitable, and war against the aggressor at this moment would save Spain, the world's battered vanguard. And if there was war, it would be better to be in its heart and have a share in it. The French might begin by putting all foreigners into concentration camps, but they would admit us to co-operation in the end, because we were the veterans of their own fight.

It dawned on me then that I was regaining control of myself. I had learned many lessons.

On the day when huge posters mobilizing several French age-classes invaded walls and hoardings, the owner of the Hôtel Delambre called me into the parlor.

"This means war. If the rest of your debt to us is not paid by Sunday, I'll go to the police about it. We can't have foreigners without any income —I've spoken about you to the police anyhow. On Monday we'll shut up the hotel and go away to the country. Paris will be bombed at once, it will be the first town they bomb."

Ilsa was in bed with 'flu. I walked through the streets of Paris without wanting to go anywhere. At the Porte d'Orléans, private cars loaded with suitcases and bundles crept forward on a broad front, blocking each other's way out of the city. The railway stations were beleaguered by crowds, sullen, silent, and uneasy. Rows of shops had shuttered doors and windows. This was panic about to break loose.

I went back to our room to look after Ilsa and to eat something. But all we had in store were a few potatoes and half a loaf of bread, infested in all its pores by the tiny red ants which clutched at their pasture and would not be shaken off. I went back into the street and asked the waiter in the Dôme to give me a glass of red wine, which I poured down my throat. He filled it afresh, absent-minded, staring past my shoulder at the stream of cars on the boulevard, cars with big trunks on their luggage-grids.

"Those swine—it's the barracks for us, and they . . . Well, we'll have to cut the throats of quite a lot of people, just as you did in Spain."

Somebody shook me by the shoulder. "Well, well, what are you doing here, Barea? And how's Ilsa? Come and have a look at my car. But where *is* Ilsa? How's life?"

It was Miguel, the Cuban, who had drifted into besieged Madrid out of curiosity, out of sympathy, and out of the urge to escape from his own empty life. In Spain he used to say that he loved Ilsa like a sister; now he insisted on seeing her at once. He was appalled at the squalor of our room, appalled at our drawn faces, and he overwhelmed me with re-proaches because I had never sought him out in Paris during the past months when he had been flinging away his money. Now, as though to punish me for my constant fear of a blind, cruel, senseless chance, this chance meeting saved us from an encounter with a hostile police. Miguel gave me the money to buy ourselves free from the hotel then and there. We knew where to go; friends who looked after the empty flat of a Nor-wegian journalist, with the right to sub-let, had offered us a room which seemed unbelievably bright, clean, and airy, but which we had been un-able to take as long as our debt tied us to the hotel. We moved in on the following morning, although the hotelkeeper suddenly asked me to stay: the Pact of Munich had been signed and he no longer thought it necessary to leave Paris and shut his hotel.

Munich destroyed Spain's last hope. It was clear beyond any doubt that no country in Europe would lift a finger to help us against Hitler and his Spanish friends. Russia would have to withdraw her assistance, already painfully reduced; her open intervention in Spain would have meant that the whole of Europe would fall on Russia herself and destroy her. For the immolation of Czechoslovakia and the weak submission of the Great Powers to Hitler's ultimatum had not provoked a wave of anger and contempt for the dictator; they had provoked a tidal wave of fear, naked fear of war and destruction, which bred the urge to deflect that war and destruction on to others.

The Frenchmen with whom I spoke were brutally open. They were ordinary men with small incomes and small ambitions, trying to build up their savings account against old age, disliking the very memory of the last war. They would have welcomed it if, after Czechoslovakia, they could have directed the dictator's greed and fury against another country which he might crush, while his feelings towards France would soften. For France was innocent. France wanted to live at peace with the whole world. The true France repudiated the guilty men, the warmongers, the militant socialists, the Communists, the Spanish Reds who tried to drag Europe into their war; the true France had signed the Munich Pact.

For a few weeks I, too, felt guiltily glad at the respite from war and made myself forget the smell of putrefaction in the country which still—for how long?—gave us hospitality. It was so great a relief to be in the new room, to learn the trick of how to make three francs provide a meal from Trudy, our generous and hard-worked hostess, and to write at leisure, to be able to think without petty fears hammering at one's brain! It was the first time since our coming to Paris that I could let Ilsa rest at her ease; soon she went to work with her old freshness, forcing me to haul the brightest colors and the sharpest pains of my childhood out of my secret mind and to give them shape in my book.

The autumn sun was dipping Paris in a golden glow. After our meal we used to walk to the Jardin du Luxembourg, slowly, like two convalescents, and sit down on a bench in the sunshine. We had to go early, for the seats filled quickly with children, nurses, and old people. We did not talk much, for to talk of the matters which occupied our thoughts was to conjure up nightmares. It was better to sit still and look at the dance of the fallow chestnut leaves in the sun-flecked avenue.

An old couple was stopping at the bench opposite ours, she small and vivacious, kicking up the sand with the ferrule of her stick, he erect and bony, with a white goatee and white, pointed, carefully waxed mustaches. Before he permitted her to sit down he dusted the seat with his silk handkerchief. She wore a dress of black, figured silk, and he carried a silver-handled cane under his arm, like an officer's baton. They spoke to each other in a soft murmur, with courteously inclined heads. When she moved her tapering fingers in their black lace mittens, they looked like the wings of a bird shaking off raindrops.

Ilsa said: "When we're as old as they, we might be rather like them. At least, it would be nice. You will be a dried-up, lean old man anyhow, and I'll do my best to become a small, wrinkled old lady. We'll take our afternoon walks in a garden, and warm ourselves in the sun, and tell each other about old times, and smile at the dreadful things that happened to us when we were younger."

"But how will you turn yourself into a little old woman?"

"Just as many others do it. My mother, for example, used to be quite as round as I am now——"

"Come, come, was she?"

"For her size I mean. Really, she was quite plump, and now she's getting fragile and shrinking very pleasantly, though I know it mostly from her photos . . ."

The old man opposite rose, lifted his hat, and stretched out his right hand.

"Look, now they'll dance a minuet!"

But the old gentleman bowed, kissed his lady's finger-tips, and walked sedately down the avenue, his silver-handled cane under his arm. Her fingers escaping from the black mittens moved like the wings of a bird that cannot fly.

"Oh—but you won't do that to me!" Ilsa exclaimed, and her eyes filled with water.

"Of course I will, I'll go to the café and sit with my cronies, and you can stay in the garden all by yourself." But then I saw that a drop had splashed on to her skirt and was spreading there, and I blinked as though grit had got under my eyelids, for no good reason whatsoever. I had to tell her childish stories, until the corners of her mouth crinkled in laughter and deepened into the question marks which made me feel happy.

I received a parcel of books from Spain: *Valor y Miedo* had been published. But I thought the publishers would not send many copies to Madrid where they belonged; Madrid was cut off from Barcelona.

I read what I had spasmodically written, with the sound of bombs in my ear, and some of it I still liked, though much now seemed of light weight. Yet it made me glad and proud to think that I had torn something straight and simple out of the whirl.

One of the first copies I gave away—the first of all was Ilsa's—went to Vicente, the shop assistant of our Spanish greengrocer. The owner himself, like most of the Spanish fruiterers in Paris, had no liking for the Republicans who wanted to control the export trade, to favor co-operatives, to raise the Spanish workers' wages, and so to curtail private profits. His assistants were Republicans for the very same reasons. Vicente had invited me to the attic where he lived with his thrifty French wife, taken me to the big storehouses in the *Halles* where Spanish packers and porters handled fruit and vegetables coming from Valencia and the Canaries, and told me of his secret fear that France was going the way of Spain, the way to Fascism or civil war. When I gave him my book, he was proud, as though it gave him a share in our fight. He dragged me to the little café near the *Halles* where the Spaniards met. There they used to collect money for the organizations, most of them under Communist leadership, which tried to bring relief to Republican Spain.

The men were shouting and swearing, smoking, drinking, and discussing the way of the world with as much swashbuckling gusto as the people in Serafín's tavern during the months before the clash. They would not admit that things could go wrong in Spain; France, yes—France was going to the dogs because those French had no fight in them, but the people of Spain would show them all. . . . They fingered the pages of my book, looked in it for words to confirm what they said, and slapped me on the back. I still spoke their language. But while I was at ease among them, I kept thinking of the other book which I was writing so as to understand why we were swayed from outburst to passivity, from faith to violence; and it chafed me.

Another of the copies was a bribe to our concierge. The manager of the block of flats in which we lived, a huge modern building with central heating and exorbitant rents, disliked our household because it consisted of foreigners. Once he came and tried to be offensive; at that time a Norwegian couple was living there as well, and the manager declared that he did not like it. The authorities would do well to keep foreigners under even stricter supervision in these turbulent times when they only caused mischief. It was lucky for us that the concierge took our part and gave good reports about us. Thus we religiously paid him his tip at the beginning of the month, because it was more important than food to us to keep him well disposed, and I took pains to do what was just as essential as the tip: I always listened to him. He would intercept me in the courtyard and begin his hardluck story. He had lost a leg in the last war, his chest had caved in, his wife had no understanding for his lost ambitions, and he had to drink so as to keep going.

"Times are bad. . . . Politics, Monsieur! If I had wanted to—now look at this." He would push me into his lodge and point at a diploma hanging on the wall. "You see, I was destined for the Bar. Yes, though I'm a humble doorkeeper now, I'm an educated man with a degree. But that cursed war!" This was his cue to turn back his trouser leg and show me his artificial leg, pink like a doll's. "Here I am, left to rot. This cursed leg ate up my last thousand francs. It hurts me to think of what I might have been." This was the moment to invite him to a glass of wine in the *bistro*. If I failed to respond, he guessed the state of my finances and invited me, because he longed to display his submerged self and to beg for the listener's admiration. Towards the end of the month, when he had consumed all the tips from all the tenants in the huge beehive, he would pounce on me when I passed and begin to talk with the supplicating eyes of a dog suffering from thirst. He would spread out cuttings describing the many battles in which he had fought as a conscript soldier, and he would open the case with his Croix de Guerre. The cross had worn out the pile of the blue velvet lining. Then he would ask, invariably: "And what do you think of it all?"

When I gave him my book, he weighed it ceremoniously in his hands and said: "Ah—the Liberty of the People! But let me tell you, we, the Frenchmen, brought Liberty into this world. It was our blood that was shed for the liberation of——" He stopped, twisted his mustache which at once dropped limply back into place, and added: "You know what I mean." His wife was gazing at him with the wondering, dark-brown eyes of a cow.

As time went on, my concierge began to speak of certain unspecified difficulties caused by the manager. The point was, there were really too many foreigners in Paris. It was not meant against us as individuals, but he did not think that the lease of the flat would be prolonged on March the 1st. The tenant was never there in person, and some people considered that it was not right to have a center of aliens in the building. We had many friends, after all, who visited us, hadn't we? Would we not rather go back to our own country?

The collapse of the Spanish front began on the eve of Christmas, at the Ebro. The way to Barcelona lay open. But Madrid still stood. The enemy launched no attack on the besieged city; he left it in the clutch of hunger and isolation. Nini Haslund had come back from her relief work in Spain and told of the despair of the mothers, of their dull, nagging, hopeless despair. But there was no surrender.

Paris had grown dark, foggy, and cold. We were alone in the flat, for our hosts had gone away to the country, fighting their own battle with misery. I had finished my new book, working in spurts when the type-writer was not blocked by the translations which helped us to live, or by Ilsa's laborious and unskilled copying of other people's manuscripts. But when the first rough version of *The Forge* was completed, I sagged. It seemed insolent to hope that it would reach and touch people who wanted to hide from their fears and from their awareness of the social rift within their own world. It might never be printed. I heard it said so often that nobody wanted to hear about anything Spanish. If so, my contribution to the battle would be futile; for writing was to me part of action, part of our war against death and for life, and not just self-expression.

I had struggled to fuse form and vision, but my words were crude be-cause I had had to break away from the conventional rhythms of our literature, if I was to evoke the sounds and images of the world which had made me and so many of my generation. Had I evoked them? I was not sure. I was a learner again, I had to learn how to tell my own truth. The conceptions of art of the professional writers did not help me; they hardly interested me. Twice a French writer had taken me along to a lit-erary gathering, but the self-conscious statements of people gyrating round one "master" here and another "master" there had only filled me with astonished boredom and an embarrassing disgust. Now it depressed me to think that I belonged nowhere and so might once again condemn myself to uselessness; and yet it was impossible to act on the beliefs of others and not on my own unless I wanted to lose whatever virtue there might be in me.

When I was very low in spirit, an unknown Spaniard rang me up. He had seen the manuscript of *The Forge,* as the reader of the French pub-lisher to whom I had sent it, and he wanted to discuss it with me. The man came, a weak man, split in himself, with his roots in the old Spain and his mind groping towards the new, afraid of the pain which the final clash inflicted on him and the others. He had not greatly liked my way of writing because, as he said, it scared him by its brutality; but he had recommended the book for publication because it had the force to release things which he and others like him kept painfully buried in themselves. I saw his excitement, his relief at the freedom of my outspokenness had given him, and I saw with amazement that he envied me. The publisher kept the book, but never answered. It no longer mattered so much, because that other man's words had told me that the book was alive.

In the last days of the year 1938, a bitter frost fell on Paris. Pipes froze in many houses. We were lucky, because the central heating in our flat still worked, and when a young Pole with whom I was friends—he was on the way to becoming a grimly realistic writer of French prose restrained by Gide's influence—rang me up to ask whether we could not rescue him and his wife from their ice cold, waterless flat, I gladly invited them to stay with us. On the next morning, two police agents called and asked for our guests; they had not informed the Commissariat of their district that they were going to spend a night away from their registered address, and it was only thanks to their satisfactory conduct so far, and to the French Army papers of the young man, that the agents refrained from arresting them. All this in pompous official language and without any civility. Then we were severely warned not to let foreigners stay with us overnight, being foreigners ourselves. Our guests would have to report to the Préfecture, and it would count greatly against them. No, they could not stay until their pipes unfroze, except with the permit of their Commissariat.

When I left the house that day, the concierge called me into his lodge: "I'm sorry, but I had to tell the police that you had people staying with you overnight who hadn't given me their papers. You see, if I hadn't told them, somebody else would have done it. The manager doesn't like me as it is. I told you things were getting difficult. Well, everyone's got to look out for himself, I say."

A few days later, I met a young Basque whom I knew slightly in the bar of the Dôme. He told me that the police had asked for his papers three times in a single night, the last time when he was with a girl friend in her Hôtel Meublé. He possessed a safe-conduct of Franco's Government, which his father, a manufacturer of San Sebastian, had procured for him at the time when he wanted to cross the frontier into France; the paper had no validity except for the Spanish frontier officials in Irun, but on seeing it, one of the French police agents had said: "Our apologies, we've nothing against you, but you see, it's high time we cleared France of all those Reds."

When we went to the Préfecture to get the prolongation of our *Récépisses,* the official subjected us to a lengthy cross-examination. Were we refugees? No, we had our passports of the Spanish Republic and could return there. Would we not register as refugees—we would not return to Spain now, would we? We would not register as refugees; we insisted on our rights as Spanish citizens. In the end he told us that we soon would be refugees anyhow, whether we liked it or not, and then our case would be reconsidered. But he granted us the prolongation of our papers—this time.

In the drab corridor I met Spaniards waiting for their turn; they told me of many who had been expelled from Paris and ordered to provinces in the north of France. Then I saw a familiar face: "He looks worried!"

"Didn't you know they'd arrested him and kept him locked up a few days, just because they knew he'd been a Minister of the *Generalitat?*"

It was Ventura i Gassols, the Catalan poet whom intellectual Paris had fêted a few years before. He scuttled down the stairs, a hunted animal. The gray house smelled of rot.

How could I have been fool enough to think that they, those officials and their bosses, would admit us to co-operation in the war once it reached France? They were preparing the Maginot Line of their caste, and we were the enemy to them. They would try to use the war as their tool. In the end it would devour them and their country. And we would have to pay the price first. But I did not want to become the cannon-fodder of a French Fascism. I would not let ourselves be caught in the trap, doubly defeated.

If we wanted to live and fight, and not to rot and be hunted, we had to leave France. Get out of the trap. Go to England—a desperate effort would get us the money, even if we had to ask friends again—and stay there, free. Not to Latin-America, for our war was fought in Europe. But away from this stench of decay.

There, within the flaky, stale-smelling walls of the Préfecture, I was possessed by the urge to escape into freedom. The noises of the city, dulled by the thick walls, hammered at the back of my skull, and the horrors of senseless destruction were closing in on me again.

The plain-clothes man bowed and said: "Passports, please."

As I fumbled in my pocket, I felt my forehead and the palms of my hands go damp. The dread of the last few weeks, when the pack was hunting in full cry, sat in my marrow. And this was our last meeting with the French police.

The man looked perfunctorily at the papers and put his rubber stamps on one after the other of our passports. Then he handed them back,

thanked us politely, and shut the door of our compartment with consider-
ate care. The wheels of the fast train were humming, and we kept silence,
Ilsa and I, looking at each other. This time, we belonged to the lucky
ones; international laws and treaties were still valid for us. Yet the vision
of thousands and thousands of others filled the compartment, until I saw
nothing else.

Since the end of January the Spanish frontier had been a broken dam,
through which the flood of refugees and routed soldiers poured into
France. On January the 26th Barcelona had fallen to Franco. The exodus
from all the towns and villages along the coast had begun. Women, children, men, beasts, struggling along the roads, through frozen fields, in the
deadly snows of the mountains. Pitiless planes overhead, a blood-drunk
army pressing from the back, and a small band of soldiers checking its
advance, pushed back inexorably and still fighting on, face to the enemy.
Poor people with pitiful bundles, fortunate people in overloaded cars
cleaving their way through the packed highways, and at the gates of
France an endless queue of exhausted fugitives waiting for admission into
safety. Admission into the concentration camps which this France had
prepared for free men: barbed wire, black sentries, abuse, and robbery, and
disease, and the first bunches of refugees herded together without roof or
shelter, shivering in the cruel February winds.

Was all France blind? Did Frenchmen not see that one day—soon—
they would call upon those Spaniards to fight for French liberty? Or was
it that France had given up her own liberty?

The deck of the small steamer was almost deserted. The sea was
choppy, most of the passengers had disappeared, Ilsa had gone to lie
down in the cabin. A spare, wiry Englishman was sitting on one of the
hatches, his feet dangling, and seemed to enjoy the spray which the wind
drove into his face. I was sheltering from the gale behind a bulkhead, together with two of the sailors. We exchanged cigarettes, and I began to
talk, I had to talk. I spoke about the fight of Spain, and they asked many
questions. In the end I was carried away by my scorching anger and
poured out all my grievances against France. I asked the two, face to
face, the questions I had asked myself:

"Are the French blind, or have they given up their own liberty?"

The two men looked gravely at me. One of them had clear blue eyes
and a fresh, boyish face, the other had deep-set, black eyes, rough-hewn
features and a bare, hairy chest. Then they spoke together, in one breath
and with almost identical words:

"Oh no, we shall fight. The others are the ones who won't fight." And their stress on the words "the others" sank a deep gulf between the two Frances. The older one added:

"Look, comrade, don't go away from France in bitterness. We'll fight together yet."

The coast of Dieppe was fading behind us.

Rose Farm House   *Autumn, 1944*
Mapledurham
Oxfordshire